ISBN 978-1-332-00329-7
PIBN 10266671

FB &c Ltd, Dalton House, 60 Windsor Avenue, London, SW19 2RR.
Company number 08720141. Registered in England and Wales.

BLACK'S

PICTURESQUE TOURIST

OF

SCOTLAND.

Harriette E. Hart
From her dear
little Grandniece
Harriette Hart Haswell

id not give it to you
gave me pictures for it
Little Hellen

Wm. John Gibbon

Sarah

[illegible]

Picture by the Rev. Jo[illegible]omson, the property of [illegible] Tait Esq.

TO LOCH SCAVAIG, SKYE.

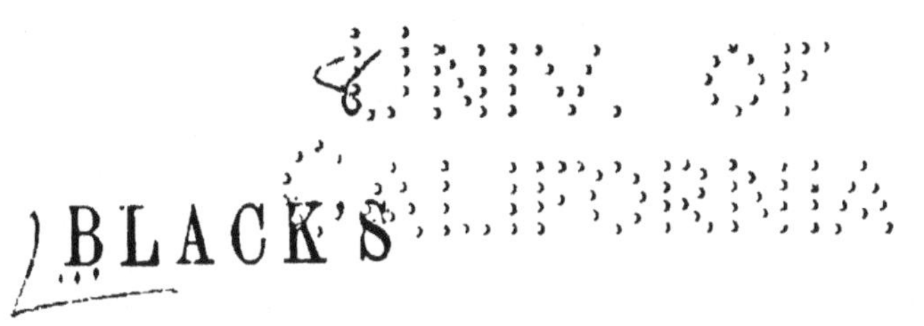

BLACK'S PICTURESQUE TOURIST OF SCOTLAND.

NINTH EDITION.

EDINBURGH:
ADAM AND CHARLES BLACK, 6 NORTH BRIDGE,
BOOKSELLERS AND PUBLISHERS TO THE QUEEN.

MDCCCLII.

PREFACE

TO THE NINTH EDITION.

In plan and execution the present volume differs from most works published with similar intent. Eloquence, or ambitious eulogium of the scenery to which the volume is meant to be a guide, has been studiously suppressed. A plain and intelligible account is given of those localities most worthy of the attention of strangers, and of the means by which they can be reached; the measure of admiration with which they must be contemplated is not prescribed. By adopting this course, space has been found for the incorporation of a large amount of Traditionary, Historical, and Literary Illustration, by which a recollection of the scenery will be more permanently fixed in the memory of the tourist, than by any original description of its features which the author could himself have given.

Neither labour nor expense has been spared to give the work the greatest possible degree of accuracy. To secure this object, the several sheets, in their progress through the press, have been transmitted to individuals conversant with the topography of the respective districts; while the descriptions of Edinburgh, Glasgow, and Aberdeen, have been wholly contributed by natives of these cities.

The expense of travelling, and the gratuities to servants at hotels, are subjects so materially influenced by the habits of the traveller, and the style of the establish-

ment at which he sojourns, that it is difficult to afford precise information in regard to them. At the same time, the Publishers have reason to believe that a few particulars on these heads will be generally acceptable to tourists, and they have accordingly embodied, in the following note, the result of the enquiries which they judged it proper to make upon the subject.

The improvements made upon every edition since the work first appeared, have been numerous and important. The present edition has been enlarged by Tours in Dumfriesshire and Galloway, in Ross-shire, and in Sutherland, while many of the other Tours have been re-constructed for the purpose of accommodating them to the altered means of locomotion by which Tourists are conducted over the ground. To the Illustrations also, several additions have been made. Among these, a Map of Central Scotland, on an enlarged scale, will be found of very great value, while the Railway Charts now comprehend every Railway in Scotland. A variety of Woodcuts, also introduced for the first time into the present edition, will be found to impart to the text both interest and ornament. The naming of the Hotels in the several towns and districts described, has been welcomed as valuable information; it is accordingly continued in the present edition.

For the favourable reception the work continues to meet with, the Publishers return their best thanks. They, at the same time, express their acknowledgments to the public press for numerous laudatory notices, which, if not unmerited by *former* editions, will be found to be still better deserved by the *present.*

TRAVELLING EXPENSES.

THE expense necessarily attendant upon travelling must be admitted to be a considerable drawback from its pleasures. Still the evil is inevitable; and it may be satisfactory to tourists to be able to estimate the price to be paid for their enjoyment.

The following scale shows the average charge for the several items which enter into the traveller's bill. The prices in the *first* division of the scale are rarely exceeded in any of the Inns in the smaller towns in Scotland; while in some villages, charges even more moderate may sometimes be met with. The prices in the *second* division show the charges in Hotels of the highest class in Edinburgh.

Breakfast, 1/6 to 2/	2/ to 3/
Dinner, 2/ to 3/	3/ to 4/
Tea, 1/6 to 2/	2/ to 3/
Supper, 1/6 to 2/	According to what is ordered.
Port or Sherry, per bottle, 5/	6/
Porter or Ale, per bottle, /6 to 1/	1/
Brandy, per gill, 1/6	2/
Whisky, per gill, /9	1/
Bed, 1/6 to 3/	3/6 to 4/

*** If the Traveller require his table to be furnished beyond the ordinary scale of comfort, he must be prepared for a proportionate increase of charge.

In the inferior country Inns, Wine, Brandy, and Malt Liquor are frequently not to be met with, or, if kept, will probably be of indifferent quality.

Posting, 1s. 6d. per mile; postboy, 3d. per mile.
A one-horse four-wheeled carriage, 1s. per mile, or 15s. per day.
A gig, 10s. 6d. to 12s. per day.
A riding-horse, 6s. or 7s.; a pony, 5s. per day.

*** In large towns the charges for carriages and riding-horses are about 20 per cent above those here quoted. Where the hire is for several successive days, an abatement may be expected. The posting is the same in town and country.

The payment of the gratuities to servants at Inns is a source of great annoyance to travellers. It would very larg contribute to the tourist's comfort were the charges under this head included among the other items of the landlord's bill. Although this practice has been adopted by a few Hotel-keepers in other parts of the kingdom, it is believed that it has not yet been introduced into any of the Inns in Scotland.

To enable them to furnish tourists with some information on this subject, the publishers have applied to two Hotel-keepers of the first respectability (the one in Dublin, the other in Liverpool) by whom the practice of charging for servants is adopted, and the following are averaged from the rates charged in their establishments:

1.

A single gentleman, taking the general accommodation of the Hotel for one or two meals as a passing traveller, Waiter, 6d.; Chambermaid, 6d.; Porter or Boots, 6d. This includes the removal of any reasonable weight of luggage; but extra messages and parcels are charged separately.

2.

A single gentleman, staying a day and night, and taking his meals in the hotel, 1s. 6d. or 2s. for servants, and if he stays several days, 1s. or 1s. 6d. per day.

3.

A gentleman and his wife, occupying a sitting-room and bedroom, 2s. 6d. to 3s. 6d. per night for servants. If accompanied by sons or daughters, or other relatives, half this rate from each; but no charge for children under nine years of age.

4.

A party of four or six for one night, about 1s. 6d. each.

Upon submitting this scale to several of the most respectable Hotel-keepers in Edinburgh, they consider the rates to be a fair average. In country and village inns, even the lowest of the payments above quoted may be unnecessarily liberal, while in some of the fashionable hotels in London the highest may be considerably under par.

CONTENTS.

SIXTH TOUR.

SEVENTH TOUR.

EIGHTH TOUR.

NINTH TOUR.

TENTH TOUR.

ELEVENTH TOUR.

TWELFTH TOUR.

THIRTEENTH TOUR.

FOURTEENTH TOUR.

FIFTEENTH TOUR.

SIXTEENTH TOUR.

SEVENTEENTH TOUR.

EIGHTEENTH TOUR.

NINETEENTH TOUR.

TWENTIETH TOUR.

TWENTY-FIRST TOUR.

ROAD ITINERARY.

RAILWAY ITINERARY.

ILLUSTRATIONS.

I. MAPS, PLANS, AND RAILWAY CHARTS.

II. VIEWS OF SCENERY, &c.

*** The Engravings on Wood are distinguished by *Italics*.

TABLE OF THE DISTANCES

OF THE PRINCIPAL TOWNS IN SCOTLAND FROM EACH OTHER AND FROM LONDON, GENERALLY CALCULATED BY THE MAIL ROADS.

	EDINBURGH	Aberdeen	Arbroath	Ayr	Banff	Berwick-on-Tweed	Campbelton	Cupar Fife	Dumbarton	Dumfries	Dundee	Elgin	Falkirk	Glasgow	Greenock	Haddington	Hamilton	Inverary	Inverness	Jedburgh	John o' Groat's House	Kelso	Kirkcudbright	Lanark	Montrose	Paisley	Perth	Port Patrick	Stirling	Thurso	Wick	Wigton	DISTANCE FROM LONDON
EDINBURGH																																	392
Aberdeen	109																																501
Arbroath	60	49																															452
Ayr	77	177	128																														394
Banff	154	45	94	222																													546
Berwick-on-Tweed	56	164	115	132	209																												337
Campbelton	177	276	233	60	283	232																											529
Cupar Fife	30	79	80	107	124	85	181																										429
Dumbarton	58	150	106	47	195	113	108	81																									410
Dumfries	71	180	131	59	240	108	205	101	86																								338
Dundee	43	66	17	116	111	96	181	13	89	114																							435
Elgin	169	68	99	206	84	224	231	125	180	240	112																						561
Falkirk	24	127	84	56	159	79	156	54	37	88	67	157																					416
Glasgow	44	143	100	33	175	99	133	74	14	72	83	173	23																				396
Greenock	66	165	122	46	197	121	111	96	12	94	105	195	45	22																			418
Haddington	17	126	77	94	171	38	194	47	75	88	60	186	41	61	83																		375
Hamilton	37	146	97	38	186	92	134	58	23	61	80	184	22	11	33	54																	381
Inverary	104	169	125	93	207	159	73	108	46	132	108	173	83	60	38	121	71																456
Inverness	157	104	153	195	75	212	208	136	148	228	136	41	146	162	184	174	173	135															549
Jedburgh	47	156	107	98	201	33	222	77	103	73	90	216	71	89	111	46	78	149	204														354
John o' Groat's	314	235	284	326	206	369	339	294	279	365	294	172	277	293	315	331	304	266	131	361													706
Kelso	43	152	103	120	212	23	220	73	101	83	86	212	67	87	109	86	80	147	200	10	357												368
Kirkcudbright	99	208	159	64	253	135	115	129	112	26	142	268	121	98	120	116	90	157	256	102	391	112											364
Lanark	31	140	91	51	185	86	158	61	39	58	74	199	32	25	47	48	14	85	187	64	318	62	82										375
Montrose	72	37	12	149	82	127	210	42	119	143	29	93	96	112	134	89	123	187	135	119	266	115	171	103									464
Paisley	52	151	108	34	183	107	127	82	9	80	91	181	31	8	16	69	19	54	170	97	301	95	106	83	120								407
Perth	40	83	89	94	126	95	159	22	68	111	22	129	45	61	83	57	72	86	114	87	272	83	139	71	51	69							432
Port Patrick	183	242	193	56	264	183	60	163	103	78	172	262	112	89	111	150	92	149	251	135	382	126	55	95	201	90	150						421
Stirling	35	116	73	60	148	90	153	47	34	99	56	146	11	27	49	52	38	80	135	82	266	78	125	37	85	85	34	116					427
Thurso	316	263	312	354	234	371	367	295	307	387	295	200	305	321	343	333	332	294	159	363	20	359	415	381	294	329	273	410	294				708
Wick	295	242	291	333	213	350	346	274	286	366	274	179	284	300	322	312	311	278	138	342	19	338	394	310	273	308	252	389	273	21			687
Wigton	105	214	165	50	258	106	93	135	97	55	148	256	121	83	95	122	84	143	245	128	404	138	31	70	176	83	144	87	110	403	383		395
Carlisle	92	201	151	92	246	88	180	122	109	37	135	261	116	95	117	109	84	155	249	53	388	63	63	74	164	106	132	120	110	408	387	94	301

☞ The names of the various towns are arranged at each end of the line of figures, and the angle where the perpendicular and horizontal lines meet, gives the distance of the respective towns from each other.

THE

PICTURESQUE TOURIST

OF

SCOTLAND.

ORIGIN OF THE NAME—EXTENT—GENERAL ASPECT—NATURAL DIVISIONS—MOUNTAINS—VALES—RIVERS—LAKES—MINERAL PRODUCE AND SPRINGS—CLIMATE—AGRICULTURE—ANIMAL KINGDOM—FISHERIES—MANUFACTURES—COMMERCE—INTERNAL COMMUNICATION REVENUE—CONSTITUTION—RELIGIOUS INSTITUTIONS—UNIVERSITIES AND SCHOOLS—ADMINISTRATION OF JUSTICE—POPULATION.

SCOTLAND is the northern and smaller division of the Island of Great Britain. The origin of the term is involved in much obscurity. That part of the country which lies beyond the Firths of Forth and Clyde received from the Romans the appellation of Caledonia, and its inhabitants were denominated Caledonians. They were afterwards known by the name of Picts, and from them the country was for some centuries called Pictland. The term Scotland began to come into use, for the first time, in the eleventh century, and this name is supposed to have been derived from a colony of Scots, who had previously left Ireland, and planted themselves in Argyleshire and the West Highlands.

EXTENT.—The longest line that can be drawn in Scotland, is from its most southerly point, the Mull of Galloway, in lat. 54° 38′ N., long. 4° 50′ W., to Dunnet Head, its most northerly point, in lat. 58° 40′ 30″ N., long. 3° 29′ W., or about 285 miles; but the longest line that can be drawn in about the same parallel of longitude, is from the

A

former point to Cape Wrath, in lat. 58° 36′ N., long. 4° 56′ W., a distance of 275 miles. The breadth is extremely various. From Buchanness point to the point of Ardnamurchan in Argyleshire, the distance is 160 miles; but from the bottom of Loch Broom to the Firth of Dornoch, it is only twenty-four miles. The whole coast is so much penetrated by arms of the sea, that there is only one spot throughout its whole circuit upwards of forty miles from the shore. The area of the mainland is computed at 25,520 square miles of land, and 494 of fresh water lakes; the islands are supposed to contain about 4080 square miles of land, and about 144 of water.

General Aspect.—The surface of the country is distinguished for variety, and, compared with England, it is, generally speaking, rugged and mountainous. It is supposed, that estimating the whole extent of the country, exclusive of lakes, at 19,000,000 acres, scarcely so many as 6,000,000 are arable—that is, less than one-third; whereas in England, the proportion of arable land to the entire extent of the country exceeds three-fourths. With the exception of a few tracts of rich alluvial land along the courses of the great rivers, Scotland has no extensive tracts of level ground, the surface of the country being generally varied with hill and dale.

Natural Divisions.—Scotland is naturally divided into Highlands and Lowlands. The former division comprehends, besides the Hebrides, the Orkney and Shetland islands, the counties of Argyle, Inverness, Nairn, Ross, Cromarty, Sutherland, and Caithness, with parts of Dumbarton, Stirling, Perth, Forfar, Kincardine, Aberdeen, Banff, and Moray or Elgin. The Highlands, again, are divided into two unequal portions, by the chain of lakes occupying the Glenmore-nan-albin, or "Great glen of Caledonia," stretching north-east and south-west across the island, from Inverness to Fort-William, now connected together, and forming the Caledonian Canal. The northern division of the Highlands is decidedly the more barren and unproductive of the two, though the other division contains the highest mountains. In the eastern parts of Ross and Cromarty there are level tracts of considerable fertility. The Lowland division of the kingdom, though comparatively flat, comprises also a great deal of mountainous country.

MOUNTAINS.—Of the Highland mountains, the most celebrated is the chain of the Grampians. It commences on the south side of Loch Etive in Argyleshire, and terminates between Stonehaven and the mouth of the Dee on the eastern coast. The most elevated part of this range lies at the head of the Dee. Ben Macdui, the highest mountain in Scotland, rises to the height of 4418 feet, and the adjoining mountains of Cairngorm, Cairntoul, and Ben Avon, are respectively 4050, 4245, and 3967 feet high. The other principal summits of the Grampian chain are, Schehallion, near the east end of Loch Rannoch, 3613 feet above the level of the sea; Ben Lawers, on the north side of Loch Tay, 3945; Ben More, at the head of Glendochart, 3818; Ben Lomond, on the side of Loch Lomond, 3191; and Ben Cruachan, at the head of Loch Awe, 3390. Ben Nevis, till recently reputed the highest of the British mountains, lies immediately to the east of Fort-William, being separated from the Grampians by the moor of Rannoch; it rises 4416 feet above the mean level of the sea,* and its circumference at the base is supposed to exceed twenty-four miles. To the south of the Grampians, and running parallel to them across the island, there is a chain of hills divided by the valleys of the Tay and Forth into three distinct portions, and bearing the names of the Sidlaw, Ochil, and Campsie hills. The low country between them and the Grampians is called the valley of Strathmore. In the Lowland division of the country, the Cheviots form the principal range. These hills are situated partly in England and partly in Scotland. They separate Northumberland from Roxburghshire, stretch through the latter county in a westerly direction, keeping to the north of Liddesdale, then bending north-west towards

* The height of Ben Nevis, as here given, was obtained by Mr. David Stevenson, civil engineer, from careful barometric observations made simultaneously on the top of Ben Nevis and at Corpach Loch on 15th August 1844, and the calculations were made by Mr. William Swan, teacher of mathematics, Edinburgh.

the junction of the counties of Roxburgh, Selkirk and Dumfries, they unite with the Lowther Hills. This extensive group, which, near the above-mentioned junction, has Ettrick water for its eastern boundary, spreads over the southern portion of the counties of Selkirk, Peebles, and Lanark, and the north of Dumfries-shire, and in the west of the latter county joins the ridges, which, passing through Kirkcudbrightshire, Wigtonshire, and the south of Ayrshire, terminate at Loch Ryan in the Irish Channel. Of these hills the highest lie on the confines of the counties of Dumfries, Peebles, Lanark, and Selkirk; Broadlaw, in the parish of Tweedsmuir, the most elevated mountain in the south of Scotland, is 2741 feet above the level of the sea; Hartfell, contiguous to Broadlaw, is 2635 feet above the level of the sea, and several of the neighbouring hills rise to the height of about 2000 feet.

VALES.—The most important level tracts in Scotland are the Carse of Stirling and Falkirk, which occupies the country on both sides the Forth, from Borrowstounness on the south, and Kincardine on the north, westward to Gartmore; the tract between Dundee and Perth, bounded by the Sidlaw hills on the north, and the Tay on the south, denominated the Carse of Gowrie; the Merse of Berwickshire, extending from Leader water along the Tweed to Berwick; and the valley of Strathmore, which comprises a considerable portion of the counties of Perth and Angus, stretching from Methven in the former to the vicinity of Laurencekirk in Kincardineshire, and from thence, under the name of *the How of the Mearns*, to within a short distance of Stonehaven. Besides these, there are several smaller straths, such as Teviotdale in Roxburghshire, Tynedale in East-Lothian, and *the How of Fife.*

RIVERS.—The principal rivers of Scotland are, the Tweed, the Forth, the Tay, the Spey, and the Clyde. The Tweed rises in Tweedsmuir about six miles from Moffat. It runs first north-east to Peebles, then east, with a little inclination to the south, to Melrose; it next passes Kelso and Coldstream, and pursuing a north-easterly direction, falls into the sea at Berwick. During the latter part of its course, the

Tweed forms the boundary between England and Scotland. The descent from its source to Peebles is 1000 feet, and thence to Berwick about 500 feet more. Including windings, its length is reckoned at rather more than 100 miles. Its principal tributaries are, the Ettrick, which it receives near Selkirk ; the Gala a little above, and the Leader a little below Melrose ; the Teviot at Kelso ; the Till at Tillmouth ; and the Adder near Berwick. The salmon fisheries at Berwick are very productive. The extent of country drained by the Tweed is 1687 square miles.

The Forth rises on the east side of Ben Lomond, and runs in an easterly direction, with many windings, till it unites with the Firth of Forth at Kincardine. Its most important tributary is the Teith, which it receives a short way above Stirling. It drains 793 square miles.

The Tay conveys to the sea a greater quantity of water than any other river in Britain. It has its source in the western extremity of Perthshire, in the district of Breadalbane, on the frontiers of Lorn in Argyleshire. At first it receives the name of the Fillan. After a winding course of eight or nine miles it spreads itself out into Loch Dochart, and, under the appellation of the Dochart, flows in an easterly direction through the vale of Glendochart, at the eastern extremity of which, having previously received the waters of the Lochy, it expands into the beautiful long narrow lake, called Loch Tay. Issuing thence, it speedily receives a great augmentation by the river Lyon, and running north and east at Logierait, about eight miles above Dunkeld, it is joined by the Tummel. It now takes a direction more towards the south, to Dunkeld, where, on its right bank, it receives the beautiful river Bran. On leaving Dunkeld, it runs east to Kinclaven, and after receiving a considerable augmentation to the volume of its waters by the accession of the Isla, the Shochie, and the Almond, it flows in a southwesterly course to Perth. At the foot of the vale of Strathearn, it receives on its right bank its last great tributary, the Earn, and gradually expanding its waters, it flows in a north-easterly direction past Newburgh, where it assumes the appearance of a Firth or estuary. Ten miles from the

German ocean it passes Dundee, and finally unites its waters to the sea, between Tentsmoor Point and Buttonness. The Tay is celebrated for its salmon fisheries, the value of which is between £10,000 and £11,000 per annum. The river is navigable for vessels of 400 tons burden, as far as Perth, thirty-two miles from the German ocean. Its drainage is 2283 square miles, and its mean discharge below the junction of the Earn, has been ascertained by Mr. David Stevenson, to be 273,117 cubic feet per minute. That of the Thames is stated at only 80,220 cubic feet per minute, or less than one-third that of the Tay.

The Spey is the most rapid of the Scottish rivers, and, next to the Tay, discharges the greatest quantity of water. It has its source in Loch Spey, within about six miles of the head of Loch Lochy. It runs in a north-easterly direction through Badenoch and Strathspey to Fochabers, below which it falls into the Moray Firth, at Garmouth. During its course, it receives numerous mountain streams, but no important tributary. From its source to its mouth, the distance is about seventy-five miles; but following its windings, its course is about ninety-six miles. Owing to the origin and course of its tributary waters, the Spey is very liable to sudden and destructive inundations. It flows through the best wooded part of the Highlands, and affords a water-carriage for the produce of the extensive woods of Glenmore and Strathspey, large quantities of which are floated down to the seaport of Garmouth. It drains 1234 square miles.

The Clyde is, in a commercial point of view, the most important river of Scotland. It has its origin in the highest part of the southern mountain land, at no great distance from the sources of the Tweed and the Annan. It flows at first in a northerly direction, with a slight inclination to the east, as far as Biggar. Being joined by the Douglas, near Harperfield, it takes a north-west course by Lanark, Hamilton, and Glasgow, falling into the Firth of Clyde below Dumbarton. Following its windings, the course of the Clyde, from its source to Dumbarton, is about seventy-three miles, but the length of the river, in a direct line, is only about fifty-two miles. Its principal tributaries are the Douglas, Nethan, Avon, Mouse, Kelvin, Cart, and Leven. The extent of its drainage, exclusive of the Leven, is 945 square miles. Of the celebrated falls of the Clyde, two are above, and two below Lanark; the uppermost is Bonnington Linn, the height of which is about thirty feet; the second fall is Corra Linn, where the water dashes over the rock in three distinct leaps; Dundaff Fall is ten feet high, and at Stonebyres there are three distinct falls, altogether measuring about seventy-six feet in height. At high water the Clyde is navigable for the largest class of merchant vessels as far as Glasgow, and large sums of money have been expended, especially of late, in improving and deepening the channel. The Forth and Clyde Canal falls into the latter river, at Dunglass, a little above Dumbarton.

LAKES.—The chief lakes of Scotland are—Loch Lomond, lying between Dumbartonshire and Stirlingshire; Loch Ness, in Inverness-shire; Loch Maree, in Ross-shire; Loch Awe, in Argyleshire; Lochs Tay, Rannoch, and Erich, in Perthshire, &c.

MINERAL PRODUCE.—The minerals of Scotland are numerous and valuable. The great coal-field of Scotland extends, with little interruption, from the eastern to the western coast. The most valuable part of this field is situated on the north and south sides of the Forth, about the average breadth of ten or twelve miles on each side, and on the north and south sides of the Clyde, ranging through Renfrewshire, part of Lanarkshire; and the north of Ayrshire. Detached coal-fields have also been found in various other parts of Scotland. Lime is very generally diffused throughout the country. Iron abounds in many parts, particularly in the coal-field. Lead-mines are wrought to a great extent at Leadhills and Wanlockhead, in Dumfries-shire. In the soil which covers these fields, particles of gold have occasionally been found; copper-ore is found at Blair Logie, Airthrie, and at Fetlar, in Orkney; antimony at Langholm; manganese in the neighbourhood of Aberdeen; silver has been wrought at Alva in Stirlingshire, in Clackmannanshire, and at Leadhills in Lanarkshire; there are extensive slate-quarries in Aberdeenshire, Argyleshire, Perthshire, and Peebles-shire; marble is found in Argyleshire, Sutherland, and the Hebrides; sandstone abounds generally throughout the country; and granite, and other primitive rocks, within the limits of the Grampians.

Mineral Springs.—There are numerous medicinal mineral springs in various parts of Scotland. "The most remarkable of these are—the sulphurous waters of *Strathpeffer*, near Dingwall, Ross-shire; *Muirtown*, in the same neighbourhood; *Moffat*, in Dumfries-shire; and *St. Bernard's*, at Stockbridge, a suburb of Edinburgh: the chalybeates of *Hartfell*, near Moffat; *Vicar's Bridge*, near Dollar, Stirlingshire; and *Bonnington*, near Edinburgh: the saline waters of *Dunblane*, near Stirling; *Airthrie*, also near Stirling; *Pitcaithly*, near Perth; and *Innerleithen*, near Peebles. At *St. Catherine's*, in the parish of Liberton, near Edinburgh, there is a spring which yields asphaltum in considerable quantities." *

Climate.—The climate of Scotland is extremely variable. Owing to its insular situation, however, neither the cold in winter, nor the heat in summer, is so intense as in similar latitudes on the continent. The annual average temperature may be estimated at from 44° to 47° of Fahrenheit. The quantity of rain which falls on the east coast of Scotland varies from 22 to 26 inches, while on the west coast, and in the Hebrides, it ranges from 35 to 46 inches. The average number of days in which either rain or snow falls in parts situated on the west coast, is about 200; on the east coast, about 145. The winds are more variable than in England, and more violent, especially about the equinoxes. Westerly winds generally prevail, especially during autumn and the early part of winter, but north-east winds are prevalent and severe during spring and the early part of summer.

Agriculture.—The soils of the various districts of Scotland are exceedingly diversified. The general average is inferior to that of England, although many of the valleys

* Malte Brun and Balbi Abridged. *Second Edition*. Edin. 1844.

are highly productive. In Berwickshire, the Lothians, Clydesdale, Fifeshire, the Carses of Stirling, Falkirk, and more particularly in the Carse of Gowrie, Strathearn, Strathmore, and Moray, there are tracts of land not inferior to any in the empire. The inferiority of the climate and soil, as compared with England, is exhibited by contrasting the phenomena of vegetation in the two countries. Notwithstanding the very advanced state of agriculture, in many districts of Scotland, the crops are not reaped with the same certainty as in England, nor do the ordinary kinds of grain arrive at the same perfection. Thus, although Scotch and English barley may be of the same weight, the former does not bring so high a price; it contains less saccharine matter, and does not yield so large a quantity of malt. Various fruits, also, which ripen in the one country, seldom arrive at maturity in the other, and never reach the same perfection; while different berries acquire in Scotland somewhat of that delicious flavour which distinguishes them in still higher parallels.

Animal Kingdom.—The domestic animals common to Scotland are the same as those of England, with some varieties in the breeds. Among the wild animals, the roe and the red-deer are most worthy of notice. The golden eagle, and other birds of prey, are found in the mountainous districts, and the country abounds with all kinds of moor-game, partridges, and water-fowl.

Fisheries.—There are many valuable fisheries in Scotland; the salmon fisheries, especially, produce a large revenue to their owners, but, during late years, they have experienced an extraordinary decline.

The herring fishery is carried on to a considerable extent on the east coast of Scotland, and there are most productive and valuable fisheries of ling and cod in the neighbourhood of the Shetland and Orkney Islands.

Manufactures.—The manufactures of Scotland, especially those of linen and cotton, are extensive and flourishing. The woollen manufacture, compared with that of England, is inconsiderable. The making of steam-engines, and every other description of machinery, as also the building of steam-boats, both of wood and iron, is carried on to a great extent, especially on the Clyde; and vast quantities of cast-iron goods are produced at Carron, Shotts, and other works.

COMMERCE.—The commerce of Scotland has increased with astonishing rapidity, especially within a comparatively recent period, and a vast trade is now carried on, particularly with America and the West Indies. It is supposed, that since 1814, the increase in the principal manufactures and trades carried on in the country, and in the number of individuals employed in them, amounts to at least 30, or 35 per cent.

INTERNAL COMMUNICATION.—Carriage roads extend over every part of the country; and "in consequence of the excellent materials which abound in all parts of Scotland, and of the greater skill and science of Scottish trustees and surveyors, the turnpike roads in Scotland are superior to those in England."* The irregularity of surface is not favourable to artificial inland navigation. Among the most important Canals are the *Caledonian Canal*, connecting the Lakes Ness, Oich, and Lochy, with the Beauly Firth on the north, and with Loch Eil on the south; the *Forth and Clyde or Great Canal*, extending from the Firth of Forth at Grangemouth, to Bowling Bay on the Firth of Clyde; and the *Union Canal*, commencing at Edinburgh, and terminating in the Great Canal at Port Downie near Falkirk. Besides these, there are several others which may be noticed in describing the localities through which they pass. Among the Railways of Scotland, completed, or in progress, the most important are—the *Edinburgh and Glasgow*, the *Glasgow and S. Western*, the *Glasgow and Greenock*, the *Dumbartonshire*, the *Caledonian*, the *North British*, the *Scottish Central*, the *Scottish Midland Junction*, the *Edinburgh, Perth, and Dundee*, the *Aberdeen*, and the *Dundee and Perth*.

REVENUE.—The increase in the revenue has fully kept pace with the increased prosperity of the country. At

* Sir H. Parnell on Roads, p. 318.

the period of the Union, the revenue amounted only to £110,606; in 1788, it was £1,090,148; in 1813, (when the Income Tax was at its height,) it amounted to £4,204,007; in 1831, notwithstanding the repeal of the Income Tax, and many other taxes, the gross revenue amounted to £5,254,624; and in 1840, although there was a farther reduction of taxation, it amounted to £5,231,727. The returns since this period, with the exception of the year 1842, have continued to exhibit a progressive increase in amount.

CONSTITUTION.—Under the Reform Act of 1832, Scotland returns fifty-three members to the imperial Parliament, of whom thirty are for the shires, and twenty-three for the cities, boroughs, and towns; twenty-seven counties return one member each, and the counties of Elgin and Nairn, Ross and Cromarty, and Clackmannan and Kinross, are combined in pairs, each of which returns one member. Of the cities, boroughs, and towns—seventy-six in number—Edinburgh and Glasgow return two members each; Aberdeen, Paisley, Dundee, Greenock, and Perth, one each; the remaining burghs and towns are combined into sets or districts, each set, jointly, sending one member. The Scottish Peers choose sixteen of their number to represent them in the House of Lords. These representative Peers, like the Commoners, hold their seats for only one Parliament.

RELIGIOUS INSTITUTIONS.—Scotland is divided into 1023 parishes, (including parishes *quoad sacra*,) each of which is provided with one minister, or, in a few instances in towns, with two. The number of parishes, *quoad sacra*, has, however, been increased of late. The stipends of the endowed clergy, with the glebe and manse, probably average from £200 to £300 a-year. The government of the Church is vested in kirk-sessions, presbyteries, synods, and the General Assembly. The number of churches belonging to Dissenters, of all denominations, amounts to 1500, besides a considerable number of missionary stations. Of this number about 730 belong to the Free Church of Scotland, which separated from the Establishment in 1843. The incomes of the Dissenting clergy are wholly derived from their congregations; they average, probably, from £120 to £130 a-year, including a house and garden. In many cases, however, the income is considerably larger.

UNIVERSITIES AND SCHOOLS.—Scotland has four Universities, that of St. Andrews, founded by Papal authority in 1413; that of Glasgow, by the same authority, in 1450; that of Aberdeen, also, with the sanction of the Pope, in 1494, though education did not commence there till 1500; and that of Edinburgh, the only one instituted since the Reformation, in 1582. None of these colleges or universities can be said to be liberally endowed. St. Andrews has eleven professorships; Glasgow twenty-two; King's College, Aberdeen, nine; Marischal College, twelve; and Edinburgh thirty-one. The aggregate number of students in these universities is at present about 2593, of which Edinburgh has 1050, Glasgow 843, Aberdeen about 550, and St. Andrews 150. In every parish there is at least one school, for teaching the ordinary branches of education. The emoluments of the schoolmaster are derived from a small annual salary, with a free house and garden, provided by the landed proprietors, and moderate school fees. Private schools, also, are very numerous, and it is supposed, on good authority, that the total number of schools of every kind in Scotland amounts to about 5500.

ADMINISTRATION OF JUSTICE.—The supreme *civil* court of Scotland, is called the Court of Session. It holds, in Edinburgh, two sessions annually. The number of judges was formerly fifteen, but is now thirteen; they are styled Lords of Session, and sit in two courts or chambers, called the first and second divisions, which form in effect, two courts of equal and independent authority. The Court of Justiciary, the supreme *criminal* court of Scotland, consists at present of six judges, who are also judges of the Court of Session. The president of the whole Court is the Lord Justice-General. The Court holds sittings in Edinburgh during the recess of the Court of Session; and twice a year, in the spring and autumn vacations, the judges hold circuits in the chief provincial towns, two going each circuit. The Court of Exchequer, for the trial of cases connected with the revenue, is now held as a separate establishment, and the duties are devolved on two of the judges of the Court of Session. There are also inferior courts of law, viz. the courts of the boroughs, of the justices of the peace, and of the sheriffs.

POPULATION.—The population of Scotland at the period of the Union, in 1707, is supposed not to have exceeded 1,050,000. In 1755, it amounted to 1,265,380; in 1831, it had increased to 2,365,114; and in 1841, to 2,628,957; of which 1,246,427 were males, and 1,382,530 females. The average population per square mile is 88.5. During the ten years ending with 1820, the increase was 16 per cent.; during the ten years ending with 1830, 13 per cent.; and during the ten years ending with 1840, 11 per cent. The population of Scotland has increased less rapidly than that of England, and much less so than that of Ireland; and, in consequence, the Scotch have "advanced much more rapidly than the English or Irish, in wealth, and in the command of the necessaries and conveniences of life. Their progress in this respect has indeed been quite astonishing. The habits, diet, dress, and other accommodations of the people, have been signally improved. It is not too much to affirm, that the peasantry of the present day are better lodged, better clothed, and better fed, than the middle classes of landowners a century ago." *

THE approach to Scotland by tourists from other countries must, of course, be determined by the particular views and circumstances of individuals. By railway the *North British* and the *Caledonian* lines are the great avenues of approach. Those who enter by the former line may diverge westward from Berwick to Kelso, Melrose, and Abbotsford, and having visited these places, proceed by railway to Edinburgh. Those who enter by the Caledonian line should continue their journey to Edinburgh or to Glasgow, as best comports with their subsequent progress. The great majority of tourists come at once to the metropolis, and to all who visit Scotland for the first time, this plan possesses many advantages. Edinburgh (with its environs) is of itself an object of very great interest and curiosity, and, by the increased facilities of travelling, is placed cheaply within a few hours' journey of the finest scenery of Perth, Stirling, Dumbarton, and Argyle shires. We shall therefore assume Edinburgh as our first great starting point, and commence our description with a notice of that city and its interesting environs.

EDINBURGH.

SITUATION—ARCHITECTURE—POPULATION—LEGAL PROFESSION—MANUFACTURES—SOCIAL ADVANTAGES.

[*Hotels*:—Douglas' Hotel, St. Andrew Square; British Hotel, 70 Queen Street; Queen's Hotel, Princes Street—First rate family hotels. Those more generally frequented by Tourists are Gibb's Royal Hotel, 53 Princes Street, opposite the Scott Monument; Waterloo Hotel, Waterloo Place; Tait's New Royal Hotel, M'Queen's Hotel, Campbell's North British Hotel, Star Hotel, Mackay's Hotel, Caledonian Hotel, Crown Hotel—all in Princes Street; London Hotel, St. Andrew Square; Regent Hotel, Waterloo Place.]

THE metropolis of Scotland is situated in the northern part of the County of Mid-Lothian, and is about two miles distant from the Firth of Forth.* Its length and breadth are nearly equal, measuring about two miles in either direction. In panoramic splendour, its site is generally admitted to be unequalled by any capital in Europe, and the prospect from the elevated points of the city and neighbourhood is of singular beauty and grandeur. The noble estuary of the Forth, expanding from River into Ocean; the solitary grandeur of Arthur's Seat; the varied park and woodland scenery which enrich the southward prospect; the pastoral acclivities of the neighbouring Pentland Hills, and the more shadowy splendours of the Lammer moors, the Ochils, and the Grampians, form some of the features of a landscape combining, in one vast expanse, the richest elements of the beautiful and the sublime.

* The precise geographical position of the centre of the city is 55° 57′ 20″ north latitude, and 3° 10′ 30″ west longitude.

"Traced like a map the landscape lies
In cultured beauty stretching wide;
There Pentland's green acclivities;
There Ocean, with its azure tide;
There Arthur's Seat; and, gleaming through
Thy southern wing, Dunedin blue!
While in the orient, Lammer's daughters,
A distant giant range, are seen,
North Berwick-Law, with cone of green,
And Bass amid the waters." *

To most of the great cities in the kingdom the approaches lie through mean and squalid suburbs, by which the stranger is gradually introduced to the more striking streets and public edifices. The avenues to Edinburgh, on the contrary, are lined with streets of a highly respectable class, the abodes of poverty being, for the most part, confined to those gigantic piles of building in the older parts of the city, where they so essentially contribute to the picturesque grandeur of the place.

The general architecture of the city is very imposing, whether we regard the picturesque disorder of the buildings in the Old Town, or the symmetrical proportions of the streets and squares in the New. Of the public edifices it may be observed, that while the greater number are distinguished by chaste design and excellent masonry, there are none of those sumptuous structures which, like St. Paul's or Westminster Abbey, York Minster, and some other of the English Provincial Cathedrals, astonish the beholder alike by their magnitude and their architectural splendour. But in no city of the kingdom is the general standard of excellence so well maintained. If there be no edifice to overwhelm the imagination by its magnificence, there are comparatively few to offend taste by their deformity or meanness of design. Above all, Edinburgh is wholly exempt from such examples of ostentatious deformity as, in London, may be seen to mingle with some of the most graceful specimens of domestic architecture in the Regent Park.

* Delta.

The resemblance between Athens and Edinburgh, which has been remarked by most travellers who have visited both capitals, has conferred upon the Scottish Metropolis the title of "The Modern Athens."* Stuart, author of "The Antiquities of Athens," was the first to draw attention to this resemblance, and his opinion has been confirmed by the testimony of many later writers. Dr. Clarke remarks, that the neighbourhood of Athens is just the Highlands of Scotland enriched with the splendid remains of art; and Mr. H. W. Williams observes, that the distant view of Athens from the Ægean Sea is extremely like that of Edinburgh from the Firth of Forth, "*though certainly the latter is considerably superior.*"

Nor are the natural or artificial beauties of the place its only attractions, for many of its localities teem with the recollections of "the majestic past," and are associated with events of deep historical importance. Other of its localities have been invested with an interest no less engrossing by the transcendent genius of Sir Walter Scott, whose novels have not only refreshed and embellished the incidents of history, but have conferred on many a spot, formerly unknown to fame, a reputation as enduring as the annals of history itself.

In literary eminence, also, Edinburgh claims a distinguished place. At the commencement of the present century, its University displayed an array of contemporaneous talent unequalled by any similar institution either before or since,† and the present professors continue honourably to maintain its scientific and literary reputation.

The population of Edinburgh and Leith, at the Union in 1707, was estimated at 35,000; in 1755, at 57,195; and in

* In one of those altercations with which Lords Brougham and Campbell occasionally enliven the discussions in the Upper House of Parliament, it was stated by the former that the epithet "Modern Athens" was resented by the inhabitants of Edinburgh as a mockery or an insult. So far as our own experience goes, we have never heard of any of our townsmen quarrelling with the epithet.

† We have only to remind our readers of the names of Robertson, Playfair, Black, Cullen, Robison, Blair, Dugald Stewart, Gregory, and Monro, to vindicate what otherwise might appear a sweeping assertion.

1775, at 70,430. The population of the city and suburbs, *exclusive of Leith*, according to the decennial census since 1801, has been—in 1801, 66,544; in 1811, 81,784; in 1821, 112,235; in 1831, 136,301; and in 1841, 138,182.*

POPULATION RETURNS OF 1841 FOR EDINBURGH AND ITS SUBURBS.				
OCCUPATIONS.	MALES.		FEMALES.	
	20 years of age and upwards.	Under 20 years of age.	20 years of age and upwards.	Under 20 years of age.
Persons engaged in professions, commerce, trade, and agriculture, .	30,431	6,476	16,016	4,990
Persons of independent means, . .	1,013	74	5,127	241
Alms-people, pensioners, paupers, and beggars, ...	431	239	710	186
Persons in barns, boats, and barges; lunatics, and prisoners in gaol,	255	147	299	85
Residue of population, ...	691	21,556	24,790	24,425
TOTAL POPULATION, ...	32,821	28,492	46,942	29,927

Distinguishing males from females, the above table shows an excess of the latter amounting to 15,556. Probably no great city in the kingdom exhibits such a numerical disproportion in the sexes. This circumstance is mainly to be attributed to the stationary or retrograde state of industrial occupation in the town, the young men being obliged to seek for employment in other fields of enterprise, while the females, less adventurous, and less able to indulge the spirit of adventure where it exists, are compelled to remain 'cabin'd, cribb'd, confin'd,' in their native town. The numerical preponderance of the gentler sex may further be accounted for by the fact that an unusually large proportion of the inhabitants of Edinburgh are in circumstances enabling them to employ one or more domestic servants, of whom the great proportion are females.

A comparison of the population returns of Edinburgh, with those of five other of the large towns of the kingdom, will enable the reader to form some idea of the proportions which the professional and other liberally educated classes bear to the other orders of society. The returns for 1831 admitting of a more accurate classification than those of

* These are the numbers according to the *Parochial* enumerations. Within the *Parliamentary* boundary the population is 140,241.

1841, we adopt the former as being more convenient for our present purpose.

NAMES OF TOWNS AND THEIR SUBURBS.	TOTAL POPULATION.	MALES TWENTY YEARS OF AGE.					MALE SERVANTS.	FEMALE SERVANTS.
		Employed in Manufactures, or in making Manufacg. Machiny.	Employed in Retail or Handicraft Trades.	Capitalists, Bankers, Professional, and other liberally educated Men.	Labourers employed in Labour not Agricultural.	Other Males (except Servants.)		
EDINBURGH and Leith.	161,909	792	19,764	7463	4448	2296	1422	12,429
GLASGOW.	202,426	19,913	18,832	2723	574	4012	946	8006
LIVERPOOL and Toxteth Park.	189,242	359	21,208	5201	16,095	1214	363	9033
MANCHEST. and Salford.	182,812	15,342	17,931	2821	7629	1695	398	3985
BRISTOL and Barton-Regis.	103,886	415	11,270	2654	7312	1867	814	5702
BIRMINGHAM.	146,986	5028	19,469	2388	5292	1371	966	5233

This table, compiled from parliamentary documents, not only demonstrates the large proportion borne by the educated ranks to the general mass of the population, but from the number of male and female domestic servants, it is also obvious that the average number of families in comfortable circumstances must exceed that of any of the other large towns of the empire.* It must not, however, be concluded that there are many of the inhabitants of Edinburgh in circumstances of great opulence; in this respect it probably cannot vie with the other towns in the table, but competence is as generally possessed and comfort as widely diffused as in any other community of like magnitude.

The prosperity of the city essentially depends upon its College and Schools, and still more essentially upon the Courts of Judicature. The former attract many strangers

* According to the census of 1841, the number of domestic servants was 14,381, of whom 1614 were males, and 12,767 females. The increase in the number of this class during the ten years, therefore, appears to be 503—or considerably more than one-fourth of the entire increase in the population of the city.

who desire to secure for their families a liberal education at a moderate expense; the latter afford employment for the gentlemen of the Legal Profession, whose number is so great that they may be said to form at least one-third of the population in the higher and middle ranks of society.*

As it has no very extensive manufactures, the city is exempt from those sudden mercantile convulsions productive of so much misery in many other of the great towns

* The great family of Lawyers may be divided into the following classes. The first class consists of the Judges of the Court of Session, generally styled LORDS OF SESSION. Their nomination is with the Crown: they are now invariably chosen from among the Advocates, and, before their appointment, they must have been practising at the bar for at least five years. Their number was formerly 15, but is now reduced to 13. The salaries of the ordinary judges are £3000 a-year each, and those of the Lord Justice-Clerk and Lord President are £4000 and £4500 respectively. The ADVOCATES (*Anglice* Barristers) form the second class. They are united into a Society or Incorporation called the *Faculty of Advocates*, and possess the privilege of pleading before every Court in Scotland, and also in Scotch appeals before the House of Lords. The present number of the body is about 440, but there are not one-third of them in practice, and probably not one-sixth of them subsist solely by their professional gains. A considerable number of them are gentlemen wholly independent of their profession, who have joined the body on account of the status which they acquire from the learning and accomplishment of its members. The next class consists of the WRITERS TO THE SIGNET, who also form an Incorporation. They were originally called *Clerks to the Signet*, from their having been employed in the Secretary of State's office in preparing summonses, and other writs which received the Royal Signet, and they have still the sole privilege of preparing such writs. They are in other respects similar to the English Attorneys or Solicitors, and they are the oldest, most numerous, and most wealthy body of Law Practitioners in Scotland. Before admission to the body, an apprenticeship of five years is required, and an attendance of two Sessions at one of the Universities, independently of the Law Classes. The number of the Society is at present about 650, of whom about 400 are in practice. The SOLICITORS BEFORE THE SUPREME COURT, and ADVOCATES' FIRST CLERKS, form another section of this class, their duties being the same as those of Writers to the Signet, with the exception of their not being entitled to sign writs passing the Signet. These three classes, along with certain functionaries connected with the Court, form the College of Justice, which possesses certain privileges, the members being, until lately, exempted from most of the local taxes, and they are still exempt from the annuity levied for payment of the stipend of the Clergy of Edinburgh. They are not amenable to the jurisdiction of any inferior Court, excepting the Small Debt Court held by the Sheriff. The Solicitors at Law, (who practise before the inferior Courts,) the Accountants, and others, who pass under the more general name of Writers, are also included in the great family of Lawyers, but their distinctive peculiarities we think it unnecessary to mention here.

of the kingdom. Printing and publishing are carried on to a large extent. In this department of industry Edinburgh far surpasses all the towns of the kingdom, London only excepted; many of the most valuable and popular works of the age emanating from the Edinburgh press.* Printing papers are manufactured to a large extent in the neighbourhood, but none of the mills are in the immediate vicinity of the city. Although there are some other branches of manufacture, they are, for the most part, on an insignificant scale.

As a place of family residence, Edinburgh possesses many advantages. The climate, although it cannot be called mild or genial, is yet eminently salubrious; and favourable, not only to longevity, but to the development of the mental and physical powers. The annual quantity of rain is moderate, compared with the fall upon the western coast; for while the average in Edinburgh is about 23½, in Glasgow it is about 29.65. The violent winds, to which the city is exposed by its elevated situation, are by no means unfavourable to general health, as they carry the benefit of a thorough ventilation into the close-built lanes and alleys of the Old Town. The facilities of education, and the advantages of cultivated society, have been already alluded to. In the former of these particulars, we believe it to be unequalled in the kingdom, and in the latter it can be surpassed by London alone.

The markets are liberally supplied with all the necessaries and luxuries of the table. White fish are more especially abundant, cod, haddocks, and, at certain seasons, herrings, being sold at a very low price. Coal of good quality is found in the immediate neighbourhood of the city, and

* The Edinburgh Review, the North British Review, Blackwood's Magazine, Tait's Magazine, the Medical Journal, the Journal of Agriculture, and the Philosophical Journal, are some of the more important periodical publications. In circulation, it is worthy of remark, that both Blackwood's and Tait's Magazines far exceed any of their London contemporaries.

Chambers's Journal is also deserving of notice, as being the first and most extensively circulated of the periodicals of its class.

There are eleven newspapers, of which one is published thrice a-week, five twice a-week, and the rest weekly.

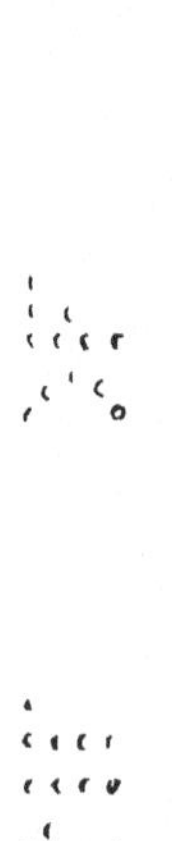

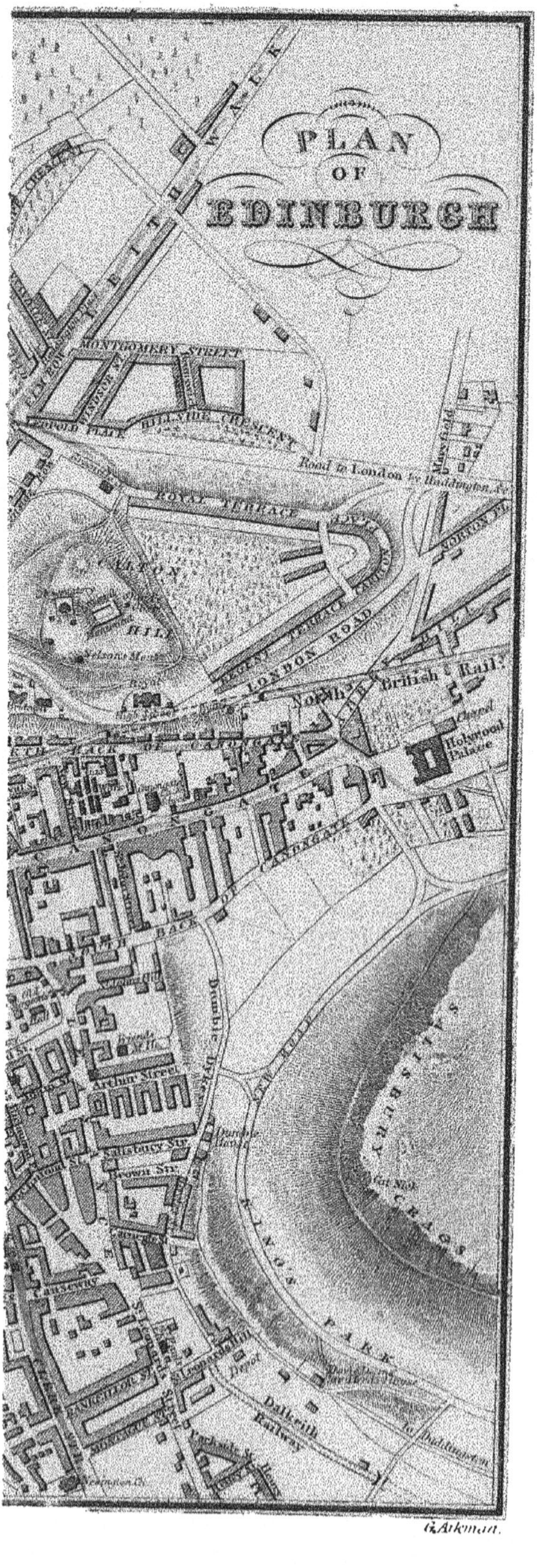

PLAN OF EDINBURGH

G. Aikman.

the recent extension of the works of the Water Company now furnishes the inhabitants with a copious supply of excellent water. Upon the whole, it would be difficult to name a city which unites so many social advantages, and where a person of cultivated mind and moderate fortune could pass his time more agreeably.

The most convenient mode of imparting information to strangers, is to select a particular district of the city to be perambulated, describing the objects of interest on the way. With this view, we shall visit all the more important public buildings and institutions in successive walks, adding in notes such collateral or subordinate information, as may appear necessary to convey a more accurate idea of the city and its institutions, as well as other matter which may tend to enliven the dulness of dry topographical details.

WALK FIRST.*

REGISTER HOUSE—THEATRE-ROYAL—STAMP-OFFICE—POST-OFFICE—PRISON—BRIDEWELL—CALTON HILL—STEWART'S MONUMENT—OBSERVATORY—PLAYFAIR'S MONUMENT—CAMERA OBSCURA—NELSON'S MONUMENT—NATIONAL MONUMENT—HIGH SCHOOL—BURNS'S MONUMENT—HOLYROOD PALACE AND ABBEY—ARTHUR'S SEAT—HOUSE OF JOHN KNOX—NORTH BRIDGE.

THE central situation of the building, and the large number of hotels in its neighbourhood, points out

THE REGISTER HOUSE

as an appropriate starting point. This handsome edifice, designed by the celebrated Robert Adam, is the Depository of the Public Records.† It forms a square of 200 feet,

* The several Walks are indicated by different colours on the Map of the City prefixed. Walk First is coloured *Red*. When the *continued* line of colour is exchanged for a *dotted* line, it is to be understood that tourists who cannot accomplish the whole distance may omit the dotted portion of the Walk.

† This important establishment includes various offices, such as the offices of the Clerks and Extractors of the Court of Session, of the Jury Court, and of the Court of Justiciary, the office of the Great and Privy Seal, of the Chancery, the Lord Lyon's office, the Bill-Chamber, &c. But it is most celebrated for the

surmounted by a dome of fifty feet diameter. It contains upwards of 100 apartments for the transaction of public

different Registers which are there kept, and from which it derives its name. The most important and useful of these are the Registers of Sasines, of Inhibitions, and of Adjudications.

When a person wishes either to dispose absolutely of a landed estate in Scotland, or to grant a security over it (such as an heritable bond), it is necessary for him not only to grant a conveyance of the property to the purchaser or creditor, as the case may be, but also to give him Infeftment or Sasine, which is a symbolical delivery of the land. An instrument of Sasine is then written out by a notary-public, which must be recorded in the Register of Sasines. The date of recording is held to be the date of the Sasine, and the party whose Sasine is *first recorded* is preferred to the property. The Sasine may be recorded either in the General Register for all Scotland, which is kept in the Register House at Edinburgh, or in the particular Register for the County where the lands lie. These County Registers are transmitted at stated periods to the Keeper of the Records in Edinburgh.

This is the manner in which a person *voluntarily* divests himself of his lands: but there are also two kinds of diligence—Inhibition and Adjudication—by which an individual's heritable property may be affected without his consent. By the former, a debtor is prohibited from conveying or burdening his property to the prejudice of the creditor using the inhibition; by the latter, he is divested of the property, which, by a decree of the Court, is declared to belong to his creditor, in satisfaction of his debt. An inhibition must be executed, and with the execution of it recorded within forty days of its date, either in the General Register of Inhibitions at Edinburgh, or in the particular Register for the County, which, like the County Registers of Sasines, are transmitted at stated periods to the Keeper of the Records at Edinburgh. An abbreviate of a decree of adjudication must be recorded within sixty days of its date, in a register kept in the Register House for that purpose, called the Register of Abbreviates of Adjudication.

A person, therefore, who wishes either to purchase a property, or make a loan over it, may, by a search of the Register of Sasines, Inhibitions, and Adjudications, ascertain whether there has been any previous sale or conveyance of it by the proprietor or his predecessors—to what extent it may be burdened with debts—whether the proprietor has been prohibited by inhibition from granting any voluntary conveyance—or whether there has been any judicial assignation of it by adjudication. It is a principle of the Scotch law, that no party who has possessed a property upon an heritable title for forty years shall be disquieted in his possession thereafter; and, also, that any party who may have possessed a title to a property without insisting in or prosecuting it for a period of forty years shall be held to have abandoned his right. A forty years' search of the records, showing that no incumbrances exist, is therefore generally considered sufficient evidence that the property is not liable to any burden or ground of eviction, and that any one may with safety either purchase it or lend money on its security. No such assurance of the safety of a transaction, relative to landed property, can be obtained in England, nor probably in any other country in Europe. The consequence is, that Scotch mortgages form a very favourite investment with those capitalists who are more anxious to secure the safety of the capital itself, than a high rate of interest.

business. Among these the great room, in which the older records are deposited, is distinguished for its handsome proportions. Admission can only be obtained by an introduction to some of the public officers. In front of the building will stand the fine EQUESTRIAN STATUE of the DUKE OF WELLINGTON, by Steele, and on the opposite side of the street is

THE THEATRE-ROYAL.

Its exterior is plain almost to meanness, but its internal accommodation is excellent. Although theatrical amusements are not very warmly supported in the city, the management of the theatre is most efficient, and the regular company of a highly respectable order.*

Proceeding due east, we enter Waterloo Place, and on the right pass successively the STAMP OFFICE and the POST OFFICE. The lightness of the open colonnades on either side of the street are generally much admired by English strangers. It was upon entering this street, and contemplating the Calton Hill before him, that George IV. exclaimed, in royal rapture, "How superb!" Still advancing in the same direction, we reach the stair leading to the Calton Hill, from the top of which may be seen, in the churchyard across the street, the circular tower erected as a monument to David Hume the Historian. In the same churchyard stands an obelisk erected in 1845 to the memory of Muir, Palmer, Skirving, Gerrald, and Margarot, who suffered banishment for their efforts in the cause of popular freedom in 1794. However worthy the object, it may well be questioned whether human ingenuity could have devised a structure worse fitted for such a site, or more uncongenial to the surrounding architecture. The GAOL is immediately to the east of the churchyard, and a little farther along, in the same direction, is BRIDEWELL. These institutions are now consolidated into one prison. Strangers are admitted only when accompanied by a member of the Prison-Board.

* A smaller theatre, under the same management, is open during the summer months. It stands at the head of Leith Walk, but possesses no architectural attraction.

Upon the left hand, in ascending the second flight of steps to the hill, is the graceful MONUMENT TO DUGALD STEWART, a reproduction, with some variations, of the Choragic monument of Lysicrates. For the design of this monument, Edinburgh is indebted to the classical taste of Mr. Playfair. Close by are THE OBSERVATORY, and MONUMENT to PROFESSOR PLAYFAIR. The unshapely building, occupying a prominent position a little to the west, is the OLD OBSERVATORY. Upon the summit of the hill stands NELSON'S MONUMENT, a structure more ponderous than elegant, "modelled exactly after a Dutch skipper's spy-glass, or a butter-churn,"* but which, though wholly destitute of grandeur of design, becomes impressive from its magnitude and elevated site. The prospect from the top of the monument is very fine; the admission-fee is threepence. Near Nelson's Monument are the twelve columns of the NATIONAL MONUMENT, a structure intended to commemorate the heroes who fell at Waterloo. The splendour of the projected building (which was to be a literal reproduc-

tion of the Parthenon) was worthy of so patriotic a cause, but, unfortunately, the architectural ambition of the projectors was far in advance of the pecuniary means at their

* The Modern Athens. By a Modern Greek. London, 1825.

G. Aikman

HIGH SCHOOL EDINBURGH.

disposal, and the monument consequently remains unfinished. It cannot fail to be lamented, not only by all Scotsmen, but by every man of taste, that this attempt to restore one of the "glories of the antique world," upon a site worthy of its fame, should thus be defeated by the want of funds. So far as the building has proceeded, the workmanship is masterly, affording a very fine example of Edinburgh masonry. The view with which our text is illustrated represents the existing condition of this modern ruin.

On the southern slope of the hill, overlooking the buildings of the Old Town,

THE HIGH SCHOOL

occupies a site worthy of its architectural beauty. The business of the school is conducted by a Rector, four Classical Masters, Teachers of French and German, of Writing, Arithmetic, and Mathematics, and of Fencing and Gymnastics. Of these the first five have a small endowment from the city, in addition to the Class-fees. Although essentially a classical seminary, due consideration is given to those collateral branches of learning which form a necessary part of a liberal education. The extent of the building affords ample accommodation for conducting the business of instruction upon the most approved principles; and the play-ground, extending to nearly two acres, commands a fine prospect of the Old Town, Arthur's Seat, and the adjacent country.* Opposite the High School, close upon

* In 1823, the increasing population of the city appeared to demand the institution of another seminary for the same branches of learning as the High School. THE NEW ACADEMY was accordingly then founded in the northern suburbs of the city by an influential body of the inhabitants, and its situation renders it more convenient for those residing in that neighbourhood. In both institutions the instruction of the pupils is conducted with the utmost zeal and success, many of them, after completing their curriculum of study, carrying off the highest honours in the Universities of Oxford and Cambridge. Still more recently has been instituted THE SOUTHERN ACADEMY, for the convenience of the inhabitants of that quarter of the city. Here also the instruction of the pupils is most judiciously superintended. To the admirable mental culture these institutions afford may principally be imputed the advanced intelligence which distinguishes the great body of the inhabitants of the Scottish Metropolis, a large proportion of the children of the higher and middle classes receiv-

the road side, stands BURNS'S MONUMENT. The statue of the Poet by Flaxman, which for some time adorned the interior, has now been placed in the University Library.

From this point a descent may be made bv a footpath to the North Back of the Canongate, at the Lower end of which the stranger will reach

HOLYROOD PALACE.

This ancient residence of Scottish Royalty is a handsome building of a quadrangular form, with a central court ninety-four feet square. Its front is flanked with double castellated towers, imparting to the building that military character which the events of Scottish History have so often proved to have been requisite in her Royal residences.

The changes which from time to time the edifice has undergone render it a matter of difficulty to affix a precise date to any part of it. The towers of the north-west corner, built by James V., are understood to be the most ancient portion of the present building. In 1822, previous to the visit of George IV., some improvements were made in its internal accommodation, and since that time its walls have undergone a thorough repair at the expense of the Crown. The most interesting relic is the BED OF QUEEN MARY, which remains in the same state as when last occupied by that unhappy Princess. The CLOSET, where the murderers of Rizzio surprised their victim, is also an object of interest to visiters. This bloody tragedy was acted on the 9th of March 1566. "The Queen was seated at supper in a small cabinet adjoining to her bedroom, with the Countess of Argyle, Rizzio, and one or two other persons. Darnley suddenly entered the apartment, and, without addressing or saluting the company, gazed on Rizzio with a sullen and vindictive look; after him followed Lord Ruthven, pale and ghastly, having risen from a bed of long

ing their education in one or other of these seminaries. Besides the public Institutions, there are many admirably conducted private schools. Those interested in the instruction of the humbler ranks would do well to visit Dr. BELL'S SCHOOL in Niddry Street, where a very large number of children of both sexes receive the benefit of a useful education.

QUEEN MARY'S BED-CHAMBER.

sickness to be chief actor in this savage deed; other armed men appeared behind. Ruthven called upon Rizzio to come forth from a place which he was unworthy to hold. The miserable Italian, perceiving he was the destined victim of this violent intrusion, started up, and seizing the Queen by the skirts of her gown, implored her protection. Mary was speedily forced by the King from his hold. George Douglas, a bastard of the Angus family, snatched the King's own dagger from his side, and struck Rizzio a blow; he was then dragged into the outer apartment, and slain with fifty-six wounds. The Queen exhausted herself in prayers and entreaties for the wretched man's life; but when she was at length told that her servant was slain, she said, 'I will then dry my tears, and study revenge.' During the perpetration of this murder, Morton, the chancellor of the kingdom, whose duty it was to enforce the laws of the realm, kept the doors of the Palace with 160 armed men, to ensure the perpetration of the murder."*

Stains are still shown at the door of the apartment, said to be produced by the blood of the murdered man.† The

* SCOTT'S *Scotland*, vol. ii., p. 105.

† A pleasant story, suggested by these reputed blood-marks, occurs in the introductory chapter to the Second Series of Chronicles of the Canongate. Our readers, we are assured, will thank us for enlivening our narrative by here introducing it.

"My long habitation in the neighbourhood," says Mr. Chrystal Croftangry, "and the quiet respectability of my habits, have given me a sort of intimacy with good Mrs. Policy, the housekeeper in that most interesting part of the old building, called Queen Mary's Apartments. But a circumstance which lately happened has conferred upon me greater privileges; so that, indeed, I might, I believe, venture on the exploit of Chatelet, who was executed for being found secreted at midnight in the very bedchamber of Scotland's mistress.

"It chanced, that the good lady I have mentioned, was, in the discharge of her function, showing the apartments to a Cockney from London;—not one of your quiet, dull, commonplace visitors, who gape, yawn, and listen with an acquiescent *umph*, to the information doled out by the provincial cicerone. No such thing—this was the brisk alert agent of a great house in the city, who missed no opportunity of doing business, as he termed it—that is, of putting off the goods of his employers, and improving his own account of commission. He had fidgeted through the suite of apartments, without finding the least opportunity to touch upon that which he considered as the principal end of his existence. Even the story of Rizzio's assassination presented no ideas to this emissary of commerce, until the housekeeper appealed, in support of her narrative, to the dusky stains of blood upon the floor.

largest apartment in the Palace is the Picture Gallery, which measures 150 feet long, by 27 broad. Upon the walls of this room are suspended the portraits of 106 Scottish Kings, in a style of art truly barbarous. They appear to be " mostly by the same hand, painted either from the ima-

" 'These are the stains,' she said: 'nothing will remove them from the place —there they have been for two hundred and fifty years—and there they will remain while the floor is left standing—neither water nor any thing else will ever remove them from that spot.'

" Now, our Cockney, amongst other articles, sold Scouring Drops, as they are called, and a stain of two hundred and fifty years' standing was interesting to him, not because it had been caused by the blood of a Queen's favourite, slain in her apartment, but because it offered so admirable an opportunity to prove the efficacy of his unequalled Detergent Elixir. Down on his knees went our friend, but neither in horror nor devotion.

" 'Two hundred and fifty years, ma'am, and nothing take it away? Why, if it had been five hundred, I have something in my pocket will fetch it out in five minutes. D'ye see this elixir, ma'am? I will show you the stain vanish in a moment.'

" Accordingly, wetting one end of his handkerchief with the all-deterging specific, he began to rub away on the planks, without heeding the remonstrances of Mrs. Policy. She, good soul, stood at first in astonishment, like the Abbess in St. Bridget's, when a profane visitant drank up the vial of brandy which had long passed muster among the relics of the cloister for the tears of the blessed saint. The venerable guardian of St. Bridget probably expected the interference of her patroness—She of Holy Rood might, perhaps, hope that David Rizzio's spectre would arise to prevent the profanation. But Mrs. Policy stood not long in the silence of horror. She uplifted her voice, and screamed as loudly as Queen Mary herself, when the dreadful deed was in the act of perpetration—

'Harrow now out! and walawa!' she cried.

" I happened to be taking my morning walk in the adjoining gallery, pondering in my mind why the kings of Scotland, who hung around me, should be each and every one painted with a nose like the knocker of a door, when, lo! the walls once more re-echoed with such shrieks, as formerly were as often heard in the Scottish Palaces as were sounds of revelry and music. Somewhat surprised at such an alarm in a place so solitary, I hastened to the spot, and found the well-meaning traveller scrubbing the floor like a housemaid, while Mrs. Policy, dragging him by the skirts of the coat, in vain endeavoured to divert him from his sacrilegious purpose. It cost me some trouble to explain to the zealous purifier of silk stockings, embroidered waistcoats, broad cloth, and deal planks, that there were such things in the world as stains which ought to remain indelible, on account of the associations with which they are connected. Our good friend viewed every thing of the kind only as the means of displaying the virtue of his vaunted commodity. He comprehended, however. that he would not be permitted to proceed to exemplify its powers on the present occasion, as two or three inhabitants appeared, who, like me, threatened to maintain the housekeeper's side of the question. He therefore took his leave, muttering that he had always heard the Scots were a nasty people, but

gination, or porters hired to sit for the purpose."* In the olden time, many a scene of courtly gaiety has enlivened this gloomy hall; among the last were the balls given by Prince Charles Edward in 1745. The election of the representative Peers of Scotland and the levees and entertainments given by the Lord High Commissioner to the General Assembly of the Church of Scotland, are now the only ceremonies performed within its walls. In the south side of the quadrangle is the Hall of State fitted up for the levees of George IV. in 1822; and in the eastern side is the suite of apartments occupied by Charles X. (of France) and his family in 1830-3. Her present Majesty has rescued the Palace from the neglect into which it had fallen, by making it her halting place when visiting her Highland residence. The rooms are shown to strangers by the domestics of the Duke of Hamilton, hereditary keeper. Three different persons are employed in exhibiting the Palace and Abbey, the gratuities being left to the discretion of visitors. Various attempts have been made by the Magistrates and Council of the city to induce the Duke of Hamilton to sanction the exaction of a stated fee of small amount, or to make some other arrangement by which the exhibition should be placed on a more satisfactory footing. These attempts having been unsuccessful, the Municipal body passed a resolution expressive of their opinion, that the payment of 1s. by each party not exceeding six, to each of the exhibitors, should be regarded as adequate remuneration. It may at the same time be observed, that the payment of even this sum is wholly dependent on the pleasure of visitors, as Mr. Hume, when referring in the House of Commons to the estimate for the repairs of the Royal Palaces in Scotland, observed, that "he held in his hand a letter from the Duke of Hamilton, stating that orders had

had no idea they carried it so far as to choose to have the floors of their palaces blood-boltered, like Banquo's ghost, when to remove them would have cost but a hundred drops of the Infallible Detergent Elixir, prepared and sold by Messrs. Scrub and Rub, in five shilling and ten shilling bottles, each bottle being marked with the initials of the inventor, to counterfeit which would be to incur the pains of forgery."

* Humphrey Clinker.

been given for the opening of Holyrood Palace free of charge to the public."

On the north side of the Palace are the ruins of the ABBEY OF HOLYROODHOUSE, founded in 1128, by David I., a prince whose prodigal liberality to the clergy drew from James VI. the pithy observation that he was "a sair sanct for the Crown."* Of this building nothing now remains but the mouldering ruins of the chapel, situated immediately behind the palace. "It was fitted up by Charles I. as a chapel royal, that it might serve as a model of the English form of worship, which he was anxious to introduce into Scotland. He was himself crowned in it in 1633. James II. (VII. of Scotland) afterwards rendered it into a model of Catholic worship, to equally little purpose. Since the fall of the roof in 1768, it has been a ruin."† In the south-east corner are deposited the remains of David II., James II., James V., and Magdalen his Queen, Henry Lord Darnley, and other illustrious persons. The precincts of the Abbey, including Arthur's Seat and Salisbury Crags, are a sanctuary for insolvent debtors. The limit of the privileged territory, on the side next the town, extends to about a hundred yards from the Palace.‡

The immediate proximity of Arthur's Seat may induce many tourists to ascend the hill.§ Its height is 822 feet

* The legend connected with its foundation is as follows:—The pious David, while hunting in the forest of Drumsheuch, was placed in the utmost peril by the attack of a stag. When defending himself from his assailant, a cross miraculously descended from heaven into his hand, upon seeing which the stag fled in dismay. The sequel is more credible. In a dream which visited the slumbers of the monarch, he was commanded to erect an abbey on the spot of his remarkable preservation; and, in obedience to the heavenly mandate, he founded the Abbey of Holyroodhouse.

† CHAMBERS' *Picture of Scotland.*

‡ In Croftangrie, a narrow lane close by the Abbey, is a house said to have been occupied by the Regent Murray.

§ "A nobler contrast there can hardly exist than that of the huge city, dark with the smoke of ages, and groaning with the various sounds of active industry or idle revel, and the lofty and craggy hill, silent and solitary as the grave; one exhibiting the full tide of existence, pressing and precipitating itself forward with the force of an inundation; the other resembling some time-worn anchorite, whose life passes as silent and unobserved as the slender rill, which escapes unheard, and scarce seen, from the fountain of his patron saint. The city resembles the busy temple, where the modern Comus and Mammon hold their

above the level of the sea. The ascent, which is neither difficult nor dangerous, may be made either by the footpath leading past St. Anthony's well, with St. Anthony's Chapel on the left; or by following Victoria Road, commencing at the northern base of the hill, to the point presenting the easiest access to the summit. This point is reached after passing Dunsapie Loch, on the left of the road, a spot as sequestered as if there were no such city as Edinburgh within a distance of 50 miles. Descending again to the road, the tourist may prosecute the beautiful walk round the hill, and return to the city by the south side; or he may retrace his steps and proceed up the Canongate from Holyrood.

If the footpath ascent be preferred, the pedestrian proceeds up the face of the hill, passing on the left the ruins of St. Anthony's Chapel,* while upon the right is the semicircular ridge of bold and precipitous rocks known by the name of Salisbury Crags. The walk along the top of these Crags commands beautiful prospects of the city, as also

court, and thousands sacrifice ease, independence, and virtue itself, at their shrine; the misty and lonely mountain seems as a throne to the majestic but terrible genius of feudal times, where the same divinities dispensed coronets and domains to those who had heads to devise, and arms to execute, bold enterprises.—SIR WALTER SCOTT—*Introduction to the Chronicles of the Canongate.*

* The spot where Jeanie Deans is represented to have met with the ruffian Robertson may be seen in ascending the hill, although no remains of the cairn are now visible. "It was situated," says the novelist, "in the depth of the valley behind Salisbury Crags, which has for a background the north-western shoulder of the mountain, called Arthur's Seat, on whose descent still remain the ruins of what was once a chapel, or hermitage, dedicated to Saint Anthony the Eremite. A better site for such a building could hardly have been selected; for the chapel, situated among the rude and pathless cliffs, lies in a desert, even in the immediate vicinity of a rich, populous, and tumultuous capital; and the hum of the city might mingle with the orisons of the recluses, conveying as little of worldly interest as if it had been the roar of the distant ocean. Beneath the steep ascent on which these ruins are still visible was, and perhaps is still pointed out, the place where the wretch Nicol Muschat had closed a long scene of cruelty towards his unfortunate wife, by murdering her with circumstances of uncommon barbarity. The execration in which the man's crime was held extended itself to the place where it was perpetrated, which was marked by a small *cairn,* or heap of stones, composed of those which each passenger had thrown there in testimony of abhorrence, and on the principle, it would seem, of the ancient British malediction, 'May you have a cairn for your burial-place.'"—*Heart of Mid-Lothian.*

does the promenade immediately below.* From this walk may be seen the site of the cottage of Davie Deans, and other objects rendered imperishably interesting by the novels of Sir Walter Scott.

Retracing our steps to Holyrood, and proceeding up the Canongate, we reach, upon the right, a narrow archway conducting to a court known by the name of the WHITE HORSE CLOSE, a singular looking group of houses, which, in ancient times, was a well-frequented *hostelrie*. The White Horse Inn is understood to be the oldest place of the kind in the city, of which the premises preserve, in any measure, their original integrity. It is now partitioned into dwelling-houses of the lowest class. A little further up the street, on the opposite side, is QUEENSBERRY HOUSE, a large dull looking structure, erected by William, first Duke of Queensberry. Charles, the third Duke, was born here in 1698, and his sprightly Duchess, Lady Catharine Hyde, here patronised the poet Gay. The building is now converted into a "House of Refuge for the Destitute." Continuing to ascend the street, we pass, upon the right hand, the un-

* "If I were to choose a spot from which the rising or setting sun could be seen to the greatest possible advantage, it would be that wild path winding around the foot of the high belt of semi-circular rocks, called Salisbury Crags, and marking the verge of the steep descent which slopes down into the glen on the south-eastern side of the City of Edinburgh. The prospect, in its general outline, commands a close-built, high-piled city, stretching itself out in a form which, to a romantic imagination, may be supposed to represent that of a dragon; now a noble arm of the sea, with its rocks, isles, distant shores, and boundary of mountains; and now a fair and fertile champaign country, varied with hill, dale, and rock, and skirted by the picturesque ridge of the Pentland mountains. But as the path gently circles around the base of the cliffs, the prospect, composed as it is of these enchanting and sublime objects, changes at every step, and presents them blended with, or divided from each other, in every possible variety which can gratify the eye and the imagination. When a piece of scenery so beautiful, yet so varied—so exciting by its intricacy, and yet so sublime—is lighted up by the tints of morning or of evening, and displays all that variety of shadowy depth, exchanged with partial brilliancy, which gives character even to the tamest of landscapes, the effect approaches near to enchantment. This path used to be my favourite evening and morning resort when engaged with a favourite author or new subject of study."—*Heart of Mid-Lothian.*

The solid and commodious pathway which has now superseded the winding footpath above described was suggested by this glowing eulogy of the surrounding landscape.

gainly fabric called the CANONGATE KIRK, and next reach the Court-Room and Jail of the Canongate. In a niche of the latter building are painted the arms of the Canongate, with the motto, "*Sic itur ad astra,*" as if the worthy inhabitants of this ancient burgh regarded the prison as the surest avenue to heaven. A little further up the street, on the left, is MORAY HOUSE, the ancient mansion of the Earls of Moray, erected in 1618. Oliver Cromwell, on his first visit to Edinburgh, in 1648, took up his residence here, and established friendly relations with the leaders of the Covenanters. From the balcony in front of the building, the Marquis of Argyle and his family saw the Marquis of Montrose conducted to prison, from whence he was shortly afterwards led to execution. The house is now occupied as the Normal School of the Free Church. Still ascending the street, we pass upon the right and left, Leith Wynd and St. Mary's Wynd, two narrow streets, dedicated to the sale of old clothes. At the head of the Netherbow, where it expands into the High Street, stands the HOUSE OF JOHN KNOX. The building having fallen into a very dilapidated state, the public authorities, in 1849, condemned it as unsafe, and ordered it to be taken down ; but a subscription for its preservation having been originated by some of the more public-spirited of the citizens, the calamity and reproach of destroying this interesting memorial of the great Reformer have been averted. In its restoration the most scrupulous care was taken to preserve every feature of the original building, and this fortunately proved less difficult than had been imagined, as, on taking off the external coating of decayed lath and plaster, it was found that the main features of the ancient edifice consist of substantial masonry and oaken timbers, which now promise, with ordinary care, to last for centuries. The removal of some of the extraneous modern additions brought to light several interesting features of the original edifice, and, in particular, an elegantly sculptured slab, with a coat of arms and initials, closely corresponding in ornamental details to a tablet, bearing the arms of the Queen Regent, Mary de

CANONGATE JAIL.

Guise, formerly on her house at Leith. Over the door is the following admonitory inscription :—

Lufe.God.abobe.al.and.your.nichbour.as.your.self.

and close beneath the window from which KNOX is said to have preached to the populace there has long existed a rude effigy of the Reformer stuck upon the corner in the attitude of addressing the passers by. The woodcut in

the text represents the building before the recent repairs, and the reader, by comparing it with the structure itself, will be enabled to judge how perfectly this restoration has been effected. Pursuing his way up the High Street, the stupendous height of many of the houses, and the air of antique majesty, which, in spite of some modern innovations, still distinguishes the street, cannot fail to strike the attention of the tourist. From either side descend numerous lanes or *closes* of a width frequently limited to six

CHALMERS'S CLOSE—HIGH STREET.

feet, and so steep as to be of very laborious ascent. In these closes are the squalid abodes of some of the lowest of the population.

Upon reaching the North Bridge, our first walk will terminate by returning to the Register Office. If the stranger desires to prolong it, he will continue to ascend the High Street, commencing with the Tron Church. For the sake of arrangement, however, we must designate the next division of his progress the Second Walk.

WALK SECOND.*

TRON CHURCH—ROYAL EXCHANGE—ST. GILES'S CATHEDRAL—PARLIAMENT HOUSE—ADVOCATES' LIBRARY—SIGNET LIBRARY—COUNTY HALL — BANK OF SCOTLAND — CASTLE — GEORGE IV. BRIDGE HERIOT'S HOSPITAL.

PROCEEDING as before from the Register Office, the stranger will now walk along the North Bridge. This bridge was founded in 1763, and completed in 1769. On the 3d of August in the latter year, the arches of three vaults in the south abutment, in consequence of an error in construction, gave way with a tremendous crash, and filled the whole city with alarm. Five persons were killed by the accident. There is a floating prediction that a similar catastrophe is once more destined to occur. From the parapet, on each side, is an extensive view of the city towards the east and the west. For architectural effect, the buildings upon the Calton Hill are perhaps more advantageously grouped in the view from the northern end of the open space of this bridge, than from any other point, although the most prominent deformity on the hill—the Martyrs' Monument—is offensively conspicuous. In the spacious area seen immediately below, when looking over the western parapet,

* This Walk is coloured *green* on the Map.

are the termini of the Edinburgh and Glasgow, the Edinburgh, Perth, and Dundee, and the North British Railways. The same area also contains the fruit and vegetable markets. From these, an ascent by stairs conducts to the fish, butcher, and poultry markets, which are situated upon successive terraces communicating with each other. The terminus of the North British Railway extends to the area on the east side of the bridge. Proceeding to the upper end of the North Bridge, the stranger again reaches the High Street, part of which he traversed in the preceding walk. Its length from the Castle to Holyrood Palace is about a mile.* At the point where the High Street and the North and South Bridges cross each other, stands the Tron Church, an edifice of no architectural pretension. It derived its name from a *tron* or weighing beam in its immediate neighbourhood, to which, in former times, it was customary to nail false notaries and other malefactors by the ears. Its clock is provided with a dial plate of dimmed glass, which is lighted with gas from the inside after nightfall.

Ascending the High Street,

THE ROYAL EXCHANGE BUILDINGS

stand upon the right hand side of the way, opposite St. Giles's Cathedral. The Council Chamber for the meetings of the Magistracy, and various other apartments for the transaction of municipal business, occupy the side of the quadrangle opposite the entrance. Parties proposing to visit the Crown Room in the Castle, will here obtain orders of admission on the terms mentioned on page 50 of the present work. The spot where the city Cross formerly stood

* Although we have here given the general designation of High Street to this imposing line of buildings, its various divisions, commencing at the Castle, are severally known by the names *Castle Hill, Lawnmarket, High Street, Netherbow* and *Canongate*. A more stirring spectacle can scarcely be imagined than the progress of Her Majesty along this street, from Holyrood to the Castle. From ground to roof the windows of these gigantic dwellings were crowded with fair and happy faces, while the advance of the Royal Pair was heralded by the waving of thousands of white handkerchiefs, and by the enthusiastic cheering of the populace, who lined the street on either side, and of the various public bodies who occupied the temporary platforms along the line of progress.

is now indicated by a radiated pavement about twenty-five yards from the entrance to the Exchange. It was demolished in 1756. On the morning of the day when the workmen began their labours, "some gentlemen who had spent the night over a social bottle, caused wine and glasses be carried thither, mounted the ancient fabric, and solemnly drank its dirge."*

ST. GILES'S CATHEDRAL

is nearly opposite the Royal Exchange. It derives its name from its patron, St. Giles, abbot and confessor, and

* "Dun-Edin's Cross, a pillar'd stone,
Rose on a turret octagon;
But now is razed that monument
Whence royal edict rang,
And voice of Scotland's law was sent
In glorious trumpet clang.
O! be his tomb as lead to lead;
Upon its dull destroyer's head.
A minstrel's malison is said."—

Marmion, canto v. st. 25.

tutelar saint of Edinburgh.* The date of its foundation is unknown. It is first mentioned in the year 1359, in a charter of David II. In 1466, it was made a collegiate church, and no fewer than forty altars were at this period supported within its walls. The Scottish poet, Gavin Douglas, (the translator of Virgil,) was for some time Provost of St. Giles. After the Reformation it was partitioned into four places of worship, and the sacred vessels and relics which it contained, including the arm-bone referred to in the preceding note, were seized by the Magistrates of the City, and the proceeds of their sale applied to the repairing of the building. In 1603, before the departure of James VI. to take possession of the throne of England, he attended divine service in this church, after which he delivered a farewell address to his Scottish subjects, assuring them of his unalterable affection. "His words were often interrupted by the tears of the whole audience, who, though they exulted at the King's prosperity, were melted into sorrow by these tender declarations."† On the 13th October 1643, the Solemn League and Covenant was sworn to and subscribed within its walls by the Committee of Estates of Parliament, the Commission of the Church, and the English Commission. The Regent Murray and the Marquis of Montrose are interred near the centre of the south side of the church,

* Mr. Stark, in his very accurate work, relates that the legend regarding St. Giles, describes him as "a native of Greece, born in the sixth century. On the death of his parents, he gave all his estate to the poor, and travelled into France, where he retired into the deep recess of a wilderness, near the conflux of the Rhone with the sea, and continued there for three years, living upon the spontaneous produce of the earth and the milk of a doe. Having obtained the reputation of extraordinary sanctity, various miracles were attributed to him; and he founded a monastery in Languedoc, long after known by the name of St. Giles. In the reign of James II., Mr. Preston of Gourton, a gentleman whose descendants still possess an estate in the county of Edinburgh, procured a supposed arm-bone of this holy man, which relic he most piously bequeathed to the Church of St. Giles in Edinburgh. In gratitude for this invaluable donation, the magistrates of the city, in 1454, considering that the said bone was 'freely left to oure moyer kirk of Saint Gele of Edinburgh, withoutyn ony condition makyn,' granted a charter in favour of Mr. Preston's heirs, by which the nearest heir of the name of Preston was entitled to the honour of carrying it in all public processions. This honour the family of Preston continued to enjoy till the Reformation."—*Picture of Edinburgh*, p. 217.

† ROBERTSON'S *History of Scotland*.

and on the outside of its northern wall is the monument of Napier of Merchiston, the inventor of logarithms.

The cathedral is now divided into three places of worship, viz. the High Church, the Tolbooth Church, and a Hall, originally intended for the meetings of the General Assembly, but which, after its completion, was found to be unfit for the purpose. In the High Church the Magistrates of the City, and the Judges of the Court of Session, attend divine service in their official robes. The patronage of these, as well as of all the other city parish churches, is vested in the Magistrates and Town Council. The remains of John Knox, the intrepid Ecclesiastical Reformer, were deposited in the cemetery of St. Giles, which formerly occupied the ground where the buildings of the Parliament Square now stand.

So lately as the year 1817, all the spaces between the buttresses of the church were occupied by small shops called the *krames*, grafted upon the walls of the building ; the unholy fires of the shopkeepers begriming with their smoke the whole external surface of the sacred edifice. The annexed engraving represents this curious alliance between the sacred and profane, while the wood-cut introduced into the text exhibits the building in its present state. With the exception of the spire, the whole of the external walls of the Cathedral have in recent years been renovated—a circumstance which has materially impaired the venerable aspect of the building.

In the centre of the Parliament Square, of which the Cathedral just described may be said to form the northern side, stands THE EQUESTRIAN STATUE OF CHARLES II., which, in vigour of design and general effect, still maintains its rank as the best specimen of metal statuary which Edinburgh possesses.

The Police Office, the Chambers of the Court of Exchequer, the Parliament House, and the Libraries of the Faculty of Advocates and of the Writers to the Signet, form the eastern, western, and southern sides of the Square.

THE PARLIAMENT HOUSE

is situated in the south-west angle. The large hall, now

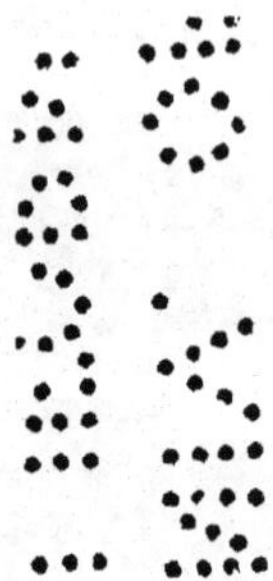

known by the name of the *Outer-House*, is the place in which the Scottish Parliament met before the Union. This hall is 122 feet long by 49 broad. Its roof is of oak, arched and handsomely finished. It contains two statues—one of Henry Dundas, the first Lord Melville, and the other of that eminent lawyer, Lord President Blair, who died in 1811. At the south end of the Outer-House are four small chambers or Courts, in which the Lords Ordinary sit. Entering from the east side, are two larger Courts of modern and elegant structure, appropriated to the First and Second Divisions of the Court, before whom are tried those cases which are of unusual importance or difficulty, or where the judgment of a Lord Ordinary has been brought under review of the Court by a reclaimer or appeal. Adjoining to the Court-Rooms of the Divisions is another Court-Room of nearly similar appearance, in which sits the High Court of Justiciary, the supreme criminal tribunal of Scotland.

In session time, and during the hours of business, the Outer-House presents a very animated scene. As all the Courts open into it, it affords a very convenient promenade or lounging place for those counsel or agents whose cases are not then actually going on in Court. The well-employed advocates may be seen flitting from bar to bar, or Court to Court, while agents whose causes have just been called, may be observed pressing through the crowd, with anxious face and hurried step, looking out for the counsel, whose absence from the debate might be fatal to their clients. Occasionally may be seen some unfortunate litigant, listening with all reverence and humility, to an opinion on the merits of his case from one of the fathers of the bar, his countenance reflecting the alternate lights and shadows of hope and apprehension. The less employed and unemployed counsel and agents, and a number of loungers who make this hall a place of resort, may be seen in groups conversing together, in every variety of tone and manner, from the gravity of consultation to the gaiety of uncontrolled merriment.*

* For an account of the various classes of Law Practitioners, see the foot-note, page 19.

THE ADVOCATES' LIBRARY

adjoins the Parliament House, with which it has a communication. It contains the most valuable collection of books in Scotland, the printed works amounting to 150,000 volumes, and the manuscripts to 1700. The collection of Scottish poetry is exceedingly rare and curious. The volumes in this department amount to nearly 400, and the number is receiving constant additions from the laudable ambition of the "Faculty," and the zeal of their librarian, to augment its treasures. Of the manuscripts, the most valuable are those relating to the civil and ecclesiastical history of Scotland. The funds of the Library are chiefly derived from the fees paid by each advocate, upon his entering as a member of the Faculty. It is also one of the five libraries which receive from Stationers' Hall a copy of every new work published in Great Britain or Ireland. No public institution in Great Britain is conducted with greater liberality. Strangers are freely admitted without introduction; and no one who is at all known, is ever denied the privilege of resorting to, and of reading or writing in the library. The members are entitled to borrow twenty-five volumes at one time, and to lend any of the books so borrowed to their friends. The literary wealth of the library is at present deposited in a suite of apartments neither spacious, elegant, nor commodious. It is proposed to build a new library in the neighbourhood for their reception. The office of principal librarian has been held by men eminently distinguished in the world of letters, Thomas Ruddiman, David Hume, and Adam Ferguson, having honoured the institution by filling this situation. More recently the office was held by David Irving, L L.D., an accomplished scholar and learned civilian, and it is at present filled by Mr. S. Halkett, a very eminent linguist.

THE SIGNET LIBRARY

is also immediately adjoining to the Parliament House. It

possesses two handsome rooms, one of which was acquired a few years ago from the Advocates' Library. These rooms, more especially the upper one, are well worthy the attention of strangers. This library is peculiarly rich in the department of history, more especially in British and Irish history. The total number of volumes it contains may be estimated at 50,000. It is supported exclusively by the contributions of the Writers to Her Majesty's Signet, and the same liberality which distinguishes the Advocates' Library, also prevails in the management of its affairs. The present librarian, Mr. David Laing, is distinguished by the extent and accuracy of his bibliographical knowledge. He also possesses that general acquaintance with literature which forms one of the most valuable qualifications for the office which he holds.

The County Hall stands at the western termination of the Libraries above described. The general plan is taken from the Temple of Erectheus at Athens, and the principal entrance, from the Choragic Monument of Thrasyllus. The Hall is decorated with a statue of Lord Chief Baron Dundas, by Chantrey.

The Old Tolbooth, sometimes called by the inhabitants

"The Heart of Mid-Lothian," and which, under this name, has become so renowned in the novel of Sir Walter Scott, formerly stood in the middle of the High Street, at the north-west corner of St. Giles's Church.* This gloomy looking building was built in 1561. From that period till the year 1640, it served for the accommodation of Parliament and the Courts of Justice, as well as for the confinement of prisoners; but after the erection of the present Parliament House, it was employed only as a prison. Its situation, jammed as it was into the middle of one of the chief thoroughfares of the city, was signally inconvenient, and in 1817, when the New Prison was prepared for the reception of inmates, the ancient pile of the Tolbooth was demolished. The great entrance-door, with its ponderous padlock and key, were removed to Abbotsford, the seat of Sir Walter Scott, where they are now to be seen, with the other curiosities of the place.†

Proceeding up the High Street, we pass, upon the left. George the Fourth's Bridge, and on the right, Bank Street, at the foot of which stands THE BANK OF SCOTLAND, an edifice of high architectural merit, erected at an expense of £75,000.‡ The fine gothic building on the left, the

* A few years ago a chartist orator, in addressing an audience upon the Calton Hill, commenced with the inauspicious phrase, "Men of the Heart of Mid-Lothian!" The compliment, which unquestionably belongs to the class called "left-handed," was, of course, acknowledged by an unanimous burst of laughter from the crowd.

† Alluding to the removal of these relics, Sir Walter observes, "It is not without interest, that we see the gateway through which so much of the stormy politics of a rude age, and the vice and misery of later times, had found their passage, now occupied in the service of rural economy. Last year, to complete the change, a tom-tit was pleased to build her nest within the lock of the Tolbooth—a strong temptation to have committed a sonnet, had the author, like Tony Lumpkin, been in a concatenation accordingly."

‡ The Bank of Scotland has the merit of having originated and established the distinctive principles of the Scottish Banking System. It is the earliest establishment of the kind in Scotland, having been incorporated by Act of the Scottish Parliament in 1695. The capital of the Bank—originally £100,000—is now £1,500,000; of which sum £1,000,000 has been paid up. In the year 1704, it commenced the issue of £1 notes—a practice universally adopted by Scottish Banks till the passing of Sir Robert Peel's bill of 1844, which limits the number of banks privileged to issue notes to those established at the period of the enactment

foundation stone of which was laid during the recent visit of Her Majesty, is VICTORIA HALL, erected as a place of meeting for the General Assembly of the Church of Scotland, and also used as one of the city churches. The noble spire of this building, which rises to the height of 241 feet, is one of the finest modern ornaments of the city, and from its commanding position there is scarcely any point from which it is not conspicuously seen. The length of the building from east to west is 141 feet. The design is by Mr. Gillespie Graham. At the head of the High Street, upon a precipitous rocky eminence, stands

THE CASTLE,

the most prominent building in the city, and one of the four fortresses which, by the Articles of Union, are to be kept constantly fortified.* The period of its foundation is unknown. There is no doubt, however, that it can boast a more remote antiquity than any other part of the city, and that it has formed the nucleus around which Edinburgh has arisen. The earliest name by which it is recognised in history, is *Castrum Puellarum*, or "The Camp of the Maidens," from the daughters of the Pictish kings being educated and brought up within its walls. It consists of a series of irregular fortifications, and although, before the invention of gunpowder, it might be considered impregnable, it is now a place of more apparent than real strength.

With the exception of the *Bank of Scotland*, the *Royal Bank of Scotland*, and the *British Linen Company*, all of which possess large capitals, there are no chartered banking associations in Scotland *with limited responsibility*. In all the other institutions of the kind, *the partners are jointly and severally liable for the debts of the company, to the whole extent of their fortunes*. And when, in addition to this security, it is considered that there is no limitation to the number of partners of which a banking company of Scotland may consist, and that the public records afford the means of ascertaining with absolute certainty, the real and heritable estate of which the partners may be possessed, it is obvious that the banking establishments of the country possess a solidity of basis highly advantageous to the community at large. "Whatever may be the defects of the Scotch Banking System," says Mr. M'Culloch, "it is probably superior to every other system hitherto established."

* The other fortresses included in this provision, are the Castles of Dumbarton, Blackness, and Stirling.

It can be approached only upon the eastern side. The other three sides are very precipitous ; some parts, as an English friend of our own observed, being *more than perpendicular.* Its elevation is 383 feet above the level of the sea, and, from various parts of the fortifications, a magnificent view of the surrounding country may be obtained. It contains accommodation for 2000 soldiers, and its armoury affords space for 30,000 stand of arms. Facing the north-east is the principal or Half-Moon Battery, mounted with twelve, eighteen, and twenty-four pounders, the only use of which, in these piping times of peace, is to fire on holidays and occasions of public rejoicing. The architectural effect of the Castle has been much marred by a clumsy pile of barracks on its western side, which, observes Sir Walter Scott, would be honoured by a comparison with the most vulgar cotton-mill.

In the earlier periods of Scottish history, this fortress experienced the vicissitudes common to the times, and was frequently taken and re-taken by various conflicting parties. In the present work, we can only advert to one or two of the more striking events in its annals.

In 1296, during the contest for the crown between Bruce and Baliol, it was besieged and taken by the English. It still remained in their possession in 1313, at which time it was strongly garrisoned and commanded by Piers Leland, a Lombard. This governor, having fallen under the suspicion of the garrison, was thrown into a dungeon, and another appointed to the command, in whose fidelity they had complete confidence. It has frequently been remarked, that in capturing fortresses, those attacks are generally most successful which are made upon points where the attempt appears the most desperate. Such was the case in the example now to be narrated. Randolph, Earl of Moray, was one day surveying the gigantic rock, and probably contemplating the possibility of a successful assault upon the fortress, when he was accosted by one of his men-at-arms with the question, " Do you think it impracticable, my lord ?" Randolph turned his eyes upon the querist, a man a little past the prime of life, but of a firm, well-knit figure, and bearing in his bright eye, and bold and open brow, indications of an intrepidity which had already made him remarkable in the Scottish army.

"Do you mean the rock, Francis?"* said the earl; "perhaps not, if we could borrow the wings of our gallant hawks."

"There are wings," replied Francis, with a thoughtful smile, "as strong, as buoyant, and as daring. My father was keeper of yonder fortress."

"What of that? you speak in riddles."

"I was then young, reckless, high-hearted; I was mewed up in that convent-like castle; my mistress was in the plain below—"

"Well, what then?"

"'Sdeath, my Lord, can you not imagine that I speak of the wings of love? Every night I descended that steep at the witching hour, and every morning before the dawn I crept back to my barracks. I constructed a light twelve-foot ladder, by means of which I was able to pass the places that are perpendicular; and so well, at length, did I become acquainted with the route, that in the darkest and stormiest night, I found my way as easily as when the moonlight enabled me to see my love in the distance, waiting for me at her cottage door."

"You are a daring, desperate, noble fellow, Francis! However, your motive is now gone; your mistress—"

"She is dead: say no more; but another has taken her place."

"Ay, ay, it's the soldier's way. Women will die, or even grow old; and what are we to do? Come, who is your mistress now?"

"MY COUNTRY! What I have done for love, I can do again for honour; and what *I* can accomplish, you, noble Randolph, and many of our comrades, can do far better.

* The soldier's name was William Frank. Mr. Leitch Ritchie here uses the novelist's license in dealing with the name, and in throwing the story into the form of a dialogue, but the events are strictly in accordance with the historical narrative.

Give me thirty picked men, and a twelve-foot ladder. and the fortress is our own!"

The Earl of Moray, whatever his real thoughts of the enterprise might have been, was not the man to refuse such a challenge. A ladder was provided, and thirty men chosen from the troops; and in the middle of a dark night, the party, commanded by Randolph himself, and guided by William Francis, set forth on their desperate enterprise.

By catching at crag after crag, and digging their fingers into the interstices of the rocks, they succeeded in mounting a considerable way; but the weather was now so thick, they could receive but little assistance from their eyes; and thus they continued to climb, almost in utter darkness, like men struggling up a precipice in the nightmare. They at length reached a shelving table of the cliff, above which the ascent, for ten or twelve feet, was perpendicular; and having fixed their ladder, the whole party lay down to recover breath.

From this place they could hear the tread and voices of the "check-watches" or patrol above; and surrounded by the perils of such a moment, it is not wonderful that some illusions may have mingled with their thoughts. They even imagined that they were seen from the battlements; although, being themselves unable to see the warders, this was highly improbable. It became evident, notwithstanding, from the words they caught here and there, in the pauses of the night-wind, that the conversation of the English soldiers above, related to a surprise of the castle; and, at length, these appalling words broke like thunder on their ears: "Stand! I see you well!" A fragment of the rock was hurled down at the same instant; and, as rushing from crag to crag, it bounded over their heads, Randolph and his brave followers, in this wild, helpless, and extraordinary situation, felt the damp of mortal terror gathering upon their brow, as they clung, with a death-grip, to the precipice.

The startled echoes of the rock were at length silent, and so were the voices above. The adventurers paused, listening breathless; no sound was heard but the sighing of the wind, and the measured tread of the sentinel, who had resumed his walk. The men thought they were in a dream, and no wonder; for the incident just mentioned, which is related by Barbour, was one of the most singular coincidences that ever occurred. The shout of the sentinel, and the missile he had thrown, were merely a boyish freak; and while listening to the echoes of the rock, he had not the smallest idea that the sounds which gave pleasure to him, carried terror, and almost despair, into the hearts of the enemy.

The adventurers, half uncertain whether they were not the victims of some illusion, determined that it was as safe to go on as to turn back; and pursuing their laborious and dangerous path, they at length reached the bottom of the wall. This last barrier they scaled by means of their ladder; and leaping down among the astonished check-watches, they cried their war-cry, and, in the midst of answering shouts of "treason! treason!" notwithstanding the desperate resistance of the garrison, captured the Castle of Edinburgh.*

Robert Bruce then entirely demolished its fortifications, that it might not again be occupied by a hostile power. The wisdom of this policy was subsequently proved by the conduct of Edward III. who, on his return from Perth, caused it to be rebuilt and strongly garrisoned. But his possession of it was destined to be of short duration. One of those stratagems characteristic of the adventurous spirit of the times, was successfully resorted to for its deliverance. In 1341, Sir William Douglas, with three other gentlemen, waited upon the governor. One of them, professing to be an English merchant, informed him that he had a vessel in the Forth richly laden with wine, beer, and biscuits exquisitely spiced, and produced at the same time samples of the cargo. The governor, pleased with their quality, agreed for the purchase of the whole, which the pretended captain requested permission to deliver early next day, to avoid interruption from the Scots. He accordingly arrived at the

* HEATH's Picturesque Annual. *Scott and Scotland*, pp. 174-7.

time appointed, attended by a dozen of armed followers, disguised as seamen, and the gates being opened for the reception of the provisions, they contrived, just in the entrance, to overturn one of the carriages, thus effectually preventing the closing of the gates. The porter and guards were then put to the sword, and the assailants being reinforced by Douglas and his party, who lay in ambush near the entrance, the English garrison was overpowered, and expelled from the castle.

During the reign of Queen Mary, when the country was distracted by intestine wars, this fortress was gallantly defended for the Queen by Kirkaldy of Grange. The rest of Scotland had submitted to the authority of Morton the Regent, Kirkaldy alone, with a few brave associates, remaining faithful to the cause of his Royal Mistress. Morton was unable, with the troops at his command, to reduce the garrison, but Elizabeth having sent Sir William Drury to his aid with 1500 foot, and a train of artillery, trenches were opened, and approaches regularly carried on against the castle. For three and thirty days Kirkaldy gallantly resisted the combined forces of the Scots and English, nor did he demand a parley till the fortifications were battered down, and the wells were dried up or choked with rubbish. Even then, with a heroism truly chivalrous, he determined rather to fall gloriously behind the ramparts, than surrender to his enemies. But his garrison were not animated with the same heroic courage. Rising in a mutiny, they compelled him to capitulate. Drury, in the name of his mistress, engaged that he should be honourably treated; but Elizabeth, insensible alike to the claims of valour, and to the pledged honour of her own officer, surrendered Kirkaldy to the Regent, who, *with her consent*, hanged the gallant soldier and his brother at the Cross, on the 3d of August 1573.

In 1650, the castle was besieged by the Parliamentary army under Cromwell; and capitulated on honourable terms. In 1745, although Prince Charles Stuart held possession of the city, he did not attempt the reduction of the castle. In modern times, some of the prisoners, during the French war, were confined within its walls. The SCOTTISH

REGALIA are exhibited in the Crown Room every day from twelve till three o'clock. Visitors are gratuitously admitted by an order from the Lord Provost, which may be obtained by applying at the City Chambers between twelve and three o'clock. Persons procuring orders are required to sign their names and places of residence in a book kept in the City Chambers for this purpose, and the order is available only upon that day on which it is dated. These insignia of Scottish Royalty consist of a Crown, a Sceptre, and a Sword of State.* Along with them is also shown the Lord Trea-

* "Taking these articles in connection with the great historical events and personages that enter into the composition of their present value, it is impossible to look upon them without emotions of singular interest, while, at the same time, their essential littleness excites wonder at the mighty circumstances and destinies which have been determined by the possession or the want of possession of what they emblematize and represent. *For* this diadem did Bruce liberate his country; *with* it, his son nearly occasioned its ruin. It purchased for Scotland the benefit of the mature sagacity of Robert II.—did not save Robert III. from a death of grief—procured, perhaps, the assassination of James I.—instigated James IV. to successful rebellion against his father, whose violent death was expiated by his own. Its dignity was proudly increased by James V. who was yet more unfortunate, perhaps, in his end, than a long list of unfortunate predecessors. It was worn by the devoted head of Mary, who found it the occasion of woes and calamities unnumbered and unexampled It was placed

surer's Rod of Office, found deposited in the same strong oak chest in which the Regalia were discovered. The room where Queen Mary gave birth to James VI., in whom the crowns of England and Scotland were united, will be an object of interest to many strangers. The gigantic piece of artillery, called MONS MEG, after the man who cast it, and his wife Meg, is mounted on a carriage on the Bomb Battery. It was employed at the siege of Norham, and afterwards burst when firing a salute to the Duke of York in 1682, since which time it has never been repaired. On the north side of the esplanade stands the Statue of the late Duke of York, erected to commemorate his services as Commander-in-Chief of the Forces. A cannon-ball, said to have been shot from the castle in 1745, may be seen sticking in the gable wall of the house on the south side of the entrance to the esplanade.

In returning from the Castle, an opening upon the left, immediately upon leaving the esplanade, conducts to the house of Allan Ramsay, the author of "The Gentle Shepherd," a pastoral drama of charming simplicity, and still highly popular among the rural population of Scotland.

The stranger will now retrace his steps to

GEORGE IV. BRIDGE,

which spans the Cowgate, and forms an important feature in the modern improvements of the city. At its northern end is the WEST BOW, which, before the erection of this bridge, presented an aspect highly interesting to the lover

upon the infant brow of her son, to the exclusion of herself from all its glories and advantages, but not the conclusion of the distresses in which it had involved her. Her unfortunate grandson, for its sake, visited Scotland, and had it placed upon his head with magnificent ceremonies; but the nation whose sovereignty it gave him was the first to rebel against his authority, and work his destruction. The Presbyterian solemnity with which it was given to Charles II. was only a preface to the disasters of Worcester; and afterwards it was remembered by this monarch, little to the advantage of Scotland, that it had been placed upon his head with conditions and restrictions which wounded at once his pride and his conscience. It was worn by no other monarch, and the period of its disuse seems to have been the epoch from which we may reckon the happiness of our monarchs, and the revival of our national prosperity."—CHAMBERS' *Walks in Edinburgh*, p. 49.

of antique buildings. Although now a place of small consideration, it is not 100 years since the Assembly Rooms of Edinburgh were situate within its precincts. Before the erection of the North and South Bridges, it was also the principal avenue by which wheel carriages reached the more elevated streets of the city. It "has been ascended by Anne of Denmark, James I., and Charles I., by Oliver Cromwell, Charles II., and James II. How different the avenue by which George IV. entered the city!"* But the West Bow has also been the scene of many more mournful processions. Previous to the year 1785, criminals were conducted through the Bow to the place of execution in the Grassmarket, and the murderers of Porteous, after securing their victim, hurried him down this street to meet the fate they had destined for him.† The spot where the city gibbet stood is now indicated by a cross upon the causeway of the

* CHAMBERS' *Traditions of Edinburgh*, vol. i., p. 140

† The murder of Captain Porteous forms an event so memorable, not only in the annals of the city, but in what may be termed the philosophy of mobs, that a brief account of the event may not be unacceptable. We need hardly remind our readers that it forms one of the most striking incidents in the Heart of Mid-Lothian.

John Porteous was the son of a tailor in Edinburgh; his father intended to breed him up to his own trade, but the youthful profligacy of the son defeated the parent's prudent intention, and he enlisted into the Scotch corps at that time in the service of the States of Holland. Here he learned military discipline, and upon returning to his own country in 1715, his services were engaged by the magistrates of Edinburgh to discipline the City Guard. For such a task he was eminently qualified, not only by his military education, but by his natural activity and resolution; and, in spite of the profligacy of his character, he received a captain's commission in the corps.

The duty of the Edinburgh City Guard was to preserve the public peace when any tumult was apprehended. They consisted principally of discharged veterans, who, when off duty, worked at their respective trades. To the rabble they were objects of mingled derision and dislike, and the numerous indignities they suffered, rendered them somewhat morose and austere in temper. At public executions they generally surrounded the scaffold, and it was on an occasion of this kind that Porteous, their captain, committed the outrage for which he paid the penalty of his life.

The criminal, on the occasion in question, had excited the commiseration of the populace by the disinterested courage he displayed in achieving the escape of his accomplice. At this time it was customary to conduct prisoners under sentence of death to attend divine service in the Tolbooth Church. Wilson, the criminal above alluded to, and Robertson, his companion in crime, had reached the church, guarded by four soldiers, when Wilson suddenly seized one of the

market-place, in the middle of the street, between No. 104 on the one side, and No. 123 on the other ; the centre of

guards in each hand, and a third with his teeth, and shouted to his accomplice to fly for his life. Robertson immediately fled and effected his escape. This circumstance naturally excited a strong feeling of sympathy for Wilson; and the magistrates, fearing an attempt at rescue, had requested the presence of a detachment of infantry in a street adjoining that where the execution was to take place, for the purpose of intimidating the populace. The introduction of another military force than his own into a quarter of the city where no drums but his were ever beat, highly incensed Captain Porteous, and aggravated the ferocity of a temper naturally surly and brutal. Contrary to the apprehension of the authorities, the execution was allowed to pass undisturbed; but the dead body had hung only a short time upon the gibbet when a tumult arose among the multitude—stones and other missiles where thrown at Porteous and his men, and one of the populace, more adventurous than the rest, sprung upon the scaffold, and cut the rope by which the criminal was suspended.

Porteous was exasperated to frenzy by this outrage on his authority, and leaping from the scaffold, he seized the musket of one of the guards, gave the word to fire, and discharging his piece, shot the man dead upon the spot. Several of his soldiers also, having obeyed his order to fire, six or seven persons were killed, and many others wounded. The mob still continuing their attack, another volley was fired upon them, by which several others fell, and the scene of violence only closed when Porteous and his soldiers reached the guard-house in the High Street. For his reckless and sanguinary conduct in this affair, Captain Porteous was arraigned before the High Court of Justiciary, and sentence of death was passed upon him. His execution was appointed to take place on the 8th of September 1736.

The day of doom arrived, and the ample area of the Grassmarket was crowded in every part with a countless multitude, drawn together to gratify their revenge or satisfy their sense of justice by the spectacle of the execution. But their vengeance met with a temporary disappointment. The hour of execution was already past, without the appearance of the criminal, and the expectant multitude began to interchange suspicions that a reprieve might have arrived. Deep and universal was the groan of indignation which arose from the crowd, when they learned that such was indeed the fact. The case having been represented to her Majesty Queen Caroline, she intimated her royal pleasure that the prisoner should be reprieved for six weeks. The shout of disappointed revenge was followed by suppressed mutterings and communings among the crowd, but no act of violence was committed; they saw the gallows taken down, and then gradually dispersed to their respective homes and occupations.

Night ushered in another scene of the drama. A drum was heard beating to arms, and the populace promptly answered its summons by turning out into the streets. Their numbers rapidly increased, and, separating into different parties, they took possession of the city gates, posting sentinels for their security. They then disarmed the City Guard, and, having thus possessed themselves of weapons, they were the uncontrolled masters of the city. During the progress of the riot, various efforts were made to communicate with the castle, but the vigilance of the insurgents defeated all such attempts. The Tolbooth was now invested, and a strong party of the rioters having surrounded it, another party proceeded to break up the doors. For a considerable time the

the cross covering the precise spot in which the socket-stone of the gallows-tree was sunk. Behind the remaining houses of the Bow, and approached by an entry through them, stands the HOUSE OF MAJOR WEIR, the celebrated necromancer, who, along with his sister, suffered death for witchcraft in 1670. The fate of Weir is chiefly remarkable from his being a man of some condition (the son of a gentleman, and his mother a lady of family in Clydesdale), which was rarely the case with those who were the victims of such accusations. Whether the crimes which he confessed were the diseased fancies of temporary derangement, or whether he was in reality a man of atrociously depraved life, does not very clearly appear. After his condemnation, he doggedly refused to have recourse to prayer, "arguing, that as he had no hope whatever of escaping Satan, there was no need

great strength of the place rendered their efforts fruitless, but, having brought fire to their aid, they burned the door and rushed into the prison.

Porteous, elated with his escape from the sentence he so richly merited, was regaling a party of his boon companions within the building, when the assault was made upon its gates. The wretched man well knew the hatred with which he was regarded by the populace, and was at no loss to comprehend the motive for their violence. Escape seemed impossible. The chimney was the only place of concealment that occurred to him, and scrambling into it, he supported himself by laying hold of the bars of iron with which the chimneys of a prison-house are crossed to prevent the escape of criminals. But his enemies soon dragged him from his hiding-place, and, hurrying him along the streets, they brought him to the very spot, where, that morning, he ought to have paid the forfeit of his life. The want of a rope was now the sole obstacle to the accomplishment of their purpose, and this want was soon supplied by breaking open a shop where the article was sold; a dyer's pole served in room of a gallows, and from it they suspended the unhappy man. Having thus propitiated the spirit of offended justice, they threw down the weapons of which they had possessed themselves, and quietly dispersed to their respective homes.

It has been justly observed, that the murder of Porteous has more the character of a conspiracy than of a riot. The whole proceedings of the insurgents were marked by a cool and deliberate intrepidity, quite at variance with the accustomed conduct of rioters. No violence was perpetrated either upon person or property, save the single act of vengeance executed upon Porteous. So studious were the insurgents to avoid every appearance of prædial outrage, that a guinea was left upon the counter of the shop from which they took the rope to hang their victim. None of the offenders were ever discovered, although Government made the most strenuous exertions, and offered large rewards for their apprehension. There can be little doubt, however, that many of the participators in that night's transactions were of a class unaccustomed to mingle in scenes of vulgar tumult.

of incensing him by vain efforts at repentance."* The house, ever after the death of Weir, enjoyed the reputation of being haunted, and so general was the horror entertained for the crimes of the man and the terrors of his abode, that, till the present century, no family was ever found hardy enough to occupy the house as a residence.

In the Grassmarket—situated, as we have already mentioned, at the foot of the Bow—a weekly market is held on Wednesday, for grain and horses. The new building on the south side is the Corn Market. At its south-west corner it is entered by the WEST PORT, the scene of the appalling atrocities of the monster Burke. As the name of this wretched man has now become the current term to distinguish the crime for which he suffered, we need scarcely remind our readers that his victims were destroyed by strangling, and that his object was not to possess himself of their property, for they were all of a humble rank in life, but to convert their bodies into a source of gain by selling them to the anatomist.

Proceeding along the Bridge, Heriot's Hospital will be seen occupying a fine situation on the right. At the southern end of the Bridge, upon the right hand, is the entrance to THE GREYFRIARS' CHURCHYARD, in ancient times the garden belonging to the monastery of Greyfriars, which was situated in the Grassmarket. In this churchyard are interred George Buchanan, the accomplished Latin poet, and preceptor of James VI., Allan Ramsay, the Scottish poet, Principal Robertson, the historian, Dr. Black, the distinguished chemist, Dr. Hugh Blair, Colin Maclaurin, Dr. M'Crie, the biographer of Knox, and other eminent men. The two Churches in the burying-ground, known by the name of Old Greyfriars, and New Greyfriars, were completely destroyed by fire in January 1845. Of the former, Principal Robertson was pastor for many years. Leaving the churchyard, and advancing a few yards up the Candlemaker Row, a broad road will be seen upon the right conducting to the CHARITY WORKHOUSE. The grounds around the house are laid out as a kitchen garden for the establish-

* SIR WALTER SCOTT'S *Letters on Demonology and Witchcraft*, p. 330.

ED NBURGH CASTLE FROM THE GRASSMARKET.

ment, and the inmates are frequently employed in its cultivation. The house itself is a large building of the plainest description. The funds by which the institution is supported are derived from an assessment on house property, collections at the church-doors, and occasional donations and voluntary contributions from the citizens. The average number of inmates is about 750.*

After passing the Work-House the stranger will take the road to the right, and in a few minutes he will reach the gate of

HERIOT'S HOSPITAL.

This handsome edifice, one of the proudest ornaments of the city, owes its foundation to George Heriot, jeweller to James VI., whose name will probably be more familiar to the ear of strangers as the "jingling Geordie" of "The Fortunes of Nigel."† The design, which is attributed to Inigo Jones, is in that mixed style which dates its origin from the reign of Elizabeth, examples of which are afforded by Drumlanrig Castle in Dumfries-shire, Northumberland House in the Strand, and many other edifices throughout the kingdom. Its form is quadrangular, the sides each measuring 162 feet, and enclosing a court of 92 feet square. The building was commenced in 1628, and completed in 1660, and the erection is said to have cost £27,000. The chapel, occupying the south side of the quadrangle, a few years ago presented nothing but a clay floor and bare walls, round which there was a stone seat, to accommodate the boys when assembled for morning and evening service. It is now fitted up in a very different style, and with its splendid pulpit, fine oaken carvings, richly adorned ceiling, and beautifully stained glass windows, forms one of the principal attractions of the place. The object of this splen-

* Besides this institution, the parish of St. Cuthberts and the Canongate have each a house for the reception of paupers, with peculiar funds, and separate boards of management.

† "For the wealth God has sent me, it shall not want inheritors while there are orphan lads in Auld Reekie."—*Fortunes of Nigel, Chapter IV.*

A brief outline of the benevolent founder's history is given in the Note to Chapter II. of the same work.

ARKET,

North Bridge

did institution is the maintenance and education of "poor and fatherless boys," or boys whose parents are in indigent circumstances, "freemen's sons of the town of Edinburgh," of whom 180 are accommodated within its walls. The course of instruction consists of English, Latin, Greek, Writing, Arithmetic, Book-keeping, Mathematics, and Geography. To these branches have recently been added French, Drawing, the Elements of Music, and Practical Mechanics. Boys are admitted between the age of seven and ten, and generally leave at fourteen, unless superior scholarship appears to fit them for prosecuting some of the learned professions, in which case the period of their stay is extended, with the view of preparing them for the studies of the University. All the boys, upon leaving the hospital, receive a bible, and other useful books, with two suits of clothes of their own choice. Those going out as apprentices are allowed £10 annually for five years, and £5 at the termination of their apprenticeship. Those destined for any of the learned professions are sent to college for four years, during which period they receive £30 a year. In 1836, an act was obtained from Parliament, empowering the Governors to extend the benefits of the Institution, and employ their surplus funds in establishing Free Schools in the different parishes of the city. Ten of these schools are already in full operation, in which very nearly 3000 children, of both sexes, are instructed in the usual branches of a parochial education, the females being, in addition, taught sewing and knitting. This great scheme of instruction, when complete, must prove of incalculable benefit to the community, as the advantages of a substantial education will be brought within the reach of every citizen, however humble. In addition to these liberal provisions for the instruction of youth, there are also ten bursaries, or exhibitions, open to the competition of young men not connected with the institution. The successful competitors for these bursaries receive £20 *per annum*, for four years. The princely provision thus made for the welfare of his countrymen, amply justifies the sentiment put into the mouth of the founder by Sir Walter Scott, "I think mine own estate and memory, as I shall order it, has a fair chance of outliving those of greater men." The management is vested in the Town Council and Clergy of the City, and visitors are admitted by an order from any of the Governors.

Retracing our steps to the entrance of the Charity Work-House, the Meadow Walk will be seen exactly opposite. In a field, upon the right hand, a short way down the walk, stands

GEORGE WATSON'S HOSPITAL.

This hospital is for the benefit of the children and grandchildren of decayed merchants of the city of Edinburgh. The building is plain, but commodious. Boys are received into this hospital between seven and ten, and remain till fifteen years of age. The number of boys amount to about eighty, and the education they receive very much resembles that of Heriot's Hospital. Each boy, after leaving the hospital, receives £10 a-year for five years ; and, upon attaining the age of twenty-five, if unmarried and well-conducted, he receives a further sum of £50. Such as evince "an extraordinary genius for letters," receive £20 a-year, for four years, and £17 a-year, during the two succeeding years. The management is vested in the Master, Assistants, and Treasurer of the Merchant Company of Edinburgh, the ministers of the Old Church, and five members of the Town Council. A little to the west of George Watson's Hospital, stands the Merchant Maiden Hospital, but as it does not come within the scope of any of our walks, we think it better to include the description of it, and of the other more important hospitals which we do not pass in our progress, in a foot-note.*

* *The Merchant Maiden Hospital* was founded in 1695, for the maintenance and education of the daughters of merchant burgesses in the city. Nearly 100 girls are maintained in this hospital. They are admitted between seven and eleven years of age, and leave at seventeen. The course of instruction includes English, Writing, Arithmetic, Geography, French, Music, Drawing, Dancing, and Needle-work. Upon leaving the hospital, each girl receives £9, 6s. 8d. The original edifice stood in Bristo Street; the present building is agreeably situated in Laurieston, a little to the west of George Watson's Hospital.

The Trades' Maiden Hospital stands on the south side of Argyle Square. The girls eligible for admission into this institution, are the daughters of decayed

Immediately adjoining to the Meadows, on the south-west, are Bruntsfield Links (*Anglice* Downs), where many of the inhabitants are accustomed to amuse themselves with

tradesmen. It supports about 50 girls, who are admitted at the same age, and instructed in the same branches as in the Merchant Maiden Hospital. They go out at the age of seventeen, each girl receiving £5, 11s. and a bible.

The Orphan Hospital maintains and educates about 100 children of both sexes. The old building, situated near Trinity College Church, was abandoned as unhealthy, and a handsome new edifice was erected in 1833, on the property of Dean. The benefits of the institution are extended to the whole of Scotland.

John Watson's Institution is a spacious and showy edifice, also situated on the property of Dean. The purpose of the endowment, is the maintenance and education of destitute children. About 120 children are maintained in it. They are admitted between the ages of five and eight, and leave at fourteen.

Cauvin's Hospital is pleasantly situated at Duddingston, a village about a mile and a half to the east of Edinburgh. The children enjoying the benefit of this institution are "the sons of respectable but poor teachers," and "of poor but honest farmers;" whom failing, "the sons of respectable master printers or booksellers," and "of respectable servants in the agricultural line." Twenty boys are maintained in it. They are admissible from six to eight years of age, and are retained in the hospital for six years.

Trinity College Hospital, the oldest charitable institution in the city. Was founded in 1461 by Mary of Gueldres. It stood at the foot of the lane called Leith Wynd, but the ground being purchased by the North British Railway Company, the inmates have been removed to Moray House, which has been comfortably fitted up for their reception. Its benefits are conferred on "burgesses, their wives or children not married, nor under the age of fifty years." Forty persons are maintained within the walls of the hospital, and about ninety out-pensioners receive £6 a-year.

Gillespie's Hospital enjoys a fine situation on the south-west confines of the city. The founder was a tobacconist in Edinburgh, who devoted the greater part of his property to endow an hospital for the maintenance of indigent old men and women, and for the elementary education of 100 poor boys. The number of the aged inmates is between thirty and forty. None are admitted under the age of fifty-five, a preference being given to servants of the founder, or persons of his name.

Donaldson's Hospital—probably the finest building in Scotland, certainly the finest of modern date—stands on a piece of ground to the westward of the city, about half a mile along the Glasgow Road from the Edinburgh and Glasgow Railway Station at the Hay-Weights. The founder was a printer in Edinburgh, who died in 1830, and bequeathed the greater part of his estate, amounting to nearly £200,000, for the purpose of building and maintaining an hospital for poor boys and girls. Of these there will be accommodation for about 300. The building is from the design of Mr. W. H. Playfair, whose reputation would securely rest on this structure alone, if Scotland were not fortunate enough to possess numerous other examples of his taste and genius.

Stewart's Hospital.—Another institution for the maintenance of poor boys, now being erected, for which Mr. Daniel Stewart of the Exchequer, who died in 1814, left about £13,000 and some houses in the Old Town.

the national game of golf. The game is played with a club and ball. The club is formed of ash, flexible and finely

tapered, measuring from three to four feet long, according to the player's height or length of arm. The head is faced

Chalmers' Hospital.—For the erection and endowment of an hospital under this name, "for the sick and hurt," Chalmers, a plumber, who died in 1836, has left the sum of £30,000.

Besides the endowments for the relief of the destitute, there are many other charitable associations maintained by private subscription. Among them may be mentioned, The House of Refuge—The House of Industry—The Strangers' Friend Society—The Blind Asylum—The Deaf and Dumb Institution—The Night Asylum for the Houseless—The Society for Relief of the Destitute Sick—The Society for the Relief of Indigent Old Men, and two similar institutions for the Relief of Indigent Old Women—The Seamen's Friend Society—and the Society for Clothing the Industrious Poor.

There are also many public Dispensaries, and a Lying-in Hospital, where medicines and medical attendance are gratuitously afforded to the poor; but a further enumeration of such institutions does not appear to be required for the purposes of the present work.

with horn and loaded with lead. The ball is about the size of a common tennis ball, made of feathers, compressed very firmly into a hard and slightly elastic leathern cover. The game consists in striking the ball successively into a certain number of small holes, about a quarter of a mile apart, the player who does so in the smallest number of strokes being the victor. Each player carries an assortment of clubs varying in elasticity, and thus adapted to the distance the ball is to be driven, the best club for a long stroke being laid aside for one less elastic when the distance becomes shortened. An expert player will strike a ball from 130 to 200 yards.* The *Thistle Golf Club of Edinburgh* have their arms, crest, and uniform. The last consists of a single-breasted scarlet coat, with green collar, and plain gilt buttons, white trousers, and a badge bearing the device of the thistle upon the left breast.

Returning from the Links to that point of the Meadows where the walks cross each other, the stranger will be in the immediate neighbourhood of

GEORGE'S SQUARE.

This is the only large square in the Old Town. Towards the close of the last century, it was the principal place of residence of the higher ranks; the Duchess of Gordon, the Countess of Sutherland, the Countess of Glasgow, Viscount Duncan, the Hon. Henry Erskine, and many other persons of rank, residing there. The house of Walter Scott, Esq., W.S., father of the novelist, was on the west side of the Square.

Passing along Charles Street and Bristo Street, and turning to the right into Lothian Street, two places of worship will be observed upon the left hand—the one a Roman Catholic and the other a Baptist Chapel—the two being built upon a mutual gable. Proceeding along Lothian

* Among the most memorable feats in the annals of golfing is that of a player who struck a ball over the top of St. Giles's steeple from a point within the Parliament Square. Another player, still alive, struck his ball over Melville's Monument, which, from the ground to the head of the statue, measures 150 feet.

Street and South College Street, and then turning to the right a short distance along Nicolson Street, the stranger will arrive in front of the fine portico of

THE ROYAL COLLEGE OF SURGEONS.

In classic elegance, few buildings will be found to surpass this handsome structure, although its effect is much impaired by the uncongenial architecture of the surrounding houses. The principal portion of the building is occupied with an extensive museum of anatomical and surgical preparations. The arrangement is, in every respect, admirable, and a praiseworthy liberality is exhibited in the admission of strangers. Although, by the strict letter of the regulations, a member's order is requisite, yet even this form is, in most cases, dispensed with. A little further south, on the same side of the street, is the Asylum for the Industrious Blind.

Returning northward, the next object of importance is

THE UNIVERSITY.

No regular University existed in Edinburgh till the year 1582, although, long previous to this period, teachers of philosophy and divinity had been established in the city. On the 24th of April of that year, King James VI. issued the charter for its foundation, and in the following year the course of instruction was commenced. By the liberality of James, and private benefactions, the University rapidly advanced in importance, and, as its revenues increased, its sphere of usefulness was extended by the addition of new professorships, till, in the 18th century, it attained a celebrity unsurpassed by any academical institution in Europe.

The present structure is of modern erection. The old buildings were both unsightly and incommodious, and a subscription having been set on foot, the foundation of the present handsome and spacious edifice was laid in 1789. The local subscriptions, however, were insufficient to accomplish the object; and, upon the case being brought before Parliament, an annual grant of £10,000 was obtained to complete the undertaking. The plan is by Mr.

Robert Adam, with some subsequent modifications, principally in the internal arrangement, by Mr. W. H. Playfair. The buildings are of a quadrangular form, the sides measuring 358 by 255 feet, with a spacious court in the centre. The eastern front is adorned with a portico, supported by Doric columns, twenty-six feet in height, each formed of a single block of stone.

No test of any description is required from the students; they are not resident within the College, nor are they distinguished by any peculiarity of dress. In pursuing their studies they are at perfect liberty to select the classes they attend—a certain curriculum of study is, however, requisite in taking degrees in Medicine and Art, those who intend to qualify for a degree in the latter being required to attend the Classes of Humanity, Greek, Logic, Rhetoric, Moral Philosophy, Natural Philosophy, and Mathematics. The number of students attending the University during the present session (1844–45,) is 1050.

There are 34 foundations for bursaries, the benefit of which is extended to 80 students. The greater number of these bursaries do not exceed in value £10 per annum, their aggregate amount being only £1172 a-year.

The Museum contains a large collection of specimens in the various departments of Natural History. The Ornithological department is peculiarly valuable, both from its extent and admirable classification. Visiters are admitted upon payment of one shilling each. There is also an Anatomical Museum, where the professional visiter will be highly interested by the variety and beauty of the preparations.

The Library occupies the south side of the building. The principal apartment is equally distinguished by the symmetry of its proportions, the chasteness of its decorations, and its admirable adaptation to the purpose for which it is intended. It is incomparably the finest library-room in Scotland—measuring 187 feet in length, by 50 in breadth, with an arched roof from 50 to 58 feet high. The monument of Burns by Flaxman graces the west end of the room.

Proceeding northward, upon leaving the University,

THE ROYAL INFIRMARY

is situated in the first street upon the right. A detailed account of this institution does not appear to be necessary in the present work. Besides the relief afforded to patients, clinical lectures, or discourses on the cases in the several wards, are delivered within the walls by certain Professors of the University. The professor of clinical surgery also lectures upon the more important surgical cases in the wards under his inspection. Besides the professorial lectures, the ordinary physicians and surgeons of the institution deliver clinical discourses on the cases under their immediate care. Journals are regularly kept, recording the symptoms, progress, and result of the cases, with the various remedies employed. To these journals the students have access.

The fees paid by students for the right to attend the medical and surgical practice in the Hospital, are five guineas for an annual, or twelve guineas for a perpetual ticket.

Proceeding along the South Bridge, an open railing, for a short distance on either side, affords a view of the Cowgate, with which the tourist will, in all probability, have no wish to cultivate a closer acquaintance. The Register House will again come into view on reaching the Tron Church, thus terminating our Second Walk.

WALK THIRD.*

SCOTT MONUMENT—ROYAL INSTITUTION—NEW CLUB—ST. JOHN'S CHAPEL—ST. CUTHBERT'S CHURCH—CHARLOTTE SQUARE—ST. GEORGE'S CHURCH—DEAN BRIDGE—AINSLIE PLACE—MORAY PLACE—HERIOT ROW—PITT MONUMENT—GEORGE FOURTH'S MONUMENT—ASSEMBLY ROOMS—PHYSICIANS' HALL—ST. ANDREW'S SQUARE—MELVILLE MONUMENT—ROYAL BANK.

In this walk we shall conduct the stranger through the principal streets of the New Town, adverting to all the more striking objects in our progress.

* This Walk is coloured *yellow* on the Map.

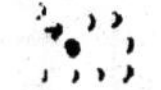

G. M. Kemp inv. et del. — R. Scott sculpsit

THE SCOTT MONUMENT

Proceeding to the westward, the buildings of the High Street will be seen upon the left, towering to the heavens like the habitations of a race of Titans. These buildings, standing upon a steep and lofty ridge, with tributary lanes or closes descending abruptly to the valley beneath, produce an effect highly picturesque and majestic. The interjacent valley, extending westward to the end of Princes Street, along which the Edinburgh and Glasgow Railway now passes, was formerly a stagnant pond or marsh, known by the name of the Nor-Loch. The

MONUMENT TO SIR WALTER SCOTT,*

of which an engraving illustrates our text, will be observed within the railing of the pleasure-grounds opposite the foot of St. David Street. The design was furnished by George M. Kemp, an architect wholly unknown to fame until declared the successful competitor for this honour, and who died before the structure was completed. The foundation was laid on the 15th of August 1840, and the building was finished in 1844. Its height is 200 feet 6 inches, and its cost was £15,650. A stair of 287 steps conducts to the gallery at the top. In each front of the Monument, above the principal arch, are six small niches, making a total of 24 in the main structure, besides 32 others in the piers and abutment towers. These niches are to be occupied by sculptural impersonations of the characters, historical and fanciful, pourtrayed in the writings of Sir Walter. The following statues fill the four principal niches which crown the four lowest arches. In the northern niche facing Princes Street is the statue of Prince Charles (from *Waverley*) drawing his sword. In the eastern niche, on the side next the Calton Hill, is Meg Merrilees (from *Guy Mannering*) breaking the sapling over the head of Lucy Bertram. In the southern niche, next the Old Town, is the statue of the *Lady of the Lake* stepping from a boat to the shore ; and, in the western niche, is the *Last Minstrel* playing on his harp. Other statues

* To the galleries of the Scott Monument, the charge for admission is sixpence for each person.

for the remaining niches are in progress. The following is the inscription on the plate placed under the foundation-stone :—

THIS GRAVEN PLATE,
DEPOSITED IN THE BASE OF A VOTIVE BUILDING
ON THE FIFTEENTH DAY OF AUGUST IN THE YEAR OF CHRIST 1840,
AND NEVER LIKELY TO SEE THE LIGHT AGAIN
TILL ALL THE SURROUNDING STRUCTURES ARE CRUMBLED TO DUST
BY THE DECAY OF TIME, OR BY HUMAN OR ELEMENTAL VIOLENCE,
MAY THEN TESTIFY TO A DISTANT POSTERITY THAT
HIS COUNTRYMEN BEGAN ON THAT DAY
TO RAISE AN EFFIGY AND ARCHITECTURAL MONUMENT
TO THE MEMORY OF SIR WALTER SCOTT, BART.,
WHOSE ADMIRABLE WRITINGS WERE THEN ALLOWED
TO HAVE GIVEN MORE DELIGHT AND SUGGESTED BETTER FEELING
TO A LARGER CLASS OF READERS IN EVERY RANK OF SOCIETY
THAN THOSE OF ANY OTHER AUTHOR,
WITH THE EXCEPTION OF SHAKESPEARE ALONE:
AND WHICH WERE THEREFORE THOUGHT LIKELY TO BE REMEMBERED
LONG AFTER THIS ACT OF GRATITUDE,
ON THE PART OF THE FIRST GENERATION OF HIS ADMIRERS,
SHOULD BE FORGOTTEN.

HE WAS BORN AT EDINBURGH 15TH AUGUST 1771;
AND DIED AT ABBOTSFORD 21ST SEPTEMBER 1832.

Fine though the structure be, it may be questioned whether the site is the best that could have been chosen; and whether the Old Town would not have been a more congenial atmosphere for such a memorial. In its present situation, the effect of its mass is to depress and overpower every surrounding object, the Castle Rock itself not excepted. The marble statue of Scott, by Steell—a fine work of art, and a most faithful likeness—was placed in the monument on the 15th of August 1846.

The Earthen Mound, formed by the deposition of the rubbish accumulated in digging the foundations of the houses in the New Town, is a convenient avenue between the New Town and the Old. Had circumstances admitted of the communication being effected by a handsome arched bridge instead of this shapeless accumulation of earth, another fine feature might have been added to the architecture of the city. Sir Walter Scott, in his "Provincial Antiquities," bitterly denounces the narrowness of spirit which led to the formation of this Mound, speaking of it as " that huge deformity which now extends its lumpish length betwixt Bank Street and Hanover Street, the most hopeless and irremediable error which has been committed in the course of the improvements of Edinburgh, and which, when the view which it has interrupted is contrasted with that which it presents, is, and must be, a subject of constant regret and provocation." At the time Sir Walter penned this invective, the rubbish of which the Mound is composed met the eye in all its naked deformity. The shrubbery which now adorns the slopes has deprived the censure of much of its force, although it can never cease to be lamented that such an opportunity to add another grace to the architecture of the city should be for ever lost. The FREE CHURCH COLLEGE, a fine structure, occupies a commanding position at the head of the Mound; its two towers, when viewed from the middle of Hanover Street, deriving a crowning grace from the spire of Victoria Hall beyond it. If there were sermons in stones, the architectural harmony existing between the two buildings might rebuke the discord which has too much prevailed between the religious bodies to which they respectively belong. At the northern extremity of the Mound stands

THE ROYAL INSTITUTION,

one of the handsomest modern buildings of which Edinburgh can boast. The expense of driving the piles upon which this fine structure is built, exceeded £1600. The Royal Society, the Royal Institution for the Encouragement of the Fine Arts in Scotland, and the Board of Trustees for the Improvement of Manufactures, have apartments within its walls. The paintings of the Scottish Artists are exhibited in the Institution during the spring months,* but

* The works of the Scottish Artists, of which by far the larger portion of the collection consists, form of themselves a gallery well fitted to instruct and elevate the public taste; but in addition to these, the exhibition generally includes some of the choicest modern pictures from the private galleries of the generous and opulent collectors of England. Several paintings of great beauty, comprehending specimens of Wilkie, Etty, Turner, Maclise, Stanfield, Roberts, and other eminent Artists, have thus been made familiar to the eyes of thousands who would never have seen them in the residences of their proprietors The

the new building about to be erected a little to the south of the present structure will be employed for this purpose upon its completion. The Royal Society holds its meetings once a fortnight during the winter months, when papers connected with the varied departments of science and learning, falling within the scope of the Society's plan, are read by the several members.

Continuing our walk towards the west, we pass on the right THE NEW CLUB, an association of Noblemen and Gentlemen, partaking of the character of a joint-stock Hotel and Reading Room, for the exclusive accommodation of members. These are elected by ballot, the number being limited to 660. The entrance-money is thirty-five guineas, and the annual subscription five guineas.

The frowning grandeur of the Castle Rock now becomes very imposing, and presents a striking contrast to the tranquil beauty of the green sward and shrubberies of the valley beneath. These pleasure grounds, endowed with natural features of the most varied character, and improved by all the resources of modern horticulture, form one of the chief ornaments of the City.

Upon reaching the west end of Princes Street, ST. JOHN'S CHAPEL and ST. CUTHBERT'S CHURCH will be seen upon the left, the former an elegant structure of the florid Gothic order, the latter an unsightly pile of huge dimensions, with

exhibition of such works has exercised a sensible influence on the taste of the community. The altered views of the general public in regard to the works of Turner, afford convincing evidence that a more enlightened connoisseurship is beginning to extend itself even to the middle ranks of Edinburgh society. When these mighty creations of genius were first submitted to view in the Institution, they were either disregarded, or made the subject of ridicule by a large proportion of visitors. The voice of the scoffer is now silenced, and we find instead the enthusiastic worship of enlightened votaries.

"The Association for the Promotion of the Fine Arts in Scotland"—the first of the Art-Unions established in this country—is in a flourishing condition. To its animating influence must mainly be attributed the improved condition of Art and Artists in Scotland. Previous to its foundation, the patronage of Art was at the lowest ebb. The annual subscriptions to the Association now exceed £5000; and this system of co-operation in support of Art, instead of extinguishing private patronage, has given it a wholesome stimulus, the certainty that a large number of the pictures annually exhibited for sale will be purchased by the Association for distribution among its members, lending a quickening impulse both to private collectors and to publishers to compete in the acquisition.

a double gallery.* St. John's is one of the places of worship belonging to the Scottish Episcopal Communion, and is embellished with all those graces of internal and external architecture, by which the English Church usually distinguishes the edifices dedicated to her religious service.†

Turning to the north, the stranger will now enter Charlotte Square, a spacious quadrangle of excellent houses. In the centre of its western side stands St. George's Church, the handsomest modern place of worship in the Scotch Establishment. Its erection cost £33,000.

After passing along the narrow lane by the side of St. George's, and through Charlotte Place, the stranger will turn to the right, and proceed by Melville Place, Randolph Crescent, and Lynedoch Place, to

THE DEAN BRIDGE.

A fine view is commanded from the bridge. Among the more striking objects is Donaldson's Hospital, (page 59.) Trinity Chapel, one of the Episcopal places of worship, stands at the north end of the bridge. The roadway passes at the great height of 106 feet above the bed of the stream.‡ The arches are four in number, each 96 feet span,

* "A circumstance happened with respect to this Church, and to more than one besides, which singularly illustrates the proverb, that Scotsmen are ever wise behind the hand. When the heritors had chosen the cheapest, or at least the ugliest, plan which was laid before them, had seen it executed, and were at leisure to contemplate the ground cumbered with a great heavy oblong barn, with huge disproportioned windows, they repented of the enormity which they had sanctioned, and endeavoured to repair their error by building a steeple, in a style of ornamented and florid architecture; as if the absurd finery of such an appendage could relieve the heaviness of the principal building, which it only rendered more deformed by the contrast."—Sir Walter Scott's *Provincial Antiquities.*

† The other Episcopal Chapels in Edinburgh are, St. Paul's, York Place, a Gothic structure of singular elegance; St. George's, also in York Place, a small but commodious place of worship; St. James's, Broughton Place; St. Paul's, Carrubber's Close; St. Peter's Roxburgh Place; Trinity Chapel, near the Dean Bridge; St. Thomas's, Rutland Street; and St. Columba's, Castle Hill.

‡ This is the stream which Richie Moniplies, in the Fortunes of Nigel, represents as a navigable river, superior to the Thames. Strangers, who have seen both, will be enabled to estimate how far Richie's patriotism had obscured his power of memory.

"I suppose you will tell me next," (said Master Heriot) "that you have at Edinburgh as fine a navigable river as the Thames, with all its shipping?"—"The

the breadth between the parapets being 39 feet, and the total length of the bridge 447 feet. The design was furnished by the late Mr. Telford.

As no object of any interest occurs on the river side, the stranger may retrace his steps to Randolph Crescent, through which he will pass to Great Stuart Street, Ainslie Place, and

MORAY PLACE.

This is the quarter of the city most celebrated for the architectural magnificence of its buildings. The ground is the property of the Earl of Moray, and the various streets, squares, and crescents erected upon it, are in accordance with a uniform plan designed by Mr. Gillespie Graham, architect.* By some persons it has been objected that the simplicity of style, and massiveness of structure, which particularly distinguish these buildings, impart an aspect of solemnity and gloom repugnant to the character of domestic architecture. Even the harmony of design and uniformity of plan have offended some critics. "The New Town of Edinburgh," says Dr. James Johnson, in his work entitled 'The Recess,' "is beautifully monotonous, and magnificently dull." Until philosophers shall succeed in establishing a uniform standard of taste, it will be vain to contend with such cavillers; we may only observe, that the massive dignity of the architecture in this quarter of the city, has called forth the admiration of the large majority of intelligent visiters. Nor is the substantial comfort of the dwellings to be overlooked. The walls are of the most solid and durable masonry; both the building materials and workmanship being of the best description. The house, No. 24, which the stranger passes in following the line of route we have adopted, was the residence of the late Lord Jeffrey.

The rent of the houses in Moray Place, varies from £140 to £160, and in Ainslie Place, from £100 to £130.

Thames!" exclaimed Richie, in a tone of ineffable contempt, "God bless your honour's judgment, we have at Edinburgh the Water of Leith and the Nor-Loch!"

* The annual *feu-duty* or ground-rent of the houses, in this quarter of the city, varies from 20s. to 40s. per foot of frontage.

Leaving Moray Place by Darnaway Street, the stranger is introduced to another *suite* of those pleasure grounds, which tend so much to beautify the city. Ascending the first opening on the right (Wemyss Place), we reach Queen Street, which overlooks the pleasure grounds. Through the openings formed by the streets running to the north, a noble prospect is obtained of the Firth of Forth, the shores of Fife, and the Ochil Hills, and in some states of the atmosphere, the peaks of the Grampians may be seen in the distance. Proceeding eastward along Queen Street, the first opening on the right is Castle Street, in which street the house numbered 39, was the town residence of Sir Walter Scott. The house is now occupied by Professor Napier, editor of the Edinburgh Review. Continuing his progress up Castle Street, the stranger reaches George's Street, and looking eastward, he will observe

THE PITT STATUE

occupying the spot where George's Street is intersected by Frederick Street. The statue is executed by Chantrey, and is regarded as a very favourable specimen of his bronzes. Still continuing to proceed eastward, THE ASSEMBLY ROOMS will be seen upon the right. Their external appearance is plain and unpretending, the only approach to ornament being the four Doric columns, doing duty as a portico in the front of the building. In these Rooms are held the public Assemblies and Concerts,* and other meetings of

* Although there is no want either of taste or capacity for music in Scotland, the inhabitants of Edinburgh cannot be said to be distinguished for their practical devotion to the art. Vocal music in parts, or concerted instrumental music, is rarely met with in private society; the Glee Club, and the associations formed from time to time, for orchestral music, being almost wholly dependent upon the professional musicians. The higher styles of ecclesiastical music may be said to be unknown, except from the performances at the three musical festivals held at the distant intervals of 1815, 1824, and 1844. The organ is excluded both from the churches of the Establishment and from the chapels of the most numerous of the Dissenting bodies, and in few congregations is there even a band of professional singers. The psalmody is, for the most part, led by the precentor alone, who is followed by the whole congregation, vociferating the melody, "without remorse or mitigation of voice." The want of chorus-singers, arising from the abject state of sacred music, is a formidable obstacle to holding a musical festival in the city; and although efforts have been making, by some

various kinds. The Music-room, a recent addition to the original edifice, forms the largest of the apartments, and is fitted up in a style of great splendour. It measures 108 feet long, by 91 broad. The courtesy of Messrs. Burn and Bryce, the architects, has enabled us to give a ground plan,

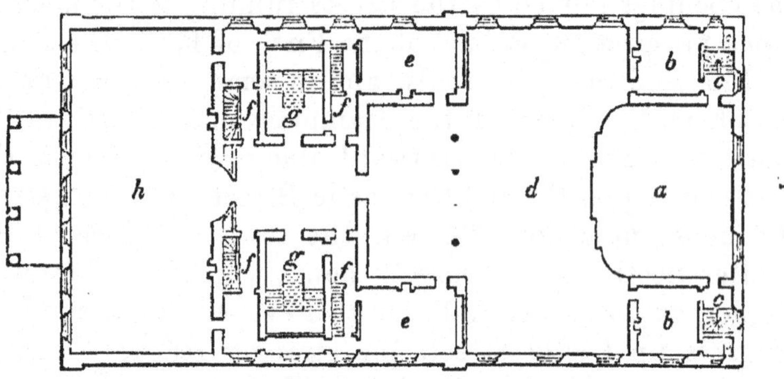

a, Orchestra.
b b, Musicians' Rooms.
c c, Staircases.
d, Music Hall.
e e. Ladies' Robing Room.
f f, Private Staircases.
g g g, Entrance Stairs and Lobby.
h, Assembly Room.

exhibiting the proportions of this noble room, the expense of which, including the organ, exceeded £10,000. The principal Ballroom is 92 feet long, 42 feet wide, and 40 feet high. There are also various other apartments of smaller dimensions. A little to the east, where Hanover Street intersects George street, stands

GEORGE IV. STATUE,

also executed by Chantrey, but wholly unworthy of the

of the professional vocalists, to discipline a body of singers to supply this want, by which a considerable measure of proficiency has been attained, Edinburgh is still immeasurably behind the cathedral towns, and even some of the manufacturing towns of England, in that indispensable requisite of the oratorio—an efficient chorus.

The introduction of the 'Wilhem *Method*,' and the 'Mainzerian *System*,' must be admitted to have diffused, to a considerable extent, an elementary knowledge of music among the middle and lower ranks; and so far, they are deserving of praise. Whether the temporary enthusiasm kindled by these instructors of "the million," will result in a real advance of musical skill and science, is still to be determined.

The Professional Society of Edinburgh includes, among its members, many highly respectable musicians; but the more liberal encouragement held out in London, to the first order of talent, deprives the city of most of its best professors in this as well as other walks of art.

fame of that gifted artist. There is gross affectation in the head, in the manner of extending the sceptre, and, in fact, in the whole air of the figure. These defects, when named to him by a friend, were frankly acknowledged by Chantrey, who stated that, in his original design, both the head and the sceptred hand were in very different attitudes, but that he had been compelled to alter them to their present position by the express command of his sovereign. The fine building forming the north-east corner of the intersecting streets is the Edinburgh and Glasgow Bank; and, on the opposite side of George's Street, in the house No. 24, is the Museum of the Antiquarian Society, to which strangers are admitted by an order from any of the members. Among the relics of antiquity preserved in this collection may be mentioned the colours carried by the Covenanters during the civil war; the stool which Jenny Geddes, in her zeal against Prelacy, launched at the head of the Bishop of Edinburgh in St. Giles's Church; and the *Maiden*, or Scottish Guillotine, with which the Earl of Morton, the Marquis of Argyle, Sir Robert Spottiswood, and many other distinguished persons, were beheaded.*

Continuing our progress eastward, ST. ANDREW'S CHURCH stands upon the left. It possesses a portico, supported by four Corinthian columns, and a handsome spire rising to the height of 168 feet, remarkable for its lightness of design and elegance of proportion. The showy building on the opposite side is the Commercial Bank of Scotland.

THE MELVILLE MONUMENT,

which graces the centre of St. Andrew's Square, was erected to the memory of the late Lord Melville. It rises 136

* It is very generally believed that it was the Earl of Morton who introduced the Maiden into Scotland. This opinion, however, has been proved to be erroneous, entries in the Council Records showing that it was in use long before his time. Michael Wing-the-wind, in "The Abbot," refers to this instrument during his conversation with Adam Woodcock in Holyrood Palace. "Herod's daughter," says Michael, "who did such execution with her foot and ancle, danced not men's heads off more cleanly than this Maiden of Morton. 'Tis an axe, man—an axe, which falls of itself like a sash window, and never gives the headsman the trouble to wield it."

feet in height, to which the statue adds other 14 feet. The design is that of the Trajan column, the shaft being fluted, instead of ornamented with sculpture as in the ancient model.

In the third flat (*Anglice* floor) of the house in the north-west corner of the Square (No. 21), Lord Brougham was born; and the house directly opposite, in the south-west corner, with entrance from St. David Street, was the residence of David Hume.

In the centre of the east side of the Square, standing apart from the other buildings, is the Royal Bank. In front of the Bank is an equestrian Statue of the Earl of Hopetoun. On the same side is the British Linen Company's Bank, a structure most luxurious in the richness of its ornament.

Passing through St. Andrew's Street, we again reach Princes Street, and terminate our Third Walk by returning to the Register House.

WALK FOURTH.*

ROYAL TERRACE—LEITH WALK—(LEITH—NEWHAVEN)—INVERLEITH ROW—EXPERIMENTAL GARDENS—BOTANIC GARDENS.

In the three preceding Walks we have exhausted most of the objects of interest in the city; and if the stranger should with them close his perambulations, he sacrifices very little worthy of notice. But in order to render our Hand-book more complete, we find it necessary to give a short description of Leith, and a passing notice of Newhaven. By omitting both of these places, the circuit of the present walk is very materially abridged, without any corresponding diminution of its interest. We shall therefore print the description of Leith and Newhaven in a smaller type, that the reader may more readily distinguish the portion of the text which relates to them, and which may be read or passed over at pleasure.

Proceeding from the Register House down Greenside

* This Walk is coloured *blue* on the Map.

Street, nothing worthy of remark occurs till we reach the head of LEITH WALK, one of the most splendid roads in the kingdom. Turning to the right at this point, a noble range of buildings, called the ROYAL TERRACE, partly obscured by an unsightly church of recent erection, will be seen occupying the northern side of the Calton Hill. These buildings command a magnificent prospect of the Firth of Forth and the opposite shores, with all the interjacent country.

Tourists proposing to visit Leith will continue their progress down Leith Walk. Omnibuses ply between Edinburgh and Leith every quarter of an hour; and as there is nothing of peculiar interest to be seen upon the way, time will be saved by taking advantage of one of these vehicles as they pass.

LEITH,

The sea-port of Edinburgh, is distant about a mile and a half from the centre of the metropolis. It was not only the first, but, for several centuries, the only port in Scotland, traces of its existence being found in documents of the 12th century. During its early history, few places have so often been the scene of military operations. In 1313, all the vessels in the harbour were burned by the English, and in 1410 a similar act of vengeance was repeated. "In 1544, the town was plundered and burned, its pier destroyed, and its shipping carried off, by the Earl of Hertford, to avenge the insult which Henry VIII. conceived the Scotch had offered him by refusing to betroth their young queen, Mary, to his son Prince Edward. Three years subsequent to this, it was again plundered and burned by the English, under Hertford, then Duke of Somerset, and its whole shipping, together with all that in the Forth, entirely annihilated by the English admiral, Lord Clinton. Four years after this, the town was fortified by Desse, a French general, who came over with 6000 men to assist the Queen-Regent in suppressing the Reformation. On the completion of these fortifications, which consisted in throwing a strong and high wall, with towers at intervals, around the town, the Queen-Regent took up her residence there, and, surrounded with her countrymen, hoped to be able to maintain her authority in the kingdom. These measures, however, had only the effect of widening the breach between her and her subjects, till they finally took up arms, and besieged her in her stronghold. In October 1559, the

Lords of the Congregation invested Leith with an army, but, after various ineffectual attempts to gain access to the town by scaling the walls, they were driven back with great slaughter by a desperate sally of the besieged.

"In the month of April in the succeeding year, the forces of the Congregation again invested the town, being now aided by an army of 6000 men, under Lord Grey of Wilton, despatched to their assistance by Elizabeth. On this occasion, the contest was protracted and sanguinary. For two months, during which the town suffered dreadfully from famine, as well as from the more violent casualties of war, the struggle continued, without any decisive advantage being gained by either side; at the end of that period, both parties being heartily tired of the contest, a treaty was entered into, by which it was stipulated that the French should evacuate the kingdom, that they should be allowed to embark unmolested, and that the English army should, upon the same day, begin its march to England. Immediately after the conclusion of this treaty, the walls of Leith were demolished by order of the Town Council of Edinburgh, and no vestige of them now remains."* In 1561, when Queen Mary came from France to take possession of the throne of her ancestors, she landed upon the pier of Leith; but of this pier no vestiges now remain. In 1650, the town was occupied by Cromwell, who exacted an assessment from the inhabitants. In 1715, the citadel was taken by a party of the adherents of the Stuart family, but, upon being threatened by the Duke of Argyle, it was speedily evacuated. George IV., upon visiting Scotland in 1822, landed at a spot a little to the north of the New Drawbridge, where an inscribed plate has been inserted in the pavement to commemorate the event.

Leith presents few antiquities of any interest. Among those which remain, may be mentioned the Parish Church of South Leith, a Gothic edifice, built previous to the year 1496, and the old church of North Leith, founded in 1493. In the Links, upon the south-east side of the Town, may be seen several mounds, raised for the purpose of planting cannon, by the besieging army, in 1560.

The town "is for the most part irregularly and confusedly built, and a great portion of it is extremely filthy, crowded, and inelegant. Some parts of it, again, are the reverse of this, being spacious, cleanly, and handsome. Such are two or three of the modern streets, and various ranges of private dwellings, erected of late years on the eastern and western skirts of the town.

"The modern public buildings worthy of remark are the Exchange Buildings, a large and elegant structure in the Grecian style of architecture, containing a spacious and handsome assembly-room, a commodious hotel, and public reading-room. The expense of the

* *Encyclopædia Britannica*, Seventh Edition. Article LEITH.

erection was £16,000. The Custom-House, situated in North Leith, is also a very handsome building; it was erected in 1812, at an expense of £12,000. The premises of the Leith branch of the National Bank occupy a neat little edifice, erected in 1805-6. The New Court House, by far the most elegant building in the town, forms altogether, whether the chasteness of the design or the neatness of the workmanship be considered, a very favourable specimen of modern architecture on a small scale."* The Parish Church of North Leith is a handsome though unpretending structure, surmounted by a tasteful spire;—the living is one of the best in the Church of Scotland.

The chief manufactures are ropes and cordage, sail-cloth, bottles, soap, and candles. There are several breweries and a distillery, and ship-building is carried on to a considerable extent.

Leith is the most important naval station on the east coast of Scotland, and a considerable traffic is carried on at the port, the gross revenues of which average above £20,000 a-year: but "it is universally admitted that the harbour, in its present state, is very inadequate to the accommodation of the trade of Edinburgh and of the Firth of Forth, especially to the important branches of steam navigation and the ferry communication between the opposite shores of the Firth."† Large sums have been expended, from time to time, with the view of improving the harbour and docks, but they are still considered inadequate to the trade. Government, in the arrangement of the affairs of the City of Edinburgh, by an Act passed in July 1838, made provision for making extensive improvements in the harbour, a portion of which have been carried into effect. The pier, which is a fine work, forms an excellent promenade.

Leith, with Musselburgh, Portobello, and Newhaven, returns a Member to Parliament. The population amounted, in 1841, to 26,026.

NEWHAVEN

Is a small fishing village, situate about a mile farther up the Forth than Leith. It possesses a stone and a chain pier, but neither the one nor the other has sufficient depth of water to admit of the approach of steamers of large size. The London boats, accordingly, now land and take on board their passengers at Granton, a little farther up the Firth, where a low-water pier has recently been constructed by the Duke of Buccleuch. It was at this pier that Her Majesty, on her recent gracious visit, landed and re-embarked.

* *Encyclopædia Britannica.*

† Parliamentary Report, July 1835.

The inhabitants of Newhaven are a laborious and hardy race. They form a distinct community, rarely intermarrying with any other class. The male inhabitants are almost all fishermen, and the females are constantly occupied in vending the produce of their husbands' industry in the markets or streets of Edinburgh.

When provoked, the *fishwives* display resources of abuse quite equal to their Billingsgate contemporaries. They are also celebrated for the exorbitant prices they demand for their goods, not unfrequently asking three or four times the sum they finally consent to take. Other traders, when purchasers are cheapening their wares, or offering a price which they consider much below their value, are therefore in the habit of saying, "What! would you mak' a fishwife o' me?" Although a very hard-working people, they rarely indulge in an excessive use of ardent spirits. The quantity they consume is, indeed, very considerable, but the prodigious loads with which they are burdened, may be allowed to form some apology for the occasional use of such a stimulus, and their constant exercise in the open air appears to prevent any injurious effects from following the indulgence. They are for the most part, tidy in their habits, and, in these days, when one dull uniformity pervades the dress of all classes, it is refreshing to the lover of the picturesque to contemplate the gaudy garb of the rosy, hearty, mirth-making fishwife.

The Edinburgh, Leith, and Granton Railway affords the means of returning to Edinburgh in seven minutes. At the Newhaven end, the terminus is at Trinity, a little to the west of the village, and there is another at Granton Pier. At Edinburgh, the terminus is in the valley at the east end of Princes Street, but passengers may leave the carriages at the station-house at the foot of Scotland Street, before entering the tunnel. Those who take the latter course will proceed in a straight line by Dublin Street and Duke Street to St. Andrew Square, where they may visit the statue of Sir Walter Scott, described on p. 82, and conclude their walk as therein pointed out.*

Returning to the head of Broughton Street, the neat Gothic front of the Roman Catholic Chapel will be observed on the west side of the street, close by the Adelphi Theatre. At the end of York Place stands St. Paul's Chapel, an elegant Gothic structure, one of the places of worship of the Episcopal Communion. Continuing to proceed down Broughton Street, the stranger will next pass the chapel of the sect called Rowites, whose vagaries made so much noise in the religious world some years ago. Immediately contiguous to this place of worship, is Albany Street Chapel, belonging to the Independents. At the corner of Broughton Place is St. James's Chapel, an Episcopal place of worship, and at the east end of the same street is the principal chapel of the United Secession, the most numerous dissenting body in Scotland, with the exception of the Free Church, which, although essentially a community of Dissenters, is not yet reconciled to the name. Continuing to proceed northwards, by Mansfield Place and Bellevue Crescent, St. Mary's Church will be seen terminating the northern extremity of the latter street. It is one of the neatest of the Edinburgh Churches, possessing a portico and spire, respectable in design and of excellent masonry. Immediately beyond the Church is the entrance to the Newhaven Railway. At the northern end of Claremont Street—(the range of lofty houses opposite St. Mary's Church)—are the Zoological Gardens. They are pleasantly situated, and laid out with good taste. Although the collection is only of recent formation, it is already con-

* Those tourists who visit Leith and Newhaven, and do not return by railway, will require to invert the order of the subsequent pages of this walk, so that the succession of the objects described may accord with the progress of their route. The following will be the order in which the objects will occur, supposing the stranger to return the direct road to Edinburgh:—Botanic Gardens, Canonmills, St. Mary's Church, St. James's Chapel, Albany Street Chapel, St. Paul's Chapel, Roman Catholic Chapel.

siderable, and is constantly receiving additions. The adventurous spirit which carries Scotsmen to the remotest corners of the globe, has tended in no small degree to enrich the collection, many of the fine specimens which it contains having been presented by natives of Scotland travelling, or permanently resident in foreign countries.

From St. Mary's Church the road now declines towards the village of Canonmills. After passing this squalid suburb,* the stranger crosses the Water of Leith, by Canonmills Bridge. Upon his left he will observe some massive and singular looking buildings, erected, some years ago, by an Oil Gas Company. The speculation was soon abandoned as an unprofitable one, and the buildings are now occupied as warehouses. At the further end of Howard Place is situated the CALEDONIAN HORTICULTURAL SOCIETY'S GARDEN, a beautiful and interesting piece of ground, containing 10 imperial acres, and commanding one of the finest views of Edinburgh from the north. Strangers are admitted by orders from members of the Society, or on application to Mr. W. W. Evans, the Curator of the garden.†

* The general character of the place has one redeeming feature. Dr. Neill's pleasant suburban residence, "like a jewel of gold in a swine's snout," is situated on the confines of the village. The proprietor is a distinguished botanist and naturalist, his gardens displaying a variety of botanical rarities, as well as many choice living specimens of interesting objects in the animal kingdom.

† The Caledonian Horticultural Society was established in 1809, since which period large sums have been annually expended in the production of new fruits, flowers, and vegetables, and in perfecting and bringing to maturity those already introduced. In the centre of the garden stands a spacious and elegant hall for the meetings of the Society, adorned with a marble bust, by Steele, of the Secretary, Dr. Neill; and in front of the hall, a fine lawn is laid out, as a promenade ground; where several exhibitions of exotic plants annually take place, attended by all the beauty and fashion of the city. The garden is arranged into various compartments, having soils suited for the different collections placed in them. The raised belts which surround and intersect the garden are occupied as an Arboretum, and contain authentic named specimens of all the newer kinds of trees and shrubs. There is an Apple orchard containing specimens of upwards of 900 named varieties; and a pear orchard, containing upwards of 450 named varieties. The collections also contain 85 varieties of Plums, 25 of Cherries, 27 of Currants, and 30 of Raspberries. The kinds of Strawberries are very numerous, extending to no fewer than 120 sorts, and of Gooseberries the collection is still greater, exceeding 400 kinds. One of the chief objects of the garden is also to exhibit the most approved kinds of culinary vegetables in a growing state, duly tallied, so as to form a school for the infor-

Upon the same side of Inverleith Road, considerably farther along, is the ROYAL BOTANIC GARDEN. To this noble garden, strangers are freely admitted, but the hot-houses are open to the public only on Saturday, between the hours of twelve and four.

The garden embraces an extent of 14½ English acres, and presents every facility for prosecuting the study of Botany.*

It is surrounded by trees on the west, south, and eastern

mation of those visiting the garden; and to test such novelties or rarities as may from time to time be recommended, to make trial of various manures, and to exhibit different modes of culture.

* Immediately upon his entrance to the grounds, the stranger is struck with the luxuriance and vigour of the evergreens, to the cultivation of which Mr. Wm. M'Nab, the late able curator, devoted much attention. On the southern side of the garden there is a large collection of hardy plants arranged according to the Natural System of Jussieu, such as *ferns, grasses, labiate, cruciform, leguminous, umbelliferous*, and *composite plants*, &c. Close to this collection is a small pond containing rushes, water lilies, &c., and a ditch containing those plants which thrive best in such a situation. To the north of this arrangement is a collection of British plants, arranged according to the Linnæan or artificial system, with the name attached to each species. On the eastern side are the plants indigenous to Scotland, and on the west, a few which are found in England and Ireland but not in Scotland. A little to the east of this British arrangement, is a collection of roses. Proceeding northwards, we come to a general collection of hardy evergreens, chiefly exotic; to the east of which is a collection of Medical plants, with the names and natural orders attached. We then reach the Greenhouses. These contain a large collection of exotics, which thrive admirably. The western division contains *heaths, epacrideæ, dryandras, proteas, grevilleas, diosmas*, &c., while in the eastern division, we have a stove with a northern exposure, in which *epiphytes* are cultivated with great success. The peculiar forms of these plants, and their remarkable mode of growth, attract the attention of all.

In the other greenhouses of the front range, there are many interesting plants; among these may be noticed *Plantains*, which bear fruit well, *Papaw tree, Pitcher-plant, Papyrus, Indian rubber fig, cacti, cinnamon, tea plants, camphor tree, Astrapæa*, some of the *Fig* tribe growing suspended in the air, *amaryllides, arums, euphorbias*, &c. In front of this range of houses is a piece of ground on which many of the plants of warmer regions, such as *palms, acacias*, &c., are cultivated in the open air, being carefully protected during winter. Behind these houses is a smaller range in which numerous seedlings are cultivated, and a large Palm-house, about 45 feet high, in which are found *Plantains* and *Bananas, Sago Palms, Fan Palms, European Palms, Cabbage Palms, Date Palms, Coco Nut Trees, Sugar Cane, Bamboos, Screw Pine*, &c. The houses are heated partly by hot water and partly by steam. From the top of the boiler-house there is a very fine view of Edinburgh. Against the high northern wall of the garden, having a south aspect, many valuable exotics are trained, as, *Magnolias, Acacias, Edwardsias, Camellias, Myrtles, Eucalypti*, &c. On the north aspect of the south boundary wall, the Damask Rhododendrons are trained, and flower freely every year.

sides, and among these, there are some of considerable interest. Many of them were removed, in their full grown state, from the former garden in Leith Walk, and under the judicious management of the late Mr. M'Nab, they have all succeeded. To the west of the general European collection is an old Yew, which has been twice transplanted, having been transferred, first, from the Old Physic Gardens, below the North Bridge, to the garden in Leith Walk, and afterwards removed to its present situation. Beside the collection of British plants is a magnetic observatory, superintended by the Professor of Natural Philosophy. The class-room of the Professor of Botany, and the house of the superintendent, are situated on the right-hand side of the entrance. A little further down the road, on the opposite side, is the entrance to the burying-ground of the Edinburgh Cemetery Company. The grounds are laid out with much taste, and the company has conferred an important benefit on the community by affording the means of sepulture in such a spot at extremely moderate charges.

In returning, the stranger may vary his route by turning to the right, immediately after recrossing Canonmills Bridge, and proceeding by Huntly Street, Brandon Street, Pitt Street, and Dundas Street, to Queen Street. Turning to the left along Queen Street, he will pass St. David's Street on the right, and proceed up St. Andrew's Street, the next opening on the same side of the way. On the left hand, upon entering St. Andrew's Square, he may step into the passage No. 31, at the end of which, immediately in front of the door to the premises of Mr. Cadell the publisher, is placed a statue of Sir Walter Scott cut in freestone by Greenshields, a self-taught Lanarkshire artist. The likeness is very striking, and the unaffected character and homely manner of the great novelist are so faithfully expressed, that a friend of Sir Walter's, upon seeing it, exclaimed, "This is not a statue of the man, but his petrifaction."

Resuming his progress along the side of the Square, the stranger will again reach Princes Street, and, turning to the left, will regain the Register House, thus terminating our Fourth Walk.

The objects of interest in the City being now exhausted, we proceed to introduce the tourist to some spots in the vicinity more particularly worthy of notice. Among these we may observe that Roslin is regarded as the most attrac-tive, although we have commenced with Habbie's Howe, as the best geographical arrangement.

Before proceeding to describe these places, it may be of advantage that the means of conveyance from Edinburgh to various important towns and villages should be commu-nicated to tourists. Information under this head is accor-dingly condensed in the following table :—

CONVEYANCES FROM EDINBURGH.

Railways to

Aberdeen.	Dundee & Cupar.	Gorebridge.	London.
Bathgate.	Dunfermline.	Granton.	Midcalder.
Berwick.	Dunse.	Haddington.	Melrose.
Birmingham.	Ecclefechan.	Hawick.	Musselburgh.
Bridge of Allan.	Falkirk.	Kirkcaldy.	Newcastle.
Carlisle.	Forfar.	Lanark.	Perth.
Dalkeith.	Galashiels.	Leith.	Portobello.
Dunbar.	Glasgow.	Linlithgow.	Stirling.

Coaches from Croall's Office, 10 *Princes Street, to*

Corstorphine, every afternoon
Dalkeith, 4 or 5 times daily.
Dunfermline by Queensferry, morning and afternoon.
Elie (Fife).
Innerleithen, every morning.
Lasswade, 5 or 6 times daily
Leven, every forenoon.
Linton, every afternoon.
Musselburgh, 3 or 4 times daily.
Peebles, every morning and after-noon.
Pennicuick, 3 or 4 times daily.
Portobello, every hour.
Ratho, every afternoon.
Roslin, once every forenoon in summer months, returning in the after-noon.

Steamers from Granton Pier to

Aberdeen direct, daily, generally at 6 a.m.
Inverness and Moray Firth, every Tuesday and Thursday, calling at Aberdeen, Banff, Lossiemouth, Burghead, Nairn, Cromarty, and Fort-George.
Kirkwall and Lerwick, calling at Wick, every Friday morning.
London, every Wednesday and Satur-day afternoon.
Newcastle (from Leith), every Wed-nesday and Saturday afternoon.
Stirling, every day, according to tide. (Office for inquiry 10 Princes St.)
Wick and Thurso, calling at Aberdeen, every Monday at 2 o'clock.
Montrose and Peterhead, every Wed-nesday and Saturday, returning Tuesday and Friday.

From Leith to

Dundee, every Wednesday and Sa-turday, returning Tuesday and Friday.

For further particulars, tourists are referred to Harthill's and Murray's Time Tables.

ENVIRONS OF EDINBURGH.

HABBIE'S HOWE. *

A very delightful excursion may be made from Edinburgh to Newhall, distant about twelve miles, supposed, with great probability, to be the scene of Allan Ramsay's celebrated pastoral, "The Gentle Shepherd."

Leaving Edinburgh by Bruntsfield Links, the tourist passes on the right MERCHISTON CASTLE, the birth-place of the celebrated Napier, the inventor of Logarithms. A little further on is the village of Morningside, and a number of villas and country boxes. Two miles from Edinburgh is the hermitage of Braid, (J. Gordon, Esq. of Clunie,) situated at the bottom of a narrow and thickly wooded dell, through which a small rivulet, called the Braid Burn, strays. The road now skirts the rocky eminences called the Hills of Braid, which command a beautiful view of Edinburgh, with the Firth of Forth, and the shores of Fife in the background. The more northern side, called Blackford Hill, the property of Richard Trotter, Esq. of Mortonhall, is the spot mentioned in "Marmion."

"Still on the spot Lord Marmion stay'd,
For fairer scene he ne'er survey'd," &c.

The space of ground which extends from the bottom of Blackford Hill to the suburbs of Edinburgh was formerly denominated the Borough Moor. Here James IV. arrayed his army, previous to his departure on the fatal expedition which terminated in the Battle of Flodden. The HARE STONE, in which the Royal Standard was fixed, is still to be seen built into the wall, which runs along the side of the footpath at the place called Boroughmoor-head. On the right, at some distance, are Dreghorn, (A. Trotter, Esq.,) the village of Colinton, delightfully situated at the bottom of the Pentland Hills, and Colinton House, (Lord Dunfermline.) About five miles from Edinburgh, on the

* Tourists visiting Habbie's Howe must engage a vehicle for the purpose, as there is no regular convevance.

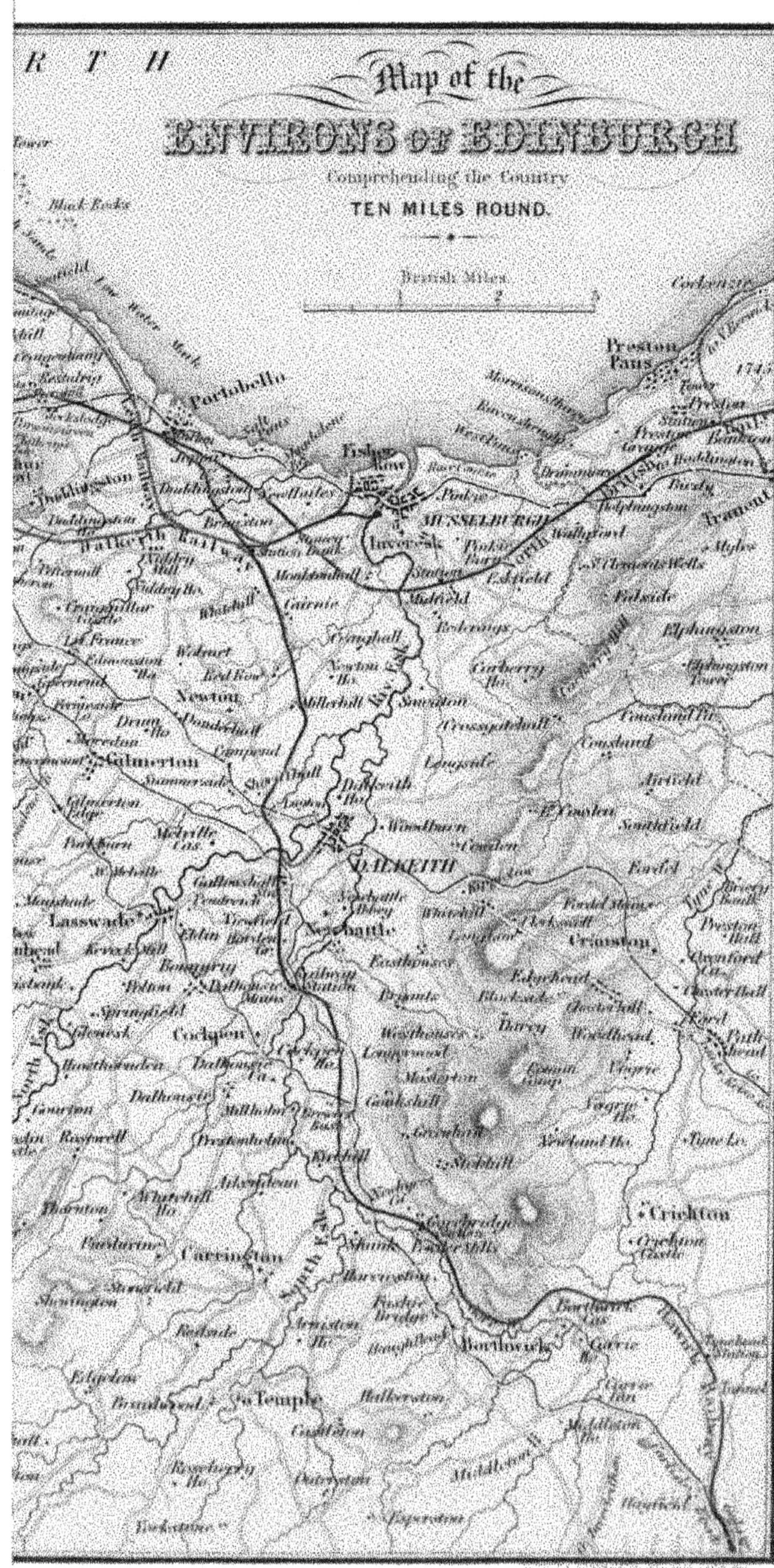
Map of the
ENVIRONS OF EDINBURGH
Comprehending the Country
TEN MILES ROUND.
British Miles
Portobello
Fisher Row
MUSSELBURGH
Inveresk
Preston Pans
Dalkeith Railway
DALKEITH
Newbattle
Lasswade
Gilmerton
Newton
Cockpen
Carrington
Temple
Borthwick
Crichton
Cranston
Duddingston
Tranent
Elphingston
Falside
Wallyford
Carberry Ho.
Pinkie
Melville Cas.
Dalhousie Cas.
Hawthornden
Arniston Ho.
Borthwick Cas.
Crichton Castle
Middleton Ho.
Rosebery Ho.
North Esk
South Esk

southern slope of the Pentland Hills is WOODHOUSELEE, the seat of James Tytler, Esq., surrounded by fine woods. The ancient house of the same name, once the property of Bothwellhaugh, the assassin of the Regent Murray, was four miles distant from the present site. Woodhouselee had been bestowed upon Sir James Ballenden, one of the Regent's favourites, who seized the house, and turned out Lady Bothwellhaugh naked, in a cold night, into the open fields, where, before next morning, she became furiously mad.* The road now passes the hamlet of Upper Howgate, and a little farther on Glencorse Church, embosomed in a wood. On the right is the vale of Glencorse, watered by a little rill, called Logan Water, or, more commonly, Glencorse Burn. The head of this valley is supposed by some to be the scene of Allan Ramsay's pastoral drama, "The Gentle Shepherd," but the appearance of the scenery, as well as the absence of all the localities noticed by Ramsay, render this opinion extremely improbable. The sequestered pastoral character of this valley, however, renders it well worthy of a visit. After crossing Glencorse Burn, the road passes House-of-Muir, in the neighbourhood of which is the place where the Covenanters were defeated, 28th November 1666. Passing through the village of Silver Burn, the road reaches

NEWHALL,

on the banks of the North Esk, about three miles from Pennycuik House, and twelve south-west from Edinburgh. Newhall is now the property of Robert Brown, Esq. At the era of Ramsay's drama, it belonged to Dr. Alexander Pennycuik, a poet and antiquary. In 1703, it passed into the hands of Sir David Forbes, a distinguished lawyer ; and, in Ramsay's time, was the property of Mr. John Forbes, son to Sir David, and cousin-german to the celebrated President Forbes of Culloden. The scenery around Newhall answers most minutely to the description in the drama. Near the house, on the north side of the vale, there is a

* This event forms the subject of Sir Walter Scott's fine ballad of "Cadyow Castle," which will be found quoted entire in the SEVENTH TOUR.

crag (called the Harbour Crag, from having afforded refuge to the Covenanters), which closely corresponds with the "craggy bield" described in the first scene of the first act.

Farther up the vale, a variety of other scenes, corresponding to the descriptions of the poet, are to be met with.

PENNYCUIK HOUSE, the seat of Sir George Clerk, Bart., is well worthy of a visit. The neighbouring scenery is extremely beautiful, and the pleasure-grounds are highly ornamented. The house contains an extensive and excellent collection of paintings, with a number of Roman antiquities found in Britain, and, amongst other curiosities, the buff-coat worn by Dundee at the battle of Killiecrankie.

ROSLIN.

HAWTHORNDEN—MELVILLE CASTLE—DALKEITH PALACE—NEWBATTLE ABBEY—DALHOUSIE CASTLE—BORTHWICK AND CRICHTON CASTLES—CRAIGMILLAR CASTLE—HOPETOUN HOUSE.

During summer, a coach leaves 10 Princes Street for Roslin at 11 o'clock A. M., returning at 3 P. M.

If the Roslin coach should be full, parties may go by the Lasswade coach to Loanhead, where they are within a mile and a half of Roslin.

The Chapel and Castle are exhibited to strangers every day; and there is a small inn with stabling at Roslin.

Borthwick and Crichton Castles are most easily reached by the North British Railway, leaving the line at Gorebridge Station.

Hopetoun House is most easily reached by coach from 10 Princes Street.

Another interesting scene, that well deserves a visit, is ROSLIN CHAPEL, situated about seven miles from Edinburgh, on the banks of the North Esk. The vale of Roslin is one of those sequestered dells, abounding with all the romantic varieties of cliff, copsewood, and waterfall. Its Gothic Chapel is an exquisitely decorated specimen of ecclesiastical architecture, founded in 1446, by William St. Clair, Earl of Orkney, and Lord of Roslin. At the Revolution of 1688, part of it was defaced by a mob from Edinburgh, but it was repaired in the following century by General St. Clair; and a restoration of its more dilapidated parts has recently been made by the present Earl. "This building," says Mr. Britton, "may be pronounced unique,

PENNYCU K HOUSE.

and I am confident it will be found curious, elaborate, and singularly interesting. The Chapel of King's College, St. George, and Henry VII., are all conformable to the styles of the respective ages when they were erected; and these styles display a gradual advancement in lightness and pro-

fusion of ornament: but the CHAPEL OF ROSLIN combines the solidity of the Norman with the minute decorations of the latest species of the Tudor age. It is impossible to designate the architecture of this building by any given or familiar term: for the variety and eccentricity of its parts are not to be defined by any words of common acceptation." The nave is bold and lofty, enclosed, as usual, by side aisles, the pillars and arches of which display a profusion of ornament, executed in the most beautiful manner. The "Prentice's Pillar" in particular, with its finely sculptured foliage, is a piece of exquisite workmanship. It is said that the master-builder of the Chapel, being unable to execute the design of this pillar from the plans in his possession, proceeded to Rome, that he might see a column of a similar description which had been executed in that city. During his absence, his apprentice proceeded with the execution of the design, and, upon the master's return, he found this finely ornamented column completed. Stung with envy at this proof of the superior ability of his apprentice, he struck him a blow with his mallet, and killed him on the spot. Upon the architrave uniting the Prentice's Pillar to a smaller one, is the following sententious inscription from the book of Apocryphal Scripture, called Esdras;—"*Forte est vinum, fortior est rex, fortiores sunt mulieres; super omnia vincit veritas.*" Beneath the Chapel lie the Barons of Roslin, all of whom, till the time of James VII., were buried in complete armour.*

* This circumstance, as well as the superstitious belief that, on the night before the death of any of these barons, the chapel appeared in flames, is beautifully described by Sir Walter Scott, in his exquisite ballad of Rosabelle:

O listen, listen, ladies gay!
No haughty feats of arms I tell;
Soft is the note, and sad the lay,
That mourns the lovely Rosabelle.

"Moor, moor the barge, ye gallant crew!
And, gentle ladye, deign to stay!
Rest thee in Castle Ravensheuch,
Nor tempt the stormy firth to day.

"The blackening wave is edged with white:
To inch and rock the sea-mews fly;
The fishers have heard the Water-Sprite,
Whose screams forbode that wreck is nigh.

"Last night the gifted Seer did view
A wet shroud swathed round ladye gay!
Then stay thee, Fair, in Ravensheuch;
Why cross the gloomy firth to day?"

"'Tis not because Lord Lindesay's heir
To-night at Roslin leads the ball,
But that my ladye-mother there
Sits lonely in her castle-hall.

"'Tis not because the ring they ride—
And Lindesay at the ring rides well—
But that my sire the wine will chide,
If 'tis not fill'd by Rosabelle."

O'er Roslin, all that dreary night,
A wondrous blaze was seen to gleam;
'Twas broader than the watch-fire's light,
And redder than the bright moon-beam.

It glared on Roslin's castled rock,
It ruddied all the copsewood glen;
'Twas seen from Dryden's groves of oak,
And seen from cavern'd Hawthornden.

Seem'd all on fire that chapel proud,
Where Roslin's chiefs uncoffin'd lie,
Each baron, for a sable shroud,
Sheathed in his iron panoply.

Seem'd all on fire within, around,
Deep sacristy and altar's pale;
Shone every pillar foliage bound,
And glimmer'd all the dead men's mail.

Blazed battlement and pinnet high,
Blazed every rose-carved buttress fair—
So still they blaze, when fate is nigh
The lordly line of high St. Clair.

There are twenty of Roslin's barons bold
Lie buried within that proud chapelle;
Each one the holy vault doth hold—
But the sea holds lovely Rosabelle.

And each St. Clair was buried there,
With candle, with book, and with knell;
But the sea caves rung, and the wild winds
The dirge of lovely Rosabelle. [sung.

There is no stated fee for admission to the Chapel, but the exhibiter expects a small gratuity.*

The mouldering ruin of Roslin Castle, with its tremeu dous triple tier of vaults, stands upon a peninsular rock overhanging the picturesque glen of the Esk, and is accessible only by a bridge of great height, thrown over a deep cut in the solid rock, which separates it from the adjacent ground. This Castle, the origin of which is involved in obscurity, was long the abode of the proud family of the St. Clairs, Earls of Caithness and Orkney. In 1544, it was burned down by the Earl of Hertford; and, in 1650, it surrendered to General Monck. About sixty or seventy years ago, the comparatively modern mansion, which has been erected amidst the ruins of the old castle, was inhabited by a genuine Scottish laird of the old stamp, the lineal descendant of the high race who first founded the pile, and the last male of their long line. He was captain of the Royal Company of Archers, and Hereditary Grand Master of the Scottish Masons. At his death, the estate descended to Sir James Erskine St. Clair, father of the present Earl of Rosslyn, who now represents the family.

The neighbouring moor of Roslin was the scene of a celebrated battle, fought 24th February 1302, in which the Scots, under Comyn, then guardian of the kingdom, and Simon Fraser, attacked and defeated three divisions of the English on the same day.†

* Hawthornden being open to strangers *only on Wednesdays*, (as directed on page 90,) and Dalkeith Palace *only on Wednesdays and Saturdays*, Wednesday is the only day upon which *all the three places* can be seen, and tourists will, therefore, endeavour to devote this day to the purpose.

† "Three triumphs in a day!
Three hosts subdued by one!
Three armies scattered like the spray
Beneath one summer sun.—
Who, pausing 'mid this solitude
Of rocky streams and leafy trees,
Who, gazing o'er this quiet wood,
Would ever dream of these?
Or have a thought that ought intrude,
Save birds and humming bees."

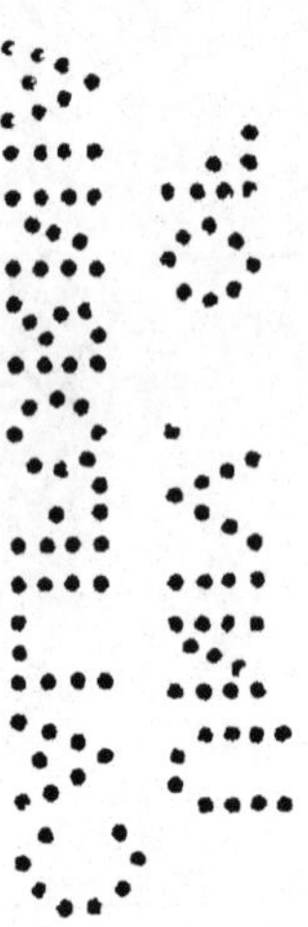

After leaving Roslin, we pass the caves of Gorton, situated in the front of a high cliff on the southern side of the stream. These caverns, during the reign of David II., while Scotland was overrun by the English, afforded shelter to the gallant Sir Alexander Ramsay of Dalwolsey, with a band of chosen patriots.

Passing through scenery of great natural beauty, the footpath down the river conducts the tourist to

HAWTHORNDEN,

the classical habitation of the poet Drummond, the friend of Shakspeare and Jonson; it is now the property of Sir James Walker Drummond. "This romantic spot seems to have been formed by nature in one of her happiest moments. All the materials that compose the picturesque seem here combined in endless variety: stupendous rocks, rich and varied in colours, hanging in threatening aspect, crowned with trees that expose their bare branching roots; here the gentle birch hanging midway, and there the oak, bending its stubborn branches, meeting each other; huge fragments of rocks impede the rapid flow of the stream, that hurries brawling along unseen, but heard far beneath, mingling in the breeze that gently agitates the wood." Being built with some view to defence, the house rises from the very edge of the grey cliff, which descends sheer down to the stream. An inscription on the front of the building testifies that it was repaired by the poet in 1638. It is well known that Ben Jonson walked from London, on foot, to visit Drummond, and lived several weeks with him at Hawthorndon. Under the mansion are several subterraneous caves, hewn out of the solid rock with great labour, and connected with each other by long passages; in the courtyard there is a well of prodigious depth, which communicates with them. These caverns are supposed to have been constructed as places of refuge, when the public calamities rendered the ordinary habitations unsafe. The walks around the house are peculiarly fine, but without a special order from the proprietor, admission to them is limited to Wednesday of each week. Visitors from Edinburgh gene-

MELVILLE CASTLE.

rally engage a vehicle to the house, walking up the glen, and meeting their carriage again at Roslin.

Farther down the river is the pretty village of LASSWADE, the name of which is said to be derived from a *lass*, who, in former times, waded across the stream, carrying upon her back those whose circumstances enabled them to purchase the luxury of such a conveyance. In a cottage in the vicinity Sir Walter Scott spent some of the happiest years of his life. At a short distance is

MELVILLE CASTLE,

the seat of Viscount Melville. The building was erected by the celebrated Harry Dundas, first Viscount Melville. The park contains some fine wood. Two miles farther is the town of DALKEITH, in which is held the most extensive grain market in Scotland. In its immediate neighbourhood, situated on an overhanging bank of the North Esk, a little to the east of the town, stands

DALKEITH PALACE,

a seat of the Duke of Buccleuch. It is a large, but by no means elegant, structure, surrounded by an extensive park, through which the rivers of North and South Esk flow, and unite their streams a short way below the house. The first proprietors of Dalkeith upon record are the Grahams; from them it passed, in the reign of David II., by a daughter, into the possession of Sir William Douglas, ancestor of the Earls of Morton. In the reign of Queen Mary, Dalkeith was the head-quarters of the celebrated Regent Morton, and, after resigning his regency, he retired to this stronghold, which, from the general idea entertained of his character, acquired, at that time, the expressive name of the Lion's Den. In the year 1642, the estate was purchased from the Earl of Morton by Francis, Earl of Buccleuch. Anne, Duchess of Buccleuch and Monmouth, after the execution of her unhappy husband, substituted the modern for the ancient mansion, and lived here in royal state, and, for more than a century, it has formed the residence of the Buccleuch family. Since the union of the crowns, Dalkeith

House has thrice been the temporary residence of royalty, —namely, of King Charles, in 1633, of George IV., in 1822. and of her present Majesty, in 1842. It is worthy of notice, that Froissart, the historian of chivalry, visited the Earl of Douglas, and lived with him several weeks at the Castle of Dalkeith. There is a popular belief current, that the treasure unrighteously amassed by the Regent Morton lies hidden somewhere among the vaults of the ancient building; but Godscroft assures us, that it was expended by the Earl of Angus in supporting the companions of his exile in England, and that, when it was exhausted, the Earl generously exclaimed, "Is it, then, all gone? let it go; I never looked it should have done so much good!" Dalkeith Palace is shown to strangers, when the family is not residing there, on Wednesday and Saturday. The environs of Dalkeith are interesting, and the tourist may be conveyed thither from Edinburgh, by the North British Railway, several times a-day.*

About a mile south-west from Dalkeith, on the northern bank of the South Esk, is

NEWBATTLE ABBEY,

a seat of the Marquis of Lothian. This mansion stands on

* The beautiful scenes through which the North and South Esk flow, and the various seats that adorn the banks of these streams, are very happily described by Sir Walter Scott in his ballad of the Grey Brother:—

"Sweet are the paths,—Oh, passing sweet!
By Esk's fair streams that run,
O'er airy steep, through copsewoods deep,
Impervious to the sun.

There the rapt poet's step may rove,
And yield the Muse the day,
There Beauty, led by timid Love,
May shun the tell-tale ray.

From that fair dome where suit is paid,
By blast of bugle free, †
To Auchindinny's hazel glade,
And haunted Woodhouselee.

Who knows not Melville's beechy grove,
And Roslin's rocky glen,
Dalkeith, which all the virtues love,
And classic Hawthornden?"

† Pennycuik. See ante, p. 84.

the spot formerly occupied by the Abbey of Newbattle, founded by David I. for a community of Cistertian monks. An ancestor of the present noble proprietor was the last abbot, and his son, Mark Ker, got the possessions of the abbey erected into a temporal lordship in the year 1591. The house contains a number of fine paintings and curious manuscripts, and the lawn is interspersed with some straggling trees of great size.

About two miles farther up the South Esk is

DALHOUSIE CASTLE,

a modernized building in the castellated form. The original structure was of vast antiquity and great strength. The present possessor, the Earl of Dalhousie, is the lineal descendant of the celebrated Sir Alexander Ramsay. The scenery around Dalhousie is romantic and beautiful.

Passing Arniston, the residence of the celebrated family of Dundas, the tourist, at the distance of about eleven miles from Edinburgh, comes in sight of Borthwick Castle, an ancient and stately tower, rising out of the centre of a small but well cultivated valley, watered by a stream called the Gore. This interesting fortress is in the form of a double tower, seventy-four feet in length, sixty-eight in breadth, and ninety feet in height from the area to the battlements. It occupies a knoll, surrounded by the small river, and is enclosed within an outer court, fortified by a strong outward wall, having flanking towers at the angles. The interior of the castle is exceedingly interesting. The hall is a stately and magnificent apartment, the ceiling of which consists of a smooth vault of ashler work. Three stairs, ascending at the angles of the building, gave access to the separate stories; one is quite ruinous, but the others are still tolerably entire. The license for building Borthwick Castle was granted by James I. to Sir William Borthwick, 2d June 1430. It was to Borthwick that Queen Mary retired with Bothwell, three weeks after her unfortunate marriage with that nobleman, and from which she was obliged, a few days afterwards, to flee to Dunbar in the disguise of a page. During the civil war, Borthwick held out gallantly against the victorious Cromwell, and surrendered at last upon honourable terms. The effect of Cromwell's battery still remains, his fire having destroyed a part of the freestone facing of the eastern side of the castle. Borthwick is now the property of John Borthwick, Esq. of Crookstone, a claimant of the ancient peerage of Borthwick, which has remained in abeyance since the death of the ninth Lord Borthwick, in the reign of Charles II. The valley of Borthwick is a sober, peaceful, sequestered, and exquisitely rural spot, and its manse and church, farm-houses and cottages, are in complete harmony with its prevailing character. In the manse of Borthwick, Dr. Robertson, the historian, was born.

A mile and a quarter to the eastward of Borthwick Castle, and within sight of its battlements, stands CRICHTON CASTLE, on the banks of the Tyne, twelve and a half miles south from Edinburgh, and about two miles above the village of Pathhead, on the Lauder road. The footpath which leads from Borthwick to Crichton meanders delightfully through natural pastures and rushy meadows, among dwarf hazel, and alder and blackthorn bushes, broom and brackens, till walled in by a nearly impenetrable wilderness of furze roughly clothing the bank. The waters divide hereabouts,—the infant Tyne running eastward, while Borthwick burn, descending from the southward heights, flows west till it falls into the Esk. Crichton Castle was built at different periods, and forms, on the whole, one large square pile, enclosing an interior court-yard. A strong old tower, which forms the east side of the quadrangle, seems to have been the original part of the building. The northern quarter, which appears to be the most modern, is built in a style of remarkable elegance. The description of the castle given by Sir Walter Scott, in his poem of Marmion, is so minutely accurate, that we transcribe it in preference to any remarks of our own.

That Castle rises on the steep
  Of the green vale of Tyne;
And, far beneath, where slow they creep
From pool to eddy, dark and deep,

Where alders moist, and willows weep,
  You hear her streams repine.
The towers in different ages rose;
Their various architecture shows
  The builders' various hands;
A mighty mass, that could oppose,
When deadliest hatred fired its foes,
  The vengeful Douglas' bands.

Crichtoun! though now thy miry court
  But pens the lazy steer and sheep,
  Thy turrets rude, and totter'd Keep,
Have been the minstrel's loved resort.
Oft have I traced within thy fort,
  Of mouldering shields the mystic sense,
  Scutcheons of honour, or pretence,
Quarter'd in old armorial sort,
  Remains of rude magnificence.
Nor wholly yet hath time defaced
  Thy lordly gallery fair;
Nor yet the stony cord unbraced,
Whose twisted knots with roses laced,
  Adorn thy ruin'd stair.
Still rises, unimpair'd, below,
The court-yard's graceful portico;
Above its cornice, row and row
  Of fair-hewn facets richly show
    Their pointed diamond form,
  Though there but houseless cattle go,
    To shield them from the storm.
  And, shuddering, still may we explore,
    Where oft whilom were captives pent,
  The darkness of thy Massy More;*
    Or, from thy grass-grown battlement,
May trace in undulating line,
The sluggish mazes of the Tyne.

Crichton was the patrimonial estate and residence of the celebrated Sir William Crichton, Chancellor of Scotland, whose influence during the minority of James II., contributed so much to destroy the formidable power of the Douglas family. On the forfeiture of William, third Lord Crichton, the castle and barony of Crichton was granted to Sir John Ramsay, a favourite of James III. The defeat

* The pit or prison vault.

and death of James involved the ruin of Ramsay. He in his turn was proscribed, exiled, and his estate forfeited, and the castle and lordship of Crichton were granted anew to Patrick Hepburn, third Lord Hales, who was created Earl of Bothwell. He was ancestor of the infamous James Earl of Bothwell, who exercised such an unhappy influence over the fortunes of Queen Mary. On his outlawry, Crichton was conferred by James VI. on his kinsman Francis Stewart, Earl of Bothwell, so noted for the constant train of conspiracies and insurrections in which he was engaged. Since that period, Crichton has passed through the hands of about a dozen proprietors, and is now the property of William Burn Callender, Esq. The ancient church of Crichton still exists, at the distance of half a mile to the north of the castle. It is a small but venerable building in the shape of a cross, with a low and truncated belfry. The west end has been left unfinished.

Returning to the road, about half a mile from Pathhead, stands OXENFORD CASTLE, a residence of the Earl of Stair. It is situate on the north bank of the Tyne, in the midst of an extensive park.

About three miles south from Edinburgh are the ruins of CRAIGMILLAR CASTLE, situate on the top of a gentle eminence, and surrounded with some fine old trees. "There is nothing to show at what age or by what hand it is built;"* but the rampart wall which surrounds the castle appears, from a date preserved on it, to have been built in 1427. Craigmillar, with other fortresses in Mid-Lothian, was burned by the English after Pinkey fight in 1555, and Captain Grose surmises, with great plausibility, that much of the building, as it now appears, was erected when the castle was repaired after that event.

In point of architecture and accommodation, Craigmillar surpasses the generality of Scottish Castles. It consists of a strong tower, flanked with turrets, and connected with inferior buildings. There is an outer court in front, defended by the battlemented wall already mentioned, and beyond these there was an exterior wall, and in some places

* CHALMERS'S *Caledonia*, vol. ii. p. 570.

a deep ditch or moat. In 1813, a human skeleton was found enclosed, in an upright position, in a crevice of the vaulting of the castle. Upon being exposed to the air, it shortly crumbled to dust.

Being so near Edinburgh, Craigmillar was often occupied as a royal residence. Here John Earl of Mar, younger brother of James III., was imprisoned in 1477. James V. occupied it occasionally during his minority, and it was so often the residence of Queen Mary, that the adjacent village acquired the name of Little France, from her French guards being quartered there.

The castle and estate of Craigmillar were acquired by Sir Simon Preston in 1374, from one John de Capella, and they continued in the possession of the Preston family till about the period of the Revolution, when they were purchased by Sir Thomas Gilmour, the great lawyer, to whose descendant, Walter Little Gilmour, Esq., they still belong.

FIRST TOUR.

EDINBURGH TO MELROSE, ABBOTSFORD, AND DRYBURGH, BY RAILWAY.

NORTH BRITISH RAILWAY.

Edinburgh and Hawick (Branch).

Miles.	STATIONS.	Miles.	STATIONS.
	Edinburgh.	38½	Newstead.
	Leith (by Coach to Portobello.)	40½	Newtown St. Boswells.
3	Portobello.		49½ Roxburgh (per Branch).
4½	Niddry.		52 Wallace-Nick for Kelso (do.)
8	Dalkeith.		
8	Gallowshall or Eskbank.		*Branch of York, Newcastle, and Berwick Railway, (Kelso to Berwick).*
9	Dalhousie.		Kelso.
12	Gorebridge.		Sprouston.
13	Fushio Bridge.		Carham.
16	Tyne-head.		Cornhill, for Coldstream.
19½	Heriot.		Norham.
22¾	Fountainhall.		Velvethall.
27	Stow.		Tweedmouth, for Berwick.
30	Bowland Bridge.	45½	New Belses.
33½	Galashiels.	49	Hassendean.
37½	Melrose.	53	Hawick.

Coaches in connection with this Branch:—To Jedburgh from New Belses; to Selkirk from Galashiels; to Kelso from Wallace-Nick.

There is another Coach, not in connection with the Railway, to Jedburgh from Newtown St. Boswells Station.

Directions to accomplish this Tour, returning to Edinburgh same Day.

Notice.—From and after the 20th of August, Abbotsford House is shewn only on Wednesdays and Fridays, from two till five P.M. During the earlier part of the year, it is generally shewn when Mr. Lockhart's family is from home.

Leave Edinburgh by an early train on the Hawick Branch of the North British Railway: station at Waverley Bridge. Take a return ticket for Melrose, distant from Edinburgh thirty-seven miles, and which is reached in about two hours.

1. Visit the ruins of Melrose Abbey. Abbotsford is two miles westward, and Dryburgh four miles eastward of Melrose.
2. Walk, or hire a vehicle to Abbotsford, the interior of which is shewn to strangers.
3. Return to Melrose, from which proceed by same conveyance, or by railway to Newtown St. Boswells Station, from which Dryburgh is about a mile distant.
4. Return to Melrose, and take the evening train to Edinburgh.

NORTH BRITISH & BERWICK & KELSO RAILWAYS.

(EDINBURGH TO HAWICK.) (HAWICK TO BERWICK.)

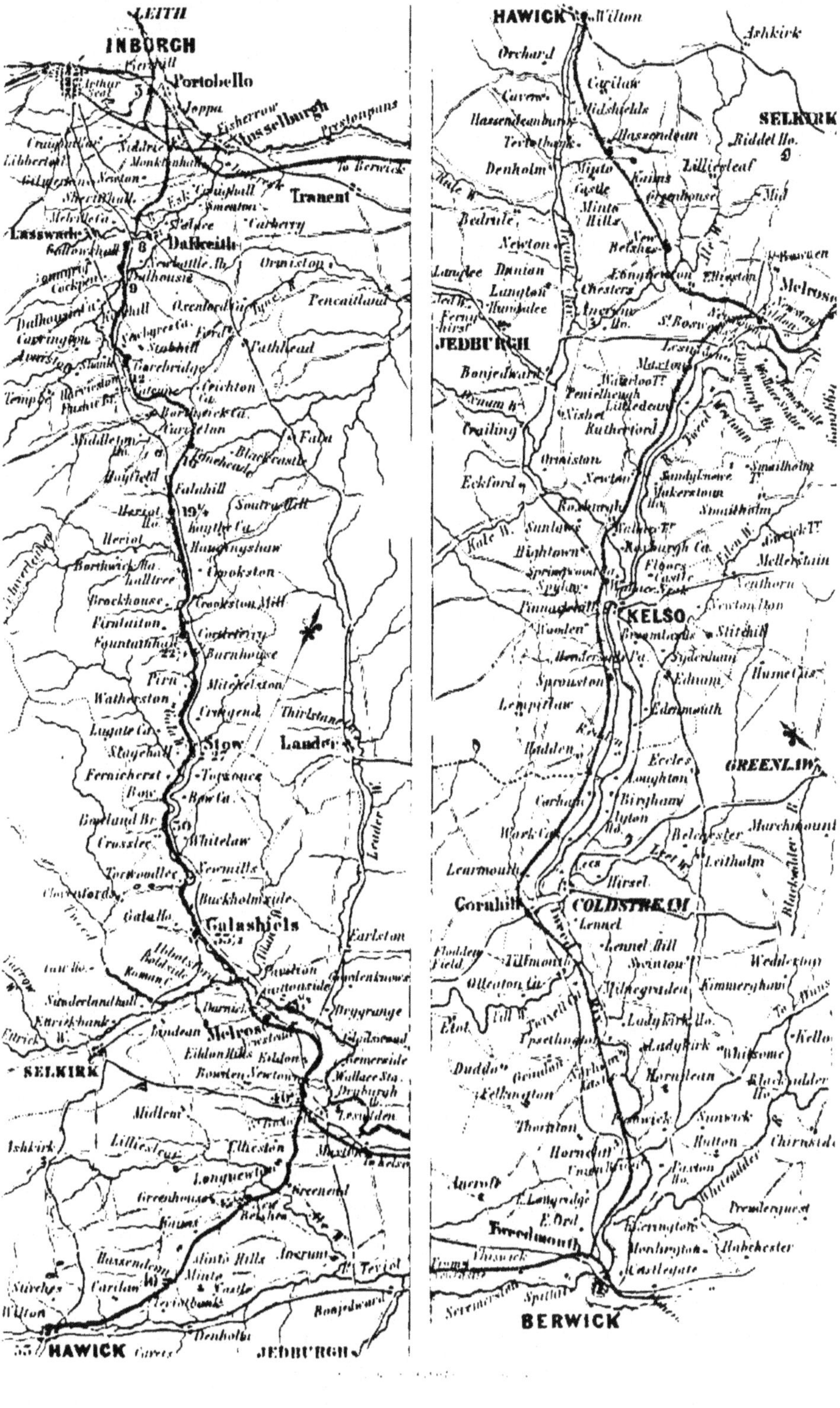

FROM EDINBURGH TO MELROSE BY RAILWAY.

The scenery of the country traversed by the Hawick Branch of the North British Railway is very pleasing.

On emerging from the tunnel, shortly after leaving the station at Edinburgh, a fine view is obtained, on the right, of Arthur's Seat, Holyrood Palace, and ruins of St. Anthony's Chapel. Passing Portobello—the principal watering-place of the inhabitants of Edinburgh—and the village of Dalkeith, both on the left, the line skirts the grounds of Dalhousie Castle, affording in its progress a beautiful prospect of the Pentland Hills to the right. Close to Gorebridge Station, on the left, are the ruins of Gorebridge Castle. A little beyond the Station, after passing through two short tunnels, a glance may be had of Arniston House, (R. Dundas, Esq.) on the right. About two miles further on, we come in sight of Borthwick village and the ruins of Borthwick Castle on the right, and those of Crichton Castle on the left, both beautifully situated in the valley of the Tyne. (For description, see page 94). A little beyond Heriot Station, to the left, is Crookston (J. Borthwick, Esq.)

Proceeding onwards, we reach Stow Station, opposite the ancient and irregular village of the same name, situated in the middle of a district which formerly bore the name of We-dale (the Vale of Wo). The whole of this territory belonged at one time to the Bishops of St. Andrews, and many of their charters are dated from We-dale. The line now crosses the Lugate Water by a viaduct, and reaches Crosslec, on the confines of the county of Roxburgh. The river Gala here forms the boundary between the counties of Roxburgh and Selkirk, and the alder, birch, and hazel, are found in abundance on its banks. The "Braw Lads of Gala Water," are celebrated in Burns's well-known beautiful lyric of that name. In the immediate neighbourhood, but not visible from the line, is Torwoodlee, the fine mansion of Pringle of Torwoodlee, situated in the midst of stately trees, upon a fine terrace overhanging the Gala. A few hundred yards to the west of the modern mansion are the ruins of the old house, jutting out from the side of a hill.

At a little distance to the west of the ruin, lies the family burying-ground, embowered in the midst of a dark grove. The Pringles of Torwoodlee are a very old family, and celebrated in Border story. Their representative, in the reign of Charles II., was peculiarly obnoxious to Government, on account of his exertions in the cause of the Covenant, and his concern in Argyle's rebellion. Within a mile of his house, on different sides of the vale of Gala, were two old towers, called Buckholm and Blindlee, occupied by two of his inveterate enemies, who are said to have kept continual watch over his motions, in order to find occasion to accuse him to Government. At the distance of 33½ miles from Edinburgh, the train reaches the manufacturing town of

GALASHIELS.

[*Inns*:—The Bridge Inn; The Commercial; Victoria Hotel; Railway Hotel.]

Galashiels is situated on the banks of the Gala, about a mile above its junction with the Tweed. It contains about 4000 inhabitants, principally engaged in the production of woollen cloths. About sixty years ago, Galashiels was only a small village, occupying part of the higher ground near the church, and extending within the park, where the ruins of the old court-house still remain, towards the baronial mansion of Gala. A few weavers contented themselves with exercising their individual industry; but by degrees union and enterprise enlarged the demand, and devised new means of meeting it. Mills were built—at first on a small scale, but by increasing prosperity were enlarged and multiplied, and a populous town soon covered the green fields beside the Gala. Originally the only species of manufacture was a coarse woollen cloth, called "Galashiels gray," the wool employed being the produce of the surrounding hills; but now the goods manufactured chiefly consist of fancy articles, such as tartans, tweeds, and shawls of the finest texture and most brilliant colours, while the wool is principally imported from Van Diemen's Land. Within the last few years the town and its manufactures have increased with even greater rapidity than at any former period. The mills have grown to four times their original size; large new premises have been erected; the water force of the Gala has been exhausted, and, though the distance from coal is great, recourse has been had to the aid of steam.

The town is partly in Selkirkshire, and partly in Roxburgh. Galashiels proper is a burgh of barony, under the family of Gala. which now bears the name of Scott, though representing the ancient Pringles, the ancestor of Mr. Scott having married the heiress of that baronial house, and succeeded to its fortunes in 1623. An old pear-tree exists near the house, on which the destined bride is said to have been amusing herself in youthful frolics whilst the marriage-contract was signed.

In 1813, Mr. Richard Lees, manufacturer, assisted by a blacksmith, constructed a wire bridge over the Gala, being the first specimen of this American invention erected in the old world. It was destroyed by a flood in autumn 1838, but another has been erected in its place. The higher ground of the parish is traversed by the remains of an ancient wall, supposed to be the Catrail, and near it at Rink, on an eminence, is an old British Camp. From Galashiels a coach runs in connection with the railway to

SELKIRK.

[*Inns*:—Mitchell's Inn; The Fleece Inn.]

Selkirk is situated on a piece of high ground overhanging the Ettrick. It is a neat town, and the beautiful woods surrounding the Haining, the seat of the late Robert Pringle, Esq., of Clifton, now belonging to his sister, Mrs. Douglas of Edderstone, form an excellent background to it. The population of the burgh is 2593. It gives the title of Earl to a branch of the Douglas family.

A party of the citizens of Selkirk, under the command of their town-clerk, William Brydone, behaved with great gallantry at the battle of Flodden, when, in revenge for their brave conduct, the English entirely destroyed the town by fire. A pennon, taken from an English leader by a person of the name of Fletcher, is still kept in Selkirk by the successive Deacons of the weavers, and Brydone's sword is still in the possession of his lineal descendants. The well-known pathetic ballad of "The Flowers of the Forest," was composed on the loss sustained by the inhabitants of Ettrick Forest at the fatal battle of Flodden. The principal trade carried on in Selkirk at the time of the battle, and for centuries afterwards, was the manufacture of thin or *single-soled* shoes.* Hence, to be made a souter of Selkirk is the ordinary phrase for being created a burgess, and a *birse* or hog's bristle is always attached to the seal of the ticket. Of late the manufactures of Galashiels have found their way to Selkirk. Large mills have been erected on the Ettrick ; the old decaying burgh seems to have revived its youth ; new buildings are seen rising in and around a town which was long thought to have been in a hopeless state of decay, and the population has greatly increased. The line crosses the Tweed at the village of Bridgend. To the right are seen the woods of Abbotsford, and to the left "The Pavilion," the beautiful mansion of Lord Somerville, situated on the banks of the Allan Water (described page 113). The small village of Bridgend received its name from a bridge erected over the Tweed by David I., to afford a passage to the Abbey of Melrose. It consisted of four piers, upon which lay planks of wood ; and in the middle pillar was a gateway large enough for a carriage to pass through, and over that a room in which the toll-keeper resided. It was at a ford below this bridge that the adventure with the White Lady of Avenel befell Father Philip, the sacristan of the Monastery. (See Monastery, vol. i.) From this bridge the Girthgate, a path to the sanctuary of Soutra, runs up the valley of Allan Water, and over the moors to Soutra Hill. The Eildon Hills now rise majestically on the right, and shortly afterwards the train arrives at

MELROSE.

[*Inns*:—The George Hotel; Thomson's Hotel; King's Arms; Railway Hotel.]

Melrose is situated on the Tweed, near the base of the

* Up wi' the Souters o' Selkirk,
And down wi' the Earl o' Hume;
And up wi' a' the braw lads
That sew the single-soled shoon.

Eildon Hills. It is thirty-seven miles from Edinburgh, twelve from Jedburgh, and fourteen from Kelso. "The vale of the Tweed is everywhere fertile and beautiful, and here grandeur is combined with beauty and fertility. The eye is presented with a wide range of pleasing and impressive scenery—of villages and hamlets—the river winding rapidly among smiling fields and orchards, the town with its groves, and gardens, and neat rural church, wooded acclivities, and steep pastoral slopes crowned with the shapely summits of majestic hills, forming a richly diversified and striking panorama, not to speak of the elegant and graceful remains of the ancient Abbey, the sight of which conveys a deep interest to the mind, carries it back through ages and events long past, and leads to sober reflections on the vicissitudes of human affairs, and the instability of human institutions."* Near the village are the remains of the famous Abbey, which affords the finest specimen of Gothic architecture and Gothic sculpture ever reared in this country. The stone of which it is built, though it has resisted the weather for so many ages, retains perfect sharpness, so that even the most minute ornaments seem as entire as when newly wrought. The other buildings being completely destroyed, the ruins of the church alone remain to attest the ancient magnificence of this celebrated monastery. It is in the usual form of a Latin cross, with a square tower in the centre, eighty-four feet in height, of which only the west side is standing. The parts now remaining of this structure are the choir and transept—the west side, and part of the north and south walls of the great tower, part of the nave, nearly the whole of the southmost aisle, and part of the north aisle. The west gable being in ruins, the principal entrance is by a richly moulded Gothic portal in the south transept. Over this doorway is a magnificent window, twenty-four feet in height and sixteen in breadth, divided by four bars or mullions, which branch out or interlace each other at the top in a variety of graceful curves. The stone work of the whole window yet remains perfect. Over this window are nine niches, and two on each buttress,

* *Monastic Annals of Teviotdale*, p. 190.

which formerly contained images of our Saviour and his Apostles. Beneath the window is a statue of John Baptist, with his eye directed upward, as if looking upon the image of Christ above. The carving upon the pedestals and canopies of the niches exhibits a variety of quaint figures and devices. The buttresses and pinnacles on the east and west sides of the same transept present a curious diversity of sculptured forms of plants and animals. On the south-east side are a great many musicians admirably cut. In the south wall of the nave are eight beautiful windows, each sixteen feet in height and eight in breadth, having upright mullions of stone with rich tracery. These windows light eight small square chapels of uniform dimensions, which run along the south side of the nave, and are separated from each other by thin partition walls of stone. The west end of the nave, and five of the chapels included in it, are now roofless. The end next the central tower is arched over—the side aisles and chapels, with their original Gothic roof, and the middle avenue with a plain vault thrown over it in 1618, at which time this part of the building was fitted up as a parish church. The choir or chancel, which is built in the form of half a Greek cross, displays the finest architectural taste. The eastern window in particular is uncommonly elegant and beautiful. Sir Walter Scott, in describing this part of the building, says—

" The moon on the east oriel shone
Through slender shafts of shapely stone
By foliaged tracery combined :
Thou would'st have thought some fairy's hand
'Twixt poplars straight the osier wand
In many a freakish knot had twined ;
Then framed a spell when the work was done,
And changed the willow wreaths to stone."

The original beautifully fretted and sculptured stone roof of the east end of the chancel is still standing, and rises high

" On pillars lofty, and light, and small,
The keystone that lock'd each ribbed aisle,
Was a fleur-de-lys or a quatre-feuille :
The corbells were carved grotesque and grim,

Drawn by W. H. Townsend. Engraved by Wm Chapman.

MELROSE ABBEY.

And the pillars with cluster'd shafts so trim,
With base and with capital flourished around,
Seemed bundles of lances which garlands had bound."

The outside of the fabric is everywhere profusely embellished with niches having canopies of an elegant design exquisitely carved, and some of them still containing statues.

The cloisters formed a quadrangle on the north-west side of the church. The door of entrance from the cloisters to the church is on the north side, close by the west wall of the transept, and is exquisitely carved. The foliage upon the capitals of the pilasters on each side is so nicely chiselled, that a straw can be made to penetrate through the interstices between the leaves and stalks. Through this door the "monk of St. Mary's aisle," in the Lay of the Last Minstrel, is said to have conducted William of Deloraine to the grave of Michael Scott, after conducting him through the cloister. The best views of the Abbey are obtained from the south-east corner of the churchyard, and from the grounds of Prior Bank (W. Tait, Esq.) But, in the words of Sir W. Scott,

"If thou would'st view fair Melrose aright,
Go visit it by the pale moonlight;
For the gay beams of lightsome day
Gild, but to flout, the ruins grey.
When the broken arches are black in night,
And each shafted oriel glimmers white;
When the cold light's uncertain shower
Streams on the ruin'd central tower;
When buttress and buttress, alternately,
Seem framed of ebon and ivory;
When silver edges the imagery,
And the scrolls that teach thee to live and die;
When distant Tweed is heard to rave,
And the owlet to hoot o'er the dead man's grave,
Then go—but go alone the while—
Then view St. David's ruin'd pile;
And, home returning, soothly swear,
Was never scene so sad and fair!"

Within the Abbey lie the remains of many a gallant warrior and venerable priest. A large slab of polished marble, of a greenish-black colour, with petrified shells imbedded in it, is believed to cover the dust of Alexander II., who was interred beside the high altar under the east window. Here, also, the heart of King Robert Bruce is supposed to have been deposited, after Douglas had made an unsuccessful attempt to carry it to the Holy Land. Many of the powerful family of Douglas were interred in this church—among these were William Douglas, "the dark knight of Liddisdale," who tarnished his laurels by the barbarous murder of his companion in arms, the gallant Sir Alexander Ramsay, and was himself killed by his god-son and chief, William Earl of Douglas, while hunting in Ettrick Forest; and James, second Earl of Douglas, who fell at the celebrated battle of Otterburn. Their tombs, which occupied two crypts near the high altar, were defaced by the English, under Sir Ralph Evers and Sir Brian Latoun—an insult which was signally avenged by their descendant, the Earl of Angus, at the battle of Ancrum Moor.

Melrose Abbey was founded by David I., by whom it was munificently endowed. The foundation was laid in 1136, but the building was not completed till 1146, when it was dedicated to the Virgin Mary. The monks were of the reformed class called Cistertians. They were brought from the Abbey of Rievalle, in the North Riding of Yorkshire, and were the first of this order who came into Scotland. It was destroyed by the English in their retreat under Edward II. in 1322, and, four years after, Robert Bruce gave £2000 sterling to rebuild it. This sum, equal to £50,000 of the money of the present day, was raised chiefly from the baronies of Cessford and Eckford, forfeited by Sir Roger de Mowbray, and the lands of Nesbit, Longnewton, Maxton, and Caverton, forfeited by William Lord Soulis. The present beautiful fabric, which is still the object of general admiration in its ruins, was then raised in a style of graceful magnificence, that entitles it to be classed among the most perfect works of the best age of that description of ecclesiastical architecture to which it belongs. In 1385, it was burnt by Richard II.; in 1545, it was despoiled by Evers and Latoun; and, again, in the same year, it was destroyed by the Earl of Hertford. At the period of the Reformation it suffered severely, from the misdirected zeal of the Reformers.* Its chief dilapidations, however, must be attributed to the hostile incursions of the English, and to the wanton mischief or sordid utilitarianism of later times.† The estates of the abbey were granted by Queen Mary in 1566 to James Hepburn, Earl of Bothwell, by whose forfeiture in 1567, they reverted again to the Crown, and the usufruct, with the title of Commendator, was conferred, the following year, upon James Douglas, second son to Sir William Douglas of Lochleven.‡ In 1609, the abbey and its possessions were erected into a temporal lordship for Sir John Ramsay, who had been created Viscount Haddington, for his service in preserving James VI. from the treasonable attempt of the Earl of Gowrie. Lord Haddingtou, who was afterwards created Earl of Holderness, appears to have disposed of the possessions belonging to the lordship of Melrose, since we find that they were granted by charter to Sir Thomas Hamilton, ("Tam o' the Cowgate,") a celebrated lawyer, who was created Earl of Melrose in 1619, and afterwards Earl of Haddington. Part of the lands were granted to Walter Scott, Earl of Buccleuch; and his descendants, about the beginning of the eighteenth century, acquired by purchase the remainder of the Abbey lands included in the lordship of Melrose, which still form a part of the extensive possessions of the same noble family.

At the abolition of heritable jurisdictions in 1747, the Lady Isabella Scott was allowed the sum of £1200 sterling, as compensation for her right to the bailiery of Melrose.

* The following verse, from a once popular ballad, shows that, at the time of the Reformation, the inmates of this Abbey shared in the general reproach of *sensuality* and *irregularity* thrown upon the Romish churchmen:—

" The monks of Melrose made gude kail
On Fridays when they fasted;
Nor wanted they gude beef and ale,
As lang's their neighbours' lasted."

† The same remark is applicable to the dilapidations of the other monasteries of Teviotdale. In some instances the heritors seem to have availed themselves of the venerable ruins as a quarry for materials to build or repair modern churches and schools. Fragments of sculptured stones frequently occur in private dwellings. A better spirit now generally prevails.

‡ *Monastic Annals of Teviotdale*, p. 245.

When King David I. laid the foundations of Melrose Abbey, the ground on which Melrose now stands was occupied by a village called Fordel. The present village is an extremely curious and antique place, and has evidently been, in a great measure, built out of the ruins of the abbey. In the centre of the village stands a cross, about twenty feet high, supposed to be coeval with the abbey. There is a ridge in a field near the town, called the Corse-rig, which the proprietor of the field holds upon the sole condition that he shall keep up the cross.

In the vicinity of Melrose are the Eildon hills, the *Tremontium* of the Romans.* Opposite to the village, a wire bridge leads across the Tweed, to the scattered little village of Gattonside, with its numerous orchards. A short way farther down the river, on a peninsula formed by a remarkable sweep of the Tweed, stood the ancient monastery of Old Melrose. The estate of Old Melrose was long possessed by a family of the name of Ormestoun. It is now the property of Adam Fairholme, Esq. of Chapel.

EXCURSIONS FROM MELROSE.

1. MELROSE TO ABBOTSFORD.

Leave Melrose by the road which proceeds eastwards by the Established and Free Churches, to the village of Darnick, where there is an ancient tower, built during the fifteenth century. Between Darnick and Bridgend is a place called Skinnersfield (a corruption of Skirmishfield), where a battle was fought in 1526 between the Earl of Angus and the Laird of Buccleuch, for possession of the person of James V., which terminated in favour of Angus.†

* It is said that Eildon hills were once an uniform cone, and that the summit was formed into the three picturesque peaks, into which it is now divided, by the spirit, for whom Michael Scott was under the necessity of finding constant employment.—See *Lay of the Last Minstrel*, canto ii., stanza 13.

† The Earl of Angus, with his reluctant ward, had slept at Melrose, and the clans of Home and Kerr, under the Lord Home, and the Barons of Cessford

A little above the junction of the Gala with the Tweed, stands

ABBOTSFORD,

the seat of Sir Walter Scott, Bart., situated on a bank overhanging the south side of the Tweed, which at this place makes a beautiful sweep around the declivity on which the house stands. Further up the river, on the opposite bank, venerable trees, scattered over a considerable space, indicate

and Fairnihirst, had taken their leave of the king, when, in the grey of the morning, Buccleuch and his band of cavalry, comprehending a large body of Elliots, Armstrongs, and other broken clans, were discovered, hanging like a thunder cloud upon the neighbouring hill of Haliden. The encounter was fierce and obstinate, but the Homes and Kerrs, returning at the noise of the battle, bore down and dispersed the left wing of Buccleuch's little army. The hired banditti fled on all sides, but the chief himself, surrounded by his clan, fought desperately in the retreat. The Laird of Cessford, chief of the Roxburgh Kerrs, pursued the chase fiercely, till, at the bottom of a steep path, Elliot of Stobbs turned and slew him, with a stroke of his lance. When Cessford fell, the pursuit ceased, but his death, with those of Buccleuch's friends who fell in the action, to the number of eighty, occasioned a deadly feud betwixt the clans of Scott and Kerr, which cost much blood upon the marches.—See *Introduction to Minstrelsy of the Scottish Border*, and *Lay of the Last Minstrel*.

the site of the old mansion and village of Boldside, of which a fisherman's cottage is now the only representative. Below the Selkirk road may be seen the site of its church, and the haunted churchyard extended along the face of the bank. Immediately opposite, at the extremity of his property, Sir Walter had a bower overhanging the Tweed, where he frequently sat musing during the heat of the day. Boldside is referred to in Lockhart's Life of Scott. Abbotsford is now occupied by Mr. Hope, who married Sir Walter Scott's grand-daughter. When he is at home strangers are admitted on Wednesdays and Fridays, and daily during his absence.*

Abbotsford is a house of very extraordinary proportions, and though irregular as a whole, it produces a very striking effect. The entrance to the house is by a porchway, adorned with petrified stags' horns, into a hall, which is perhaps the most interesting of all the apartments. The walls are pannelled with richly carved oak from the palace of Dunfermline, and the roof consists of painted arches of the same material. Round the cornice there is a line of coats-armorial richly blazoned, belonging to the families who kept the borders—as the Douglasses, Kers, Scotts, Turnbulls, Maxwells, Chisholms, Elliots, and Armstrongs. The floor is of black and white marble from the Hebrides, and the walls are hung with ancient armour, and various specimens of military implements. From the hall strangers are conducted to the armoury, which runs quite across the house, and communicates with the drawing-room on the one side, and the dining-room on the other. The drawing-room is a lofty saloon with wood of cedar. Its antique ebony furniture, carved cabinets, &c., are all of beautiful workmanship. The dining-room is a very handsome apartment, with a roof of black oak richly carved. It contains a fine collection of pictures; the most interesting of which are the head of Queen Mary in a charger the day after she was beheaded, and a full length portrait of Lord Essex, of Oliver Cromwell, Claverhouse, Charles II., Charles XII. of Sweden, and, among several family pictures, one of Sir Walter's

* No specific sum can be prescribed as the gratuity payable to domestics in such cases. The amount will necessarily vary between prince and peasant, but 1s. for a single individual, and 2s. 6d. for parties not exceeding six, may be regarded as fair medium payments.

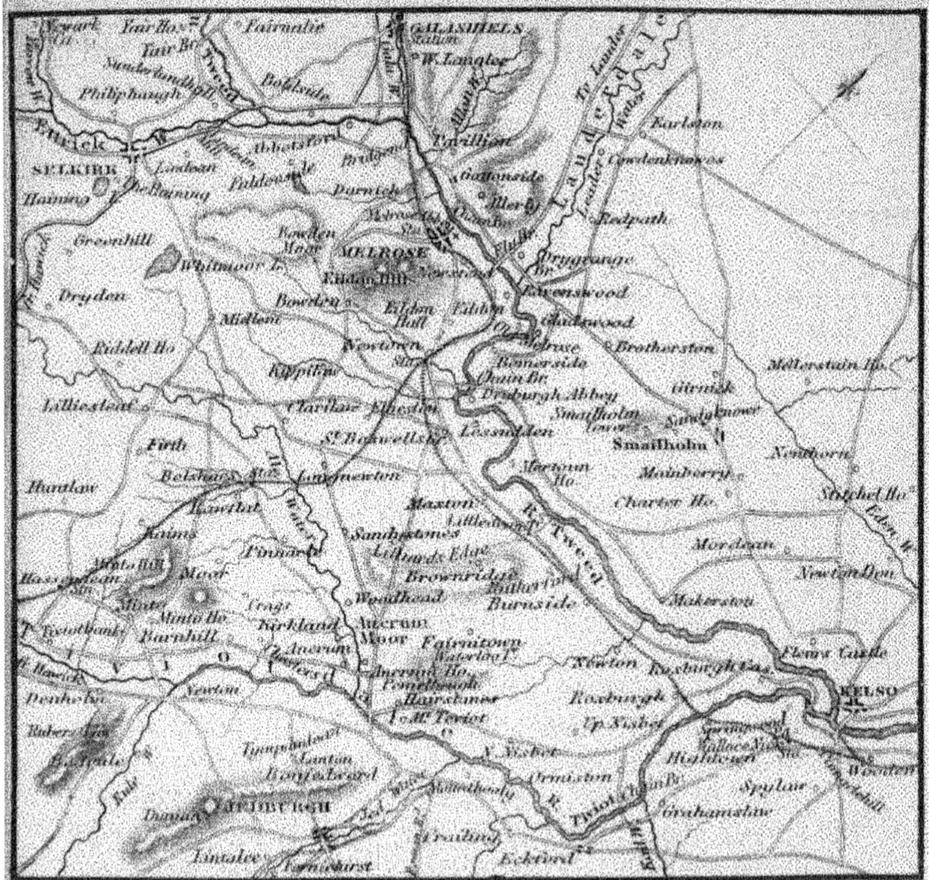

CHART OF THE VALES OF TEVIOT AND TWEED.

great-grandfather, who allowed his beard to grow after the execution of Charles I. The breakfast parlour is a small and neat apartment, overlooking the Tweed on the one side, and the wild hills of Ettrick and Yarrow on the other. It contains a beautiful and valuable collection of water-colour drawings, chiefly by Turner, and Thomson of Duddingstone, the designs for the magnificent work entitled "Provincial Antiquities of Scotland." The library, which is the largest of all the apartments, is a magnificent room, fifty feet by sixty. The roof is of carved oak, chiefly after models from Roslin. The collection of books in this room amounts to about 20,000 volumes, many of them extremely rare and valuable. From the library there is a communication with the study, a room of about twenty-five feet square by twenty feet high, containing of what is properly called furniture nothing but a small writing-table in the centre, a plain arm-chair covered with black leather, and a single chair besides. There are a few books, chiefly for reference, and a light gallery of tracery work runs round three sides of the room, which contains only one window, so that the place is rather sombre. From this room you enter a small closet, containing what must be viewed by all with the deepest interest—the body-clothes worn by Sir Walter previous to his decease.* The external walls of the house, as well as those of the adjoining garden, are enriched with many old carved stones, which have originally figured in other and very different situations. The door of the old tolbooth of Edinburgh, the pulpit from which Ralph Erskine preached, and various other curious and interesting relics, may also be seen. Through the whole extent of the surrounding forests there are a number of beautiful winding walks, and near the waterfalls in the deep ravines are benches or bowers commanding the most picturesque views. The mansion of Abbotsford and its woods have been entirely created by its late proprietor, who, when he purchased the ground about thirty years ago, found it occupied by a small onstead called "Cartley Hole." The first purchase was made from the late Dr. Douglas of Galashiels. It is said that the money was paid by instalments, and that the letter enclosing the last remittance contained these lines·

"Noo the gowd's thine,
And the land's mine."

Various other "pendicles" were purchased at different times from the neighbouring bonnet-lairds, at prices greatly above

* "After showing us the principal rooms, the woman opened a small closet adjoining the study, in which hung the last clothes that Sir Walter had worn. There was the broad-skirted blue coat with large buttons, the plaid trowsers, the heavy shoes, the broad-rimmed hat, and stout walking-stick,—the dress in which he rambled about in the morning, and which he laid off when he took to his bed in his last illness. She took down the coat, and gave it a shake and a wipe of the collar, as if he were waiting to put it on again!"—WILLIS'S *Pencillings by the Way.*

their real value. In December 1830, the library, museum, plate, and furniture of every description, were presented to Sir Walter as a free gift by his creditors, and he afterwards bequeathed the same to his eldest son, burdened with a sum of £5000 to be divided among his younger children. The proceeds of a subscription set on foot in London a considerable time ago, have been applied to the payment of this debt, thus enabling the trustees to entail the library and museum as an heir-loom in the family.

A little to the east of Abbotsford, on the opposite bank of the river, below the junction of the Gala, the Allan or Elwand water runs into the Tweed. There can be little doubt that the vale of the Allan is the true "Glendearg" of the Monastery.* The banks on each side are steep, and rise boldly over the eccentric stream which jets from rock to rock, rendering it absolutely necessary for the traveller to cross and recross it, as he pursues his way up the bottom of the narrow valley. "The hills also rise at some places abruptly over the little glen, displaying at intervals the grey rock overhung with wood, and farther up rises the mountain in purple majesty—the dark rich hue contrasting beautifully with the thickets of oak and birch, the mountain ashes and thorns, the alders and quivering aspens which chequered and varied the descent, and not less with the dark green velvet turf which composed the level part of the narrow glen."

* "When we had ridden a little time on the moors, he said to me rather pointedly, 'I am going to show you something that I think will interest you;' and presently, in a wild corner of the hills, he halted us at a place where stood three small ancient towers, or castellated houses, in ruins, at short distances from each other. It was plain, upon the slightest consideration of the topography, that one (perhaps any one) of these was the tower of Glendearg, where so many romantic and marvellous adventures happen in the Monastery. While we looked at this forlorn group, I said to Sir Walter that they were what Burns called 'ghaist-alluring edifices.' 'Yes,' he answered carelessly, 'I dare say there are many stories about them.' As we returned, by a different route, he made me dismount and take a footpath through a part of Lord Somerville's grounds, where the Elland runs through a beautiful little valley, the stream winding between level borders of the brightest green sward, which narrow or widen as the steep sides of the glen advance or recede. The place is called the Fairy Dean, and it required no cicerone to tell, that the glen was that in which Father Eustace, in the Monastery, is intercepted by the White Lady of Avenel." —*Letter of Mr. Adolphus*—LOCKHART'S *Life of Scott*, vol. v.

2. MELROSE TO DRYBURGH ABBEY.

The most direct way to Dryburgh Abbey is either by road or railway to Newtown St. Boswells, from which the road turns directly to the left. At a short distance from the station is a toll-bar, where the road, overhung with trees, turns again to the left, and conducts to the banks of the Tweed. The tourist is here ferried across for a penny to the other side, on reaching which, a ten minutes' walk brings him to Dryburgh Abbey.

By the other road, which is by far the most picturesque, the tourist is conducted, by the village of Newstead, across the Tweed to Drygrange Bridge, two miles below Melrose, where the Leader pours its waters from the north, through a beautiful wooded vale to join the Tweed. The view from the Bemerside road, near Gladswood, is one of the most beautiful and interesting in the south of Scotland. From no other point can the eye command with equal advantage the whole vale of Melrose; and if the tourist should have time to proceed by this route, he should by no means neglect to take this view on his way to Dryburgh. In the immediate vicinity is Drygrange (John Tod, Esq.), beautifully situated. About a mile and a half from Drygrange is the house of Cowdenknowes (Dr. Home), standing on the east bank of the Leader, at the foot of the hill of Cowdenknowes, celebrated in song for its "bonny, bonny broom." A mile farther up the Leader is the village of Earlstoun, anciently Erceldoune, the dwelling of Thomas Learmont, commonly called Thomas the Rhymer, in whom, as in the mighty men of old,

——— the honour'd name
Of prophet and of poet was the same.

The remains of the Rhymer's Tower are still pointed out, in the midst of a beautiful haugh, on the east side of the Leader. A little further on, in the vicinity of Dryburgh, is the mansion of Bemerside, the lands and barony of which have been in the possession of the Haigs since the time of Malcolm IV. The following rhyme respecting this family, which testifies to the confident belief of the country people in the perpetual lineal succession of the Haigs, is ascribed to no less venerable and infallible an authority than Thomas the Rhymer, whose patrimonial territory was not far from Bemerside.

> "Tide, tide, whate'er betide,
> There'll ay be Haigs in Bemerside."

The great-grandfather of the present Mr. Haig had twelve daughters, before his wife brought him a male-heir. The common people trembled for the credit of their favourite soothsayer. But at length the birth of a son confirmed their belief in the prophecy beyond a shadow of doubt.*

Four miles from Melrose, on the north bank of the Tweed, within the county of Berwick, stand the picturesque ruins of

DRYBURGH ABBEY,

on a richly wooded haugh, round which the river makes a fine circuitous sweep. The situation is eminently beautiful, and both the abbey, and the modern mansion-house of the proprietor, are completely embosomed in wood.* The finest view of the ruins is from the "Braeheads," behind the village of Lessuden. Dryburgh Abbey was founded in 1150, during the reign of David I., by Hugh de Moreville, Lord of Lauderdale, Constable of Scotland, upon a site which is supposed to have been originally a place of Druidical worship. The monks were of the Premonstratensian order, and were brought from the abbey founded at Alnwick a short time before. Edward II., in his retreat from the unsuccessful invasion of Scotland in 1322, encamped in the grounds of Dryburgh, and, setting fire to the monastery, burnt it to the ground. Robert I. contributed liberally towards its repair, but it has been doubted whether it was ever fully restored to its original magnificence. In 1544, the abbey was again destroyed by a hostile incursion of the English, under Sir George Bowes and Sir Brian Layton. The principal remains of the building are, the western gable of the nave of the church, the ends of the transept, part of the choir, and

* The guide lives in a cottage near the entrance. The gratuity we have suggested as payment for the exhibition of Abbotsford, viz., 1s. for a single person, and 2s. 6d. for parties not exceeding six, should be sufficient here.

a portion of the domestic buildings. In St. Mary's aisle, which is by far the most beautiful part of the ruin, Sir Walter Scott was buried, 26th September 1832, in the burying-ground of his ancestors, the Haliburtons of Newmains, the ancient proprietors of the abbey. On each side are the tombs of his wife and only son, the late Colonel Scott. The ruins are almost completely overgrown with foliage. In 1604, James VI. granted Dryburgh Abbey to John, Earl of Mar, and he afterwards erected it into a temporal lordship and peerage, with the title of Lord Cardross, conferring it upon the same Earl, who made it over to his third son, Henry, ancestor of the Earl of Buchan. The abbey was subsequently sold to the Haliburtons of Mertoun, from whom it was purchased by Colonel Tod, whose heirs sold it to the Earl of Buchan in 1786. The Earl at his death, bequeathed it to his son, Sir David Erskine, at whose death, in 1837, it reverted to the Buchan family.

In the immediate vicinity of the abbey is the neat mansion-house of Dryburgh, surrounded by stately trees. At a short distance, is a chain suspension-bridge over the Tweed, erected in 1818, at the expense of the late Earl of Buchan, but rendered impassable by a storm in January 1840, and never since repaired. On a rising-ground at the end of the bridge, is a circular temple dedicated to the Muses, surmounted by a bust of Thomson, the author of the "Seasons." Farther up, on a rocky eminence overlooking the river, is a colossal statue of the Scottish patriot Wallace. The whole prospect around is eminently beautiful, embracing both wood and water, mountain and rock scenery.*

Tourists employing vehicles for this excursion cannot proceed the one way and return the other, as there is no way of crossing the Tweed at Dryburgh except by small ferry boats.

The principal Hotels at Melrose are "The George," and

* Connected with Dryburgh is the following story, told by Sir Walter Scott in his Border Minstrelsy:—"Soon after the Rebellion in 1745, an unfortunate female wanderer took up her residence in a dark vault among the ruins of Dryburgh Abbey, which, during the day, she never quitted. When night fell, she

"Thomson's," where excellent accommodation may be had, and vehicles hired for visiting the places of interest in the vicinity.

3. MELROSE—JEDBURGH—HAWICK.

Returning to Melrose by Railway.

From Melrose, tourists may reach Jedburgh by coach either from Newtown St. Boswells or New Belses stations, both on the line of railway from Melrose to Hawick.

Supposing that the former is the point from which the tourist chooses to diverge, having informed himself of the proper hour of the coaches starting, he takes the train to Newtown St. Boswells station. Proceeding from thence southwards by coach, a beautiful view is obtained of Dryburgh Abbey and the course of the Tweed. A few miles farther on, the road passes ANCRUM MOOR, where the Earl of Angus routed the English in 1545. During the year 1544, Sir Ralph Eure and Sir Brian Layton committed the most dreadful ravages upon the Scottish frontiers. As a reward for their services, the English monarch promised to the two barons a feudal grant of the country which they had thus reduced to a desert; upon hearing which, Archibald Douglas, the seventh Earl of Angus, is said to have sworn to write the deed of investiture upon their skins, with sharp pens, and

issued from this miserable habitation, and went to the house of Mr. Haliburton of Newmains, or to that of Mr. Erskine of Shielfield, two gentlemen of the neighbourhood. From their charity she obtained such necessaries as she could be prevailed on to accept. At twelve, each night, she lighted her candle and returning to her vault, assuring her neighbours that, during her absence, her habitation was arranged by a spirit, to whom she gave the uncouth appellation of Fatlips, and whom she described as a little man, wearing heavy iron shoes, with which he trampled the clay floor of the vault, to dispel the damps. This circumstance caused her to be regarded, by the well informed, with compassion, as deranged in her understanding, and, by the vulgar, with some degree of terror. The cause of her adopting this extraordinary mode of life she would never explain. It was, however, believed to have been occasioned by a vow, that, during the absence of a man to whom she was attached, she would never look upon the sun. Her lover never returned. He fell during the civil war of 1745-6, and she never more would behold the light of day. The vault, or rather dungeon, in which this unfortunate woman lived and died, passes still by the name of the supernatural being with which its gloom was tenanted by her disturbed imagination."

bloody ink, in resentment for their having defaced the tombs of his ancestors at Melrose. In 1545, Eure and Layton again entered Scotland with an army of upwards of 5000 men, and even exceeded their former cruelty. As they returned towards Jedburgh, they were overtaken by Angus at the head of 1000 horse, who was shortly after joined by the famous Norman Lesley with a body of Fife-men. While the Scottish general was hesitating whether to advance or retire, Sir Walter Scott of Buccleuch came up at full speed with a small but chosen body of his retainers, and by his advice, an immediate attack was made. The battle was commenced upon a piece of low flat ground, near Penielheugh,* and, just as it began, a heron, roused from the marshes by the tumult, soared away betwixt the encountering armies. "O!" exclaimed Angus, "that I had here my white gosshawk, that we might all yoke at once!" The Scots obtained a complete victory, Sir Ralph Eure and his son, together with Sir Brian Layton and 800 Englishmen, many of whom were persons of rank, falling in the engagement. A mile beyond this, on the right, the road passes Ancrum House, (Sir William Scott, Bart.,) and on the opposite bank of the Ale, is the village of Ancrum. At the manse of Ancrum, Thomson the poet spent much of his time with Mr. Cranstoun, the clergyman of the parish. A short way beyond, at some distance on the left, is Mount Teviot, a seat of the Marquis of Lothian, whose second title is Earl of Ancrum. On the right, two miles up the Teviot, is Chesters, (W. Ogilvie, Esq.) The tourist now crosses the Teviot by Ancrum Bridge. A short way beyond, on the right, is Tympandean, with the ruins of an ancient tower, and a mile farther on the left is Bonjedward, an ancient Roman station. The Roman road here crossed the Jed, and is still in a state of preservation from the Jed to the Border hills. At the distance of another mile, in the deep vale of the sylvan Jed, the tourist enters the royal burgh of

JEDBURGH.

[*Inns*:—The Spread Eagle; The Thistle; The Harrow.]

Jedburgh is situated in the midst of gardens and venerable

* Penielheugh is the hill upon which the Waterloo Monument is built.

orchards, and environed with wooded and precipitous banks. This is a place of great antiquity; the village of old Jedworth, about four miles above the present town, having been founded by Ecgred, Bishop of Lindisfarn, A.D. 845. St. Kenoch was Abbot of Jedburgh, A.D. 1000, and its royal castle is mentioned in the earliest Scottish annals. It appears to have been a royal burgh even in the time of David I. It was the chief town on the middle marches. Defended by its castle and numerous towers, and, surrounded by the fastnesses of its forest, it was frequently the rendezvous of the Scottish armies, and was as frequently assailed, pillaged, and burnt, by the English.

Its importance declined from the union of the two crowns, and though it has in modern times revived, it has never reached any great extent either in population or trade. The population within the Parliamentary boundary in 1841, was 3277, being about 300 less than in 1831. It is the county town of Roxburghshire, the seat of the circuit court of justiciary and of a presbytery. Its weekly market is on Tuesday, and it has besides several good annual fairs and monthly markets for cattle.

Many interesting objects of antiquity were destroyed during the last century, such as St. David's tower—the gateway of the ancient bridge of the Canongate—and the cross, an interesting edifice, on which, according to Bannatyne, the magistrates, having espoused the cause of James VI., compelled the heralds of Mary, after suffering unseemly chastisement, to eat their proclamation. The principal object of curiosity is the remains of the Abbey. It was enlarged and richly endowed by David I., and other munificent patrons about the year 1118, or 1147. At one period, its powerful abbots disputed, though unsuccessfully, the jurisdiction of the Bishops of Glasgow, who generally resided at Ancrum in the neighbourhood. It suffered frequently in the English wars, especially from the invasions of Edward I. and Edward III. It sustained a siege of two hours under the artillery of the Earl of Surrey, at the storming of Jedburgh, in the reign of Henry VIII., and the traces of the flames are still visible on its ruined walls. It suffered subsequent dilapidation from the forces of the Earl of Hertford; and in common with the other monasteries of Teviotdale, does not appear to have been inhabited at the time of the Reformation. The monks were Canons regular or Augustine friars, brought from Beauvais in France.

At the Reformation, the lands of the Abbey were converted into a temporal lordship, with the title of Lord Jedburgh, in favour of Sir Andrew Ker of Ferniehirst, and they are now possessed by his descendant, the Marquis of Lothian. It is a magnificent ruin, and is considered the most perfect and beautiful specimen of the Saxon and early Gothic in Scotland. The principal parts now remaining are, the nave, nearly the whole of the choir, with the south aisle, the centre tower, and the north transept, which is entire, and has long been set apart as a burial-place for the family of the Marquis of Lothian. In the western gable is a door of exceedingly beautiful workmanship. But the most curious and interesting part of it is the Norman door, which entered from the cloisters on the south, of exquisitely delicate and beautiful workmanship: the finer portions of sculpture are rapidly decaying. Over the intersection of the nave and transept, rises a massive square tower, with irregular turrets and belfry, to the height of 100 feet. The west end is fitted up as a parish church, in a most barbarous and unseemly style. Some public-spirited individuals have lately expended a considerable sum in repairing the decayed parts of the building, so as to prevent farther dilapidation.

The best view of the Abbey is obtained from the banks of the river. The Castle of Jedburgh, situated on an eminence at the town head, was a favourite residence of our early Scottish kings, from the time of David I. to Alexander III.* Malcolm the fourth died there—Alexander III. married there, with unusual pomp, October 14, 1285, Jolande, daughter of the Count de Dreux, on which occasion the festivities of the evening are said to have been interrupted by the sudden and ominous appearance of a spectre, which,

* "Jeda's ancient walls, once seat of kings."
HAMILTON *of Bangor.*

entering the dance, filled the gay company with consternation. The importance of this castle may be estimated from the circumstance of its always ranking in the treaties with England, along with Roxburgh, Edinburgh, and Stirling, and from the fact, that when the Scottish government determined to destroy it, it was meditated to impose a tax of two pennies on every hearth in Scotland, as the only means of accomplishing so arduous an undertaking. The site of this ancient fortress is now occupied by a new jail, from the top of which there is a beautiful view of the town and neighbourhood.

In the lower part of the town, may be still seen the old mansion occupied by Queen Mary, and where she lay sick for several weeks after her visit to Bothwell, at Hermitage. She rode from Jedburgh to Hermitage, and returned on the same day, a distance of about 40 miles; she was in consequence thrown into a violent fever, and her life for some time despaired of.

The rich soil and mild climate of Jedburgh renders it peculiarly congenial to horticulture; delicate plants and fruits succeeding in the open air, which in other places require to be placed under glass. Many of the pear trees are of great size and antiquity, and bear immense crops, which are disposed of through an extensive district. The best kinds are French, and may probably have been planted by the Monks.

The inhabitants of Jedburgh, in ancient times, were a warlike race, and were celebrated for their dexterity in handling a particular sort of partisan; which, therefore, got the name of the "Jethart staff." Their timely aid is said to have turned the fortune of the day at the skirmish of Reidswire. Their proud war-cry was, "Jethart's here."* Their arms are a mounted trooper advancing to the charge, with the motto, "Strenue et prospere." They have still in preservation some ancient trophies taken from the English, particularly a flag or pennon taken at Bannockburn. The ordinary proverb of "Jethart justice,"

* "Then raise the slogan with ane shout,
"Fy, Tindaill to it! Jedbrugh's here."
Raid of Reidswire.

where men were said to be hanged first and tried afterwards, appears to have taken its rise from some instances of summary justice executed on the Border marauders.*

In the south aisle of the Abbey, then used as the Grammar School, the poet Thomson, whose father was translated from Ednam to Southdean on the Jed, when the poet was only two years old, received the rudiments of his education. It is not generally known that when he attended Edinburgh University, he did so as the bursar of the Presbytery of Jedburgh. The celebrated Samuel Rutherford is also said to have been educated here. Dr. Somerville, historian of William and Anne, was upwards of fifty years minister of Jedburgh, and in the manse was born the amiable and highly gifted Mrs. Somerville. Sir David Brewster is also a native of Jedburgh.

The environs of Jedburgh abound in rich woodland scenes, and the walk through the picturesque woods and groves which adorn the precipitous banks of the winding Jed, is especially delightful.† On the banks of the Jed, at Hundalee, Lintalee, and Mossburnford, are caves dug out of the rock, supposed to have been used as hiding-places in ancient warfare. In the neighbourhood are the remains of numerous camps; but the most remarkable is the camp of Lintalee, little more than a mile from the town, where Douglas, as described in Barbour's Bruce, lay for the defence of Scotland, during the absence of the king in Ireland, and where in a desperate personal encounter he slew the English commander the Earl of Brittany, at the head of his army, and routed the whole with great slaughter—an achievement commemorated in the armorial bearings of the Douglas family. Jed forest was conferred on Douglas by Bruce, the regality of which was sold to the crown by the Duke of Douglas. The forest lands still belong to Lord Douglas. A short distance from the town, the half ruinous

* There is a similar English proverb concerning Lydford:—

"I oft have heard of Lydford law,
Where in the morn men hang and draw,
And sit in judgment after."

BROWN'S *Poems*.

† "Eden scenes on crystal Jed."

BURNS.

castle of Ferniehirst, the ancient seat of the Kerrs, occupies a romantic situation on the right bank of the river. It was built by Sir Thomas Kerr in 1490, and was taken by the English in 1523, and again, after the battle of Pinkie. The family of Kerr settled at Kerrsheugh in the 13th century, and from this place the Marquis of Lothian takes his title as a British Peer. About a mile northward from the castle grows a large oak tree, called, on account of its great size, "the king of the wood," and at the side of the ruin stands another, equally large, called "the capon tree." Both trees are noticed in Gilpin's Forest Scenery.

From Jedburgh to Hawick there is a fine drive of about ten miles along the bank of the Teviot. The vale of the Rule intervenes, as also the chief hills of Teviotdale, the Dunian, and Ruberslaw. The whole course of the Teviot between these towns is studded on each side with cottages and mansions, the most distinguished of which is Minto House. The Earl of Minto's grounds and Minto Crags are most easily reached by leaving the railway at Hassendean Station, walking from thence, by a very pleasant road, through the village of Minto to the Lodge. By the liberality of the noble proprietor, the grounds are accessible to all parties desirous of seeing them, every day, Sundays excepted. The mansion—a large, commodious house—is surrounded with beautiful grounds, studded with some noble old trees. At no great distance from the house are Minto Crags, a romantic assemblage of cliffs which rise suddenly above the vale of Teviot. A small platform on a projecting crag, commanding a most beautiful prospect, is termed *Barnhill's Bed.* This Barnhill is said to have been a robber or outlaw. There are remains of a strong tower beneath the rocks, where he is supposed to have dwelt, and from which he derived his name. On the summit of the crags are the fragments of another ancient tower in a picturesque situation.* Nearly opposite to Minto House lies

* "On Minto Crags the moon-beams glint,
Where Barnhill hew'd his bed of flint,
Who flung his outlaw'd limbs to rest,
Where falcons hang their giddy nest,
'Mid cliffs from whence his eagle eye
For many a league his prey could spy,
Cliffs, doubling, on their echoes borne,
The terrors of the robber's horn;
Cliffs which for many a later year
The warbling Doric reed shall hear,
When some sad swain shall teach the grove,
Ambition is no cure for love."

Lay of the Last Minstrel.

the pleasant village of Denholm, the birthplace of Dr. John Leyden, and a little farther to the west, Cavers, the seat of J. Douglas, Esq. Situated upon a haugh, at the junction of the Slitterick and Teviot, is the thriving town of

HAWICK.

[*Inns*:—The Tower; The Commercial; The Crown.]

Hawick is a burgh of regality, and is of considerable antiquity, and its inhabitants are principally engaged in manufactures. Hawick has made a considerable figure in Border history, and from its proximity to the Border, has frequently suffered severely from the inroads of the English. The Slitterick is crossed by a bridge of peculiarly antique construction, and at the head of the town is a moat-hill, where the brave Sir Alexander Ramsay was acting in his capacity of Sheriff of Teviotdale, when he was seized by Sir William Douglas, the "dark knight of Liddisdale," and plunged into one of the dungeons of Hermitage Castle, where he perished of hunger. Hawick is noted among topers for its "gill." A *Hawick gill* is well known in Scotland to be half a mutchkin, equal to two gills.* On the right bank of the Teviot, about two miles above Hawick, stands the ancient tower of Goldielands, one of the most entire now extant upon the Border. The proprietors of this tower belonged to the clan of Scott. The last of them is said to have been hanged over his own gate, for march treason. About a mile farther up the river, on the opposite bank, stands the celebrated tower of Branxholm, the principal scene of the "Lay of the Last Minstrel," and during the 15th and 16th centuries the residence of the Buccleuch family. Branxholm was famous of yore for the charms of a *bonnie lass*, whose beauty has been celebrated by Ramsay in a ballad beginning

"As I came in by Teviot side,
And by the braes o' Branksome,
There first I saw my bloomin' bride,
Young, smiling, sweet, and handsome."†

---

* "Weel she loo'ed a Hawick gill,
And leuch to see a tappit hen."
Andrew and his Cuttie Gun.
[A tappit hen is a frothing measure of claret.]

† The bonnie lass was daughter to a woman nicknamed Jean the Ranter, who

Nearly opposite Goldielands Tower the Teviot is joined by Borthwick water. At the head of a narrow valley formed by this stream, stands Harden Castle, a long-shaped plain looking structure, interesting as a specimen of an ancient Border fortress. The carved stucco work upon the ceiling of the old hall is well worth attention. The lobby is paved with marble; and the mantel-piece of one of the rooms is surmounted with an earl's coronet, and the letters, W. E. T. wreathed together, signifying "Walter Earl of Tarras," a title which, in 1660, was conferred for life upon Walter Scott of Highchester, the husband of Mary Countess of Buccleuch. In front of the house there is a dark precipitous dell, covered on both sides with beautiful trees; in the recesses of which the freebooting lairds of former times were said to have kept their spoil.* From Hawick the tourist may return by railway to Melrose or Edinburgh.

kept an ale-house at the Hamlet, near Branxholm Castle. A young officer named Maitland, who happened to be quartered somewhere in the neighbourhood, saw, loved, and married her. So strange was such an alliance deemed in those days, that it was imputed to the influence of witchcraft.

* "Where Bortho hoarse, that loads the meads with sand,
Rolls her red tide to Teviot's western strand,
Through slaty hills whose sides are shagged with thorn,
Where springs in scatter'd tufts the dark green corn,
Towers wood-girt Harden, far above the vale,
And clouds of ravens o'er the turrets sail;
A hardy race who never shrunk from war,
The *Scott* to rival realms a mighty bar,
Here fix'd his mountain home, a wide domain,
And rich the soil had purple heath been grain;
But what the niggard ground of wealth denied,
From fields more bless'd his fearless arm supplied."

LEYDEN'S *Scenes of Infancy*.

"Wide lay his lands round Oakwood tower
And wide round haunted Castle Ower;
High over Borthwick's mountain flood,
His wood-embosomed mansion stood,
In the dark glen so deep below,
The herds of plunder'd England low."

Lay of the Last Minstrel, c. iv.

4. MELROSE—SELKIRK—VALES OF ETTRICK AND YARROW—ST. MARY'S LOCH—MOFFAT.

To accomplish this tour it is necessary, as there is no stage-coach, either to hire a conveyance or walk from Melrose to Moffat. At Moffat the tourist has the Caledonian Railway at his service, and may proceed by it either to Edinburgh, Glasgow, or Carlisle. Leaving Melrose by the road which proceeds westwards by Abbotsford, about three miles from Selkirk, the Ettrick flows into the Tweed at Sunderland Hall, where bridges are thrown over both rivers. Near this spot is the secluded burying-ground of Lindean, with the ruins of its church. Here the body of the "dark Knight of Liddisdale" rested on its way from Ettrick Forest, where he was murdered, to Melrose Abbey, where he was buried. The road now enters Selkirkshire, and leads the tourist along the south bank of the Ettrick to the town of Selkirk, described at page 101.

Leaving Selkirk, the tourist crosses the bridge over the Ettrick, and turns up the north bank. The plain on the northern side of the river is Philiphaugh, the scene of the defeat of the Marquis of Montrose, by General Leslie, 13th September 1645. Montrose himself had taken up his quarters, with his cavalry, in the town of Selkirk, while his infantry, amounting to about twelve or fifteen hundred men, were posted on Philiphaugh. Leslie arrived at Melrose the evening before the engagement, and next morning, favoured by a thick mist, he reached Montrose's encampment without being descried by a single scout. The surprisal was complete, and when the Marquis, who had been alarmed by the noise of the firing, reached the scene of the battle, he beheld his army dispersed in irretrievable rout. After a desperate but unavailing attempt to retrieve the fortune of the day, he cut his way through a body of Leslie's troopers, and fled up Yarrow and over Minchmoor towards Peebles. This defeat destroyed the fruit of Montrose's six splendid victories, and effectually ruined the royal cause in Scotland. The estate of Philiphaugh is the property of W. Murray, Esq., the descendant of the "Outlaw Murray," commemorated in the beautiful ballad of that name. At the head of Philiphaugh the Yarrow comes out, from Newark's "birken bower," to join the Ettrick. At the confluence of these streams, about a mile above Selkirk, is Carterhaugh, the supposed scene of the fairy ballad of "Tamlane." The vale of Yarrow parts off from the head of Philiphaugh towards the right, that of Ettrick towards the left. The whole of this tract of country was, not many centuries ago, covered with wood, and its popular designation still is "The Forest," of which no vestige is now to be seen.

> "The scenes are desert now, and bare,
> Where flourished once a forest fair,
> Up pathless Ettrick and on Yarrow,
> Where erst the outlaw drew his arrow."
>
> SCOTT.

Turning up the vale of Ettrick, the first object of interest that occurs is Oakwood, the residence of the hero of the ballad called

"The Dowie Dens of Yarrow," and, from time immemorial, the property of the Scotts of Harden; it is supposed, also, to have been the mansion of the famous wizard Michael Scott. Two or three miles farther up the glen is the village of Ettrick-brig-end, and about six miles above, the remains of the Tower of Tushielaw may be discerned upon the hill which rises from the north bank of the river. Tushielaw was the residence of the celebrated freebooter Adam Scott, called the King of the Border, who was hanged by James V. in the course of that memorable expedition in 1529, which proved fatal to Johnnie Armstrong, Cockburn of Henderland, and many other marauders; the elm tree on which he was hanged still exists among the ruins. Opposite to Tushielaw the Rankleburn joins the Ettrick. The vale of Rankleburn contains the lonely farm of Buccleuch, supposed to have been the original property of the noble family of that name. There are remains of a church and burial ground, and of a kiln and mill in this district, but no traces of a baronial mansion. Farther up are the ruins of Thirlestane Castle, and close by, the modern mansion of Thirlestane, the seat of Lord Napier, the lineal descendant of the old family of the Scotts of Thirlestane, as well as of the still more famous one of the Napiers of Merchiston. Sir John Scott of Thirlestane, his paternal ancestor, was the only chief willing to follow James V. in his invasion of England, when the rest of the Scottish nobles, encamped at Fala, obstinately refused to take part in the expedition. In memory of his fidelity, James granted to his family a charter of arms, entitling them to bear a border of fleurs-de-luce similar to the tressure in the royal arms, with a bundle of spears for the crest, motto, "ready, aye ready."—(See *Lay of the Last Minstrel*, canto iv.) Thirlestane is surrounded with extensive plantations, and its late noble and benevolent owner employed for many years his whole time and talents in carrying on, at great expense, important improvements in this district. About a mile farther up stand the kirk and hamlet of Ettrick. A cottage near the sacred edifice is pointed out as the birth-place of the Ettrick Shepherd. The celebrated Thomas Boston was minister of Ettrick, and, in the church-yard, a handsome monument has been erected to his memory, since the commencement of the present century.

Crossing the hills which bound the vale of Ettrick on the right, the tourist descends into the celebrated vale of Yarrow. At the head of the vale is the solitary sheet of water called ST. MARY'S LOCH, four miles long, and nearly one broad.

——"lone St. Mary's silent lake.
—————— nor fen nor sedge
Pollute the pure lake's crystal edge.
Abrupt and sheer the mountains sink,
At once upon the level brink:
And just a trace of silver sand
Marks where the water meets the land

Far in the mirror bright and blue
Each hill's huge outline you may view;
Shaggy with heath, but lonely bare,
Nor tree, nor bush, nor brake, is there,
Save where of land yon slender line
Bears 'thwart the lake the scatter'd pine.
Yet even this nakedness has power,
And aids the feeling of the hour:
Nor thicket, dell, nor copse you spy,
Where living thing concealed might lie;
There's nothing left to fancy's guess,
You see that all is loneliness;
And silence aids—though the steep hills
Send to the lake a thousand rills:
In summer tide so soft they weep,
The sound but lulls the ear asleep;
Your horse's hoof-tread sounds too rude,
So stilly is the solitude." *

The river Yarrow flows from the east end, and a small stream connects the Loch of the Lowes with its western extremity. In the winter it is still frequented by flights of wild swans; hence Wordsworth's lines:

" The swans on sweet St. Mary's Lake
Float double—swan and shadow!

In the neighbourhood is the farm of Blackhouse, adjacent to which are the remains of a very ancient tower in a wild and solitary glen, upon a torrent named Douglas Burn, which issues from the hills on the north, and joins the Yarrow, after passing a craggy rock, called the Douglas-craig. This wild scene, now a part of the Traquair estate, formed one of the most ancient possessions of the renowned family of Douglas, and is said by popular tradition to be the scene of the fine old ballad of "The Douglas Tragedy." Near the eastern extremity of St. Mary's Loch are the ruins of Dryhope Tower, the birth-place of Mary Scott, famous by the traditional name of the "Flower of Yarrow," and a mile westward is the ancient burying-ground of St. Mary's Kirk, but the Church has long ago disappeared.

" Though in feudal strife, a foe
Hath laid Our Lady's chapel low,
Yet still beneath the hallow'd soil
The peasant rests him from his toil,
And, dying, bids his bones be laid
Where erst his simple fathers pray'd."†

A funeral in a spot so very retired has an uncommonly striking effect. At a short distance to the north of the burial-ground, is a small mound, said by tradition to be the grave of Mass John Birnam, the former tenant of the chaplainry.

* *Marmion.* Introduction to Canto II.
† *Marmion.* Introduction to Canto II.

"That wizard priest, whose bones are thrust
From company of holy dust."

In the adjacent vale of Megget is Henderland Castle, the residence of Cockburn, a border freebooter, who was hanged over the gate of his own tower by James V. Tradition says that Cockburn was surprised by the king while sitting at dinner. A mountain torrent, called Henderland Burn, rushes impetuously from the hills through a rocky chasm, named the Dow-glen, and passes near the site of the tower. To the recesses of this glen the wife of Cockburn is said to have retreated during the execution of her husband, and a place, called the *Lady's Seat,* is still shown, where she is said to have striven to drown, amid the roar of a foaming cataract, the tumultuous noise which announced the close of his existence. The beautiful pathetic ballad, entitled "The Lament of the Border Widow," was composed on this event. On the south side of St. Mary's Loch is a hill called the Merecleuchhead, over which there is a scarcely visible track, termed the King's Road, leading over the hills into Ettrick.* At the head of the Loch of the Lowes, on the east, is Riskenhope, and on the west Chapelhope, the scene of the tale of "The Brownie of Bodsbeck." A few miles farther on through the hills is a small house, formerly an inn, called Birkhill, opposite the door of which Claverhouse shot four Covenanters, whose grave-stones were discernible in Ettrick churchyard a few years ago. Opposite the house at Birkhill is a hill called the Watch Hill, from the circumstance of the Covenanters stationing one of their number there, to give notice of the approach of the soldiers; and a little below is a hideous gully, containing a waterfall, called Dobbs Linn, and a cave which served as a place of retreat for the persecuted remnant. Near the head of Moffat Water is the "dark LOCH SKENE," a mountain lake of considerable size, pre-eminent over all lakes of the south of Scotland for the impressive gloom and sterility that surround it. The stream which forms its outlet, after a short and hurried course, falls from a cataract of immense height, and gloomy grandeur, called from its appearance THE GREY MARE'S TAIL. The water is precipitated over a dark rugged precipice, about 300 feet high. A little way from the foot of the cataract is a sort of trench, called "The Giant's Grave," which has evidently been a battery designed to command the pass. The character of the surrounding scenery is uncommonly savage and gloomy, and the *earn,* or Scottish eagle, has for many ages built its nest yearly upon an islet in Loch Skene. This rude

* An old song opens with this stanza:

"The King rade round the Merecleuchhead,
Booted and spurr'd, as we a' did see;
Syne dined wi' a lass at Mossfennan yett.
A little below the Logan Lee.

and savage scene is well described in the introduction to the second canto of Marmion.

"There eagles scream from isle to shore;
Down all the rocks the torrents roar;
O'er the black waves incessant driven,
Dark mists infect the summer heaven;
Through the rude barriers of the lake
Away its hurrying waters break
Faster and whiter, dash and curl,
Till down yon dark abyss they hurl.
Rises the fog-smoke, white as snow,
Thunders the viewless stream below.

——————— the bottom of the den,
Where, deep deep down and far within,
Toils with the rocks the roaring linn;
Then issuing forth one foamy wave,
And wheeling round the Giant's Grave
White as the snowy charger's tail,
Drives down the pass of Moffatdale."

The vale of Moffat, although less celebrated for its literary associations, is by no means inferior in picturesque attraction to its more favoured rivals, the Ettrick and Yarrow. To within a short distance from the village of Moffat the valley is strictly pastoral; and although its upper extremity, from its great elevation, is not unfrequently shrouded in mist, a day of sunshine discloses scenery of a highly pleasing and romantic character.

MOFFAT.

[*Inns*:—The Annandale Arms; The Star.]

The village of Moffat is situated on an elevation of about 370 feet above the sea, in a pastoral valley of the same name, near the junction of the Moffat, Leader, and Annan waters. With a gentle declivity to the south, it is protected on the north and east by a range of lofty flat-backed mountains, forming the highest south of the Forth. Hartfell, from which the range takes its name, is 2635 feet, and Broadland, 2741 feet high. It is much resorted to in summer on account of its healthy situation, and the two mineral springs, Moffat Well and Hartfell Spa, in its vicinity, the former being of a sulphurous, and the latter of a chalybeate character. The water of the well sparkles like champagne when taken from the fountain; and from the time of its discovery, 200 years ago, has maintained its character for the cure of many diseases. There are a number of neat lodging-houses in and near the village for the accommodation of visitors. From this the tourist may proceed by the Caledonian Railway to Edinburgh, Glasgow, or Carlisle.

5. MELROSE—KELSO—COLDSTREAM—BERWICK-ON-TWEED.

By Railway.

Leaving Melrose, the first station we arrive at is Newstead, at the village of the same name. Near it is a Roman camp. A little beyond Newstead, on the left, is Ravenswood House. On the same side, a little farther on, but not visible from the line, is Old Melrose.

NEWTOWN ST. BOSWELLS STATION.

[*Inn*:—Gavenlock's. A coach to Jedburgh.]

Here the main line to Hawick branches off on the right. Not far from the station, on the left, is the village of Newtown. The old village of St. Boswells appears to have stood in the vicinity of the Church, where the foundations of houses are occasionally discovered in the operations of agriculture. In the banks are many copious springs, and several of them form beautiful petrifactions. Hard by is the village of Lessuden, formerly a place of some importance, for, when burned by the English in 1544, it contained sixteen strong towers. On the Green is held the fair of St. Boswells, the principal market for sheep and lambs in the south of Scotland. Black cattle are also sold, although their number is not considerable; but the show of horns is generally so fine that buyers attend from all parts both of the north of England and south of Scotland. Two miles from St. Boswells is the village of Maxton, and, on the opposite side of the river, in a delightful situation, is Mer-

ballad of the "Eve of St. John;" and interesting from its having been the object which largely contributed to kindle the genius and inspire the style of the distinguished Scottish minstrel. The poet resided for some time, while a boy, at the neighbouring farm-house of Sandy-knowe, then inhabited by his paternal grandfather, and he has beautifully described the scenery in one of his preliminary epistles to Marmion.* The Tower is a high square building, surrounded by an outer wall, now ruinous. The circuit of the outer court being defended, on three sides, by a precipice and morass, is accessible only from the west by a steep and rocky path. The apartments are placed one above another, and communicate by a narrow stair. From the elevated situation of Smailholm Tower, it is seen many miles in every direction. It formerly belonged to the Pringles of Whytbank, and is now the property of Lord Polwarth. Continuing along the line, amidst the richest scenery, the tourist enjoys frequent glimpses of the river Tweed, with its wooded banks. Passing Newtown Don, (Sir Wm. Don, Bart.) we reach

ROXBURGH STATION.

On the left is Roxburgh village, and on the right, upon a grassy knoll, are the scanty remains of the famous CASTLE OF ROXBURGH, situate near the junction of the Tweed and Teviot, which here approach so close as to form a narrow isthmus. Roxburgh Castle was formerly a fortress of

taken by his army, under the direction of his widow. The spot where James was killed, by the bursting of a cannon, is marked by a holly tree, which grows upon the opposite bank of the Tweed. Nearly opposite to the ruins of the Castle, on the left bank of the river, is FLEURS CASTLE, the seat of the Duke of Roxburghe, commanding a fine view of the surrounding country. Extensive alterations and repairs have lately been made on this building, which render it one of the most stately specimens of the Tudor style in Scotland. On the Haugh, upon the south side of the river, is held, on the 5th of August, St. James's Fair, the greatest fair, next to St. Boswell's, in the south of Scotland. Proceeding onward, the tourist reaches Wallace Nick Station, 15 miles from Melrose, from which an omnibus conveys passengers to

KELSO.

[*Inns*:—The Cross Keys; The Queen's Head.]

This town occupies a beautiful situation on the margin of the Tweed, and consists of four principal streets, and a spacious square or market-place, in which stand the town-hall, erected in 1816, and many well-built houses, with elegant shops. Kelso is the residence of a number of people in easy circumstances, who live in a style of considerable elegance. It carries on a good inland trade, and has a weekly market and four annual fairs.* Its population is 5328. The most prominent object in Kelso is the venerable abbey, a noble specimen of the solid and majestic style of architecture called the Saxon or early Norman. The monks were of a reformed class of the Benedictines, first established at Tiron in France, and hence called Tironenses. David I., when Earl of Huntingdon, introduced the Tironenses into Scotland, and settled them near his castle at Selkirk, in the year 1113. The principal residence of the kings of Scotland, at this period, was the Castle of Roxburgh; and when David succeeded to the Scottish crown, after the death of his brother, in 1124, he removed the convent from Selkirk to Kelso, within view of his royal castle. The foundation of the

* Kelso is a burgh of barony, governed, under the general police Act, by a bailie and sixteen Commissioners. It is one of the cleanest and best lighted towns in Scotland.

church was laid on the 3d of May 1128. In consequence of its vicinity to the English border, Kelso suffered severely during the wars between the two countries, and the monastery was frequently laid waste by fire. It was reduced to its present ruinous state by the English, under the Earl of Hertford, in 1545. The only parts now remaining are the walls of the transepts, the centre tower, and west end, and a small part of the choir. After the Reformation, a low gloomy vault was thrown over the transept, to make it serve as a parish church, and it continued to be used for this purpose till 1771, when one Sunday, during divine service, the congregation were alarmed by the falling of a piece of plaster from the roof, and hurried out in terror, believing that the vault over their heads was giving way; and this, together with an ancient prophecy, attributed to Thomas the Rhymer, "that the kirk should fall when at the fullest," caused the church to be deserted, and it has never since had an opportunity of tumbling on a full congregation. The ruins were disencumbered of the rude modern masonry, by the good taste of William Duke of Roxburghe, and his successor Duke James, and, in 1823, the decayed parts were strengthened and repaired by subscription. After the Reformation, the principal part of the estates of this rich abbey were held *in commendam* by Sir John Maitland, the ancestor of the Earl of Lauderdale, who exchanged it with Francis Stewart, afterwards Earl of Bothwell, for the priory of Coldinghame. This nobleman, for his repeated treasons, was attainted in 1592, and the lands and possessions of Kelso abbey were finally conferred upon Sir Robert Ker of Cessford, and they are still enjoyed by his descendant, the Duke of Roxburghe.

The environs of Kelso are singularly beautiful. They are thus described by Leyden, in his *Scenes of Infancy*.

"Bosom'd in woods where mighty rivers run,
Kelso's fair vale expands before the sun,
Its rising downs in vernal beauty swell,
And, fring'd with hazel, winds each flowery dell,
Green spangled plains to dimpling lawns succeed,
And Tempe rises on the banks of Tweed,
Blue o'er the river Kelso's shadow lies,
And copse-clad isles amid the waters rise."

The most admired view is from the bridge, looking up the river. In this view are comprehended the junction of the Tweed and Teviot, and the ruins of Roxburgh Castle; in front, the Palace of Fleurs, with its lawns sloping to the river's edge, and sheltered by lofty trees behind. On the south bank of the Teviot are the woods and mansion of Springwood Park, (Sir George Douglas, Bart.,) and close by is the fine bridge across the stream. On the right is the town, extended along the banks of the Tweed; nearer is Ednam House, and immediately beyond are the lofty ruins of the Abbey. In the background are the hills of Stitchel and Mellerstain—the castle of Home—the picturesque summits of the Eildon Hills, Penielheugh, &c. An excellent view may also be obtained of the district around Kelso, from the top of an eminence, on the south bank of the river, called Pinnacle-hill; and a third, equally interesting, from the building appropriated as a Museum and Library, situated on an elevation termed the Terrace.*

About two miles north from Kelso, on the banks of the Eden, is the village of EDNAM, the birth-place of the poet Thomson, near to which a monument has been erected to his memory. A little to the west, is Newton-Don, the seat of Sir William Don, Bart.; and two miles farther to the north is Stitchel, the mansion of Sir John Pringle, Bart. A short way beyond, on a considerable eminence, commanding a view of the whole Merse and a great deal of Roxburghshire, is Home Castle, once the residence of the ancient and powerful family of that name. After the battle of Pinkie, 1547, it was taken by the English, under the Duke of Somerset, and again, during the time of the Commonwealth, it was besieged and taken by Oliver Cromwell. Three miles to the west is Mellerstain House, the seat of George Baillie, Esq., of Jerviswood, surrounded by extensive plantations.

The line from Kelso to Berwick, which is a branch of the

* From Kelso a road leads to Jedburgh, by the villages of Maxwellheugh and Heaton, the beautiful banks of the Kale, Grahamslaw, where there are some remarkable caves, the villages of Eckford and Crailing, Crailing house, (J. Paton, Esq.,) formerly the seat of the noble family of Cranstoun, and Bonjedward, (Archibald Jerdon, Esq.)

York, Newcastle, and Berwick Railway, follows along the southern banks of the Tweed to Berwick. At the distance of two miles, are the Station and village of Sprouston, where passengers may also leave for Kelso; the line here enters the Merse, or Berwickshire. On the left is seen the Tweed, which now forms the boundary between England and Scotland. To the left of Carham Station is Carham Church, with Carham Hall. A mile and a half farther, on the same side, are the ruins of Wark Castle, celebrated in Border history. A mile farther, on the left, is the Hirsel, the seat of the Earl of Home; the park contains some fine preserves. Nine miles from Kelso, the train stops at Cornhill Station, where passengers leave for

COLDSTREAM.

[*Inns*:—The Newcastle Arms; The Commercial.]

Coldstream occupies an elevated situation on the north bank of the Tweed, which is here crossed by a handsome bridge. The population of the town is about 3000. In consequence of its proximity to England, Coldstream, like Gretna Green, is celebrated for its irregular marriages. In the principal inn Lord Brougham was married. During the winter of 1659-60, General Monck resided in Coldstream before he marched into England to restore Charles II., and here he raised a horse regiment, which is still denominated the Coldstream Guards. On the bank of the Tweed, to the west of the town, is Lees, the beautiful seat of Sir William Marjoribanks, Bart. About a mile and a half to the east of the town are the ruins of the Church of Lennel, which was the name of the parish before Coldstream existed. Near it is Lennel House (Earl of Haddington), in which the venerable Patrick Brydone, author of "Travels in Sicily and Malta," spent the latter years of his long life.* Following the course of the river, we come to Tillmouth, where the Till, a deep, dark, and sullen stream, flows into the Tweed.† On its banks stands Twisel Castle (Sir Francis

* There are two roads from Coldstream to Berwick, one along the north bank and one along the south bank of the Tweed. The latter is the more interesting, and is generally preferred.

† The different characteristics of the two rivers are pointed out in the following rhyme:—

Blake, Bart.) Beneath the castle, the ancient bridge is still standing by which the English crossed the Till before the battle of Flodden.* The glen is romantic and delightful, with steep banks on each side, covered with copsewood. On the opposite bank of the Tweed is Milne-Graden, (the late Admiral Sir David Milne, Bart.,) once the seat of the Kerrs of Graden, and, at an earlier period, the residence of the chief of a Border clan, known by the name of Graden.† A little to the north-east is the village of Swinton. The estate of Swinton is remarkable, as having been, with only two very brief interruptions, the property of one family since the days of the Anglo-Saxon monarchy. The first of the Swintons acquired the name and the estate, as a reward for the bravery which he displayed in clearing the country of the wild swine which then infested it. The family have produced many distinguished warriors. At the battle of Beaugé, in France, Thomas Duke of Clarence, brother to Henry V., was unhorsed by Sir John Swinton of Swinton, who distinguished him by a coronet of precious stones which he wore around his helmet.‡ The brave conduct of another of this warlike family, at the battle of Homildon Hill, in 1402, has been dramatized by Sir Walter Scott,

Tweed said to Till,
" What gars ye rin sae still ?"
Till said to Tweed,
" Though ye rin wi' speed,
And I rin slaw,
Yet, where ye drown ae man
I drown twa !"

—————— " They cross'd
The Till, by Twisel Bridge.
High sight it is, and haughty, while
They dive into the deep defile;
Beneath the cavern'd cliff they fall,
Beneath the castle's airy wall.
By rock, by oak, by hawthorn tree,
Troop after troop are disappearing;
Troop after troop their banners rearing,
Upon the eastern bank you see,
Still pouring down the rocky den,
Where flows the sullen Till,
And, rising from the dim wood glen
Standards on standards, men on men,
In slow succession still,
And sweeping o'er the Gothic arch,
And pressing on, in ceaseless march,
To gain the opposing hill."

Marmion, c. vi.

† SIR WALTER SCOTT's *Border Antiquities*, p. 152.

‡ " And Swinton laid the lance in rest
That tamed, of yore, the sparkling crest
Of Clarence's Plantagenet."

Lay of the Last Minstrel, c. v., s. 4.

whose grandmother was the daughter of Sir John Swinton of Swinton. To the left is seen Ladykirk Church—an ancient Gothic building, said to have been erected by James IV., in consequence of a vow made to the Virgin, when he found himself in great danger while crossing the Tweed, by a ford in the neighbourhood. By this ford the English and Scottish armies made their mutual invasions, before the bridge of Berwick was erected. The adjacent field, called Hollywell Haugh, was the place where Edward I. met the Scottish nobility, to settle the dispute between Bruce and Baliol, relative to the crown of Scotland. On the opposite bank of the Tweed stands the celebrated CASTLE of NORHAM.*

* "The ruinous castle of Norham (anciently called Ubbanford) is situated on the southern bank of the Tweed, about six miles above Berwick, and where that river is still the boundary between England and Scotland. The extent of its ruins, as well as its historical importance, shows it to have been a place of magnificence, as well as strength. Edward I. resided there when he was created umpire of the dispute concerning the Scottish succession. It was repeatedly taken and retaken during the wars between England and Scotland; and, indeed, scarce any happened, in which it had not a principal share. Norham Castle is situated on a steep bank, which overhangs the river. The repeated sieges which the castle had sustained, rendered frequent repairs necessary."

EDINBURGH to PEEBLES, SELKIRK, MELROSE, KELSO & BERWICK

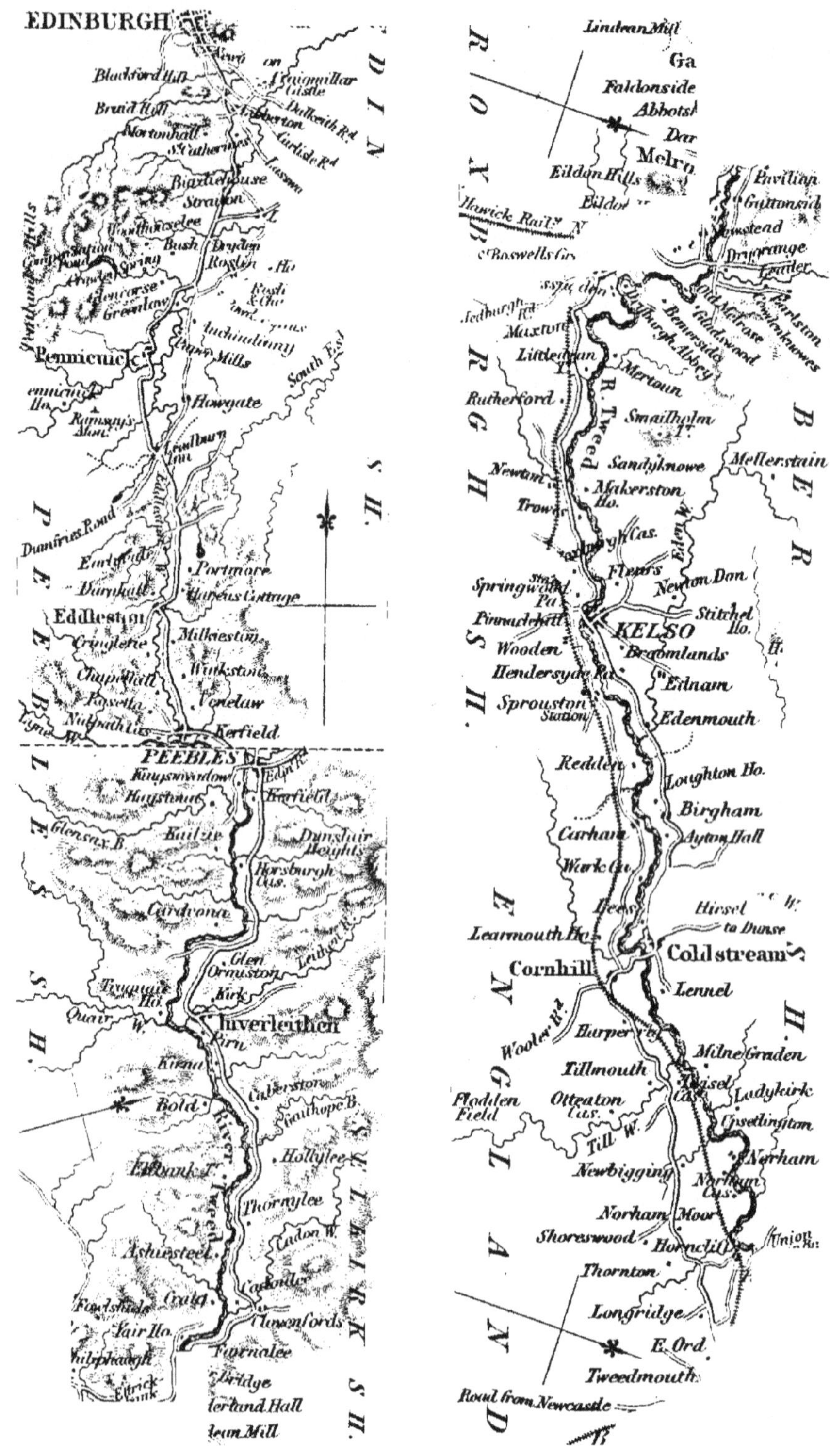

About four miles from Berwick, is Paxton House, the seat of Forman Home, Esq., which contains a fine collection of pictures. In the immediate neighbourhood, the Tweed is crossed by the Union Wire Suspension Bridge, constructed in 1820, by Captain Samuel Brown. Its length is 437 feet; width, 18; height of piers above low-water mark, 69; and is one of the finest structures of that kind in this part of Scotland. Near Paxton, the Tweed is joined by the Whitadder, the principal river which flows through Berwickshire; on its banks, a few miles to the north-west, is Ninewells, the paternal seat of David Hume.

Passing Velvet Hall Station and Halidon Hill, the scene of a battle in 1333, between the English and the Scots, in which the latter were defeated, the train arrives at Tweedmouth Station. To the left, at the other end of the bridge across the Tweed, is Berwick-on-Tweed.

SECOND TOUR.

EDINBURGH TO PEEBLES BY COACH.

Leave Edinburgh by Nicolson Street, and proceed by Liberton and Pennycuik, (as per Itinerary, page 502). Twenty-two miles from Edinburgh, is the royal burgh and county town of

PEEBLES.

[*Inns*:—The Tontine.]

Peebles is beautifully situated on the banks of the river Tweed. It is a town of great antiquity, and must, from a very early period, have been a seat of population, as is indicated by its name, which, in British, signifies shielings or dwelling-places; it is certain that at the end of the eleventh century there were at this place, a village, a church, a mill, and a brewhouse. The population of the burgh within the Royalty at last census, was 1908. Owing to its situation in the midst of a fine hunting country, and on the direct road to the royal forest of Ettrick, it became at an early period the occasional residence of the Kings of Scotland, and is the scene of the celebrated poem of James I., entitled "*Peblis to the Play.*" On account of its sequestered situation, this town figures little in Scottish history, and seems to have taken no part in any great historical event. It was, however, burnt and laid waste oftener than once during the invasions of the English. Peebles is divided into two districts—the old and new town. A bridge of great antiquity, consisting of five arches, connects the town with an extensive suburb on the opposite bank. The appearance of the whole is very pleasing, and the surrounding scenery is extremely beautiful. Peebles is a town possessed of very little commerce or manufacture. It has a weekly market, and seven annual fairs. At the end of the fifteenth century Peebles possessed no fewer than eleven places of worship, out of which the remains of only two are now visible. There is a large edifice of a castellated appearance still existing, known to have belonged to the Queensberry family, which is believed to be the scene of a highly romantic incident thus related by Sir Walter Scott. There is a tradition in Tweeddale. that when Nidpath Castle, near Peebles, was inhabited by the Earls of March, a mutual passion subsisted between a daughter of that noble family, and a son of the Laird of Tushielaw, in Ettrick forest. As the alliance was thought unsuitable by her parents, the young man went abroad. During his absence the young lady fell into a consumption, and at length, as the only means of saving her life, her father consented that her lover should be recalled. On the day when he was expected to pass through Peebles, on the road to Tushielaw, the young lady, though much exhausted, caused herself to be carried to the balcony of a house in Peebles, belonging to the family, that she might see him as he rode past. Her anxiety and eagerness gave such force to her organs, that she is said to have distinguished his horse's footsteps at an incredible distance. But Tushielaw, unprepared for the change in her appearance, and not expecting to see her in that place, rode on without recognizing her, or even slackening his pace. The lady was unable to support the shock, and, after a short struggle, died in the arms of her attendants.

The vale of the Tweed, both above and below Peebles, contained a chain of strong castles to serve as a defence against the incursions of English marauders. These castles were built in the shape of square towers, and usually consisted of three stories—the lower one on the ground floor being vaulted, and appropriated to the reception of horses and cattle in times of danger. They were built alternately on both sides of the river, and in a continued view of each other. A fire kindled on the top of these towers was the signal of an incursion, and, in this manner, a tract of country seventy miles long, from Berwick to the Bield, and fifty broad, was alarmed in a few hours.

"A score of fires, I ween,
From height, and hill, and cliff were seen,
Each with warlike tidings fraught,
Each from each the signal caught;
Each after each they glanced in sight,
As stars arise upon the night;
They gleam'd on many a dusky tarn,
Haunted by the lonely earn,*
On many a cairn's grey pyramid,
Where urns of mighty chiefs lie hid."

Lay of the Last Minstrel.

The strongest and the most entire of these fortresses is NIDPATH CASTLE, situated about a mile west from the town of Peebles, on a rock projecting over the north bank of the Tweed, which here runs through a deep narrow glen, once well wooded on both sides. Nidpath was at one time the chief residence of the powerful family of the Frasers, from whom the families of Lovat and Salton in the north are descended. The last of the family in the male line was Sir Simon Fraser, the staunch friend of Wallace, who, in 1302, along with Comyn, then guardian of the kingdom, defeated three divisions of the English on the same day, on Roslin Moor. Sir Simon left two daughters co-heiresses, one of whom married Hay of Yester, an ancestor of the Marquis of Tweeddale. The second Earl of Tweeddale garrisoned Nidpath, in 1636, for the service of Charles II., and it held out longer against Cromwell than any place south of the

* The Scottish Eagle.

Forth. The Tweeddale family were so much impoverished by their exertions in the royal cause, that they were obliged, before the end of the reign of Charles II., to dispose of their barony of Nidpath to William, first Duke of Queensberry, who purchased it for his son the first Earl of March. On the death of the last Duke of Queensberry in 1810, the Earl of Wemyss, as heir of entail, succeeded to the Nidpath estate. The castle is now falling fast to decay. It was formerly approached by an avenue of fine trees, all of which were cut down by the late Duke of Queensberry to impoverish the estate before it descended to the heir of entail. The poet, Wordsworth, has spoken of this conduct with just indignation in the following sonnet :—

" Degenerate Douglas ! oh, the unworthy Lord !
Whom mere despite of heart could so far please,
And love of havoc, (for with such disease
Fame taxes him,) that he could send forth word
To level with the dust a noble horde,
A brotherhood of venerable Trees,
Leaving an ancient dome, and towers like these,
Beggar'd and outraged !—Many hearts deplored
The fate of those old Trees ; and oft, with pain,
The traveller, at this day, will stop and gaze
On wrongs which Nature scarcely seems to heed :
For shelter'd places, bosoms, nooks, and bays,
And the pure mountains, and the gentle Tweed,
And the green silent pastures, yet remain."

From Peebles a pleasant excursion may be made to Innerleithen, six miles distant. The road proceeds along the northern bank of the Tweed by Kerfield (Gillespie, Esq.), on the opposite bank of the river, King's Meadows and Hayston, (Sir Adam Hay, Bart.)—the ruins of Horsburgh Castle, the property of the ancient family of the Horsburghs, now resident at Pirn—Kailzie, (R. N. Campbell, Esq.), Nether Horsburgh, (Campbell, Esq.), Cardrona, the seat of the old family of Williamson, and Glenormiston House, (W. Chambers, Esq.) Six miles below Peebles, and about a quarter of a mile from the mouth of Leithen water, is

INNERLEITHEN.

[*Inns* :—Riddle's Inn.]

This village occupies a pleasant situation at the bottom of a sequestered dell, environed on the east and west by high and partially wooded hills, and having the Tweed rolling in front. Till little more than thirty years ago, Innerleithen was one of the smallest and most primitive hamlets in this pastoral district. But about the beginning of the present century, its mineral spring began to attract notice, and it has now become a favourite watering-place, much frequented in the summer and autumn by visiters from Edinburgh. The healthiness of the climate—the beauty of the situation—its proximity to St. Mary's Loch in Yarrow, the Tweed, and various trouting streams, as well as other advantages connected with its locality, render Innerleithen a very delightful residence. A handsome wooden bridge leads across the Tweed to the hamlet of Traquair and Traquair House, the seat of the Earl of Traquair. At a short distance, at the base of a hill overlooking the lawn, a few birch trees may be seen, the scanty remains of the famed "Bush aboon Traquair." A few years ago an association was instituted at Innerleithen, called the St. Ronan's Border Club, consisting of a number of gentlemen connected with all parts of the country, who hold an annual festival for the performance of games and gymnastic exercises.

At a short distance from Innerleithen, is Pirn; and three miles farther on, entering Selkirkshire, is Holylee (Ballantyne, Esq.) A mile beyond, on the opposite side of the river, are the ruins of Elibank Tower, from which Lord Elibank takes his title. Two miles farther on is Ashiestiel (Col. Russell), once the residence of Sir Walter Scott. A mile beyond this the road crosses Caddon Water, and at the village of Clovenfords, joins the road from Edinburgh to Selkirk. Two miles beyond, it passes the old mansion-house of Fairnielee, now almost in ruins, and Yair, the seat of Alexander Pringle, Esq., of Whitbank, one of the loveliest spots in Scotland, closely surrounded by hills most luxuriantly wooded. The road then crosses the Tweed at Yair Bridge, and, two miles farther on, the Ettrick, and enters Selkirk (for description see p. 101).

THIRD TOUR.

EDINBURGH, HADDINGTON, DUNBAR, BERWICK, BY NORTH BRITISH RAILWAY.

EDINBURGH TO BERWICK.

Miles.	STATIONS.	Miles.	STATIONS.
	Edinburgh.	23½	Linton.
3	Portobello.	29	Dunbar.
6½	Inveresk.	33½	Innerwick.
10	Tranent.	37	Cockburnspath.
13½	Longniddry.	41½	Grant's House.
	18 *Arr.* Haddington (per Bran.)	46½	Reston.
17½	Drem.		50½ *Arr.* Chirnside (per Bran.)
	20 *Arr.* Dirleton (per Branch).		55 Dunse. (do.)
	23 North Berwick (do.)	50½	Ayton.
		52	Burnmouth.
21	East Fortune.	58	Berwick.

SHORTLY after leaving Edinburgh Station at Waverley Bridge, the tourist, on emerging from the tunnel through the Calton Hill, obtains a fine view of Salisbury Crags, Arthur's Seat, and St. Anthony's Chapel, to the right. Passing Jock's Lodge and Piershill Barracks, the train reaches

PORTOBELLO,

[*Inns*:—Storie's Hotel.]

a bathing village and favourite summer residence of the citizens of Edinburgh. A great number of elegant new streets have been built in the village, and hot and cold baths were erected in 1807. A mile and a-half further on, there is a branch line from Niddry Station to the town of

MUSSELBURGH,

[*Inns*:—The King's Arms.]

connected with Fisherrow by three bridges, the oldest of which is supposed to have been built by the Romans. Musselburgh, including Fisherrow, is an ancient burgh of regality, and unites with Portobello, Leith, and Newhaven

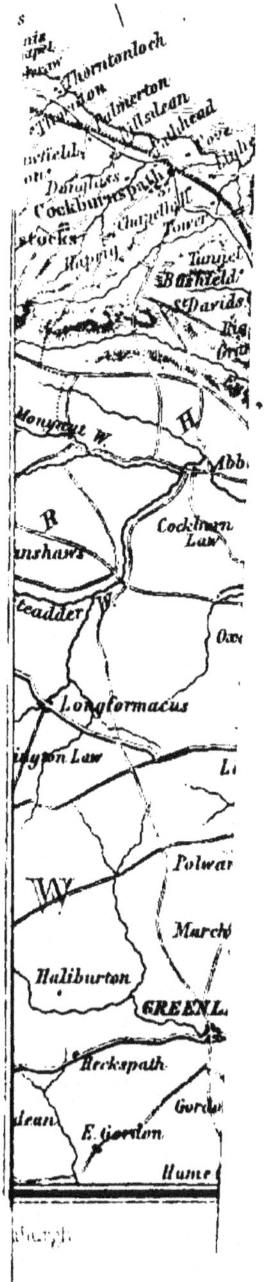

Thorntonloch
Palmerton
Cockburnspath
Tower
Cockburn Law
Longformacus
Haliburton
Heckspath
E. Gordon
Hume

in returning a member to Parliament. The population of the town, within the Parliamentary boundary, is 6366. The lordship and regality of Musselburgh were granted by James VI. to his chancellor, Lord Thirlestane, an ancestor of the Earls of Lauderdale. From them it was purchased in 1709 by Anne, Duchess of Buccleuch and Monmouth, and it still continues in the family of Buccleuch, along with the superiority of the burgh. The great Randolph, Earl of Moray, the nephew of Bruce, and regent of the kingdom, died, it is supposed of poison, in Musselburgh, in 1332. On Musselburgh links, an extensive plain between the town and the sea, the Edinburgh races, formerly held at Leith, are run. On this plain, in 1638, the Marquis of Hamilton, representing Charles I., met the Covenanting party; and here Oliver Cromwell, in 1650, quartered his infantry, while the cavalry were lodged in the town. In a garden, at the east end of Musselburgh, is a small cell, covered by a mound, the only remains now existing of a religious establishment, called the chapel of Loretto. After the Reformation, the materials of the ruined chapel were employed in building the present jail. For this sacrilegious act, it is said the inhabitants of Musselburgh were annually excommunicated at Rome till the end of the last century. At the east end of Musselburgh is Pinkie House, the seat of Sir John Hope, Bart., interesting for its many historical associations. It was originally a country mansion of the Abbot of Dunfermline, but was converted into its present shape at the beginning of the seventeenth century by Alexander Seton, Earl of Dunfermline. Inveresk Station, 6½ miles. About half a mile southward at Pinkieburn, on the east side of the Esk, is the spot where, in 1547, the battle of Pinkie was fought, in which the Scottish army was defeated by the English, commanded by the Duke of Somerset. Southward, to the right, is Carberry Hill, where, in 1567, Queen Mary surrendered to the insurgent nobles.*

* In the year 1728, a woman named Maggy Dickson, resident in Inveresk, was tried and condemned for child-murder, and duly (as was thought) executed in the Grassmarket of Edinburgh. When the dreadful ceremony was over, poor Maggy's friends put her body into a chest, and drove it away, in a cart, to

Proceeding onwards to the left, on the sea-coast, is Preston Grange (Sir George Suttie, Bart.) and on the right Dolphingston village, with its castle in ruins.

Tranent Station, 10 miles. Upon the left is Preston Tower, formerly the residence of the Hamiltons of Preston. On the coast is the village of Prestonpans. In this neighbourhood, 21st September 1745, was fought the memorable battle between the royal forces under Sir John Cope, and the Highland Army under Prince Charles Stuart. Near Tranent is Bankton House (—— M'Dowall, Esq.), which belonged to Colonel Gardiner, who fell nobly fighting for his country, close beside the wall of the park attached to his own residence. To the right is the ancient village of

TRANENT.

[*Inns*:—The Plough.]

It is mentioned in a charter of the 12th century under the name of Travernent. Proceeding by the Railway, to the left, is Seton House, which stands on the site of the once princely palace of Seton, for many centuries the seat of the Setons, Earls of Wintoun.* The last Earl was attainted

Musselburgh. When about two miles from town, the cart was stopped at a place called Peffermill, and the relations adjourned to a tavern for refreshment. On coming out of the house, what was their astonishment to see Maggy sitting up in the chest, having been restored to life by the motion of the cart. They took her home to Musselburgh, and she was soon entirely recovered. Sir Walter Scott, in the "Heart of Mid-Lothian," makes Madge Wildfire speak of "half-hangit Maggie Dickson, that cried saut mony a day after she had been hangit; her voice was roupit and hoarse, and her neck was a wee agee, or ye wad hae ken'd nae odds on her, frae ony other sautwife."—*Waverley Novels*, vol. xiii. p. 26.

* The Setons were one of the most distinguished Scottish families, whether in respect of wealth, antiquity of descent, or splendour of alliance. They took their original name from their habitation, Seaton, "the dwelling by the sea," where, it is said, their founder was settled by King David I. About the middle of the fourteenth century, the estate descended to Margaret Seton, who married Allan de Wyntoun, a neighbouring baron. This match was so displeasing to her own relations, that it occasioned a deadly feud, in consequence of which, we are assured by Fordun, no fewer than a hundred ploughs were put off work. George, the fifth Lord Seton, who lived in the time of Queen Mary, was one of her most attached friends, and it was to his castle of Niddry that she repaired, after her escape from Lochleven. He was grand-master of the household, in which capacity he had a picture painted of himself, with his official baton, and the following motto :—

on account of his concern in the rebellion of 1715. After his attainder the furniture of the palace was sold by the Commissioners of Enquiry, and, about forty years since, the building itself was removed, and the present mansion erected on its site. At a little distance from the house stands the Collegiate Church of Seton, which is now all that remains to attest the splendour of the family. It is a handsome little Gothic edifice, still nearly entire. There are also visible some monuments of the ancient lords of Seton fast mouldering into decay. Longniddry Station, 13½ miles. The Laird of Longniddry was a zealous reformer, and had John Knox for the tutor of his children. The ruins of the family chapel, in which Knox preached, are still pointed out. Northward, near the coast, is Gosford House, a mansion of the Earl of Wemyss. About three miles from Tranent, is Gladsmuir, noted as the birth-

In adversitate patiens;
In prosperitate benevolus.
Hazard, yet forward.

He declined to be promoted to an earldom, which Queen Mary offered him. On his refusing this honour, Mary wrote, or caused to be written, the following lines:—

Sunt comites, ducesque, alii sunt denique reges;
Sethoni dominum sit satis esse mihi.

Which may thus be rendered:—

Earl, duke, or king, be thou that list to be;
Seton, thy lordship is enough for me.

After the battle of Langside, Lord Seton was obliged to retire abroad for safety; and was in exile for two years, during which he was reduced to the necessity of driving a waggon in Flanders for his subsistence. His picture in this occupation, and the garb belonging to it, was painted at the lower end of the gallery in the ancient palace of Seton. In the time of James VI. the Seton family attained the dignity of Earl of Wintoun, and continued to flourish until the time of George, the fifth and last who enjoyed that dignity, and the large fortune which was annexed to it. In 1715, this unfortunate nobleman entered into the rebellion, and joined the Viscount of Kenmore with a fine troop of horse. He behaved with spirit and gallantry in the affair of the barricades at Preston; and afterwards, when waiting his fate in the Tower, made his escape by sawing through, with great ingenuity, the bars of the windows. He ended his motley life at Rome, in 1749, and with him closed the long and illustrious line of Seton, whose male descendants have, by intermarriage, come to represent the great houses of Gordon, Aboyne, and Eglinton. Their estate was forfeited, and has since passed through several hands.—*Provincial Antiquities*, by Sir Walter Scott, p. 97. See also *The Abbot*, vol. i., p. 277.

The Earl of Eglinton was lately served heir to the title of Earl of Wintoun.

place of George Heriot, founder of the Hospital at Edinburgh. Dr. Robertson was clergyman of this parish, and here he composed his History of Scotland. To the left is seen a column in the distance, rising conspicuously from the top of the highest of the Garleton hills, raised by the grateful tenantry to commemorate the virtues of the fourth Earl of Hopetoun. From Longniddry there is a branch line to Haddington. Passing on the right, Elvingston (R. Ainslie, Esq.), and on the left, Huntington (J. Ainslie, Esq.), and Alderston (J. Aitchison, Esq.); and on the right Letham (Sir T. B. Hepburn, Bart.), and Clerkington (General Sir Robert Houstoun, Bart.), the tourist will observe a monument of granite, raised as a tribute of regret and affection to the late Robert Ferguson of Raith. Eighteen miles from Edinburgh is the county town of

HADDINGTON.

[*Inns:*—The George; The Black Bull.]

Haddington occupies an agreeable situation on the north bank of the Tyne, the burgh, within the parliamentary boundary, containing 3777 inhabitants. The precise period at which Haddington became a royal burgh is unknown, its ancient records being lost; but it is known to be of very great antiquity, and is supposed to have received its name from Ada Countess of Northumberland, who founded a nunnery here in 1178. It has been several times burnt by the English or by accident, and has twice suffered greatly from an inundation of the Tyne. On the south side of the town is the Franciscan Church, a noble old Gothic building, partly in ruins. Fordun says, that on account of its splendour it was called the "Lamp of Lothian." The great tower and choir are roofless, and fast falling into decay, but the chancel is still in repair as a parish church. It is alleged that the celebrated John Knox was born in a house about a hundred feet to the east of the church. Haddington is chiefly remarkable in the present day for its grain market, one of the most extensive in Scotland. About a mile to the south of Haddington is Lennoxlove or Lethington, a seat of Lord Blantyre. It consists of a massive old tower, erected by the Giffords, with a modern addition, and is surrounded by a grove of lofty aged trees. Lethington came into the possession of the Lauderdale family by purchase about the middle of the fourteenth century, and was for some time the chief residence of that family. It was there that the celebrated Secretary Lethington lived, and one of its alleys, which he frequented, is still called the Politician's Walk.* Within sight of Lethington stands the mansion-house of Coalstoun, a seat of the Earl of Dalhousie, whose mother was the heiress of the ancient family of Broun of Coalstoun.†

To the north of Haddington lies the little village of Athelstaneford, which, in the early part of the last century, had for its ministers successively two poets—Robert Blair, author of "The Grave," and John Home, the author of "Douglas."

From Haddington, the course of the London Road proceeds eastward by Amisfield, and Stevenston House (Sir J. G. Sinclair, Baronet). Overhanging the south bank of the Tyne, are the ruins of Hailes Castle (Sir C. Ferguson, Baronet), which formerly belonged to the Hepburns, and was the chief residence of Queen Mary during her connexion with Bothwell. South of the castle rises Traprain Law, a rocky hill, anciently called Dunpender Law.

* Lethington contains several fine portraits, particularly a full-length, by Lely, of Frances Theresa Stuart, Duchess of Lennox, the most admired beauty of the court of Charles II. She was a daughter of Walter Stuart, M.D., a son of the first Lord Blantyre; and Lethington got the additional name of Lennox-love, from being a compliment to her from her husband. It is stated by Grammont, that the King caused this lady to be represented as the emblematical figure *Britannia* on the coin of the realm.

† One of the Brouns of Coalstoun, about 300 years ago, married a daughter of John third Lord Yester, with whom he obtained in dowry a pear, with the assurance that, as long as the pear was preserved, the family would be attended with unfailing prosperity. This celebrated pear is still preserved in a silver box. At no great distance, in the neighbourhood of Gifford, is Yester House, the elegant seat of the Marquis of Tweeddale, the descendant of the wizard Lord who enchanted the Coalstoun pear. The ancient Castle of Yester stood nearer the Lammermuir Hills, and the remains of it are still to be seen on a peninsula, formed by two streams. It contained a capacious cavern, called in the country Bo' Hall, *i. e.* Hobgoblin Hall, supposed to have been formed by magical art. The reader will not need to be reminded of the use made of the Goblin Hall and the wizard Lord in the poem of "Marmion," canto iii.

Resuming the line of railway from Longniddry, we proceed by Ballencrieff to Drem Station, 17½ miles. From this there is a branch line to the village of

NORTH BERWICK.*

[*Inns*:—M'Donald's.]

* About seven miles north-west of Dunbar, and two and a half eastward from North Berwick, are the ruins of the famous Castle of Tantallon. From the land side they are scarcely visible, till the visiter, surmounting a height which conceals them, finds himself close under the external walls. The description of this castle given in the poem of Marmion, renders any account of our own unnecessary.

——————" Tantallon vast
Broad, massive, high, and stretching far,
And held impregnable in war,
On a projecting rock it rose,
And round three sides the ocean flows,
The fourth did battled walls enclose,
And double mound and fosse;
By narrow drawbridge, outworks strong,
Through studded gates, an entrance long,
To the main court they cross.
It was a wide and stately square,
Around were lodgings fit and fair,
And towers of various form,
Which on the court projected far,
And broke its lines quadrangular;
Here was square keep, there turret high,
Or pinnacle that sought the sky,
Whence oft the warder could descry
The gathering ocean storm.

c. v., st. 33.

Tantallon was a principal stronghold of the Douglas family; and when the Earl of Angus was banished in 1526, it continued to hold out against James V. The king went in person against it, and, for its reduction, borrowed from the Castle of Dunbar, then belonging to the Duke of Albany, two great cannons, whose names, Pitscottie informs us, were "Thrawn-mouth'd Mow and her Marrow;" also, "two great bocards, and two moyan, two double falcons, and four quarter falcons," for the safe guiding and re-delivery of which three lords were laid in pawn at Dunbar. Yet, notwithstanding all this apparatus, James was forced to raise the siege, and only afterwards obtained possession of Tantallon by treaty with the governor, Simon Panango. Tantallon was at length "dung down" by the Covenanters; its lord, the Marquis of Douglas, being a favourer of the royal cause. About the beginning of the eighteenth century, the Marquis, afterwards Duke of Douglas, sold the estate of North Berwick, with the castle of Tantallon, to Sir Hew Dalrymple, President of the Court of Session, and they now remain in the possession of his descendant, Sir Hew H. Dalrymple, Bart., of Bargeny and North Berwick.

Two miles north from Tantallon lies the Bass Island, or rather Rock, rising

Linton Station, 23½ miles. To the left is the village of LINTON.—[*Inns:*—Red Lion.]—The Kirk of Preston, and Smeaton House (Sir T. B. Hepburn, Bart.), are seen at a little distance on the left bank of the Tyne. The train next passes Phantassie (T. Mitchell Innes, Esq.), noted in the annals of agriculture as the residence of the late John Rennie, the celebrated engineer, who was born at Phantassie, and educated in this neighbourhood. At some distance, on the left, situate on the estuary of the Tyne, is Tyningham House, the noble mansion of the Earl of Haddington, surrounded by venerable woods and a spacious park * On the right, to the south of the London Road, is Biel (Mrs. Ferguson), with its extensive plantations and charming walks. Immediately below the mansion-house, formerly the residence of Lord Presmennan, a beautiful sheet of water, called Presmennan Lake, has recently been formed, by throwing an artificial mound across a small rivulet which descends from the Lammermuir Hills. The privilege of perambulating the grounds is permitted by the kindness

400 feet sheer out of the sea. The Bass is about a mile in circumference, and is conical on the one side, presenting, on the other, an abrupt and overhanging precipice. It is remarkable for its immense quantities of sea-fowl, chiefly solan geese. Upon the top of the rock gushes out a spring of clear water, and there is verdure enough to support a few sheep. The Bass was long the stronghold of a family of the name of Lauder, one of whom distinguished himself as a compatriot of Wallace. The castle, situated on the south side of the island, is now ruinous. In 1671, it was sold by the Lauder family, for £4000, to Charles II., by whom it was converted into a royal fortress and state prison. Many of the most eminent of the Covenanters were confined here. At the Revolution, it was the last stronghold in Great Britain that held out for James VII.; but, after a resistance of several months, the garrison were at last compelled to surrender, by the failure of their supplies of provisions. The Bass is now the property of Sir Hew Hamilton Dalrymple, Bart. This remarkable rock is visited in summer by numerous pleasure parties. In order to perform the visit, it is necessary to apply for a boat either at North Berwick, or at Canty Bay, near Tantallon.

* In the Tyningham grounds are some magnificent holly hedges. "One of these hedges," says Mr. Miller, in his "Popular Philosophy," "is no less than twenty-five feet high and eighteen broad; and the length of what is denominated the Holly Walks, lying chiefly between two hedges of fifteen feet high and eleven broad, is no less than thirty-five chains eighty links, English measure."

of the proprietrix, who also allows the use of a boat upon the lake to the numerous summer parties who visit it. Beyond, on the right, is Belton Place (Captain Hay, R. N.), and on the left Nineware House (James Hamilton, Esq.) A short way farther on is the village of Belton-ford, a mile farther West Barns, and half a mile beyond it the beautifully situated village of Belhaven, from which Lord Belhaven takes his title. Near the village is excellent sea-bathing; and a sulphurous Spa was lately discovered in its neighbourhood. The train now passes on the left Winterfield (Colonel Anderson), Belhaven Church, and an old tower called Knockenhair, used, during last war, as a signal station. On the right, at a little distance, is Lochend House (Sir George Warrender, Bart.) Still farther off, on the same side, are Bower House (General Carfrae), and Spott (James Sprott, Esq.), their plantations imparting a sylvan variety to a rich corn-field country. Twenty-nine miles from Edinburgh, is the royal burgh and seaport town of

DUNBAR.

[*Inns:*—The George.]

The name is supposed to be derived from two Celtic words, signifying the Castle on the extremity. Its population was 3014 at last census. It was created a royal burgh by David II., ostensibly to prevent English merchants from bringing into and carrying out of the kingdom wool, hides, and other commodities, without the payment of custom. The only public building worthy of notice is the church, erected in 1819, on the site of the old collegiate church, the first of the kind founded in Scotland. It contains a most splendid marble monument to Sir George Home, created Earl of Dunbar and March by James VI. At the entrance to the town from the west, there are the remains of a monastery of the Grey Friars. Dunbar could also boast of a convent of the White Friars; but the record says they were *banished to Peebles* for their *immorality*. The coast in the neighbourhood of Dunbar is remarkably perilous, and the entrance to the harbour is rocky and difficult. Oliver Cromwell contributed three hundred pounds towards the erection of the eastern pier; another pier on the west has been lately built, and a dry dock has also been constructed. A large addition has been made to the harbour, at the joint expense of the town and the Fishery Board. The cost has been about £14,000. A grain market is held every Monday, and a cattle market the first Monday of every month. Dunbar House, the residence of the Earl of Lauderdale, stands at the north end of the principal street. About two hundred yards north from Dunbar House stands the celebrated Castle of Dunbar. Its antiquity is unknown, but so early as 1070 it was given, with the adjacent manor, by Malcolm Canmore, to Patrick Earl of Northumberland, a princely noble, who fled from England at the Conquest, and became the progenitor of the family of Cospatricks, Earls of Dunbar and March. This once formidable fortress has passed through many varieties of fortune, but the most memorable incident in its history was the gallant and successful defence made by *Black Agnes*, Countess of March, against an English army under the Earl of Salisbury. When the battering engines of the besiegers flung massive stones on the battlements, she caused her maidens, as if in scorn, to wipe away the dust with their handkerchiefs; and when the Earl of Salisbury commanded a huge military engine, called a *sow*, to be advanced to the foot of the walls, she, in a scoffing rhyme, advised him to take good care of his sow, for she would make her farrow her pigs. She then ordered an enormous rock to be discharged on the engine, which crushed it to pieces.* On another occasion, an arrow shot by an

* A similar story is told of Judge Bankes's lady, while holding out Corffe Castle against the Parliament forces. The incident is thus alluded to by Mr. W. Stewart Rose, in his poem addressed to Corffe Castle:—

"'Twas when you rear'd, 'mid sap and siege,
The banner of your rightful liege,
At your she-captain's call;
Who, miracle of womankind!
Lent mettle to the meanest hind
That mann'd her castle wall.

What

archer of her train struck to the heart an English knight, through his complete suit of armour,—"There goes one of my lady's tiring-pins," said the Earl of Salisbury, "the Countess' love-shafts pierce to the heart." After a successful defence, which lasted six weeks, the siege was abandoned by the English troops. George, tenth Earl of Dunbar and March, on a quarrel with Alexander, Duke of Albany, brother of James III., retreated into England. His large estate was thereupon forfeited, and, with Dunbar Castle, passed into the hands of the Duke of Albany, to whom on his memorable escape from Edinburgh Castle, it afforded shelter till he departed for France. In the year 1567, Queen Mary conferred the keeping of this important stronghold on the infamous Bothwell; and here she twice found shelter—once, after the murder of Rizzio; and a second time, when she made her escape from Borthwick Castle, in the disguise of a page. After her surrender at Carberry Hill, Dunbar Castle was taken, and completely destroyed by the Regent Murray. It is now the property of the Earl of Lauderdale, who is also superior, in right of the Earl of March.

Near the town of Dunbar were fought two battles, in both of which the Scots were defeated—one in 1296, when Baliol was defeated by the forces of Edward I.; the other in 1650, when the Scottish army, under General Leslie, was routed with great slaughter at Doonhill, by Cromwell. This battle is still remembered by the people of Scotland under the opprobrious epithet of "the race of Dunbar," or "the Tyesday's chase;" the engagement having taken place on a Tuesday. An eminence, lying about two miles south from the town, gives its name to the latter battle, and the former was in the same direction, but a little nearer.

Perhaps no part of the British coast affords a richer treat to the geologist, than that lying between Belhaven and St. Abb's Head. Over the whole of it, Hutton and Playfair,

What time the banded zealots swore,
Long foil'd thy banner'd towers, before
Their fearful entrance made,
To rase thy walls with plough and harrow,
Yet oft the wild sow cast her farrow,
And well the boar was bay'd."

and Sir James Hall, have very frequently wandered ; and, from its phenomena, some of their favourite theories derive their clearest illustrations. The Emperor of Russia, when he visited Dunbar as Prince Nicholas, was so charmed with a singularly beautiful formation of basalt that presents itself at the entrance of the harbour, as to direct that specimens of it should be conveyed to Russia.

Leaving Dunbar, the tourist passes, on the left, Broxmouth Park, formerly the head-quarters of Cromwell at the battle of Doonhill, but now the site of a large mansion belonging to the Duke of Roxburghe. Innerwick Station, 33½ miles. A mile to the south is Thurston (Hunter, Esq.) A short way beyond, on the right, are the ruins of Innerwick Castle, situated on the edge of a precipitous glen; and, on the opposite side of the glen, stands Thornton Tower: the former the fortalice of a Hamilton, and the latter of a Hume. Innerwick was burnt by the English, and Thornton blown up with gunpowder, during Somerset's expedition. Cockburnspath Station, 37 miles. To the right is the village of Cockburnspath (a corruption of Colbrandspath.) A mile beyond the village, and on the left, close to the road, is the ancient tower of Cockburnspath, now the property of Sir J. Hall of Dunglas. Dunglas House, the splendid mansion of Sir John Hall, embosomed amid beautiful plantations, is well deserving the tourist's notice.* The tract of country through which the line now passes is high and flat, but broken at little distances by numerous deep and

* Dunglas House stands on the site of the old castle, which was originally a fortress of the Earls of Home, and still gives their second title to that family. After the attainder of the Earl of Home, in 1516, it passed into the hands of the Douglases. It was destroyed by Somerset, in 1548, but was again rebuilt and enlarged. It was finally destroyed in 1640, on which occasion the Earl of Haddington, and a number of other persons of distinction, were killed by the explosion of the powder magazine. The old parish church stands near Dunglas House. Great good taste is displayed in the manner the ruin is preserved as the family mausoleum.

narrow ravines, each of which has a small stream at tho bottom running towards the sea. The most remarkable of these ravines is the Peaths, over which the celebrated Peaths or Pease bridge was thrown in 1786, when it was the post road. This singular structure is 123 feet in height, 300 feet in length, and sixteen feet wide. The post road now crosses the glen, about a quarter of a mile above the bridge. In former times, the Peaths was a most important pass, and Oliver Cromwell describes it in his dispatch to the Parliament, after the battle of Dunbar, as a place "where one man to hinder, is better than twelve to make way." Grant's House Station, 41½ miles. Five miles farther is Reston Station, 46½ miles. From this, coaches run in connection with the Railway to Chirnside and Dunse. From the village of Reston, a road turns off on the left to the beautiful village of Coldingham—[*Inns:* The Anchor; Mrs. Thomson's.]* Proceeding along the banks

* Coldingham is situated upon a small eminence, in the centre of a fine valley, at a short distance from the sea. It is remarkable for the ruins of its priory, so celebrated in Border history. The monastery was established by St. Abb, in the seventh century, and is said to have been the first in Scotland. The buildings were once of great magnificence and extent, but, of late years, they have been greatly dilapidated, by the rapacious license of the people in taking away stones, for the purpose of building their own houses, so that only a few detached fragments now remain. About fifty years ago, in taking down a tower at the south-west corner, the skeleton of a nun was found standing upright in a hollow of the wall, no doubt a victim to a breach of her vows.

North-east of Coldingham about two miles, is the celebrated promontory called St. Abb's Head. It consists of two hills, the western of which is occupied by an observatory; the eastern, called the Kirkhill, still exhibits the remains of a monastery and a church. The savage and dreary character of the scenery is exceedingly striking. The neighbouring promontory of Fast Castle derives its name from an ancient baronial fortress, built upon the very point of the precipitous headland. Fast Castle is the Wolf's Crag of the "Bride of Lammermoor," and is thus described in that tragic tale:—"The roar of the sea had long announced their approach to the cliffs, on the summit of which, like the nest of some sea-eagle, the founder of the fortalice had perched his eyry. The pale moon, which had hitherto been contending with flitting clouds, now shone out, and gave them a view of the solitary and naked tower, situated on a projecting cliff, that beetled on the German Ocean. On three sides, the rock was precipitous; on the fourth, which was that towards the land, it had been originally fenced by an artificial ditch and drawbridge, but the latter was broken down and ruinous, and the former had been in part filled up, so as to allow passage for a horseman into the narrow court-yard, encircled on two sides with low

of the Eye, the tourist reaches Ayton Station, $50\frac{1}{2}$ miles. Ayton House (Mitchell Innes, Esq.) stands to the east of the village. The banks of the Eye afford some fine scenery. At its confluence with the sea stands the seaport and fishing town of Eyemouth. This town was formerly notorious for the smuggling carried on by its inhabitants, but of late years the contraband trade has been entirely suppressed.* Burnmouth Station, 52 miles. At the bottom of a deep ravine, on the sea coast, is the romantic little fishing village of Burnmouth, the well-situated, and formerly well-frequented haunt of the smuggler. Ten miles farther, the tourist passes the ruins of Lamerton Kirk, where, in 1503, Margaret, daughter of

offices and stables, partly ruinous, and closed on the landward front by a low embattled wall, while the remaining side of the quadrangle was occupied by the tower itself, which, tall and narrow, and built of a greyish stone, stood glimmering in the moonlight, like the sheeted spectre of some huge giant. A wilder, or more disconsolate dwelling, it was perhaps difficult to conceive. The sombrous and heavy sound of the billows, successively dashing against the rocky beach, at a profound distance beneath, was, to the ear, what the landscape was to the eye—a symbol of unvaried and monotonous melancholy, not unmingled with horror." That castle was, in former days, a place of retreat of the great Earls of Home. Notwithstanding its strength, it was repeatedly taken and recaptured during the Border wars. About the close of the sixteenth century, it became the stronghold of the celebrated Logan of Restalrig, so famous for his share in the Gowrie Conspiracy; and it was to this place that the conspirators intended to convey the king, after getting possession of his person. There is a contract existing in the charter chest of Lord Napier, between this Logan and the celebrated Napier of Merchiston, setting forth, that, as Fast Castle was supposed to contain a quantity of hidden treasure, Napier was to make search for the same by divination, and, for his reward, was to have the third of what was found, and to have his expenses paid in whatever event. Fast Castle now belongs to Sir J. Hall of Dunglas. The precipitous rocks on this coast are inhabited by an immense number of sea-fowl, and a number of young men in the neighbourhood occasionally scale these dreadful and dizzy heights, in order to steal the eggs of the birds. Strange to say, an accident does not occur among them, perhaps, once in a century.

* "I stood upon Eyemouth fort,
And guess ye what I saw?
Fairnieside and Flemington,
Newhouses and Cocklaw.
The Fairy Folk o' Fosterland,
The witches o' Edincraw,
The rye rigs o' Reston,
And Dunse dings a'."

Old Rhyme.

Henry VII., was married by proxy to James IV.—a marriage which ultimately led to the union of the crowns. At a distance of fifty-eight miles from Edinburgh, the train reaches the town of

BERWICK-ON-TWEED.

[*Inns*:—The Red Lion; The King's Arms; The Salmon.]

Berwick is situated upon a gentle declivity close by the German Ocean on the north side of the river Tweed. It is a well-built town, with spacious streets, and is surrounded by walls which only of late ceased to be regularly fortified. The population amounts to about 10,000. It is governed by a mayor, recorder, and justices, and sends two members to Parliament. The trade of the port is considerable. Berwick occupies a prominent place in the history of the Border wars, and has been often taken and retaken both by the Scots and English. It was finally ceded to the English in 1482, and, since then, has remained subject to the laws of England, though forming, politically, a distinct territory. Its castle, so celebrated in the early history of these kingdoms, is now a shapeless ruin.

James IV.—a mar-
union of the crowns.
Edinburgh, the

ED.

The Salmon.]

vity close by the
e river Tweed. It is
and is surrounded
regularly fortified.
00. It is governed
sends two members
is considerable. Ber-
history of the Bor-
retaken both by the
to the English in
subject to the laws of
a distinct territory.
history of these king-

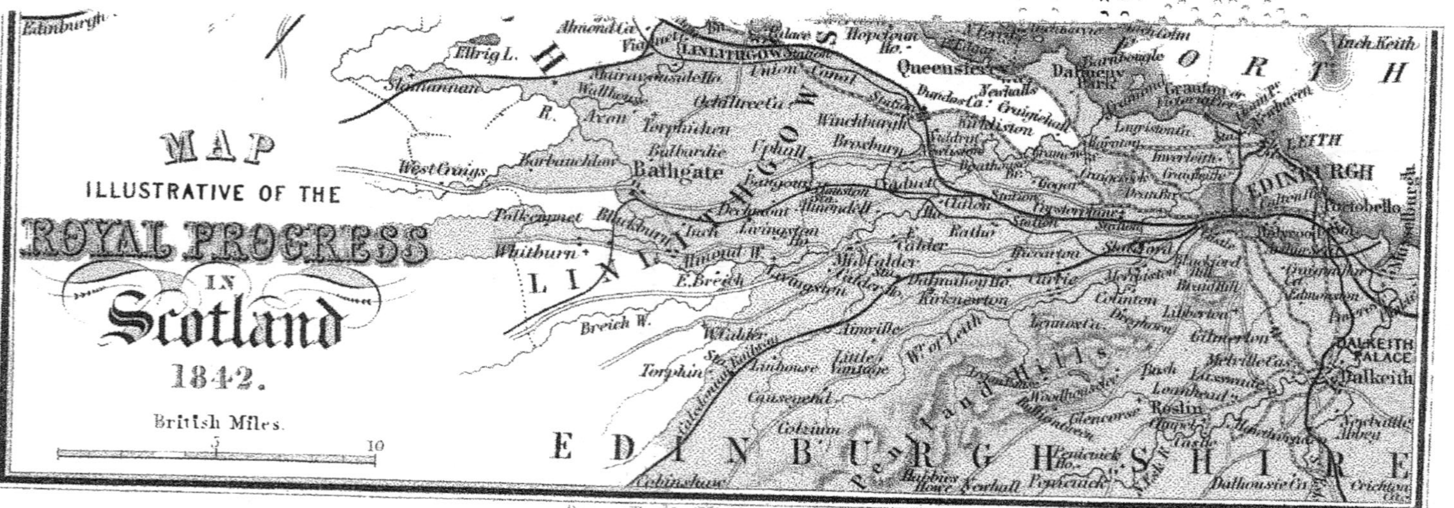
MAP
ILLUSTRATIVE OF THE
ROYAL PROGRESS
IN
Scotland
1842.
British Miles.
5
10
Edinburgh
Ellrig L.
Slamannan
West Craigs
Bathgate
Torphichen
Bathgate
Polkemmet
Whitburn
E. Breich
Breich W.
Torphin
LINLITHGOW
Queensferry
Dalmeny Park
Winchburgh
Broxburn
Uphall
Kirkliston
LEITH
EDINBURGH
Portobello
Musselburgh
Currie
Colinton
Liberton
Gilmerton
DALKEITH PALACE
Dalkeith
Roslin
Penicuick
Causewend
Cobinshaw
Crichton
Dalhousie
Newbattle Abbey
Mid Calder
Dalmahoy Ho.
Kirknewton
Pentland Hills
F O R T H
Inch Keith
E D I N B U R G H S H I R E
Drawn & Engd. by J. Bartholomew Edinr.

FOURTH TOUR.

*** The Map of the Royal Progress annexed exhibits the various routes from Edinburgh to Stirling. The Scottish Central line of Railway branches off from the Edinburgh and Glasgow Railway at the Greenhill Junction (4½ miles beyond Falkirk), and from Polmont Junction 3 miles before reaching Falkirk, from which it proceeds to Stirling and Perth.

Her Majesty's first Route is indicated on the Map by a conspicuous double line dotted in the centre.

EDINBURGH—LINLITHGOW—FALKIRK—STIRLING—BY THE EDINBURGH AND GLASGOW, AND SCOTTISH CENTRAL RAILWAYS.

EDINBURGH TO STIRLING BY RAILWAY.			
Miles.	Stations.	Miles.	Stations.
	Edinburgh.	17½	Linlithgow.
3½	Corstorphine.	22¼	Polmont Junction.
5½	Gogar.	25¼	Falkirk.
8½	Ratho.	29	Greenhill Junction.
12	Winchburgh.	36	Stirling.

LEAVING Edinburgh by Princes Street, Corstorphine Hill, richly wooded and studded with villas, is seen on the right, and the Pentland Hills on the left. Three miles from Edinburgh is the village of Corstorphine. At about seven miles farther the line crosses a very fine viaduct over the Almond water, and enters Linlithgowshire. To the right are seen the grounds of Newliston (Hog, Esq.), formerly the seat of the great Earl of Stair, who is said to have caused the woods around the house to be planted so as to resemble the position of the troops at the battle of Dettingen, where he commanded under George II.* A short dis-

* "During the rebellion of 1745, the route of the Highland Army having brought them near Newliston, an alarm arose in the Councils of Prince Charles, lest the MacDonalds of Glencoe should sieze the opportunity of marking their recollection of the massacre of Glencoe, by burning or plundering the house of the descendant of their persecutor; and it was agreed that a guard should be posted to protect the house of Lord Stair. MacDonald of Glencoe heard the resolution, and deemed his honour and that of his clan concerned. He demanded an audience of Charles Edward, and, admitting the propriety of placing a guard on a house so obnoxious to the feelings of the Highland army, and to those of his own clan in particular, he demanded, as a matter of right rather than of favour, that the protecting guard should be supplied by the MacDonalds of Glencoe. The request of the high-spirited chieftain was granted

tance beyond, to the right, a glance may be had of the ruins of Niddry Castle, where Queen Mary passed the first night after her escape from Lochleven. It was then the property of the Earl of Seton—it now belongs to the Earl of Hopetoun. In the immediate neighbourhood is the village of Winchburgh, where Edward II. first halted in his flight from the battle of Bannockburn. About eighteen miles from Edinburgh, on the margin of a beautiful lake, is the ancient royal burgh and county town of

LINLITHGOW.*

[*Inns*:—The Star and Garter.]

So early as the beginning of the twelfth century, Linlithgow was one of the principal burghs in the kingdom. It contains a considerable number of old fashioned houses, many of which belonged of old to the knights of St. John, who had their preceptory at Torphichen, in this county.

The most interesting object in Linlithgow is the Palace, a massive quadrangular edifice, situated upon an eminence which advances a little way into the lake. It occupies about an acre of ground, and, though in ruins, is still a picturesque and beautiful object.† The internal architecture is extremely elegant, but the exterior has a heavy appear-

and the MacDonalds guarded from the slightest injury the house of the cruel and crafty statesman who had devised and directed the massacre of their ancestor."—*Tales of a Grandfather*, vol. iv. p. 23.

It was in the family of the first Lord Stair, that the tragic incident occurred which forms the groundwork of Sir Walter Scott's tale of the "Bride of Lammermoor."

* Popularly denominated "the faithful town of Linlithgow."

† "Of all the palaces so fair
Built for the royal dwelling
In Scotland, far beyond compare
Linlithgow is excelling.
And in its park in genial June,
How sweet the merry linnet's tune,
How blyth the blackbird's lay!
The wild buck *bells* from thorny brake,
The coot dives merry on the lake,—
The saddest heart might pleasure take
To see a scene so gay."
Marmion, c. iv., st. 15.

ance from the want of windows. Over the interior of the grand gate is a niche which was formerly filled by a statue of Pope Julius II., who presented James V. with the sword of state, which still forms part of the regalia. It was destroyed during the last century by a blacksmith, who had heard popery inveighed against in the neighbouring church. Above this entrance was the Parliament Hall, once a splendid apartment, with a beautifully ornamented chimney at one end, and underneath it, has been a magnificent piazza. This part of the palace is understood to have been begun by James IV., and finished and ornamented by his successor. The west side of the palace is the most ancient, and contains the room where the unfortunate Queen Mary was born.*

In one of the vaults below, James III. found shelter when he was in danger of assassination from some of his rebellious subjects. The north side of the quadrangle is the most modern, having been built by James VI. shortly after his visit to Scotland in 1617. In the centre of the court are the elaborately carved ruins of the Palace Well, a once beautiful and ingenious work, erected by James V. It was destroyed by the royal army in 1746.

The nucleus of the Palace seems to have been a tower or fort, first built by Edward I., who inhabited it in person a whole winter. It was taken and demolished by Bruce in 1307.† It appears, however, to have been rebuilt by the

* Her father, who then lay on his deathbed at Falkland, on being told of her birth, replied, "Is it so?" reflecting on the alliance which had placed the Stuart family on the throne, "then God's will be done! It came with a lass, and it will go with a lass." With these words he turned his face to the wall, and died of a broken heart.

† It was taken in the following remarkable way:—The garrison was supplied with hay by a neighbouring rustic, of the name of Binnock or Binning, who favoured the interest of Bruce. "Binnock had been ordered by the English governor to furnish some cart-loads of hay, of which they were in want. He promised to bring it accordingly; but the night before he drove the hay to the castle, he stationed a party of his friends, as well armed as possible, near the entrance, where they could not be seen by the garrison, and gave them directions that they should come to his assistance as soon as they should hear him cry a signal, which was to be,—'Call all, call all!' Then he loaded a great waggon with hay; but in the waggon he placed eight strong men, well armed, lying flat on their breasts, and covered over with hay, so that they could not be

English during the minority of David II., but was again burnt down in 1424. The palace was finally reduced to its present ruinous condition by Hawley's dragoons, who were quartered in it on the night of the 31st of January 1746. In the morning, when they were preparing to depart, the dastardly scoundrels were observed deliberately throwing the ashes of the fires into the straw on which they had lain. The whole palace was speedily in a blaze, and it has ever since remained an empty and blackened ruin.* A grant has been made by Government to renew some of the stairs, and to arrest the farther progress of dilapidation.

The Church, a venerable and impressive structure, stands between the Palace and the town, and may be regarded as one of the finest and most entire specimens of Gothic architecture in Scotland. It was dedicated to the archangel Michael, who was also considered the patron saint of

seen. He himself walked carelessly beside the waggon; and he chose the stoutest and bravest of his servants to be the driver, who carried at his belt a strong axe or hatchet. In this way Binnock approached the castle early in the morning; and the watchman, who only saw two men, Binnock being one of them, with a cart of hay, which they expected, opened the gates, and raised up the portcullis, to permit them to enter the castle. But as soon as the cart had gotten under the gateway, Binnock made a sign to his servant, who, with his axe, suddenly cut asunder the *soam*, that is, the yoke which fastens the horses to the cart, and the horses, finding themselves free, naturally started forward, the cart remaining behind under the arch of the gate. At the same moment, Binnock cried, as loud as he could, 'Call all, call all!' and, drawing the sword which he had under his country habit, he killed the porter. The armed men then jumped up from under the hay where they lay concealed, and rushed on the English guard. The Englishmen tried to shut the gates, but they could not, because the cart of hay remained in the gateway, and prevented the folding-doors from being closed. The portcullis was also let fall, but the grating was caught on the cart, and so could not drop to the ground. The men who were in ambush near the gate, hearing the cry, 'Call all, call all!' ran to assist those who had leapt out from amongst the hay; the castle was taken, and all the Englishmen killed or made prisoners. King Robert rewarded Binnock by bestowing on him an estate, which his posterity long afterwards enjoyed. The Binnings of Wallyford, descended from that person, still bear in their coat armorial a wain loaded with hay, with the motto, 'Virtute doloque.'—*Tales of a Grandfather*, vol. i., p. 139.

* "They halted at Linlithgow, distinguished by its ancient palace, which, sixty years since, was entire and habitable, and whose venerable ruins, *not quite sixty years since*, very narrowly escaped the unworthy fate of being converted into a barrack for French prisoners. May repose and blessings attend the ashes of the patriotic statesman (President Blair) who, amongst his last services to Scotland, interposed to prevent this profanation."—*Waverley*, vol. i., p. 92.

LINLITHGOW PALACE.

the town. The Church was founded by David I., but was ornamented chiefly by George Crichton, Bishop of Dunkeld. It is now divided by a partition wall, and the eastern half alone is used as a place of worship. It was in an aisle in this Church, according to tradition, that James IV. was sitting when he saw the strange apparition which warned him against his fatal expedition to England.* In front of the Town-house stands the Cross Well, a very curious and elegant erection. The present edifice was built in 1807, but it is said to be an exact fac-simile of the original, erected in 1620. The sculpture is very elaborate, and the water is made to pour in great profusion from the mouths of a multitude of grotesque figures. The vast copiousness of

* The story is told by Pitscottie with characteristic simplicity:—"The king came to Lithgow, where he happened to be for the time at the Council, very sad and dolorous, making his devotion to God to send him good chance and fortune in his voyage. In this meantime, there came a man, clad in a blue gown, in at the kirk door, and belted about him in a roll of linen cloth; a pair of brotikings (buskings) on his feet, to the great of his legs; with all other hose and clothes conformed thereto; but he had nothing on his head, but syde (long) red yellow hair behind, and on his haffits (cheeks) which wan down to his shoulders; but his forehead was bald and bare. He seemed to be a man of two-and-fifty years, with a great pike-staff in his hand, and came first forward among the lords, crying and speiring (asking) for the king, saying he desired to speak with him. While, at the last, he came where the king was sitting in the desk at his prayers; but, when he saw the king, he made him little reverence or salutation, but leaned down grofling on the desk before him, and said to him in this manner, as after follows:—'Sir king, my mother hath sent me to you, desiring you not to pass, at this time, where thou art purposed; for if thou does, thou wilt not fare well in thy journey, nor none that passes with thee. Further, she bade thee mell (meddle) with no woman, nor use their counsel, nor let them touch thy body, nor thou theirs; for if thou do it, thou wilt be confounded and brought to shame.'

"By this man had spoken thir words unto the king's grace, the evening song was near done, and the king paused on thir words, studying to give him an answer; but in the meantime, before the king's eyes, and in the presence of all the lords that were about him for the time, this man vanished away, and could no wise be seen or comprehended, but vanished away as he had been a blink of the sun, or a whip of the whirlwind, and could no more be seen. I heard say, Sir David Lindesay, lyon-herauld, and John Inglis, the marshal, who were, at that time, young men, and special servants to the king's grace, were standing presently beside the king, who thought to have laid hands on this man, that they might have speired further tidings at him; but all for nought, they could not touch him; for he vanished away betwixt them, and was no more seen." There can be little doubt that the supposed apparition was a contrivance of the queen to deter James from his impolitic warfare.

water at Linlithgow is alluded to in the following well-known rhyme:—

> "Glasgow for bells,
> Lithgow for wells,
> Fa'kirk for beans and peas,
> Peebles for clashes and lees."

It was in Linlithgow that David Hamilton of Bothwellhaugh, on the 23d of January 1570, shot the Regent Murray, when passing through the town, in revenge for a private injury. The house from which the shot was fired belonged to the Archbishop of St. Andrews. It was taken down a number of years ago, and replaced by a modern edifice.

During the plague of 1645, Linlithgow happening to be comparatively free of the infection, the Palace and Church were used by the Courts of Justice and the members of the University of Edinburgh as their meeting places. At the Restoration, the inhabitants of Linlithgow burned the Solemn League and Covenant amidst great rejoicing. The ringleader in this affair was one Ramsay, the minister of the parish, who had formerly been a zealous supporter of the Covenant. In Linlithgow is still kept up the old custom of riding the marches. The town has derived considerable advantage from the Union Canal, which passes along the high grounds immediately to the south. Leather is the staple commodity of the place; linen and woollen manufactures are also carried on to a considerable extent. The population of the burgh within the Parliamentary boundary in 1841, was 3872.

Proceeding westward from Linlithgow, the line crosses the viaduct over the Avon, and enters Stirlingshire. On the face of an eminence overlooking the wide carse of the same name, is the town of

FALKIRK.

[*Inns*:—The Red Lion.]

It was a town of some note in the early part of the eleventh century. The old church, which was demolished about thirty years ago, was erected in 1057. The original name of the town was *Eglishbreckk*, signifying "the speckled church," in allusion, it is supposed, to the colour of the stones. In the churchyard are shown the graves of two celebrated Scottish heroes—Sir John Graham, the friend of Wallace, and Sir John Stewart of Bonkill, both of whom fell fighting bravely against the English at the battle of Falkirk, in 1298. Over the former a monument was erected with an inscription, which has been renewed three times since his death. It at present stands thus :—

Mente Manuque Potens, et Vallae Fidus Achates,
Conditur Hic Gramus, Bello Interfectus ab Anglis.

TRANSLATION.

Here lyes Sir John the Grame, baith wight and wise,
Ane of the chiefs who rescewit Scotland thrise,
Ane better knight not to the world was lent,
Nor was gude Grame of truth and hardiment.

In the churchyard is also to be seen the monument of two brave officers, Sir Robert Monro of Foulis, and his brother, Dr. Monro, who were killed in the second battle of Falkirk, January 17, 1746. Falkirk is noted for its great cattle markets or *trysts*, held thrice a-year, to which a vast number of black cattle are brought from the Highlands and Islands.

About two miles north of the town are the celebrated Carron Iron Works, the largest manufactory of the kind in the world.

Near Grahamston—the suburb of Falkirk where the Railway Station is built—a battle was fought, in 1298, between the forces of Edward I. and the Scots, under Wallace and Sir John Graham, in which the latter were defeated. The battle of Falkirk-muir, between the royal forces, under General Hawley, and the Highlanders, in which the latter gained a complete victory, was fought on the high ground lying to the south-west of the town. Hawley had suffered himself to be detained at Callander House by the wit and gaiety of the Countess of Kilmarnock (whose husband was with the Prince's army,) until the Highlanders had taken up an advantageous position, and were ready to attack his army.

The consequence of this negligence, coupled with an incapacity to act, was, that his troops were thrown into confusion, and completely routed.*

The view from the eminence on which the battle was fought is remarkably extensive, varied, and beautiful.

Passengers from Edinburgh to Stirling sometimes branch off from Polmont Junction, at others from Greenhill Junction. By the first arrangement the Glasgow passengers are met at Larbert Station, by the second at Greenhill. Near Larbert Station are the church and village of Larbert, and Larbert House. In Larbert Kirk, Bruce, the famous Abyssinian traveller, lies interred. Kinnaird, his patrimonial estate, is at no great distance. A mile and a half farther on, the line passes through the remains of the Torwood Forest, where Sir William Wallace is said to have found shelter in a tree when pursued by his enemies. At Torwood-head, Mr. Cargill, in 1680, excommunicated Charles II., the Duke of York, and the ministry. About four miles farther on, is the Station and village of Bannockburn, remarkable for its manufac-

* "Hawley had not a better head, and certainly a much worse heart, than Sir John Cope, who was a humane, good-tempered man. The new general ridiculed severely the conduct of his predecessor, and remembering that he had seen, in 1715, the left wing of the Highlanders broken by a charge of the Duke of Argyle's horse, which came upon them across a morass, he resolved to manœuvre in the same manner. He forgot, however, a material circumstance—that the morass at Sheriffmuir was hard frozen, which made some difference in favour of the cavalry. Hawley's manœuvre, as commanded and executed, plunged a great part of his dragoons up to the saddle-laps in a bog, where the Highlanders cut them to pieces with so little trouble, that, as one of the performers assured us, the feat was as easy as slicing *bacon*. The gallantry of some of the English regiments beat off the Highland charge on another point, and, amid a tempest of wind and rain which has been seldom equalled, the field presented the singular prospect of two armies flying different ways at the same moment. The king's troops, however, ran fastest and farthest, and were the last to recover their courage; indeed, they retreated that night to Falkirk, leaving their guns, burning their tents, and striking a new panic into the British nation, which was but just recovering from the flutter excited by what, in olden times, would have been called the Raid of Derby. In the drawing-room which took place at Saint James's on the day the news arrived, all countenances were marked with doubt and apprehension, excepting those of George the Second, the Earl of Stair, and Sir John Cope, who was radiant with joy at Hawley's discomfiture. Indeed, the idea of the two generals was so closely connected, that a noble peer of Scotland, upon the same day, addressed Sir John Cope by the title of General Hawley, to the no small amusement of those who heard the *quid pro quo*."—SIR WALTER SCOTT'S *Prose Works*, vol. xix., p. 303.

tories of tartans and carpets. To the left of the line, between Bannockburn and St. Ninians, and about a mile distant from Stirling, is the scene of the famous battle, the Marathon of the North, fought June 24th, 1314, between the English army of 100,000 men, under Edward II., and the Scottish army of 30,000, commanded by Robert Bruce, in which the former were signally defeated, with the loss of 30,000 men, and 700 barons and knights. The Scottish army extended in a north-easterly direction from the brook of Bannock, which was so rugged and broken as to cover the right flank effectually, to the village of St. Ninians, probably in the line of the present road from Stirling to Kilsyth. The royal standard was pitched, according to tradition, in a stone having a round hole for its reception, and thence called the Bore-Stone. The remaining fragment of this stone, protected from the depredations of strangers by a frame-work of iron, is still shown on the top of a small eminence called Brocks Brae, to the south-west of St. Ninians. To the northward, where there is a morass called Halberd's Bog, Bruce fortified his position against cavalry by digging a number of pits so close together as to resemble the cells in a honeycomb. They were slightly covered with brushwood and green sods, so as not to be obvious to an impetuous enemy.* It was in the immediate

* On the evening before the battle a personal encounter took place between Bruce and Sir Henry de Bohun, a gallant English knight, the issue of which had a great effect upon the spirits of both armies. It is thus recorded by Sir Walter Scott, in "The Lord of the Isles:"—

"Dash'd from the ranks Sir Henry Boune,—
He spurr'd his steed, he couched his lance,
And darted on the Bruce at once.—
As motionless as rocks that bide
The wrath of the advancing tide,
The Bruce stood fast. Each heart beat high,
And dazzled was each gazing eye.—
The heart had hardly time to think,
The eye-lid scarcely time to wink,
While on the king, like flash of flame,
Spurr'd to full speed the war-horse came!—
The partridge may the falcon mock,
If that slight palfrey stand the shock.—
But, swerving from the knight's career,
Just as they met, Bruce shunn'd the spear;
Onward the baffled warrior bore
His course—but soon his course was o'er,—

neighbourhood of this spot that the heat of the contest took place. A short time ago one of the workmen employed in draining the moss discovered an old sword about three feet below the surface. Formerly there were two large stones, erected in the lower extremity of a lawn which fronts a villa near the village of Newhouse, about a quarter of a mile from the south part of Stirling, marking the spot where a skirmish took place between Randolph Earl of Moray, and a party of English commanded by Sir Robert Clifford.* The stones have been removed, but the place is still popularly called Randals-field.

High in his stirrups stood the king,
And gave his battle-axe the swing;
Right on De Boune, the whiles he pass'd,
Fell that stern blow—the first—the last!—
Such strength upon the blow was put,
The helmet crash'd like hazel-nut,
The axe-shaft, with its brazen clasp,
Was shiver'd to the gauntlet grasp;
Springs from the blow the startled horse;
Drops to the plain the lifeless corse,
First of that fatal field, how soon,
How sudden fell the fierce De Boune."

The Scottish leaders remonstrated with the king upon his temerity; he only answered, "I have broken my good battle-axe." The English vanguard retreated, after witnessing this single combat.

* Bruce had enjoined Randolph, who commanded the left wing of his army, to be vigilant in preventing any advanced parties of the English from throwing succours into the Castle of Stirling. Eight hundred horsemen, commanded by Sir Robert Clifford, were detached from the English army; they made a circuit by the low grounds to the east, and approached the Castle. The king perceived their motion, and coming up to Randolph, angrily exclaimed, "Thoughtless man! you have suffered the enemy to pass. Randolph hastened to repair his fault, or perish. As he advanced, the English cavalry wheeled to attack him. Randolph drew up his troops in a circular form, with their spears resting on the ground, and protended on every side. At the first onset, Sir William Daynecourt, an English commander of distinguished note, was slain. The enemy, far superior in numbers to Randolph, environed him, and pressed hard on his little band; Douglas saw his jeopardy, and requested the king's permission to go and succour him. "You shall not move from your ground," cried the king, "let Randolph extricate himself as he best may, I will not alter my order of battle, and lose the advantage of my position."—"In truth," replied Douglas, "I cannot stand by and see Randolph perish, and, therefore, with your leave, I must aid him." The king unwillingly consented, and Douglas flew to the assistance of his friend. While approaching, he perceived that the English were falling into disorder, and that the perseverance of Randolph had prevailed over their impetuous courage. "Halt!" cried Douglas, "those brave men have repulsed the enemy, let us not diminish their glory by sharing it."—DALRYMPLE's *Annals of Scotland*.

About a mile from the field of battle, in another direction, is a place called the Bloody Folds, where the Earl of Gloucester is said to have made a stand, and died gallantly at the head of his own military tenants and vassals. There is also a place in this neighbourhood called Ingram's Crook, which is supposed to have derived its name from Sir Ingram Umfraville, one of the English commanders. In the rear of the position occupied by the Scottish army is the Gillies' Hill, which derived its name from the following circumstance:—In a valley westward of this hill, Bruce stationed his baggage, under the charge of the gillies or servants and retainers of the camp. At the critical moment when the English line was wavering, these gillies, prompted either by the enthusiasm of the moment, or the desire of plunder, assumed, in a tumultuary manner, such arms as they found nearest, and showed themselves on the hill like a new army advancing to battle. The English taking these for a fresh body of troops, were seized with a panic, and fled in every direction.

About a mile westward from the field of Bannockburn, was fought, in 1488, the battle of Sauchieburn, in which James III. was defeated and slain. The Barons of Scotland, being dissatisfied with the government of the king, rose in rebellion against him, and drew into their party the king's eldest son, then a youth of fifteen, afterwards James IV. The unfortunate monarch, with inferior numbers, attacked the army of the insurgents. The consequences proved most calamitous. The royal forces, after an obstinate struggle, gave way, and the king, flying from the field, fell from his horse as it started at a woman and water-pitcher near the village of Millton. He was carried into the mill in a state of insensibility by the miller and his wife, without being recognised. On recovering his senses he asked for a priest, to whom he might make confession. One of his pursuers coming up, exclaimed, "I am a priest," and, approaching the unfortunate monarch, who was lying in a corner of the mill, stabbed him several times to the heart. James IV. was seized with deep remorse for his conduct in this affair, which manifested itself in severe acts of penance, among

Drawn by G. Cattermole — Engraved by W. Forrest

STIRLING CASTLE.

Edinburgh, Published Sept. 1, 1846, by Adam & Charles Black, 27 North Bridge.

others, in wearing a ho
he added certain
St. Ninians, or, as it
a thriving village a
steeple stands separate
mediate vicinity. The
magazine by the High
blown up; but though
the steeple remained
tourist enters the

Stirling is delightfully
Forth, and bears in its
resemblance to Edinburg
most interesting
Castle, the first founda
of antiquity. It was
protracted sieges, dur
for the independence
residence about the
Stuart, and was long
monarchs. It was the
V.; and James VI. and
baptized in it. The
is in the form of a quad
part of the fortress. The
square are the oldest
ments is still called
the assassination of Will
of James II., after he
On the west side of
which was originally a

* So little had the prince been
was almost a stranger to his
fore him, a few days after the
perhaps, with some
are you my father?"
am not your father
† "
‡ Douglas

others, in wearing a heavy iron belt, to the weight of which he added certain ounces every year as long as he lived.*

St. Ninians, or, as it is commonly called, St. Ringans, is a thriving village a short way south from Stirling. Its steeple stands separate from the church, which is in its immediate vicinity. The old church, being used as a powder magazine by the Highlanders in 1746, was accidentally blown up; but though the church was completely destroyed, the steeple remained uninjured. A mile farther on, the tourist enters the royal burgh of

STIRLING.

[*Inns*:—The Royal Hotel; The Golden Lion.]

Stirling is delightfully situated on an eminence near the river Forth, and bears in its external appearance a considerable resemblance to Edinburgh, though on a smaller scale. The most interesting and conspicuous object in Stirling is the Castle, the first foundation of which is lost in the darkness of antiquity. It was frequently taken and retaken after protracted sieges, during the wars which were carried on for the independence of Scotland. It became a royal residence about the time of the accession of the house of Stuart, and was long the favourite abode of the Scottish monarchs. It was the birthplace of James II. and James V.; and James VI. and his eldest son Prince Henry were baptized in it. The palace, which was built by James V., is in the form of a quadrangle, and occupies the south-east part of the fortress. The buildings on the south side of the square are the oldest part of the Castle. One of the apartments is still called Douglas's Room, in consequence of the assassination of William Earl of Douglas by the hand of James II., after he had granted him a safe-conduct.†

On the west side of the square is a long low building, which was originally a chapel, and is now used as a store-

* So little had the prince been accustomed to his father's company, that he was almost a stranger to his person; for when Sir Andrew Wood appeared before him, a few days after the battle, struck with his stately appearance, or, perhaps, with some resemblance he bore to the late king, he asked him, "Sir, are you my father?" To which the admiral, bursting into tears, replied, "I am not your father, but I was your father's true servant."

† "Ye towers! within whose circuit dread,
A Douglas by his sovereign bled."

Lady of the Lake.

room and armoury. This building was erected by James VI., and was the scene of the baptism of his son Prince Henry. Underneath the exterior wall, on the west, a narrow road leads from the town, and descends the precipice behind the Castle. This is called Ballangeich, a Gaelic word signifying " windy pass," which is remarkable as having furnished the fictitious name adopted by James V. in the various disguises which he was in the habit of assuming, for the purpose of seeing that justice was regularly administered, and frequently also from the less justifiable motive of gallantry.* To the north of the Castle is a small

* The two excellent comic songs, entitled " The Gaberlunzie man," and " We'll gae nae mair a roving," are said to have been founded on the success of this monarch's amorous adventures, when travelling in the disguise of a beggar. The following anecdotes respecting this frolicsome prince, are given by Sir Walter Scott :—

" Another adventure, which had nearly cost James his life, is said to have taken place at the village of Cramond, near Edinburgh, where he had rendered his addresses acceptable to a pretty girl of the lower rank. Four or five persons, whether relations or lovers of his mistress is uncertain, beset the disguised monarch, as he returned from his rendezvous. Naturally gallant, and an admirable master of his weapon, the king took post on the high and narrow bridge over the Almond river, and defended himself bravely with his sword. A peasant, who was thrashing in a neighbouring barn, came out upon the noise, and whether moved by compassion or by natural gallantry, took the weaker side, and laid about with his flail so effectually, as to disperse the assailants, well threshed, even according to the letter. He then conducted the king into his barn, where his guest requested a bason and towel, to remove the stains of the broil. This being procured with difficulty, James employed himself in learning what was the summit of his deliverer's earthly wishes, and found that they were bounded by the desire of possessing, in property, the farm of Braehead, upon which he laboured as a bondsman. The lands chanced to belong to the Crown; and James directed him to come to the Palace of Holy-Rood, and inquire for the Guidman (*i. e.* farmer) of Ballangeich, a name by which he was known in his excursions, and which answered to *Il Bondocani* of Haroun Alraschid. He presented himself accordingly, and found with due astonishment that he had saved his monarch's life, and that he was to be gratified with a Crown-charter of the lands of Braehead, under the service of presenting an ewer, bason, and towel, for the king to wash his hands, when he shall happen to pass the Bridge of Cramond. In 1822, when George IV. came to Scotland, the descendant of this John Howison of Braehead, who still possesses the estate which was given to his ancestor, appeared at a solemn festival, and offered his Majesty water from a silver ewer."

Another of James's frolics is thus narrated by Mr. Campbell, from the Statistical Account. " Being once benighted when out a hunting, and separated from his attendants, he happened to enter a cottage in the midst of a moor, at the foot of the Ochil hills, near Alloa, where, unknown, he was kindly received. In order to regale their unexpected guest, the *gude-man* (*i. e.* landlord, farmer) desired the *gude-wife* to fetch the hen that roosted nearest the cock, which is

mount on which executions commonly took place.* On this eminence, and within sight of their Castle of Doune

always the plumpest, for the stranger's supper. The king, highly pleased with his night's lodging, and hospitable entertainment, told mine host, at parting, that he should be glad to return his civility, and requested that, the first time he came to Stirling, he would call at the castle, and enquire for the *gude-man of Ballangeich.* Donaldson, the landlord, did not fail to call on the *gude-man of Ballangeich,* when his astonishment, at finding that the king had been his guest, afforded no small amusement to the merry monarch and his courtiers; and, to carry on the pleasantry, he was thenceforth designated by James with the title of King of the Moors, which name and designation have descended from father to son ever since; and they have continued in possession of the identical spot, the property of Mr. Erskine of Mar, till very lately, when this gentleman, with reluctance, turned out the descendant and representative of the King of the Moors, on account of his Majesty's invincible indolence, and great dislike to reform or innovation of any kind, although, from the spirited example of his neighbour tenants on the same estate, he is convinced similar exertion would promote his advantage."

The following anecdote is extracted from the genealogical work of Buchanan of Auchmar, upon Scottish surnames:—

"This John Buchanan of Auchmar and Arnpryor was afterwards termed King of Kippen,† upon the following account:—King James V., a very sociable, debonair prince, residing at Stirling, in Buchanan of Arnpryor's time, carriers were very frequently passing along the common road, being near Arnpryor's house, with necessaries for the use of the king's family, and he having some extraordinary occasion, ordered one of these carriers to leave his load at his house and he would pay him for it; which the carrier refused to do, telling him he was the king's carrier, and his load was for his majesty's use. To which Arnpryor seemed to have small regard, compelling the carrier, in the end, to leave his load; telling him, if King James was king of Scotland, he was king of Kippen, so that it was reasonable he should share with his neighbour king in some of these loads so frequently carried that road. The carrier representing this usage, and telling the story as Arnpryor spoke it, to some of the king's servants, it came at length to his majesty's ears, who, shortly thereafter, with a few attendants, came to visit his neighbour king, who was, in the meantime, at dinner. King James having sent a servant to demand access, was denied the same by a tall fellow with a battle-axe, who stood porter at the gate, telling there could be no access till dinner was over. This answer not satisfying the king, he sent to demand access a second time; upon which he was desired by the porter to desist, otherwise he would find cause to repent his rudeness. His majesty finding this method would not do, desired the porter to tell his master that the good-man of Ballangeich desired to speak with the King of Kippen. The porter telling Arnpryor so much, he in all humble manner, came and received the king, and having entertained him with much sumptuousness and jollity, became so agreeable to King James, that he allowed him to take so much of any provision he found carrying that road as he had occasion for; and, seeing he made the first visit, desired Arnpryor in a few days to return him a second at Stirling, which he performed, and continued in very much favour with the king, always thereafter being termed King of Kippen while he lived."

* "Thou, O sad and fatal mound,
That oft has heard the death-axe sound.
Lady of the Lake.

† A small district of Perthshire.

and their extensive possessions, Murdoch Duke of Albany, Duncan Earl of Lennox, his father-in-law, and his two sons, Walter and Alexander Stuart, were beheaded in 1424. The execution of Walter Stuart is supposed, with great probability, to be the groundwork of the beautiful pathetic ballad of "Young Waters." This "heading-hill" now commonly bears the name of Hurley-Hacket, from its being the scene of an amusement practised by James V. when a boy, and his courtiers, which consisted in sliding in some sort of chair from top to bottom of the bank. On the south side of the Castle Hill is a small piece of ground called the Valley, with a rock on the south side denominated the Ladies' Rock. On this spot tournaments used to be held. The view from the Castle Hill is remarkably magnificent. To the north and east are the Ochil hills, and the windings of the Forth through the Carse of Stirling, with its fertile fields, luxuriant woods, and stately mansions. On the west lies the vale of Menteith, bounded by the Highland mountains. The Campsie hills close the horizon to the south. and in the foreground, on the east, are the town, the Abbey Craig, and the ruins of Cambuskenneth Abbey, and, in a clear day, the Castle of Edinburgh and Arthur's Seat are seen. Stirling Castle is one of the four fortresses of Scotland, which, by the articles of the Union, are always to be kept in repair. It is now used as a barrack. South-west of the Castle lies the King's Park, and to the east of it are the King's Gardens, which, though now unenclosed, and reduced to the condition of a marshy pasture, still retain the fantastic forms into which they had been thrown by the gardeners of ancient times.

The Greyfriars or Franciscan church of Stirling was erected in 1494 by James IV., and some additions were made to it by Cardinal Beaton. It is a handsome Gothic building, and, since the Reformation, has been divided into two places of worship, called the East and West Churches. In this church the Earl of Arran, Regent of the kingdom, abjured Romanism in 1543 ; it was also the scene of the coronation of James VI., on the 29th July 1597, when John Knox preached the coronation sermon. The celebrated

ST RLING CASTLE FROM THE LADY'S ROCK.

Ebenezer Erskine, founder of the Secession Church, was one of the ministers of the West Church.

To the north of the church stand the ruins of a haggard-looking building called Mar's Work. It was built by the Earl of Mar out of the ruins of Cambuskenneth Abbey. This conduct excited much popular dissatisfaction, in allusion to which the Earl caused several inscriptions, in the form of distiches, to be affixed to his house. Three of these inscriptions may still be decyphered and severally run thus :—

Speik forth and spair nocht ;
Consider weel, and cair nocht.

The moir I stand in oppin hitht,
My faultis more subject ar to sitht.

I pray all luikars on this luging,
With gentle e to gif their juging.

In the immediate neighbourhood of this building is a fine piece of architecture in the old Scottish style, called Argyle's Lodging, which was built by Sir William Alexander, the first Earl of Stirling, whose arms are elaborately sculptured above the door.* It afterwards passed into the hands of the Argyle family, and is now used as a military hospital.

Stirling has long been celebrated for its schools, and also for the number of its hospitals or residences for decayed persons. By an act of the Scottish Parliament in 1437, Stirling was appointed to be the place for keeping the Jug, or standard of dry measure, from which all others through-

* The Earl of Stirling was one of those men who, to literary habits, add a keen relish for the pursuits of active life. He was the originator of the project for the colonization of Nova Scotia, and had the entire management of the scheme. He was the author of several volumes of poetry, which at one time obtained considerable praise, Lithgow styling him "true castalian fire ;" Drayton, "my Alexander ;" and King James, "my philosophical poet." Indeed, so great a favourite was he with the pedantic monarch, whose learning, doubtless, was not seldom the theme of his skilful flattery, that he obtained large grants of land and lordships both in North America and Scotland, as well as the privilege of coining for the latter country a species of base copper money called *turners*. It is said that when he inscribed the motto, *Per mare et terras*, upon his house in Stirling, his countrymen punningly read it, *Per metre et turners*, in allusion to his double capacity as maker of verses and coin.

out the country were appointed to be taken, while the Firlot was given to Linlithgow, the Ell to Edinburgh, the Reel to Perth, and the Pound to Lanark. The Stirling Jug is still preserved with great care. In 1841, the population of the town was 8029. Stirling Bridge was long a structure of great importance, having been, till lately, almost the only access into the northern part of Scotland for wheeled carriages. The old bridge is still standing, and viewed from the new bridge, by which it has been superseded, it forms a picturesque and interesting object. The erection of the new structure cost £17,000. The outside facing is of greenstone from the neighbouring cliff of Abbey Craig. At a very early period there was a wooden bridge over the Forth, about half a mile above the present structure, which was the scene of one of the most gallant achievements of Sir William Wallace, on the 13th of September 1297. An English army of 50,000 foot and 1000 horse, commanded by Cressingham, advanced towards Stirling in quest of Wallace, who, on his part, having collected an army of 40,000 men, marched southward to dispute the passage of the Forth. He posted his army near Cambuskenneth, allowing only a part of them to be seen. The English hurried across the river, to attack the Scots. After a considerable number of them had thus passed over, and the bridge was crowded with those who were following, Wallace charged those who had crossed with his whole strength, slew a very great number, and drove the rest into the river Forth, where the greater part were drowned. The remainder of the English army, who were left on the southern bank of the river, fled in great confusion, having first set fire to the wooden bridge, that the Scots might not pursue them. Cressingham himself was among the slain, and his rapine and oppression had rendered him so detestable to the Scots, that they are said to have flayed off his skin and cut it in pieces to make girths for their horses.

The Agricultural Museum of the Messrs. Drummond is well worthy of a visit. The extent of the collection would do credit to a town ten times the size of Stirling, and the liberality with which it is exhibited is most creditable to the proprietors.

The steel engraving of Stirling Castle, with which our text is illustrated, represents the scene in Waverley, where the party of Balmawhapple, upon passing the fortress, are saluted by a bullet from its walls. The artist has selected the moment when the valorous laird returns the compliment by discharging his pistol at the inhospitable rock.

From Stirling, the Scottish Central Railway proceeds by the Bridge of Allan, Dunblane, Greenloaning, and Auchterarder, to Perth, where it joins the Scottish Midland to Forfar and Arbroath.

FIFTH TOUR.

*** The Map of the Royal Progress facing page 159, illustrates this Tour.

FROM EDINBURGH TO STIRLING BY STEAMBOAT.*

LOOKING straight across the Firth, leaving Granton Pier, the burgh of Burntisland may be observed directly opposite. Shortly after leaving Granton, may be seen Lauriston Castle, formerly the property of John Law, the projector of the Mississippi scheme, and sold by his descendant Marshal Lauriston about 30 years ago. On the north shore is the village of Aberdour, and near it the seat of the Earl of Morton, who is known here by the title of "the Gudeman of Aberdour." North of the Castle is the mansion-house of Hillside. A little farther on is the island of Inch Colm, with the remains of a monastery, founded, in 1123, by Alexander I. To the north of this is Dalgetty Church,

* Steamboats sail for Alloa and Stirling every day from Granton Pier. Coaches to the boat run from No. 10, Princes Street, where correct information as to the hours of sailing may be obtained.

near which is Otterstoun Loch, with the mansion-houses of Otterstoun and Cockairney, the property of Sir Robert Moubray, on its sweetly-wooded banks. On the south shore, at the mouth of the river Almond, stand the village of Cramond, and Cramond House, (Lady Torphichen,) and a little farther west is Dalmeny Park, the seat of the Earl of Rosebery. Near it are the ruins of Barnbougle Castle, an ancient seat of the family of the Moubrays. Directly opposite is Donibristle, a seat of the Earl of Moray, the scene of the atrocious murder, by the Earl of Huntly, of the youthful Earl of Moray, son-in-law of the celebrated Regent Murray.* A short way to the westward lies the

* The Earl of Huntly, head of the powerful family of Gordon, had chanced to have some feudal differences with the Earl of Murray, in the course of which John Gordon, a brother of Gordon of Cluny, was killed by a shot from Murray's castle of Darnaway. This was enough to make the two families irreconcilable enemies, even if they had been otherwise on friendly terms. About 1591-2, an accusation was brought against Murray, for having given some countenance or assistance to Stewart, Earl of Bothwell, in a recent treasonable exploit. King James, without recollecting, perhaps, the hostility between the two Earls, sent Huntly with a commission to bring the Earl of Murray to his presence. Huntly probably rejoiced in the errand, as giving him an opportunity of revenging himself on his feudal enemy. He beset the house of Donibristle, on the northern shore of the Forth, and summoned Murray to surrender. In reply, a gun was fired, which mortally wounded one of the Gordons. The assailants proceeded to set fire to the house; when Dunbar, sheriff of the county of Moray, said to the Earl, 'Let us not stay to be burnt in the flaming house: I will go out foremost, and the Gordons, taking me for your Lordship, will kill me, while you escape in the confusion.' They rushed out among their enemies accordingly, and Dunbar was slain. But his death did not save his friend, as he had generously intended. Murray, indeed, escaped for the moment, but as he fled towards the rocks of the sea-shore, he was traced by the silken tassels attached to his head-piece, which had taken fire as he broke out among the flames. By this means, his pursuers followed him down amongst the cliffs, near the sea; and Gordon of Buckie, who is said to have been the first that overtook him, wounded him mortally. As Murray was gasping in the last agony, Huntly came up; and it is alleged, by tradition, that Gordon pointed his dirk against the person of his chief, saying, 'By heaven! my Lord, you shall be as deep in as I;' and so he compelled him to wound Murray whilst he was dying. Huntly, with a wavering hand, struck the expiring Earl on the face. Thinking of his superior beauty, even in that moment of parting life, Murray stammered out the dying words, 'You have spoiled a better face than your own.'

"After this deed of violence, Huntly did not choose to return to Edinburgh, but departed for the north. He took refuge, for the moment, in the castle of Ravenscraig, belonging to the Lord Sinclair, who told him, with a mixture of

ancient burgh of Inverkeithing. On the two coasts are the towns of North and South Queensferry; and, in the strait between them, is the fortified islet of Inchgarvie. On a rocky promontory, on the north shore, are the ruins of Rosyth Castle, once the seat of the Stuarts of Rosyth, a branch of the Royal House of Scotland, from whom it is said the mother of Oliver Cromwell was descended. Half a mile beyond Inchgarvie is Port Edgar, where George IV. embarked, after a visit to the Earl of Hopetoun, 29th August 1822. On an eminence, beyond South Queensferry, is Dundas Castle, the original seat of the Dundas family before the eleventh century, and still the residence of their lineal descendant, Dundas of that Ilk. Farther on, upon the same side, and about a mile from the shore, is Hopetoun House, the splendid mansion of the Earl of Hopetoun; and on a peninsula to the westward, stands Blackness Castle, one of the four fortresses which, by the Articles of the Union, are to be kept constantly garrisoned. Close by the village of Charleston, on the north side of the Forth, stands Broomhall, the seat of the Earl of Elgin. Farther on is Crombie Point and Crombie House, then the village of Torryburn, next Torry House (Captain Erskine Wemyss of Wemyss Castle) and Newmills village. Returning to the south coast, and proceeding westward, may be seen in succession Carriden

Scottish caution and hospitality, that he was welcome to come in, but would have been twice as welcome to have passed by. Gordon, when a long period had passed by, avowed his contrition for the guilt he had incurred."—*Tales of a Grandfather*, vol. ii., p. 191.

Upon this tragical circumstance, the following beautiful ballad is founded:—

"Ye Highlands and ye Lawlands,
Oh, where have ye been?
They hae slain the Earl o' Murray,
And lain him on the green.

Now, wae be to you, Huntly!
And wherefore did ye sae?
I bade you bring him wi' you,
But forbade you him to slae."

He was a braw gallant,
And he rade at the ring;
And the bonnie Earl o' Murray,
Oh! he micht ha' been a king.

He was a braw gallant,
And he rade at the glave;
And the bonnie Earl o' Murray,
Oh! he was the Queen's luve!

Oh! lang will his lady
Look ower the Castle Doune,
Ere she see the Earl o' Murray
Come sounding through the toun."

House,* (James Hope, Esq.,) Kirkgrange Salt Pans, Borrowstounness, Kinneil House, the property of the Duke of Hamilton, for some time the residence of the late Professor Dugald Stewart; and Grangemouth, situated at the mouth of Carron Water. On the north side is Valleyfield, (Lady Baird Preston,) and near it the ancient and decayed burgh of Culross, (pronounced *Cooris.*)† The inhabitants are a remarkably primitive set of people. Immediately behind it are the ruins of a Cistertian abbey, founded in 1217 by Malcolm Earl of Fife. At the Reformation, its possessions were conferred upon Sir James Colville, who was created Lord Colville of Culross. From the family of Colville it passed to the Earls of Dundonald, who sold it to the late Sir Robert Preston, Bart. A little farther on is Blair Castle, (Alison, Esq.,) and about a mile beyond this is Sands House, (Johnstone, Esq.,) after which the tourist reaches the town and shipping port of Kincardine. Near it stand the ruins of the ancient castle of Tulliallan, formerly the property of the knights of Blackadder, and Tulliallan Castle, the residence of Baroness Keith and Count Flahault, built by the late Admiral Lord Keith, the father of the present proprietrix, who is also the lineal representative of one of the most ancient families in Scotland—the Mercers of Aldie. On the opposite side is Higgin's Nook, (J. Burn Murdoch, Esq.,) and beyond it, upon a height, Airth Castle, (Graham, Esq.,) near which there is a square tower, built in 1298, previous to the battle

* In a house, close upon the shore, which now serves as a sort of lodge to this property, the famous Colonel Gardiner, who fell at the battle of Prestonpans, was born.

† Culross was famous for the manufacture of *girdles*, the round iron plates on which the people of Scotland bake their barley and oaten bread. "The hammermen of Edinburgh are no' that bad at girdles for carcakes, neither, though the Cu'ross hammermen have the gree for that."—*Heart of Mid-Lothian*, vol. ii., p. 254.

Culross was also celebrated for its salt-pans and coal mines. In the reign of James VI. the coal-mines were worked a great way under the bed of the Forth, and the coals were shipped at a mound which defended from the water the mouth of a subterraneous communication with the coal-pit. James VI., when on a visit to the proprietor, Sir George Bruce, being conducted, by his own desire, into the coal-pit, was led to ascend from it by the mound, when it was high tide. Seeing himself surrounded, on all sides, by water, he apprehended a plot, and bawled out "Treason," but Sir George soon dispelled his Majesty's fears, by handing him into an elegant pinnace that was lying alongside.

of Falkirk. The castle contains original portraits of the celebrated Graham of Claverhouse, Viscount Dundee; and of the admirable Crichton. About a mile to the west is Dunmore House, a castellated structure, the residence of the Earl of Dunmore. Nearly opposite, upon the right, is Kennet House, the seat of Robert Bruce, Esq. of Kennet. Farther on, upon the same side, is Clackmannan, the capital of the small county of that name; and to the west of the town, delightfully situated on an eminence, is Clackmannan Tower, said to have been built by Robert Bruce. It is now the property of the Earl of Zetland. Close beside the tower once stood the palace of Robert Bruce, and family house of Bruce of Clackmannan, now demolished. This was the residence of the old Jacobite lady, Mrs. Bruce of Clackmannan, who is mentioned in Currie's Life of Burns as having knighted that poet with a sword which belonged to Bruce. The sword and a helmet which had also belonged to the hero are now in the possession of Lord Elgin, who represents the family of Bruce, and are to be seen at Broomhall, near Dunfermline. About a mile beyond Clackmannan, and in the neighbourhood of extensive collieries and distilleries, is the town of ALLOA.—[*Inns:*—Royal Oak Hotel; Crown Inn; Ship Inn.]—Near the town, and in the midst of a fine park, stands Alloa House, the ancient seat of the family of Erskine, Earls of Mar, and the subject of a fine Scottish air. The principal part of the building was destroyed by fire about twenty years ago, but there is still standing the original tower, an erection of the thirteenth century. It is ninety feet high, and the walls are eleven feet thick. At Alloa commence those remarkable windings called the "Links of Forth." These windings of the river form a great number of beautiful peninsulas, which, being of a very luxuriant and fertile soil, gave rise to the old rhyme,—

> "The lairdship o' the bonnie Links o' Forth
> Is better than an earldom o' the North."

The distance by land from Alloa to Stirling Bridge is only six miles, while by water it is twelve. On the same

hills, from their proximity, now assume an air of imposing grandeur, and Stirling Castle forms a magnificent feature in the landscape. Beyond Tullibody, on the same side, is Cambus village, at the mouth of the Devon. The vale of the Devon is famed for its romantic beauty, and for the striking cascades formed by the river. Nearly opposite Cambus is Polmaise, (Murray, Esq.) Farther on, upon the right, are the ruins of Cambuskenneth Abbey, situated on one of the peninsular plains formed by the windings of the river. It was founded by David I., in 1147, for canons regular of the order of St. Augustine, and was one of the richest and most extensive abbeys in Scotland. At the Reformation, its possessions were bestowed by James VI. on the Earl of Mar; but about the year 1737 it was purchased by the Town Council of Stirling, for the benefit of Cowan's Hospital. Of the once extensive fabric of the Abbey, nothing now exists except a few broken walls and a tower, which was the belfry. On the right is seen the Abbey Craig, and soon after the tourist reaches Stirling.

From Stirling a pleasant episodical tour may be made to Castle Campbell, the Rumbling Brig, and the Devil's Caldron.

Leaving Stirling, the tourist has on his left the soft green pastoral yet lofty hills of the Ochil range, with their magnificent wooded glades and warm sunward slopes, consisting of intermingling copse, cornfields, and meadows, while on the right is a rich and level country, bounded by the Forth, now entwining its silver links and spreading into a noble estuary. The most southerly of the Ochil hills is Damyat, famous for the extensive and splendid view obtained from its summit. In its neighbourhood is Bencleuch, which shoots up into a tall rocky point, called Craigleith, remarkable in ancient times for the production of falcons. In a hollow near this, the snow often lies far into the summer. The people give it the picturesque name of Lady Alva's Web. Three miles from Stirling the tourist reaches the beautiful village of Blairlogie, and four miles beyond it the village of Alva, which was formerly remarkable for its silver mines. Alva House, the residence of Johnstone of Alva, stands on an eminence projecting from the base of the Woodhill.* Three miles from Alva is Tilli-

* "Oh, Alva woods are bonnie,
Tillicoultry hills are fair,
But when I think o' the bonnie braes o' Menstrie,
It mak's my heart aye sair."—*Fairy Rhyme.*

The village of Menstrie lies two miles west of Alva. Menstrie House was the seat of the Earl of Stirling.

coultry, and at the distance of other 3 miles (being in all 13 miles from Stirling) is the village of Dollar.—[*Inns:*—Castle Campbell Inn.]—At Dollar there is an extensive academy, founded by a person of the name of Macnab, a native of the parish, who had realized a large fortune in London. It is a handsome Grecian building, and is furnished with good masters for the various branches of education. In the neighbourhood is the remarkable ruin of Castle Campbell, occupying a wild and romantic situation on the top of a high and almost insulated rock. The only access to the castle is by an isthmus connecting the mount with the hill behind. The mount on which it is situated is nearly encompassed on all sides by thick bosky woods, and mountain rivulets descending on either side, unite at the base. Immediately behind rises a vast amphitheatre of wooded hills. Castle Campbell is a place of great antiquity. The precise period at which it came into the possession of the Argyle family is not certainly known. In 1493, an act of Parliament was passed for changing the name of "the castle called the Gloume,"* to Castle Campbell, and it continued to be a possession of the great clan family of Argyle, till about thirty years ago, upon the death of the late Duke, it was sold to the late Mr. Tait of Harvieston. It is said that John Knox resided in Castle Campbell, under the protection of Archibald, the fourth Earl, who was the first of the Scottish nobility that publicly embraced the Protestant religion. Castle Campbell was destroyed in 1645. "The feudal hatred of Montrose, and of the clans composing the strength of his army, the vindictive resentment also of the Ogilvies for the destruction of "the bonnie House of Airlie," and that of the Stirlingshire cavaliers for that of Menstrie, doomed this magnificent pile to flames and ruin. The destruction of many a meaner habitation by the same unscrupulous and unsparing spirit of vengeance has been long forgotten, but the majestic remains of Castle Campbell still excite a sigh in those that view them, over the miseries of civil war."† About two miles above Dollar is an interesting spot where the Devon forms a series of cascades, one of which is called the Caldron Linn.‡ The river here suddenly enters

* The ancient name of the castle, it is often said, was the Castle of Gloom. The mountain streams that flow on the different sides are still called, the one the Water of Care, the other the Burn of Sorrow; and, after the junction in front of the castle, they traverse the valley of Dollar, or Dolour. The proper etymologists, however, tell a different tale. The old Gaelic name of the stronghold was *Cock Leum*, or Mad Leap. The glen of Care, was the glen of *Caer* or castle, a British word; and Dollar is simply *Dalor*, the high field.—CHAMBERS' *Gazetteer*, vol i., 191.

† *Tales of a Grandfather*, vol. iii., p. 12.

‡ Instead of the usual route, pedestrians, in coming from Dollar, should strike off the high road soon after they get above *Vicar's Bridge*, and take along a path to the right, leading to *Cowden* and *Muckart Mill*, and from thence by

a deep gulf, where, finding itself confined, it has, by continual efforts against the sides, worked out a cavity resembling a large caldron. From this gulf the water works its way through an aperture beneath the surface into a lower cavity, where it is covered with a constant foam. The water then works its way into a third caldron, out of which it is precipitated by a sheer fall of forty-four feet. The best view of this magnificent scene is from the bottom of the fall. About a mile farther up the vale, the rocks on each side rise to the height of eighty-six feet, and the banks of the stream are contracted in such a manner, that a bridge of twenty-five feet span connects them. A handsome new bridge has lately been erected above the old one, from the bed of the stream a hundred and twenty feet. On account of the rocky nature of the channel, the river here makes a violent noise, hence the name of the Rumbling Bridge.* A few hundred yards farther up, there is another cascade, called the Devil's Mill, where the water vibrating from one side to another of the pool, and constantly beating against the sides of the rock, produces an intermittent noise like that of a mill in motion. The whole of the scenes around these remarkable cascades are of the most romantic kind, and strikingly different from all other Scottish scenery. "The clear winding Devon," as almost every reader will recollect, has been celebrated by Burns in his beautiful lyric, "The Banks of the Devon." Miss Charlotte Hamilton, (afterwards Mrs. Adair,) the lady on whom this song was composed, was at that time residing at Harvieston, near Dollar.

The tourist may, if he choose, proceed by the Crook of Devon to Kinross, and thence to Edinburgh,—a route of which he will find the principal part described in the tour from Edinburgh to Perth; or he may proceed to Dunfermline, and thence to North Queensferry, by a route much more agreeable, and only two miles longer.

A short but pleasant excursion may also be made from Stirling to Dunblane, distant six miles, and to the Roman Camp at Ardoch, twelve miles distant.

the *Blair Hill*, to the Caldron Linn. This is a short *cut*, which keeps near the river by a far more romantic line than the turnpike road.

* A short distance from the Rumbling Bridge is Aldie Castle, the ancient seat of the Mercers of Aldie, now represented by Baroness Keith. At Aldie, a man on being hanged for the slight offence of stealing a *caup fu' o' corn*, is said to have uttered a malediction upon the family, to the effect that the estate of Aldie should never be inherited by a male heir for nineteen generations. It is a somewhat singular coincidence, that this has already so far taken effect,—Lady Keith being the daughter of an heiress, who was the grand-daughter and successor to another heiress, and being herself the mother of several daughters but of no male child. The slogan or war cry of the Mercers of Aldie, was "The grit pule."

Leaving Stirling, the tourist crosses the Forth by the new Railway Bridge. A short way farther up the river is the Old Bridge, a very antique structure. General Blakeney, the governor of the Castle, in 1745, caused the south arch to be destroyed, to interrupt the march of the Highlanders. On this bridge Archbishop Hamilton of St. Andrews, the last Roman Catholic Archbishop of Scotland, was hanged in 1571, in full pontificals, for his alleged accession to the assassination of Regent Murray. The tourist now passes, on the right, the village of Causewayhead, backed by the Abbey Crag. In the vicinity is Airthrey Castle, (Lord Abercromby). Three miles from Stirling is the pretty little village of the BRIDGE OF ALLAN, (*Inns:* Philp's Hotel; Barr's Hotel), much resorted to in summer on account of a mineral well in the neighbourhood. In the vicinity is Keir, (W. Stirling, Esq.,) and a mile and a half beyond it, the road passes Kippenross, the seat of Stirling of Kippendavie. In the lawn is a plane-tree, supposed to be the largest in the kingdom. It is 42 feet in circumference at the ground, 100 feet high, and 467 years old. A little beyond Kippenross, on the banks of the beautiful little river Allan, is the ancient cathedral city of

DUNBLANE.

[*Inns:* —Kinross'.]

The cathedral, which was founded in 1142, and richly endowed by David I., is still tolerably entire. The east end is fitted up, in an elegant style, as a parish church. The prebendal stalls of richly carved dark oak, have fortunately been preserved. Several of the Bishops of Dunblane were distinguished persons, but the most celebrated of them was the good Bishop Leighton, afterwards Archbishop of Glasgow, who founded a library here, which has been greatly increased by subsequent literary donations. The mineral spring at Cromlix, in the vicinity of Dunblane, is frequented by many.

About two miles east by north of Dunblane is Sheriffmuir, the scene of the battle which was fought in 1715 between the Earl of Mar, and the royal forces under the Duke of Argyle. In this engagement the left wing of each army was defeated, and the right of each was victorious; but the fruits of the victory remained with the Duke of Argyle.† Near the western extremity of the muir is

* Popularly characterized as "drucken Dumblane."

† A number of noblemen and gentlemen, on both sides, were slain in this engagement; among others, the Earls of Forfar and Strathmore, the chieftain of Clanronald, &c. The body of the gallant young Earl of Strathmore was found on the field, watched by a faithful old domestic, who, being asked the name of the person whose body he waited upon with so much care, made this striking reply, "He was a man yesterday." "There was mair *tint* (lost) at Sheriffmuir," is a common proverb in Scotland. It is told, that a Highlander lamented that, at the battle of Sheriffmuir, he had "lost his father and his mother, and a gude buff belt, weal worth them baith." Burns has made this battle the subject of a song replete with humour.

Kippendavie, (—Stirling, Esq.,) and four miles beyond is Greenloaning. A mile and a half farther on, the tourist reaches Ardoch House, the seat of Major William Moray Stirling. Within his parks is the celebrated Roman Camp of Ardoch, esteemed the most entire in the kingdom. General Wade's military road passes over one of its sides. The measure of the whole area is 1060 feet by 900, and it is calculated to have contained no fewer than 20,000 men. There appear to have been three or four ditches, and as many rampart walls surrounding the camp. The prætorium, which rises above the level of the camp, but is not precisely in the centre, forms a regular square, each side being exactly twenty yards. The camp is defended on the south-east side by a deep morass, and on the west side by the banks of the water of Knaick, which rises perpendicularly to the height of about fifty feet. In the immediate vicinity there are two other encampments more slightly fortified.

The Tourist may proceed from Greenloaning Station to Perth or Stirling by Scottish Central Railway, or from the same station, by coach to Crieff.

Proceeding towards Perth, the scenery expands, and the country becomes highly cultivated. On the left, at a short distance, on the brow of a low hill, is the straggling village of Auchterarder, celebrated as the place where the events occurred which ended in the disruption of the Scotch Church, and produced the Free Church of Scotland. The next station is Dunning, between which and the village of the same name, is Duncrub, the seat of Lord Rollo.

At Forteviot there are some interesting Pictish remains. The palace with which they are said to have been connected has been long since washed away by the May Water, which here forms a junction with the River Earn. Half way between this and Forgandenny Station, there is a good view of Dupplin Castle, the seat of the Earl of Kinnoul. Passing Forgandenny Station, and the village of the same name on the right, we cross the Earn, and enter Moncrieff tunnel, 1¼ mile in length, blasted at an expense of 250,000 lbs. of gunpowder. On emerging from this, in the course of a few minutes, we see stretched before us, with panoramic effect, the beautiful city of Perth.

SIXTH TOUR.

STIRLING—DOUNE—CALLANDER—THE TROSACHS—LOCH KATRINE—LOCH LOMOND.

THERE are two roads which lead from Stirling to Doune, the first stage on the way to Loch Katrine—one crosses the Forth by Stirling Bridge, and proceeds along the east bank of the Teith, passing, in succession, the beautiful village of Bridge of Allan, and the neat parish church of Lecropt, built in the Gothic style; the other, proceeding up the valley of the Forth, passes the house of Craigforth, (Hon. C. F. Stuart,) and, two miles from Stirling, crosses the river at the bridge of Drip. At the distance of about four miles from Stirling, the road passes Ochtertyre, (Dundas, Esq.,) once the residence of Mr. J. Ramsay, the friend of Blacklock, of Burns, and of Scott; a mile and a half farther on, the road passes the mansion of Blair-Drummond, (Home Drummond, Esq.,) embosomed in fine woods and plantations. About sixty or seventy years ago, the celebrated Lord Kames became proprietor of this estate, and commenced that series of operations, by which what was once a bleak and marshy moor has been turned into rich corn-fields.* The road now crosses the Teith, by a fine old bridge built by Robert Spittal, tailor to Queen Margaret, widow of James IV., whence a fine view of Doune Castle is obtained; and, about nine miles from Stirling, enters the village of

DOUNE.

[*Inns*:—M'Intyre's.]

Just before crossing the bridge, and on the left hand, are Deanston Works, one of the most extensive cotton factories in Scotland. They are driven by the Water of the Teith, which is led for upwards of a mile in a capacious mill-lead, and propels four stupendous overshot wheels, 36 feet in diameter and II in breadth, which perform their stately revolutions under one spacious roof. The works are under

* The removal of Blair-Drummond Moss is probably the most extensive agricultural enterprise ever undertaken in this country. Underneath the moss, at a depth varying from six to sixteen feet, lay a stratum of fine clay of a most productive quality, if a plan could be devised for relieving it from the superincumbent turf. This was accomplished by obtaining a command of water sufficient to wash the whole away into the river Forth. A wheel, twenty-eight feet in diameter and eight feet wide, propelled by a running stream, was employed to raise part of the water, by which it was driven to the level of the moss. This was accomplished by means of a simple mechanical arrangement, the water by driving the wheel being actually employed in raising itself, a duty which it performed at the rate of six and a half tons per minute. The water thus lifted was directed into channels cut in the moss, along the sides of which men were stationed, cutting the moss into pieces and tumbling it into the current of water, by which it was floated into the river. Fifteen hundred acres of fine land have thus been added to the estate of the present proprietor.

admirable regulation, and a visit to the clean village of Deanston, which is in their immediate neighbourhood, and inhabited entirely by the work people, may interest some tourists. These noble works owe their well merited celebrity to their late manager, Mr. James Smith. The village of Doune was, in former times, celebrated for the manufacture of Highland pistols. The ruins of Doune Castle, a massive and extensive fortress, supposed to have been built about the fourteenth century, are situated on the point of a steep and narrow green bank, washed on one side by the Teith, and on the other by the Ardoch. It was anciently the seat of the Earls of Monteith; but, about the beginning of the fifteenth century, it was forfeited to the Crown, and became the favourite residence of the two successive Dukes of Albany, who governed Scotland during the captivity of James I.; Queen Margaret, and the unfortunate Queen Mary, are also said frequently to have resided in this fortress. It was held for Prince Charles during the rebellion of 1745, and here he disposed his prisoners taken at Falkirk, and, among the rest, the author of the tragedy of Douglas.* Doune Castle has long been the

* "This noble ruin," says Sir Walter Scott, "holds a commanding station on the banks of the river Teith, and has been one of the largest castles in Scotland. Murdoch, Duke of Albany, the founder of this stately pile, was beheaded on the Castlehill of Stirling, from which he might see the towers of Doune, the monument of his fallen greatness. In 1745-6, a garrison, on the part of the Chevalier, was put into the castle, then less ruinous than at present. It was commanded by Mr. Stewart of Balloch, as governor for Prince Charles; who was a man of property, near Callander. This castle became, at that time, the actual scene of a romantic escape made by John Home, the author of Douglas, and by some other prisoners, who, having been taken at the battle of Falkirk, were confined there by the insurgents. The poet, who had, in his own mind, a large stock of that romantic and enthusiastic spirit of adventure which he has described as animating the youthful hero of his drama, devised and undertook the perilous enterprise of escaping from his prison. He inspired his companions with his sentiments, and when every attempt at open force was deemed hopeless, they resolved to twist their bed-clothes into ropes, and thus to descend. Four persons, with Home himself, reached the ground in safety. But the rope broke with the fifth, who was a tall, lusty man. The sixth was Thomas Barrow, a brave young Englishman, a particular friend of Home's. Determined to take the risk, even in such unfavourable circumstances, Barrow committed himself to the broken rope, slid down on it as far as it could assist him, and then let himself drop. His friends beneath succeeded in breaking his fall. Nevertheless he dislocated his ankle, and had several of his ribs broken. His com-

property of the Earls of Moray, who derive it from their second title of Lord Doune. About a mile to the north-

panions, however, were able to bear him off in safety. The Highlanders next morning sought for their prisoners with great activity. An old gentleman told the author he remembered seeing the commander Stewart,

'Bloody with spurring, fiery red with haste,'

riding furiously through the country in quest of the fugitives."—*Note, Waverley.*

west, the Earl of Moray has a mansion named Doune Lodge, formerly designated Cambus-Wallace, when it was the property of the Edmonstones. At the distance of three miles westward from Doune, on the opposite side of the river, is Lanrick Castle, (Jardine, Esq.,) formerly the seat of Sir Evan Murray M'Gregor, chieftain of Clan-Gregor, and three miles farther on is Cambusmore, (A. Buchanan, Esq.,) where Sir Walter Scott, in his juvenile days, spent some months, for several summers.* Sixteen miles from Stirling, at the foot of the chain of mountains which forms the Highland boundary, is the village of

CALLANDER.

[*Inns*:—M'Gregor's; The Eagle; Campbell's.]

From Callander there are coaches to the Trosachs and to Stirling. Although not within the boundary of the Highlands, "yet, from having been so long in the near neighbourhood, it has caught much of the very best part of the Highland character. Few hills out of the Highlands, (if these, indeed, be out of it,) exhibit bolder bosoms of wooded crag

* He has given a striking sketch of the most interesting objects on his route, in his description of Fitzjames's ride, after the combat with Roderick Dhu :—

They dashed that rapid torrent through,
And up Carhonie's hill they flew;
Still at the gallop prick'd the knight,
His merry-men follow'd as they might.
Along thy banks, swift Teith! they ride,
And in the race they mock thy tide;
Torry and Lendrick now are past,
And Deanstoun lies behind them cast;
They rise, the banner'd towers of Doune,
They sink in distant woodland soon;
Blair-Drummond sees the hoofs strike fire,
They sweep like breeze through Ochertyre;
They mark just glance and disappear
The lofty brow of ancient Keir;
They bathe their coursers' sweltering sides,
Dark Forth! amid thy sluggish tides,
And on the opposing shore take ground,
With splash, with scramble, and with bound.
Right-hand they leave thy cliffs, Craig-Forth!
And soon the bulwark of the North,
Grey Stirling, with her towers and town,
Upon their fleet career look'd down."

Lady of the Lake, c. v., st. 18.

and pastoral enclosure, than those which overhang the village, securing it from the blasts of the east and the north,

and receding in grand perspective far back in the sky."* To the westward two little rivers, issuing respectively from Loch Lubnaig and Loch Venachar, unite and form the Teith. At the east end of the village there is a neat villa, the property of Lady Willoughby D'Eresby. The Falls of Bracklinn, a mile and half to the north-east of the village, form one of the most attractive objects in this vicinity. They consist in a series of short falls, shelving rapids, and dark linns, formed by the Keltie Burn. Above a chasm where the brook precipitates itself from a height of at least

* CHRISTOPHER NORTH, in *Blackwood's Magazine*. Vol. xx., p. 402.

fifty feet, there is thrown a rustic foot-bridge, of about three feet in breadth, which is scarcely to be crossed by a stranger without awe and apprehension. The magnificent mountain Benledi, 3000 feet in height, which closes the prospect towards the west, forms the most striking feature of the scenery in this neighbourhood.*

There are two roads which lead from Callander to the Trosachs—the north and south roads; of these, the former is the more picturesque. Passing the valley of Bochastle, the house of Leny, (Hamilton, Esq.), and the rapids of Carchonzie, the tourist reaches "Coilantogle Ford," about

* At Callander, a road much frequented by tourists, leads, in a northerly direction, to Lochearn-Head, (fourteen miles,) by the Pass of Leny, Loch Lubnaig, and Balquidder. At the distance of two miles from Callander, the river Leny forms several fine cascades which will well repay the tourist for the trouble of alighting from his vehicle and climbing the low wall on the road-side. The scenery of the Pass is very rich and beautiful. It is thus described in the opening scene of the Legend of Montrose:—"Their course had been, for some time, along the banks of a lake, whose deep waters reflected the crimson beams of the western sun. The broken path, which they pursued with some difficulty, was, in some places, shaded by ancient birches and oak-trees, and, in others, overhung by fragments of huge rock. Elsewhere, the hill, which formed the northern side of this beautiful sheet of water, arose in steep, but less precipitous acclivity, and was arrayed in heath of the darkest purple." The scenery in this district has been celebrated by the same illustrious pen, in the Lady of the Lake. It was up the Pass of Leny that the cross of fire was carried by young Angus of Duncraggan.

"Benledi saw the Cross of Fire;
It glanced like lightning up Strath-Ire;
O'er hill and dale the summons flew,
Nor rest, nor pause young Angus knew;
The tear that gathered in his eye
He left the mountain breeze to dry;
Until, where Teith's young waters roll,
Betwixt him and a wooded knoll,
That graced the sable strath with green,
The chapel of St. Bride was seen."

Here the cross is delivered to Norman of Armandave, who starts off with it along the shores of Loch Lubnaig, and away toward the distant district of Balquidder. The chapel of St. Bride stood on a small romantic knoll, between the opening of the Pass of Leny and Loch Lubnaig, and Strath-Ire is situated at the south end, and along the eastern side of Loch Lubnaig; Armandave is on the west side of the loch. By the side of Lubnaig is Ardhullary, a house built for a Highland retreat, by Bruce the Abyssinian traveller, in which it is said he wrote the account of his travels. In the churchyard of Balquidder Rob Roy was interred, beneath a stone, marked only with a fir-tree crossed by a sword, supporting a crown. "The braes of Balquither" have been celebrated in song.

two and a half miles from Callander. This is the scene of the combat between Fitzjames and Roderick Dhu. Loch Venachar is four miles long, Loch Achray a mile and a half, the space between the lochs about half a mile, and from the western extremity of the latter to Loch Katrine, one mile, making the whole distance between Callander and Loch Katrine from nine to ten miles. Lanrick Mead, the mustering-place of Clan Alpin, lies on the north side of Loch Venachar. Soon after, the tourist passes, a little to the left, the hamlet of Duncraggan, the huts of which

> "Peep like moss-grown rocks half seen,
> Half hidden in the copse so green."

In one of these a double bedded-room is fitted up for the reception of tourists, and, if a humble scale of accommodation will satisfy thē wayfarer, it may be prudent that he should avail himself of its shelter, lest he should find the inn full.

The Bridge of Turk* crosses the water, which, descending from Glenfinlas, joins the Teith between Lochs Venachar and Achray; and a mile and a half further on, is the inn of Ardcheanochrochan, (M'Gregor's) beautifully situate on the side of Loch Achray.† The tourist is now in the Trosachs (*Troschen*, bristled territory,) the road which

* Here a path strikes off, on the right, to Glenfinlas, once a royal hunting forest; it is now the property of the Earl of Moray, and is inhabited by a primitive race of farmers, all Stewarts. In times of yore, it was chiefly inhabited by the Macgregors. Glenfinlas is the scene of Sir Walter Scott's ballad entitled, "Glenfinlas; or, Lord Ronald's Coronach."

† The crowds of tourists visiting the Trosachs, during the summer months, make it a matter of great uncertainty whether accommodation can be obtained at the inn. The usual effects of monopoly will also be experienced, and the civilities are nicely proportioned to the means the tourist is supposed to possess for compensating them. The boats upon Loch Katrine belong to the inn, and after paying the regular fare, (2s. 6d.) the boatmen proceed to extort gratuities from the passengers, which they state (with what truth we know not) to be the only remuneration they receive for their services. The charge of these Highland gillies, for conveying luggage from the inn to the loch, is also most extravagant. The distance is about a mile, and three shillings have been occasionally extorted for carrying a small parcel this trifling distance. These practices, it must be admitted are calculated, in a high degree, to uphold the ancient reputation of Loch Katrine, or, with more correctness of etymology, Loch Kateran, which being interpreted, signifieth *The Loch of the Robbers.*

"High on the south, huge Benvenue
Down on the lake in masses threw
Crags, knolls, and mounds confusedly hurled,
The fragments of an earlier world;
A wildering forest, feather'd o'er
His ruin'd sides and summit hoar;
While on the north, through middle air,
Benan heav'd high his forehead bare."*

In the defile of Beal-an-Duine, (where Fitzjames lost his "gallant grey,") we are in the heart of the great gorge.† Then appears a narrow inlet, and a moment afterwards Loch Katrine itself bursts upon our view, the Alps of Ar-

* *Lady of the Lake*, c. i., s. 14.

† "A skirmish actually took place at a pass thus called, in the Trosachs, and closed with the remarkable incident mentioned in the 'Lady of the Lake.' It was greatly posterior in date to the reign of James V.

"In this roughly wooded island,* the country people secreted their wives and children, and their most valuable effects, from the rapacity of Cromwell's soldiers, during their inroad into this country in the time of the republic. These invaders, not venturing to ascend by the ladders along the side of the lake, took a more circuitous road, through the heart of the Trosachs, the most frequented path at that time, which penetrated the wilderness about half way between Binean and the lake, by a tract called Yea-chailleach, or the old Wife's Bog.

"In one of the defiles of this by-road, the men of the country at that time hung upon the rear of the invading enemy, and shot one of Cromwell's men, whose grave marks the scene of action, and gives name to that pass.† In revenge of this insult, the soldiers resolved to plunder the island, to violate the women, and put the children to death. With this brutal intention, one of the party, more expert than the rest, swam towards the island, to fetch the boat to his comrades, which had carried the women to their asylum, and lay moored in one of the creeks. His companions stood on the shore of the mainland, in full view of all that was to pass, waiting anxiously for his return with the boat. But, just as the swimmer had got to the nearest point of the island, and was laying hold of a black rock to get on shore, a heroine, who stood on the very point where he meant to land, hastily snatching a dagger from below her apron, with one stroke severed his head from the body. His party, seeing this disaster, and relinquishing all future hope of revenge or conquest, made the best of their way out of their perilous situation. This amazon's great-grandson lives at Bridge of Turk, who, besides others, attests the anecdote."—*Sketch of the Scenery near Callander*. Stirling, 1806, p. 20. I have only to add to this account, that the heroine's name was Helen Stuart.—*Notes to the Lady of the Lake*, p. 53.

* That at the eastern extremity of Loch Katrine, called "Ellen's Isle."

† Beallach-an-duine.

roquhar towering in the distance. Loch Katrine is of a serpentine form, encircled by lofty mountains, and is ten miles in length, attaining, in some places, a breadth of two miles. The scenery which fringes it at its eastern extremity is precisely of the same wild character as the Trosachs. Near the eastern shore there is an island exactly corresponding with the description of the residence of Douglas, in the Lady of the Lake. A cottage was erected upon it by Lady Willoughby D'Eresby, which, a few years ago, was accidentally burnt down. Coir-nan-Uriskin, "the Den of the Goblin," is marked by a deep vertical gash in the face of one of the extensive ramifications of Benvenue, overhanging the lake. It is surrounded with stupendous rocks, and overshaded by birch trees, mingled with oaks, the spontaneous production of the mountain, even where its cliffs appear denuded of soil. Above the eastern hollow is the pass of Beal-ach-nam-Bo, a magnificent glade overhung with birch trees. By this pass, in the days of blackmail and reavers, cattle were driven across the shoulder of the hill.

The following striking description of the Trosachs is given by Sir Walter Scott, in the Lady of the Lake:—

" The western waves of ebbing day
Roll'd o'er the glen their level way;
Each purple peak, each flinty spire,
Was bathed in floods of living fire.
But not a setting beam could glow
Within the dark ravines below,
Where twined the path, in shadow hid,
Round many a rocky pyramid,
Shooting abruptly from the dell
Its thunder-splinter'd pinnacle;
Round many an insulated mass,
The native bulwarks of the pass,
Huge as the tower which builders vain
Presumptuous piled on Shinar's plain.
The rocky summits, split and rent,
Form'd turret, dome, or battlement,
Or seem'd fantastically set
With cupola or minaret,
Wild crests as pagod ever deck'd,
Or mosque of eastern architect.
Nor were these earth-borne castles bare,
Nor lack'd they many a banner fair:
For, from their shiver'd brows display'd,
Far o'er the unfathomable glade,
All twinkling with the dew-drops sheen,
The briar rose fell in streamers green,
And creeping shrubs of thousand dyes,
Waved in the west wind's summer sighs.

" Boon nature scatter'd free and wild,
Each plant or flower, the mountain's child.
Here eglantine embalm'd the air,
Hawthorn and hazel mingled there:
The primrose pale, and violet flower,
Found in each cliff a narrow bower;
Foxglove and nightshade, side by side,
Emblems of punishment and pride,
Group'd their dark hues with every stain
The weather-beaten crags retain.
With boughs that quaked at every breath,
Grey birch and aspen wept beneath;
Aloft, the ash and warrior oak
Cast anchor in the rifted rock:
And, higher yet, the pine-tree hung
His shatter'd trunk, and frequent flung,
Where seem'd the cliffs to meet on high,
His boughs athwart the narrow'd sky,
Highest of all, where white peaks glanced,
Where glist'ning streamers waved and danced
The wanderer's eye could barely view
The summer heaven's delicious blue;
So wondrous wild, the whole might seem
The scenery of a fairy dream."

The district of Menteith, only a few miles to the south of the Trosachs, comprehends a range of scenery little inferior in beauty. It contains the lake of Menteith, Aberfoyle, Loch Ard, and Loch Chon, and is approached from Stirling by Ochtertyre, Kincardine, and Ruskie. The lake of Menteith is a circular sheet of water, about five miles in circumference, adorned with ancient woods. It possesses an aspect of placid beauty rather than of grandeur, and the forms of the surrounding hills are neither bold nor striking, but present a gentle undulating line to the eye of the spectator. In the centre of the lake are two small islands called Inchmachome, or the Isle of Rest,* and Talla, or the Earl's Isle. The former, which is the larger and more easterly island, consists of about five acres, and contains the ruins of a Priory, where Queen Mary resided during the invasion of the English in 1547, before she was removed to France. This priory was founded, about the year 1238, by Walter Cumming, second son of William Cumming, Earl of Buchan. He obtained, by grant from the Crown, the extensive district of Badenoch, and by marriage with the Countess of Menteith, he became Earl of Menteith. After his death, Walter Stewart, brother of Alexander, High-Steward of Scotland, obtained a grant of the title and estates of Menteith, in right of his wife, the younger sister of the Countess of Menteith. His second son was Sir John of Ruskie, properly called Stewart, but usually Menteith, the betrayer of the patriot Wallace. In the choir of the church is an ancient tombstone, supposed to be that of Walter Stewart. A writ granted by Robert Bruce, at this place, in April 1310, is recorded in the Chartulary of Arbroath. The buildings connected with this monastery are supposed to have been destroyed at the Reformation. The island of Inchmachome is now the property of his Grace the Duke of Montrose. The principal proprietors around the lake are his Grace, General Graham Stirling, and Mr. Erskine of Cardross. The smaller island contains the remains of the Castle of the Grahams, Earls of Menteith, a race long extinct.† They

* "The world's gay scenes thou must resign,
Stranger, when youth has past;
Oh! were such bless'd asylum thine,
As this—*The Isle of Rest!*"

† "The Earls of Menteith, you must know, had a castle, situated upon an island in the lake, or loch, as it is called, of the same name. But though this residence, which occupied almost the whole of the islet, upon which its ruins still exist, was a strong and safe place of abode, and adapted accordingly to such perilous times, it had this inconvenience, that the stables and other domestic offices were constructed on the banks of the lake, and were, therefore, in some sort defenceless.

"It happened upon a time that there was to be a great entertainment in the castle, and a number of the Grahams were assembled. The occasion, it is said, was a marriage in the family. To prepare for this feast, much provision was got ready, and in particular, a great deal of poultry had been collected. While the feast was preparing, an unhappy chance brought Donald of the

had their garden on the isle of the Priory, and their pleasure-grounds on the neighbouring shore, which is still beautifully adorned with oak, Spanish chestnut, and plane trees of ancient growth. Some of the chestnuts are seventeen feet in circumference at six feet above the ground, and must be above three centuries old. Gartmore House, (Graham, Esq.,) lies to the west, and Rednock House, the seat of General Graham Stirling, to the east of the lake. Callander is distant seven miles. Proceeding westward, at the distance of four miles, the traveller reaches Aberfoyle, the scene of so many of the incidents in the novel of Rob Roy,* where the tourist will find a tolerable inn. At the Clachan of Aberfoyle is the junction of the Duchray and Forth, here called Avondhu, or the Black River. Under the rocky precipice on the north lies the Pass of Aberfoyle, the scene of the defeat of a party of Cromwell's troops by Graham of Duchray.† Loch Ard is a small lake, or rather two lakes,

Hammer to the side of the lake, returning at the head of a band of hungry followers, whom he was conducting homewards to the West Highlands, after some of his usual excursions into Stirlingshire. Seeing so much good victuals ready, and being possessed of an excellent appetite, the Western Highlanders neither asked questions, nor waited for an invitation, but devoured all the provisions that had been prepared for the Grahams, and then went on their way rejoicing through the difficult and dangerous path which leads from the banks of the Loch of Menteith, through the mountains, to the side of Loch Katrine.

"The Grahams were filled with the highest indignation. The company who were assembled at the castle of Menteith, headed by the earl himself, hastily took to their boats, and, disembarking on the northern side of the lake, pursued with all speed the marauders and their leader. They came up with Donald's party in the gorge of a pass, near a rock, called Craig-Vad, or the Wolf's Cliff. The battle then began, and was continued with much fury till night. The Earl or Menteith, and many of his noble kinsmen, fell, while Donald, favoured by darkness, escaped with a single attendant. The Grahams obtained, from the cause of the quarrel, the nick-name of Gramoch-an-Garrigh, or Grahams of the Hens."—*Tales of a Grandfather*, vol. ii., pp. 317-19.

* "To the left lay the valley, down which the Forth wandered on its easterly course, surrounding the beautiful detached hill, with all its garland of woods. On the right, amid a profusion of thickets, knolls, and crags, lay the bed of a broad mountain lake, lightly curled into tiny waves by the breath of the morning breeze, each glittering in its course under the influence of the sunbeams. High hills, rocks, and banks, waving with natural forests of birch and oak, formed the borders of this enchanting sheet of water; and, as their leaves rustled to the wind and twinkled in the sun, gave to the depth of solitude a sort of life and vivacity."—*Rob Roy*, vol. ii., p. 202.

† "Our route, though leading towards the lake, had hitherto been so much shaded by wood, that we only from time to time obtained a glimpse of that beautiful sheet of water. But the road now suddenly emerged from the forest ground, and, winding close by the margin of the loch, afforded us a full view of its spacious mirror, which now, the breeze having totally subsided, reflected in still magnificence the high, dark, heathy mountains, huge grey rocks, and shaggy banks, by which it is encircled. The hills now sunk on its margin so closely, and were so broken and precipitous, as to afford no passage except just

connected by a stream of 200 yards in length, beautifully situated in the middle of a fertile valley. The shores of the loch, though not remarkable for height, are so broken up into rocky and wooded eminences, here running into, and there retreating from each other, as to form some of the most beautiful landscape combinations of which Scotland can boast, and there is more than one spot which bears a striking resemblance to the Trosachs and Loch Katrine. A delightful view of the upper loch is obtained from a rising ground near its lower extremity. Looking westward, Ben Lomond is seen in the background. On the right is the lofty mountain of Benoghrie. In the foreground is Loch Ard itself, three miles in length, and one and an eighth in breadth. The road conducts along the verge of the lake, under a ledge of rock from thirty to fifty feet high. If a person standing immediately under this rock, towards its western extremity, pronounces with a firm voice a line of ten syllables, it is returned first from the opposite side of the lake, and then with equal distinctness from the wood on the east. But the day must be perfectly calm, and the lake as smooth as glass. A gnarled trunk of an oak overhanging the rock is that from which Bailie Nicol Jarvie was suspended by the skirts. In the upper loch is a rocky islet, on which are the mouldering ruins of a stronghold of Murdoch, Duke of Albany. Near the head of the lake, on the northern side, behind the House of Ledeard, is the romantic waterfall, thus accurately described in Waverley:—"It was not so remarkable either for great height or quantity of water, as for the beautiful accompaniments which made the spot interesting. After a broken cataract of about twenty feet, the stream was received in a large natural basin filled to the brim with water, which, where the bubbles of the fall subsided, was so exquisitely clear, that although it was of great depth, the eye could discern each pebble at the bottom. Eddying round this reservoir, the brook found its way as if over a broken part of the ledge, and formed a second fall, which seemed to seek the very abyss; then wheeling out beneath from among the smooth dark rocks, which it had polished for ages, it wandered murmuring down the glen, forming the stream up which Waverley had just ascended." A footpath strikes off towards Benlomond, by which the tourist may cross the hill and reach Rowardennan, on the banks of Loch Lomond; or he may proceed from Aberfoyle Inn, by Gartmore and Drymen, to Dumbarton, a distance of twenty-two miles. It is customary for travellers, after visiting the two lochs above named, to cross over the hill from Aberfoyle to the Trosachs, a distance of only five miles, but the pedestrian will do well to pursue the road along

upon the narrow line of the track which we occupied, and which was overhung with rocks, from which we might have been destroyed merely by rolling down stones, without much possibility of offering resistance."—*Rob Roy*, vol. ii., p. 208. A road has now been formed along the northern margin of the lake.

the margin of Loch Chon, a secluded sheet of water three miles in length, hemmed in by fine sloping hills feathered with natural coppice wood. This road will conduct him, after leaving the loch, into the pathway leading from Loch Katrine to Inversnaid on Loch Lomond.

A steamer now regularly plies on Loch Katrine during the summer months, sailing at such times as enables the passengers to meet the steamer on Loch Lomond. From June till the end of September, the boat generally makes two trips a-day from each end of the Loch, but as the hours of sailing, and the number of trips, are occasionally changed, we think it better to leave the tourist to obtain local information on the subject.*

"In sailing along you discover many arms of the lake—here a bold headland, where black rocks dip in unfathomable water—there the white sand in the bottom of a bay, bleached for ages by the waves. In walking on the north side, the road is sometimes cut through the face of the solid rock, which rises upwards of 200 feet perpendicular above the lake, which, before the rock was cut, had to be mounted by a kind of natural ladder. Every rock has its echo, every grove is vocal with the harmony of birds, or by the airs of women and children gathering nuts in their season. Down the side of the opposite mountain, after a shower of rain, flow an hundred white streams, which rush with incredible noise and velocity into the lake. On one side, the water-eagle sits in majesty undisturbed on his well-known rock, in sight of his nest on the top of Benvenue; the heron stalks among the reeds in search of his prey, and the sportive ducks gambol in the waters or dive below. On the other, the wild goats climb where they have scarce room for the soles of their feet, and the wild birds, perched on exalted trees and pinnacles, look down with composed indifference on man. The scene is closed by a west view of the lake,

* An abortive attempt was made to establish a steamer on Loch Katrine in 1843. The enterprise naturally met with the strenuous opposition of the boatmen who row the oar-boats on the lake, and the steamer had plied only a few days when, during the night of the 18th July, it disappeared, and has never since been heard of. Although there can be no doubt that this daring outrage must have been the work of several accomplices, the perpetrators were neve discovered.

Honour'd and bless'd be the ever-green Pine!
Long may the Tree, in his banner that glances,
Flourish, the shelter and grace of our line!
Heaven send it happy dew,
Earth lend it sap anew,
Gaily to bourgeon, and broadly to grow,
While every Highland glen
Sends our shout back agen,
'Roderigh Vich Alpine dhu, ho! ieroe!'

"Ours is no sapling, chance-sown by the fountain,
Blooming at Beltane, in winter to fade;
When the whirlwind has stripp'd every leaf on the mountain,
The more shall Clan-Alpine exhult in her shade.
Moor'd in the rifted rock,
Proof to the tempest's shock,
Firmer he roots him the ruder it blow;
Menteith and Breadalbane, then,
Echo his praise agen,
'Roderigh Vich Alpine dhu, ho! ieroe!'

"Proudly our pibroch has thrilled in Glen Fruin,
And Bannochar's groans to our slogan replied:
Glen Luss and Ross-dhu, they are smoking in ruin,
And the best of Loch-Lomond lie dead on her side.
Widow and Saxon maid,
Long shall lament our raid,
Think of Clan-Alpine with fear and with woe;
Lennox and Leven-glen
Shake when they hear agen,
"Roderigh Vich Alpine dhu, ho! ieroe!'

"Row, vassals, row, for the pride of the Highlands,
Stretch to your oars, for the ever-green Pine!
O! that the rose-bud that graces yon islands
Were wreathed in a garland around him to twine!

• *Statistical Account of Scotland.*

O that some seedling gem,
Worthy such noble stem,
Honour'd and blest in their shadow might grow !
Loud should Clan-Alpine then
Ring from the deepmost glen,
'Roderigh Vich Alpine dhu, ho ! ieroe !'"

From the west end of the lake, a wild valley, traversed by a rugged pathway about five miles long, affords a communication with Loch Lomond, upon which it opens at Inversnaid Mill, where the steamboat, which every day plies along Loch Lomond, takes in the Loch Katrine tourists.* The small lake, Arklet, lies in the hollow near this pathway. In one of the smoky huts in the valley between Loch Katrine and Loch Lomond may be seen a long Spanish musket, six feet and a half in length, once the property of Rob Roy, whose original residence was in this lone vale. Near at hand is the hut where it is said Helen MacGregor, Rob Roy's wife, first saw the light. Beside the way are the ruins of Inversnaid Fort, erected by Government in 1713 to check the MacGregors. In descending to the margin of Loch Lomond, the stranger cannot fail to be struck with

* A flock of shaggy Highland ponies is in attendance, to convey travellers across this moorland region, and a pony cart to carry their luggage. The extortion and incivility to which tourists are subjected, at this stage of their progress, are a reproach to Scotland. A recent sufferer thus addresses the editor of a Glasgow paper on the subject:—

"On being landed at the hill of Inversnaid, we as usual took our departure for Loch Katrine, mounted on the Highland ponies which awaited us. I shall say nothing of the charge, four shillings each,) which certainly appeared rather high for a ride of five miles on the back of such cattle; but I feel bound to mention the conduct of the boatmen, and others, who formed an escort to our party. They came provided with a small pony cart, which carries the luggage across, and here their extortion began. On reaching the margin of Loch Katrine, one gentleman, who had not the precaution to make a bargain with them, was charged eight shillings for the carriage of a few articles; another party five shillings; and so on in proportion. The sun was fast sinking, and, under the pretence of refreshing themselves, the whole party sat smoking and drinking for above an hour, deaf to all the entreaties which were made to them, and at length, with rudeness and extreme reluctance, at half-past five o'clock, set out: so that, by the time we reached the Trosachs, it was quite dark, and we reached the crowded inn, only to be obliged to take horses and hurry away ten miles to Callander. The consequence of this was, that we not only lost the view of the lovely scenery through which we passed, but the comfort, and even the health of our party, were endangered, by night travelling and its accompaniments."

Were this a solitary instance we should not have quoted it here; but having personally experienced the annoyance, and many of our friends having suffered in the same way, we have no hesitation in cautioning travellers to make an express bargain before they avail themselves of either ponies or cart. For a pony, we regard 2s. 6d. a moderate, and 3s. 6d. a liberal hire.

O C H I O M U

[illegible]

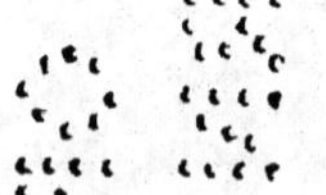

admiration at the sublimity of the mountains which hang over the opposite shore, and round the mouth of the narrow glen of Inveruglas. While the tourist is in the midst of the country of the MacGregors, he may be gratified by the perusal of Sir Walter Scott's splendid lyric, "the Gathering of Clan-Gregor:"

"The moon's on the lake, and the mist's on the brae,
And the clan has a name that is nameless by day;
Then gather, gather, gather, Gregalich!

Our signal for fight, that from monarchs we drew,
Must be heard but by night in our vengeful haloo!
Then haloo, Gregalich! haloo, Gregalich!

Glen Orchy's proud mountains, Coalchuirn and her towers,
Glenstrae and Glenlyon no longer are ours;
We're landless, landless, landless, Gregalich!

But, doom'd and devoted by vassal and lord,
Macgregor has still both his heart and his sword!
Then courage, courage, courage, Gregalich!

If they rob us of name, and pursue us with beagles,
Give their roofs to the flame, and their flesh to the eagles!
Then vengeance, vengeance, vengeance, Gregalich!

While there's leaves on the forest, or foam on the river,
Macgregor, despite them, shall flourish for ever!
Come then, Gregalich! come then, Gregalich!

Through the depths of Loch Katrine the steed shall career,
O'er the peak of Ben Lomond the galley shall steer;
And the rocks of Craig-Royston like icicles melt,
Ere our wrongs be forgot, or our vengeance unfelt!
Then gather, gather, gather, Gregalich!"

It is said that General Wolf once resided in Inversnaid Fort. At Inversnaid Mill there is a little rivulet and a cataract, the scene of Wordsworth's beautiful poem to the "Highland Girl." Tourists may await the arrival of the steamer on Loch Lomond at the inn recently established.

Loch Lomond ("the lake full of islands"), is unquestionably the pride of Scottish lakes. "This noble lake, boasting innumerable beautiful islands of every varying form and outline which fancy can frame—its northern extremity narrowing until it is lost among dusky and retreating mountains, while, gradually widening as it extends to the southward, it spreads its base around the indentures and promontories of a fair and fertile land, affords one of the most surprising, beautiful, and sublime spectacles in nature.* Its upper extremity is not unworthy of comparison with the finest views on Loch Awe, while there are points in the same division not dissimilar to the more striking parts of the Trosachs, and fully equal to them in wild grandeur.† After taking on board the tourists from Loch Katrine, the steamboat visits the upper part of the lake, which is there narrowed and hemmed in by the neighbouring mountains. At the northern extremity is Inverarnan Inn, and the wide elevated valley called Glenfalloch. From this tourists may proceed northwards by coach, according to the routes described at the end of this tour. Three miles from the upper end is a small wooded island called Eilan Vhou, and two miles farther south, another called Inveruglas, on each of which are the ruins of a stronghold of the family of Macfarlane. The slogan of this clan was "Loch Sloy," a small lake between Loch Long and Loch Lomond. At the distance of other three miles, on the western shore, is Tarbet Inn, the landing place for those who intend to proceed to Arrochar and Loch Long; or to catch the mail from Glasgow to Inverary, *via* Arrochar, Glencroe, and Rest-and-be-Thankful.‡ Farther south, a projecting headland is seen on the right, where is the ferry of Inveruglas to Rowardennan Inn, the usual starting point for those who desire to ascend to the top of Ben Lomond. This mountain is the property of the Duke of Montrose. It rises 3210 feet above the level of the lake, which is thirty-two feet above the level of the sea. The

* *Rob Roy.*

† The length of Loch Lomond is about twenty-three miles, its breadth, where greatest, at the southern extremity, is five miles, from which it gradually grows narrower, till it terminates in a prolonged stripe of water. The depth varies considerably; south of Luss it is rarely more than twenty fathoms, in the northern part it ranges from 60 to 100, and, in the places where deepest, never freezes. The total superficies of the lake is about 20,000 acres. About two-thirds of the loch, and most of the islands, are in the county of Dumbarton, the rest, with the right bank, are in the county of Stirling.

‡ During summer a coach runs from Tarbet to Crieff and Killin—one of the finest drives in Scotland—its hour of starting being timed to the arrival of the mail.

distance from the inn to the top of the mountain is six miles of continued ascent. The view from the summit is varied and most extensive, comprehending the counties of Lanark, Renfrew, and Ayr, the Firth of Clyde, and the islands of Arran and Bute, to the south, and the counties of Stirling and the Lothians, with the windings of the Forth, and the Castles of Stirling and Edinburgh, to the east. About three and a half miles from Inveruglas, is Luss, a delightful little village, situated on a promontory which juts into the lake. One of the finest points for enjoying the scenery of Loch Lomond and the environs of Luss is Stonehill, to the north of the village. Near Luss is Rossdow, the splendid residence of Sir James Colquhoun, Bart. In the vicinity of the mansion is a tower of the ancient Castle of the family of Luss, the last heiress of which married Colquhoun of Colquhoun. A short way farther on are the ruins of the Castle of Banachra, overhanging the entrance to Glen Fruin.* This castle was anciently the residence of the Colquhouns, and here the chief of that clan was basely murdered, in 1640, by one of the Macfarlanes. Near it is the lofty hill of Dunfion, or the hill of Fingal, according to tradition one of the hunting-seats of that hero From Luss southward, the breadth of the lake expands rapidly, and the surface of the water is studded with

"All the fairy crowds
Of islands that together lie
As quietly as spots of sky
Among the evening clouds."

* It was in Glen Fruin, or the Glen of Sorrow, that the celebrated battle took place between the Macgregors and Colquhouns, fraught with such fatal consequences to both parties. There had been a long and deadly feud between the Macgregors and the Laird of Luss, head of the family of Colquhoun. At length the parties met in the vale of Glen Fruin. The battle was obstinately contested, but in the end the Macgregors came off victorious, slaying two hundred of the Colquhouns, and making many prisoners. It is said, that after the battle the Macgregors murdered about eighty youths, who had been led by curiosity to view the fight. A partial representation of these transactions having been made to James VI., letters of fire and sword were issued against the Clan-Gregor. Their lands were confiscated, their very name proscribed, and, being driven to such extremity, they became notorious for acts of daring reprisal. Their legal rights were restored to them in 1755. For many interesting particulars in the history of the Macgregor clan, the reader may consult the Introduction to Rob Roy.

The islands of Loch Lomond are about thirty in number, and ten of these are of considerable extent.

After leaving Luss, the boat passes, in succession, Inch-Cruin, or the Round Island, (formerly a retreat for lunatics,) Inch Moan, or the Peat Island, Inch Fadn, (the long island,) Inch Tavanagh, to the south of which the ruins of Galbraith Castle start up from the water, Inch Lonaig, (used as a deer-park by the family of Luss,) Inch Carachan, Buck Inch, Inch Cardach, and Inch Cailliach, the Island of Women, so called from its having been the site of a nunnery. Inch Cailliach formerly gave name to the parish of Buchanan. The church belonging to the nunnery was long used as the place of worship for the parish of Buchanan, but scarcely any vestiges of it now remain; the burial-ground, which contains the family places of sepulture of several neighbouring clans, still continues to be used; the monuments of the Lairds of Macgregor, and of other families claiming a descent from the old Scottish King Alpine, are most remarkable.

> "The shafts and limbs were rods of yew,
> Whose parents, in Inch Cailliach, wave
> Their shadows o'er Clan-Alpine's grave,
> And, answering Lomond's breezes deep,
> Soothe many a chieftain's endless sleep."
>
> *Lady of the Lake*, c. iii., *and notes*.

At the north-east corner of Inch Cailliach, passengers are often landed at Beal'maha, a celebrated Highland pass.* Here some tourists choose to land, to pursue their journey through the pass, and along the banks of the loch to Rowardennan. The steamboat next approaches the little island of Clar-Inch, from which the Buchanans took their slogan or war-cry. The last island is a long narrow one, named Inch Murrin, the largest island in Loch Lomond. It is finely clothed with wood, and is employed as a deer-park by the Duke of Montrose. At its southern extremity there is an old ruined fortalice, called Lennox Castle, formerly a residence of the Earls of Lennox. Here Isabel Duchess of Albany, daughter of Duncan Earl of Lennox, resided after

* *The Lady of the Lake*, canto iv., st. 4.

the death of her husband, Murdoch, Duke of Albany, and of her two sons, and her father, who were executed after the restoration of James I., in 1424. See ante, p. 173. On the east side of the lake are the ruins of Buturich Castle, farther south is Balloch Castle (Buchanan, Esq.), and near it, on the margin of the lake, stood the ancient castle of Balloch, a stronghold of the once powerful family of Lennox; its site and moat are still visible. The steamboat now returns to Balloch, where the train is waiting to convey the passengers to Bowling, and from thence a steamboat lands them in Glasgow the same evening.

SIXTH TOUR—BRANCH A.

GLASGOW TO THE HIGHLANDS BY DUMBARTONSHIRE RAILWAY AND LOCH LOMOND.

The scenery of Loch Lomond has been rendered so accessible by the opening of the Dumbartonshire Railway, that tourists will in many instances prefer visiting it from Glasgow. For the benefit of such, we append the following sketch of routes which this new means of communication has rendered more available than heretofore.

GLASGOW TO THE HEAD OF LOCH LOMOND.

Proceed from Glasgow by one of the Castle steamers to the new railway pier at Bowling, and from thence to railway station adjacent. The new quay at Bowling will be found to be exceedingly convenient at all states of the tide. The train stops at Dumbarton, Renton, and Alexandria stations. On reaching Balloch, the quay is on a level with the terminus, and the steamer on a level with the quay, so that no effort is necessary to step out of the carriage into the Loch Lomond steamers. As soon as the passengers are on board, the steamer sets off, along the eastern shore of the loch, threading her way amongst the picturesque wooded islets which dot the lower expanse of the Queen of Scottish Lakes. The steamer calls at Tarbet, the landing-place for Inverary, and Inversnaid, the landing-place for Loch Katrine and the Trosachs, after which it proceeds to Inverarnan, at the head of the loch. By returning to Glasgow the same way, one is enabled to visit Loch Lomond, and enjoy the beauties of the lovely and picturesque scenery between Glasgow Bridge and the base of the lofty Benlomond, in seven hours.

From Inverarnan Inn, at the head of Loch Lomond, there are three favourite Routes through the Highlands, each of which may be travelled, during the summer season, by the Breadalbane and Benvoirlich coaches, which run in connexion with the steamer on Loch Lomond.

FIRST ROUTE—The Breadalbane coach proceeds by way of Glenfalloch to Crianlarich. From thence by Strathfillan, the Holy Pool, the King's Field, and Benmore, to Tyndrum. Hills of Glenorchy, through the Marquis of Breadalbane's deer forest of the Black Mount, the moors of Rannoch, the Hill of Schehallion, King's House Inn, and the Royal Forest, passing near General Wade's old military road, known as the Devil's Staircase, through the wild scenery of Glencoe, Ballachulish, and along the banks of Loch Linnhe to Fort-William, situated at the foot of Ben Nevis.

From this, tourists may proceed by the Caledonian Canal to Inverness.

SECOND ROUTE—The other Breadalbane coach proceeds the same way to Crianlarich. From that it branches off by Strathfillan, Glendochart, and Lochanour, foot of the lofty Benmore, Coirchaorach, the birth-place of Rob Roy, Loch Dochart, Killin, the ruins of Finlarig Castle, the northern shore of Loch Tay, the base of Ben Lawers, village of Kenmore, and Taymouth Castle to Aberfeldy. Coaches in connection proceed from this—*1st.* By Dunkeld to Perth. *2d.* By Glen Ogle and Killin to Callander, the Trosachs, and Stirling. *3d.* By Glenalmond and Amulree to Crieff.

THIRD ROUTE—The Benvoirlich coach proceeds in the same way from Inverarnan to Crianlarich. Then it takes the road down Glendochart and Glen Ogle, by Lochearnhead, Benvoirlich, St. Fillans, and Comrie, to Crieff.

CONVEYANCES FROM GLASGOW.

Railway Trains to

Airdrie.	Coatbridge.	Hamilton.	Lockerbie.
Ardrossan.	Cumnock.	Irvine.	London.
Ayr.	Dumfries.	Kilmarnock.	Muirkirk.
Barrhead.	Dunblane.	Kirkintilloch.	Paisley.
Bridge of Allan.	Edinburgh.	Lanark.	Perth.
Campsie.	Falkirk.	Linlithgow.	Stirling.
Carlisle.	Galston.	Loch Lomond.	Troon
Castlecary.	Greenock.		

2. Clyde Steamers.

(As the hours of the Steamers change monthly, and the Coach hours also frequently vary, it is necessary to inquire about them before starting, or to procure Murray's Time Tables, which contain all such changes.)

The Largs Steamers ply several times every day between Greenock, Gourock, Innerkip, Largs, Fairlie, Milport, and, generally, once every morning to Arran.

---

3. Glasgow and the Highlands.

GLASGOW—GREENOCK—OBAN—FORT-WILLIAM—INVERNESS—TOBERMORY—PORTREE—STAFFA—IONA.

Summer arrangements (unless prevented by some unforeseen occurrence).

From Glasgow to Oban, Fort-William, and Inverness, from Glasgow Bridge by Greenock. Pioneer, every Monday, Wednesday, and Friday, at 6 morning, and from Greenock about a quarter to 8 o'clock, arriving at Oban about 4 p.m., at Lochiel Arms' Hotel, Bannavie, the same evening, and Inverness on afternoon of following day.

From Glasgow to Oban, Fort-William, and Inverness, direct every Monday and Thursday.

From Glasgow to Oban every lawful day at 6 a.m.

From Glasgow to Oban and Tobermory, every Tuesday and Friday.

From Glasgow for Oban, Tobermory, and Portree, Duntroon Castle, every Friday morning at 8 o'clock, with goods and passengers. Passengers leaving Glasgow by the Pioneer on Friday morning at 6 o'clock, may join the Duntroon Castle at Oban the following morning.

From Inverness for Glasgow, by Corpach, Fort-William, Oban, Rothesay, Dunoon, and Greenock, every Monday, Wednesday, and Friday, arriving at Glasgow the following afternoon, calling at the Fall of Foyers.

From Oban for Glasgow, calling at Rothesay, Dunoon, and Greenock, every lawful morning.

From Portree (Skye) and Tobermory for Glasgow, the Duntroon Castle, from Portree, every Tuesday morning at 6 o'clock.

From Oban for Staffa and Iona, Tuesday, Thursday, and Saturday (weather permitting), returning to Oban same evening.

*** *Carriages and Horses taken by the Swift Boats, provided there are persons in charge to drive along the Crinan Canal.*

Office, 14 Jamaica Street, Glasgow.

---

4. Glasgow and the Highlands *via* the Crinan Canal and Inverness.

To Oban, Tobermory, and Salen, Loch Sunart, every alternate Tuesday at 6 morning.

To Oban, Ballachulish, Fort-William, every alternate Monday at 12 noon.

From Salen, Loch Sunart, and Tobermory, to Oban, Greenock, and Glasgow, every Wednesday about noon.

From Inverness and Fort-William to Oban, Greenock, and Glasgow, every alternate Thursday, at 6 A.M.

*** The MAID will call at Ballachulish, near Glencoe, on her way to Fort-William only. Passengers by this vessel will avoid the transhipping of luggage at either end of the Crinan Canal.

Glasgow to Tobermory or Fort-William, cabin, 6s.

OFFICE, 20 ST. ENOCH SQUARE.

---

5. GLASGOW, OBAN, FORT-WILLIAM, AND INVERNESS.

BY THE CLYDE, LOCHLOMOND, TYNDRUM, GLENCOE, LOCHABER, CALEDONIAN CANAL, AND FALL OF FOYERS.

The MARQUIS OF BREADALBANE, four-horse coach, starts from Glasgow for Fort-William and Oban, at ¼ to 7 A.M., from 28 Argyll Street, for the Clyde Steamer; from Fort-William for Glencoe, Lochlomond, and Glasgow, at 6 A.M., from Oban for Dalmally, Lochlomond, and Glasgow, at 7 A.M.; from Oban to Fort-William, by Dalmally and Glencoe, at 7 A.M.; from Fort-William to Oban, by Glencoe and Dalmally, at 6. A. M.; from Fort-William to Inverness, per Steamer on the Caledonian Canal, and from Inverness to Fort-William, per steamers on the Canal, where passengers may take out their seat from the Coach Guard on board.

For further information apply at WYLIE & LOCHHEAD'S 28 Argyle Street, Glasgow; in Inverness, Oban, and Fort-William, at the BREADALBANE COACH AND STEAM OFFICES.

---

6. LOCHLOMOND AND LOCH KATRINE, AND NORTH AND WEST HIGHLANDS.

The Steamers PRINCE ALBERT and WATER WITCH, sail from Balloch, in connection with Dumbarton steamers and railway, thrice a-day.

EXCURSIONS FROM GLASGOW.

Daily excursions to the head of Lochlomond and back, leaving Glasgow with the 7 A.M., or 9.15 A.M., Dumbarton steamers. Fares from Glasgow and back, 4s.

Daily afternoon excursions to the head of Lochlomond, leaving Glasgow with the 4 P.M. Dumbarton steamer, and returning the following morning to Balloch, in time for the 10.45 train to Glasgow. Parties leaving on Saturday can return on Monday. Fares from Glasgow and back, 4s.

Daily excursions, in connection with the 7 A.M. steamer from Glasgow to Balloch, Lochlomond steamer from Balloch to top of Loch and back to Tarbet. Arrochar boat from Arrochar to Glasgow. Fares (exclusive of the land part betwixt Tarbet and Arrochar) for the whole round, from Glasgow and back, 4s.

Daily excursions in connection with the Arrochar boat from Glasgow, at 9.15 A.M., Tarbet on Lochlomond to Balloch about 3.30 P.M., and Balloch to Glasgow at 5.50 P.M. Fares (exclusive of the land part between Arrochar and Tarbet) for the whole round, from Glasgow and back, 4s.

The Loch-Katrine steamer, ROB ROY, is now sailing every lawful day in connection with Lochlomond steamers. Leaving Trossachs at 8.30 A.M., 12.30 noon, and 3 P.M. Leaving Coulbarns at 10 A.M., 2 P.M., and 4.30 P.M.

Coaches run from Stirling to Trossachs, by Callender, every morning, and return in the evening.

Coaches also start from Inverarnan daily in connection with the steamers on Lochlomond—to Oban by Lochawe; to Inverness, by Glencoe and Fort William; to Aberfeldy, by Killin and Kenmure; to Creiff, by Glenogle; and also from Tarbet to Oban, by Glencrow.

Dumbarton, July, 1851.

---

8. GLASGOW TO AYR, GIRVAN, STRANRAER, BELFAST, AND CAMPBELTOWN.

From Glasgow to Stranraer every Friday, returning on Wednesdays. Hours vary.

From Stranraer to Belfast every Monday, returning on Tuesday. Hours vary.

From Ayr to Stranraer every Tuesday, Thursday, and Saturday, returning on Monday, Thursday, and Friday; calling off Girvan and Ballantrae, weather permitting.

From Ayr to Girvan every Monday, returning on Tuesday.

From Ayr to Campbeltown, calling off Kildonan and Clauchog Shore, south end of Arran, weather permitting, every Monday and Friday, returning on Tuesday and Saturday.

---

9. THE CAMPBELTOWN STEAMERS.

To and from Glasgow and Campbeltown every day, Fridays and Sundays excepted. Hours vary.

---

10. GLASGOW, AYR, GIRVAN, AND STRANRAER.

From Stranraer to Ayr thrice a-week. *From Ayr to Girvan* and *from Girvan to Ayr and Glasgow* once a-week.

---

11. GLASGOW, OBAN, TOBERMORY, SKYE.

To Stornoway, calling at Oban, Tobermory, Arisaig, Armadale, Glenelg, Kyleakin, Broadford and Portee, the Steamer 'Glow-worm,' which leaves and returns once a-week.

12. Dumbarton Steamers.

Between Glasgow and Dumbarton at 7, 9.15, 11 A.M. and 1, 4, 6 P.M. In connection with railway, to Balloch, Lochlomond.

To Helensburgh at 7.15, 10, 11, A.M. and 12, 3, 4, and 5, P.M.

To Gairloch-head. *Summer Hours*—7.15 A.M. and 3 and 4 P.M. (and Sat. 5 P.M.)

---

14. Glasgow and Liverpool.

To and from Liverpool every day at 2 P.M.; Rail at 5 P.M.

*** The steamers sailing from Liverpool or Glasgow on Thursday, call (weather permitting) at Ramsay, Isle of Man.

---

15. Glasgow and Fleetwood.

To and from Fleetwood, in connection with the Lancashire and Yorkshire railways every Monday and Friday.

Coaches from Glasgow to

Blantyre, from Tontine.
Bothwell, from Tontine.
Comrie, in connection with Scottish Central Railway.
Drymen, thrice a-week, from 38 Ingram Street.
Highlands, see page 206.
Holytown, from 10 Argyle Street.
Killin and Lochearnhead, &c., in connection with Scot. Central Bail.
Kilbride, from Tontine.
Larkhall, from 84 Trongate.
Lesmahagow, from 84 Trongate.
Oban, Fort-William, &c., see page 206.
Renfrew, from 84 Trongate.
Strathaven, from 84 Trongate.
Strathaven, by Kilbride, from Tontine.
Stonehouse, from 84 Trongate.
St. Fillan's, &c., in connection with Scottish Central Railway.

Inverary Coach.

A very fine drive may be had by the Mail from Glasgow to Inverary, *via* Dumbarton, Balloch, Banks of Loch Lomond, Tarbet, Arrochar, Loch Long, Glencroe, and Cairndow. This route commands a fine view of Ben Lomond.

In summer the Crieff and Killin Mail joins this at Tarbet. Its line of road is also very inviting to lovers of the picturesque.

Campsie Coach. (During Summer).

The Rob Roy coach leaves Campsie at a quarter before 9 o'clock morning arriving at Aberfoyle at half-past 11 o'clock; starting, on return from Aberfoyle, at three-quarters past 4 o'clock, arriving at Campsie in time for the train for Glasgow, and the Edinburgh train at Campsie Junction, thus allowing upwards of five hours to view the splendid scenery at Aberfoyle. Passengers from Glasgow leave the Queen Street Station at a quarter past 8 o'clock, and Edinburgh at half-past 6 o'clock morning, arriving at Campsie Junction in time to catch the train which runs in connection with the coach.

Fares from Glasgow. First class and inside, 5s. 8d.; first class and outside, 4s. 8d.; third class and outside, 3s. 10d. From Campsie, inside, 4s.; outside, 3s.

PLAN OF GLASGOW
Monkland Canal
NECROPOLIS
Knox's Monument
DRYGATE
Cattle Market
ROAD
GALLOWGATE
KING ST
CALTON
KIRK ST
Stevenson St
Millroad St
Rose St
Calton Ch.
GREAT HAMILTON
MONTEITH ROW
CANNING ST
CLYDE
HIGH GREEN
Nelson's Monument
BRIDGETON
KING'S PARK
FLESHERS HAUGH
Proposed Cemetery
College
Hunterian Museum
Macfarlane's Obs.
Barracks
1500 Yards.

GLASGOW.

SITUATION—HISTORICAL NOTICES—GENERAL STATISTICS OF POPULATION — COMMERCE AND MANUFACTURES — EDUCATION AND LITERATURE — CHARITABLE AND RELIGIOUS INSTITUTIONS, ETC.

[*Hotels*: Carricks's; The Wellington; The Globe; The George; Comrie's Royal—all in George Square. The Buck's Head and Tontine, in Argyle Street.

Glasgow, the commercial metropolis of Scotland, and, in wealth, population, and manufacturing and commercial importance, the third city in the United Kingdom, is situate in Lanarkshire, in the lower part of the basin of the Clyde; about twenty miles from the Atlantic Ocean, and nearly double that distance from the German Sea.

St. Mungo, or, as he has also been styled, St. Kentigern, is the reputed founder of the city. Its annals from the time of its foundation—supposed to have been about the year 560—to the early part of the twelfth century, are involved in the obscurity which overshadows nearly the whole contemporary history of those rude ages, the first fact of importance which emerges from the clouds of its earlier history, being the erection of its noble Cathedral. This fine old minster was erected by John Achaius, Bishop of Glasgow, in 1133, or, according to M'Ure, in 1136, in the reign of David the First, whose pious largesses to the clergy obtained for him the name and honours of a saint.

About forty years after the building of the Cathedral, William the Lion granted a charter for holding a "weekly mercat" in Glasgow, and afterwards erected it into a burgh of regality.

Four times during the fourteenth, and five times during the seventeenth century the town was ravished by the plague, and the loathsome disease of leprosy also long prevailed—some lepers having been confined in a house in the suburbs of Gorbals so late as 1589. The population, in 1660 was 14,678; in 1831 it amounted to 202,426; in 1841 to 280,682; and in 1851 it had reached 358,926.

Previous to 1775, the mercantile capital and enterprise of Glasgow were almost wholly employed in the tobacco trade. Large fortunes were made, and the city still exhibits evidences of the wealth and social importance of the "Tobacco Lords," as they were termed; some of the finest private dwellings in the city, and several elegant streets, being the splendid relics of their former civic grandeur and importance. The interruption which the war of the American Revolution gave to this traffic, turned the attention of the citizens to the manufacture of cotton goods, then feebly developing its latent energies in Lancashire, and to this branch of manufacture Glasgow chiefly owes her pre-eminence as a commercial and manufacturing city.

In 1451, application was made to the Pope for a bull to establish a university, and eight years afterwards a member of the illustrious house of Hamilton bequeathed four acres of ground, with a tenement of houses, for the same purpose; and thus this noble educational institution was established, and after encountering many difficulties arising from the unsettled character of the times, from its origin to near the end of the seventeenth century, rose into fame, importance, and utility. It is a corporate body, and is governed by a chancellor, rector, and dean. The number of students is at present about 843. The Hunterian Museum, attached to the College, is rich in various departments of natural history, particularly in anatomical preparations, and in coins and medals. The whole has been valued at £70,000. The Grammar or High School, for elementary classical education, is supported by the Corporation, on whom its superintendence devolves. It costs the city about £1000 per annum. Of late years, the range of elementary instruction has been extended, and various modern languages, besides drawing and mathematics, are taught. The number of scholars for the last year was 1357.

Anderson's University was founded in 1795, by Professor Anderson, chiefly for the promotion of physical science. Its lectures are well attended, and there is an excellent museum attached to this institution. In Hanover Street, running from George Square to the north, stands the Mechanic's

Institution, the lectures of which are numerously attended; attached to it is an excellent library, with a valuable scientific apparatus; and they have, together with the Mechanic's class in Anderson's University, perhaps the most beautiful and extensive series of models of steam-engines and machines of various kinds to be found in any similar institution in the country. In 1763, the illustrious James Watt began that memorable series of experiments in mechanical science which issued in the successful application of steam as a great motive power, and about fifty years after Mr. Henry Bell launched on the Clyde the first steam-vessel ever seen in this country. To the labours and discoveries of these eminent men, Glasgow may be said to owe her present eminent position as a manufacturing and commercial community. Monuments to perpetuate their memory have been erected by their grateful fellow-citizens. That of the former is placed in George's Square, in the centre of the city, and the latter at Dunglass, on the Clyde, eleven miles below the town, in a fine commanding situation.

Glasgow is also rich in many religious, charitable, and philanthropic institutions, which are supported by annual donations to the extent of £50,000. Among the most recent establishments of this kind are, the Asylum for the Houseless Poor, and the House of Refuge for Indigent and Orphan Boys.* An institution for the reception of Destitute Young Females has also recently been erected.

In a commercial community like that of Glasgow, the learned professions bear a small proportion to those engaged in the pursuits of trade and commerce; but although the chief springs of action are to be found in the stimulants of commercial and manufacturing enterprise, the character of the population is that of intellectual activity, and eagerness for the acquisition of general and available knowledge.

* A new edifice, on a large scale, is intended to be erected for the above establishment, on the north side of the city; not far from which a large handsome building has been raised as an Asylum for Old Men, in the Rottenrow.

WALK FIRST.*

GEORGE'S SQUARE—MONUMENT TO SIR WALTER SCOTT—STATUES OF SIR JOHN MOORE AND JAMES WATT—ROYAL EXCHANGE—EQUESTRIAN STATUE OF THE DUKE OF WELLINGTON—ROYAL BANK—QUEEN STREET—ARGYLE STREET—ARCADE—DUNLOP STREET—THEATRE-ROYAL—MILLER STREET—GLASSFORD STREET—STOCKWELL—HUTCHESON'S HOSPITAL—CANDLERIGGS, AND BAZAAR—TRON STEEPLE—CROSS—TONTINE BUILDINGS—EQUESTRIAN STATUE OF WILLIAM THE THIRD—TOWN HALL—CROSS STEEPLE—SALTMARKET—ST. ANDREW'S SQUARE, AND CHURCH—BRIDGEGATE—COURTHOUSES AND JAIL—HUTCHESON'S BRIDGE—GREEN—NELSON'S MONUMENT—LONDON STREET—HIGH STREET—COLLEGE BUILDINGS—BRIDEWELL—BELL OF THE BRAE—INFIRMARY—CATHEDRAL—NECROPOLIS—ASYLUM FOR THE BLIND—GEORGE'S STREET.

In point of picturesque situation Glasgow must suffer in a comparison with Edinburgh; yet, if the tourist will put himself under our guidance for a short time, we promise to shew him one of the finest cities in the British dominions, which, even in a mere landscape point of view, presents a series of pictures of equal beauty and interest. We shall adopt the same method we have found so convenient in perambulating Edinburgh, and conduct the stranger in a succession of walks through the busy city.

Suppose the tourist, then, snugly deposited in one of the excellent hotels in George's Square, one of the most central places in the city, and from which, as from a common centre, we shall commence our examination of the memorabilia of this great commercial emporium of the west.

Sallying from any of the various respectable hotels† in this spacious and handsome square—which of itself, from the elegance and agreeable bustle of its area, attracts attention from a stranger—the first object which strikes the

* In conformity with the plan adopted in our description of Edinburgh, the reader will find that the several walks through Glasgow are each distinguished by a different line of colour in the map of the city affixed. Walk First is coloured *red*. Strangers whose time is limited may omit those parts of the route indicated by a *dotted* line.

† There are five excellent hotels in George Square—the George Hotel, Comrie's, the Royal Hotel, the Star Hotel, and the Wellington Hotel; at any of which the stranger is sure of the best entertainment, as the old sign hath it, for "man and horse." Besides these, there are various taverns and eating-houses of the best description.

eye, is the monument recently erected to Sir Walter Scott. It is in the form of a fluted Doric column, about eighty feet in height, with a colossal statue of the great Minstrel on the top. The figure is half enveloped in a shepherd's plaid,* and the expression of the countenance is characterised by that air of *bonhommie* and shrewd sense which distinguished that illustrious individual. Directly in front of Sir Walter's pillar there is a fine pedestrian statue, in bronze, by Flaxman, of the lamented Sir John Moore, who was a native of Glasgow. To the right of Sir John Moore's statue, in the south-west angle of the square, there is also a noble figure of James Watt, in bronze, and of colossal magnitude. It is intended, as opportunity offers, to place the statues and monuments of other eminent men around the inclosed area of this handsome square, which is ornamented with shrubberies and walks, so that in process of time it will become a sort of open Pantheon, dedicated to the illustrious dead. Standing on the north side of the square, the spectator has before him one of the finest architectural vistas in the city. On the right, the bold spire of St. George's Church, 162 feet in height, catches the eye, surmounting a building, obviously too small for such a vast superstructure. Somewhat nearer, on the same side, is the Dissenting Chapel in which the celebrated Dr. Wardlaw officiates — an elegant building, of Grecian chasteness of conception. To the right and left a noble street, George's Street, extends for about half a mile, without presenting any other objects of especial interest. Looking to the south, the lofty colonnade of the Royal Exchange† appears, towards which imposing mass of building we shall now conduct the tourist. It stands in Queen Street, at the termination of Ingram Street, one of the finest openings in the city. This splendid fabric is built in the florid Corinthian

* It is somewhat unfortunate, that the plaid is placed on the wrong arm.

† The colonnade of the Royal Exchange is one of the boldest and most imposing architectural objects in the kingdom; and consists of a double range of fluted Corinthian pillars of great height. As a whole, the Royal Exchange of Glasgow is one of the most striking edifices in the empire, the general effect of which is grand and impressive, though some of the details may be liable to the objections of a refined criticism.

style of architecture, and is surmounted by a lantern, which forms one of the most conspicuous objects in the city. The News Room is one of the most striking apartments in the kingdom, about 100 feet long, by 40 broad, with a richly ornamented oval roof, supported by fluted Corinthian columns. The Royal Exchange is placed in the centre of a noble area, two sides of which are lined with splendid and uniform ranges of buildings, but simpler in design than the Exchange, and occupied as warehouses, shops, and counting-houses. Behind it is the Royal Bank, which is much admired by good judges, for the elegant simplicity and chasteness of its design. It is built after the model of a celebrated Greek temple. On each side of the Bank, two superb Doric arches, of bold and imposing character, afford access to Buchanan Street, also one of the principal streets in the city, in fact, the Regent Street of Glasgow. In front of the Royal Exchange has recently been placed, a colossal equestrian statue, in bronze, of the Duke of Wellington, executed by the Baron Marochetti, a French Artist. The countenance of the Duke, which is a portrait, possesses considerable calmness and dignity, but the head and neck of the horse are extravagantly overcharged with a theatrical air wholly inconsistent with elevated expression, while its body furnishes no bad example of the condition of the animal known to the veterinary surgeon as "hide-bound," a tension of the skin, rendering its movements stiff and painful, if not impracticable. The best part of the performance consists of the four elaborate alto relievos, representing the field of Waterloo, and three other designs, which adorn the four sides of the pedestal.

Proceeding down Queen Street, one of the great thoroughfares and most animated avenues in the city, a noble square of buildings will be observed in course of erection for the proprietors of the National Bank of Scotland, who are to occupy part of it as an office. When completed, it will be one of the most imposing ranges of buildings in the city. At its northern extremity, in the north-west corner of George's Square, is the terminus of the Edinburgh and Glasgow Railway, where the stranger emerges into the main artery of Glasgow, here called Argyle Street, but which bears

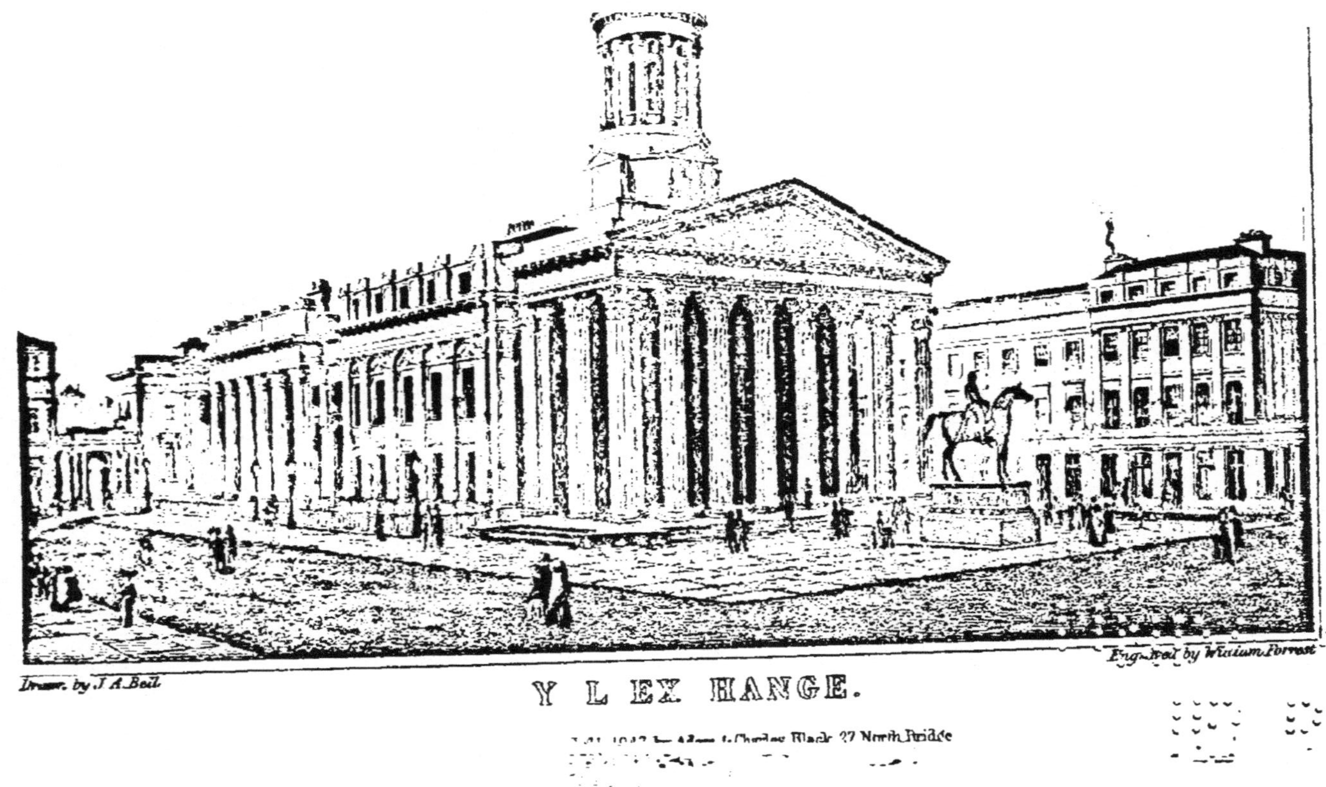

Drawn by J. A. Bell

Engraved by William Forrest

Y L EX HANGE.

[illegible] by Adam & Charles Black 27 North Bridge

the names of the Trongate and Gallowgate, towards its eastern extremities. Taking in the whole extent of this noble avenue, from east to west, it exhibits a continuation of street upwards of two miles in length.

Turning towards the east, the stranger finds himself involved in the bustle and animation of one of the most crowded thoroughfares in Europe, through which the stream of human existence flows at all hours of the day, and in all seasons, with undiminished volume and velocity. The general character of the buildings is plain, and there is no attempt at plan or uniformity of arrangement. An ancient tenement or two, with its narrow pointed gables and steep roofs, occasionally attracts the eye, and forms a fine contrast to the modern elegance of the shops below. On the left, a handsome entrance gives access to a covered Arcade, extending from this point to Buchanan Street, and containing numerous handsome shops, with a gay crowd of pedestrians at all hours. On the right, the first opening is Dunlop Street, containing the Theatre-Royal, a recent erection, but by no means very chaste or happy in its style. There was formerly a handsome theatre in Queen Street, which was destroyed by fire about ten years ago. Opposite is Miller Street, in which were formerly the stately mansions of the old Virginian merchants, but which are now occupied as places of business. Virginia Street, on the same side, is a narrow, but handsome thoroughfare, in which the City of Glasgow Bank, formerly occupied by the Union Bank of Scotland, is the most conspicuous building. It is built after the model of the Temple of Jupiter Stator at Rome, and is one of the most chaste and elegant buildings in the city. On the left, the next opening of any importance is Glassford Street, broad, and handsome in the style of its buildings, especially in that lately occupied as the Ship Bank. Here the new Post-Office is located, a plain but handsome structure, with no architectural pretensions, and greatly inferior in its public accommodations to the increasing wants of the community. In Wilson Street, one of the finest street vistas in the city, are located the New County Buildings, a splendid and imposing pile, of great extent, and of a character equally simple and majestic. Opposite Glassford Street, and running to the right towards the river, is the Stockwell, one of the oldest streets in the city. A few old tenements still show their venerable fronts here, but the remorseless march of improvement has recently swept away some of the finest. Sixty years ago, this was one of the chief avenues of the city, and the principal approach from the south, by the old bridge of Glasgow. Excepting Hutcheson Street, with its fine hospital of that name, at the upper end surmounted by an elegant tapering spire,* and Candleriggs Street, terminated by St. David's Church and Tower, and containing the New City Hall, one of the largest rooms in the kingdom, and capable of containing 4000 persons, the Bazaar, a large general market, covered in, and containing extensive accommodation—the stranger will pass several other streets of no great importance, and observe, on the right, a rather puny but venerable-looking spire, the Tron Steeple, which finely breaks the monotony of the long line of street which he has just traversed. On the right side, opposite the Candleriggs, is King Street, an old and well-frequented opening, containing the public markets for beef, mutton, fish, and vegetables, now nearly entirely disused. It terminates in the Bridgegate, a fine old street, irregular in its appearance, and of considerable breadth in some parts. An old steeple, of remarkably good proportions, rises up behind it, which anciently formed part of the building used as a hall for the merchants of Glasgow, but which has long ago been pulled down. Eighty years ago, this street was inhabited by the most respectable classes of citizens, and contained many handsome buildings. Many lanes or closes run off from it on either side, inhabited by a numerous and rather turbulent population, of the poorest classes. Some very old buildings are still to be found in

* This building is erected on the site of the old hospital, founded by two brothers, whose statues are placed in the front of the edifice, and who left considerable property for its support, chiefly in ground on the south side of the river, and on which the extensive suburb of Hutchesontown is built. A number of poor boys receive a gratis education from its funds, besides being supported otherwise. In Candleriggs Street are situate also the extensive wholesale and retail warehouses of the Messrs. Campbell, said to be one of the largest commercial establishments in the kingdom, and worthy of a visit, from the excellence of its interior arrangements.

these closes, whose appearance tells a tale of other times, but the dun and squalid character of its present occupants, does not invite a lengthened examination of these remnants of antiquity. Returning to the Trongate, a little further on is the Cross of Glasgow, forming a centre and termination to the Trongate, the Gallowgate, (a continuation of this street,) the High Street, and the Saltmarket. There is an equestrian statue of William the Third placed here, of no great merit as a work of art.

A noble range of building, (represented in the above cut,) with a superb piazza under it, extends in front, denominated the Tontine, from having been built upon that principle. There is a fine large News Room here, which was formerly known by the appellation of the Coffee-Room, and, until the New Exchange was erected, was the great focus of business and politics. The ancient jail of the burgh stood exactly at the corner of the High Street and Trongate. Criminals were executed formerly in front of this building. On its site a heavy, tasteless pile of buildings has been erected, occupied by shops and warehouses. The old Court-houses also stood here, but they have been removed to the New Jail buildings, at the foot of the Saltmarket. The Town-Hall, however, a fine apartment, containing portraits of some of the Scottish and English sovereigns, besides a very fine marble statue of William Pitt, by Chantrey, still remains. The Cross Steeple, too, a relic of the ancient civic splendour of this part of the city, and in itself an interesting object, survives still. Leaving the ancient Cross of Glasgow we next enter the Saltmarket, not now, alas ! as in the palmy days of Bailie Nicol Jarvie, the domicile of bailies, and other civic dignitaries, but occupied with a busy population of inferior shopkeepers and trades-people. The lower part, and some portions of the neighbourhood, form the Monmouth Street and Rag Fair of Glasgow, being chiefly occupied with furniture brokers and old clothes dealers. On the left is St. Andrew's Square, the buildings of which are characterized by an elegant simplicity and chaste regularity of architecture. The greater part of the area of this square is occupied with St. Andrew's Church, the largest, and, in many respects, the finest Church in the city, the portico of which, for lightness and elevation, is much admired. On the right is the Bridgegate, of which notice has already been taken. Here stood anciently several fine old buildings of some historical note ; in one of them Cromwell is said to have lodged when in Glasgow ; but, with many other ancient tenements in this street, it has long since fallen a victim to the progress of time and improvement. The stranger now emerges into a fine broad esplanade, with the Public Park or Green stretching away to the left, and the imposing pile of buildings forming the

Court-houses and Jail, on the right. These elegant buildings are in the Grecian style of architecture. The front is chaste and simple, but thought rather low for its length. From the vast increase of the city and its population, these buildings are now found to be deficient in extent, and an extensive range of building, as already noticed, has been erected in Wilson Street, for the purpose of affording suitable accommodation to the County and City Courts. On the right of the Court-houses is the river Clyde, crossed at this point by Hutcheson's Bridge, commenced in 1829, and finished in 1833. The design was given by Mr. Robert Stevenson of Edinburgh, the distinguished engineer of the Bell Rock Lighthouse. At the time when it was built the arches were the flattest that had ever been executed, being segments of a circle whose radius is 65 feet. The erection cost £22,000. A carriage drive extends around the Green, which is about two miles and a quarter in circumference. Passing up the Green, on the left, is the fine obelisk erected to the memory of Nelson, 143 feet in height. When the tide is at the full, the brimming waters of the Clyde appear at this point to great advantage, and there is a fine landscape view down the river, with the four bridges in the distance, and the variety of buildings, public and private, on the opposite banks. On the south side, vast ranges of chimneys appear, indicating the *locale* of some of the largest spinning and weaving factories in the city. The same appearances are beheld to the north-east, whilst, on the south and south-east appear, at a few miles' distance, the beautiful slopes of the Cathkin Braes, adorned with fine plantations, and gentlemen's seats. The Green is diversified with walks, some of which are shaded by noble rows of trees, and being the common property of the inhabitants, and much used for the washing and bleaching of clothes, there are several fountains of fine spring water, round which abundance of damsels may be seen clustering with their *boynes* and pitchers. The north side of this fine pleasure-ground, termed the Calton Green, rises a little, and has a handsome row of dwelling-houses lining one side of it, called Monteith Row, which, from their elevation and beauty of situation, are amongst the pleasantest in the city. Leaving the Green, (on the west and north surrounded for most of its length, by an iron railing,) by the North-west Gate, and crossing Charlotte Street, a quiet, dull-looking street, with some fine old mansions in it, we enter London Street, a broad and handsome avenue, but, considering its immediate vicinity to the Cross, the centre of the city, sorely bungled, being in a half-built and disgraceful state of dilapidation. Arrived again at the Cross, let us take a passing glance at the Gallowgate, the name of the eastern section of the main street of the city, which begins at this point. It is irregular, both in the appearance of its buildings and in its width, sometimes steep and narrow, broad, and winding. It contains large barracks for foot soldiers, and, near its easterly extremity, the Cattle-market, one of the most interesting sights of Glasgow. It occupies 30,000 square yards, and is admirably and even elegantly laid out, for its especial objects. The tower of St. John's Church is the most prominent feature in this part of the city, which, exhibiting no other objects of peculiar interest to a stranger, we shall return from this hasty sally, and proceed due north, up the ancient avenue of the High Street, which may be considered as the backbone of the skeleton of the old city.

The buildings in this fine old street are many of them venerable from their antiquity; but the presence of new ones on every side, indicates the rapid disappearance of the ancient characteristics of this part of the city. On every side, numerous *closes*, or narrow lanes, appear teeming with population, and alive with the hum and stir of active life. They are inhabited chiefly by the lower classes, and, in many of them, as well as in those in the Saltmarket and Bridgegate, the inmates are densely wedged together, which circumstance co-operating with other fatal causes, has tended to foster the elements of contagious diseases, and to lower the average duration of life of the poorer classes in the city. Proceeding up the street, and passing one or two inferior streets, there is on the right, a long range of venerable monastic-looking buildings, with a fine stone balcony in front. These are the buildings of the University, the external aspect of which harmonizes well with the grave purposes to which they are devoted. In the first of the three inner courts, there is a fine old staircase, much admired for its stately elegance. The buildings are old, and imposing in their appearance, but some of the older portions, having been taken down a few years ago, have been replaced by others of a character wholly foreign to the original style, thus marring the harmony, and disturbing the uniformity and propriety of the structure. Behind is the Hunterian Museum, a splendid edifice of the Grecian character.

It is understood that the College grounds and buildings have been, or are about to be purchased, by a railway company, for a terminus, and the College is to be rebuilt in a fine situation to the west of the city.

A little above the College is Duke Street, a fine opening to the east, and containing the City and County Bridewell, a large and striking mass of buildings in the old Saxon style of Architecture.* The High Street becomes here rather steep and narrow, with a considerable curve, and is called the Bell of the Brae. Here, in the year 1300, a severe action took place betwixt the English, commanded by Percy and Bishop Beik, and the Scots, by the Scottish champion—Wallace; in which the former were defeated with the loss of their commander. Within these thirty years, this part of the High Street contained the oldest and most curious-looking buildings in the city, but almost the whole of these ancient tenements have been pulled down, and replaced by others of the most ordinary character. At the top of this ascent, on the right, is the

* This establishment is justly celebrated for the superior excellence and economy of its arrangements and management. It contains ample accommodation and means of classification for nearly 300 prisoners, by whose labour its expenses are almost wholly defrayed. Each prisoner, it is calculated, costs the community no more than £1, 10s. per annum, so judicious is the system pursued.

Drygate, and on the left the Rottenrow; both of them very old streets, and still exhibiting sundry venerable-looking buildings, the relics of their ancient grandeur and importance. A few yards further we reach a large open space, containing in front, the Infirmary, a large and elegant building, of a composite character of architecture, and light and airy in appearance; and a little to the right, the huge mass of the Cathedral at once arrests and detains the eye of the stranger. Having already in the historical and introductory matter, briefly noticed this noble relic of antiquity, we shall merely observe farther, that it is surrounded by a vast churchyard, in which the bones of many generations rest from their labours; besides this, it contains a great many rich and ancient monumental tombs of the worthies of the old city, and the grave dignitaries of church and state in the days of other times.—The Glasgow Infirmary, including the recent additions made to it for a Fever Hospital, is a very large building. The extent of its accommodation may be inferred from the fact, that 6272 patients were admitted during the year 1837-1838. It bears a high character, not merely for the matured excellence of its arrangements, but the superior character of its medical school.* A building, in the worst possible taste, stands a little to the right of these two fine specimens of ancient and modern architecture, which is the Barony Church. Betwixt this eye-sore and the wall of the Cathedral burying-ground, which is lined with ancient sepulchral monuments, a narrow path conducts to the Bridge of Sighs, so called from its affording access to the new Glasgow Necropolis, anciently called the Fir Park. With a fine bold arch, the bridge spans the brawling rivulet, called the Molindinar Burn, which, after being collected into a small dam or lake, dashes briskly over an artificial cascade down a steep ravine, imparting a character of life and cheerfulness to a spot consecrated to the most solemn associations. The

* Its affairs are managed by twenty-five Directors, ten of whom are elected by the subscribers of two guineas a-year; the others are elected by the various public bodies of the city. The Members for the city are also *ex officio* Directors.

bold and rocky eminence which forms the Necropolis shoots suddenly up to the height of from 200 to 300 feet, forming, with its fine shrubberies, a noble background to the Cathedral. A splendid gateway, in the Italian style, appears in front, and the entire surface of the rock, bristling with columns, and every variety of monumental erection, some of them peculiarly happy and chaste in style, is divided into walks. The fine statue of Knox on the summit, and one erected to the memory of Mr. William M'Gavin, with the monument to the late Rev. Dr. Dick of Glasgow, are particularly conspicuous, and will instantly attract the eye of the stranger.* It is said to be intended ultimately to carry a tunnel through the hill from south to north, and to form galleries and chambers in the solid rock, so as to form a vast crypt, in addition to the cemetery above. From the summit, 250 feet above the level of the Clyde, the Great Reformer just mentioned looks grimly down on one of the most striking scenes that can well be imagined. The huge mass of the venerable Cathedral, surrounded by the crumbling remains and memorials of twenty-five generations, stands still and solemn at his feet, like the awful Genius of the Past; whilst the vast city stretches away in long lines and perspectives in every direction, intersected by the broad and brimming Clyde, and the uplands of Lanarkshire and Renfrewshire, with the Dumbartonshire and Argyleshire hills, forming a noble frame to the picture.† Descending from this elevated site, we shall retrace our steps down the High Street, and, striking to the right, enter George's Street, a broad and handsome opening, but, with the exception of the buildings of Anderson's University,

* Since these were erected, a marble statue of the late Mr. Charles Tennant of St. Rollox has been placed in the grounds, and a splendid mausoleum is in course of erection to the memory of Major Monteith, which, from the rich and florid style of its workmanship, and its bold imposing look and situation, will form one of the most striking objects in this noble garden of the dead.

† A little to the west of the Cathedral is the Asylum for the Blind, an establishment of great merit in its arrangements. The inmates are employed in various ways, and manufacture articles of use or ornament to a considerable extent, which are disposed of for the benefit of the institution. The new method of printing for the blind has been carried here to great perfection. Generally speaking, any respectable inn-keeper knows how to procure an order of admission for this and any other public institution in Glasgow.

which are respectable but plain in appearance, and the New High School behind them, a large building, equally devoid of architectural attraction, it offers no particular inducement to the tourist to linger on its pavements, and he now finds himself again in George's Square, ready, after brief repose, for

WALK SECOND.*

BUCHANAN STREET—VIEW FROM THE TOP OF ST. VINCENT STREET—WEST GEORGE STREET—REGENT STREET—BATH STREET—CLELAND TESTIMONIAL—LUNATIC ASYLUM—SAUCHIEHALL ROAD—GARNET HILL—FINE VIEW FROM THE TOP—WOODSIDE CRESCENT—BOTANIC GARDEN—ELMBANK CRESCENT—INDIA STREET—ST. VINCENT STREET—BLYTHSWOOD SQUARE.

TURNING to the right, and still continuing in George Street, now called West George Street, which, after passing round St. George's Church, continues its course for nearly half a mile further, till it is lost in Blythswood Square, the tourist enters Buchanan Street. Here it may be proper to observe, that four great lines of street run west from Buchanan Street, parallel to each other, two of them for nearly a mile in length—St. Vincent Street, West George Street, Regent Street, and Bath Street. The first and last named are the longest and finest. Turning north, we shall follow the easy ascent of Buchanan Street, and when at the top, we recommend a brief pause, to take a hasty look behind. The eye courses down the long vista of a spacious street, lined with handsome buildings, and in the lower half crowded with a gay population, for we have already mentioned that this is the Regent Street (London) of Glasgow. It is finely terminated by St. Enoch's Church, standing in the Square of that name; and beyond, in the distance, the green slopes of the Renfrewshire uplands appear above the houses, giving a rich and half rural character to the view. A few yards further on, we reach Sauchie-

* This walk is coloured *yellow* on the Map.

hall Street, or road, at the corner of which stands a handsome pile of buildings, denominated the Cleland Testimonial, from having been built and presented to the eminent statist of that name, by his friends in Glasgow, on his retirement from the public service of the city, after having been for many years superintendent of public works. From this point, the lofty dome of the New Town's Hospital, or Poor's House, meets the eye. This is one of the largest and finest buildings belonging to the city of Glasgow. From an octagonal centre four wings diverge, of three storeys in height, and the style of the whole building is impressive and striking. Its accommodation is very extensive, and the grounds contain about four acres.* Sauchiehall Road is lined with handsome rows of houses, and is very broad for the first half of its length. As the tourist proceeds, he finds, on the left, various handsome streets, opening into it from the south, forming part of the new town, and chiefly occupied by the wealthier classes. On the right, an elevated ridge accompanies him, containing many handsome villas, and intersected with streets. This is called Garnet Hill, and should be specially visited by the picturesque tourist, as it commands a noble view from its summit. To the north and north-west, bold ranges of hills appear at a few miles' distance ; and, faintly looming on the horizon, the lofty peaks of the Argyleshire and Perthshire mountains are seen ; nearer, the masts of vessels on the Forth and Clyde Canal appear, in the basin at Port-Dundas, with a rich undulating surface, crowded with villas, private dwellings, and the tall chimneys of numerous public works. Returning to Sauchiehall Street, the tourist arrives at Woodside Crescent, and is struck with surprise at the number and elegance of the fine streets, rows, and terraces, intermixed with ornamental shrubberies, which attract his eye. This part of the suburbs

* This building, formerly a Lunatic Asylum, has lately been purchased by the directors of the Town's Hospital, for the accommodation of the poor of the city. A new Lunatic Asylum is now erected to the west of the city, for which purpose sixty-six acres of land have been obtained, to meet the fast-growing popularity of this estimable institution. This new Asylum is an enormous pile of building, in the Saxo-Gothic style, and being happily placed on a rising ground, arrests the eye of the traveller as he approaches from the west.

is the most recently built, and is at present the most fashionable quarter for what are called self contained houses. In this neighbourhood was formerly the Royal Botanic Garden, which was recently removed to the great Western Road, about two miles from the city. It occupies a fine elevated situation, sloping down on the north to the waters of the Kelvin, whilst, on the south, the New Observatory stands out a conspicuous object, on a green swelling elevation of considerable height. Public promenades occur every week on the Saturday evenings of summer; admission, a sixpence, and at all times access can be had for the same money.

Retracing our steps, we shall strike down the first opening on the right, into Elmbank Crescent, a very handsome row of houses, but only half built. Passing through a new street just begun, called India Street, containing a few very handsome buildings, in the stately but somewhat stiff style of Louis the Fourteenth's time, the stranger finds himself at the western extremity of St. Vincent Street, here called Greenhill Place. Proceeding citywards, along this noble street, and ascending gradually, on the right is Blysthwood Square, the buildings of which, from their lofty position and elegant exterior, form one of the finest and most prominent objects to the stranger approaching Glasgow from the west. The view from this square, to the south and west, is very fine, but on the north, it is intercepted by the more commanding ridge of Garnet Hill. Returning to St. Vincent Street, the stranger finds himself descending gradually, with elegant masses of building on each side, and a noble street vista of great length before him. On the left is a handsome building, recently fitted up as a club-house, but there being no particular object to detain the eye, we shall suppose the tourist once more deposited in George's Square, in the north-west angle of which this noble opening has its termination.

WALK THIRD.*

INGRAM STREET — ASSEMBLY ROOMS — OLD BRIDGE OF GLASGOW — POOR'S HOUSE — CATHOLIC CHAPEL — CUSTOM HOUSE — GORBALS CHURCH—CARLTON PLACE—WOODEN OR SERVICE BRIDGE—GLASGOW BRIDGE—VIEW FROM BROOMIELAW—HARBOUR—SHIPPING, STEAM-VESSELS, ETC.—SUBURBS OF LAURIESTON, TRADESTON, AND HUTCHESONTOWN—BARONY OF GORBALS—PAISLEY CANAL.

LEAVING George Square again, and proceeding down Queen Street on the left, the eye glancing along Ingram Street, rests on the fine portico of the Assembly Rooms,† standing boldly forward, with the grave old College steeple in the distance, looking demurely down on the bustle and animation of this great business thoroughfare. A splendid pile of building has recently been erected at the west end of this street, opposite to the Exchange, intended for the British Linen Company's Bank. This range of building forms one of the most striking objects in the city. Entering Argyle Street once more, and threading our way eastward, through the busy crowd, to the Stockwell, we request the stranger to dash with us down this avenue towards the river, and there being no objects of any note on the route, but those which have been already seen and commented on, we find ourselves on the Old Bridge of Glasgow. This bridge was built in 1345, and was the first stone bridge erected in Glasgow. It has been twice widened, and the last time in a very elegant and ingenious manner, by adding footpaths, supported by cast-iron frames of a tasteful character, from a design by the late Mr. Telford. It is about to be taken down and rebuilt, the deepening of the river rendering this

* This walk is coloured *green* on the map.

† The Assembly Rooms is one of the finest edifices in the city, taken in connexion with the buildings on each side. The principal room—now converted into an Athenæum—is 80 feet long, 35 feet wide, and 27 in height, with a tastefully painted ceiling. Nearly opposite to the Assembly Rooms is the Union Bank of Scotland, recently erected, a fine building, though faulty in some of its details. The portico in front is surmounted by six colossal statues of allegorical personages.

necessary, as well as the interests of the river navigation. Looking up the stream, the back and one side of the Jail buildings are seen on the left, with the Green sloping beautifully down to the river. The view downwards is still finer: two bridges (the nearest, a very fine and perfectly level one, of wood, from a design by Mr. Stevenson of Edinburgh) span the glittering waters of the river. Next to it, is the Roman Catholic chapel, one of the most striking modern buildings in the Gothic style of architecture in the kingdom. It is of large dimensions, and is elegantly fitted up. Beyond it a little way is the New Custom-House, a respectable looking building. On the left bank of the river, the spire of the Gorbals Church breaks the uniformity of the outline in a pleasing manner, and two fine masses of buildings, East and West Carlton Place, from their simplicity, good taste, and happy elevation, confer a peculiar dignity upon this part of the river vista. Proceeding along this noble street, Glasgow or Broomielaw Bridge, designed by the late Mr. Telford, next demands the attention of the tasteful stranger. It is one of the finest bridges in Europe—500 feet in length, and sixty feet wide, being seven feet wider than London Bridge. It is cased with Aberdeen granite, and consists of seven arches, whilst the curve is so slight as scarcely to be observed. It forms a superb entrance to the city from the south, and from it one of the finest river harbour views in the United Kingdom may be obtained. To the south, a fine broad avenue stretches away till it is lost in the country. On the right is the Broomielaw Street, at least a mile long, with a fine ample margin to the river, and long ranges of covered sheds, and other harbour appurtenances. A noble basin, from three to four hundred feet wide and about a mile in length, with its range of quays, is before the eye, crowded with vessels of every description, from eight hundred tons burden to the smallest coasting craft, whilst steam-vessels are perpetually sending up clouds of smoke or steam, and dashing in or out with a startling velocity and noise.

Crossing the river,* the stranger will admire the spacious and elegant streets which, as he walks along, strike his eye. Portland Street is nearly a mile in length, very broad, and lined with handsome buildings. The population on this side of the river, is understood to be about 60,000, located in Laurieston Tradeston, and Hutchesontown, all in the Barony of Gorbals. The terminus of the Ayr, Paisley, and Greenock Railway is on this side, close to Glasgow Bridge, and, half a mile to the south, is the basin of the Johnstone and Paisley Canal ; to which places light and swift passage-boats depart, almost every hour, during the summer. Arrived at the old bridge of Glasgow again, the stranger, before crossing, will probably cast one lingering look on the river, and noble view on either side, after which, retracing his steps up Stockwell Street, he may, if he please, return to George's Square, by Glassford Street, Ingram Street, and the Royal Exchange, thus passing through the most crowded and interesting business thoroughfares of the city.

* There are always several steam-vessels of the largest class lying in the river to get in their machinery, and there is a powerful crane, capable of raising thirty tons, for lifting the heavy boilers, &c. on board; a much larger one is preparing, expected to be the most powerful in Britain. Glasgow has attained great celebrity as a manufactory of marine steam-engines, and, indeed, of machinery of every description. The depth of water at the Broomielaw at spring tides is now from 14 to 16 feet, and it is proposed by the Trustees of the harbour and river, to deepen to the extent of 20 feet at neap tides, no obstacles existing, according to the report of the engineer, to prevent such a result being obtained. It is also intended to widen the river, for ten or twelve miles down, to from 300 to 400 feet wide, the width to increase downwards; to bevel off the banks on either side, and to remove every other obstacle to the freedom of the navigation; so that, in a few years, with wet docks, for which a large space of ground on the south side, immediately below the suburb of Tradeston, has recently been purchased, Glasgow will possess one of the most spacious and convenient harbours in the kingdom. From July 1837 to July 1838, 4600 sailing vessels of every description, arrived and departed from the harbour, with a tonnage of 214,471 tons; and the steam tonnage on the river during the same period was 731,028 tons; these latter vessels made 7850 trips in the same time. The revenue from the harbour and river in 1839 was £43,287, 16s. 10d.; customs levied in 1839, £468,974, 12s. 2d.; and post-office revenue, £47,527, 7s. 7d.

SEVENTH TOUR.

GLASGOW—HAMILTON—BOTHWELL CASTLE AND BRIDGE—LANARK—FALLS OF CLYDE.

CALEDONIAN RAILWAY.—GLASGOW AND HAMILTON SECTION.

MILES.	STATIONS.
	Glasgow, South Side.
2	Rutherglen.
4	Cambuslang.
7½	Blantyre.
10	Hamilton.

This tour may conveniently be made by the Caledonian Railway Branch line to Hamilton, from which the tourist may proceed on foot to visit Bothwell Castle, Bothwell Bridge, and Hamilton Palace. He may then walk through the Duke of Hamilton's grounds for about two miles, and, crossing the Clyde, reach Motherwell Station, on the main line, 16 miles from Glasgow. From thence he is carried on by Carluke to Lanark, 29 miles from Glasgow. From Lanark—after visiting the Falls of Clyde—he may proceed by railway to Edinburgh, to Glasgow, or to Carlisle.

The Falls may also be conveniently visited from Edinburgh, taking the Caledonian Railway to Lanark, (30 miles), and afterwards either returning to Edinburgh, or reversing the route above described.

LEAVING Glasgow by the railway the train proceeds eastward by Rutherglen and Blantyre, to

HAMILTON

[*Inns*:—Bruce Arms.]
Omnibus to Railway Station.

Hamilton is the capital of the Middle Ward of Lanarkshire, and a burgh of regality, dependent on the Duke of Hamilton; it contains about 6000 inhabitants, of whom a considerable

SEVENTH TOUR.

GLASGOW to HAMILTON, LANARK, & THE FALLS OF CLYDE.

Riv. Clyde
Hyndford
Bonnington Ho.
Bonnington Linn
Corra Linn
LANARK
New Lanark
Stonebyres Linn
Carluke
Dalserf
Hamilton
Bothwell
Blantyre
Cambuslang
Rutherglen

EIGHTH TOUR.

GLASGOW, DUMBARTON, HELENSBURGH GREENOCK, DUNOON, ROTHSAY.

Govan
Partick
Renfrew
Kilpatrick
Dumbarton
Port Glasgow
Helensburgh
GREENOCK
Gourock
Dunoon
Inverkip
Rothsay

number are engaged in weaving. The town has been much improved by the recent erection of a new bridge, called Cadzow Bridge, opening into a street of the same name. The principal object of attraction, in this vicinity, is Hamilton Palace, the seat of the Duke of Hamilton, which stands on a plain between the town and the river. It is a magnificent structure, and has been greatly enlarged and improved by the present Duke. Its interior is extremely splendid, and contains a magnificent collection of paintings, supposed to be the best in Scotland. The most celebrated of these is *Daniel in the Lions' Den*, by Rubens.* Among other curiosities, Hamilton Palace contains the carbine with which Bothwellhaugh shot the Regent Murray.

Near Hamilton is the river Avon, a tributary of the Clyde. The vale which this stream waters is adorned with gorgeous old wood, and several ancient and modern mansions, the most famous of which is Cadyow or Cadzow Castle, the ancient baronial residence of the family of Hamilton, situated upon the precipitous banks of the Avon, about two miles above its junction with the Clyde. It was dismantled in the conclusion of the civil wars, during the reign of the unfortunate Mary. The situation of the ruins, embosomed in wood, darkened by ivy and creeping shrubs, and overhanging the brawling torrent, is romantic in the highest degree. In the immediate vicinity of Cadyow is a grove of immense oaks, the remains of the Caledonian forest, which anciently extended through the south of Scotland,

* On this splendid picture Wordsworth has composed the following sonnet :—

"Amid a fertile region, green with wood
And fresh with rivers, well doth it become
The ducal Owner, in his palace-home
To naturalize this tawny Lion brood;
Children of Art, that claim strange brotherhood
(Couched in their den) with those that roam at large
Over the burning wilderness, and charge
The wind with terror while they roar for food.
Satiate are *these*; and still—to eye and ear:
Hence, while we gaze, a more enduring fear!
Yet is the Prophet calm, nor would the cave
Daunt him—if his companions now be-drowsed,
Outstretched and listless, were by hunger roused:
Man placed him here, and God, he knows, can save."

from the Eastern to the Atlantic Ocean. Some of these trees measure twenty-five feet and upwards in circumference, and the state of decay in which they now appear, shows that they may have witnessed the rites of the Druids. The whole scenery is included in the magnificent park of the Duke of Hamilton. The famous breed of Scottish wild cattle, milk-white in colour, with black muzzles, horns, and hoofs, are still preserved in this forest. They were expelled about 1760, on account of their ferocity, but have since been restored.* The following description of their habits is abridged from an article, by the Rev. W. Patrick, in the Quarterly Journal of Agriculture :—

"I am inclined to believe that the Hamilton breed of cattle is the oldest in Scotland, or perhaps in Britain. Although Lord Tankerville has said they have 'no wild habits,' I am convinced from personal observation, that this is one of their peculiar features. In browsing their extensive pasture, they always keep close together, never scattering or straggling over it, a peculiarity which does not belong to the Kyloe, or any other breed, from the wildest or most inhospitable regions of the Highlands. The white cows are also remarkable for their systematic manner of feeding. At different periods of the year their tactics are different, but by those acquainted with their habits they are always found about the same part of the forest at the same hour of the day. In the height of summer, they always bivouac for the night towards the northern extremity of the forest; from this point they start in the morning, and browse to the southern extremity, and return at sunset to their old rendezvous; and during these perambulations they always feed *en masse*.

"The bulls are seldom ill-natured, but when they are so, they display a disposition more than ordinarily savage, cunning, pertinacious, and revengeful. A poor bird-catcher, when exercising his vocation among the 'Old Oaks,' as the park is familiarly called, chanced to be attacked by a savage bull. By great exertion he gained a tree before his assailant made up to him. Here he had occasion to observe the habits of the animal. It did not roar or bellow, but

SCOTTISH WILD OX.

* See notes to the ballad of Cadyow Castle, in the Border Minstrelsy.

merely grunted, the whole body quivered with passion and savage rage, and he frequently attacked the tree with his head and hoofs. Finding all to no purpose, he left off the vain attempt, began to browse, and removed to some distance from the tree. The bird-catcher tried to descend, but this watchful Cerberus was again instantly at his post, and it was not till after six hours' imprisonment, and various bouts at 'bo-peep' as above, that the unfortunate man was relieved by some shepherds with their dogs. A writer's apprentice, who had been at the village of Quarter on business, and who returned by the 'Oaks' as a 'near-hand cut,' was also attacked by one of these savage brutes, near the northern extremity of the forest. He was fortunate, however, in getting up a tree, but was watched by the bull, and kept there during the whole of the night, and till near two o'clock next day.

"These animals are never taken and killed like other cattle, but are always shot in the field. I once went to see a bull and some cows destroyed in this manner—not by any means for the sake of the sight—but to observe the manner and habits of the animal under peculiar circumstances. When the shooters approached, they, as usual, scampered off in a body, then stood still, tossed their heads on high, and seemed to snuff the wind; the manœuvre was often repeated, till they got so hard pressed, (and seemingly having a sort of half-idea of the tragedy which was to be performed,) they at length ran furiously in a mass, always preferring the sides of the fence and sheltered situations, and dexterously taking advantage of any inequality in the ground, or other circumstances, to conceal themselves from the assailing foe. In their flight, the bulls, or stronger of the flock, always took the lead; a smoke ascended from them which could be seen at a great distance; and they were often so close together, like sheep, that a carpet would have covered them. The cows which had young, on the first 'tug of war,' all retreated to the thickets where their calves were concealed; from prudential motives, they are never, if possible, molested. These and other wild habits I can testify to be inherent in the race, and are well known to all who have an opportunity of acquainting themselves with them."

Sir Walter Scott has made Cadyow Castle the subject of the following magnificent ballad, the perusal of which must gratify every lover of poetry and of historical recollections:—

"'Tis night—the shade of keep and spire
  Obscurely dance on Evan's stream;
And on the wave the warder's fire
  Is chequering the moonlight beam.

Fades slow their light; the east is grey:
  The weary warder leaves his tower;
Steeds snort; uncoupled stag-hounds bay,
  And merry hunters quit the bower.

The draw-bridge falls—they hurry out—
  Clatters each plank and swinging chain,
As, dashing o'er, the jovial rout
  Urge the shy steed, and slack the rein.

First of his troop, the chief rode on;
  His shouting merry-men throng behind;
The steed of princely Hamilton
  Was fleeter than the mountain wind.

From

From the thick copse the roe-bucks bound,
 The startled red-deer scuds the plain,
For the hoarse bugle's warrior-sound
 Has roused their mountain haunts again.

Through the huge oaks of Evandale,
 Whose limbs a thousand years have worn,
What sullen roar comes down the gale,
 And drowns the hunter's pealing horn?

Mightiest of all the beasts of chase,
 That roam in woody Caledon,
Crashing the forest in his race,
 The Mountain Bull comes thundering on!

Fierce, on the hunter's quiver'd band,
 He rolls his eyes of swarthy glow,
Spurns, with black hoof and horn, the sand,
 And tosses high his mane of snow.

Aim'd well, the chieftain's lance has flown;
 Struggling in blood, the savage lies;
His roar is sunk in hollow groan—
 Sound, merry huntsmen! sound the *pryse!* *

Tis noon—against the knotted oak
 The hunters rest the idle spear;
Curls through the trees the slender smoke,
 Where yeomen dight the woodland cheer.

Proudly the chieftain mark'd his clan,
 On greenwood lap all careless thrown,
Yet miss'd his eye the boldest man,
 That bore the name of Hamilton.

'Why fills not Bothwellhaugh his place,
 Still wont our weal and woe to share?
Why comes he not our sport to grace?
 Why shares he not our hunter's fare?'—

Stern Claud replied, with darkening face,
 (Grey Paisley's haughty lord was he,)
'At merry feast, or buxom chase,
 No more the warrior wilt thou see.

'Few suns have set since Woodhouselee
 Saw Bothwellhaugh's bright goblets foam,
When to his hearth, in social glee,
 The war-worn soldier turn'd him home.

'There, wan from her maternal throes,
 His Margaret, beautiful and mild,
Sate in her bower, a pallid rose,
 And peaceful nursed her new-born child.

'O change accursed! past are those days;
 False Murray's ruthless spoilers came,
And, for the hearth's domestic blaze,
 Ascends destruction's volumed flame.

'What sheeted phantom wanders wild,
 Where mountain Eske through woodland flows,
Her arms enfold a shadowy child—
 Oh, is it she, the pallid rose?

'The wilder'd traveller sees her glide,
 And hears her feeble voice with awe—
"Revenge," she cries, "on Murray's pride!
 And woe for injured Bothwellhaugh!"'

He ceased—and cries of rage and grief
 Burst mingling from the kindred band,
And half arose the kindling chief,
 And half unsheathed his Arran brand.

But who, o'er bush, o'er stream and rock,
 Rides headlong with resistless speed,
Whose bloody poniard's frantic stroke
 Drives to the leap his jaded steed?

Whose cheek is pale, whose eye-balls glare,
 As one some vision'd sight that saw;
Whose hands are bloody, loose his hair?—
 'Tis he! 'tis he! 'tis Bothwellhaugh!

From gory selle † and reeling steed
 Sprung the fierce horseman with a bound,
And, reeking from the recent deed,
 He dash'd his carbine on the ground.

Sternly he spoke—''Tis sweet to hear
 In good greenwood the bugle blown,
But sweeter to Revenge's ear
 To drink a tyrant's dying groan.

'Your slaughter'd quarry proudly trode,
 At dawning morn, o'er dale and down,
But prouder base-born Murray rode
 Through old Linlithgow's crowded town

'From the wild Border's humbled side
 In haughty triumph marched he,
While Knox relax'd his bigot pride,
 And smiled the traitorous pomp to see.

'But can stern Power, with all his vaunt,
 Or Pomp, with all her courtly glare,
The settled heart of Vengeance daunt,
 Or change the purpose of Despair?

'With hackbut bent, ‡ my secret stand,
 Dark as the purposed deed, I chose,
And mark'd, where, mingling in his band,
 Troop'd Scottish pikes, and English bows.

'Dark Morton, girt with many a spear,
 Murder's foul minion, led the van;
And clash'd their broad-swords in the rear
 The wild Macfarlanes' plaided clan.

'Glencairn and stout Parkhead were nigh,
 Obsequious at their regent's rein,
And haggard Lindesay's iron eye,
 That saw fair Mary weep in vain.

'Mid pennon'd spears, a steely grove,
 Proud Murray's plumage floated high;
Scarce could his trampling charger move,
 So close the minions crowded nigh.

'From the raised visor's shade his eye,
 Dark-rolling, glanced the ranks along,
And his steel truncheon, waved on high,
 Seem'd marshalling the iron throng.

'But yet his sadden'd brow confess'd
 A passing shade of doubt and awe;
Some fiend was whispering in his breast,
 "Beware of injured Bothwellhaugh!"

* The note blown at the death of the game.

† Saddle. A word used by Spencer, and other ancient authors.

‡ Gun cocked.

'The death-shot parts—the charger springs—
Wild rises tumult's startling roar!
And Murray's plumy helmet rings—
Rings on the ground to rise no more.

'What joy the raptured youth can feel,
To hear her love the loved one tell,—
Or he who broaches on his steel
The wolf, by whom his infant fell!

'But dearer to my injured eye,
To see in dust proud Murray roll;
And mine was ten times treble joy
To hear him groan his felon soul.

'My Margaret's spectre glided near:
With pride her bleeding victim saw;
And shriek'd in his death-deafen'd ear,
"Remember injured Bothwellhaugh!"

'Then speed thee, noble Chaterherault!
Spread to the wind thy banner'd tree!
Each warrior bend his Clydesdale bow—
Murray is fallen, and Scotland free.'

Vaults every warrior to his steed;
Loud bugles join their wild acclaim—
'Murray is fallen, and Scotland freed!
Couch Arran! couch thy spear of flame!'"

Opposite Cadyow is Chatelherault, built by the Duke of Hamilton, without regard to interior comfort, as a representation of the beautiful edifice on the estate and dukedom of the same name in France, possessed, in ancient times, by his Grace's ancestors.*

A mile and a half from Hamilton the Clyde is crossed by

BOTHWELL BRIDGE,

The scene of the famous battle which took place in 1679, between the Royal forces, under the Duke of Monmouth, and the Covenanters. The Royal army moved towards Hamilton, and reached Bothwell-moor on the 22d of June. The insurgents were encamped chiefly in the Duke of Hamilton's park, along the Clyde, which separated the two armies. Bothwell Bridge was then long and narrow, having a portal in the middle, with gates, which the Covenanters shut and barricadoed with stones and loads of timber. This important post was defended by 300 of their best men, under Hackston of Rathillet and Hall of Haughhead. The more moderate of the insurgents waited upon Monmouth, to offer terms, and obtained a promise that he would interpose with his Majesty in their behalf, on condition of their immediately dispersing themselves, and yielding up their arms. The Cameronian party, however, would accede to no terms with an uncovenanted king, and, while they were debating on the Duke's proposal, his field pieces

* The banks of the south Calder, which lie at no great distance from Hamilton, are extremely romantic, and adorned with a number of fine seats, the most remarkable of which are Wishaw Castle, (Lord Belhaven,) Coltness, (Henry Houldsworth Esq.,) Murdieston, (Admiral Sir A. Inglis Cochrane,) Allanton, (Sir Henry Steuart, Bart.) &c.

were already planted on the eastern side of the river, to cover the attack of the foot-guards, who were led on by Lord Livingstone, to force the bridge. Here Hackston maintained his post with zeal and courage, nor was it until all his ammunition was expended, and every support denied him by the general, that he reluctantly abandoned the important pass. When his party were drawn back, the Duke's army, with their cannon in front, slowly defiled along the bridge, and formed in line of battle as they came over the river. The Duke commanded the foot, and Claverhouse the Cavalry. It would seem that these movements could not have been performed without at least some loss, had the enemy been serious in opposing them. But the insurgents were otherwise employed. With the strangest delusion that ever fell upon devoted beings, they chose these precious moments to cashier their officers, and elect others in their room. In this important operation, they were at length disturbed by the Duke's cannon, at the very first discharge of which, the horse of the Covenanters wheeled and rode off, breaking and trampling down the ranks of the infantry in their flight. Monmouth humanely issued orders to stop the effusion of blood, but Claverhouse, burning to avenge his defeat, and the death of his cornet and kinsman, at Drumclog, made great slaughter among the fugitives, of whom 400 were slain. These events are thus described in *Clyde*, a poem by Wilson, reprinted in *Scottish Descriptive Poems*, edited by Dr. Leyden, Edinburgh, 1803 :—

"Where Bothwell's Bridge connects the margin steep,
And Clyde below runs silent, strong, and deep,
The hardy peasant, by oppression driven
To battle, deem'd his cause the cause of Heaven;
Unskill'd in arms, with useless courage stood,
While gentle Monmouth grieved to shed his blood;
But fierce Dundee, inflamed with deadly hate,
In vengeance for the great Montrose's fate,
Set loose the sword, and to the hero's shade
A barbarous hecatomb of victims paid." *

* See notes to the ballad of "The Battle of Bothwell Bridge," in the Border Minstrelsy. The reader cannot but remember the spirited description given of this engagement in the novel of Old Mortality.

Many of the fugitives found shelter in the wooded parks around Hamilton Palace.

Great changes have now been made on the scene of the engagement. The gateway, gate, and house of the bridge-ward were long ago removed. The original breadth of the bridge was twelve feet; but, in 1826, twenty-two feet were added to its breadth, the hollow which once lay at the Hamilton extremity was filled up, and an alteration was also made in the road, at the other end. The open park in which the Covenanters were posted, is now changed into enclosed fields and plantations, and the moor upon which the royal army advanced to the engagement, is now a cultivated and beautiful region.

The level grounds, which stretch away from Bothwell Bridge along the north-east bank of the river, once formed the patrimonial estate of Hamilton of Bothwellhaugh, the assassin of the Regent Murray.

A little farther on are Bothwell village and church. The old church, part of which is still standing, is the remains of an ancient Gothic fabric, cased all over with a thin coating of stone. Within its walls, the unfortunate Robert Duke of Rothesay, who was afterwards starved to death by his uncle the Duke of Albany, in Falkland Palace, was married to a daughter of Archibald the Grim, Earl of Douglas.

About a mile and half onwards are the magnificent ruins of

BOTHWELL CASTLE.

This noble structure is built of red freestone, and consists of a large oblong quadrangle, flanked, towards the south, by two huge circular towers, and covering an area of 234 feet in length, and ninety-nine feet in breadth. The origin of the castle is unknown, and its name was unheard of, until the time of Wallace, when it is said to have belonged to Sir Andrew Murray of Bothwell, who, with Lord William Douglas, was the first nobleman to join the Scottish hero in the assertion of his country's independence, and the last to forsake him after the failure of his patriotic attempt. After Murray's outlawry his estate of Bothwell was for-

BOTHWELL CASTLE.

feited, and conferred by Edward I. on Aylmer de Valence, second Earl of Pembroke, commander of his forces in Scotland. In this fortress a number of the English nobility took refuge after the battle of Bannockburn, but were speedily obliged to surrender. Bruce bestowed Bothwell Castle on Andrew Murray who had married that monarch's sister. It next came into the possession of Archibald the Grim, Earl of Douglas, who married the granddaughter of Andrew Murray. After the forfeiture of the Douglases in 1445, it was successively possessed by the Crichtons, John Ramsay, a favourite of James III., and the Hepburns, Earls of Bothwell. After the forfeiture of the infamous nobleman of that name, it passed through several hands, till it at last reverted to the noble family of Douglas. The present residence of Lord Douglas is a plain mansion, standing on a beautiful lawn, near the old castle. It was built by the young Earl of Forfar, who was killed at the battle of Sheriffmuir.* The scenery around Bothwell Castle is remarkably splendid, and is adorned with luxuriant natural wood. The Clyde here makes a beautiful sweep, and forms the fine semicircular declivity called Bothwell Bank, celebrated in Scottish song. The following interesting anecdote, quoted from a work entitled "Verstegan's Restitution of Decayed Intelligence," printed at Antwerp in 1605, is a proof of the antiquity of at least the air to which the song of "Bothwell Bank" is sung :—

"So fell it out of late years, that an English gentleman, travelling in Palestine, not far from Jerusalem, as he passed through a country town, he heard, by chance, a woman sitting at her door dandling her child, to sing, *Bothwell Bank, thou blumest fair*. The gentleman hereat wondered, and forthwith, in English, saluted the woman, who joyfully answered him, and said, she was right glad there to see a gentleman of our isle; and told him that she was a Scottish woman, and came first from Scotland to Venice, and from Venice thither, where her fortune was to be the wife of an officer under the Turk; who being at that instant absent, and very soon to return, she entreated the gentleman to stay there until his return. The which he did; and she, for country sake, to show herself the more kind and bountiful unto him, told her husband, at his homecoming, that the gentleman was her kinsman; whereupon her husband entertained him very kindly, and, at his departure, gave him diverse things of good value."

Directly opposite to Bothwell Castle, on the south bank of the Clyde, are the ruins of Blantyre Priory, situated on the brink of a perpendicular rock.

Leaving Hamilton, the tourist may proceed to Motherwell Station of the Caledonian Railway, two miles distant, and by rail be carried on to Lanark; or he may pursue the road along the river side. Adopting the latter plan, he crosses the Avon half a mile from Hamilton. On the opposite bank of the Clyde is Dalziel House, surrounded by fine plantations, giving an imposing effect to the landscape. The views now obtained of the river and the surrounding scenery are extremely fine. About a mile beyond Avon Bridge, the road strikes off the Carlisle road, leading towards Douglasdale, and gradually descending towards the margin of the river. On the opposite bank is Cambusnethan, (Lockhart, Esq.,) a fine castellated mansion, seated on a beautiful lawn, partly shaded by splendid lime trees. This district, which has earned the name of "The Orchard of Scotland," or "The Fruit Lands," is eminently worthy of its appellation, presenting, as it does, "one uninterrupted series of grove, garden, and orchard—a billowy ocean of foliage, waving in the summer wind, and glowing under the summer sun." During spring, the luxuriance of the blossom, and during autumn, the teeming abundance of the fruit, contribute to render this one of the most delightful drives in Scotland. Six miles from Hamilton, the Edinburgh road to Ayr crosses the Clyde at Garrion Bridge, which derives its name from a seat of Lord Belhaven's, in the immediate vicinity. A mile beyond, is the delightful bower-like village of Dalserf, celebrated for its excellent orchards. On the left is Dalserf House, (Campbell,) and, on the right, Millburn House, (Watkins, Esq.) On the opposite bank of the river is Brownlee, (Harvie, Esq.,) and the stately mansion of Mauldslie Castle, the seat of the last Earl of Hyndford.* A little farther on is Milton-Lockhart, (W. Lockhart, Esq., M.P.,) a handsome edifice in the Tudor style, standing on a fine promontory, with delightful sloping banks and gardens; and Waygateshaw, (Steel, Esq.,) once the residence of the notorious Major Weir and his sister, condemned for witchcraft in the seventeenth century. Two miles and a half beyond Dalserf, the tourist crosses the river Nethan, at Nethanfoot, by a bridge. On the right, near the junction of the Nethan and the Clyde, are the ruins of the Castle of Craignethan, or Draphane, situated on a single rock, overhanging the former stream. Craignethan appears to have been, at one time, a most extensive and important fortress. It was the seat of Sir James Hamilton, called the Bastard of Arran, a man noted for his sanguinary character, in the reign of James V.; and here Queen Mary lodged for a few days, after her escape from Lochleven. Craignethan has furnished the author of "Old Mortality" with his description of Tillietudlem.† It is now the property of Lord Douglas. The scenery around the castle exhibits a striking mixture of the sublime and beautiful. A short way beyond, on the north bank of the river is Carfin House, (Nisbet, Esq.,) and, soon after, the road enters the plantations of Stonebyres, (Monteith, Esq.) The channel of the river now

* Robert Bruce granted ten merks sterling out of his mills at Mauldslie for the purpose of keeping a lamp constantly burning upon St. Machute's tomb at Lesmahagow. The lamp was kept burning till the Reformation.

† "One morning, during his visit to Bothwell, was spent on an excursion to the ruins of Craignethan Castle, when the poet expressed such rapture with the scenery, that his hosts urged him to accept, for his lifetime, the use of a small habitable house, enclosed within the circuit of the ancient walls."—*Lockhart's Life of Scott*, v. i., p. 307.

becomes rugged and confined, and the banks more precipitous; and, in a short time, the tourist reaches **THE FALL OF STONEBYRES**, the first of

THE FALLS OF THE CLYDE,

in approaching from the west * The river here makes three distinct falls, being broken by two projecting rocks. The scene is uncommonly magnificent.†

Passing, on the left, Sunnyside Lodge, (A. Gillespie, Esq.,) and, on the right, Kirkfield, (Steel, Esq.,) and other elegant villas, the tourist, at the distance of a mile from the fall of Stonebyres, crosses the Clyde by an ancient bridge of three arches.

Twenty-five miles from Glasgow, and thirty-two from Edinburgh, is the county town and royal burgh of

LANARK.‡

[*Inns:* The Clydesdale.]
Coach to Douglas. Omnibus to the Railway Station.

Lanark is a town of no great importance in itself; till lately it was extremely dull, but the extension of the cotton-works

* The approach is by a path laid out by the well known Robert Owen.

† An interesting spectacle is afforded by the efforts of the salmon, during the spawning season, to surmount this obstacle to their further progress. It is scarcely necessary to say that these efforts are quite unavailing.

‡ It is said that the burgh of Lanark was till very recent times so poor that the single butcher of the town, who also exercised the calling of a weaver, in order to fill up his spare time, would never venture upon the speculation of killing a sheep till every part of the animal was ordered beforehand. When he felt disposed to engage in such an enterprise, he usually prevailed upon the minister, the provost, and the town-council to take shares! but when no person came forward to bespeak the fourth quarter, the sheep received a respite till better times should cast up. The bellman or *skellyman*, as he is there called, used often to go through the streets of Lanark with advertisements such as are embodied in the following popular rhyme:—

Bell-ell-ell!
There's a fat sheep to kill!
A leg for the provost,
  Another for the priest,
The bailies and deacons
  They'll tak the neist;
And if the fourth leg we cannot sell,
The sheep it maun leeve and gae back to the hill!

CHAMBERS' *Rhymes of Scotland*, p. 140.

F OF THE E AT STONEBYRES.

in its neighbourhood, and the erection of several good public buildings, have considerably improved its appearance; while its vicinity to the falls of Clyde, and its accessability from all quarters by means of the Caledonian Railway, make it a favourite place of resort for strangers during the summer months. It was in Lanark that the Scottish hero Wallace commenced his glorious exertions to free his country from a foreign yoke, and tradition points out a number of localities in the vicinity, identified with his name and exploits.* A statue of the hero is placed in a niche above the principal entrance to the parish church.

About a quarter of a mile to the east of the town, are the ruins of the very ancient church of Lanark, surrounded by the parish burying-ground.

There are a number of handsome seats in the neighbourhood of Lanark, the most splendid of which are Carstairs House, the seat of Henry Monteith, Esq., and Lee House, the seat of Sir Norman Macdonald Lockhart, Bart.

In visiting the Falls of Clyde from Lanark, the tourist should at once proceed to the uppermost, called BONNINGTON LINN, two miles from Lanark. A romantic path leads to it, through the grounds of Bonnington House, (Sir Charles Ross.) Above this cataract the river moves very slowly, but all at once it bends towards the north-east, and throws itself over a perpendicular rock of about thirty feet, into a deep hollow or basin. A dense mist continually hovers over this boiling caldron. Immediately below the first fall, the river hurries along with prodigious rapidity, boiling and foaming over its narrow and rocky channel. The banks

* Here "Wallace had many frays with Englishmen; but his first serious exploit, according to the Minstrel and general historical tradition, was the killing of young Selby, the son of the English constable of Dundee. Wallace was walking along the street, sprucely dressed in green, when Selby, a swaggering youth, came up to him with three or four companions. 'Abide, Scot,' he cried; 'who grathed you, I would like to know, in so gay a weed; an Irish cloak on your back, a Scots whittle in your belt, and rough rulzions on your feet, were fitter for your kind to wear. I will have that knife from you.' He made a step as if to take the knife, when Wallace drew it, grasped him by the collar, and ran it into him. Ere he could be seized by Selby's companions he escaped."

are very steep, and, at one point, the river struggles through a chasm of not more than four feet, where it may be stepped over. Half a mile below Bonnington Linn is CORRA LINN, the grandest of the falls, where the river takes three distinct leaps, making altogether a height of about eighty-four feet. The best view of this magnificent fall, is from the semicircular seat on the verge of the cliff opposite. There is also a rustic staircase, leading to the bottom of the Falls, partly formed of wood, and partly cut out of the solid rock, from which the cataract has a very magnificent effect. Above is a pavilion, erected in 1708, by Sir James Carmichael, then of Bonnington, which commands a fine view, and which is fitted up with mirrors, so arranged as to give the cataract the appearance of being precipitated upon the spectator. Upon a rock above the fall, on the opposite side of the river, is the old Castle of Cora; and, to the right of this castle, is Cora House, the seat of the late George Cranstoun, Esq., half hid by trees.

About half a mile below Corra Linn is the celebrated village of New Lanark, originally established in the year 1783 by the benevolent David Dale of Glasgow, father-in-law of Robert Owen. The inhabitants, who amount to about 2500, are exclusively engaged in cotton-spinning.

In Bonnington House are preserved two relics of Sir William Wallace, a portrait of the hero, and a very curious chair on which he is said to have sat.

No traveller should leave this district without visiting Cartland Crags on Mouse Water, about a mile west from Lanark. The stream flows through a deep chasm, apparently formed by an earthquake, instead of following what seems a much more natural channel a little farther to the east. The rocky banks on both sides rise to the height of about 400 feet. A few years ago a bridge was thrown across this narrow chasm, consisting of three arches of the height of 128 feet. At a little distance below is a narrow old bridge, supposed to be of Roman origin. On the north side of the stream, a few yards above the new bridge, is a cave in the face of the rock, termed "Wallace's Cave," which is pointed out by tradition as the hiding-place of that hero after he had slain Haselrig the English Sheriff.

About a mile and a half westward from Lanark, on the south side of the Mouse, is the ancient house of Jerviswood, the seat of the illustrious patriot who was murdered under the forms of law during the infamous government of Charles II. The attainder of Jerviswood was reversed by the Convention Parliament at the Revolution. On the opposite bank of the stream, situated amidst extensive plantations, is Cleghorn, the seat of Allan Elliot Lockhart, Esq., of Borthwickbrae.

About three miles below Lanark, on the north bank of the Clyde, is Lee House, the seat of Sir Norman Macdonald Lockhart, Bart. It is a fine mansion, lately modernized in the castellated style, and contains a good collection of pictures. Here is kept the famous Lee Penny, the use made of which by Sir Walter Scott, in his splendid tale of "The Talisman," must be familiar to every reader. The following curious extract is given in a note to that tale :—

"Quhilk day, amongst the referries of the Brethren of the Ministry of Lanark, it was proponed to the Synod that Gavin Hamilton of Raploch had pursueit an Complaint before them against Sir James Lockhart of Lee, anent the superstitious using of an Stone, set in silver, for the curing of deseased Cattle, q[lk] the said Gavin affirmed could not be lawfully usit, and that they had deferrit to give ony decisioune thairin till the advice of the Assemblie might be had concerning the same. The Assemblie having inquirit of the manner of using thereof, and particularly understood, be examination of the said Laird of Lee, and otherwise, that the custom is only to cast the stone in some water, and give the deceasit Cattle thereof to drink, and that the same is done without using any words, such as Charmers and Sorcerers use in their unlawful practices ; and considering that in nature thair are many things seen to work strange effects, whereof no human wit can give a reason, it having pleast God to give to stones and herbs a speciall vertue for healing of many infirmities in man and beast, advises the Brethren to surcease thair process, as therein they perceive no ground of Offence, and admonishes the said Laird of Lee, in using of the said stone, to take heid that it be usit hereafter with the least scandal that possibly maybe. Extract out of the Books of the Assemblie, holden at Glasgow, and subscribed at their command. —M. Robert Young, Clerk to the Assemblie at Glasgow"

In the grounds of Lee there is a huge oak tree, which is so completely hollowed out by age that it can hold half a dozen individuals standing upright.

The tourist may proceed from Lanark to Edinburgh, Glasgow, or Carlisle, by Caledonian Railway.

EIGHTH TOUR.

*** There are two sets of steamers which ply down the Clyde; both proceed, in the same way to Gourock. From Gourock, the one keeps the left side and continues its route by way of Largs and Millport to Arran or Ardrossan, the other takes the right side by way of Dunoon to Rothesay and Lochgilphead. This division is therefore adopted in the present route.

The steamers for Largs and Millport, Dunoon and Rothesay, sail from Glasgow almost every hour during the summer months, but those which continue their course *all the way* either to Arran, Ardrossan, or Lochgilphead, not oftener than once every day.

A chart of this Tour will be found facing page 232, and an Itinerary of the Glasgow and Greenock Railway, of which the tourist may perhaps avail himself, at the end of the volume.

GLASGOW—DUMBARTON—PORT-GLASGOW—HELENSBURGH
GREENOCK.
I. GOUROCK—LARGS—MILLPORT—ARRAN—ARDROSSAN.
II. GOUROCK—DUNOON—ROTHESAY—LOCHGILPHEAD—OBAN.

STARTING from Broomielaw in one of the steamboats which ply on the river, a few minutes' sail brings the passengers to the mouth of the Kelvin, a stream celebrated in Scottish song. The village on the left is Govan. On both sides of the river there is a series of pleasant suburban villas. About two miles below Govan, on the same side of the river, is Shieldhall, and on the right is Jordanhill, the seat of James Smith, Esq. A little farther down the river, and on the same side, is Scotstoun, the seat of Miss Oswald. On the left is Elderslie House, the seat of Archibald Speirs, Esq.; and about a mile farther down is Blythswood House, the seat of Archibald Campbell, Esq. Between the two last mentioned places is Renfrew Ferry, where a near view may be obtained of the ancient burgh of Renfrew. The appearance of the town is mean and antiquated. In the neighbourhood, Somerled, Thane of Argyle and Lord of the Isles, who had rebelled against Malcolm IV., was defeated and slain in the year 1164. The barony of Renfrew was the first possession of the Stuart family in Scotland. It gives the title of Baron to the Prince of Wales. The collected waters of the two Carts and the Gryfe flow into the Clyde at Inchinnan, about a mile below Renfrew. Near Inchinnan Bridge, the Earl of Argyle was taken prisoner in 1685. On the left, near the river, is the old mansion-house of Erskine, anciently the seat of the Earls of Mar, and latterly of the Blantyre family. Robert, eleventh Lord Blantyre, who perished accidentally in the commotions at Brussels, in 1830, erected the new princely mansion which crowns the rising ground a little farther down. The tourist is now half-way between Glasgow and Greenock. The river has expanded greatly, and assumed the appearance of a lake, apparently closed in front. The lofty heights on the right are the Kilpatrick Hills, and the village in the narrow plain between them and the river is Kilpatrick, supposed to have been the birth-place of St. Patrick, the tutelar saint of Ireland. The little bay in front of Kilpatrick is Bowling Bay. Near Bowling Inn may be perceived the mouth of the Great Junction Canal, which unites the east and west coasts of Scotland, by means of the Firths of Forth and Clyde. At a short distance below, on the right, is the little promontory of Dunglass Point, the western termination of Antoninus' Wall or Graham's Dyke, with the ruins of Dunglass Castle, formerly the property of the Colquhouns of Luss, but now belonging to Buchanan of Auchintorlie. On this spot, a monument has lately been erected to the late Henry Bell, who introduced steam-navigation on the Clyde. On the left, in the distance, are seen the church and manse of Erskine ; Bishopton House, (Lord Blantyre) ; Drums, (Captain Darroch.) On the opposite side are Milton Island, Milton House, and Printworks, ( ) ; Dumbuck House, (Geils, Esq.) ; at the foot of Dumbuck Hill (*Hill of Roes*) Garshake, (Dixon, Esq.) ; Chapel Green, Silverton Hill, and the town of

DUMBARTON.

[*Inns*:—The King's Arms ; The Elephant.]

Dumbarton Rock rises from the point of junction of the Leven and Clyde, to the height of 560 feet, measuring a mile in circumference, terminating in two sharp points, one higher than the other, and studded over with houses and batteries. Previous to his being sent to England, Wallace was confined for some time in this castle, the governor of which was the infamous Sir John Menteith, who betrayed him. The highest peak of the rock is still denominated "Wallace's Seat," and a part of the castle "Wallace's Tower." In one of the apartments, a huge two-handed sword said to have belonged to that hero, is still shown. At the union of Scotland with England, this was one of the four fortresses stipulated to be kept up ; and, accordingly, it is still in repair, and occupied by a garrison.* Opposite

* During the wars which desolated Scotland in the reign of Queen Mary, this formidable fortress was taken in the following remarkable way, by Captain Crawford of Jordanhill, a distinguished adherent of the King's party :—" He took advantage of a misty and moonless night to bring to the foot of the castle-rock, the scaling ladders which he had provided, choosing for his terrible experiment the place where the rock was highest, and where, of course, less pains were taken to keep a regular guard. This choice was fortunate ; for the first ladder broke with the weight of the men who attempted to mount, and the noise of the fall must have betrayed them, had there been any sentinel within hearing. Crawford, assisted by a soldier who had deserted from the castle and was acting as his guide, renewed the attempt in person, and having scrambled up to a projecting ledge of rock where there was some footing, contrived to make fast the ladder, by tying it to the roots of a tree, which grew about midway up the rock. Here they found a small flat surface, sufficient, however, to afford footing to the whole party, which was, of course, very few in number. In scaling the second precipice, another accident took place :—One of the party, subject to epileptic fits, was seized by one of these attacks, brought on perhaps by terror while he was in the act of climbing up the ladder. His illness made it impossible for him either to ascend or descend. To have slain the man would have been a cruel expedient, besides that the fall of his body from the ladder

to Dumbarton Castle, on the left is West Sea Bank; and beyond the Leven, on the right, is Leven Grove. Two miles farther, on the left, is Finlayston, formerly the family mansion of the Earls of Glencairn, now the seat of Graham of Gartmore; on the right, are Clyde Bank and Clyde Cottage. Approaching Port-Glasgow, we reach the Castle of Newark, which, after having belonged, in succession, to a branch of the Maxwells, and to the Belhaven family, is now the property of Lady Shaw Stewart. PORT-GLASGOW was founded, in 1668, by the merchants of Glasgow, for the embarkation and disembarkation of goods; but since the river was deepened, its importance has much declined. On the opposite shore of the Clyde are the remains of an ancient castle, believed to have been that of Cardross, in which Robert Bruce breathed his last. For several miles the shore is thickly studded with villas, among which are Ardarden House, Ardmore House, Camis-Eskan, Kilmahew Castle, and Drumfork House, all on the right side of the Firth. Three and a half miles from Dumbarton is the Kirk of Cardross, with its little attendant village. Five miles further along the shore, at the opening of the Gare Loch, is HELENSBURGH.—{*Inns:* The Baths Inn; The Tontine.}—Coach from the Tontine Hotel to Luss about 9 A.M., in connection with Lochlomond steamer, returning in the evening in time to meet the steamers on the Clyde. Two miles and a half further are the village and kirk of Row, which is the parish church of Helensburgh. The promontory opposite to Helensburgh, between the Gare Loch and Loch Long, is occupied by the mansion and beautiful grounds of Roseneath, a seat of the Argyle family. This palace, built in the Italian style, occupies the site of a fine old castle, which was burnt down in 1802. After a sail from Glasgow of about two hours and a half, the steamer reaches the large and populous seaport of

might have alarmed the garrison. Crawford caused him, therefore, to be tied to the ladder; then all the rest descending, they turned the ladder, and thus mounted with ease over the belly of the epileptic person. When the party gained the summit they slew the sentinel ere he had time to give the alarm, and easily surprised the slumbering garrison, who had trusted too much to the security of their castle to keep good watch. This exploit of Crawford may compare with any thing of the kind which we read of in history."

GREENOCK.

[*Inns*:—The Tontine; The Buck's Head; The White Hart.]

Close upon the quay stands the Custom-house, an elegant and commodious building, while streets extend over the rising ground behind. There are also several fine buildings in Cathcart Street and towards the west end of the

town. The situation of Greenock is both beautiful and convenient for commerce. Whin-hill, the rising ground at the back of the town, commands a noble prospect, and the view from the quay, the mountains of Argyleshire and Dumbartonshire rising on the opposite side, is perhaps the finest commanded by any seaport in the kingdom. In the admirably managed factory of the Shawswater Cotton Spinning Company, is the largest water-wheel in Britain, measuring seventy feet in diameter. Its majestic revolutions are fitted to impress the spectator with feelings of admiration and awe. This town was the birth-place of Watt; its population in 1841 was 36,936. Leaving Greenock, the steamer makes direct for Kempock Point, passing many villas on the shore. About three miles below Greenock, occupying both sides of Kempock Point, is the village of

GOUROCK.

[*Inns* :—The Royal Arms; The Wheat Sheaf.]

It commands a noble sea-view, and the walks along the shore towards the Cloch are very beautiful.

I. GOUROCK—LARGS—MILLPORT—ARRAN—AND ARDROSSAN.*

About a quarter of a mile off shore, the Comet steamboat was run down by the Ayr steampacket, October 21, 1825, when upwards of fifty individuals found a watery grave. Two miles further along this coast, is the old ruin of Leven Tower, crowning a fine eminence. About three miles below Gourock, the coast bends to the south at the Cloch Lighthouse, one of the most important beacons on the Clyde. A little below stands Ardgowan, the seat of Sir R. M. Shaw Stewart, Bart. A short way farther on, at the bottom of a small bay, is the little sequestered village of INNERKIP.—[*Inns* :—Innerkip Inn; George Main's.]—Two miles further on is Kelly House, and Wemyss, the pretty watering place, beautifully situated in the Bay of the same name. The countes of Renfrew and Ayr are here divided by Kellyburn. About a mile and a half farther on is Skelmorlie Castle, a seat of the Earl of Eglinton. The next promontory is Knock Point, on rounding which we pass Brisbane House, (Sir T. McD. Brisbane,) and come in sight of

LARGS.

[*Inns* :—The White Hart; The Anchor.]

The battle of Largs, between the Scottish army and that of Haeo, King of Norway, in which the latter was defeated with great slaughter, took place in 1263, on a large plain upon the seashore to the south of the village. Steering between the Great Cumbray island and the mainland, the steamer passes, at a short distance from Largs, Kelburne Castle, (Earl of Glasgow) embosomed in trees, and two or three miles further on, halts at the village of Fairlie, from

* For the continuation of the route from Gourock to Rothesay and Lochgilphead, see page 262.

which it crosses to the Great Cumbray island. In a bay at the south-east corner of the island, lies the sea-bathing village of

MILLPORT.

[*Inns:*—Millport Inn; Cumbrae Inn.]

TOUR ROUND ARRAN.

Passing between the southern point of the Island of Bute, and the Little Cumbray,† the towering heights of Arran burst upon the view. Presenting their full dimensions from the shore to their summits, and being congregated together in one stupendous group, few scenes can be more magnificent and impressive than these mountains. "Many are bare precipices from their very foundations; and the greater number raise their naked tops to the sky in stupendous pyramids and spires of rough granite, appearing to the beholder as if they had but yesterday been upheaved from their primitive beds, below the bottom of the ocean."‡

The steamer makes a halt at Corrie, a small village which derives its name from the remarkable corrie or valley on the hill immediately behind it; and while it skirts along the shores of the island, which teem with the picturesque and beautiful, the tourist is favoured with

* From Millport, another steamer leaving Glasgow at a different hour, proceeds to Ardrossan. Sailing between the Little Cumbray and the coast of Ayr, it passes Hunterston (Robert Hunter, Esq.,) and about four miles further on, reaches the ruins of Portincross Castle, situated on the edge of a rocky promontory called Fairlie Head. This castle is said to have been used as a temporary residence by the first Stewart Kings, on their way to Brodick in Arran, and Dundonald in Kyle. Its situation is singularly wild and picturesque, and the view it commands, in which the island of Arran forms the most striking feature, is beautifully varied and extensive. On doubling Fairlie Head, and keeping the coast for about five miles, we reach the seaport town of ARDROSSAN.—[*Inns:*—The Eglinton Arms.]—Excellent baths have been constructed, which attract a number of visitors, and there is one expressly for the use of the poor, for which no charge is made. It has a safe and spacious harbour, and a population of about 3500. From Ardrossan there is a daily steamer to Arran, during the summer months, and the railway affords the tourist an opportunity of reaching Ayr, or of returning to Glasgow, in a short space of time.

† "Where Cumbray's isles with verdant link
Close the fair entrance of the Clyde;
The woods of Bute, no more descried,
Are gone."
(LORD OF THE ISLES, *Canto V.*)

‡ *Statistical account of Scotland.*

an advantageous view of Goatfell from the sea, although from the similarity of contour in many of the surrounding peaks, it is not, at first sight, so easily distinguished. The steamer now rounds Merkland Point, and enters the beautiful bay of Brodick, where tourists generally disembark. There is a comfortable little inn at the village, where guides may be engaged for ascending Goatfell, and vehicles for visiting the places of interest throughout the island.

Arran forms part of the county of Bute, is 20 miles in length, by from 8 to 11 in breadth, and contains a superficial area of 165 square miles, or 105,814 acres, of which about 14,431 are cultivated. With the exception of a few farms, the whole island belongs to the Duke of Hamilton. Its population in 1841 was 6181.

The island is chiefly distinguished for its geological interest and the beauty of its scenery. "Although," observes Dr. Macculloch, "in every sense, a hilly island, its character is in this respect unequal, and in the northern and southern halves strongly contrasted. The high and serrated forms of the northern division are peculiarly striking; presenting a rugged mountainous character unequalled in Scotland, except by the Cuchullin hills in Skye. These mountains are also exceedingly elegant in their outline; and though not attaining to quite 3000 feet of elevation, yet, from their independence, and from their rising immediately out of the sea, their alpine effect is equalled by that of very few mountainous tracts in Scotland, of even much greater altitude. The southern hilly division is a tame undulating land without features, and there are not many parts which are strictly level, except in the Machrie Glen, on the west side, and on the shores of Brodick Bay. Though the shores are generally rocky, and commonly steep, they rarely rise into cliffs; but in most places the hills spring at once from the sea, leaving, however, a narrow belt of flat and green land in many places, which forms a natural road of communication nearly all round the island, agreeable, alike for its beauty, and for the access it affords to the various picturesque scenes of the island, which are chiefly found on its sea margin."

The scenery about Glen Sannox, extending southwards to the two bays of Brodick and Lamlash, is that which will chiefly engage the attention of the traveller. Its characteristic features are beautifully described by Sir Walter Scott, in the "Lord of the Isles," when Father Augustine is sent by Lord Douglas with a message to Bruce from Lochranza, "across the hills to Brodick Bay."

"Through birchen copse he wander'd slow
Stunted and sapless, thin and low;
By many a mountain stream he pass'd,
From the tall cliffs in tumult cast,
Dashing to foam their waters dun,
And sparkling in the summer's sun,

Round his grey head the wild curlew
In many a fearless circle flew.
O'er chasms he passed where fractures wide
Crav'd wary eye and ample stride;
He cross'd his brow beside the stone,*
Where Druids erst heard victims groan,
And at the cairns upon the wild,
O'er many a heathen hero piled."

There are only four roads in Arran. The first makes the circuit of the island, the second cuts through its centre from Blackwater foot to Brodick, the third crosses its southerly part from Bein na Carrigan to Lamlash, and the fourth connects the latter two together from Glen Scoradail to Clachan Glen. Confining ourselves to the first of these, we shall continue the route round the island, diverging only occasionally from the beaten track, when any object sufficiently attractive, either inland or to the sea-shore, shall induce us to do so.

From its situation, and the many objects of interest and beauty in its immediate vicinity, we shall commence with Brodick Bay, a beautifully curved plain, girt with a beach of sand and ornamented with neat cottages and villas, flourishing plantations, and cultivated fields, which, as they retire inwards, are met by the wildly contrasting valleys of Glenrosa, Glensheraig, and Glencloy. To the north is Brodick Castle, while Goatfell rises majestic in the rear.

Brodick Castle, beautifully situated on an eminence surrounded by waving plantations, remained in ruins until the year 1845, when its noble proprietor, the Duke of Hamilton, completed, with great good taste, its reconstruction on the model of the ancient fortress. At the time of the memorable interregnum when Edward I. was endeavouring to crush the spirited efforts of Wallace and Bruce for the independence of their country, it was taken and held by the English under Sir John Hastings. It did not, however, remain long in their possession; "for James, Lord Douglas, who accompanied Bruce to his retreat in Rachrin, seems in the spring of 1306 to have tired of his abode there, and set out accordingly, in the phrase of the times, to see what adventure God would send him. Sir Robert Boyd accompanied him; and his knowledge of the localities of Arran appears to have directed his course thither. They landed in the island privately, and appear to have laid an ambush for Sir John Hastings, the English Governor of Brodick, and surprised a considerable supply of arms and provisions, and nearly took the castle itself. . . . . When they were

* "The Isle of Arran, like those of Man and Anglesea, abounds with many relics of heathen, or probably Druidical superstition. There are high erect columns of unhewn stone, the most early of all monuments, the circles of rude stones, commonly entitled Druidical, and the cairns or sepulchral piles, within which are usually found urns enclosing ashes.

ioined by Bruce, it seems probable that they had gained Brodick Castle. At least tradition says that from the battlements of the tower he saw the supposed signal fire on Turnberry nook."*

After the settlement of the Scottish crown by Bruce, the castle of Brodick, as well as the greater part of Arran, was the property of the High Steward of Scotland, who, by failure of male-heirs to Bruce, succeeded to the throne under the title of Robert II. In 1455, it was stormed and levelled to the ground by the Earl of Ross, who had espoused the cause of the Earl of Douglas against his sovereign. Its next possessor was Sir Thomas Boyd, a court favourite, who married King James I.'s eldest sister, who received from that monarch the earldom of Arran as her marriage dowry. On the disgrace of the Boyds, Sir Thomas was divorced from his royal spouse, and the princess's hand, with her earldom of Arran, bestowed upon Lord Hamilton, in whose hands, with the exception of a few interruptions, it has remained until this day.

Goatfell, which forms so prominent a feature in the aspect of the island, is 2959 feet high, and rises immediately behind Brodick Inn, from which a footpath, to the east of Cnocan Burn,† conducts the tourist for a considerable way upwards, to a mill-dam. Having gained this point, without descending into the valley which runs along the bottom of the principal peak, and keeping well upon the ridge to the right, the remaining part of the ascent, (which is by far the most difficult,) will be easier accomplished than by any other way. Wild though the mountain is, its ascent is by no means so difficult as it appears to be, and with the aid of a guide can be accomplished in the space of two hours. The view from the summit on a clear day, amply repays the labour of reaching it. "The jagged and spiry peaks of the surrounding mountains, the dark hollows and deep shady corries into which the rays of the sun scarcely ever penetrate, the open swelling hills beyond, the winding shores of Lochfine, and the broad Firth of Clyde studded with its peaceful and fertile islands, the rugged islands of Argyleshire, the gentle curves of the hills of the Western islands," and the blue shores of the Green Isle, "their outlines softened in the distance, form a scene of most surpassing grandeur and loveliness."‡

Deep embosomed between the lofty mountains Goatfell and Ben Noosh, lies the beautiful valley of Glenrosa, celebrated for the impressive character of its scenery. Delightful excursions can also be made to Glensheraig and Glencloy, which are both in the immediate

* Lord of the Isles.

† The best geological route is by the bed of this stream.

‡ Ramsay's Geology of the Island of Arran, a hand-book which will be found of great use to those who wish to become practically acquainted with the geological phenomena of the island.

vicinity of Brodick. In Glencloy are the remains of an ancient fort, which tradition points out as having afforded shelter to Bruce's partisans, who had arrived in Arran before himself, while Brodick Castle was in the possession of the English; and at the head of the glen there are also the remains of a Druidical circle.

About five miles from Brodick, in the middle of a beautiful semicircular bay, lies the neat little village of Lamlash. Sheltered by the Holy Island—an irregular cone 900 feet high—this bay forms an excellent harbour for the accommodation of ships of all sizes, while its surrounding scenery cannot be beheld without delight by all lovers of the picturesque.

The Holy Isle was once the site of an ancient cathedral, said to have been founded by St. Molios, a disciple of St. Columba, who not considering the discipline of Iona sufficiently rigid, retired for greater seclusion, to this lonely isle, whence he carried the light of Christianity among the Pagan inhabitants of Arran. The cave in which the saint resided is still to be seen on the sea-shore. In the interior of it there is a shelf of rock said to have been his bed, and on the roof a Runic inscription, mentioning his name and office. He is said to have died at the advanced age of 120 years, at Lochranza, where he spent the latter part of his life, and where his remains still repose in the burying-ground at Clachan. Retiring behind the village of Lamlash are Glens Alaster and Meneadmar, at the head of which may be seen the remains of an ancient Druidical sepulchral cairn, measuring 200 feet in circumference. It is believed to cover the ashes of those who fell in a battle fought upon the spot, as on removing some of the stones, several stone coffins were found buried underneath. At the southerly point of the bay, about 3 miles from Lamlash, is King's-cross Point, whence Robert Bruce is said to have embarked for the coast of Carrick. On the other side of the Point is Whiting Bay, and a mile from Learg-a-Beg is the valley of Glen Ashdale, where there are two beautiful cascades, one above a hundred, the other above fifty feet high. When the stream is swelled by rains, one may pass dry between the larger cascade and the rock over which it falls.

From Learg-a-Beg, a splendid range of lofty precipices occupies the shore to the ruins of Kildonan Castle. "Like the Benan cliffs, the place is still and solitary. A rough and difficult footpath forms the only track beneath the cliffs; and as the tourist warily winds along, he will hear no sound save the dash of the breaking waves, the shrill cries of the waterfowl, and the incessant cawing of the rooks, which float in airy circles round the verge of the overhanging cliffs."* Opposite Kildonan Castle is the small island of Pladda, with its lighthouse. About a mile further on, to the north-east of

* Ramsay's Geological Tour in Arran.

the farm of Auchinlew, a most picturesque waterfall called Eeiss-a-Mor dashes over a lofty precipice into a magnificent amphitheatre of perpendicular cliffs. On the north side of the road, before coming to Benan, a stream descends in a fine cascade from a ravine above, to the depth of about seventy feet. On the coast, between Benan-head and the Torlin Water, situated among a vast range of columnar cliffs, called the Struye Rocks, there is a huge cavern, called the Monster's Cave, measuring 110 feet long, 40 feet broad, and 80 high. After crossing the Torlin Water, we reach Lag, where there is a small inn. About a mile from the inn, a road strikes off to the right hand, crossing the island, through Glen Scoradail, to Lamlash. Continuing along the coast, the road crosses Sloadridh Water, along the base of a mass of rounded hills, called Leac-a-Breac, and reaches Kilpatrick, where there is a cave, called the Preaching Cave. About a mile from the road, at Blackwaterfoot,* is the basaltic promontory of Drumidoon, near which there are a number of water-worn caves, one of which, called the King's Cave, is famed for having been the residence of the patriot Bruce on his first arrival in the island. On the wall at the entrance are inscribed the letters M. D. R.; and at the southern extremity is still to be seen a rudely cut hunting-scene, said to have been executed by the fugitive monarch, as a representation of his own condition when this lonely cavern was the place of his abode. It is 114 feet long, 44 broad, and 47½ high. Some of the other caves are equally large; one is called the King's Kitchen; another his cellar; and a third his stable. The hill above the caves is called the King's Hill, from its connexion with Bruce. At the northern side of this hill, on the farm of Tormore, are the remains of a very perfect and interesting Druidical circle, called Sindhe choir Thionn, or Fingal's Cauldron-seat. To one of these stones, pierced through with a hole, Fingal tied his favourite dog Bran. The road now continues along the coast, crossing the Mauchrie† and Iorsa waters. From this to Loch Ranza, the only objects of particular interest are, a solitary mountain tarn in the silent recesses of Beinn Mhorroinn, the most picturesque lake in the island, lying in a deep hollow, called Corrie an Lochan; and on the road at North Thunder-

* The remains of a large cairn or tumulus are to be seen here; but, owing to the large number of stones which have been carried away, it is now very much diminished in size. To the north of it, there is another, said to mark the spot where Fingal held his court of justice.

† The pass over the river Mauchrie is "renowned for the dilemma of a poor woman, who, being tempted by the narrowness of the ravine to step across, succeeded in making the first movement, but took fright when it became necessary to move the other foot, and remained in a posture equally ludicrous and dangerous, until some chance passenger assisted her to extricate herself. It is said she remained there some hours."—*Note to Lord of the Isles.*

gay, where there are two remarkable masses of contorted schist, which have fallen from the cliff upon the shore. Continuing along the shores of Catacol Bay, and passing the glen of the same name, the road turns round Choillembor Point, and brings us at length to "Fair Loch Ranza," where

> "Wreaths of cottage-smoke are upward curl'd
> From the lone hamlet, which her inland bay
> And circling mountains sever from the world."—

It is about a mile in length, and, during the fishing-season, is a place of great resort, 300 boats sometimes lying at anchor in the bay at the same time.*

The ruins of Loch Ranza Castle stand upon a small peninsula near the entrance of the Loch. This castle is not heard of until the year 1380, when it is enumerated among the Royal Castles, as a hunting seat of the Scottish sovereigns. The roof having fallen in, it is now fast falling into decay. Near this, in the burying ground of Clachan, are interred the remains of good St. Molios, who died here at the advanced age of 120. The figure of the saint is sculptured on his tombstone, which is said to have been brought from Iona. The ruins of the convent of St. Bride, celebrated in the "Lord of the Isles," as the lonely abode of the maid of Lorn, occupied a site near the castle:

> "In that lone convent's silent cell,
> The lovely Maid of Lorn remain'd,
> Unnamed, unknown, while Scotland far
> Resounded with the din of war;
> And many a month and many a day,
> In calm seclusion wore away."

---

* Sir Walter Scott, in his fourth canto to the "Lord of the Isles," gives the following beautiful description of the view on Bruce's approach to Loch Ranza, from the Island of Rachrin, where he had lain concealed:—

> "Now launch'd once more, the inland sea
> They furrow with fair augury,
> And steer from Arran's isle.
> The sun, ere yet he sunk behind
> Ben Ghoil, 'the Mountain of the Wind,'
> Gave his grim peaks a greeting kind,
> And bade Loch Ranza smile.
> Thither their destined course they drew;
> It seem'd the isle her monarch knew,
> So brilliant was the landward view,
> The ocean so serene;
> Each puny wave in diamonds roll'd
> O'er the calm deep, where hues of gold
> With azure strove, and green.
> The hill, the vale, the tree, the tower,
> Glow'd with the tints of evening's hour,
> The beech was silver sheen;
> The wind breathed soft as lover's sigh,
> And oft renewed, seem'd oft to die,
> With breathless stop between.
> O who, with speech of war and woes,
> Would wish to break the soft repose
> Of such enchanting scene!
> * * *
> To land King Robert lightly sprung,
> And thrice aloud his bugle rung
> With note prolong'd and varied strain.
> Till bold Ben Ghoil replied again."

But now unfortunately all trace of this interesting place is completely swept away. There is a small inn here for the accommodation of travellers. To the back of the loch is Beu Ghoil, and the two beautiful glens, Chalmadael and Eeis na bearradh. At the head of the latter gleu is a small loch called Loch Davie. The road runs along the southern shore of Loch Ranza, and leaving the coast strikes through the former of these glens to Corrie. Diverging, however, from the road, a two miles' walk from Loch Ranza along the coast, will bring the tourist to Scriden, the most northerly point of Arran. Here a most striking scene presents itself. The cliffs having given way, and rolled down the hill, have fallen in confused masses on the shore, rendering it necessary, in following the line of coast, to climb over the rocks by a rough and winding passage. Near the summit of the hill there is a chasm, not more than a yard broad, and so deep, that the bottom is lost in darkness. The edge being covered with heath, the aperture is so much hidden that the utmost caution should be used in approaching it. There are also many similar rents of a smaller size on the same mountain. Near Scriden point, is the Cock of Arran, a large stone on the beach, forming a well known landmark for seamen. Formerly, when viewed from the sea, it resembled a cock crowing ; hence its name. Having been decapitated, however, it is now deprived of this distinguishing feature. A mile from the Cock, are the grey ruins of some deserted saltpans, which, standing, as they do, amidst a scene of solitude on the unfrequented shore, lend an additional charm to the still and lonely landscape. About two miles from Sannox, the eye of the traveller is suddenly arrested by a scene as imposing as it is unexpected, known by the name of the Fallen Rocks. An immense cliff of old red sandstone, which overhung the brow of the hill, seems suddenly to have given way, and the entire slope is covered with huge irregular masses of rock, hurled from above in the wildest and most tumultuous confusion. It is not known when this fall occurred; but there is a tradition, that the noise of the descent was heard in the Isle of Bute. About a mile from the Fallen Rocks we regain the road at North Glen Sannox, and a short way further on, the famed Glen Sannox is presented to the view. This beautiful glen is separated from Glen Rosa by a rocky ridge, and is surrounded by high hills on all sides—to the north by Suithi Fheargus, or Fergus' Seat;* to the south by the steep conical hill Ciodhua Oigh,

* There is a tradition, that when Fergus the First made a survey of his kingdom, he visited Arran in the course of his wanderings; and that he might at once obtain a view of the island, the monarch and his attendants climbed this lofty hill, when, to refresh themselves after the fatigue, they sat down to dine. Hence the name.

or the Maiden's Breast; while it is closed, to the east, by lofty Cir Mhor and Ceum na Cailleach, or the Carlin's Step. This glen is admitted by almost all to be the finest in the island, and is justly characterized by MacCulloch as "the sublime in magnitude and simplicity, obscurity and silence." As the traveller pursues his lonely path, he is ever induced to pause and gaze around him in silent admiration of the wild and desolate scene. No sound of man strikes his ear, save the tramp of his own footsteps; and no sign of life is heard but the distant bleating of the moorland sheep, or the wild shriek of the eagle, soaring above his eyrie in Ciormhor. Reluctantly retracing our steps, and gaining the road, after proceeding a short way, we observe, between the road and the sea, two large boulders of granite, which have rolled down from the neighbouring heights; after passing these we are not long of reaching Corrie, where there is a small inn. At a short distance from Corrie, there is a small cascade, formed by the Locherim Burn; and further on, another more conspicuous, called the White Water, dashes down the mountain side, presenting one unbroken line of white and sparkling foam. Passing Maolden Hill, and turning Merkland Point, we again come in sight of our head-quarters at Brodick, having completed the circuit of the island.

II. GOUROCK—DUNOON—ROTHESAY—LOCHGILPHEAD.

Returning to Gourock, straight opposite on the coast of Argyle, is the Holy Loch, surrounded by steep and picturesque hills. On its eastern shore, at the mouth of the loch is the village, and now much frequented summer residence of STRONE [Strone Hotel], and a little further up, on the same side, the beautiful watering-place of KILMUN [*Inns*:—M'Murtrie's]. Here may still be seen the ruins of the Collegiate Church, founded in 1442 by Sir Duncan Campbell of Loch Awe, ancestor of the Argyle family, and where they have their burying-place. Opposite Kilmun is the village of Sandbank, after calling at which, the steamer passes the beautiful house of Mr. Hunter of Hafton, and rounding the point, comes in sight of DUNOON—[*Inns*:—The Wellington.]—one of the largest and most fashionable summer residences on the west coast. The Castle of Dunoon was once a royal residence, and a strong fortress.* An ex-

* The hereditary keepership of it was conferred by Robert Bruce on the family of Sir Colin Campbell of Loch Awe, an ancestor of the Duke of Argyle. It was the residence of the Argyle family in 1673, but from the commencement of the eighteenth century was allowed to fall into a state of ruin, and nothing but a wall now remains.

tensive and beautiful prospect is commanded from its site. From Dunoon or Kilmun there is a very pleasant road by Loch Eck and Strachur (Lord Murray) to Inverary. Tourists may go this way either by private conveyance, or by the mail-gig from Kilmun. On leaving Dunoon, the steamer skirts along Bawkie Bay. The peninsula of Cowal ends a few miles lower at Toward Point, where there is a lighthouse, besides a large modern edifice, Toward Castle, the seat of James Finlay, Esq. On the neighbouring height, on the right, are seen the venerable ruins of Toward Castle, the ancient seat of the Lamonts. Turning Toward Point, we enter Rothesay Bay, and in a short time reach the pleasant town of ROTHESAY—{*Inns:*—The Bute Arms.}—The town consists of neat streets, and the views from various elevated points around it, are extremely beautiful. The ancient royal castle of Rothesay, the favourite residence of Robert III., is one of the finest ruins in Scotland.* The western side of the Bay of Rothesay commands a noble view of the entrance to the Kyles of Bute, the crooked strait which divides Argyleshire from Bute, and the mouth of Loch Strevin, with the shores of Cowal. About two miles from Rothesay, the steamboat passes Port Bannatyne, a beautiful village encircling the bottom of Kames Bay. In the immediate vicinity stands Kames Castle, an old fortified mansion still inhabited. Between Rothesay and Kilchattan Bay stands Mount Stewart, the seat of the Marquis of Bute, surrounded by fine woods. Etterick Bay, on the west side of the island, is often visited on account of its picturesque scenery. After passing the mouth of Loch Strevin, the channel rapidly narrows. Between the ferry and the entrance of Loch Ridden, it is contracted by four islands. The passage, though narrow and intricate, is exceedingly interesting. Leaving the entrance to Loch Ridden, on the right, the steamer emerges into the open space between Ard Lamont Point on the mainland, and Etterick Bay in Bute, from which the heights of Arran are seen to great advantage. On entering Loch Pyne, the steamer passes on the

* It was burned down by the Earl of Argyle in 1685. The closet in which Robert III. died is still pointed out. Rothesay gave the title of Duke to the eldest son of the Scottish kings, as it still does to the heir-apparent of the British crown.

left the islet of Inchmarnock, with the ruins of a chapel, and soon after another islet, called Slate Island. On the left is the wild and rugged peninsula of Cantire, joined to South Knapdale by a very narrow isthmus, formed by the western and eastern Lochs of Tarbet. These two salt-water lakes or bays, into the eastern of which we now enter, encroach so far into the land, and the extremities come so near each other, that there is not a mile of land to divide them. Bruce on his way from Rachrin is said to have drawn his bark across this isthmus.

> "Up Tarbet's western lake they bore,
> Then dragg'd their bark the isthmus o'er,
> As far as Kilmconnel's shore,
> Upon the eastern bay."*

In the immediate vicinity is the Castle of Tarbet, now in ruins. Here the Earl of Argyle kept his troops previous to his unsuccessful descent upon the Lowlands in 1685. Leaving Tarbet, and pursuing our course northward, we pass Barmore Island, and shortly after come in sight of the village of LOCHGILPHEAD.—[*Inns* :—Ardrishaig Inn.] The Crinan Canal, formed to avoid the circuitous passage of 70 miles round the Mull of Cantire, is nine miles in length, with no fewer than fifteen locks. On entering the canal, a good view is obtained of Lochgilphead and Kilmory, the seat of Sir John Ord. Two miles from the sea-lock, on the left, is Auchindarroch, (Campbell, Esq.,) after which the canal passes through an extensive tract of marshy uninteresting country. Passing the village of Bellanach, we enter the Bay of Crinan. Upon the right is the modernized Castle of Duntroon, (Malcolm, Esq.,) and northward, on the same side, Loch Craignish, a fine arm of the sea, intersected by a chain of beautiful little islands, covered with ancient oak-trees. The steamboat proceeds through the Dorishtmore, or Great Gate, between the point of Craignish, and one of the chain of islets just mentioned. Islay, Jura, and Scarba, are now in sight. Between the latter two islands is the celebrated whirlpool of Corrivreckan. On the south are the

* Lord of the Isles. Canto IV.

shores of Knapdale, and to the north the islands of Shuna and Luing, with Loch Melfort opening to the right. Two miles from the point of Luing is Blackmill Bay, opposite to which is the island of Lunga. Three miles further north is the slate islet of Balnahuay, and farther to the west the Garveloch Isles. The sound of Cuan runs between the northern extremity of Luing and the island of Seil. The length of this beautiful and diversified passage is about three miles. On the west side of Seil is the circular islet of Easdale, celebrated for its slate quarries. After passing Easdale and the point of Ardincaple, Loch Feochan opens on the right, disclosing to view the broad-shouldered and double-peaked Ben Cruachan. To the north is the Island of Kerrara, and the ruins of Gylen Castle. This island forms a natural break-water to the bay and village of

OBAN.

[*Inns*:—The Caledonian; The King's Arms; The Argyle; Barr's.]

The high cliffs on the north side of the bay terminate

in a rocky promontory, surmounted by DUNOLLY CASTLE, an

ivy-clad square keep, the ancient seat of the M'Dougalls of Lorn, whose representative resides here in Dunolly House. A little to the north of Dunolly stands the Castle of Dunstaffnage, "an irregular four-sided building, placed upon a rugged mass of conglomerate rock, the sides of which have been partially picked away so as to produce a more precipitous descent beneath the walls. Its circumference is said to be about 400 feet, and the battlements are still high and of tenacious strength." In consequence of its having been occasionally possessed by the early Scottish Kings, Dunstaffnage Castle is ranked as one of the royal palaces of Scotland. From this ancient seat of royalty, it is said, the Coronation stone, now in Westminster Abbey, was transferred by Kenneth II. to Scone.

NINTH TOUR.

GLASGOW—INVERARY—LOCH AWE—DALMALLY—TAYNUILT—OBAN.

The tourist has his choice of several routes to Inverary. He may proceed *via* Dumbarton, Balloch, Loch Lomond side, Tarbet, Arroquhar, Glencroe, Rest-and-be-Thankful, and Cairndow, (the Mail Route)—or by steamer, *via* Loch Long, Loch Goil and St. Catharine's;—or by Rothesay, Tarbet, and Lochgilphead.

Supposing him to take the first route, he proceeds by the mail or steamboat to Tarbet, on the west side of Loch Lomond.

From this point to Arroquhar, on the shore of Loch Long, is a delightful walk of about half an hour, across the isthmus which lies between Loch Lomond and Loch Long. The inn of Arroquhar is twenty-two miles from Dumbarton. Loch Long is an arm of the sea, about twenty-four miles in length. In 1263, the Norwegians, who invaded Scotland, and were ultimately defeated at Largs, sailed up this loch with a fleet of sixty vessels, ravaging the country on all sides, and, on reaching the head of the loch, they drew their boats across the isthmus into Loch Lomond, and committed the same depredations on its shores. Near the head of Loch Long is a fantastic peak, called Ben Arthur or the Cobbler, from its grotesque resemblance to a shoemaker at work. Arroquhar was formerly the seat of the chief of the clan Macfarlane, it is now the property of Sir James Colquhoun of Luss. Starting from the inn at this spot, the tourist winds round the head of Loch Long, and crossing the water of Taing, enters Argyleshire. The road now skirts the western shore of Loch Long, till within a few yards of Ardgarten House, (Campbell, Esq.) where it turns to the right, and enters the vale of Glencroe—a desolate but magnificent glen about six miles in length, guarded on the right by the bold and fantastic peak of Ben Arthur. A steep path conducts the traveller to the summit of the pass, where there is a stone seat, with the inscription, "Rest and be thankful."* The road now gradually descends, passing, on the

* On this resting-place Wordsworth has composed the following sonnet:—

"Doubling and doubling with laborious walk,
Who, that has gain'd at length the wish'd-for Height,
This brief, this simple way-side Call can slight,
And rest not thankful? Whether cheer'd by talk
With some loved friend, or by the unseen hawk
Whistling to clouds and sky-born streams, that shine
At the sun's outbreak, as, with light divine,
Ere they descend to nourish root and stalk
Of valley flowers. Nor, while the limbs repose,
Will we forget that, as the fowl can keep
Absolute stillness, poised aloft in air,
And fishes front, unmoved, the torrent's sweep,
So may the Soul, through powers that Faith bestows,
Win rest, and ease, and peace, with bliss that angels share."

left, a small sheet of water, called Loch Restal, and enters the lonely valley of Glenkinglas. Passing through this solitary vale, at the distance of about three miles, the tourist is gladdened with a view of Loch Eyne. The road now passes, on the right, the farm-house of Strowan, and on the left, Ardkinglass, (Callander, Esq.) and shortly after reaches the inn of Cairndow, (thirty-six miles from Dumbarton,) where there is a ferry across Loch Fyne. Crossing the ferry, the distance to Inverary is six and a half miles. If the tourist should prefer to go round by the head of the loch, the distance is nine and a half miles.

The second route to Inverary leads the tourist up Loch Goil, which branches off from Loch Long. The peninsular group of rugged mountains which separate them is called Argyle's Bowling Green. The shores are bold and magnificent. On the margin of the loch are situated the ruins of Carrick Castle, an ancient seat of the Dunmore family. From Loch Goil Head a road leads through a wild valley, called Hell's Glen, to St. Catharine's, a distance of seven miles, whence the tourist may proceed across Loch Eyne (four miles) to Inverary.

By the third, and much the longest route, the tourist proceeds to Rothesay, then through the Kyles of Bute, and into the long arm of the sea called Loch Eyne. (See p. 264.)

INVERARY.

[*Inns*:—The Argyll Arms; The George; Walker's.]

Coach to Tarbet from Walker's (commencing in August) every morning at 7 o'clock (breakfast being ready at Cairndow on the arrival of the coach), returning from Tarbet every afternoon one hour after the steamer's arrival.

The county town of Argyleshire stands at the lower end of a small bay, where the river Aray falls into Loch Fyne. It was erected into a royal burgh, in 1648, by Charles I. while he was a prisoner in Carisbrook Castle. An obelisk has been erected in a garden beside the church, to commemorate the execution of several gentlemen of the name of Campbell, who suffered here in 1685, for their opposition to Popery. Its staple trade is the herring fishery—the herrings of Loch Eyne being celebrated for their superior excellence. Large sums of money have been laid out by the Dukes of Argyle in improving and adorning the town and neighbourhood. Inverary unites with Oban, Campbelton, Irvine, and Ayr, in electing a member of Parliament.

The most interesting object in this vicinity is Inverary Castle, the seat of the Duke of Argyle. The edifice was commenced by Duke Archibald, in 1748, after a plan by Adam. It is built of chlorite-slate, and consists of two storeys and a sunk floor, flanked with round overtopping towers, and surmounted with a square winged pavilion. In the Hall are preserved about 100 muskets, which were "out in the forty-five," and in one of the rooms is some very beautiful tapestry, which the old lady who exhibits it, states to have been "made by the goblins, wha' are a' dead now." The mansion contains nothing else of peculiar interest to strangers. The view from the hill of Duniquoich is very fine, and the rides and the walks through the grounds are extensive and picturesque.

From Inverary a road leads through Glen Aray, to Loch

Awe, a distance of nine miles. After leaving the pleasure-grounds round Inverary Castle, the tourist will find little to attract his attention till he reaches the head of the glen, and begins to descend towards Cladich, when the beautiful expanse of Loch Awe breaks upon his view. Loch Awe is about twenty-four miles in length, and varies from one and a half to two and a half in breadth. The mingled grandeur and beauty of the scenery are scarcely equalled in Britain.

Loch Awe is surrounded by lofty mountains of a rude and savage aspect, the highest of which (Ben Cruachan) rises to the height of 3400 feet, while its base, which reaches to Loch Etive, occupies an area of twenty square miles. Its towering proportions give a striking character to the scenery at the eastern extremity of Loch Awe. The sloping banks of the lake are richly clothed with natural wood. The river Awe flows from its northern side, and pours its waters into Loch Etive at Bunawe. The gully or hollow, known by the name of the *Brender*, through which the river flows, is exceedingly grand. There are about twenty-four little islands in Loch Awe, some of them beautifully crowned with trees. On one of these islets, (Inishail, or the Beautiful Isle,) are the ruins of a small nunnery of the Cistercian order. It was suppressed at the Reformation, and its possessions were erected into a temporal lordship in favour of Hay, Abbot of Inchaffray, who abjured the Roman Catholic faith. The old churchyard in this island contains a number of ancient tomb-stones, curiously carved. The MacArthurs formerly inhabited the shores of Loch Awe, opposite the island, and numerous stones in the churchyard bear the names of individuals of that ancient race. On Innes Fraoch, or the Heather Isle, are the ruins of an ancient castle of the chief of the MacNaughtons. This isle was the Hesperides of the Highlands, and is fabled to have derived its name from Fraoch, an adventurous lover, who, attempting to gratify the longing of the fair Meyo for the delicious fruit of the isle, encountered and destroyed the serpent by which it was guarded, but perished himself in the conflict. The point of land which runs into the lake immediately beyond the village of Cladich, is called Innistrynich, or the

Island of the Druids, and is the property of Mr. M'Allister of Innistrynich, who is an extensive proprietor on the opposite shore of the lake. The island of Fraoch, with the contiguous lands, were granted, in 1267, to Gilbert MacNaughton, by Alexander III. The MacNaughtons formed part of the force of MacDougal, Lord of Lorn, when he attacked Robert Bruce at Dalrigh, near Tyndrum. It is stated by Barbour, that MacNaughton pointed out to the Lord of Lorn the deeds of valour which Bruce performed in this memorable retreat, with the highest expressions of admiration. "It seems to give thee pleasure," said Lorn, "that he makes such havoc among our friends."—"Not so, by my faith," replied MacNaughton; "but be he friend or foe who achieves high deeds of chivalry, men should bear faithful witness to his valour; and never have I heard of one who, by his knightly feats, has extricated himself from such dangers as have this day surrounded Bruce." The MacNaughtons, an ancient Highland tribe, are supposed to have derived their origin from one Naughton, a distinguished warrior in the reign of Malcolm IV., who received various grants of lands from the Lord of Lochers, as a reward for the services which he rendered to him in his wars with the M'Dougals of Lorn. It is said by Buchanan of Auchmar, that "the ancestors or chiefs of this surname are reported to have been, for some ages, thanes of Loch Tay, and also to be possessed of a great estate betwixt the south side of Loch Fyne and Lochers, parts of which are Glenera, Glenshira, and Glenfine." The chief of the clan, in the reigns of Charles I. and II., was Sir Alexander MacNaughton, a stanch royalist. At the Reformation, he was knighted, and received a liberal pension, as a reward for his services. His circumstances, however, became embarrassed, and the family estates were seized by his creditors for debts, it is said, no way equivalent to their value. His great-grandson was a custom-house officer on the east coast.

At the eastern extremity of Loch Awe, at the base of Ben Cruachan, the conjoined waters of two rivers, the Strae and the Orchy, descend from their respective glens, and empty themselves into the lake. On a slightly elevated neck of land at the head of the lake, where the Orchy flows into it, stand the ruins of the celebrated castle of KILCHURN, or more properly Coalchuirn. The great tower is said to have been erected in 1443, by the lady of Sir Colin Campbell, the Black Knight of Rhodes, second son of Sir Duncan Campbell of Loch Awe, ancestor of the Argyle family. Sir Colin acquired by marriage a considerable portion of the estates of the family of Lorn, and was the founder of the powerful family of Breadalbane. He was absent on a crusade when his lady erected this noble pile, which (says Macculloch), "in the Western Highlands at least, claims the pre-eminence, no less from its magnitude and the integrity of its ruins, than from the very picturesque arrangements of the building." For the pencil of the artist few finer subjects can be found in Scotland than these ruins present. So late as 1745, Kilchurn was garrisoned by the King's troops, and all the exterior and greater part of the interior walls are still entire.*

* Our space will not admit of our quoting the whole of Wordsworth's fine Address to Kilchurn Castle, but we give the introductory part of the poem and the prose extract with which it is prefaced.

"From the top of the hill a most impressive scene opened upon our view,—a ruined castle on an island, (for an island the flood had made it,) at some distance from the shore, backed by a cove of the mountain Cruachan, down which came a foaming stream. The castle occupied every foot of the island that was visible to us, appearing to rise out of the water,—mists rested upon the mountain side, with spots of sunshine; there was a mild desolation, in the low grounds, a solemn grandeur in the mountains, and the castle was wild, yet stately—not dismantled of turrets—nor the walls broken down, though obviously a ruin."—*Extract from the Journal of my Companion.*

Child of loud-throated War! the mountain stream
Roars in thy hearing: but thy hour of rest
Is come, and thou art silent in thy age;
Save when the winds sweep by, and sounds are caught
Ambiguous, neither wholly thine nor theirs,
Oh! there is life that breathes not: powers there are
That touch each other to the quick in modes
Which the gross world no sense hath to perceive,
No soul to dream of. What art thou, from care
Cast off—abandon'd by thy rugged Sire,
Nor by soft Peace adopted; though, in place
And in dimension, such that thou mightst seem
But a mere footstool to yon sovereign Lord,
Huge Cruachan, (a thing that meaner hills

Might

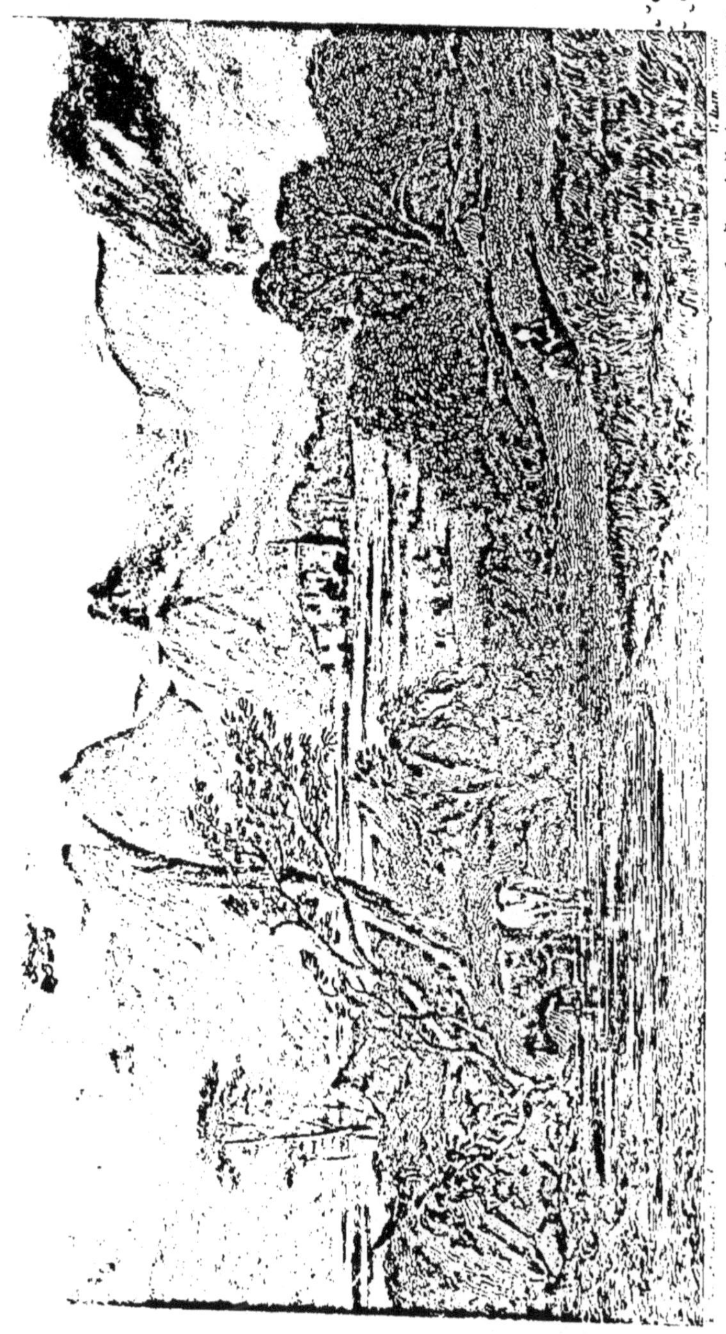

There is a good inn at Dalmally, near the head of the lake, and from it there is a beautiful view of the vale of Glenorchy. The old church of Glenorchy is of great antiquity, and the churchyard contains many ancient gravestones. The road from Dalmally to Taynuilt passes the new church of Glenorchy, and makes a long circuit round the head of the lake. Pedestrians may shorten the distance and pleasantly diversify their journey by crossing the lake in a boat. Two miles from Dalmally, we cross the river Strae, which descends from Glenstrae on the right. The whole of this district was at one time possessed by the Clan-Gregor, but they have long been deprived of all their possessions around Loch Awe, and may now say, in the words of the poet—

"Glenorchy's proud mountains, Coalchuirn and her towers,
Glenstrae and Glenlyon no longer are ours,
We're landless, landless, Gregalich !"*

In later times, this district fell into the hands of the Campbells, and often afforded them shelter in times of danger. "It's a far cry to Lochow," was the slogan of the clan, indicating the impossibility of reaching them in these

Might crush, nor know that it had suffer'd harm ;)
Yet he, not loth, in favour of thy claims
To reverence, suspends his own ; submitting
All that the God of Nature hath conferr'd,
All that he holds in common with the stars,
To the memorial majesty of Time
Impersonated in thy calm decay !"

* "In the early part of the 17th century, a young man of the name of Lamont, travelling from Cowal, in Argyleshire, to Fort-William, fell in with the son of a chieftain of the Clan Macgregor, resident in Glenstrae, while on a shooting excursion. Having adjourned to a public-house, a dispute arose, which terminated in a scuffle, in which Macgregor was mortally stabbed. Lamont instantly escaping, was closely pursued. Descrying a house, he sped thither for shelter: unquestioned, the host assured him of protection. Those in pursuit coming up, communicated the startling intelligence that the fugitive was the murderer of the eldest son of the family. Macgregor, however, faithful to his word, conducted the young man to Loch Fyne, and saw him safe across. His clemency and magnanimity were not without their recompence. Not long after, the Clan-Gregor were proscribed; when Lamont received the aged chieftain to his house, and, by every act of kindness to him and his relatives, sought to supply the place of him of whose support he had been the means of bereaving them."—*Anderson's Guide to the Highlands.*

remote fastnesses. Passing the farm-house of Corry, the road now skirts the tremendous base of Ben Cruachan, and leaving behind the majestic lake, descends the course of the foaming and rapid river Awe. The rocks and precipioes which stoop down perpendicularly on the path, exhibit some remains of the wood which once clothed them, but which has, in later times, been felled to supply the iron furnaces at Bunawe. The whole of this pass is singularly wild, particularly near the bridge which has been thrown across the impetuous river. Here was fought the celebrated battle between Robert Bruce and John of Lorn, chief of the M'Dougals, in which that warlike clan were almost destroyed. The bridge of Awe is the scene of Sir Walter Scott's beautiful tale of the Highland Widow.* About two miles onwards we cross an old bridge, and pass the church of Muckarn on the right. On the south side of Loch Etive, fourteen miles from Dalmally, is the Inn of Taynuilt. About a mile to the north is the village of Bunawe, where there is a ferry across Loch Etive, and an extensive iron furnace, which has been wrought since the middle of last century, by a Lancashire company. The portion of Loch Etive above Bunawe, possesses a high degree of simple and sequestered grandeur. Bunawe is the point from which the ascent to Ben Cruachan can be best effected. The prospect from the top of the mountain is remarkably extensive and interesting. Leaving Taynuilt, the road, at the distance of four miles, descends to the shore of Loch Etive, beautifully fringed with wood. On

* The following description is given of the spot where her cottage stood:—"We fixed our eyes with interest on one large oak, which grew on the left hand towards the river. It seemed a tree of extraordinary magnitude and picturesque beauty, and stood just where there appeared to be a few roods of open ground lying among huge stones, which had rolled down from the mountain. To add to the romance of the situation, the spot of clear ground extended round the foot of a proud-browed rock, from the summit of which leaped a mountain stream in a fall of sixty feet, in which it was dissolved into foam and dew. At the bottom of the fall, the rivulet with difficulty collected, like a routed general, its dispersed forces, and, as if tamed by its descent, found a noiseless passage through the heath to join the Awe."

the north side of the Loch, about three miles from Taynuilt, are seen Ardchattan House, and the ruins of Ardchattan Priory, covered with luxuriant ivy, and o'ercanopied by trees. The Priory, where Robert Bruce held a Parliament, was built by John MacDougal in the thirteenth century, and was burnt by Colkitto during Montrose's Wars. In the distance are seen the dark mountains of Mull and Morven, and the green island of Lismore. The latter is entirely composed of limestone. Three miles farther is Connel Ferry, where, from the narrowness of the passage, and a reef of sunken rocks, a very turbulent rapid is occasioned at particular states of the tide. In the immediate vicinity, antiquaries have placed the apocryphal Pictish capital of Beregonium. There is also a vitrified fort. Two miles beyond Connel Ferry, at the entrance of Loch Etive, are the ruins of Dunstaffnage Castle. They occupy the summit of a perpendicular rock near the extremity of a low peninsular flat projection from the southern shore. Dunstaffnage was inhabited by the MacDougals till 1448, when it was taken by Bruce after his victory at the Pass of Awe. It is now a royal castle, the Duke of Argyle being hereditary keeper. From Dunstaffnage, the celebrated stone on which our Scottish monarchs used to be crowned was transported to Scone, whence it was removed to England by Edward I., and is now deposited beneath the coronation chair in the chapel of Edward the Confessor, in Westminster Abbey. At a little distance from the castle is a small roofless chapel, where one of the Scottish kings is said to have been buried. Three miles from Dunstaffnage is the pleasant thriving village of OBAN, situated at the head of a fine bay. From the heights in the neighbourhood, magnificent sea views may be obtained; and the road which skirts the shore to the southward is overhung by romantic cliffs. In the vicinity is Dunolly Castle, the ancient fortress of the MacDougals of Lorn, situated on the point of a rocky promontory, at the northern extremity of the bay. Near it is Dunolly House, inhabited by the representative of that once powerful family.*

* "Nothing can be more wildly beautiful than the situation of Dunolly. The ruins are situated upon a bold and precipitous promontory overhanging Loch

TOURISTS visiting Skye generally start from Glasgow by steamer, or if they have previously reached Oban by either of the routes described in the Eighth and Ninth Tours, they may embark from that village when the steamer touches there.

Supposing Glasgow to be the starting point, the route as far as Oban will be found already described in the Eighth Tour. Proceeding from the finely sheltered bay of Oban, with the island of Kerrera on our left, the Castle of Dunolly will be observed proudly seated on a rugged steep. For an engraving of this Castle we refer the reader to the

Etive, and distant about a mile from the village and port of Oban. The principal part which remains is the donjon or keep; but fragments of other buildings, overgrown with ivy, attest that it had once been a place of importance, as large, apparently, as Ardtornish or Dunstaffnage. These fragments enclose a court-yard, of which the keep probably formed one side; the entrance being by a steep ascent from the neck of the isthmus, formerly cut across by a moat, and defended, doubtless, by outworks and a drawbridge. Beneath the castle stands the present mansion of the family, having on the one hand Loch Etive, with its islands and mountains, on the other two romantic eminences tufted with copsewood. There are other accompaniments suited to the scene; in particular, a huge upright pillar or detached fragment of that sort of rock called plum-pudding stone, upon the shore, about a quarter of a mile from the castle. It is called *Clachna-cau*, or the Dog's Pillar, because Fingal is said to have used it as a stake to which he bound his celebrated dog, Bran. Others say, that when the Lord of the Isles came upon a visit to the Lord of Lorn, the dogs brought for his sport were kept beside this pillar. Upon the whole, a more delightful and romantic spot can scarce be conceived; and it receives a moral interest from the considerations attached to the residence of a family once powerful enough to confront and defeat Robert Bruce, and now sunk into the shade of private life. It is at present possessed by Patrick MacDougall, Esq., the lineal and undisputed representative of the ancient Lords of Lorn. The heir of Dunolly fell in Spain, fighting under the Duke of Wellington—a death well becoming his ancestry.'—*Lord of the Isles.*

end of the Eighth Tour. Rounding the point of Kerrera the steamer stretches across the Sound of Mull. On approaching the entrance of the Sound, soon after leaving Lismore Lighthouse, we pass the "Lady's Rock," where Maclean of Duart exposed his wife at low water to be drowned by the returning tide. His cruelty was disappointed by some fishermen, who, hearing her cries, rescued her from her impending fate, and restored her to her friends. A little onwards we reach Duart Castle, now the property of Campbell of Fossil, and on the opposite side, projecting from the Morven shore, are the ruins of the Castle of Ardtornish, in former times a chief residence of the Lords of the Isles. The steamer next passes the opening of Loch Aline, and four miles beyond it the Castle of Aros may be observed on the leftward shore. The wild situations of these fortresses, and their limited accommodation, afford a striking contrast to the spacious castles of the south. They are supposed to date their origin from the period of the prostration of the Norwegian power, when Haco, King of Norway, was defeated at the battle of Largs, and when many of the island chieftains assumed an independent sway.

Proceeding onwards, we pass upon the Morven shore the estate of Drimnin. On the Mull side, the coast is high and precipitous, and finely clothed with natural wood. Passing Aros House, seated on a lofty terrace, and surrounded by extensive plantations, the steamer next reaches Tobermory, where it generally anchors for the night, but sails in the morning so early as to make it imprudent to sleep on shore, even although the accommodation were more inviting than it is. Upon leaving the bay of Tobermory, and crossing the mouth of Loch Sunart—which extends twenty miles among the hills to the eastward—the steamer begins to feel the full swell of the Atlantic. To the westward are the islands of Coll and Tiree. The heaviest sea throughout the voyage will be felt in doubling Ardnamurchan Point, and a stiff breeze from the westward is, at this point, apt to poison the pleasures of the picturesque. The steamer then touches at Faskadle, and afterwards passes the mouth of Loch Moydart, into which the fresh waters of Loch Shiel discharge themselves by the river of the same name. On a rocky promontory on the shore of Loch Moydart, stand the ruins of Castle Tyrim, an ancient stronghold of Clanranald, burned by its proprietor in 1715, before he set out to join the Earl of Mar, prior to the battle of Sheriffmuir. This act of arson he resorted to, that the castle might not fall into the hands of his hereditary enemies, the Campbells, during his absence. The barren promontory on which the castle stands, and a small wooded island near it, are the last remaining territorial possessions of Clanranald.

On the left may be seen the islands of Eig, Rum, and Canna, and further northward the Cuchullin (*pron.* Coolin,) hills of Skye rear their storm-shattered summits to the clouds. On the mainland will be observed the fine rugged outline of the Moydart hills. Pursuing our voyage, we pass in succession Loch Aynort, Loch Nuagh, and Arasaig Point, (at the last of which passengers are landed,) and enter the sound of Sleat. Armadale Castle, the seat of Lord Macdonald, " Lord of the Isles," the largest proprietor in Skye, will be seen occupying a fine situation on a gentle slope, about a quarter of a mile from the shore. It is surrounded on all sides by thriving plantations, which, with the woods of Dunvegan in the district of Kilmuir, may be said to form the whole woodland scenery of the island.

Having passed on the mainland side the outlets of Loch Morrer and Loch Nevish, the ruins of Knock Castle, in Skye, may be discerned seated on a rocky promontory projecting into the sea. The steamer next passes the mouth of Loch Hourn, another of those arms of the sea by which the western coast of Scotland is so much indented. The whole mountains around Loch Hourn are lofty and picturesque, sweeping down in grand lines towards the water's edge. Guarding the mouth of the loch stands the lofty Ben Screel, a mountain of very noble outline. The tourist will be aided in distinguishing it by the accompanying woodcut.

Approaching Khyle Rhea, a view may be obtained, on the right, of the church and ruined barracks of Bernera, built as a military station to maintain the authority of the Hanoverian Government among the Celts. A strong current prevails at Khyle Rhea, which makes it necessary for vessels to avail themselves of the tide in passing the strait. On either side of the ferry, there is an inn—an acceptable shelter in such a country, although the internal comforts are not of the highest order. Passing the narrows, the steamer reaches Loch Alsh—another arm of the sea—which, at its upper extremity, divides into the lateral branches of Loch Loung and Loch Duich. At the head of Loch Alsh, between the two subsidiary branches, stand the ruins of Eilan Donan Castle, the ancient stronghold of the Mackenzies of Kintail, built, in the time of Alexander II., as a defence against the Northmen. Passing Castle Moil, we reach the harbour of Kyle Akin, with a substantial pier, built by Lord Macdonald and the Parliamentary Commissioners. The steamer shortly after reaches Broadford, a scattered village, from which the access to the Spar Cave, Loch Coruisk, and the Cuchullin Mountains—the objects for which Skye is chiefly visited—is easier than from any other landing place at which the steamer touches. In reaching these objects, and terminating the day's journey by walking through Glen Sligachan, the tourist must be prepared to endure considerable fatigue; for unless he invades the hospitality of some of the few inhabitants of the district, he has no resting-place between Broadford and Sligachan Inn. The toil of the journey makes it also desirable that he should start early in the morning of a long summer's day, with a sufficient supply of provisions, and a flask of whisky—the latter to be reserved for use where it will most be required, in passing through Glen Sligachan.

The first object to be visited is the Spar Cave of Strathaird; and as candles must be carried from Broadford to light its recesses, the tourist may provide himself with these at the Inn. Perhaps he may also be inclined to hire a pony or a cart to carry him the first stage of his journey, and thus diminish the fatigues of the day. Having made all the preliminary arrangements, he proceeds along the river side towards Torrin, a small cluster of cottar-houses six miles to the westward of Broadford. Five miles from Broadford, at a short distance from the road side, upon the right, he passes the house of the minister of Strath. Nothing of picturesque interest occurring to arrest his progress, a two hours' walk along an excellent road brings the tourist to Torrin, where a boat must be engaged to carry him to the cave. The distance will take four oars two hours' rowing. On the right will be observed Blabhein, (*pron.* Blaven) which contends with the Cuchullins for the honour of being the highest mountain in Skye, and is little inferior to them in the wildness of its scenery;* and, at a short distance from the shore, is Kirkibost, the residence of Dr. Macalister, whom

* The ascent of Blaven may be made either from Broadford or Sligachan, but in neither case should it be attempted without a guide; for not only is it beset with dangerous and impracticable crags and precipices, but it is peculiarly liable to be suddenly enveloped in the mists which ascend from the low ground or from the sea. From either of the two places named, the tourist may devote an entire day to the ascent and the return homewards, although, with a concurrence of every favourable circumstance, and with great powers of enduring fatigue, it might be possible to include it with the excursion to the Spar Cave, Coruisk, and Glen Sligachan.

many a benighted traveller has to thank for the kindly shelter of his hospitable roof. Next passing the farm-house of Kilmarie, and coasting along the rocky shore, the boat at length reaches the mouth of the celebrated Spar Cave of Strathaird, where the tourist disembarks to explore its recesses. A description of the interior in the Notes to the "Lord of the Isles" will be so much more acceptable to our readers than any original account we could supply, that we reprint it in an abridged form, with such slight variations or additions as the present state of the Cave appears to require. The entrance lies through an opening in the rock-bound shore, and at first the appearance is rude and unpromising; but an advance of a few yards unfolds the splendour of the scene, the roof, floor, and walls appearing to be sheeted with marble, partly smooth, partly rough with frostwork and rustic ornaments, and partly seeming to be wrought into statuary. The floor, which forms a steep ascent, may be fancifully compared to a sheet of water, which, while it rushed whitening and foaming down a declivity, has been suddenly arrested and consolidated by the spell of an enchanter. At the summit of the ascent, the cave opens into a splendid gallery, adorned with dazzling crystallizations, and finally descends with rapidity to the brink of a pool of beautifully limpid water, which forms the internal boundary of the cave. The groups of combined figures, projecting or embossed, by which the pool is surrounded, are exquisitely elegant and fanciful, and might indeed give hints to the statuary by their singular and romantic disposition. There is scarce a form or group on which active fancy may not trace figures or grotesque ornaments, which have been gradually moulded in this cavern by the dropping of the calcareous water hardening into petrifactions. Many of these fine groups have either been wholly destroyed, or grievously defaced, by the Vandalism of that class of tourists who cannot rest satisfied without bearing away a fragment of every thing they contemplate, be it the lava of a volcano, or the monument of a martyr. The smoke of the torches and candles has also sullied the purity of the crystallizations; but mutilated and dimmed though they be, there is yet beauty enough left amply to reward the enterprise of the tourist, and the enthusiasm of the lover of Nature.

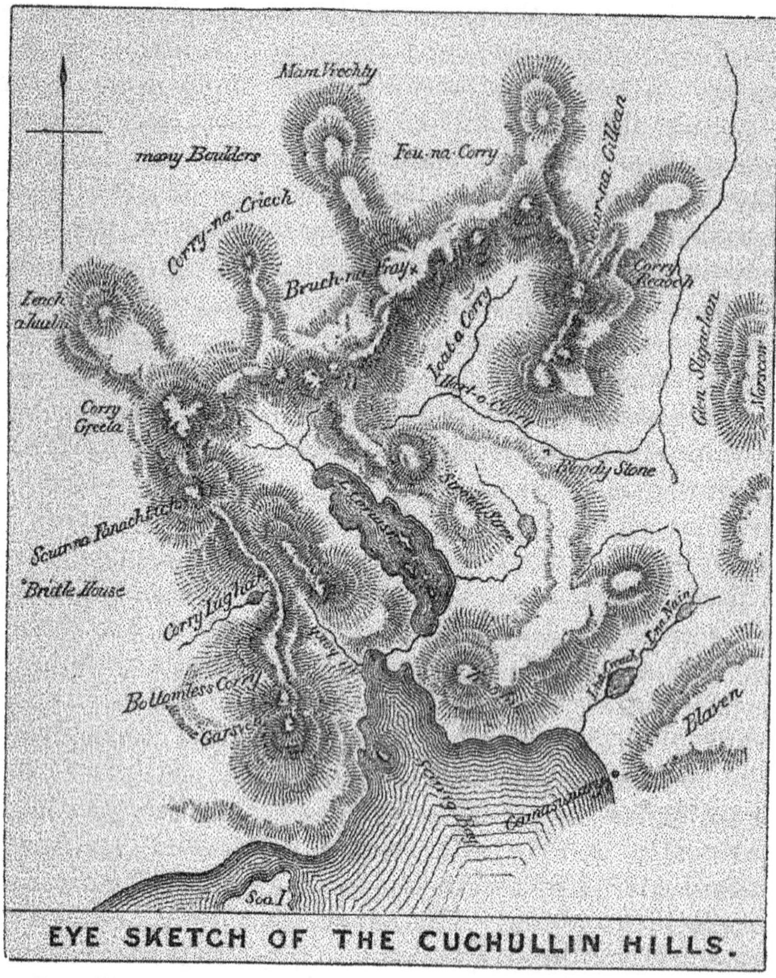

EYE SKETCH OF THE CUCHULLIN HILLS.

Leaving the Cave, and rounding Strathaird Point, the tourist enters the Bay of Scavaig, where a scene of the wildest sublimity opens upon his eye. The wild and romantic forms of the Cuchullin Hills, looming through the mist in which they are generally more or less enveloped, rear their grisly summits to the clouds, while columnar and needle-pointed rocks shoot abruptly from the bosom of the deep, forming together a scene of grandeur and of desolation altogether unequalled in any other part of the

British Isles. To reach the upper end of Loch Scavaig, at the nearest point to Loch Coruisk, will occupy the tourist about three hours from the time of leaving the Spar Cave. In the bosom of the majestic solitude before him, and only about a quarter of a mile from the landing-place, reposes the far-famed Loch Coruisk. It is approached along the course of the brawling stream which discharges the superfluous waters of Loch Coruisk into Loch Scavaig. Pursuing this track, the shores of that "dread lake" expand to the eye, and there are few who will not concur in the exclamation of the Bruce, when the deep, dark, and solemn sheet of water stretches before him·

"St. Mary! what a scene is here!
I've traversed many a mountain strand
Abroad and in my native land,
And it has been my lot to tread
Where safety, more than pleasure led;
Thus many a waste I've wandered o'er—
Clombe many a crag—cross'd many a moor—
But, by my halidome,
A scene so rude, so wild as this,
Yet so sublime in barrenness,
Ne'er did my wandering footsteps press,
Where'er I happ'd to roam."*

"The margins of the lake are composed of vast sloping rocks and gigantic stones, and these hard and herbless masses rise ridge above ridge till they blend with the higher sides and summits of the mountains, seen only partially through the racking clouds, and seeming, so unexpectedly do they appear at times above you, as if in the very act of rolling downwards. The pervading colour is an ashy brown, and there is not only a vastness, but an air of volcanic desolation about them, which we have not seen elsewhere equalled. The loftier portions of all these mountains are extremely jagged and precipitous, rising here and there into gigantic pinnacles and spires, the smallest points of which, however, would crush to atoms all the cathedrals in the earth. But the sides and bases are in many parts composed of vast rounded or tabular masses of equal-sur-

* Lord of the Isles, Canto III., stanza xiii.

faced rock, steeply inclined, indeed, but slightly granulated, so as to render walking, with due attention, easy. At least we found it so. Sir Walter Scott seems to have viewed them as more sudden in their ascent from the lake than they really are; for he describes the Cuillen mountains as rising 'so perpendicularly from the water edge, that Borrowdale, or even Glencoe, is a jest to them.' But, in truth, their lower portions are not precipitous, as there are various rocky platforms between the lake and the lofty mountain steeps, and it is these forlorn and sloping flats which constitute a pervading character of this desolate scene. Still they are steep enough, in all conscience, and whether they are or not, why should a worm of the earth gainsay the feelings of the great Magician ?"*

* WILSON'S *Voyage round the Coasts of Scotland*, vol. i., page 218.

For the small eye-sketch of Coruisk and the Cuchullins, introduced into the text, we are indebted to Professor Forbes of Edinburgh University. It was sketched by the Professor, in the course of his scientific researches, without any pretension to geometrical accuracy, to give a general idea of the disposition of the hills and valleys of the district; and is appended to a paper on the topography and geology of the Cuchullin Hills, and on the traces of ancient glaciers which they present, contributed to the *Edinburgh Philosophical Journal*. To this paper, in No. 79 of the *Journal*, the scientific reader is referred for the most satisfactory description which has yet been published of the physical features of this portion of Skye. The humbler objects of the present work admit of our availing ourselves only of the following brief extract :—

"The mountainous part of Skye, between Broadford and Loch Brittle (a distance of eleven miles,) comprises two very distinct groups of hills, as distinct in arrangement and external form as in geological composition. The group of the Red Hills (to the east) is distinguished by rounded forms, consisting of a group of dome-shaped masses crowded together and composed of a kind of syenite, in which felspar predominates. The Cuchullin range constitutes a more connected chain of craggy peaks, whose fantastic outlines, in certain positions, may perhaps vie with any in the whole world. They may be compared to those of the granite mountains of Dauphiné; and one part, in particular, resembles the Montagne de la Grave, aptly likened, by M. Elie de Beaumont, to "a gigantic nut-cracker, menacing heaven with its open jaws." This group, as we shall see, is more compact and less straggling than the other; its colour, too, is in singular contrast, varying from brown to deep green on the one side, to purple on the other, particularly after rain. Its composition is principally of hypersthene rock, which was discovered here by Dr. Macculloch, of which the excessive toughness, and its resistance to every kind of external action, whether from violence or from weather, gives much propriety to the name. The mountain of Ben Blaven stands beyond the proper limit of the Cuchullins, but in form, and evidently also in composition, it must be classed with them.

"The appearance of the Red hills, as first seen after passing the Kyles of

At the head of the lake is a quiet, grassy plain, through which the crystalline stream by which the Loch is fed meanders on its mission. The serene beauty of the spot presents a refreshing contrast to the sterile grandeur around, but when a storm brings down the floods foaming from the mountain sides, the gentle stream swells into a mighty torrent, and sweeps the plain with resistless fury.

The circuit of the lake, as Mr. Wilson observes, is by no means so difficult, as the description of Sir Walter Scott, and the distant aspect of the margin would lead the tourist to suppose. It must, however, be admitted that the *Stron-na-Stree*, on the eastern side, does rise very precipitately. The walk round cannot much exceed three miles; but the fatigue of the journey, and the length of time taken to accomplish it, make it equal to at least five miles over a good road. The lake abounds with trout, and their flavour and condition satisfied the present writer that they at least are not sufferers from the general sterility around them. The eagle may often be seen tracing its sublime circles above the serrated peaks of the Cuchullins, and the red deer—joint-heir of the wilderness—sometimes forsakes his mountain fastnesses to browse on the plain at the head of the lake.

The description of Loch Coruisk and the scenery around it, is one of the noblest passages in the Lord of the Isles. To those tourists who have not provided themselves with a copy of that poem as a companion on their tour, the quotation cannot fail to be acceptable.

• • •
—— rarely human eye has known
A scene so stern as that dread lake,
With its dark ledge of barren stone.
Seems that primeval earthquake's sway
Hath rent a strange and shatter'd way
Through the rude bosom of the hill,
And that each naked precipice,
Sable ravine, and dark abyss,
Tells of the outrage still.
The wildest glen, but this, can show
Some touch of Nature's genial glow;
On high Benmore green mosses grow,
And heath-bells bud in deep Glencroe,

Skye, recalls, in almost every detail, the groups of *Puys* of Auvergne. The absence of craters does not altogether destroy the analogy; for such mountains as Ben na Cailleach and Glamich may be perfectly compared to the Puy de Dome which has no proper crater, and of which the form is attributed to the pasty consistence of the matter during ejection, without so great an explosive force as to clear an open vent through it. The Cuchullins, as has been said, recall granitic forms, but invested with a blackness and sterility which, taken as a whole, even few active volcanoes present."

And copse on Cruchan-Ben;
But here,—above, around, below,
On mountain or in glen,
Nor tree, nor shrub, nor plant, nor flower,
Nor aught of vegetative power,
The weary eye may ken.
For all is rocks at random thrown,
Black waves, bare crags, and banks of stone,
As if were here denied
The summer sun, the spring's sweet dew,
That clothe with many a varied hue
The bleakest mountain-side.

And wilder, forward as they wound,
Were the proud cliffs and lake profound.
Huge terraces of granite black
Afforded rude and cumber'd track;
For from the mountain hoar,
Hurl'd headlong in some night of fear,
When yell'd the wolf and fled the deer,
Loose crags had toppled o'er;
And some, chance-poised and balanced, lay,
So that a stripling arm might sway
A mass no host could raise,
In Nature's rage at random thrown,
Yet trembling like the Druid's stone
On its precarious base.
The evening mists, with ceaseless change,
Now clothed the mountains' lofty range,
Now left their foreheads bare,
And round the skirts their mantle furl'd,
Or on the sable waters curl'd,
Or on the eddying breezes whirl'd,
Dispersed in middle air.
And oft, condensed, at once they lower,
When, brief and fierce, the mountain shower
Pours like a torrent down,
And when return the sun's glad beams,
Whiten'd with foam a thousand streams
Leap from the mountain's crown.

If the tourist has brought a guide from Torrin, or if any of the boatmen are qualified to act in that capacity, he may at once strike across from the head of the loch to Glen Sligachan, by the wild pass known by the name of Hart-o-Corry. If he has no guide, and is not of an adventurous disposition, he must re-embark and be landed at Camasunary, where he will be directed to the footpath conducting to Sligachan Inn. The distance from Camasunary to Sligachan is at least eight miles, and the footpath (if the rude track merits the name) is so rough, that it will occupy three or four hours to perform the journey. On the left the pedestrian passes two sheets of water, called Loch-na-Creach and Loch-na-Nain, and on his right he will perceive the precipitous side of Ben Blaven, the mountain referred to in a former page. Pursuing his route, he will observe upon the left the opening of Hart-o-Corry, and at this point he has the most striking view of the Cuchullins he will command throughout the journey. Of the numerous peaks of the Cuchullins, Scuir-na-Gillean (*the rock of the young men*) is generally regarded as the highest. As far as is known, the summit of this mountain was first reached by Professor Forbes in 1836, accompanied by a local guide who had made many previous unsuccessful attempts both alone and with strangers.* Its height was computed by Professor Forbes,

* The name of this guide is Angus Macintyre, and strangers who propose to scale the giddy height should secure his services. He may be heard of at Sligachan Inn.

by barometrical observations in 1845, and was found to be between 3200 and 3220 feet. Bruch-na-Fray is considered by the same authority to be about forty feet lower. Scuir-na-Banachtich, (*the smallpox rock*), a very acute summit of the western range, appears to the eye as elevated as Scuir-na-Gillean itself, and there is yet no evidence that it is not so. Ben Blaven is also a competitor for the honour of ranking first in altitude, and when it is considered that its less acuminated form is calculated to diminish its apparent height, we think it not improbable that it may make good its title. With the single exception of Glencoe, there is nothing on the mainland of Scotland comparable with the magnificent scene at this point of Glen Sligachan. The hills in both glens do not much differ in height, and in sterility they are nearly equal; but in the romantic grandeur of their forms, chiefly of their summits, the palm must be assigned to the Cuchullins over the hills of Glencoe. In the latter, however, there is a closer proximity of the hills to the spectator, and although the poet has sung that "distance lends enchantment to the view," we incline to believe that the near approach of these mountain masses gives them additional impressiveness.

Following the course of the river that waters this desolate valley, the tourist will reach Sligachan Inn, the accommodation of which has of late been greatly improved, rendering its roof a welcome refuge after the toils of the day. Should he wish to push on to Portree, a distance of nine and a half miles, a vehicle or ponies may be engaged at the Inn. The road presents no feature of any interest, and it is therefore of little consequence whether it is travelled by day or by night. There is an excellent road the whole way.

Portree, the capital of Skye, is situate on a steep acclivity at the side of the loch of the same name, the bay of which forms a fine land-locked natural harbour, spacious enough to contain several hundred sail. The entrance to the harbour is surrounded by bold headlands, forming the commencement of a noble range of coast scenery extending northward to the Point of Aird. The Inn affords good accommodation, and branches of the National Bank of Scotland, and of the North of Scotland Bank, are established in the village. At Portree the tourist may avail himself of the steamer to return to Glasgow, for he has now been conducted through by far the most interesting scenery of Skye. Should he desire to extend his tour to Trotternish, Vaternish, and Sleat, we shall furnish a few rapid notes to assist his progress.

PORTREE—PRINCE CHARLES'S CAVE—THE STORR—QUIRAING—POINT OF AIRD—DUNTULM CASTLE—DUNVEGAN CASTLE—BRACADALE SLIGACHAN—SCONSER—BROADFORD—KHYLE AKIN—ISLE ORONSAY—ARMADALE CASTLE.

The fine cliff scenery extending northward along the coast makes it desirable that a boat should be engaged at Portree for the first stage of the tourist's progress. Four miles from Portree, close upon the water's edge, is a cave in which Prince Charles lay for a time concealed.

National Bank of Scot-
Bank, are established
tourist may avail himself
, for he has now been
most interesting scenery of
his tour to Trotternish,
a few rapid notes to

STORR—QUIRAING—POINT
CASTLE—BRACADALE—
KYLE AKIN—ISLE ORONSAY

along the coast makes
at Portree for the first
from Portree, close upon
Charles lay for a time

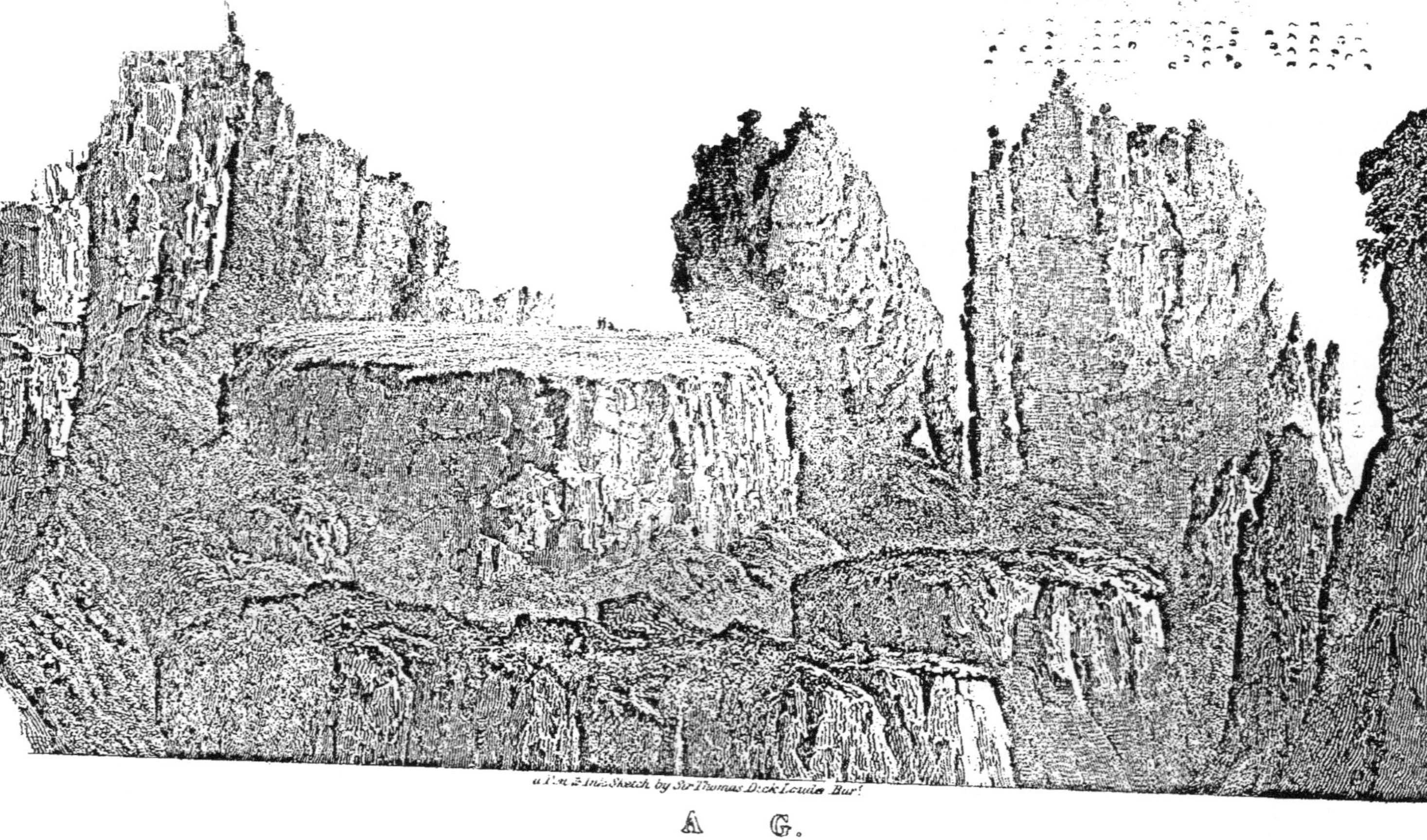

a Pen & Ink Sketch by Sir Thomas Dick Lauder Bart.

A G.

The interior presents the same richly wrought natural rock-work as adorns the cave at Strathaird, while the exuding lime-water which produces the stalactites has hardened over the entrance into a variety of graceful forms of a rich cream colour, "intermingled with the lichen-covered rock, and interwreathed with long festoons of ivy leaves of the freshest green." The ruthless hand of the spoiler here, as at Strathaird, has destroyed many of the finest stalactites. Three miles further along the coast, and about a mile and a half from the shore, is the rocky pyramidal peak called the Storr. If the tourist land here he must pursue his way over the moor to Stanchel, which is sixteen miles distant from Portree, and about eight from Storr. But to perform this journey a guide is indispensable, for the track is scarcely discernible by any eye but that of a native. From the farm-house of Stanchel

QUIRAING

is distant about a mile and a half. This remarkable scene, the boast of Trotternish, and upheld by the natives of this portion of Skye as quite equal in interest to anything in the island, is a mile and a half or two miles from Stanchel. The mountain, among the rocky barriers of which it is enclosed, is about 1000 feet in height, sloping by a declivity towards the west, but presenting north-eastwards a front of rugged precipices, varied by huge uprising columns of basalt and massy fragments of fluted rock. In other parts large spaces forming concave sections present themselves to view, ribbed by fissures and projecting seams, between which in moist weather (which is seldom wanting) streamlets descend in lengthened silvery streaks. Quiraing itself consists of a verdant platform covered with an even and unvarying turf of the finest grass, and of sufficient extent (observes the martial spirit of its Highland pastor) to contain six or seven regiments of soldiers. To readers unversed in military affairs, it may be more intelligibly described as 100 paces long by 60 broad. It is studded all round with massive columns of rock, rising up in lofty peaks, more or less acuminated, and separated by deep chasms, rendering them for the most part inaccessible. On approaching the great inlet to the platform, the passage is much obstructed by heaps of stones and rubbish, the detritus of the fractured cliffs during the waste of ages.

"But through the dark and through the cold,
And through the yawning fissures old,
Let tourist boldly press his way

Right through the quarry; and behold
A scene of soft and lovely hue!
Where blue and grey, and tender green,
Together make as sweet a scene
As ever human eye did view.

Beneath the clear blue sky he'll see
A little field of meadow ground;
But field or meadow name it not—
Call it of earth a small green plot,
With rocks encompassed round."

The entrance is guarded by an isolated pyramidal cliff, called the Needle. Having passed this rocky sentinel, the traveller gains the top of the rugged avenue; and, instead of a dark and narrow cave, he beholds the spacious opening spread before him, with the verdurous platform in its centre, to which, by a short descending path, he threads his way. He now beholds the rocks frowning aloft, and the rugged cliffs ranging themselves in circles around him. Rocky pyramids, like a bulwark, encompass the fairy plain on which he stands. The scene is felt to be a dreary solitude; yet there is a pleasing beauty in its repose. The panoramic view of the sea and intervening country is gained only in detached fragments through the rugged cliffs or the surrounding pyramids. The rocks which compose these huge columns are so streaked and variegated that the imagination of the spectator cannot fail to delineate hundreds of grotesque figures of the wildest description in their outlines. To the poetic fancy of Sir Thomas Dick Lauder, who kindly allowed the present writer to peruse the description of Quiraing in his MS. journal, this singular scene appeared "like the wonderful domain of some Polyphemean magician," while the great ravine forming the entrance seemed like the "ruined ball of some mighty Cyclops or Fingallian giant of at least 100 feet in stature." The aspect of the scene is of course materially influenced by the state of the weather; but whether streams of intercepted sunshine play among the rocky barriers, penetrating, but not illuminating their gloom; whether the clouds by enveloping their summits, leave the beholder to imagine that these manacles of rock bind earth and heaven together; or whether the mists, stalking amid the pyramids, by turns disclose and conceal their spectral forms, Quiraing must be admitted to be a scene of enchanting beauty and impressive grandeur.*

Instead of returning in the direction of Stanchel to resume his progress around the coast, the tourist may continue to follow the road that has brought him to Quiraing, till it joins the Parliamentary road a mile and a quarter from Uig. The junction of the roads is about six miles from Quiraing. We continue, however, to pursue the road along the coast. About 3½ miles from Quiraing, we reach Aird, in which district, at a place called Killmaluack, is a thatched public-house. The cliffs on this, the northern face of the island, are

* The greater part of this description of Quiraing is extracted, with some abridgment and abatement of eloquence, from the *New Statistical Account of Scotland*, vol. xiv. pp. 338-9. The engraved view is executed by Mr. Forrest, from a very graphic sketch, in pen and ink, by Sir Thomas Dick Lauder.

very majestic, and, from the sea, have a very magnificent effect. They are thus described by Mr. Wilson:—"The cliffs immediate to the sea were formed of gigantic prisms, of such large proportions as to resemble the towers of castles grouped together, each being several yards in diameter. Above these, and farther back, were some of the loftiest columns of the more ordinary thickness, we had yet observed. On the whole, the basaltic or columnar scenery of the north of Skye exceeds, in the lofty grandeur of its ranges, whatever Staffa or the Giant's Causeway can produce, although the angular forms of the two latter are more minutely finished and symmetrical." A mile and a half from Killmaluack, we reach Duntulm Castle, the ancient residence of the Macdonalds, seated on a high, rocky, and almost sea-girt point. Three miles further, on the left, stands Kilmuir Church, in the burying-ground of which, Flora Macdonald, the faithful companion of the fortunes of Prince Charles, is interred. The marble slab which was inlaid in her tombstone has been broken and carried off piecemeal by the same class of ruthless destroyers whom we have already had occasion to denounce in our description of the caves at Strathaird and Portree. Two miles further, on the right hand side of the road, is Monkstadt House, the residence of Hugh Macdonald, Esq., one of the most extensive farmers in Skye. The fertile valley extending to the north of the house is the bed of a lake which has recently been drained, the ground thus acquired being cultivated with the crooked spade peculiar to the agriculture of Skye. Mr. Macdonald is the grandnephew of Flora Macdonald, and possesses the habit-shirt worn by Prince Charles when disguised in female apparel. Three miles and a quarter from Monkstadt the tourist reaches Uig, a village of cottar farms at the head of the bay of the same name. The whole land around the bay is laid out in cultivated stripes, upon which is raised the produce which forms the chief subsistence of the inhabitants. This scattered hamlet con-

traveller reaches Dunvegan,* a distance of 11½ miles. The branch road to Dunvegan leads off the main road between the 9th and 10th milestones from Tayinlone.

DUNVEGAN CASTLE,

the family seat of Macleod of Macleod, stands upon a rock near the shore of a small bay, surrounded by woods of considerable extent, to which additions have recently been made. Though the general pile is imposing from its size and situation, the modern alterations made to improve it as a family residence, have somewhat impaired its dignity as a stronghold. The most ancient portion is said to have been built in the ninth century. Among the antiques preserved in Dunvegan, the most remarkable are the fairy flag, the horn of Rorie More, and a chalice or drinking cup of oak, mounted with silver. The last is said to have been part of the spoil taken from an Irish chief called Nial Glundubh, (*Niel of the Black Knees.*) The date in the inscription is much effaced, but it appears to be 993. The only mountains of any considerable elevation in this district of Skye are the Greater and Lesser Helvel, commonly called Macleod's Tables, from the perfectly level nature of their summits. Their height is 1700 feet.

The next stage of the tourist's journey is Struan in Bracadale, a slated public house 11¼ miles from Dunvegan.† The road skirts Loch Bracadale, and in ascending from Struan the bay presents a pleasing prospect. Half way between Struan and Sligachan the road to Talisker branches off to the right. The scenery of Talisker is highly romantic, and its soil particularly fertile. The commanding forms of the Cuchullins are again rising before us, as we approach Sligachan, which is 13¾ miles from Struan. Passing on the right the lofty conical hill called Ben Glamich, and proceeding along the shores of Loch Sligachan for 3¼ miles, we reach Sconser Inn. From Sconser to Broadford the road first skirts Loch Ainort

* Should the tourist desire to extend his researches into Vaternish, he strikes off the Dunvegan road at Fairy Bridge. Four miles from Fairy Bridge, Stein, a small village of slated houses, will be observed close by the water edge. The fertility of this spot, with its small garden farms, is a cheering contrast to the sterile wilderness through which the traveller has passed to reach it. The house of Major Macdonald, the principal proprietor of Vaternish, is about a mile further along the road, which extends to Vaternish Point.

† At Struan, a boat may be engaged by those who wish to see Macleod's Maidens, three naked basaltic pillars, shooting abruptly from the sea off the western horn of Loch Bracadale. The highest is 200, and the other two about 100 feet in height. There was at one time a fourth pillar, but it yielded to the action of the storms and the waves, and has now disappeared in the deep.

The bay of Talisker is seen to the best advantage by approaching it by water; and the tourist proceeding to Sligachan, by landing at Talisker shortens his journey by three miles.

and then the Sound of Scalpa, making a distance of 12 miles. The hillside by Scalpa Sound has a pleasant feathering of hazel and birch.

From Broadford the tourist may proceed either to Khyle Akin (8½ miles,) Khyle Rhea (12 miles,) or Isle Oronsay (12 miles.) None of the roads possesses much interest. At Khyle Akin an attempt was made, under the auspices of the late Lord Macdonald, to establish a seaport town, but the scheme entirely failed of success. It possesses, however, a respectable inn, and about a dozen good slated houses. Close to the village are the ruins of Castle Moil.

At Isle Oronsay there is a small steam-boat inn, and a commercial establishment has been founded there by the judicious enterprise of Mr. John Elder. The place derives its name from a small island, which lies so close upon the Skye coast as to form a convenient natural harbour.

Pursuing the route along the coast a road is passed on the right leading to Ord.* We next reach Knock farm on the left, and immediately adjoining it, on a rocky promontory projecting into the sea, are the ruins of Knock Castle. The country in this neighbourhood, it will be observed, presents an appearance of much higher cultivation than that through which we have hitherto passed. About two miles from Knockfin is Ostaig, the pleasant residence of Captain Macdonald, and a mile further is Armadale Castle, the seat of Lord Macdonald, and the chief mansion-house in the island. It is seated on a gentle slope, with a well-dressed lawn in front, and surrounded by woods of considerable extent. The chief ornament of the interior is a large window of painted glass in the staircase, executed at an expense of £1000, representing Somerled of the Isles, the founder of the family, who flourished in the twelfth century. The figure is in full Highland costume, armed with sword, battle-axe, and targe.

A mile and a half from Armadale Castle, is Ardvasar, a small hamlet, from the pier of which passengers can have a boat to or from the steamer. The public-house here is of a very humble kind, but the tourist who has walked over Skye may contrive to spend a night in it, for there is no other accommodation to the Point of Sleat.

* Ord is 4½ miles distant from this point. The part of the road nearest Ord lies through a pleasant valley, the sides of which have a covering of alder and of birch.

Tourists generally proceed to Oban by Lochgilphead and the Crinan Canal. There are two routes by land from Oban to Fort-William; the coast line by Connel Ferry and Appin, which is the shorter of the two, and the other by Taynuilt, Dalmally, and Glencoe. Loch Linnhe, bounded on the one hand by the craggy knolls of Appin, and on the other by the purple hills of Morven, is the commencement of that chain of salt and fresh water lakes formed into the Caledonian Canal, and presents on both sides scenery of a most romantic character. Opposite to the upper extremity of the island of Lismore, Loch Oreran branches off into the glen of that name. The first mansion to the north of this Loch is Airds, the seat of —— Rolland, Esq.; next is the ruin of Castle Stalker; Appin House, (Downie of Appin,) next occurs; and after that, at the mouth of Loch Leven, Ardshiel, (Stewart, Esq.) From Ballachulish Ferry on Loch Leven, noted for its slate quarry, the West Highland road penetrates the savage vale of Glencoe.* Coran Ferry, nine miles from Fort-William, divides Loch Linnhe from Loch Eil. On a bend of Loch Eil, near the confluence of the river Lochy, and contiguous to the village of Maryburgh, stands Fort-William—[*Inns*:—The Caledonian; The George; The Argyle Arms.]—The fort, originally erected by General Monk, and rebuilt on a smaller scale in the reign of William III., is provided with a bomb-proof magazine, and barracks to accommodate about 100 men. Ben Nevis,

* On certain days the steamer lands the passengers for Glencoe at Ballachulish Ferry. When this is not done, they must land at Coran Ferry, from which the distance to Ballachulish is four miles. A cart, said by its owner to have springs, may be hired from one of the boatmen at a charge of one shilling per mile, to carry on tourists to Ballachulish.

THE CALEDONIAN CANAL.

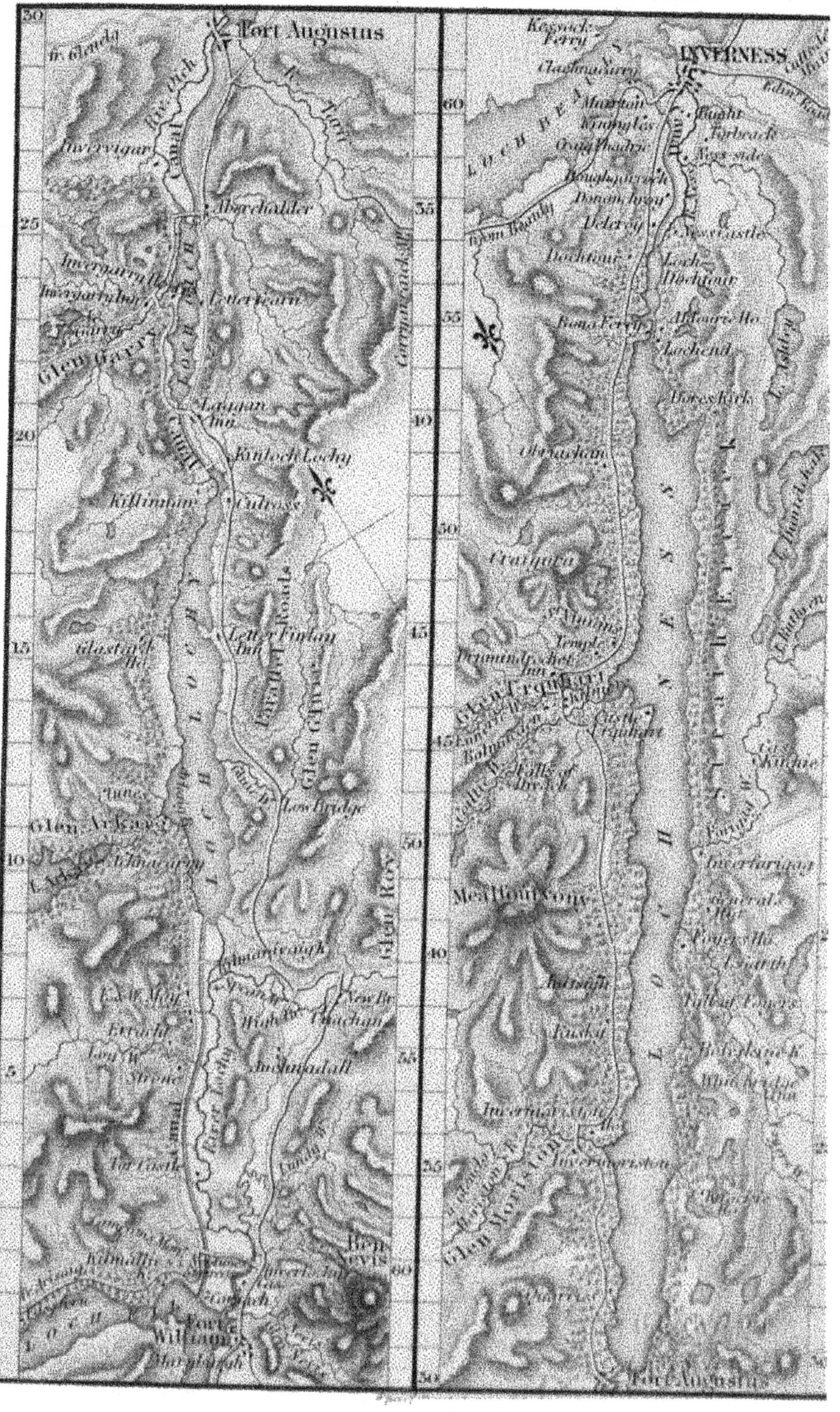

till lately considered the highest mountain in Scotland, is one of the most striking features of this neighbourhood. It rises 4416 feet above the mean level of the sea, and its circumference at the base, which, upon one side, is almost washed by the sea, is supposed to exceed twenty-four miles. "Its northern front consists of two grand distinct ascents, or terraces, the level top of the lowest of which, at an elevation of about 1700 feet, contains a wild tarn or mountain lake. The outer acclivities of this the lower part of the mountain are very steep, although covered with a short grassy sward, intermixed with heath; but at the lake this general vegetable clothing ceases. Here a strange scene of desolation presents itself. The upper and higher portion seems to meet us, as a new mountain shooting up its black porphyritic rocks through the granitic masses, along which we have hitherto made our way, and, where not absolutely precipitous, its surface is strewed with angular fragments of stone of various sizes, wedged together, and forming a singularly rugged covering, among which we look in vain for any symptoms of vegetable life, except where round some pellucid spring the rare little Alpine plants, such as Epilobium alpinum, Silene acaulis, Saxifraga stellaris and nivalis, which live only in such deserts wild, are to be found putting forth their modest blossoms, amid the encircling moss. The eagle, sallying from his eyry, may greet the approach of the wanderer, or the mournful plover, with plaintive note, salute his ear; but for those birds of the mountain the rocky wilderness were lifeless and silent as the grave; its only tenants the lightnings and the mists of heaven, and its language the voice of the storm."* A terrific precipice on the north-eastern side makes a sheer descent from the snow-capped summit of not less than 1500 feet. The tourist who is so fortunate as to ascend the mountain in a favourable state of the atmosphere, is rewarded with a prospect of remarkable extent and grandeur. Ben Lomond, Ben Cruachan, Ben More, Ben Lawers, Schehallion, and Cairngorm, rear their gigan-

* Guide to the Highlands and Islands of Scotland, by George Anderson and Peter Anderson, Esquires.

tic heads around, while other peaks, scarcely less aspiring, extend in countless number and infinite variety of form and character, to the extreme verge of the horizón.* At the distance of a mile from Fort-William stands the old Castle of Inverlochy, (now the property of Lord Abinger) near which Montrose, in 1645, achieved one of his easiest and most decisive victories. He attacked the Campbells by surprise, and with a sacrifice of only three of his men, slaughtered or drowned upwards of 1500 of Argyll's forces. A few years since, a quantity of bones were dug up on the scene of this sanguinary rout where so many fell to deck a single name. Between Inverlochy and Fort-William, the country has an aspect of stern and rugged sublimity. Hills rise over hills of all shapes and sizes, and of various hues, from the deep distant blue to the hard weather-beaten grey and dark-wooded green. A high range of limestone rocks in Glen Nevis (remarkable for the splendour of its scenery (forms a magnificent panorama of mountains, especiall; whèn lighted up by the setting sun. About three miles from the sea, on the river Lochy, are the ruinous walls of Tor Castle, the ancient seat of the Clan-Chattan. From Loch Eil to Loch Lochy the distance is eight miles. At Corpach are three locks, and, a mile beyond, a series of eight locks, called Neptune's Staircase. Each lock is 180 feet long, 40 broad, and 20 deep. Here there is a comfortable inn established, called Bannavie Inn, at which tourists

* "The ascent of Ben Nevis usually occupies three hours and a half from the base of the mountain, and the descent rather more than half that time. Some travellers go up at night, that they may enjoy the sunrise; by doing so, they run a great risk of being disappointed, as in the morning the view is generally obscured by mists, and only occasional glimpses can be caught of the glorious prospect, which is generally clearest from mid-day to six o'clock in the evening. It is imprudent for a stranger to undertake the ascent without a guide, and one can always be procured about Fort-William for seven or eight shillings. The inexperienced traveller, also, may be the better of being reminded to carry with him some wine or spirits (which, however, should be used with caution,) wherewith to qualify the spring water, which is, fortunately, abundant, and to which he will be fain to have frequent recourse, ere he attain the object of his labours. It is customary to ascend the hill on the northern side. By making a circuit to the eastward beyond Inverlochy Castle, the traveller can proceed as far as the lake on the back of a Highland pony."—*Anderson's Guide to the Highlands*, p. 268.

will be as well accommodated as at Fort-William. Passing the farms of West and East Moy, the steamer, two miles farther, enters Loch Lochy, which is ten miles in length, by about one in breadth ; near the west end there is a fine bay, called the Bay of Arkaig, at a short distance from which is Achnacarry, the mansion of Cameron of Lochiel, chief of that clan.

Between Loch Lochy and Loch Oich, is the village of Laggan. The distance between the two lochs is nearly two miles. Loch Oich is about three and a half miles long by half a mile broad, and forms the summit level of the Caledonian Canal. Near the mouth of the river Garry, which discharges itself into this loch, are the ruins of Invergarry Castle, the ancient gathering-place of the clan Macdonell. In front is a small islet with green trees, and behind, a high mountain, called *Craig an phitich*, or the Rock of the Raven, an appellation which formed the war-cry, and is still the motto of the chiefs of Glengarry.

From Loch Oich, the steamboat descends to Loch Ness, by eight locks ; the distance between the lochs being five and a half miles. At the south-western extremity of the latter, and close upon the edge of the water, stands Fort Augustus. It was built shortly after the Rebellion of 1715. In form it is quadrangular, with four bastions at the corners. The barracks contain accommodation for about 300 men, but only six privates and a sergeant are now kept in the place.

Loch Ness is nearly twenty-four miles in length, and averages a mile and a quarter in breadth. In many places it is of great depth—about 130 fathoms—and, from the uniformity of temperature maintained by this depth of water, the lake never freezes. The character of its scenery, though highly interesting, is not so varied and striking as that through which we have already conducted the tourist.

A short distance from Fort Augustus, we pass the mouth of Glenmoriston, and the beautifully situated mansion of James Murray Grant, Esquire, the proprietor. A few miles further, on the right, are Foyers House and the mouth of the river Foyers, where the steamer generally stops to afford passengers an opportunity of viewing the celebrated fall.

This famous cataract consists of two falls, of which the lower is by far the more imposing. The upper fall is about thirty feet high, twice broken in its descent; a bridge of one arch—an aerial-looking structure—being thrown over the chasm. It is seen to the best advantage from the channel of the river below the bridge. After pursuing its impetuous course for about a quarter of a mile, the stream makes its descent in a sheet of spray of dazzling whiteness into a deep and spacious linn, surrounded by gigantic rocks. The cavity of the fall is lined with a profusion of shrubs and plants, nursed by the perpetual spray. The height of this fall is variously stated, but it cannot be less than sixty feet. The banks on either side are diversified with the birch and the ash, and an undergrowth of copsewood, with those stupendous chasms and rocky eminences which confer additional grandeur on such a scene. "The Fall of Foyers," says Professor Wilson, "is the most magnificent cataract, out of all sight and hearing, in Britain. The din is quite loud enough in ordinary weather; and it is only in ordinary weather that you can approach the place from which you have a full view of all its grandeur. When the Fall is in flood—to say nothing of being drenched to the skin—you are so blinded by the sharp spray smoke, and so deafened by the dashing, and clashing, and tumbling, and rumbling thunder, that your condition is far from enviable, as you cling, 'lonely lover of nature,' to a shelf, by no means eminent for safety, above the horrid gulf. In ordinary Highland weather—meaning thereby weather neither very wet nor very dry—it is worth walking a thousand miles for one hour to behold the Fall of Foyers."* About two and

* Dr. E. D. Clarke, who visited this fall, declared it to be a finer cascade than Tivoli, and, of all he had seen, inferior only to Terni. The following lines were written by Burns upon the spot on September 5, 1787:—

"Among the heathy hills and ragged woods,
The roaring Foyers pours his mossy floods,
Till full he dashes on the rocky mounds,
Where through a shapeless breach his stream resounds,
As high in air the bursting torrents flow,
As deep recoiling surges foam below.

a half miles from this, on the left, are seen the ruins of Castle Urquhart, often noticed in the annals of the earlier Scottish monarchs, and which was the last to surrender to Edward the First. Further notice of this fine ruin will be found in our Fifteenth Tour. Glen Urquhart, which recedes behind the castle, is a beautiful Highland vale, containing many gentlemen's seats; and, at the mouth, there is a good inn called Drumnadrochet. Glen Urquhart chiefly belongs to the Earl of Seafield. At the Ferry of Bona, eight and a half miles from Drumnadrochet, the steamer enters Loch Dochfour by a narrow channel about a quarter of a mile in length. On the margin of Loch Dochfour, stands Dochfour House, the elegant mansion of E. Baillie, Esq. At the foot of the lake the steamer again enters the canal, and proceeds to Muirton, from whence there is a descent by four locks to the capacious basin of the canal, at the end of which there are two other locks, opening from the Beauly Firth.

The Caledonian Canal was finally opened in October 1822. The whole distance from the Atlantic to the German Ocean is sixty and a half miles, of which thirty-seven and a half are through natural sheets of water, and twenty-three cut as a canal. The depth of water is 17 feet when the water is at the standard level. The improvements commenced in 1843, under the direction of Mr. Walker, C.E., were finished in 1847, and, on the 1st of May, the line was opened throughout—the total cost of the works, from their commencement by Mr. Telford, in 1803, till May 1847, having exceeded £1,256,000. The steamers which keep up the communication between Glasgow and Inverness, ply almost daily from each end during the summer season. The navigation was temporarily interrupted, in the spring of 1849, by a flood of extraordinary violence. Loch Oich, fed by the swollen waters of the Garry, rose over its banks, and burst

Prone down the rock the whitening sheet descends,
And viewless echo's ear, astonish'd, rends.
Dim-seen, through rising mists and ceaseless showers,
The hoary cavern, wide-surrounding, lowers.
Still through the gap the struggling river toils,
And still below the horrid caldron boils."

into the canal, sweeping away a new stone bridge over the Oich, a few yards below the exit of the river from the loch. Loch Ness was also unusually flooded, and a breach made in the canal-bank, near Dochgarroch lock, rendered the canal impassable for a time. A third part of Inverness was under water for two days and nights, and the fine old stone bridge of seven arches, begun in 1681 and finished in 1684, was completely swept away. By persevering exertions, in a very few weeks the canal was again opened from sea to sea. George May, Esq., Clachnaharry, is the resident engineer.

For a description of Inverness, and the objects of interest in its neighbourhood, we refer to the Fifteenth Tour.

TWELFTH TOUR.

OBAN TO STAFFA AND IONA.

This excursion occupies an entire day. The fare by steamer varies from 20s. to 25s., exclusive of provisions.

In the summer and autumn months, a first-class steam-vessel is kept for the accommodation of strangers wishing to visit this far-famed spot.

After leaving Oban, the steamer passes Kerrera, a narrow rugged island, forming a natural breakwater to the bay of Oban. It was here that Alexander II. died on his expedition in 1249, and here Haco, king of Norway, met the island chieftains, who assisted him in his ill-fated descent on the coast of Scotland. Upon the south point of the island are the ruins of the Danish fort, Gylen. The boat now approaches Lismore,* a fertile island about nine miles in length and two in breadth. In ancient times it was the residence of the bishops of Argyle, who were frequently styled "Episcopi Lismorienses." Leaving Lismore on the right, the steamer enters the Sound of Mull, and passes the Lady Rock, visible only at low water, on which Maclean of Duart exposed his wife, a daughter of the second Earl of Argyle, intending that she should be swept away by the returning tide; but she was fortunately rescued by some of

* *Leosmore*, that is, "the Great Garden."

her father's people, who were passing in a boat. Maclean gave out that she had died suddenly, and was allowed to go through the ceremonial of a mock funeral, but was shortly afterwards put to death by the relations of his injured wife. This incident has been made the subject of one of Joanna Baillie's dramas—the "Family Legend." On the brink of a high cliff, on the shore of Mull, is Duart Castle, formerly the seat of the chief of the warlike and powerful clan of the Macleans. The steamer now sails along through a narrow but deep channel. On the left are the bold and mountainous shores of Mull, on the right those of that district of Argyleshire called Morven, successively indented by deep salt water lochs running up many miles inland. To the south-eastward, arise a prodigious range of mountains, among which Ben Cruachan is pre-eminent, and to the north-east is the no less huge and picturesque range of the Ardnamurchan Hills. Many ruinous castles, situated generally upon cliffs overhanging the ocean, add interest to the scene. In fine weather, a grander and more impressive scene, both from its natural beauties, and associations with ancient history and tradition, can hardly be imagined. When the weather is rough, the passage is both difficult and dangerous, from the narrowness of the channel, and in part from the numerous inland lakes, out of which sally forth a number of conflicting and thwarting tides, making the navigation perilous to open boats. The sudden flaws and gusts of wind which issue, without a moment's warning, from the mountain glens, are equally formidable ; so that, in unsettled weather, a stranger, if not much accustomed to the sea, may sometimes add to the other sublime sensations excited by the scene, that feeling of dignity which arises from a sense of danger. Opposite to Duart, on the coast of Morven, are the ruins of Ardtornish Castle,

"Where turret's airy head,
Slender and steep, and battled round,
O'erlook'd, dark Mull! thy mighty Sound,
Where thwarting tides, with mingled roar,
Part thy swarth hills from Morven's shore."*

* Lord of the Isles. *Opening Canto.*

"The situation is wild and romantic in the highest degree, having on the one hand a high and precipitous chain of rocks overhanging the sea, and, on the other, the narrow entrance to the beautiful salt water lake, called Loch Aline, which is in many places finely fringed with copsewood. The ruins of Ardtornish are not now very considerable, consisting chiefly of the remains of an old keep or tower, with fragments of outward defences. But, in former days, it was a place of great consequence, being one of the principal strongholds which the Lords of the Isles, during the period of their stormy independence, possessed upon the mainland of Argyleshire." Above the Castle of Ardtornish, is Ardtornish House, (Seller, Esq.) Another residence of the Island Kings next meets the eye in the Castle of Aros, in Mull, a powerful rock-built fortress, situated about half-way from either end of the Sound.* A short way beyond, on the Morven coast, is Killundine Castle. Holding on towards the head of the Sound, the steamer, seven miles beyond Aros, reaches Tobermory, (the well of our Lady St. Mary,) the only village of any note in Mull. It was founded in 1788, by the British Fishery Company, and is finely situated at the head of the inner recess of a well protected bay. In the immediate vicinity is Aros House, the mansion of —— Nairne, Esq. This romantic spot is well worthy the notice of the tourist. Quitting Tobermory, we pass Loch Sunart. Seven miles from Tobermory, on the Ardnamurchan coast, is the Castle of Mingarry, which

"——— sternly placed,
O'erawes the woodland and the waste."

The ruins, which are tolerably entire, are surrounded by a very high wall, forming a kind of polygon, for the purpose of adapting itself to the projecting angles of a precipice overhanging the sea, on which the castle stands. It was anciently the residence of the MacIans, a clan of Macdonalds, descended from Ian or John, a grandson of Angus

* From the village of Aros there is a road which leads across the island to Loch-na-Keal, and thence to Laggan Ulva, where there is a place of embarkation for Staffa and Iona.

Og, Lord of the Isles. Rounding the point of Callioch, the last promontory of Mull, we find ourselves moving freely on the bosom of the Atlantic, and at the same moment, if the weather is fine, the islands of Mull, including the Trishnish Isles, Tiree, Coll, Muck, Eig, and Rum, burst on the view, and, far to the north-west, the faint outlines of South Uist and Barra.* In fine weather the light-house lately erected on Skerryvore Rock may also be seen. It is a granite column 150 feet in height, and has been erected at great cost and hazard by the Commissioners of the Northern Light-houses, from the design of Alan Stevenson, Esq., engineer to the Board.

to their attention, as the most interesting and comprehensive account of the coast scenery of Scotland which has hitherto appeared.

"Fingal's Cave is indeed a most magnificent example of nature's architecture. A vast archway of nearly 70 feet in height, supporting a massive entablature of 30 feet additional, and receding for about 230 feet inwards,—the entire front, as well as the great cavernous sides, being composed of countless complicated ranges of gigantic columns, beautifully jointed, and of most symmetrical though somewhat varied forms,—the roof itself exhibiting a rich grouping of

overhanging pillars, some of snowy whiteness from the calcarcous covering by which they have become encrusted,—the whole rising from and often seen reflected by the ocean waters,—forms truly a picture of unrivalled grandeur, and one on which it is delightful to dwell even in remembrance. How often have we since recalled to mind the regularity, magnitude, and loftiness of those columns, the fine o'erhanging cliff of small prismatic basalt to which they give support, worn by the murmuring waves of many thousand years, into the semblance of some stupendous Gothic arch,

"Where thro' the long-drawn aisle and fretted vault,"

the wild waters ever urge their way,—and the receding sides of that great temple, running inwards in solemn perspective, yet ever and anon, as ocean heaves and falls, rendered visible in its far sanctuary, by the broad and flashing light reflected by the foaming surges sweeping onwards from below! Then the broken and irregular gallery which overhangs that subterranean flood, and from which, looking upwards and around, we behold the rich and varied hues of red, green, and gold, which give such splendid relief to the deep and sombre-coloured columns—the clear bright tints which sparkle beneath our feet, from the wavering yet translucent sea—the whole accompanied by the wild yet mellow and sonorous moan of each successive billow, which rises up the sides, or rolls over the finely-formed crowns of the lowlier and disjointed pillars: these are a few of the features of this exquisite and most singular scene, which cannot fail to astonish the beholder."

"Where, as to shame the temples deck'd
By skill of earthly architect,
Nature herself, it seem'd would raise
A Minster to her Maker's praise!
Not for a meaner use ascend
Her columns, or her arches bend;
Nor of a theme less solemn tells
That mighty surge that ebbs and swells,
And still, between each awful pause,
From the high vault an answer draws,
In varied tone prolong'd and high,
That mocks the organ's melody.
Nor doth its entrance front in vain
To old Iona's holy fane,
That Nature's voice might seem to say,
'Well hast thou done, frail Child of clay!
Thy humble powers that stately shrine
Task'd high and hard—but witness mine!'"*

The Boat Cave, and Mackinnon's, or the Cormorant's

* Lord *of the Isles*. c. iv., st. x.

Cave, are two others of less extent and beauty, which are usually visited after Fingal's Cave.*

Iona or Icolmkill, celebrated as an early seat of Chris-

* Professor Wilson, with Scott's description probably present to his fancy, speaks of "the pealing anthem of waves in the Cave-Cathedral of Staffa," an expression of rare felicity and beauty.

Among the numberless poetical offerings made to the glories of the place, we must content ourselves with the fine Sonnet of Wordsworth.

"Thanks for the lessons of this spot—fit school
For the presumptuous thoughts that would assign
Mechanic laws to agency divine;
And measuring heaven by earth would overrule
Infinite power. The pillar'd vestibule,
Expanding, yet precise, the roof embow'd,
Might seem designed to humble man, when proud
Of his best workmanship by plan and tool.
Down-bearing with his whole Atlantic weight
Of tide and tempest on the Structure's base,
And flashing to that Structure's topmost height,
Ocean has proved its strength, and of its grace
In calms is conscious, finding for his freight
Of softest music some responsive place."

tianity, is about nine miles to the south of Staffa. "In any other situation," says Dr. Macculloch, "the remains of Iona would be consigned to neglect and oblivion; but connected as they are with an age distinguished by the ferocity of its manners and its independence of regular government; standing a solitary monument of religion and literature, such as religion and literature then were, the mind imperceptibly recurs to the time when this island was the 'light of the western world,' 'a gem in the ocean,' and is led to contemplate with veneration its silent and ruined structures. Even at a distance, the aspect of the cathedral, insignificant as its dimensions are, produces a strong feeling of delight in him who, long coasting the rugged and barren rocks of Mull, or buffeted by turbulent waves, beholds its tower first rising out of the deep, giving to this desolate region an air of civilization, and recalling the consciousness of that human society, which, presenting elsewhere no visible traces, seems to have abandoned these rocky shores to the cormorant and the sea-gull." Iona is nearly three miles in length, and one in breadth. The origin of the celebrity of this island* is to be traced to its having become, about the year 565, the residence of Columba, an Irish Christian preacher. The monastery became, in subsequent years, the dwelling of the Cluniacenses, a class of monks who followed the rule of St. Bennet. At the Reformation, Iona, with its abbey, was annexed to the bishopric

* The following splendid and well known passage records the emotions excited in the breast of Dr. Johnson by the prospect of Iona:—"We were now treading that illustrious island which was once the luminary of the Caledonian regions, whence savage clans and roving barbarians derived the benefits of knowledge, and the blessings of religion. To abstract the mind from all local emotion would be impossible, if it were endeavoured, and would be foolish if it were possible. Whatever withdraws us from the power of our senses—whatever makes the past, the distant, or the future, predominate over the present, advances us in the dignity of thinking beings. Far from me and from my friends be such frigid philosophy as may conduct us indifferent and unmoved over any ground which has been dignified by wisdom, bravery, or virtue. That man is little to be envied whose patriotism would not gain force upon the plain of Marathon, or whose piety would not grow warmer among the ruins of Iona."

of Argyle, by James VI., in the year 1617. The celebrated ruins consist of a cathedral, a nunnery, and St. Oran's chapel. The latter, which appears to be the most ancient of these ecclesiastical remains, is of small extent (60 feet by 20) and rude architectural style, and was probably built by the Norwegians. It contains some tombs of different dates, and there are many carved stones in the pavement. The chapel of the nunnery is the next in the order of antiquity; it is in good preservation; the roof has been vaulted, and part of it still remains. The nuns were not displaced at the Reformation, but continued a long time after that event, to live together. They followed the rule of St. Augustine. The Cathedral Church of St. Mary is the principal edifice. Its form is that of a cross, the length being about 160 feet and the breadth 24. "Whatever may be its actual age it now possesses enough of 'hoar antiquity' to throw an air of solemn grandeur over the general aspect of the scene, and produces, indeed, a most imposing effect, with its massive square tower rising to the height of 70 feet above the lonesome graves, the grassy verdure of its foundations almost washed by the murmuring sea, at this time flowing gently between the lowlier shores of the Sacred Island, and the stern and rocky coast of the opposing Mull."* Most families of distinction

* Wilson's *Voyage round the Coasts of Scotland*, vol. i., p. 138.

GLASGOW, GREENOCK, KILMARNOCK & AYR
AND DUMBARTONSHIRE RAILWAYS.

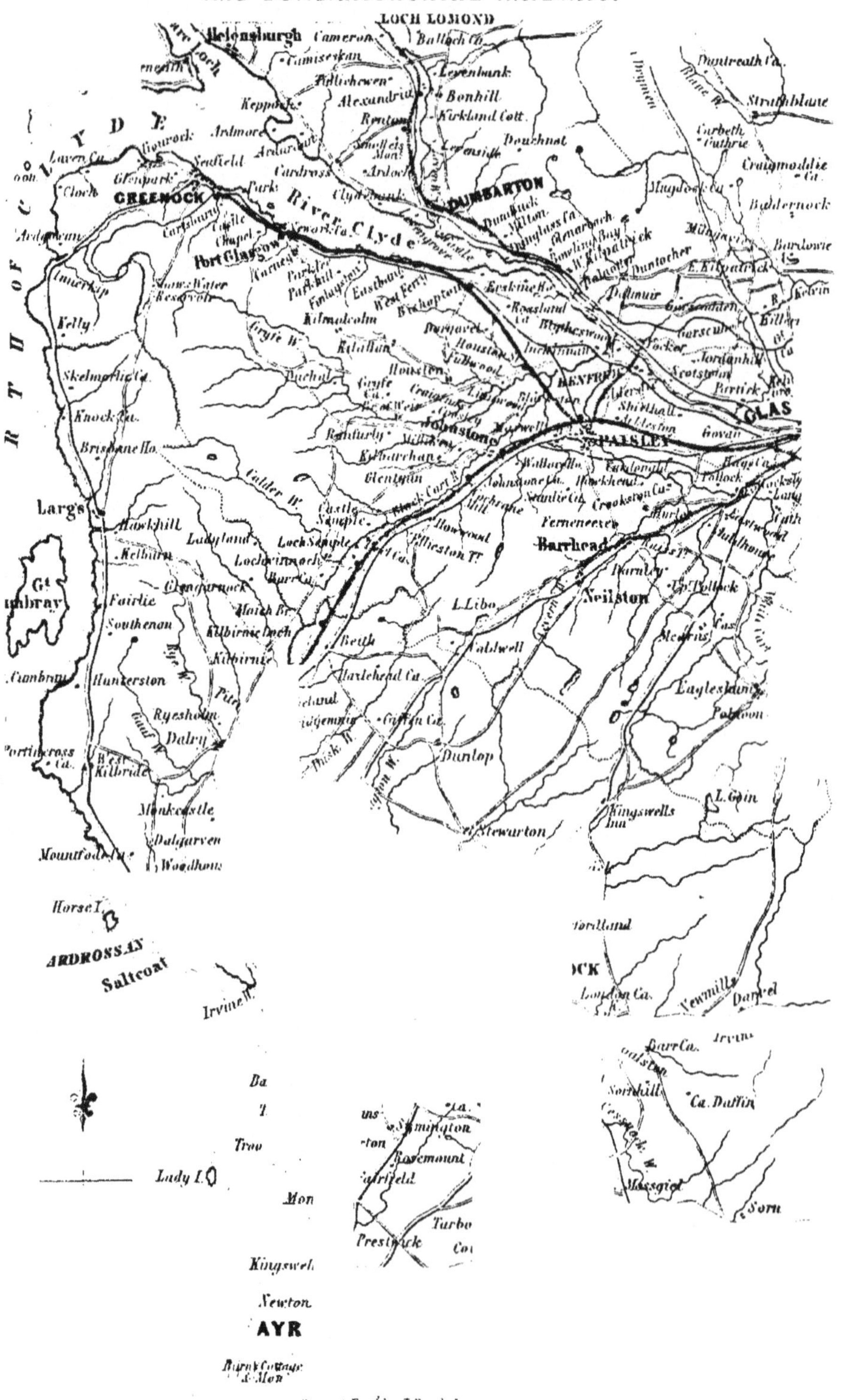

in the Highlands had burying-places here, and many erected votive chapels in different parts of the island. On the west side of Martyrs' Street is Maclean's Cross, a beautifully carved pillar, and one of the 360 stone crosses which are said to have once adorned the island; but about the year 1560, they were thrown into the sea by order of the Synod of Argyle. Iona contains 450 inhabitants, and is the property of the Duke of Argyle.

> "Homeward we turn. Isle of Columba's cell,
> Where Christian piety's soul-cheering spark
> (Kindled from Heaven between the light and dark
> Of time) shone like the morning-star,—farewell!"

THIRTEENTH TOUR.

An Itinerary of this Tour will be found at the end of the Volume.

GLASGOW—PAISLEY—KILMARNOCK—ARDROSSAN—AYR—AND THE LAND OF BURNS, BY THE GLASGOW AND AYRSHIRE RAILWAY.

The prospectus of the Railway between Glasgow and Ayrshire was issued in the spring of 1836; operations were commenced about the middle of May 1838; several portions of the line were opened at different periods; and the entire line between Glasgow and Ayr was opened on the 12th of August 1840.

The station-house at Glasgow is situate on the west side of Bridge Street, Tradestone, and very near the "Glasgow Bridge." On leaving Glasgow, the tourist passes an immense number of cotton and silk manufactories, iron-works, and other establishments of a similar kind, together with a succession of elegant villas, belonging to the wealthy merchants and manufacturers connected with the city. About half way between Glasgow and Paisley the ruins of Crookston Castle are to be seen on an eminence overhanging the south bank of the White Cart. This Castle was at one time the property of the Stewarts of Lennox, and here Queen Mary resided, when receiving the addresses of Darnley. It is now the property of Sir John Maxwell of Pollock. Seven miles from Glasgow, and 33 from Ayr, is the large manufacturing town of

PAISLEY.

[*Inns*:—The Saracen's Head.]

It is a place of great antiquity, and owes its first existence to a religious establishment founded here, about the year 1160, by Walter Stewart, the ancestor of the royal family of Scotland. The progress of the town was slow, and it was not until towards the close of last century that it assumed any appearance of importance. The original manufactures of Paisley were coarse checked linen cloth, and checked linen handkerchiefs, and these were succeeded by fabrics of a lighter and more fanciful kind. About the year 1760, the manufacture of gauze was introduced into Paisley, in imitation of the manufactures of Spitalfields. The experiment met with remarkable success, and the immense variety of elegant and richly ornamented fabrics which were issued from this place, surpassed all competition. The gauze trade now employs but few hands, and shawls of silk and cotton, plaids, scarfs, chenille and Canton crape shawls and handkerchiefs, silks, and Persian velvets, are at present the staple manufactures of the town.

Among the most interesting objects in Paisley, the Abbey Church occupies a prominent place. This magnificent building, which was dedicated to St. James and St. Mirren, suffered severely at the Reformation, and its immense revenues became the prey of several of the nobility. The chancel, which is now used as a parish church, still remains entire, along with the window of the northern transept. Attached to its south side is a small but lofty chapel, which possesses a remarkably fine echo, and contains a tomb, surmounted by a recumbent female figure, usually supposed to represent Marjory, daughter of Robert Bruce, and wife of Walter Stewart, founder of the abbey. This lady, who was mother of Robert Second, the first of the Stewart sovereigns, was killed by a fall from her horse, at a place in the neighbourhood of Paisley. The buildings connected with the abbey are the property of the Marquis of Abercorn, the representative of Claud Hamilton, the last abbot, and first temporal superior of Paisley, referred to in Sir Walter Scott's ballad of Cadyow Castle, as

> " Stern Claud ————
> Grey Paisley's haughty lord."

The population of the town, in 1841, amounted to 60,487. It returns one member to the House of Commons. A short distance from Paisley, the line passes on the left the straggling village of Elderslie. Here, near the turnpike road, is the oak in which, according to tradition, Sir William Wallace, the " Knight of Elderslie," concealed himself from the English troops. Elderslie House, which stands at a short distance, appears to be of later erection than the era of the hero. About three miles from Paisley is JOHNSTONE STATION. The town of JOHNSTONE is situated on the banks of the Black Cart. It is a thriving seat of the cotton manufacture, and contains a population of about 5900. In the vicinity of the town, to the west, is Milliken House, the seat of Sir W. M. Napier, Bart. Farther, to the north-west, is Houston House, (Speirs, Esq.) A short way farther on is the village of Kilbarchan, population 3612. The superiors of this village, in ancient times, were the Sempills of Beltrees, a family in which poetical talent was long hereditary. Sir James Sempill, ambassador to England in 1599, wrote the satire of " The Packman and the Priest." His son, Robert Sempill, was the author of the poem entitled " The Life and Death of the Piper of Kilbarchan." Francis, the son of this poet, wrote the well-known songs, " Maggie Lauder," and " She rose and loot me in." A few years ago, a statue of Habbie Simpson, the piper above-mentioned, was affixed to the steeple of the Town-Hall. After leaving the

Howood station, the line runs through a rich strath, celebrated for its beautiful scenery. On the right are the extensive and highly ornamented pleasure-grounds of Castle Semple, the seat of Colonel Harvey. On the left, above the public road to Beith, are the ruins of Elliston Tower, formerly the seat of the Sempill family. Fifteen and a half miles from Glasgow is

LOCHWINNOCH.

[*Inns*:—The Black Bull; The Buck's Head.]

The village is situated on the side of Castle Semple Loch, near the bottom of a range of hills. At a short distance to the west of it is Barr Castle, supposed to have been built in the fifteenth century. In the vicinity is Barr House, (W. Macdowell, Esq.) Castle Semple Loch is about a mile in length, and contains three wooded islets, on one of which are the remains of a fortalice erected, in ancient times, by Lord Sempill. About two and a quarter miles from Lochwinnoch, and seventeen and three quarters from Glasgow, is the town of

BEITH.

[*Inns*:—The Saracen's Head; The Commercial; The Crown; The Railway.]

In its vicinity are the ruins of Giffen Castle, formerly a possession of the Eglinton family. Proceeding onwards, near the river Garnock, are the remains of the ancient castle of Glengarnock, the property of the Earl of Glasgow, and the beautiful sheet of water called Kilbirnie Loch, extending about two miles in length, and half a mile in breadth. Nineteen and a half miles from Glasgow is KILBIRNIE, situated on the banks of the Garnock, about a mile and a half to the right of the station. Twenty-two miles from Glasgow, is

DALRY.

[*Inns*:—The Blair Arms; The White Hart.]

This thriving village is situated on an eminence, and nearly surrounded with the waters of the Garnock, Rye, and Caaf. It contains 4326 inhabitants, who are chiefly employed in weaving. From this a branch line strikes off to the left to the manufacturing town of

KILMARNOCK.

[*Inns*:—The George; The Black Bull.]

It is distinguished for its manufacture of worsted shawls, Brussels and Venetian carpets, boots, shoes, and some other articles; and its success in these manufactures has raised it to the rank of the principal town in Ayrshire for size. wealth, and population. According to the last census, the population amounted to 17,844. Within a mile north of the town, stand the ruins of Dean Castle, once the residence of the Earls of Kilmarnock. Eight and a half miles from Kilmarnock, and twenty-three and a half from Glasgow, is Stewarton. About fourteen miles from Ayr, and twenty-six from Glasgow, is

KILWINNING.

[*Inns*:—The Eglinton Arms; The Wintoun Arms.]

Kilwinning* signifies the cell of Winning, and derives its name from the circumstance of a saint named Winning having resided here in the eighth century. Hugh de Moreville, lord of Cuningham, in 1107, founded here an abbey for monks of the Tyronensian order, dedicated to Saint

* At the distance of about a mile from Kilwinning stands Eglinton Castle, the splendid mansion of the Earl of Eglinton and Wintoun, towards which public attention was recently directed by the tournament which was held in its vicinity in September 1839. — The castle was built about forty years ago, and is surrounded by extensive pleasure-grounds. The family of Montgomery is of Norman origin, and the first of the name that settled in Scotland was Robert de Montgomerie, who obtained from Walter, the High Steward of Scotland, a grant of the barony of Eaglesham, in the county of Renfrew. In the fourteenth century, Alexander de Montgomerie acquired the baronies of Eglinton and Ardrossan, by marriage with Elizabeth, daughter and sole heiress of Sir Hugh de Eglinton. At the famous battle of Otterbourne, fought in 1387, Henry Percy, the renowned Hotspur, was taken prisoner by Sir Hugh Montgomery, and, for his ransom, built the castle of Penoon or Polnoon, in Renfrewshire, which is still the property of the Eglinton family. In 1488, the representative of the family was raised to the peerage, by the title of Lord Montgomery, and in 1507-8, Hugh, the third baron, was created Earl of Eglinton. In 1582, Robert, the first Earl of Wintoun, married Lady Margaret Montgomery, eldest daughter of Hugh, third Earl of Eglinton, and the third son of that marriage, Sir Alexander Seton of Foulstruther, was adopted into the family, and became sixth Earl of Eglinton. The direct line of the Wintoun family having failed, the present Earl of Eglinton was, in January 1841, served heir to the title of Earl of Wintoun. The late Earl, Hugh, was created a British peer, by the title of Baron Ardrossan. Archibald William, the present and thirteenth Earl, was born 29th September 1812.

Winning, the ruins of which still exist. The greater part of this splendid edifice was destroyed at the Reformation, and a grant of it was made to the Earl of Glencairn; but the temporalities were erected, in 1603, into a lordship in favour of Lord Eglinton. A party of freemasons, who came from the continent to assist in the building of this monastery, were the first to introduce freemasonry into Scotland, and by means of the establishment of lodges, the knowledge of their mysteries was diffused over the rest of the country. Kilwinning is also distinguished as a seat of archery, a company of archers having been organised here in 1488. They have a custom of shooting annually for a prize at the popinjay or papingo, a practice described in the tale of Old Mortality. The population of Kilwinning is 3772. On the right a branch of the railway leads to the towns of SALTCOATS and ARDROSSAN, the former being about four miles distant, and the latter about five and a half miles. About 200 years ago, Saltcoats was inhabited by only four families, who gained their livelihood by making salt. It now contains 4000 inhabitants.

ARDROSSAN.

[*Inns*:—Eglinton Arms.]

This town, which of late has attained considerable celebrity as a watering place, is of recent origin, and its rise is owing chiefly to the public-spirited exertions of the Eglinton family. It possesses an excellent harbour, for which it was indebted to the late Earl of Eglinton, who laid out an enormous sum of money on its erection. The undertaking has now been accomplished by the present Earl.* Proceeding onward, should the atmosphere be clear, the tourist will obtain on the right, a view of the Island of Arran, with its lofty and precipitous mountains. The line next crosses the Garnoch, which here forms the boundary betwixt the parishes of Kilwinning and Irvine. A little farther on, the river Irvine is crossed by an elegant bridge of six arches. Twenty-nine and a half miles from Glasgow, and ten and a half miles from Ayr, is the royal burgh of

* Steamboats ply regularly from Ardrossan to Glasgow, Fleetwood, Arran, and Belfast.

IRVINE.

[*Inns*:—The King's Arms; The Wheat Sheaf.]

A monastery of Carmelite or White Friars was founded here in 1412. There are 124 vessels belonging to the port, which employ 1000 seamen. Irvine unites with Ayr, Campbelton, Inverary, and Oban, in returning a member to Parliament. The population in 1840 was 10,779. Irvine is remarkable for having been the temporary residence of Burns, and the birth-place of James Montgomery the poet, and John Galt the novelist. After leavng Irvine, a view is obtained, on the left, of the remains of the ancient castle of Dundonald, standing on an elevated position, about two miles distant. The situation of this castle, on the top of a beautiful hill, is singularly noble. It was the property of Robert Stewart, who, in right of his mother, Marjory Bruce, succeeded to the Scottish throne under the title of Robert II. Here he wooed and married his first wife, the beautiful Elizabeth Mure of Rowallan, and here he died in 1390. This castle gives the title of Earl to the noble family of Cochrane. The estate passed into the hands of the Earl of Eglinton in the beginning of last century; but the castle, along with the hill on which it stands, and five roods of adjoining land, still belong to the Earl of Dundonald. In the vicinity of Dundonald Castle are the remains of an ancient church dedicated to the Virgin, called Our Lady's Kirk. James IV., in passing through this part of his kingdom, uniformly made an offering at this Kirk, generally giving fourteen shillings at a time. About four and a half miles from Irvine, and six miles from Ayr, is

TROON.

[*Inns*:—Mrs. Douglas'; Maitland's; Findlay's.]

The village is situated on the right, at about half a mile from the station. The Duke of Portland is superior of this place, and under his patronage it has attained to considerable importance. It is a well-frequented watering place, and carries on a small coasting trade. The line now passes very near the sea; and in the course of a short time we observe, on the left, Fullarton House, a seat of the Duke of Portland, situate on a spacious lawn, and surrounded, except in front, with extensive woods. Three miles onward is MONKTON STATION, and village, and a mile farther, the small burgh of Prestwick; a little beyond it, the ruins of Kingscase, a charitable institution, endowed by King Robert Bruce; and, at the distance of forty miles from Glasgow, at the mouth of the river of the same name, lies the county town and royal burgh of

AYR.

[*Inns*:—The King's Arms; The Star; The Ayr Arms; The Commercial.]

Ayr was erected into a royal burgh by William the Lion. It contains a number of handsome public buildings, and many of its shops and dwelling-houses may vie in elegance with those of the metropolis. The river Ayr divides Ayr Proper from Newton and Wallacetown. The river rises on the border of the county, at the eastern extremity of the parish of Muirkirk, and after a course of about thirty miles, falls into the sea at this place. It is crossed here by two bridges, respectively termed the Auld and New Brigs, and noticed under these denominations by Burns, in his poem of "The Twa Brigs." The Auld Brig is said to have been built in the reign of Alexander III. (1249-1285) by two maiden sisters of the name of Lowe, whose effigies were consequently carved upon a stone in the eastern parapet, near the south end of the fabric. It is stated by tradition, that before the erection of this bridge, a ford, about two hundred yards farther up, called the Doocote Stream, afforded the best passage which is to be had across the river in this quarter. The new bridge was erected in 1788, chiefly through the exertions of Provost Ballantyne, the gentleman to whom Burns dedicated the poem of "The Twa Brigs." The "Dungeon Clock," alluded to in the poem, was placed at the top of an old steeple in the Sandgate, but was taken down in 1826. The "Wallace Tower" was a rude old building, which stood in the eastern part of the High Street, at the head of a lane named the Mill Vennel. It was in this tower, according to tradition, that Wallace was confined. Having become ruinous, it was taken down in

1835, and a Gothic structure erected on its site, containing at the top the clock and bells of the dungeon steeple, and ornamented in front by a statue of Wallace, executed by Mr. Thom, the well-known self-taught sculptor. Another statue of "Scotia's ill-requited chief" was placed about thirty years ago by a citizen of Ayr, on the front of a dwelling-house, which occupies the site of the ancient court-house of Ayr, supposed to have been that in which, according to Blind Harry, the Scottish lords were treacherously hanged. The fort of Ayr was built by Oliver Cromwell, in 1652, upon a level piece of ground between the town and the sea. A few fragments of the ramparts still remain, together with an old tower, which formed part of St. John's Church, founded in the twelfth century. Cromwell inclosed this church within the walls of his citadel, and turned it into an armoury, but, as a compensation to the inhabitants, he gave £150 towards the erection of the present Old Church of Ayr, on the site of a Dominican monastery, remarkable in history as the place where Robert Bruce held the Parliament which settled his succession. The only memorial now existing of this monastery is in the name of a spring called the Friar's Well, which runs through the churchyard into the river. The Old Church still contains the same seats and galleries with which it was originally fitted up.

At the north-eastern angle of the fort, close upon the harbour, is supposed to have stood the ancient Castle of Ayr, built by William the Lion. The Cross of Ayr, an elegant structure in the form of a hexagon, which stood where Sandgate Street meets High Street, was removed when the New Bridge was built in 1788.

The population of the burgh of Ayr, within the Royalty, amounted, in 1841, to 7035.

About two and a half miles to the south of Ayr, overhanging the sea, is the old castle of Greenan, of which mention is made in a charter granted towards the end of the twelfth century, in the reign of King William the Lion.

Dunure Castle stands about five miles farther along the

coast, round the heads of Ayr, and not far from the mouth of the Doon. Dunure is now a tall empty tower, occupying a commanding situation on this rugged coast. It appears

to have been the first mansion of any consequence possessed by the family of Kennedy, and was the place where, in 1570, Gilbert, fourth Earl of Cassillis, confined Allen Stewart, Commendator of the Abbey of Crossraguel; and, in order to prevail upon him to surrender his lands, roasted him before a slow fire, till pain obliged him to comply. This castle, which has been in ruins since the seventeenth century, now gives a territorial designation to a branch of the family of Kennedy, the present representative of which is T. F. Kennedy, Esq., formerly Member of Parliament for the Ayr district of burghs.

Colzean, or Colyean Castle, the principal seat of Archibald Marquis of Ailsa, and twelfth Earl of Cassillis, is situate about three miles farther along the Carrick coast, and about two miles from the village of Kirkoswald. This magnificent and picturesque mansion was built in 1777 by David tenth Earl, on the site of the old House of the Cove, erected about the middle of the sixteenth century by Sir Thomas Kennedy, second son of Gilbert Earl of Cassillis. It stands upon the verge of a great basaltic cliff overhanging the sea, and presents along the verge of a precipice "a range of lofty castellated masses, with windows in a Gothic taste, a splendid terraced garden in front, a bridge of approach and offices in corresponding style at a little distance to the left, the whole covering an area of four acres, and conveying a most imposing impression of baronial dignity, affluence, and taste." The interior of the castle contains an extensive and valuable collection of arms and armour.

The Kennedys have long held a prominent place among the aristocracy of Ayrshire. According to the old rhyme,

"'Twixt Wigton and the town o' Ayr,
Port-Patrick and the Cruives of Cree,
Nae man need think for to bide there,
Unless he court wi' Kenedie."

This powerful race was first ennobled, in 1466, by the title of Lord Kennedy; in 1510 they attained the dignity of Earls of Cassillis; and, in 1831, Archibald the twelfth Earl, was created Marquis of Ailsa. The main line of the Cassillis family became extinct in 1759, and the title and family estates became the inheritance of Sir Thomas Kennedy of Colzean, who accordingly became ninth Earl of Cassillis. He was descended from Sir T. Kennedy, who was assassinated near the town of Ayr, May 12th, 1602, by Kennedy of Bargeny, at the instigation of Mure of Auchindrane, a deed which has been made the subject of a drama by Sir Walter Scott.

Directly underneath the castle are the Coves of Colzean, six in number. According to popular report, they are a favourite haunt of fairies, and are known to have afforded shelter, after the revolution, to Sir Archibald Kennedy of Colzean, who acquired an unenviable notoriety as a *persecutor*, during the reigns of Charles II. and James VII.

Colzean and the Cove are thus alluded to by Burns, in his "Halloween :"

"Upon that night when fairies light,
On Cassillis Downan's dance,
Or ower the lays in splendid blaze,
On sprightly coursers prance,
Or for *Colzean* the route is ta'en
Beneath the moon's pale beams,
There up the *Cove*, to stray and rove,
Among the rocks and streams,
To sport that night."

TURNBERRY CASTLE,

"Where Bruce once ruled the martial ranks,
And shook the Carrick spear,"

stands a few miles to the south of Colzean. It was in the twelfth and thirteenth centuries "the principal house in Carrick, and the seat of a powerful race of native chiefs, derived from Fergus, Lord of Galloway, and designated Earls of Carrick, who possessed the supreme influence in this mountainous region previous to the rise of the Kennedies." In 1271, Robert Bruce, son of the Lord of Annandale, married the widowed Countess of Carrick, to whom the earldom had descended. From this union sprung Robert Bruce, King of Scotland, who, if not born in Turnberry Castle, must have spent many of his youthful years in it. It was in the neighbourhood of this place that a fire, accidentally kindled, was mistaken by the hero for an appointed signal, and caused him to cross the sea from Arran to Carrick, to attempt the deliverance of his country. On landing, the mistake was discovered, but he nevertheless determined to proceed with the enterprise ; and though he was not immediately successful in his exertions for the liberation of Scotland from the English yoke, he was never again forced to leave the country till this object was attained. This incident has been related both by Barbour, and by Sir Walter Scott, in the "Lord of the Isles." The latter thus describes the appearance of the "ruddy signal" kindled on Carrick shore :—

"As less and less the distance grows,
High and more high the beacon rose;
The light, that seem'd a twinkling star,
Now blazed portentous, fierce, and far.
Dark-red the heaven above it glow'd,
Dark-red the sea beneath it flow'd;
Red rose the rocks on ocean's brim
In blood-red lights her islets swim,
Wild scream the dazzled sea-fowl gave,
Dropp'd from their crags on plashing wave.
The deer to distant covert drew,
The black-cock deem'd it day, and crew.
Like some tall castle given to flame,
O'er half the land the lustre came.
* *
Wide o'er the sky the splendour glows,
As that portentous meteor rose;
Helm, axe, and falchion glitter'd bright,
And in the red and dusky light
His comrade's face each warrior saw,
Nor marvell'd it was pale with awe.
Then high in air the beams were lost,
And darkness sunk upon the coast." *

"The only tradition now remembered of the landing of Robert Bruce in Carrick, relates to the fire seen by him from the isle of Arran. It is still generally reported and religiously believed by many, that this fire was really the work of supernatural power, unassisted by the hand of any mortal being; and it is said, that for several centuries the flame rose yearly on the same hour of the same night of the year on which the king first saw it from the turrets of Brodick Castle; and some go so far as to say, that if the exact time were known it would be still seen. That this superstitious notion is very ancient, is evident from the place where the fire is said to have appeared being called the Bogle's Brae beyond the remembrance of man.

"The top of the rock on which Turnberry is built is about eighteen feet above high-water mark. The ruin, rising between forty and fifty feet above the water, has a majestic appearance from the sea. Around the Castle of Turnberry

* *Lord of the Isles*, c. v., st. 13, 14.

was a level plain of about two miles in extent, forming the Castle Park. There could be nothing more beautiful than the copsewood and verdure of this extensive meadow before it was invaded by the ploughshare."*

Turnberry is still enumerated (under the denomination of Carrick) among the royal palaces of Scotland. It is now the property of the Marquis of Ailsa.

Within sight of Turnberry, and not more than a mile from it, is the farm of Shanter, formerly the residence of Douglas Graham, the original of "Tam o' Shanter."

At a short distance is the village of Kirkoswald, at which Burns attended school for some months, in the nineteenth year of his age. In the churchyard of this village two of his characters (Tam o' Shanter and Souter Johnny) are interred.

AILSA CRAIG, a huge rock, which rises sheer out of the sea, presents a striking appearance from this shore. Its nearest distance to land is about ten miles from the coast near Girvan. It is 1103 feet in height, and about two miles in circumference at the base. The ruins of a tower, of three storeys, are to be seen perched upon it. It is the property of the Marquis of Ailsa, who takes his title as a British Peer from it. Its principal productions are solan geese, goats, and rabbits, and it is let at £30 per annum. Ailsa Craig is noticed by Burns in his song of "Duncan Gray."

BURNS' MONUMENT & COTTAGE, ALLOWAY KIRK, AND THE BRIG OF DOON.

Burns' Monument is 2¾ miles south of Ayr, 5¾ miles from Maybole, 36¾ miles from Glasgow by the Turnpike, and 42¾ by the Railway. Following the road from Ayr, a short distance from the town, there is a hill called Barnweil, which is said to have derived its name from the circumstance, that Wallace, on leaving Ayr, after having, in revenge for the treacherous slaughter of his friend, set on fire the barns in which the English soldiery were inclosed, paused on this spot to look back upon the conflagra-

* Notes to canto v. of the *Lord of the Isles.*

tion, and remarked, "The Barns o' Avr burn well." There is good reason, however, to doubt the accuracy of this traditionary etymology, and it is more likely that the name is of Celtic origin, and is descriptive of the nature of the ground. In the neighbourhood of Kirk Alloway are the various localities mentioned in "Tam o' Shanter's" route. At the distance of about one hundred and fifty yards from a bridge, called Slaphouse Bridge, is

"The Ford,
Where in the snaw the chapman smoor'd."

About one hundred yards from the "Ford," and about twenty from the road, in the plot of ground behind the house occupied by Roselle gamekeeper, is

"The meikle stane,
Whare drunken Charlie brak 's neck-bane."

Passing on the left the beautiful mansion of Roselle, (Archibald Hamilton, Esq. of Carcluie,) the tourist, at the distance of about two miles from Ayr, reaches the cottage where Burns was born on the 25th of January 1759. The original erection was a *Clay Bigging*, consisting of two apartments, the kitchen and the *spence*, or sitting-room. The cottage was built on part of seven acres of ground, of which Burns' father took a perpetual lease from Dr. Campbell, physician in Ayr, with the view of commencing business as nurseryman and gardener. Having built this house with his own hands, he married, in December 1757, Agnes Brown, the mother of the poet; and, having been engaged by Mr. Ferguson of Doonholm, as his gardener and overseer, he abandoned his design of forming a nursery, but continued to reside in the cottage till 1766. On removing to Lochlee he sold his leasehold to the Corporation of Shoemakers in Ayr, to whom the house and ground still belong. The house is now occupied as an ale-house. In the interior of the kitchen is shown a recess, where stood the bed in which the Poet was born. This bedstead may now be seen at Brownhill Inn, near Thornhill, Dumfries-shire.

About a mile and a half to the south-east of the cottage, on an eminence, stands the farm of Mount Oliphant, which

William Burns rented on leaving the cottage at Whitsuntide 1766.

Proceeding towards Burns' Monument, we perceive in a field a single tree, enclosed with a paling, the last remnant of a group which covered

> "The cairn
> Where hunters fand the murder'd bairn."

The position of the "cairn," and also of the "ford," at a distance from the highway, is accounted for by the fact, that the old road from Ayr, by which the Poet supposed his hero to have approached Alloway Kirk, was to the west of the present line. We now reach

> "Alloway's auld haunted kirk."

This interesting building has long been roofless, but the walls are pretty well preserved, and it still retains its bell at the east end. The woodwork has all been taken away to form snuff-boxes and other memorials of this celebrated spot.

In the area of the kirk, the late Lord Alloway, one of the Judges of the Court of Session, was interred; and near the gate of the churchyard is the grave of Burns' father, marked by a plain tombstone, a renewal of the original stone, which had been demolished and carried away in fragments. "The churchyard of Alloway," says Mr. Robert Chambers, "has now become fashionable with the dead as well as the living. Its little area is absolutely crowded with modern monuments, referring to persons, many of whom have been brought from considerable distances to take their rest in this doubly consecrated ground."

A few yards to the west of Alloway Kirk, a well trickles down into the Doon, where formerly stood the thorn on which

> "Mungo's mither hang'd hersel."

A few hundred yards from the kirk is the "Auld Brig" of Doon, which figures so conspicuously in the tale of Tam o' Shanter. The age of the structure is unknown, but it is evidently of great antiquity. The "New Bridge" which has been built since the time of Burns, stands about a hundred yards below the Old. The tasteful cottage between the Kirk and the Bridge belongs to Mr. David Auld, to whom the admirers of the Ayrshire bard are deeply indebted for the unwearied zeal and fine taste which he has displayed in adorning the grounds of the Monument. Close beside the end of the bridge is a neat inn for the accommodation of tourists. Directly over the bridge stands the beautiful Monument of Burns, the foundation-stone of which was laid on 25th January 1820. The project of erecting this monument originated with the late Sir Alexander Boswell of Auchinleck. It was designed by Thomas Hamilton, Esq., architect, Edinburgh, and cost upwards of £3300. The grounds around it measure about an acre and a rood, and are very tastefully laid out. In a circular apartment on the ground-floor there are exhibited several articles appropriate to the place,—various editions of the Poet's works, a snuff-box made from the woodwork of Alloway Kirk, a copy of the original portraits of Burns by Naysmith, &c., and the Bibles given by Burns to his Highland Mary. The possessor of these interesting relics having emigrated to Canada in 1834, they were purchased by a party of gentlemen in Montreal for £25, and forwarded to the Provost of Ayr, to be presented in their name to the trustees for the Monument. This was accordingly done on the 25th of January 1841, the anniversary of the Poet's birth-day. From the base of the columns, a remarkably splendid view is obtained of the surrounding scenery. In a small grotto at the south side of the enclosed ground are shown the two far-famed statues of Tam o' Shanter and Souter Johnnie by Mr. Thom of Ayr.

The Doon, to which the writings of Burns have given such celebrity, takes its rise in a lake of the same name, about eight miles in length, which is situated at the junction of the counties of Ayr and Kirkcudbright. The Doon has a course of eighteen miles, throughout which it forms the boundary between the districts of Carrick and Kyle. The scenery of the Ness Glen, through which the river runs immediately after issuing from the lake, is remarkably woody and picturesque, and is a favourite resort of *picnic* parties. Colonel M'Adam of Craigengillan, with a praiseworthy liberality, allows visiters to pass through his grounds on their way to the Loch from Dalmellington. On a small island, near the upper extremity of Loch Doon, are the ruins of an ancient castle of considerable strength, which figured in the wars between England and Scotland during the time of Robert Bruce. Sir Chrystal Seton, that hero's brother-in-law, took refuge in this fortress after the defeat at Methven, June 1306. When the castle was surrendered to the English, Sir Chrystal was taken, and barbarously put to death at Dumfries, by command of King Edward.

TARBOLTON, COILSFIELD, &c.

William Burns, on the death of his landlord, Provost Ferguson, removed from Mount Oliphant, in 1777, to Lochlee, situate in the parish of Tarbolton, and about three miles from the village of that name. While residing in this farm, Burns established a Bachelor's Club in Tarbolton, in the latter part of the year 1780; and here, in 1783, he was initiated into the mysteries of freemasonry. About two hundred yards north of the village, on the road leading to Galston, lies the scene of "Death and Dr. Hornbook." "Willie's Mill," alluded to in the poem, was the Mill of Tarbolton, situated on the Faile, about two hundred yards east of the village, and was called by the name used in the poem, in consequence of its being then occupied by William Muir, a friend of the Burns family.

About half a mile from Tarbolton stands the mansion-house of Coilsfield, designated by Burns "the Castle o' Montgomery," from its being in his time the residence of Colonel Hugh Montgomery, afterwards Earl of Eglinton. Here Mary Campbell, Burns' "Highland Mary," lived in the humble capacity of a dairymaid. In this neighbourhood, near the junction of the rivulet Faile with the Ayr, was the scene of the parting which the poet has described in such exquisite terms. In the anticipation of her marriage with Burns, Mary resolved to pay a visit to her relations in Argyleshire. Previous to her departure, she met her lover on a Sunday in May, and at their parting, "standing one on each side of a small brook, they laved their hands in the stream, and, holding a Bible between them, pronounced a vow of eternal constancy." This was their last meeting. In returning from her visit of filial duty, Mary Campbell fell sick and died at Greenock. This event produced an indelible impression on the mind of Burns, and he has given utterance to his feelings in some of the finest and most touching verses he has ever written. That "noblest of all his ballads," as the Address to "*Mary in Heaven*" has justly been designated, was composed at Ellisland, in 1789, on the anniversary of the day on which he heard of the death of his early love. According to the account given by Mrs. Burns to Mr. Lockhart, "Burns spent that day, though labouring under a cold, in the usual work of his harvest, and apparently in excellent spirits. But as the twilight deepened, he appeared to grow 'very sad about something,' and at length wandered out into the barnyard, to which his wife, in her anxiety for his health, followed him, entreating him in vain to observe that frost had set in, and to return to the fireside. On being again and again requested to do so, he always promised compliance—but still remained where he was, striding up and down slowly, and contemplating the sky, which was singularly clear and starry. At last Mrs. Burns found him stretched on a mass of straw, with his eyes fixed on a beautiful planet, 'that shone like another moon,' and prevailed on him to come in. Immediately, on entering the house, he called for his desk, and wrote exactly as they now stand, with all the ease of one copying from memory, the sublime and pathetic verses—

"Thou lingering star, with lessening ray,
That lovest to greet the early morn,
Again thou usherest in the day
My Mary from my soul was torn.

O, Mary! dear departed shade,
Where is thy place of blissful rest?
See'st thou thy lover lowly laid,
Hear'st thou the groans that rend his breast," &c.

"This," observes Mr. Carruthers in his 'Highland Notes,' "is the most beautiful and touching passage in all Burns' life. His after loves were of the earth, earthy, but his passion for Highland Mary was as pure as it was fervent and lasting. It dawned upon him at the most susceptible period of life; it let in enchantment upon scenes and objects which he had previously looked upon with coldness or aversion — it gave a fine tone of humanity to his whole moral being. Let us not admit the dictum of Byron, that 'the cold in clime are cold in blood,' since in peasant life, among the woods of Ayr, was nursed, in solitude and obscurity, a passion as deep, and thrilling, and romantic, as the loves of Tasso or Petrarch, and immeasurably beyond those of Sidney and Waller. Sacharissa and the fair ones of Arcadia must yield to the dairymaid of Montgomery Castle."*

According to unvarying tradition, Coilsfield derives its name from "Auld King Coil," who is supposed to have left his name to this whole district of Ayrshire, as well as to the rivulet of Coyl and the parish of Coylton. He is said to have been overthrown and slain in this neighbourhood, in a bloody battle with Fergus King of Scots. This statement receives some countenance from the fact, that in May 1837, several urns, and a stone grave containing some bones, were dug up in a circular mound near Coilsfield, where, according to unvarying tradition, the remains of "Auld King Coil" were deposited. Burns alludes to this tradition in his poem of "The Vision."

> "There where a sceptred Pictish shade,
> Stalk'd round his ashes lowly laid,
> I mark'd a martial race portray'd
> In colours strong;
> Bold, soldier-featured, undismay'd
> They strode along."

* *The Highland Note-Book, or Sketches and Anecdotes*, by R. CARRUTHERS, a small volume of narrative and descriptive pieces of much merit and interest, evincing throughout not only an intimate acquaintance with local history and tradition, but a fine appreciation of the beautiful and sublime in natural scenery, and a picturesqueness of style well fitted for the subjects.

The "martial race," here referred to, are the Montgomeries. Coilsfield is now the property of the Earl of Eglinton, grandson of the gentleman who possessed it in Burns' time.

MAUCHLINE, MOSSGIEL, &c.

On the death of William Burns, his widow and family removed to Mossgiel, a farm about a mile north of Mauchline, which the poet and his brother Gilbert had taken some months before the death of their father. Here Burns lived during the period of his life extending from his 25th to his 28th year, and here he wrote his principal poems. The *spence* of this farm-house is the scene described in the opening of *The Vision*, and in the *stableloft*, where he slept, many of his most admired poems were written. Mauchline, which "appropriated a large share of the notice of the poet during his residence at Mossgiel," lies about nine miles from Kilmarnock, and eleven from Ayr. It is situated on the face of a slope, about a mile from the river Ayr, and contains upwards of 1300 inhabitants. Mauchline was the scene of the *Holy Fair*, and of the *Jolly Beggars*, and here dwelt John Dow, Nanse Tinnock, "Daddy Auld," and other characters who figured conspicuously in the poet's writings. The churchyard was the scene of the *Holy Fair*, but the present church is a recent substitute for the old barn-like edifice which existed in Burns's time. Near the church is the *Whitefoord Arms* Inn, where Burns wrote, on a pane of glass, the well-known amusing epitaph on the landlord, John Dow. Nearly opposite the churchyard gate is the house of "Auld Nanse Tinnock," bearing over the door the date 1744. "It is remembered," says Mr. Chambers, "that Nancy could never understand how the poet should have talked of enjoying himself in her house three times a-week,—'the lad,' she said, 'hardly ever drank three half-mutchkins under her roof in his life.'" The cottage of *Poosie Nansie*, the scene of the "Jolly Beggars," is also pointed out. Close behind the churchyard is the house in which Mr. Gavin Hamilton, the early friend of

Burns, lived. In this house is shown the room in which Burns composed the satirical poem entitled "The Calf." This room is farther remarkable as the one in which the poet was married.

The scenes of some of Burns's most admired lyrics are to be found on the banks of the Ayr, at a short distance from Mauchline. The "Braes of Ballochmyle," the scene of his beautiful song entitled "The Lass o' Ballochmyle," are situated at the distance of about two miles from Mossgiel, and extend along the north bank of the Ayr, between the village of Catrine and Howford Bridge. They form part of the pleasure-grounds connected with Ballochmyle House, the seat of Alexander, Esq. Ballochmyle was at one time the property of the Whitefoords, an old and once powerful Ayrshire family. Colonel Allan Whitefoord, one of the members of this family, was the original of the character of Colonel Talbot, described in the novel of Waverley. Another of them, Caleb Whitefoord, "the best natured man, with the worst natured muse," has been immortalised by Goldsmith in a postscript to his witty poem entitled "Retaliation." Sir John Whitefoord, the representative of the family in the time of Burns, having been forced to part with his estate in consequence of declining circumstances, Burns wrote some plaintive verses on the occasion, referring to the grief of Maria Whitefoord, afterwards Mrs Cranstoun, on leaving the family inheritance

"Through faded groves Maria sang,
Hersel' in beauty's bloom the while,
And aye the wild-wood echoes rang,
Fareweel the braes of Ballochmyle.

Low in your wintry beds, ye flowers,
Again ye 'll flourish fresh and fair;
Ye birdies dumb in withering bowers,
Again ye 'll charm the vocal air;

But here, alas! for me nae mair
Shall birdie charm or floweret smile;
Fareweel the bonnie banks of Ayr—
Fareweel, fareweel, sweet Ballochmyle."

Ballochmyle was purchased by Claud Alexander, Esq.; and shortly after that gentleman had taken possession of the mansion, his sister Miss Wilhelmina Alexander, a famed beauty, walking out along the braes one evening in July 1786, encountered Burns, with his shoulder placed against one of the trees. The result was, that the poet, during his homeward walk, composed the well-known song entitled "The Lass of Ballochmyle." The spot where Miss Alexander met the poet is now distinguished by a rustic grotto or moss-house, ornamented with appropriate devices; and on a tablet in the back there is inscribed a fac-simile of two of the verses of the poem, as it appeared in the holograph of the author. Near Ballochmyle is the manufacturing village of Catrine, at one time the seat of Dr. Stewart, and of his son, the celebrated Professor Dugald Stewart. To them Burns alludes in the following stanza in "The Vision"

"With deep-struck reverential awe,
The learned sire and son I saw,
To Nature's God and Nature's law
They gave their lore;
This all its source and end to draw,
That to adore."

Between the villages of Tarbolton and Mauchline stands the mansion of Barskimming, occupying a romantic situation on the banks of the Ayr. The scenery of the river at this spot is remarkably beautiful. Barskimming, and its late proprietor, Lord President Miller, are thus alluded to in the above-mentioned poem:—

"Through many a wild romantic grove,
Near many a hermit-fancied cove,
Fit haunts for friendship or for love;
In musing mood,
An aged judge I saw him rove,
Dispensing good."

A short distance farther up the river, at the point where the Lugar joins the Ayr, is the spot where Burns composed the poem entitled "Man was made to mourn."

FOURTEENTH TOUR.

CARLISLE—ANNAN—DUMFRIES—THORNHILL—KIRCUDBRIGHT—WHITHORN—STRANRAER.

CARLISLE.

[*Inns*:—Bush; Coffee House; Royal Hotel.]

Carlisle, the capital of county Cumberland, and the seat of a bishopric founded by Henry I., stands on a gentle eminence, in an extensive plain, at the confluence of the Eden, Caldew, and Peteril, which nearly surround what was anciently termed "the merrie citie." The environs are rich in villas, woods, lawns, and gardens. At a short distance to the south of the town is Corby Castle, the romantic residence of Philip Howard, Esq., M.P., beautifully wooded and watered. At the commencement of the present century, the population of the town scarcely exceeded 10,000; in 1841 it had risen to 23,000, and at present it is believed to approach 26,000—partly owing to the clustered railways of which it forms a centre, and still more to the introduction of extensive cotton and other manufactures, including a biscuit-baking establishment, considered the largest north of Portsmouth, in Great Britain.

Leaving, then, "the heart of Cumberland," with its beautiful bridge of ten arches, completed in 1817, its time-worn Cathedral, where rest the ashes of Archdeacon Paley, the numerous public buildings, churches, and spires, the venerable Castle, associated with many a tale of Border feud and foray, and last, but not least, the tall chimneys, emitting plentiful volumes of smoke, the tourist crosses the Eden by the Caledonian Railway; and from that point is conveyed rapidly to the boundary, skirted by a running stream, alluded to by Home in his tragedy of "Douglas"—

> "Here an ideal line, and there a nameless brook,
> Divide the sister kingdoms."

All the world has heard of Gretna-green, now the site of a straggling village, with a roadside inn a little way beyond, long celebrated as favourite temples of Hymen; or, in other words, the scene of the runaway irregular marriages frequently denounced by the Lords of Justiciary during their Border circuits; but which, from certain peculiarities in the Scottish law of marriage, no act of Session has hitherto succeeded either in exploding or sensibly diminishing. Indefensible as the practice may be, it would be easy to append a lengthened list of *distingues* married at Gretna-green, including two Lord Chancellors (Eldon and Erskine), Sir Thomas Lethbridge, Bart., his son, and many others.

At Gretna, the tourist passes from the Caledonian to the Nithsdale, or Glasgow and South-Western Railway; and thence onward to Dumfries, *via* Dornock, Annan,* Cummertrees, Ruthwell, Mousewald, the Glen, and Kinmount,—seats of the Marquis of Queensberry, and his son and heir, Lord Drumlanrig. In this route the scenery is

* This royal burgh and parish ranks as one of the most ancient towns in Scotland. Its first charter, received from King Robert Bruce, was renewed by James V. in 1538, and again by James VI. in 1612. It is situate on the left bank of the Annan water, near its discharge into the Solway Frith, 16 miles south of Dumfries, and 79 from Edinburgh. Considerable improvements in the architecture of the town have been introduced of late years by the opening of new streets, one of the best of which leads to the railway station, and among the more ornamental modern edifices, may be classed the offices of the Commercial and British Linen Company's banks. The parish church stands at the east end of the town, and, in the opposite direction, are the town-house and market place. Closely adjoining, strangers descry a handsome bridge of three arches, crossing the Annan a short distance above its *embouchure*. The late Hugh Clapperton, and the Rev. Edward Irving, were natives of Annan, the latter of whom, after achieving name and notoriety, was ejected at a Presbyterial meeting in the parish church, by the same body that licensed him as a preacher. It was a strange scene, where hundreds heard for the first time the mutterings called the "unknown tongue"—a spectacle, in fact, which, viewed in connexion with the speeches delivered, and the judgment pronounced, few who attended can ever forget. Besides the parish church there are several other places of worship belonging to dissenting bodies. The population of Annan is 4,600; and it unites with Dumfries, Kirkcudbright, Lochmaben, and Sanquhar, in returning a representative to the House of Commons.

tame and monotonous, but relieved occasionally by cheering glimpses of the Solway Frith, and the range of hills overlooking the Cumberland and Westmoreland lake districts.

Passing Ruthwell and its manse gardens, adorned by a curious Runic column, and summer-house composed of stones indented with foot-prints of land tortoises, ere the second formation of red sandstone had cooled down, the traveller descries the ancient keep and surrounding woods of Comlongan Castle, connected with which are yew-trees of great age, and varied traces of antiquity befitting a barony which during ages has formed part of the extensive Dumfriesshire estates of the Earl of Mansfield. The traveller now approaches a twelve-mile-long morass, called Lochar Moss, through which the stream called Lochar serpentines its sluggish way. Regarding this moss a tradition has passed from sire to son, through successive generations,—

> "Ance a wood, and then a sea,
> Now a moss, and ay will be."

But the improvements already effected, and others contemplated, bid fair to falsify this ancient prediction.

DUMFRIES.

[*Inns*:—King's Arms; Commercial.]

Upon reaching the capital of the south, most strangers first find their way to St. Michael's, *alias* the old churchyard, and sometimes called the Westminster Abbey of Scotland. Among the multitudinous monumental structures on the ground, that which is erected to Robert Burns is the most important. This monument was built on the strength of a public subscription, patronised by George IV., Sir Francis Burdett, and many other members of the aristocracy in North and South Britain. The design was furnished by Thomas F. Hunt, architect, and the sculpture by Turnerelli. The emblematic marble is composed of a plough and two figures representing the genius of Scotland investing Burns, in his rustic dress and employment, with her inspiring mantle. Leaving

St. Michael's, tourists naturally wish to inspect the modest mansion in which the poet died, and in which his widow continued to live for more than thirty years after his death. The churches in the town are numerous. In connexion with the Establishment there are three; two United Secession; one Episcopalian; one Free Church; one Catholic Chapel; one Cameronian; one Independent; one Relief; and one Methodist Chapel. The town possesses a spacious academy, with ample play-ground attached; a court-house, with sheriff's, and sheriff-clerk's chambers; a new jail; and an infirmary, situated a little out of town. The town-house steeple was designed by Inigo Jones. Now, that the tanning trade has declined, the chief branch of manufactures is hosiery.

Dumfries has long been noted for its weekly cattle markets, held during the greater part of the year, and four annual fairs, for the sale of cattle, horses, and occasionally sheep. Formerly, 25,000 grown bullocks and heifers were sent to England yearly, valued at £10 each, over-head, besides the export of fatted animals sent to other quarters. The principal foreign trade is with America and the Baltic, for timber, of which the value varies from £8,000 to £10,000. The imports are coal, slate, iron, tallow, bones, guano, wine, and colonial produce. There belonged to the port, on the 1st January 1850, 150 vessels, of the aggregate burden of 10,721 tons. Customs revenue in 1849 amounted to £12,912. The town is governed by a provost, three bailies, and twenty-two councillors. Corporation revenue in 1849, £1408.

Between Dumfries and the West of Scotland the intercourse is now complete by the railway, which, in ascending Nithsdale, passes all the centres of population—Thornhill, Sanquhar, New and Old Cumnock, Mauchline, Kilmarnock, Ayr, and Paisley, onward to Glasgow. In travelling south, the line terminates at Gretna, where it joins the Caledonian, which passes on to Carlisle, and from that point by various lines to the metropolis itself.

Great and distinctly traceable as is the antiquity of

Dumfries, it was not till the twelfth century that it became a royal burgh. About seventy years afterwards, Devorgilla, daughter of Alan, last lord of Galloway, and mother of John Baliol, erected a monastery for Franciscan friars; and about the same time built a bridge across the Nith, with a view to endow, by tollage and other dues, the religious foundation. This wonderful structure consisted originally of thirteen arches, with a barrier in the centre; but for some years they have been reduced to six; and it is now only crossed by foot passengers. The vestiges of Roman arch-work excepted, it is believed to be the oldest bridge in Scotland. Castledyke ranks as a second antiquity, bearing, as it still does, its original name, although now private property, and, in proportion to extent, one of the loveliest residences in the South of Scotland. Traces of its ancient fosses still remain, and a moat on the opposite side of the river, upon which sentinels were stationed to sound the alarum in times of danger. Another strong castle stood on the site occupied, for considerably more than a century, by the new church; for as Dumfries was in some respects a Border town, defences were found indispensable in resisting the sacking forays of the English. It was at Castledykes that Comyn, one of the rivals of Bruce, resided, when a messenger of his was intercepted at Lochmaben, carrying treasonable letters to London. The future hero of Bannockburn, accompanied by the head of the Kirkpatricks, and other friends, hastened to Dumfries to demand an explanation. Bruce found "the Comyn" standing before the high altar of the Friar's Church, taxed him with the falsehood and treachery of his despatches to Edward, and, high words having arisen, he drew a dagger and assassinated his kinsman, under circumstances of great provocation. James VI. in passing through Dumfries in 1617, presented the trades with a small silver gun to foster rivalry among marksmen; but as time rolled on, and order became established, prudence counselled the discontinuance of so dangerous a pastime—(See Mayne's "Siller Gun"). In 1706 the burgesses displayed their opposition to the

Union by burning at the Cross the articles and names of the Commissioners. In 1715 they evinced great loyalty to the reigning family by fortifying the town so strongly, that the insurgents, who threatened, abandoned their intention—a service for which they paid dearly in 1745, in the shape of fines and other mulcts, on the retreat of the rebel army from England, commanded by Prince Charles in person.

Leaving Dumfries, by railway, the tourist is carried along a handsome bridge of ten arches, the effect of which is enhanced by the surrounding scenery, including the peninsular point where the Nith receives the waters of the Cluden; and where, hard by, burst into view the remains of Lincluden Abbey. The ruins attract numerous summer visitors. Close by the ruins is Lincluden House—(Hon. Mrs. Young). According to Captain Grose and other authorities, Lincluden was originally a nunnery, but in consequence of irregularities, real or imputed, became shortly after a college, and continued for centuries the abode of Beadsmen, who performed its services, dispensed its charities, and applied its revenues, until scared away by the Reformation. The chapel, although roofless, still exhibits interesting fragments in architecture, and contains a tomb erected in memory of Margaritta, one of the daughters of Alan, Lord Galloway.

About three miles above the first, the Nith is spanned by a second bridge, composed of timber, skirted on the one side by Cowhill and Portrack, the properties and seats of Admiral Johnston, and A. H. Maxwell, Esq.; and on the other by the broad and fertile holms of Dalswinton. The mansion-house stands on an elevated terrace, and behind it is the lake, rendered classical as the cradle of steam navigation. At that time it was the property of Patrick Miller, Esq., but now it belongs to James M'Alpine Leny, Esq. When Burns visited Edinburgh, on the publication of a second edition of his poems, he became acquainted with Mr. Miller, and it was on his invitation that he entered as tenant on the farm of Ellisland, then a portion of the Dalswinton estate, but disjoined a number of years ago. It was at Ellisland Col. Wm. Burns was born, and there his gifted father, among other effusions, produced two of his noblest, viz., "Tam o' Shanter," and the ode to "Mary in Heaven." Hence the interest which attaches to a spot which owes its chief external charm to the banks of Nith.

At a trifling distance from the wooden railway bridge, travellers hail the lawns, plantations, and mansion-house of Friars' Carse, where "the Ayrshire ploughman," was not unfrequently an honoured guest. It was here "the Whistle" was contested in Scandinavian fashion, and where the then resident Major Riddel, dispensed a generous hospitality. Till A.D. 1500, if not later, a community of Friars were seised in the lands, as the name implies, and hence the origin of the rustic fog-house, erected in commemoration, on one of the glazed windows of which the poet with a diamond pencil inscribed a copy of verses, "familiar as household words," and which the key-note alone will sufficiently recal:—

"Life is but a day at most,
Sprung from night; in darkness lost;
Hope not sunshine every hour,
Fear not clouds will always lower.
Stranger go; Heaven be thy guide,
Quod the Beadsman of Nidside."

Friars' Carse, like many other villas with fertile acres around, has been possessed by different proprietors and tenants during the last sixty or seventy years; and the family of one of the last of these, before removing, cut the poetical pane from its rustic site, but so clumsily, that it received considerable injury. Still the lines remained long after the hand that traced them had been mouldering in the dust; and, in consequence, the relic, at a sale in Dumfries, actually brought the sum of £15 sterling,—a high compliment to the vitality irradicable from everything connected with high original genius.

At a short distance from Friars' Carse is Blackwood—(William Copland, Esq.)—a finely situated residence.

Leaving Auldgirth, the next stage is Brownhill, now the site of a railway station, and at an earlier date a posting-house and inn.

Arriving at Closeburn Station, $11\frac{3}{4}$ miles from Dumfries, WALLACE HALL ACADEMY, so named from its founder, will be observed on the right. It is one of the most liberally endowed, and best conducted educational establishments in Scotland. The late Dr. Carson, and Professors Hunter and Gillespie of St. Andrews, were among its pupils. At a short distance are the Manse and Church, pleasantly situated. Closeburn Hall, the seat of the late Sir Charles Menteath, Bart., and recently purchased by Douglas Baird, Esq., is the adjoining property. In its vicinity is CRICKOPE LINN, a romantic dell, much visited by lovers of the picturesque. The Duchess of Buccleuch, with her titled friends, makes it a frequent place of resort in summer when residing at Drumlanrig Castle.

THORNHILL

[*Inns*:—The Buccleuch and Queensberry; The George.]

Is a thriving village 2 miles distant from Closeburn. Persons proposing to visit Drumlanrig Castle—4 miles distant—here leave the railway, and may be provided with vehicles at either of the inns. The drive is very beautiful, and the commanding supremacy of the Castle over the surrounding scenery is very striking. The parish church (Morton) will be observed on an eminence, a short distance to the right, on leaving the village; and about 2 miles distant from it, but not visible unless closely approached, are the ruins of Morton Castle. Having reached the hamlet of Carronbridge, the tourist may either continue to proceed along the public road and cross the Nith by Drumlanrig Bridge, or he may turn to the left and ford the river. If the road by the bridge be taken, the house of the head gamekeeper (J. Shaw), whose experiments and observations established the natural history of the salmon, will be seen, pleasantly situated on rising ground within Drumlanrig Park. In style of architecture Drumlanrig Castle closely approximates to Heriot's Hospital in Edinburgh, and, like that building, its design is attributed to Inigo Jones. Its inner quadrangle has been invaded by a chapel, which much disfigures its appearance. The interior possesses no very important treasures either in art or in antiquities, but it is well worth visiting for the views from the windows or the roof.

The road or railroad along the side of the Nith towards Sanquhar, forms a pleasant route. Within two miles of Sanquhar is the mansion-house of Elliock, in one of the rooms of which the admirable Crichton is said to have been born. In the neighbourhood of Sanquhar is a carpet manufactory, and within the town are the branches of two banks.

From Sanquhar the tourist may proceed by rail to New Cumnock (distant about 6 miles), from which, leaving the line, he may direct his route to Dalmellington; or, returning by rail to Thornhill, he may engage a vehicle to carry him by Penpont and Minihive into Galloway. Adopting this route, he passes through a romantic district known as the Glenkens, the mountain solitudes of which, from difficulty of access, are seldom disturbed by the wandering pedestrian. Carsphairn, a cheerful-looking little place, is the first town by this route on the road to Dalmellington and Ayr. The scenery is of a wild and bleak description for some miles, but after crossing the Deugh, which falls into the Ken, and descending from the high grounds, the country assumes a more fertile appearance, and becomes well wooded, as New Galloway, surrounded by gardens, is approached (distant from Carsphairn 12, Castle Douglas 14, Kirkcudbright 20, Dumfries 24 miles). The town consists of a single street of houses, generally of one storey, and possesses a good inn (the Kenmure Arms). The scenery in the neighbourhood is very beautiful, the river Ken here expanding into a loch, or rather a chain of lochs, about 10 miles in length, and half a mile in breadth, fringed with wood and surrounded by lofty mountains. In the vicinity is Kenmure Castle, a place of considerable antiquity. Leaving New Galloway, and crossing the Ken, on the opposite side of which there is a large inn, named the Spalding Arms, the road runs parallel to the lake, and forms a most charming route. About 7 miles beyond New

Galloway, Parton House (Miss Glendonwyn), surrounded by beautiful birch plantations, is seen to the left, and 3 miles further is the village of Crossmichael. From thence Castle Douglas is distant about 4 miles—a large, well-built, and thriving market town (distant from Kirkcudbright 10, Dumfries 18, Edinburgh 89 miles). One of the most beautiful features of the neighbourhood is Carlingwark Loch, covering a surface of 100 acres, studded with picturesque little islands covered with wood, and enlivened by numerous swans floating on its waters. About a mile to the west of the town, and visible from the road, on a small island in the Dee, stands Threave Castle, once the seat of the Black Douglasses, and the scene of many a bloody tragedy. It was built in the fourteenth century. The remains consist of a great square tower of enormous strength, partly surrounded by a wall and three small round towers. Above the main gateway may be observed a projecting block of granite, called "the hanging stone;" of which these old lords of Galloway were wont to boast that "the hanging stone of Threave never wanted its tassel." The large cannon "Mons Meg," now in Edinburgh Castle, was forged in the neighbourhood, and used by James II. at the reduction of this stronghold, in 1455. Two of the granite balls fired on that occasion were found not long since on removing some of the ruins. At a short distance to the south is Gelston Castle, a modern building, erected by the late Sir William Douglas, to whose energy and enterprise both the town and neighbourhood owe, in a great measure, their relative prosperity and beauty.*

* A pleasant excursion may be made in one day from this point, starting southward to Auchencairn, distant seven miles, a village where there is a good inn, situated near the little land-locked bay of that name. The road passes through some fine scenery, skirting the base of the rocky and picturesque hills Screel and Bengairn, and is well fringed with wood. Proceeding thence about three miles to the sea-coast, the caves of Barlocco are reached, which, although somewhat difficult of access, will repay the toil. The White Cave has an arched entrance high as the nave of a cathedral, and extends inwards to a considerable distance. When the sunbeams lighten up the interior, the effect is very fine, the rock being composed of dark red conglomerate, and the floor covered with beautifully smooth and

Leaving Castle Douglas by the coach road to Kirkcudbright, the tourist will cross the Dee at Tongland Bridge, 8 miles distant, at which point the scenery is varied and interesting. On the opposite side of the Tarff, embosomed in trees, is Compstone Castle (Lord Dundrennan), where Montgomery wrote his poem of "The Cherrie and the Slae," in 1597, the scene of which is laid in this neighbourhood.* The Dee is a stream of Highland aspect, "having a course of between forty and fifty miles, and exhibiting in its descent many features both of beauty and grandeur. Perhaps the finest part of its course are the four miles along which it forms the eastern boundary of Tongland parish. Its banks are richly wooded, and the current is in some places forced between perpendicular rocks 70 or 80 feet high. It is seen to great advantage from the old bridge, where it appears in a straight line for nearly a quarter of a mile; and the series of rocky shelves causing it to rise in successive undulations, it resembles the convolutions of an enormous serpent, while the large streaks and patches that diverge from their crests give an animation and a savage beauty which it would be hard to match in many Scottish rivers."†

Two miles distant from Tongland Bridge is Kirkcudbright—[*Inn:* Selkirk Arms.]—Distant from Gatehouse 8,

rounded pebbles of various hues. There are several other caves in the neighbourhood, but none quite so large. Continuing the route about a mile onward, Oroland House is visible on the left hand, and, passing through a fertile district for about four miles, the grey ruins of Dundrennan Abbey are seen at a short distance in a beautiful green valley. The first sight of this old building is very impressive—all about the place being so secluded and still. The portion of the ruin now standing has been thoroughly repaired by the Commissioners of Woods and Forests; it was founded in A.D. 1142. There is a small inn at the village, where refreshments may be obtained, but the tourist is recommended to proceed to Kirkcudbright, (distant 6 miles), where he will get every comfort he can desire at Mr. Tyson's Inn, "The Selkirk Arms."

* "But as I looked myne alane
I saw a river rin
Out owre a steepy rock of stane
Syne lighted in a lin.
With tumbling and rumbling
Among the rocks around,
Devalling and falling
Into a pit profound.

† Statistical Account of Scotland.

Dumfries 28, Edinburgh 83 miles. It is situated about 6 miles above the confluence of the Dee with the Solway, the river here forming an estuary. St. Mary's Isle, containing the seat of the Earl of Selkirk, now a beautifully wooded peninsula, is in the immediate vicinity. The town is surrounded with finely terraced woods and romantic walks. The parish church, erected a few years ago, at an expense of £6782, is a conspicuous object, contrasting with the ivy-covered ruins of the old castle of the Maclellans. Crossing the Dee by the ferry-boat, a good road leads to the banks of the Fleet, which passes through the Hybla of Scotland—the parish of Borgue, famous for its honey —extensive farms, stretching away on either side, until it skirts the deer-park and grounds of Cally, at the entrance to which stands the town of Gatehouse. It is well built, and surrounded by large gardens, owing its prosperity to the liberality of the Murrays of Broughton, whose princely residence, Cally, is in close proximity. The house is built of granite, after a design by Adam. The grounds are tastefully laid out, and the views from the front of the house combine, on a vast scale, all the elements of the finest landscapes, extensive ornamental gardens, shady walks, lawns studded with forest trees, forming the foreground of a picture which is filled up, on the one hand, by the heath-covered mountains, and on the other by Fleet Bay, with its islands, and in the distance the bold rocky cliffs of Wigtonshire, crested by the ruins of Cruggleton Castle. Leaving Gatehouse by the bridge crossing the Fleet, the tall old tower of Cardoness* is seen on the right, and about a mile from the road, in a secluded little valley, is the picturesque ivy-covered ruin of Anworth church, once the scene of Samuel Rutherfurd's labours. A monument, erected on a neighbouring hill to the memory of this divine, has been shattered by lightning—the fragment still remaining for a landmark to the mariners on the Solway. From Cardoness to Creetown, a distance of 12 miles, the route is one of the finest in Scotland, forming

* Its last inhabitant was Sir Godfrey M'Culloch, who, in 1697, was executed in Edinburgh for murder.

a series of ever-changing views,—the bay of Wigtown on the one hand, and the thickly wooded cliffs of Anworth and Kirkmabreck on the other. Six miles from Gatehouse, at Ravenshall, there are several singular cliffs and caverns, distinguished by their intimate connection with the smuggling scenes and characters in Scott's novel of Guy Mannering. A mile in advance, on an eminence to the right, is Kirkdale House, and five miles farther is Creetown, a small town, in the neighbourhood of which there are several valuable granite quarries, from which the new Liverpool Docks have been built. They give employment to about 300 men. In the manse of this parish, Dr. Thomas Brown, the distinguished ethical philosopher, was born 1778, and he was buried in the old churchyard here in 1820. Barholme (M'Culloch, Esq.) is passed about a mile in advance, and a ferry conducts the tourist into Wigtownshire.* The county town is distant about

* NEWTON-STEWART.—[*Inn:* Galloway Arms, Mumby].—The tourist, instead of crossing into Wigtonshire at this point, may continue the route five miles further to Newton-Stewart, where the river Cree is spanned by a handsome bridge of five arches, from which a beautiful glimpse of river scenery may be obtained. It is surrounded by swelling hills on every side, and, towering far above its neighbours, is Cairnsmuir, with its rounded summit of smooth granite, over which light fleecy clouds are generally hovering. A delightful excursion may be made from Newton-Stewart to Loch Trool, a very beautiful little lake, distant about 14 miles, to which there is a carriage road. It is about two miles long, fringed with wood, and surrounded by mountains, some of which rise to the height of 2700 to 3000 feet. The road here terminates, but the hardy pedestrian, if he wishes to enjoy some of the grander sights of nature, may penetrate into the grim solitudes of Loch Enoch. We extract from Mr. Grierson's interesting little work the following account of his ascent of Merrick—"The highest hill that rises o'er the source of Dee." The ascent was from Loch Trool. "After scrambling among huge blocks of granite for about three miles, we came to one of the most sequestered and inaccessible shepherds' dwellings in Scotland, called Kilsharg," and "provided with stout *cleekies* to steady us among the rocks and moss-bags, we then proceeded to the top of the mountain, which might be about four miles from the cottage." "The first part of our route was serious climbing, but the last two miles consisted of a gentle slope over soft verdant pasture." "The view from its summit is of the most commanding description. The whole Frith of Clyde lies, as it were, mapped before you towards the west. The weather was by no means remarkably clear; still we saw the whole

three miles from the ferry, and is seen from a considerable distance, being built on a slight eminence. Many of the houses are elegant structures. The principal street is so wide as to admit of a large bowling-green, in its centre, which adds considerably to the beauty of the town. The law and commissary courts are held here; and about a mile to the west of the town is the village of Bladenoch, famed over Galloway for its distillery; and crossing the river of that name by an old-fashioned bridge, the tract of rich country known by the name of Baldoon is seen on the left. It is divided into two farms, of about 600 acres, and is rightly named "the Garden of Galloway." Formerly it was the property of the Dunbars; and it was in Baldoon Castle, the ruins of which are still standing, that the melancholy circumstances occurred upon which the story of the Bride of Lammermoor is founded. Three miles farther, the road passes through the village of Kirkinner; and five miles farther the town of Garlieston—a lively little seaport, possessing a good harbour—from which a steamboat sails to Liverpool every week. Adjoining the town is Galloway House, the principal seat of the Earl of Galloway. The grounds are well

of Arran, with its fantastic peaks, the Mull of Kintyre, the coast of Ireland, Mull of Galloway, Benghairn, Criffell, the Moffat Hills," &c. "The adjoining mountains, Carlin's Cairn, the Mill Yeas, &c., had a sternly wild appearance." "The side of the mountain towards the north and north-east is remarkably abrupt, and falls into Loch Enoch by two prodigious leaps, which characterise its appearance from a distance, and have a fearful aspect when viewed from the brink." "Loch Enoch is in some respects one of the most remarkable lochs anywhere to be seen. It contains several islands, in one of which is a small lake, said to be well stocked with trout, and it is so indented by headlands, that keeping close to its margin would perhaps double the circumference, which may be estimated at about three miles. A more desolate, dreary, unapproachable scene, can hardly be imagined. All its shores are of granite, bleached by the storms of ages, which, in such a region, probably 1200 feet at least above the sea, must rage with tremendous fury. It is intersected by dykes of granite, resembling artificial piers;" and "some of its bays contain abundance of beautiful granite sand resembling the finest oatmeal, which is much prized for sharpening scythes, and carried to a great distance for that purpose." The tourist is cautioned to beware of fogs, for, in a region so rugged and remote from human dwellings, they would prove most bewildering and dangerous.

planned, and the carriage drives are of considerable extent. After passing these grounds towards Whithorn, the road is rather uninteresting. Whithorn, distant from Garlieston about 4 miles, from Wigtown 8, although not particularly interesting to the tourist in search of the picturesque, merits a short notice by reason of the historical associations connected with its name. It was here that Christianity was first introduced into Scotland "Bede relates that the first tribes of North Britain who turned from their idols to worship the true God, owed their conversion to the British Bishop Ninyas, or Ninian. He had studied at Rome; and on that headland of Galloway where he chose the seat of his mission, he built a church of stone, in a way unusual among the Britons.* It was dedicated by him to St. Martin of Tours, from whom he obtained masons to shape its walls after the Roman fashion. In this 'White House,' as it was named, the body of St. Ninian had its rest with the bodies of many other saints; and for ages the place continued to be famous, not only in North Britain, but throughout the Anglo-Saxon kingdoms, and among the races of Ireland. Even from Gaul, letters were sent to 'the brethren of St. Ninian at Whithorn,' written by the most accomplished scholar of the age, Alcuin, the divine and the philosopher, the historian and the poet—the confidant of Charlemagne. In more modern times, the ancient shrine was renowned as a pilgrimage whither kings and princes, churchmen and warriors, with people from many realms, came by sea and land to make their devotions."† Here St. Ninian built a church in the fourth century. Here, also, were the Priory of Whithorn and the Cathedral Church of Galloway; but of these little remain, except a ruined and roofless chancel, built about the end of the twelfth century, and occupying the site of much more ancient buildings, which had been the crypt, as it would seem, of an extensive church. It is a well-proportioned and beautiful specimen of the early English style, and within the last 30 years has been used as the parish church. The western door-

* Tradition points to a small ruin on the Isle of Whithorn, distant 2 miles, as the site of St. Ninian's church.

† Quarterly Review.

way is in fine preservation, and worthy a careful examination. The town consists of one street, running from south to north, narrow at the extremities, and extremely wide in the middle. Proceeding southward nearly 2 miles, the road passes Glasserton House (S. Stewart, Esq.) Nine miles to the north-west is Port-William, a marine village, near which is Monreith (Sir William Maxwell). The road leads the tourist along a lonely shore for eight miles, on which a habitation is scarcely to be seen; thence leaving the sea at Auchenmaly Bay and proceeding six miles through a pastoral country, it reaches Glenluce, about a mile and half from the most inland point of Luce Bay, a quiet little town of about 1000 inhabitants. To the west of the town stand the ruins of Glenluce Abbey, founded A.D. 1190, by Alan, Lord of Galloway. The original buildings must have been extensive, but the chapter-house is the only portion in fair preservation, Continuing the route to Stranraer, the road, crossing the Luce water, passes, at some distance on the right, Dunragget (Sir James D. Hay), and, 10 miles from Glenluce, reaches the large seaport of Stranraer—[*Inns:* King's Arms, and George Hotel]—beautifully situated at the head of Loch Ryan, a noble arm of the sea. It is 50 miles distant from Ayr, and 68¾ from Dumfries. It consists of three streets, parallel to the shore, and intersected by several others. The principal of these are well and handsomely built, but numerous hovels appear in the lanes and outskirts of the town. Population 5678. Stranraer may be called the capital of "*the Rhins*" of Galloway, a Gaelic word denoting the forks of which the Mull of Galloway forms the one pointed extremity, and Corsewall Lighthouse, fronting Craig Nelson, the other. Two steamers maintain a weekly communication with Glasgow, and a third with Belfast. Mail coaches between Portpatrick and Dumfries, pass through the town daily. The neighbourhood is rich in natural beauty, and possesses several gentlemen's seats. "Castle Kennedy," with its lochs and singular woods, planted in military fashion, (Culhorn, Earl of Stair,) Lochnaw Castle (Sir A. Agnew), Dunskey (Col. Blair), &c.

EDINBURGH, KINROSS, PERTH, DUNKELD, BLAIR ATHOLL.

Drawn & Engd by J. Bartholomew Edinr

FIFTEENTH TOUR.

EDINBURGH—[KINROSS—LOCH LEVEN]—PERTH—[ST. ANDREW'S—DUNDEE]—DUNKELD—BLAIR-ATHOLL—INVERNESS.

Embracing a diverging tour from Dunkeld to Kenmore, Aberfeldy, Taymouth, Killin, Lochearnhead, Comrie, and Crieff.

Tourists may reach Perth from Edinburgh in two ways—

1. By Edinburgh, Perth, and Dundee Railway, crossing the Forth—the shortest and most usual route.
2. By Scottish Central Railway by Stirling.

EDINBURGH TO PERTH BY RAILWAY.

By Edin. Perth & Dundee Line.

Miles.		STATIONS.
		Perth.
4		Bridge of Earn.
7¾		Abernethy.
10¾		Newburgh.
15½		Collessie.
	FROM DUNDEE.	Dundee.
		Broughty.
		Ferry-Port
	8	Leuchars.
	11¼	Dairsie.
	14¾	Cupar.
	17	Springfield.
20		Ladybank Junction.
21		Kingskettle.
23		Falkland Road.
26		Markinch.
28½		Thornton Junction.
31		Dysart.
32		Sinclairtown.
33		Kirkcaldy.
36½		Kinghorn.
39		Burntisland.
44		Granton.
47		Edinburgh.

By Scottish Central Line.

Miles.	STATIONS.
	Perth.
4	Forgandenny.
7	Forteviot.
9½	Dunning.
13½	Auchterarder.
18	Blackford.
22	Greenloaning.
25½	Kinbuck.
28	Dunblane.
30	Bridge of Allan
33	Stirling.
35½	Bannockburn.
41	Larbert.
45	Greenhill Junction.
75	Edinburgh.

Coaches in connection with the Edinburgh, Perth, and Dundee Line—

From Kirkcaldy to Anstruther. | From Dysart to Leven.
From Markinch to Leslie. | From Falkland to Auchtermuchty.
From Leuchars to St. Andrews.

Edinburgh to Perth, by Kinross and Lochleven.—The coach which used to run on this road has been discontinued. Tourists would require to hire from Forth Hotel, Burntisland.

EDINBURGH —(LOCH LEVEN—ST. ANDREWS)—PERTH—(DUNDEE)—DUNKELD—(DIVERGING TOUR TO ABERFELDY, TAYMOUTH, LOCHEARNHEAD, COMRIE, AND CRIEFF)—BLAIR-ATHOLL—INVERNESS.

TOURISTS adopting the first of the two lines of progress on the preceding page, upon reaching Granton, cross the Firth of Forth in the railway steamer, which lands them at

BURNTISLAND,

[*Inn*:—The Forth Hotel.]

a sea-bathing village, resorted to by the inhabitants of Edinburgh.* Proceeding from Burntisland, the line runs

* During summer there is generally a coach from the Hotel to Kinross and Lochleven. The historical is greater than the picturesque interest of the locality. If the coach should not be running, a vehicle may be hired at the Hotel. The distance is 15 miles.

On the banks of Loch Leven is the county town of

KINROSS.

[*Inns*:—The Salutation; Stocks'.]

Kinross House (Sir Graham Montgomery), erected in 1685 for the Duke of York, stands on the edge of the lake. The promontory on which it stands was once occupied by a stronghold, long the residence of the Earls of Morton. By far the most interesting object in the neighbourhood of Kinross is Loch Leven. Its form is an irregular oval, extending from ten to eleven miles in circumference. It contains four islands, the chief of which are St. Serf's Isle, near the east end, so named from its having been the site of a priory dedicated to St. Serf; and another, situated near the shore opposite Kinross, on which are the picturesque ruins of

LOCH LEVEN CASTLE,

celebrated from its being the prison-house of the unfortunate Queen Mary. Loch Leven Castle is of unknown antiquity; but it is noticed in history as early as 1334, when an unsuccessful siege was laid to it by an English army, commanded by John de Strevelin. It was anciently a royal castle, and was for some time the residence of Alexander III. It has been repeatedly used as a state prison. Patrick Graham, Archbishop of St. Andrews, and grandson of Robert III., after an unsuccessful attempt to reform the lives of the Catholic clergy, was, through their influence at Court, arrested, confined in

North

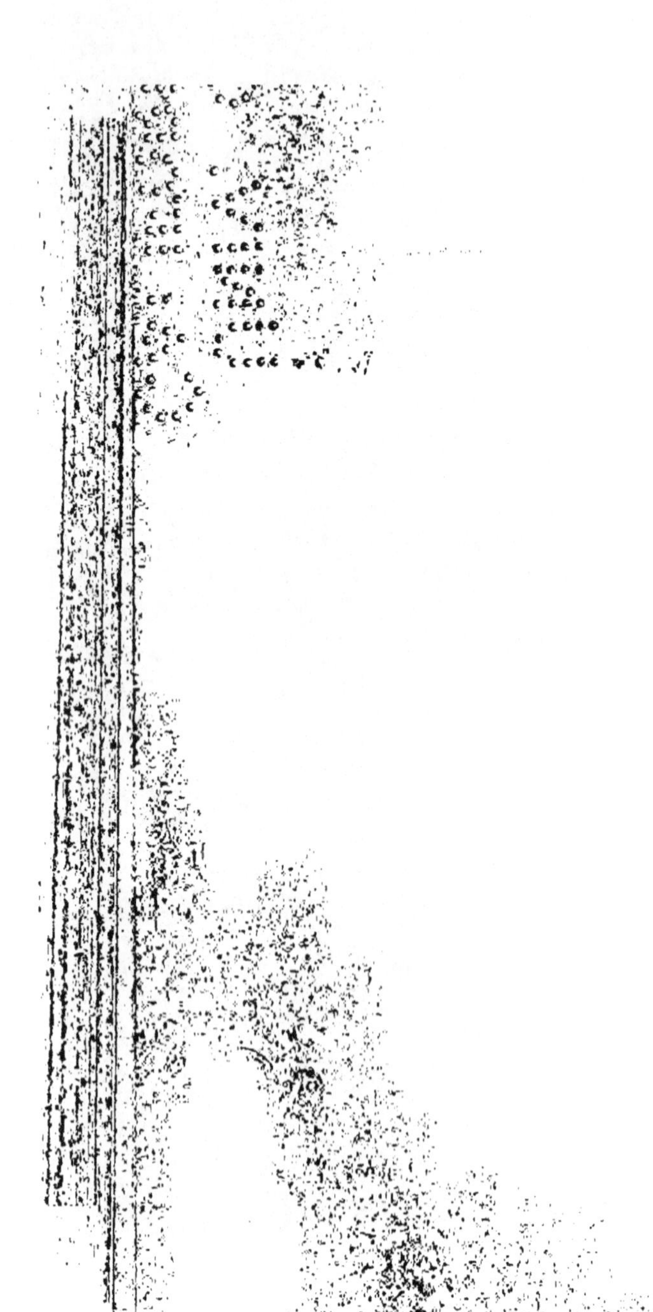

EDINBURGH, PERTH & DUNDEE RAILWAY.

along the sea-coast by Kinghorn ($10\frac{1}{2}$ miles), Kirkaldy (14 miles). In the vicinity of Kirkaldy are Raith House and grounds (Sir H. Ferguson Davie, Bart). Dysart Station (16 miles). From the line to this distance there is a

different monasteries, and at last died a prisoner in Loch Leven Castle in 1478. According to Winton's Chronicle, he was buried in the Monastery of St. Serf. In 1542, Loch Leven Castle was granted by James V. to Sir Robert Douglas, stepfather to the famous Earl of Murray; and in 1567, Queen Mary was imprisoned there after her surrender at Carberry Hill. The engraving which illustrates our text, represents Lord Lindsay and his party on the occasion of that memorable visit to Queen Mary, which terminated in her abdication of the Crown. The pennon of the ruthless baron is displayed by one of his attendants, as a signal for the boat, while he himself blows "a clamorous blast on his bugle." Queen Mary escaped from the castle, May 2, 1568, through the aid of young Douglas, and is said by general tradition to have gone ashore on the lands of Coldon, at the south side of the lake, whence she was conducted, by Lord Seton, to Niddry Castle in West Lothian. The keys of the Castle, which were thrown into the lake at the time of her escape, were recently found by a young man belonging to Kinross, who presented them to the Earl of Morton. Loch Leven is celebrated for the excellence of its trout. The rich taste and bright red colour, are derived chiefly from small crustacea and shell-fish upon which they feed. The silver grey trout is apparently the original native of the loch, and, in many respects, the finest fish of the whole. The *char* or *gelly trough*, rivalling in richness and flavour the best specimens of this kind, have of late years disappeared; and an attempt made in April 1843, by Sir W. Jardine and Mr. James Wilson, to obtain them by deep-water fishing, proved unsuccessful.* At the eastern extremity of the loch, there are some remains of the monasteries of Portmoak, and Scotland's Well. The river Leven flows from the lake on the east side, and pursues an easterly course to the Firth of Forth. The vale of the Leven is beautiful, and is ornamented with the woods around Leslie, the seat of the Earl of Rothes. About two miles from Kinross, on the Perth road, is the village of Milnathort, or Mills of Forth; and to the right, at

* The level of the loch was, some years ago, reduced $4\frac{1}{2}$ feet, by means of a deep cut at the eastern extremity, conveying the water to the river, a portion of the former channel of which is now dry; 750 acres of land were thus gained from the loch, but this was effected at so great an outlay, that the value of the land barely covered the expense of the works necessary to reclaim it.

pleasant seaward view. It now strikes off into the interior to Thornton, the junction station from which the Dunfermline line diverges. From this it continues northwards by Markinch (21 miles), Falkland (24 miles). About three miles

some distance, are the ruins of Burleigh Castle, which gave title to Lord Burleigh, attainted in 1716. Three miles to the northward the road enters Glenfarg, a romantic little valley, enclosed by the Ochils, clothed with verdure to their summits.

At the northern extremity of the glen is Ayton House (J. Murray, Esq.), and at a short distance to the right, is the ancient village of Abernethy, with its round tower. Passing some hamlets, the tourist reaches the BRIDGE OF EARN, near which is the hill of Moncreiffe, affording the first view of Perth.* It was the prospect from this hill that was greeted by the ancient Romans with the exclamation "*Ecce Tiber!* Ecce *Campus Martius!*" The Tiber rather than the Tay is the gainer by this comparison. The Tiber at Rome is much narrower than the Tay at Perth; its waters are muddy and sluggish, and its banks tame, dirty, and unclad with trees. The Tay, on the contrary, is here 500 feet in breadth, its stream deep, but of crystalline purity, and although it forms a broad and beautiful sheet of water, it is not stagnant, but flows with a perceptible current. Its eastern bank

* "One of the most beautiful points of view which Britain, or perhaps the world can afford, is, or rather we may say was, the prospect from a spot called the Wicks of Baiglie, being a species of niche at which the traveller arrived, after a long stage from Kinross, through a waste and uninteresting country, and from which, as forming a pass over the summit of a ridgy eminence which he had gradually surmounted, he beheld stretching beneath him the valley of the Tay, traversed by its ample and lordly stream; the town of Perth, with its two large meadows or Inches, its steeples, and its towers; the hills of Moncreiffe and Kinnoul faintly rising into picturesque rocks, partly clothed with woods; the rich margin of the river, studded with elegant mansions; and the distant view of the huge Grampian Mountains, the northern screen of this exquisite landscape. The alteration of the road, greatly, it must be owned, to the improvement of general intercourse, avoids this magnificent point of view, and the landscape is introduced more gradually and partially to the eye, though the approach must be still considered as extremely beautiful. There is still, we believe, a footpath left open by which the station at the Wicks of Baiglie may be approached; and the traveller by quitting his horse or equipage, and walking a few hundred yards, may still compare the real landscape with the sketch which we have attempted to give."—*Fair Maid of Perth*, vol. i., p. 21.

Sir Walter was mistaken, however, in supposing that Perth could be seen from the spot he has indicated.

from this station are the ruins of Falkland Palace. The Castle of Falkland, which existed previous to the old Palace, was the place of imprisonment of David, Duke of Rothesay, whose life was, for a time, sustained by a wet nurse conveying to him milk from her breast through a reed. The modern mansion, Falkland House (Tyndal Bruce, Esq.), pleasantly seated at the foot of Lomond Hill, is visible from the line on the left, immediately after leaving Kingskettle Station (26 miles). Ladybank Junction (27 miles). Here the line to Cupar-Fife and Dundee branches off to the right,* that for Perth to the left. Collessie Station ($31\frac{3}{4}$

rises rapidly, and for more than a mile exhibits an almost unbroken line of villas, which are seen peeping through partial openings in the masses of willows, limes, and sycamores, which cover the acclivity down to the water's edge. The fertile Carse of Gowrie,—the Firth of Tay, with the populous town of Dundee,—the City of Perth, and the beautiful valley of Strathearn, bounded by the hills of Menteith, are all distinctly seen from this eminence. Pennant calls this view "the glory of Scotland."

* CUPAR, $32\frac{1}{2}$ miles from Edinburgh is a considerable town, but the principal inducement for tourists to take the Dundee branch of the line is to visit St. Andrews. This is done by proceeding to Leuchars station (39 miles from Edinburgh) from which there is a coach to

ST. ANDREWS.

[*Inns:*—The Cross Keys; The Star Hotel; The Black Bull.]

St. Andrews was formerly a place of great importance, and was the seat of the primate of Scotland. It is entered at the west end by a massive antique portal,—preserved unimpaired,—its other extremity terminating in the ruins of the cathedral, church, and monastery. The city abounds in curious antique houses, which were once occupied by persons of rank, both in church and state, and it has an air of seclusion and quiet, which, taken in connexion with its colleges and memorials of antiquity, gives it an appearance not unlike some of the cathedral towns of England. The origin of St. Andrews is involved in obscurity, but it is justly believed to have been at a very early period the seat of a religious establishment. It was originally denominated Muckross. According to the common tradition, about the end of the fourth century it became the residence of St. Regulus, who

miles). On the right, immediately after passing Inchrye, the valley of the Tay expands to view, and a beautiful prospeet is afforded of the fertile Carse of Gowrie. Across the

was shipwrecked here. The ruins of a chapel and an entire tower, known by the name of St. Regulus, or St. Rule, are still to be seen near the cathedral. On the union of the Scottish and Pictish kingdoms, the name of the city was changed to St. Andrews. The famous priory of St. Andrews was erected by Bishop Robert, in the reign of Alexander I., about the year 1120. It was made a royal burgh by David I. in the year 1140. The charter of Malcolm II., written upon a small bit of parchment, is preserved in the tolbooth. In 1471, it was erected into an archbishoprick by Sextus IV. at the request of James IV. At what time its church became metropolitan, is not known with certainty, but it must have been at a very early period. St. Andrews contains many interesting memorials of antiquity. The chapel of St. Regulus is, without doubt, one of the oldest relics of ecclesiastical architecture in the kingdom. The tower is a square prism 108 feet in height, the side of the base being 24 feet. A winding stair leads to the summit, from which a most delightful view is obtained. The stone of which this building is composed, is of so excellent a texture, that although it has been exposed to the weather for so many centuries, it still remains quite entire and unimpaired. The chapel to the east of the tower, which was the principal one, still remains; but of a small chapel to the west, which formerly existed, there is now no trace. The cathedral was founded in the year 1159 by Bishop Arnold, but it was not finished till the time of Bishop Lamberton, who completed it in 1318. This magnificent fabric, the work of several ages, was demolished in a single day by an infuriated mob, excited by a sermon of John Knox against idolatry, preached in the parish church of St. Andrews.* It was an edifice of great extent, the

---

* This event is graphically described by Professor Tennant in his poem entitled "Papistry Stormed; or the Dinging Doun o' the Cathedral." We may give a short extract as a specimen of the poem :—

"I sing the steir, strabash, and strife,
Whan bickarin' frae the towns o' Fife
Great bangs o' bodies, thick and rife,
Gaed to Sanct Andro's town ;

"And wi' John Calvin in their heads,
And hammers in their hands, and spades,
Enraged at idols, mass, and beads,
Dang the Cathedral down.

"I wot the bruilzie then was dour,
Wi' sticks, and stanes, and bluidy clour,
Ere Papists unto Calvin's power
Gaif up their strongest places ;

And fearfu' the stramash and stour
Whan pinnacle cam down, and tow'r,
And Virgin Marys in a shower
Fell flat, and smash'd their faces.

The copper roofs that dazzlit heaven,
Were frae their rafters rent and riven,
The marble altars dasht and driven,
The cods wi' velvet laces ;

"The siller ewers and candlesticks ;
The purple stole and gowden pyx ;
And tunakyls and dalmatycks
Cam tumbling frae their cases.

"The devil stood bumbazed to see
The bonnie cosie byke where he
Had cuddlit mony a century,
Rip't up wi' sic disgraces.

Firth, Castle Huntly, Errol, and Kinfauns, successively present themselves to the eye. Newburgh Station (36¼ miles) Abernethy Station (39¼ miles). In the clean and

length being 350 feet, the breadth 65, and the transept 180 feet. The eastern gable, half of the western, part of the south side wall, and of the transept, are all that now remain of this once splendid wall.

The other religious houses in St. Andrews were the convent of the Dominicans, founded in 1274 by Bishop Wishart; the convent of Observantines, founded by Bishop Kennedy, and finished by his successor, Patrick Graham, in 1478; a collegiate church, which stood immediately above the harbour, and a priory. Slight vestiges of the latter, which was the most important of these foundations, may be traced to the south of the cathedral. It was of great extent, and richly endowed. Its boundary wall is still nearly entire, and seems to have enclosed all the east quarter of the town. The prior of St. Andrews had precedence of all abbots and priors, and on festival days had a right to wear a mitre and all Episcopal ornaments.

" Upon a rock overlooking the sea, on the north-east side of the city, are the remains of the castle. This fortress was founded about the year 1200, by Roger, one of the bishops of St. Andrews, and was repaired towards the end of the 14th century by Bishop Trail, who died in it in 1401. He was buried near the high altar of the cathedral, with this singular epitaph:—

> ' Hic fuit ecclesiae directa columna, fenestra
> Lucida, thuribulum redolens, campana sonora.'

" James III. was born in the castle. It was the residence of Cardinal Beaton, who, after the cruel execution of the celebrated reformer, George Wishart, in front of it, was afraid of the fury of the people; and his knowledge of this, joined to his apprehension of an invasion from England, induced him to strengthen the fortifications, with the view of rendering the castle impregnable. In this fortress he was surprised and assassinated by Norman Lesley, aided by fifteen others. Early in the morning of May 29, 1546, they seized on the gate of the castle, which had been left open for the workmen who were finishing the fortifications; and having placed sentinels at the door of the Cardinal's apartment, they awakened his numerous domestics one by one, and, turning them out of the castle, without violence, tumult, or injury to any other person, inflicted on Beaton the death he justly merited. The conspirators were immediately besieged in this castle by the regent, Earl of Arran; and although their strength consisted of only 150 men, they resisted his efforts for five months,

pleasantly situate village of Abernethy is a round tower, resembling those of Ireland, which have so much engaged the attention of antiquarians. Its height is 74 feet. Bridge

owing more to the unskilfulness of the attack than the strength of the place, for in 1547, the castle was reduced and demolished, and its picturesque ruins serve as a landmark to mariners."*

The University of St. Andrews—the oldest establishment of that nature in Scotland—was founded in 1411 by Bishop Wardlaw. It consisted formerly of three colleges:—1. St. Salvator's, which was founded in 1458 by Bishop Kennedy. The buildings of this college formed an extensive court or quadrangle about 230 feet long, and 180 wide, and a gateway surmounted by a spire 156 feet high. On one side is the church, on another what was the library of St. Salvator's, the third contains apartments for students, the fourth is unfinished. The buildings connected with this college have fallen into a state of decay, and a grant was made by Parliament for erecting a new structure. One half of the proposed buildings for the United College have been erected, but the rest of the funds appointed to complete the works having unfortunately been diverted to another purpose, the structure remains incomplete. 2. St. Leonard's College, which was founded by Prior Hepburn in 1532. This is now united with St. Salvator's, and the buildings sold and converted into private houses. 3. New, or St. Mary's College, which was established by Archbishop Hamilton in 1552, but the house was completed by Archbishop Beaton. The buildings of this college have lately been repaired with great taste.

In the United College the languages, philosophy, and the sciences are taught. St. Mary's, which stands in a different part of the town, is reserved exclusively for theology. The classes and discipline of the two colleges are quite distinct, each having its respective Principal and Professors. They have a common library, containing upwards of 50,000 volumes.

The Madras College was established in the year 1833, by the late Dr. Andrew Bell, a native of St. Andrews, and inventor of the monitorial system of education which bears his name, who bestowed the munificent sum of £60,000 in three per cent. stock for its establishment. The buildings, which are very splendid, stand on the site of the Blackfriars monastery, and in front of the College is the fine old ruin of the chapel connected with that monastery The course of education comprises the Classics, the English and other modern lan-

* *Encyclopædia Britannica*, seventh edition, vol. iii., p. 121.

of Earn (43 miles), a sweetly seated village, which affords accommodation to the strangers who resort to Pitcaithly Wells in the neighbourhood. It possesses a ball-room, a

guages, Mathematics, Natural Philosophy, Chemistry, Music, and Drawing. The fees being low, and in many cases not exacted, the institution has been very successful, the number of scholars averaging about eight hundred.

St. Andrews contains eight places of worship—the parish church, the college church, an episcopal, free church, secession, independent, and baptist chapel, and a new chapel in connection with the established church, which was opened in August 1840. The parish church is a spacious structure, 162 feet in length, by 63 in breadth, and is large enough to accommodate 2500 persons. It contains a lofty monument of white marble, erected in honour of Archbishop Sharpe, who, in revenge for his oppressive conduct, was murdered by some of the exasperated Covenanters. On this monument is a bas relief representing the tragical scene of the murder. To the north is situated the college church, which belongs to the united college of St. Salvator and St. Leonard. It was founded in 1458 by Bishop Kennedy, and contains a beautiful tomb of its founder, who died in 1466. It is a piece of exquisite Gothic workmanship, though much injured by time and accidents. About the year 1683, on opening this tomb, six highly ornamented silver maces were discovered, which had been concealed there in times of trouble. Three of these maces are still preserved in the university, and one was presented to each of the other three Scottish universities. The top has been ornamented by a representation of our Saviour, with angels around, and the instruments of his passion; with these are shown some silver arrows with large silver plates affixed to them, on which are inscribed the arms and names of those who were victors in the annual competitions of archery, which, after having been discontinued for half a century, were again revived in 1833. Golf is now the prevailing game in St. Andrews. It is played on a piece of ground called the Links, which stretches along the sea-shore to the extent of nearly two miles. A considerable number of golf-balls are manufactured in St. Andrews. Besides the consumption of the town, about 9000 are annually exported to various other places.

The trade of St. Andrews was once very considerable. The shipping of the port now consists of a few vessels employed in the coasting trade. The harbour is guarded by piers, and is safe and commodious; but it is difficult of access, having a narrow entrance,

library, and every other requisite convenience. Four miles farther, and the tourist reaches

PERTH.

[*Inns*:—The Royal George; The Salutation; The Star; The City.]

PERTH, an ancient royal burgh, and one of the handsomest towns in Scotland, is beautifully situated on the west bank of the Tay, 47 miles from Edinburgh. It occupies the

and being exposed to the east wind, which raises a heavy sea on the coast. The shore of the bay is low on the west side, but to the south it is precipitous, bold, and rocky; and, in severe storms, vessels are frequently driven on it and lost. St. Andrews unites with Cupar, Anstruther, Pittenweem, Crail, and Kilrenny, in returning a member to Parliament. The population of the town is 4300.

Returning to Leuchars Station and proceeding towards Dundee, the tourist is carried across the Firth of Tay, from Ferry-Port-on-Craig to Broughty Ferry.

About six miles up the Firth of Tay, on the north shore, is

DUNDEE.

[*Inns*:—Royal Hotel; British Hotel; Crown Hotel.]

Steamers:—To Perth, daily, fare 1s. To Leith, every Tuesday and Friday. To London, every Wednesday afternoon.

Dundee is the third town in Scotland in population. It is also a place of great antiquity, deriving its origin from Malcolm Canmore, and erected into a royal burgh by William the Lion. The population of the town and parish, according to the census of 1851, amounts to 78,829. The trade of Dundee has long been extensive, and has rapidly increased in late years. Its manufactures are chiefly yarns, brown and bleached linen, canvas and cotton bagging, for the home and foreign market, great quantities of which are exported directly to France, and to North and South America. This town, indeed, may be considered the principal seat of the coarse linen trade of Britain, and the great emporium for flax and hemp. In 1850, its imports of these articles amounted to 43,866 tons, value £1,350,000; and there were exported in the same year 600,000 pieces of linen goods, amounting in value to about £3,000,000. In the town and neighbourhood are about 60 spinning-mills and power-loom factories; besides several extensive iron founderies, with establishments for the manufacture of steam-engines and machinery. Ship-building is also carried on to a very considerable extent. Although the depression of trade materially

centre of a spacious plain, having two beautiful pieces of public ground called the North and South Inches extending on each side.

affected all these departments of enterprise for several years, the year 1850 has been distinguished by very general commercial prosperity.

The grandest and most important feature of Dundee is its harbour, with its magnificent wet docks, built and in progress, and a number of spacious quays, patent slip, graving dock, &c., spreading along the margin of the Tay, a mile and a half from east to west. These splendid works, up to May 1850, have cost £800,000, and yield an annual revenue of £25,000. An elegant building has been erected for the Custom House and Excise Office, with premises for the accommodation of the Harbour Trustees, and officers connected with the establishment. The number of vessels belonging to the port in December 1850 was 360, their tonnage being 60,000. Of these a few are employed in the whale fishery, and many of them in the Baltic and American Trade. The number of vessels which entered the harbour in 1849 was 4921, their tonnage 385,095. In the London trade, besides a number of schooners, there are three splendid steam vessels, of 300 horse power, each of which was built at an expense of upwards of £20,000.

A splendid bridge of ten arches and 900 feet in length, built in 1772, leads across the Tay to the north. Perth, or, as it used to be called from its church, St. Johnstoun, boasts of a high antiquity, and has been the scene of many interesting events. On account of its importance and its vicinity to the royal palace of Scone, it was long the metropolis of the kingdom before Edinburgh obtained that distinction. Here, too, the Parliaments and national assemblies were held, and many of the nobility took up their residence. Perth contains several beautiful streets and terraces, and a number of fine public buildings. The oldest of these is St. John's Church, the precise origin of which is unknown. It has undergone various modifications, and is now divided into the East, West, and Middle Churches.

ern Bank of Scotland. A little to the west of the High Street, in the Nethergate, are the remains of an old cathedral, which contained four places of worship, one of which was built in the finest Gothic style, the groining of the arches being much admired. Three of these churches were completely destroyed by fire on Sunday morning, the 3d January, 1841; measures were taken for repairing or rebuilding two of them, which are now completed. This structure is said to have been originally built by David, Earl of Huntingdon, in 1185. On the west end of these churches stands a magnificent Gothic tower, 156 feet high. There are several other churches and chapels connected with the Establishment, besides two Episcopal chapels, two elegant Roman Catholic chapels, and many other places of worship for Dissenters, who form a very considerable part of the population. Among the public institutions may be mentioned a Lunatic Asylum, an Infirmary, which has a Dispensary for out-patients, and an Orphan Institution; a Chamber of Commerce, the Society of Writers, incorporated by royal charter, and a Mechanics' Institution. Dundee has two joint-stock banking establishments, viz., the Dundee Bank, and the Eastern Bank of Scotland. Besides these, there are agencies for the Bank of Scotland, the British Linen Company, the National Bank of Scotland, and the Western Bank of Scotland. There is a native establishment for Fire Insurance, and three for Sea Insurance; also numerous agencies for fire, life, and sea offices. Three newspapers are published in the town. Unobstructed railway communication exists with all parts of the kingdom. To the south by the Edinburgh and Northern line; to the west by the Dundee and Perth; to the east by the Dundee and Arbroath; and to the north by the

ST. JOHN'S CHURCH.

The demolition of ecclesiastical architecture which accompanied the Reformation, commenced in this church, in consequence of a sermon preached by John Knox against idolatry. At the south end of the Watergate stood Gowrie

House, the scene of the mysterious incident in Scottish history called the Gowrie Conspiracy. The whole of that interesting old building has now been removed, and the site is occupied by the County Hall, a splendid structure in the Grecian style. In George Street stands a fine building, erected in 1823, in honour of Provost Marshall, in

Dundee and Newtyle railway, all these forming part of the great trunk lines from Aberdeen southward.

Dundee was in ancient times fortified with walls; but of its walls or gates, no traces now remain, except the Cowgate Port, from which Wishart the martyr is said to have preached to the people during the plague of 1544. At the period of the Reformation, it was the first town in Scotland which publicly renounced the Roman Catholic faith; and so zealous was the spirit of its Protestantism, that it acquired the name of "*the second Geneva.*" In 1651, the town was sacked, with

the lower part of which is the Public Library, and in the upper part the Museum of the Literary and Antiquarian Society, founded in 1784, and probably the finest provincial collection of the kind in Scotland. Perth also contains an excellent Academy, a Gas-work of large dimensions, a Water-house of excellent architecture, and an Infirmary equally handsome. Murray's Royal Asylum for Lunatics, erected and endowed by the benevolence of the individual whose name it bears, is a splendid building, situated on a rising ground to the east of the town. The depot, erected for the reception of prisoners during the French war, has been converted into a General Prison or Penitentiary. The present building is fitted to contain about 350 inmates, and upon the success of the present experiment depends the future enlargement of the establishment. Previous to the Reformation, Perth contained an immense number of religious houses. One of these, the Monastery of Greyfriars, stood at the end of the Speygate. In Blackfriars Monastery, which was situated at the north side of the town, James I. was assassinated by a band of conspirators. But of these and many other interesting buildings not a vestige now remains. Perth has been the scene of many important historical events. It was occupied by the English during the reign of Edward I., but was besieged and taken by Robert Bruce. In the time of the great civil war it was taken by the Marquis of Montrose after the battle of Tippermuir. In 1715, and again in 1745, it was occupied by the rebel Highland army, who there proclaimed the Pre-

circumstances of revolting cruelty, by General Monk; and so great was the amount of plunder, that each of his soldiers is said to have received £60 sterling as his share. According to tradition, the indiscriminate carnage which took place on this memorable occasion was continued till the third day, when a child was found sucking the breast of its murdered mother.*

---

* The sail up the Tay from Dundee to Perth is one of uncommon beauty, and should be taken in preference to the railway if the weather permits. Steamers ply regularly between the two cities.

tender as king. The Inches are two beautiful pieces of ground, each about a mile and a-half in circumference, affording agreeable and healthy walks to the inhabitants, and delightfully variegated with trees. On the North Inch there took place, in the reign of Robert III., that singular combat between the Clan-Kay and Clan-Chattan, which Sir Walter Scott has introduced with so much effect into his novel of the Fair Maid of Perth. The town is surrounded on all sides with the most beautiful and picturesque scenery, and the interesting objects in the neighbourhood are so numerous, that it would require a volume to notice them all. The summits of the hills of Moncreiffe and Kinnoull, to which the access is easy by carriage roads, are well worthy of a visit—the former, in particular, no tourist should omit visiting, as it affords one of the finest prospects in Scotland. At the foot of Kinnoull Hill, lies Kinfauns Castle, from which every visitor returns delighted with the natural and artificial beauties both in and around it. Scone Palace (noticed below) will amply repay the trouble of a visit ; and so will Dupplin Castle, the seat of the Earl of Kinnoull, situated about five miles west of Perth. The Dupplin Library is well known for its collection of rare and valuable editions of the classics, and the woods around the castle are magnificent. Lynedoch, also, is a favourite excursion, chiefly on account of the graves of Bessy Bell and Mary Gray, which are situate on the romantic banks of the Almond. According to the census of 1851, the population of Perth, within the Parliamentary boundary, was 23,797.

PERTH TO DUNKELD BY COACH.

Leaving Perth by the North Inch, the tourist passes on the left Few House, (Nicol, Esq.), and Tulloch Printfield ; and, at the distance of two and a half miles from Perth, on the opposite side of the Tay, he will observe Scone Palace, the seat of the Earl of Mansfield, who represents the old family of Stormont. It is an immense modern building, in the castellated style, occupying the site of the ancient palace of the kings of Scotland. Much of the old furniture

DUPP N AST E.

has been preserved in the modern house. Among other relics are a bed used by James VI., and another of a flowered crimson velvet, said to have been wrought by Queen Mary when imprisoned in Loch Leven Castle. A state bed is also shown, presented by George II. to the celebrated Lord Chief-Justice Mansfield, the subject of Pope's line :

"How many an Ovid was in Murray lost."

The gallery, which is 160 feet long, occupies the site of the old hall in which the coronations were celebrated. Charles II. was crowned in the old edifice in 1651, and the chevalier de St. George in 1715. The situation of the palace is highly picturesque, and the view from the windows of the drawing-room is most splendid. At the north side of the house is a *tumulus*, termed the Moat Hill, said to have been composed of earth from the estates of the different proprietors who here attended on the kings. The famous stone on which the Scottish monarchs were crowned was brought from Dunstaffnage to this Abbey. It was removed by Edward I. to Westminster Abbey, where it still remains, forming part of the coronation chair of the British monarchs. The Abbey of Scone was destroyed at the time of the Reformation by a mob from Dundee, and the only part now remaining is an old aisle, containing a magnificent marble monument to the memory of the first Viscount Stormont. The old market-cross of Scone still remains, surrounded by the pleasure-grounds which have been substituted in the place of the ancient village. Two and a-half miles from Perth, the road crosses the Almond near its junction with the Tay, and winds among plantations chiefly on the estate of the late Lord Lynedoch. About two miles in advance, a road leads off from the left to Redgorton and Monedie, and a few paces farther on, a road upon the right conducts to the field of Luncarty, situated on the west bank of the Tay, about four miles from Perth, the scene of a decisive battle between the Scots and Danes in the reign of Kenneth III. The Scots were at first forced to retreat, but were rallied by a peasant of the name of Hay, and his two sons, who were ploughing in the neighbourhood. By the aid of these courageous peasants, who were armed only with a yoke, the Scots obtained a complete victory. In commemoration of this circumstance, the crest of the Hays has for many centuries been a peasant carrying a yoke over his shoulder. The plain on which the battle was fought is now used as a bleachfield. A mile in advance the road crosses the fine trouting streams of Ordie and Shochie.* A little farther on, a road turns off to the right to the Linn of Campsie, where the Tay forms a magnificent cascade, and the village of Stanley, famous for its extensive spinning-mills. The tourist next passes, on the left, the ruins of a residence of the family of Nairn, and the Mill of Loak ; and nine miles from Perth, enters the village of Auchtergaven. Three miles farther on the tourist passes Murthly Castle (Sir Wm. Drummond,) a magnificent but unfinished edifice, and a short way north of it, the old castle of Murthly. In the immediate neighbourhood is Birnam Hill, 1580 feet above the level of the sea, and Birnam Wood, so famous for its connexion with the fate of Macbeth. The ancient forest has now disappeared, and been replaced by a few trees of modern growth. From the summit of the hill a magnificent prospect is commanded of the vale of the Tay, and of the extensive woods which environ Dunkeld.† The traveller now passes the village of Little Dunkeld,‡ crosses the river and enters

* Perth suffered from a nocturnal inundation of the Tay in the year 1210, and it is predicted that it will again be destroyed in a similar manner :—

" Says the Shochie to the Ordie,
  ' Where shall we meet ?'
' At the cross o' Perth,
  When a' men are fast asleep.' "

Popular Rhyme.

† Birnam Inn is a comfortable and well-frequented establishment, where the wants of tourists are equally well supplied as at the inns in Dunkeld.

‡ " O what a parish, what a terrible parish,
  O what a parish is that of Dunkell !
They hae hangit the minister, drown'd the precentor
  Dung down the steeple, and drucken the bell !
Though the steeple was down, the kirk was still stannin',
  They biggit a burn where the bell used to hang ;
A stell-pat they gat, and they brew'd Hieland whisky,
  On Sundays they drank it, and rantit and sang."

Old Song.

DUNKELD.

[*Inns*:—The Duke of Atholl's Arms; The Royal Hotel.]

Coaches to Aberfeldy, Blair-Atholl, Callander, Dunkeld Road Railway Station, Forfar, Inverness, Kenmore, Perth, Pitlochrie.

"There are few places," says Dr. Macculloch, "of which the effect is so striking as Dunkeld, when first seen on emerging from this pass, (a pass formed by the Tay, by which the traveller enters the Highlands,) nor does it owe this more to the suddenness of the view, or to its contrast with the long preceding blank, than to its own intrinsic beauty; to its magnificent bridge and its cathedral nestling among its dark woody hills; to its noble river, and to the brilliant profusion of rich ornament. The leading object in the landscape is the noble bridge standing high above the Tay. The cathedral seen above it, and relieved by the dark woods by which it is embosomed, and the town, with its congregated grey houses, add to the general mass of architecture, and thus enhance its effect in the landscape. Beyond, rise the round and rich swelling woods that skirt the river, stretching away in a long vista to the foot of Craigvinean, which, with all its forests of fir, rises a broad shadowy mass against the sky. The varied outline of Craig-y-Barns, one continuous range of darkly-wooded hill, now swelling to the light, and again subsiding in deep shadowy recesses, forms the remainder of the splendid distance. The Duke of Atholl's grounds present a succession of walks and rides in every style of beauty that can be imagined, the extent of the walks being fifty miles, and of the rides thirty. It is the property of few places, perhaps of no one in all Britain, to admit, within such a space, of such a prolongation of lines of access, and everywhere with so much variety of character and beauty."* The most interesting object in the town of Dunkeld, is the ancient and venerable cathedral. The great aisle measures 120 by 60 feet, the walls are 40 feet high, and the side aisles 12 feet wide. It is now roofless, but the choir was rebuilt

* Tourists are conducted over a portion of the grounds by guides provided by the Duke of Atholl, whose charge to *single individuals* is 2s. 6d., and to *parties* of three or more 1s. each.

and converted into a place of worship by the late Duke of Atholl, at an expense of £5000. The new church is handsomely fitted up. In the vestry there is a statue in armour, of somewhat rude workmanship, which was formerly placed at the grave of the notorious *Wolf of Badenoch*, who burned the cathedral of Elgin. The early history of this establishment is obscure, but it is understood that there was a monastery of the Culdees here, which David I. converted into a bishoprick, A.D. 1127. Among its bishops were Bishop Sinclair, celebrated for his patriotic exertions in the reign of Robert Bruce, and Gawin Douglas, famous for his poetical talents. Immediately behind the cathedral, stands the ancient mansion of the Dukes of Atholl. A magnificent new mansion was commenced by the late Duke, but his death, in 1830, has suspended the progress of the building. At the end of the cathedral are two of the first larches introduced into Britain from Switzerland in 1737. Those at Monzie were brought at the same time, and having been planted the night before, are entitled to the honour—hitherto erroneously ascribed to these—of being the oldest in Britain. The walks through the policies of Dunkeld have been pronounced, by the late Dr. E. Clarke, to be almost without a rival. The larch woods alone cover an extent of 11,000 square acres ; the number of these trees planted by the late Duke of Atholl being about twenty-seven millions, besides several millions of other sorts of trees. The tourist returns from the policies to Dunkeld by the village of Inver, in which the small thatched house long occupied by Neil Gow, the celebrated musician, may be seen. An old wooden press, said to have belonged to him, forms part of the furniture of the present tenant. Dunkeld, it will be remembered, was among the places visited by Her Majesty in 1842, on which occasion the festivities were on a scale of great splendour. The royal tent stood on the lawn to the east of the cathedral.

From the base of Craigvinean, a long wooded eminence projects, across which a path leads to Ossian's Hall, situated beside a cataract formed by a fall of the Braan. This is generally esteemed the greatest curiosity of Dunkeld. A hermitage or summer-house is placed forty feet from the bottom of the fall, and is constructed in such a manner that the cascade is entirely concealed by its walls. Opposite to the entrance is a picture of Ossian playing upon his harp, and singing the songs of other times. The pannel upon which the picture is painted, is suddenly drawn aside by the guide, disclosing the cataract foaming over its rocky barriers, and roaring with a voice of thunder. In the sides and ceiling of the apartment are numerous mirrors, exhibiting the waterfall under a variety of aspects, sometimes as if precipitating its torrents upon the spectator, sometimes inverted, as if rushing upwards into the air. About a mile higher up the Braan, is the Rumbling Bridge, which is thrown across a narrow chasm, eighty feet above the waterway. Into this gulf the Braan pours itself with great fury, foaming and roaring over the massive fragments of rock which have fallen into its channel, and casting a thick cloud of spray high above the bridge. In picturesqueness of feature this fall is probably superior to that already described. The rocks by which the river is girt in, admit of the spectator approaching close upon the torrent, and if he occupies the several points of view recommended by the guide, he may discover that a sense of danger is no inconsiderable element in producing impressions of the sublime.

"The most perfect and extensive view," says Dr. Macculloch, "of the grounds of Dunkeld, is to be obtained opposite to the village of Inver, and at a considerable elevation above the bridge of the Braan; it affords a better conception of the collected magnificence and grandeur of the whole than any other place."* A fine view may also

* From Dunkeld the tourist may go off to the east by Cluny to Blairgowrie, distant twelve miles; a route which comprises some exquisitely beautiful scenery. The road winds along the foot of the Grampians, and passes in succession the Loch of Lowe, Butterstone Loch, the Loch of Cluny, with the ancient castle of Cluny, a seat of the Earl of Airlie, on a small island near the southern shore, Forneth, (Binny, Esq.,) the Loch of Marlie, Kinloch, (Hog, Esq.,) Baleid, (Campbell, Esq.): the House of Marlie, (Farquharson, Esq.,) and the church and inn of Marlie or Kinloch, much resorted to by parties from Perth and Dunkeld. Two miles farther, on the west bank of the Ericht, is BLAIRGOWRIE.—[*Inns:*—M'Laren's.]—Near it is Craighall-Rattray, one of the most picturesquely situate mansions in Scotland, being built on the top of a perpendicular rock of great height on the banks of the Ericht.

be obtained from the cottage of Dr. Fisher, situate upon an eminence at the east end of the bridge. The proprietor politely allows strangers to enter his ground, in order to enjoy the prospect.

DUNKELD TO ABERFELDY—KENMORE—TAYMOUTH CASTLE—KILLIN—LOCHEARNHEAD—COMRIE—CRIEFF.

lower part of Glen Lyon is called, and, crossing the Lyon by a boat, he turns the corner of a hill, and all at once alights upon the lovely village of Kenmore.—[*Inns*:—M'Pherson's.]

If, however, as is usually the case, the tourist should prefer the route by Logierait and Aberfeldy, on leaving Dunkeld he crosses the Tay by a magnificent bridge of seven arches, and, a little farther on, reaches the village of Inver, where the Braan is crossed by a bridge, and a road strikes off upon the left to Amulree. Three miles beyond this, the road enters the village of Dalmarnock, then the village of Ballalachan, and a mile and a half beyond, passes Dalguise (Stewart, Esq.,) on the left. The road now leads along a wide cultivated valley, through which flow the combined waters of the Tay and Tummel. It abounds in the finest scenery, and extensive masses of larch and pine skirt the edges of the hills above. Six and a half miles from Dunkeld we pass Kinnaird House (Duke of Atholl,) and one mile further, the village of Balmacneil;—opposite this spot the Tummel falls into the Tay. On a tongue of land, formed by the confluence of these rivers, stands the village of Logierait (eight and a half miles from Dunkeld.) One mile from Balmacneil is Port village, and one mile further, Balnaguard Inn—the opening scene of Mrs. Brunton's novel, entitled "Self-Control." On the right is Eastertyre (Mrs. M'Glashan.) Across the Tay is Ballechin (Captain R. Scott,) which appears to have been the scene of the slaughter of Sir James the Rose, in the original ballad of that name. About half a mile beyond is Grandtully Arms Inn. A mile further is Eastmill, and opposite, across the Tay, Fyndynet. After passing some Highland villages, the venerable Castle of Grandtully (Sir Wm. D. Stewart, Bart.,) appears on the left, surrounded by rows of stately elms. It is an old structure, but kept in a habitable condition, and is said by Sir Walter Scott to bear a strong resemblance to the mansion of Tullyveolan in Waverley. One of the square wings is completely encompassed with ivy. Three miles from Grandtully is the village of ABERFELDY.—[*Inns:* The Breadalbane Arms; The Caledonian.]—Coaches to Perth and Dunkeld. Near this are the beautiful falls of Moness, said by Pennant to be an epitome of every thing desirable in a waterfall. The description Burns has given of these falls is not only beautiful in itself, but strikingly accurate:

"The braes ascend like lofty wa's,
The foaming stream deep roaring fa's,
O'erhung wi' fragrant spreading shaws,
The Birks of Aberfeldy.

"The hoary cliffs are crown'd wi' flowers,
White o'er the linn the burnie pours,
And rising, weets, wi' misty showers,
The Birks of Aberfeldy."

The falls are three in number; the lowest is a mile from the village, the uppermost a mile and a half. The glen is deep, and so exceedingly confined, that the trees in some places unite their branches from the opposite sides. The lowest fall consists chiefly of a series of cascades formed by a small tributary rivulet pouring down the east side of the dell. The next series consists of a succession of falls, comprising a perpendicular height of not less than a hundred feet. The last and highest cascade is a perpendicular fall of about fifty feet. Here the traveller may cross the dell by means of a rustic bridge, and return to the inn by a varied route. Opposite Aberfeldy the Tay is crossed by one of General Wade's bridges. About a mile in advance, on the north side, stands Castle Menzies, (*pron. Meengis,*) the seat of Sir Neil Menzies, the chief of that name, erected in the sixteenth century. It stands at the foot of a lofty range of rocky hills, and is surrounded by a park filled with aged trees, among which are some planes of extraordinary size. Weem Castle, the former seat of the family, was burned by Montrose. About a mile farther is Balfrax, (Marquis of Breadalbane,) and about a mile beyond, the Lyon water joins the Tay. Six miles from Aberfeldy the tourist reaches the beautiful little village of Kenmore, situated at the north-east extremity of Loch Tay. It consists of an inn, with good accommodation, and fifteen or sixteen houses, neatly white-washed, some of them embowered in ivy, honeysuckle, and sweet-briar. The most remarkable object in the vicinity of Kenmore, is

TAYMOUTH CASTLE,

the princely mansion of the Marquis of Breadalbane, with its much admired environs. The castle is a magnificent dark-grey pile of four storeys, with round corner towers, and terminating in an airy central pavilion. Its interior is splendidly fitted up, and it contains one of the best collections of paintings in Scotland. The most striking feature in the edifice is the grand staircase. The pleasure-grounds are laid out with great taste, and possess a striking combination of beauty and grandeur. The hills which confine them are luxuriantly wooded and picturesque in their outlines, and the plain below is richly adorned with old gigantic trees. The view from the hill in front of the castle is reckoned one of the finest in Scotland. On the right is Drummond Hill, and behind it the lofty Ben Lawers, with Ben More in the remote distance. On the left, two hills, partially wooded, rise from the water, one above another. In the foreground a portion of the lake is seen, with the village and church of Kenmore, and to the north of them, a light bridge spans the Tay, immediately behind which is the little wooded island of Loch Tay, with the ruins of a priory founded by Alexander I., whose Queen, Sybilla, lies interred here.* The scene is thus described in an impromptu of Robert Burns, who visited the spot in August 1787.

* The last residents in this priory were three nuns, who, once a-year, visited a fair in Kenmore, which, owing to that circumstance, is still called "Holy Women's Market."

"The outstretching lake, embosom'd 'mong the hills,
The eye with wonder and amazement fills;
The Tay, meandering sweet in infant pride;
The palace rising by his verdant side;
The lawns, wood-fringed, in nature's native taste,
The hillocks dropt in nature's careless haste;
The arches striding o'er the new-born stream,
The village glittering in the noon-tide beam."

Along the north bank of the river, there is a terrace sixteen yards wide and three miles in length, overshadowed by a row of stately beech trees, and on the opposite side, there is a similar walk extending a mile from Kenmore. These promenades are connected by a light cast-iron bridge. Taymouth Castle was first built by Sir Colin Campbell, sixth knight of Lochaw, in the year 1580. It was then, and until lately, called Balloch, from the Gaelic *bealach,* a word signifying the outlet of a lake or glen. The builder being asked why he had placed his house at the extremity of his estate, replied, "*We'll brizz yont,*" (press onward,) adding, that *he intended Ballach should in time be in the middle of it.* The possessions of the family have, however, extended in the opposite direction. They now reach from Aberfeldy, four miles eastward, to the Atlantic Ocean, a space upwards of one hundred miles, and are said to be the *longest* in Britain.

The reception of the Queen at Taymouth, on the occasion of her visit in 1842, was considered by her Majesty to be the finest thing she had seen in Scotland. On that festive occasion the majestic features of the surrounding landscape were aided by all the resources of human art and the animation of human life. Her Majesty arrived on Wednesday the 7th September, at six in the evening. Her arrival was awaited by a gathering of the powerful clan Campbell, and by thousands besides, both Celts and Sassenachs, who had crowded to the spot from all quarters of the country. As the evening advanced, a brilliant illumination gradually spread its lustre over the scene, realizing the fabled splendours of the Arabian Tales. The trunks of the trees were converted into picturesque and irregular columns of fire, and their branches became covered with clusters of sparkling rubies, emeralds, topazes, and diamonds, like the fairy fruit in the ideal gardens of the genii. The variegated lamps, hung along the wire-fence of the deer park in beautiful festoons, presented the appearance of an unsupported and aërial barrier of living fire. The fort among the woods above the Castle blazed with golden light from 40,000 coloured lamps, and ever and anon the flash of a gun gave additional momentary splendour to the woods, and the boom of its report reverberated in sublime echoes through the valley. Soaring above all, the lofty summits of the northern hills were crowned with immense bonfires, in countless numbers, so that the rugged outlines of the most distant mountains in the background were rendered

THE QUEEN PLANT NG THE SCOTCH F R TAYMOU H.

visible by their own volcanic-looking flames. To all these blazing and sparkling wonders, the intense darkness of the night gave additional effect. At ten o'clock, a salute from the battery announced the commencement of the fireworks, which were produced in the highest style of pyrotechnical art. Their display took place upon the sloping lawn that hangs towards the base of the hill, directly across the park in front of the house. There were many honest citizens of London present, who had seen the glories of Vauxhall, and who declared that they were all utterly extinguished by those of this single night at Taymouth. The dancing took place on two platforms in front of the Castle, the manly forms and energetic action of the Highlanders being exhibited to striking advantage by a blaze of torch-light.

Many were the whimsical scenes that occurred in Kenmore, Aberfeldy, and the hamlets and the houses of the surrounding districts, on this memorable occasion, from the crowds of strangers that besieged them for beds. Every floor was covered with shakedowns, and for each of these a charge of from ten shillings to a sovereign was made; and many were glad to content themselves with a chair to sit up in. The scramble for food next morning was no less than it had been for beds, and many who had never tasted porridge in their lives before, seized upon the wooden bicker that contained it, and were fain to gobble it up with the help of a horn spoon. It was pleasant to see, however, that all these inconveniences were borne with good humour, every one declaring that a sight of the glories of Taymouth would have been cheaply purchased by deprivations and hardships of tenfold greater magnitude. And, indeed, they were glories, such as, when taken together with the magnificence of the natural theatre where they were exhibited, are scarcely to be paralleled. The revelries at Kenilworth, in honour of Elizabeth, were sufficiently gorgeous; but rich as is the district in which they took place, it can no more be compared, in point of romantic effect, with that of the bold wooded mountains, the variegated plains, and the sparkling streams of Taymouth, than the homely countenance and ascetic expression of the Queen, who was a guest there, can be thought of in comparison with the lovely face that shed its smiles that night on all within the noble castle of the Marquess and Marchioness of Breadalbane.*

Leaving Kenmore and Taymouth, the tourist proceeds along the shores of the Loch to Killin, which is sixteen miles distant at the

* The above description of the festivities at Taymouth is abridged from Sir Thomas Dick Lauder's "Memorial of the Royal Progress." We lament that limited space has rendered it necessary for us to condense the picturesque and glowing style of the distinguished author, but the force of circumstances has made this Procrustean process unavoidable.

opposite extremity. Both shores abound in beautiful scenery, but the southern is preferable, on account of the view which it commands of the gigantic Ben Lawers, which borders the other side of the loch.* This road is rather longer, and considerably more hilly than that along the northern shore, but it is quite passable for a carriage. There is a good deal of cultivated ground on either side, with many rude and picturesque cottages. Two miles from Kenmore, on the south side of the lake, is the fine waterfall of Acharn, half a mile off the road. The cascade appears to be about eighty or ninety feet high, and a neat hermitage has been formed, commanding an excellent view of the fall. Midway between Kenmore and Killin, upon the north side of the lake, is the village of Lawers, containing a church and an inn. The road continues to lead along the foot of Ben Lawers, affording a fine prospect of the scenery at the head of the loch. Eight miles from Lawers, beautifully seated on the banks of the Dochart, near its junction with the Lochy, is the straggling little village of KILLIN.—[*Inns:*—Streethouse.]

Fingal's grave, in a field immediately to the north of the village, is indicated by a stone about two feet in height. Killin is deservedly admired for the varied beauty of its landscapes. The vale of the Dochart is stern and wild, but that of the Lochy is peculiarly beautiful. At the village the Dochart rushes over a strange expanse of rock, and encircles two islands, one covered with magnificent pines,

* "The northern shore of the lake presented a far more Alpine prospect than that upon which the Glover was stationed. Woods and thickets ran up the sides of the mountains, and disappeared among the sinuosities formed by the winding ravines which separated them from each other; but far above these specimens of a tolerable natural soil, arose the swart and bare mountains themselves, in the dark grey desolation proper to the season. Some were peaked, some broad-crested, some rocky and precipitous, others of a tamer outline; and the clan of Titans seemed to be commanded by their appropriate chieftains—the frowning mountain of Ben Lawers, and the still more lofty eminence of Ben Mohr, arising high above the rest, whose peaks retain a dazzling helmet of snow far into the summer season, and sometimes during the whole year. Yet the borders of this wild and silvan region, where the mountains descended upon the lake, intimated, even at that early period, many traces of human habitation. Hamlets were seen, especially on the northern margin of the lake, half hid among the little glens that poured their tributary streams into Loch Tay, which, like many earthly things, made a fair show at a distance, but, when more closely approached, were disgustful and repulsive, from their squalid want of the conveniences which even attend Indian wigwams. The magnificent bosom of the lake itself was a scene to gaze on with delight. Its noble breadth, with its termination in a full and beautiful run, was rendered yet more picturesque by one of those islets which are often happily situated in Scottish lakes. The ruins upon that isle, now almost shapeless, being overgrown with wood, rose, at the time we speak of, into the towers and pinnacles of a priory, where slumbered the remains of Sybilla, daughter of Henry I. of England, and consort of Alexander the First of Scotland."—*Fair Maid of Perth.*

K LL N AND AUCHMORE.

on one of which is the tomb of the Macnabs. From the upper end of the lower island there are three bridges across the stream. "Killin," says Dr. Macculloch, with some exaggeration, "is the most extraordinary collection of extraordinary scenery in Scotland—unlike every thing else in the country, and perhaps on earth, and a perfect picture gallery in itself, since you cannot move three yards without meeting a new landscape. A busy artist might here draw a month and not exhaust it. * * * Fir-trees, rocks, torrents, mills, bridges, and houses, under endless combinations, produce the great bulk of the middle landscape, while the distances more constantly are found in the surrounding hills, in their varied woods, in the bright expanse of the lake, and the minute ornaments of the distant valley, in the rocks and bold summit of Cailleach, and in the lofty vision of Ben Lawers, which towers, like a huge giant, to the clouds—the monarch of the scene. On the north side of Loch Tay, and about a mile and a half from the village of Killin, stand the picturesque ruins of Finlarig Castle, an ancient seat of the Breadalbane family. The castle is a narrow building of three storeys, entirely overgrown with ivy, and surrounded by venerable trees. Immediately adjoining is the family vault. The following anecdote of the olden times is related by the Messrs. Anderson in their excellent Guide to the Highlands: "On the occasion of a marriage festival at Finlarig, in years gone by, when occupied by the heir-apparent, intelligence was given to the company, which comprised the principal youth of the clan, that a party of the Macdonalds of Keppoch, who had just passed with a drove of *lifted* cattle, had refused to pay the accustomed *road* collop. Flushed with revelry, the guests indignantly sallied out and attacked the Macdonalds on the adjoining hill of Stronoclachan, but, from their irregular impetuosity, they were repulsed, and twenty young gentlemen left dead on the spot. Tidings of the affray were conveyed to Taymouth, and a reinforcement arriving, the victors were overtaken in Glenorchy, and routed, and their leader slain."

On leaving Killin the tourist proceeds up Glen Dochart and passes, on the right, the mansion house of Achlyne, a seat of the Marquis of Breadalbane. A little beyond, at a place called Leeks, a road strikes off to Crianlarich Inn, from which the tourist may either go by Tyndrum and Dalmally to Inverary, or he may descend Glenfalloch till he reach the head of Loch Lomond. The traveller now enters Glen-Ogle, a narrow and gloomy defile, hemmed in by the rocky sides of the mountains, which are here strikingly grand, rising on the one side in a succession of terraces, and on the other in a steep acclivity, surmounted by perpendicular precipices. Among these wild cliffs the eagle has built her nest for many years. At the distance of 8 miles from Killin, is the little village of LOCHEARNHEAD—[*Inns:* Walker's.]—From this point the tourist may turn southwards by Balquhidder, the burial-place of Rob Roy, and proceed through the wild pass of Loch Lubnaig and Leny to Callander, a distance of 14 miles; or he may take the route along Lochearn to St. Fillans, Comrie, and Crieff, a distance of 19½ miles. If it be his intention to visit the Trosachs and Loch Katrine from Callander, he will adopt the former route, otherwise he should embrace the opportunity of acquainting himself with the beauty of the line of road to Crieff, and the charming scenery around the town. Loch Earn is about seven miles in length, and about one mile in breadth. "Limited as are the di-

Cottage in Glen-Ogle.

mensions of Loch Earn," says Dr. Macculloch, "it is exceeded in beauty by few of our lakes, as far as it is possible for many beauties to exist in so small a space. It is a miniature and model of scenery that might well occupy ten times the space. Yet there is nothing trifling or small in the details,—nothing to diminish its grandeur of style, and tell us we are contemplating a reduced copy." This is only a brief extract from the eulogium of the learned doctor, the rest of which is rather overcharged. The passage quoted may be considered by tourists as fairly representing the claims of Lochearn to their admiration.

There are roads along each side of the loch, and in the view which they respectively command, they are very equally balanced. The coach which runs between Killin and Crieff takes the road along the north side, as the easiest for the horses. It also commands a favourable view of Ben Voirlich. The road along the south side commands the view of a more strikingly indented shore, and a greater expanse of mountain scenery. Along the latter route, a mile and a half from the inn, we come to Edinample, an ancient castellated mansion belonging to the Marquis of Breadalbane. Immediately below the road, there is a fine waterfall, formed by the Ample, a mountain stream, which pours in two perpendicular torrents over a broad rugged rock, and uniting about midway, is again precipitated over a second precipice.* The road now passes through continuous woods of oak, larch, ash, and birch. The view to the south is closed up by the huge Ben Voirlich, (*i.e.* the Great Mountain of the lake,) which rises to the height of 3300 feet. About midway between Lochearnhead and the east end of the lake is Ardvoirlich, (Robert Stewart, Esq.,) the Darlinvaroch of the *Legend of Montrose*.† The landscapes

* After passing along the bridge, a footpath will be observed on the left, leading to the best points of view below the fall.

† "During the reign of James IV., a great feud between the powerful families of Drummond and Murray divided Perthshire. The former being the most numerous and powerful, cooped up eight score of the Murrays in the kirk of Monavaird, and set fire to it. The wives and children of the ill-fated men, who had also found shelter in the church, perished by the same conflagration. One man, named David Murray, escaped by the humanity of one of the Drummonds, who received him in his arms as he leaped from amongst the flames. As King James IV. ruled with more activity than most of his predecessors, this cruel deed was severely revenged, and several of the perpetrators were beheaded at Stirling. In consequence of the prosecution against his clan, the Drummond, by whose assistance David Murray had escaped, fled to Ireland, until, by means of the person whose life he had saved, he was permitted to return to Scotland, where he and his descendants were distinguished by the name of Drummond Eirinch, or Ernoch, that is, Drummond of Ireland; and the same title was bestowed on their estate.

"The Drummond-Ernoch of James the Sixth's time was a king's forester in the forest of Glenartney, and chanced to be employed there in search of venison about the year 1588, or early in 1589. The forest was adjacent to the chief haunts of the MacGregors, or a particular race of them, known by the title of MacEagh, or Children of the Mist. They considered the forester's hunting in their vicinity as an aggression; or perhaps they had him at feud, for the apprehension or slaughter of some of their own name, or for some similar reason. This tribe of MacGregors were outlawed and persecuted, as the reader may see in the Introduction to Rob Roy; and every man's hand being against them, their hand was of course directed against every man. In short, they surprised and slew Drummond-Ernoch, cut off his head, and carried it with them, wrapt in the corner of one of their plaids.

"In the full exultation of vengeance, they stopped at the house of Ardvoirlich, and demanded refreshment, which the lady, a sister of the murdered Drummond-Ernoch, (her husband being absent,) was afraid or unwilling to refuse. She caused bread and cheese to be placed before them, and gave directions for more substantial refreshments to be prepared. While she was absent with this

to the east of the house are peculiarly beautiful. At the foot of Loch Earn, there is a small islet covered with wood, which was at one time the retreat of a bandit sept of the name of Neish. Having on one occasion plundered some of the Macnabs, a party of that clan, commanded by the chieftain's son, carried a boat from Loch

hospitable intention, the barbarians placed the head of her brother on the table, filling the mouth with bread and cheese, and bidding him eat, for many a merry meal he had eaten in that house.

"The poor woman returning, and beholding this dreadful sight, shrieked aloud, and fled into the woods, where, as described in the romance, she roamed a raving maniac, and for some time secreted herself from all living society. Some remaining instinctive feeling brought her at length to steal a glance from a distance at the maidens while they milked the cows, which, being observed, her husband, Ardvoirlich, had her conveyed back to her home, and detained her there until she gave birth to a child, of whom she had been pregnant; after which she was observed gradually to recover her mental faculties.

"Meanwhile, the outlaws had carried to the utmost their insults against the regal authority, which, indeed, as exercised, they had little reason for respecting. They bore the same bloody trophy, which they had so savagely exhibited to the lady of Ardvoirlich, into the old church of Balquhidder, nearly in the centre of their country, where the Laird of MacGregor and all his clan being convened for the purpose, laid their hands successively on the dead man's head, and swore, in heathenish and barbarous manner, to defend the author of the deed. This fierce and vindictive combination gave the late lamented Sir Alexander Boswell, Bart., subject for a spirited poem, entitled 'Clan-Alpin's Vow,' which was printed, but not published, in 1811."

We give the conclusion of the poem :—"The Clan-Gregor has met in the ancient church of Balquhidder. The head of Drummond-Ernoch is placed on the altar, covered for a time with the banner of the tribe. The chief of the tribe advances to the altar :—

"And pausing, on the banner gazed;
Then cried in scorn, his finger raised,
'This was the boon of Scotland's king;'
And with a quick and angry fling,
Tossing the pageant screen away,
The dead man's head before him lay.
Unmov'd he scann'd the visage o'er,
The clotted locks were dark with gore,
The features with convulsion grim,
The eyes contorted, sunk, and dim,
But, unappall'd, in angry mood,
With lowering brow, unmoved he stood.
Upon the head his bared right hand
He laid, the other grasp'd his brand;
Then kneeling, cried, 'To Heaven I swear
This deed of death I own, and share;
As truly, fully mine, as though
This my right hand had dealt the blow;
Come, then, our foemen, one, come all;
If to revenge this caitiff's fall
One blade is bared, one bow is drawn,
Mine everlasting peace I pawn,
To claim from them, or claim from him,
In retribution, limb for limb.
In sudden fray, or open strife,
This steel shall render life for life.'
He ceased; and at his beckoning nod,
The clansmen to the altar trod;
And not a whisper breath'd around,
And nought was heard of mortal sound,
Save from the clanking arms they bore,
That rattled on the marble floor;
And each, as he approached in haste,
Upon the scalp his right hand placed;
With livid lip, and gather'd brow,
Each uttered, in his turn, the vow.
Fierce Malcolm watch'd the passing scene,
And search'd them through with glances keen;
Then dash'd a tear-drop from his eye;
Unbid it came—he knew not why.
Exulting high, he towering stood;
'Kinsmen,' he cried, 'of Alpin's blood,
And worthy of Clan-Alpin's name,
Unstained by cowardice and shame,
E'en do, spare nocht, in time of ill
Shall be Clan-Alpin's legend still!'"

Introduction to Legend of Montrose.

LOCHEARN-HEAD.

Tay to Loch Earn, surprised the banditti by night, and put them all to the sword. In commemoration of this event, the Macnabs assumed for their crest a man's head, with the motto, "Dreadnought."

At the east end of Loch Earn, 7½ miles from Lochearnhead, stands the village of ST. FILLANS.—[*Inns:*—St. Fillan's Inn.]—Formerly a wretched hamlet, known by the name of Portmore, it has become, through the exertions of Lord and Lady Willoughby D'Eresby, on whose ground it stands, one of the sweetest spots in Scotland. It derived its name from St. Fillan, a celebrated saint who resided in this place. He was the favourite saint of Robert Bruce, and one of his arms was borne in a shrine by the Abbot of Inchaffray at the battle of Bannockburn. On the summit of a hill in this neighbourhood, called Dun Fillan, there is a well consecrated by him, which even to this day is supposed to be efficacious for the cure of many disorders. The St. Fillan Society, formed in 1819, holds occasional meetings in this place for athletic sports and performances on the bagpipe, and confers prizes on the successful competitors. The games are held on the plain immediately beyond the small bridge called St. Fillan's Bridge, and are usually attended by great numbers of persons of condition, male and female, from all parts of the Highlands. The vallev of Strathearn, which extends from this place nearly to Perth, contains many fine villas and wooded parks, and is celebrated for its beauty and fertility. Leaving St. Fillans, the Aberuchill hills upon the right are very grandly grouped, and before entering the wood-enclosed part of the road the tourist should rest his eyes on the scene. The highest peak is the summit of Birron hill. The road now winds along the banks of the river Earn, through groves of lofty trees, presenting here and there broken glimpses of the ridges of the neighbouring mountains. About 9½ miles from Lochearnhead, we pass the mansion of Duneira, the favourite seat of the late Lord Melville, with its picturesque grounds and delightful pleasure walks. It is now the property of Sir David Dundas, Bart. A little farther on, Dalchonzie (Skene, Esq.,) and Aberuchill Castle * (Major Drummond,) are seen on the right; and, 12¾ miles from Lochearnhead, or 5½ from St. Fillans, pleasantly situated on the north bank of the river Earn, at its confluence with the Ruchill, the tourist enters the village of COMRIE.—[*Inns:*—Comrie Inn.]—Comrie is by many supposed to have been the scene of the dreadful battle between Galgacus and Agricola. Half a mile south of the village are the remains of a Roman

* Aberuchill was built in 1602, and was the scene of many sanguinary battles between the Campbells and Macgregors.

Camp. Close to the village stands Comrie House (Dundas, Bart.,) on the east side of which the Lednock Water flows into the Earn. On the summit of a hill called Dunmore, a monument seventy-two feet in height has been erected to the memory of the late Lord Melville, overhanging a turbulent little stream called the "Humble Bumble." At the foot of Dunmore, there is a place called the Devil's Caldron," where the Lednock, at the farther extremity of a long, deep and narrow chasm, is precipitated into a dark and dismal gulf. From the monument there is an extensive and interesting view of the adjacent country.

Leaving Comrie, we descend towards Crieff, through a scene of the most enchanting beauty. A mile and a half beyond Comrie, we pass, on the left, Lawers House (the mansion of the late Lord Balgray,) with a fine avenue, a mile in length, on the opposite side of the road. The parks contain some of the largest pine-trees in Scotland. A mile farther on is Clathick (Colquhoun, Esq.,) and half a mile beyond (3½ from Crieff) the road passess Monievaird Kirk. On an eminence to the south of this place there is an obelisk, erected to Sir David Baird, Bart. A mile and a half beyond is

OCHTERTYRE,

(Sir William Keith Murray,) celebrated for the romantic beauty of its situation. The view commanded from the avenue of approach to the house, and from the garden around it, is truly exquisite, combining, in marvellous harmony, every attribute of beauty in landscape. Wood and water, hill and dale, are charmingly balanced in the composition. The taste displayed in distributing the wood over the fields opposite the approach, is a model well worthy of study by other proprietors. The majestic Benvoirlich closes the distance to the west. Rich as the neighbourhood of Crieff must be considered in fine scenery, the first place must be assigned to the view from Ochtertyre. A ruined tower, the remains of a fortress erected in the 13th century, by Comyn of Badenoch, stands on the bank of a sheet of water, called the Loch of Monievaird, near the mansion. The adjacent vale of the Turit exhibits a variety of romantic scenery, which has been rendered classical by the pen of Burns.* About 6¾ miles

* While on a visit to Sir William Murray at Ochtertyre, he wrote the beautiful song, "Blythe was she," on Miss Euphemia Murray of Lintrose, a lady whose beauty had acquired for her the name of "The Flower of Strathmore.'

from Comrie, delightfully situated on a slope above the river Earn, backed by hills and crags, and the Knock of Crieff, all of considerable altitude, is the town of

CRIEFF.

[*Inns*:—Drummond Arms.]

Coaches to Greenloaning Station. To Killin, by Comrie, St. Fillans, Benvoirlich, Lochearnhead.

The population of the town is about 5000. An ancient cross, of apparently great antiquity, in the middle of the central street, is worthy of notice. An educational establishment, called St. Margaret's College, for young ladies of the Episcopal communion, has recently been formed, and the salubrity of the climate of Crieff recommends it as an excellent locality for such foundations.

The environs of Crieff, as already stated, are exquisitely beautiful, and will amply repay the visit of the tourist. The view from the Old Market Park, on the northern outskirts of the town, will satisfy strangers of the truth of this, and it is most gratifying to be enabled to add that the neighbouring proprietors evince the most praiseworthy liberality in throwing open to the public the walks around their houses, and through their grounds. Two miles south from the town* is the entrance to the avenue of

DRUMMOND CASTLE,

the ancient residence of the noble family of Perth, now represented by Lady Willoughby D'Eresby. "If Drummond Castle," says Macculloch, "is not all that it might be rendered, it is still absolutely unrivalled in the low country, and only exceeded in the Highlands by Dunkeld and Blair. Placed in the most advantageous position to enjoy the magnificent and various expanse around, it looks over scenery scarcely any where equalled. With ground of the most commanding and varied forms, including water and rock, and abrupt hill and dell, and gentle undulations, its extent is princely, and its aspect that of ancient wealth and ancient power. Noble avenues, profuse woods, a waste of lawn and pasture, an unrestrained scope, everything bespeaks the carelessness of liberality and extensive possessions, while the ancient castle, its earliest part belonging to 1500, stamps on it that air of high and distant opulence which adds so deep a moral interest to the rural beauties of baronial Britain."

This ancient "keep" was visited by her Majesty on her tour

* Although the *entrance* to the avenue is only two miles from Crieff, the avenue itself adds another mile to the distance between Crieff and the Castle.

through the Highlands, on which occasion a splendid pavilion was erected for the dining hall, the accommodation within the building being but limited. Immediately in front of the principal face of the castle lie the matchless flower-gardens of Drummond, known by repute to every florist in the kingdom.

Three miles north from Crieff, on the road to Amulree, is MONZIE CASTLE, (pronounced *Monee*,) Campbell, Esq., surrounded and backed by scenery of remarkable beauty, Benvoirlich in the distance. In the grounds behind the house are the five oldest larch trees in Scotland, planted the night before those in Dunkeld, hitherto erroneously reported to have been the oldest. The circumference of the trunk of one of these trees is 19 feet 7 inches, at 3 feet from the ground. The paintings and armoury are well worthy of attention, and among the furniture is a solid mahogany cup, 14 feet 7 inches in circumference at the lip. Pursuing the route 7½ miles from Crieff, in the direction of Aberfeldy, the tourist will reach Ossian's grave, the situation of which is marked by a huge square mass of rock, surrounded by an elevated circle on the moor. One of General Wade's soldiers, called the "lang man," is buried within the same circle, and the General's road intersected it. Now, however, the road is carried *round*, not *over* the consecrated spot. The glen is very wild and desolate.

Leaving Crieff for Perth, we pass in succession Fern Tower (Lady Baird;) a mile beyond this Cultaquhey (Maxton, Esq.,) then Inchbraikie (Major Græme,) and next on the right, Abercairney, (Major W. M. Stirling). Farther on is the village of Foulis, and a mile beyond this are the ruins of the Abbey of Inchaffray, founded in 1200 by an Earl of Strathearn and his Countess, and the abbot of which carried the arm of St. Fillan at the battle of Bannockburn. A mile farther on, the road passes Gorthy, (Mercer, Esq.,) and shortly after enters the plantations of Balgowan, the seat of the late Lord Lynedoch. A little farther, the road passes on the right Tippermalloch, (R. Smyth, Esq.), and, six miles from Perth, enters the village of Methven, containing a population of about 2000.* In the immediate

* At Methven a road branches off to TRINITY COLLEGE, a large structure for the education of the clergy and youth of the Scotch Episcopal Church. It stands on the estate of George Patton, Esq. of Cairnies, who liberally granted a space of 20 imperial acres in extent for this purpose. The Rev. Charles Wordsworth, warden of the College, has also contributed the munificent sum of £7000 towards the building. It is 10 miles distant from Perth Within half a mile from the College is a comfortable inn.

Strangers proceeding from the College to Crieff should take the road by Buchanty. From Buchanty a road to the right leads to Glen-Almond House

neighbourhood stands Methven Castle (W. Smyth, Esq.) Within the grounds, visible from the road, is the Pepperwell Oak. In 1722, when David Smyth, the laird of Methven was confined in the Tower of London, under suspicion of his political opinions, a man came to his lady, Katharine Cochran, (then at Methven) supposing that she might be in want of money, and offered her 100 merks Scots for it, which she refused to take. The trunk is 18 feet in circumference. Near Methven, Robert Bruce was defeated, June 19, 1306, by the English under the command of Aymer de Valence, Earl of Pembroke. About two miles and a half from Perth, the road passes the ancient castle of Ruthven, the scene of the memorable incident known in Scottish history by the name of the *Raid of Ruthven.* The name of the building has been changed to Huntingtower, and it is now converted into a residence for workmen. A short distance to the north is Lynedoch Cottage, within the grounds of which is Burn Braes, a spot on the banks of Brauchieburn, where Bessie Bell and Mary Gray

———————" biggit a bower,
And theekit it ower wi' rashes."

Dronach Haugh, where these unfortunate beauties were buried, is about half a mile west from Lynedoch Cottage, on the banks of the river Almond.* Over their supposed grave is placed a stone, with the following inscription, "they lived—they loved—they died." The road now passes Tulloch bleachfield and printfield, and shortly after enters the town of Perth. The distance from Crieff to Perth by this road is 17 miles.

(J. Patton, Esq.), within two miles of which are the remains of a vitrified fort. Resuming the road to Crieff, a Roman camp may be observed on the left, immediately before reaching the 14th milestone. Should the tourist desire to visit Ossian's grave, already described, he turns into the Aberfeldy road (which branches to the right after passing the 14th milestone), and two miles along that road he reaches the spot. Returning to the Crieff road we pass Foulford Inn (4 miles from Crieff); and three miles from Crieff the beauties of Monzie Castle are presented on the right. The fine expanse of Strathearn then spreads before the eye, and charms the tourist on the remaining portion of the road to Crieff. By this road the distance from Perth to Crieff is 21 miles.

* The common tradition is, that Bessie Bell and Mary Gray were the daughters of two country gentlemen in the neighbourhood of Perth, and an intimate friendship subsisted between them. Bessie Bell, daughter of the Laird of Kinnaird, happened to be on a visit to Mary Gray, at her father's house of Lynedoch, when the plague of 1666 broke out. To avoid the infection, the two young ladies built themselves a bower in a very retired and romantic spot called the Burnbraes, about three-quarters of a mile westward from Lynedoch House, where they resided for some time, supplied with food, it is said, by a young gentleman of Perth, who was in love with them both. The disease was unfor-

KILLIECRANKIE—BLAIR-ATHOLL—FALLS OF BRUAR—MORAYSHIRE FLOODS—INVERNESS.

LEAVING Dunkeld, the road passes for some miles along the eastern bank of the Tay, and at the distance of five miles reaches Dowally Kirk. On the opposite side of the river are seen Dalguise, (Stewart, Esq.,) and Kinnaird House, (Duke of Atholl.) A little farther on is Moulinearn Inn. A mile farther on is Donavourd, (Macfarlane, Esq.,) on the right, and Dunfallandy, (Miss Ferguson,) on the western bank of the Tummel. A mile beyond is the village of PITLOCHRIE—[Sduard's Inn].—A little farther, on a low tongue of land formed by the junction of the Tummel and the Garry, is Faskally House (Butter, Esq.),

tunately communicated to them by their lover, and proved fatal, when, according to custom in cases of the plague, they were not buried in the ordinary parochial place of sepulture, but in a sequestered spot called Dronach Haugh, at the foot of a brae of the same name, upon the banks of the river Almond. The late Lord Lynedoch put an iron railing round the grave, and planted some yew trees beside it.

The following pathetic little ballad, which Allan Ramsay supplanted by a much inferior song, has fortunately been recovered by Mr. Kirkpatrick Sharpe:

"O Bessie Bell and Mary Gray,
They war twa bonnie lasses,
They biggit a bower on yon burn side,
And theekit it ower wi' rashes.
They theekit it ower wi' rashes green,
They theekit it ower wi' heather;
But the pest cam frae the burrows-town,
And slew them baith thegither.

They thocht to lie in Methven kirk-yard,
Amang their noble kin;
But they maun lie on Lynedoch brae,
To beek forenent the sun.
And Bessie Bell and Mary Gray,
They war twa bonnie lasses;
They biggit a bower on yon burn side.
And theekit it ower wi' rashes."

PENNANT'S *Tour*. CHAMBERS'S *Ballads*, p. 146.

surrounded by wooded hills, forming a most romantic and attractive scene.* Proceeding onward, at the distance of a mile, the traveller enters the celebrated pass of KILLIECRANKIE, which stretches for the space of a mile or more along the termination of the river Garry. The hills which, on both sides, approach very near, are covered with natural wood, and descend in rugged precipices to the deep channel of the river. At the bridge over the Garry, near the entrance of the pass, a road leads on the left to the districts of the Tummel and Rannoch. The north end of this pass is the well-known scene of the battle fought, in 1689, between the Highland clans under Viscount Dundee, and the troops of King William, commanded by General Mackay. A stone is pointed out at Urrard House, on the right, which marks the spot where Dundee received his death-wound.†

* On the estate of Faskally, upon the high ground about a mile from Pitlochrie, on the road from Dunkeld, is a pretty little waterfall called the Black Spout.

† "Dundee," says Sir John Dalrymple, "flew to the Convention, and demanded justice. The Duke of Hamilton, who wished to get rid of a troublesome adversary, treated his complaint with neglect; and in order to sting him in the tenderest part, reflected upon that courage which could be alarmed by imaginary dangers. Dundee left the house in a rage, mounted his horse, and with a troop of fifty horsemen, who had deserted to him from his regiment in England, galloped through the city. Being asked by one of his friends who stopped him, where he was going? he waved his hat, and is reported to have answered, 'Wherever the spirit of Montrose shall direct me.'"—*Memoirs*, 4to edit. vol. i. p. 287. Dundee immediately proceeded to collect the army with which he fought the battle of Killiecrankie. This incident has been commemorated by Sir W. Scott in the following spirited song:—

"To the Lords of Convention, 'twas Clavers who spoke,
Ere the King's crown go down, there are crowns to be broke,
So each cavalier, who loves honour and me,
Let him follow the bonnet of Bonnie Dundee.

Come, fill up my cup, come, fill up my can,
Come, saddle my horses, and call up my men;
Come, open the West Port, and let me gae free,
And it's room for the bonnets of bonnie Dundee.

Dundee he is mounted, he rides up the street;
The bells are rung backward, the drums they are beat;
But the Provost, douce man, said, Just e'en let him be;
The town is weel quit of that deil of Dundee.
Come, fill up, &c.

Several villas adorn the terraced sides of the valley approaching the pass, viz. Urrard House, (Alston, Esq.,) Killiecrankie Cottage, (Hay, Esq.,) Strathgarrie, (A. H. Mitchel-

As he rode down the sanctified bends of the Bow,
Each carline was flyting and shaking her pow;
But some young plants of grace, they look'd couthie and slee,
Thinking—Luck to thy bonnet, thou bonnie Dundee!
Come, fill up, &c.

With sour-featured saints the Grassmarket was pang'd,
As if half of the west had set tryst to be hang'd;
There was spite in each face, there was fear in each e'e,
As they watch'd for the bonnet of bonnie Dundee.
Come, fill up, &c.

The cowls of Kilmarnock had spits and had spears,
And lang-hafted gullies to kill cavaliers;
But they shrunk to close-heads, and the causeway left free
At a toss of the bonnet of bonnie Dundee.
Come, fill up, &c.

He spurred to the foot of the high castle rock,
And to the gay Gordon he gallantly spoke;
Let Mons Meg and her marrows three volleys let flee,
For love of the bonnet of bonnie Dundee.
Come, fill up, &c.

The Gordon has asked of him whither he goes—
Wheresoever shall guide me the soul of Montrose;
Your Grace in short space shall have tidings of me,
Or that low lies the bonnet of bonnie Dundee.
Come, fill up, &c.

There are hills beyond Pentland, and streams beyond Forth;
If there's lords in the Southland, there's chiefs in the North;
There are wild dunniewassals three thousand times three,
Will cry *Hoich!* for the bonnet of bonnie Dundee.
Come, fill up, &c.

Away to the hills, to the woods, to the rocks,
Ere I own a usurper, I'll couch with the fox:
And tremble, false Whigs, though triumphant ye be,
You have not seen the last of my bonnet and me.
Come, fill up, &c.

He waved his proud arm, and the trumpets were blown,
The kettle drums clash'd, and the horsemen rode on,
Till on Ravelston crags, and on Clermiston lee,
Died away the wild war-note of bonnie Dundee.

Come, fill up my cup, come, fill up my can,
Come saddle my horses, and call up my men;
Fling all your gates open, and let me gae free,
For 'tis up with the bonnets of bonnie Dundee."

son, Esq.), &c. Passing Lude (M'Inroy, Esq.) the road descends into the valley, and crosses the river at the Bridge of Tilt, where there is a neat village.—[*Inns* :— The Atholl Arms; The Bridge of Tilt.]—The beauties of Glen Tilt, and the Falls of Fender, will amply repay a visit. A little farther on, the road reaches the village and inn of Blair, the latter commodious and well conducted; and, in the neighbourhood, the noble old castle of Blair, now called Atholl House, the ancient residence of the Dukes of that name. It is a long narrow building of three storeys. It was formerly much higher, and a place of considerable strength, but was reduced in height in consequence of the attacks of the Highlanders in 1716. In September 1844, Her Majesty sojourned for nearly three weeks at Blair Castle, visiting the falls of Bruar, the pass of Killiecrankie, the falls of Tummel, and the other picturesque scenery with which the neighbourhood abounds. Blair is celebrated for its noble old woods.

In the immediate neighbourhood there are many interesting waterfalls. Three miles to the westward are those of Bruar. The streamlet makes several distinct falls, and rushes through a rough perpendicular channel above which the sloping banks are covered with a fir plantation formed by the late Duke of Atholl, in compliance with the request of Burns in the well-known "Petition." And now, according to the poet's wish—

"lofty firs and ashes cool,
The lowly banks o'erspread,
And view deep-bending in the pool,
Their shadow's watery bed!

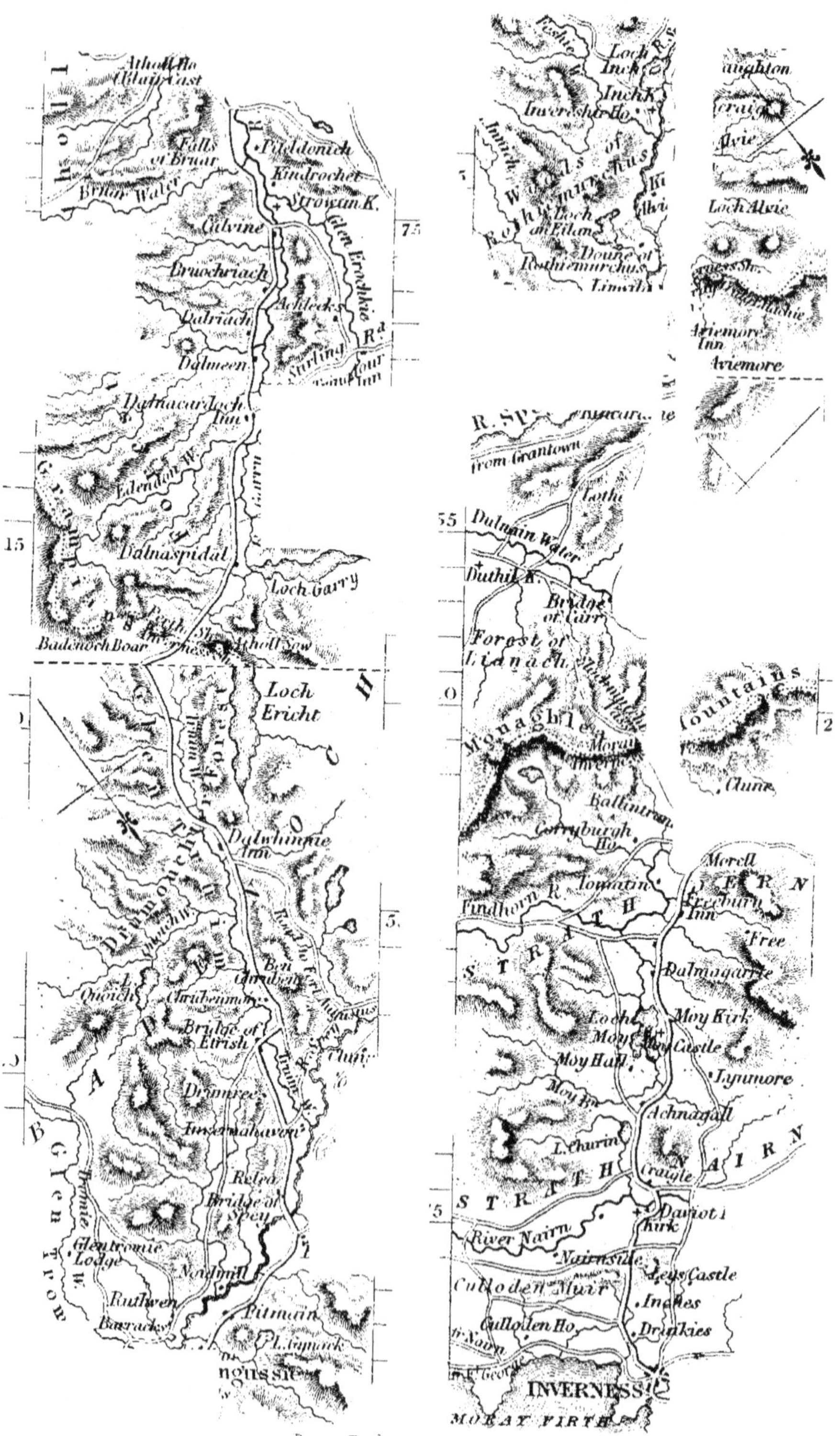

Drawn & Engd. by J. Bartholomew, Edinr.

> 'Here fragrant birks in woodbines drest,
> The craggy cliffs adorn,
> And for the little songster's nest,
> The close embow'ring thorn."

A walk has been cut through the plantation, and a number of fantastic little grottoes erected, and a carriage-road leads as far as the second set of falls. From Blair-Atholl, a road leads through Glen Tilt, and over a wild mountainous district, to the Braes of Mar. Leaving Blair-Atholl, the tourist passes through a wild Alpine territory, and, proceeding along the banks of the Garry, at the distance of ten miles and a half, reaches the inn of Dalnacardoch. The country between Dalnacardoch and Dalwhinnie, (thirteen miles,) presents a most desolate and cheerless aspect. Half way there are two mountains, named the Badenoch *Boar* and the Atholl *Sow*, at which the mountain streams part in opposite directions, some running eastward to join the Truim and the Spey, while others fall into the Tay. This spot is the proper separation between the counties of Inverness and Perth. The savage pass between Dalnacardoch and Dalwhinnie is called Drumouchter. The inn of Dalwhinnie is surrounded by a young plantation, the only green and pleasing object on which the eye can rest for many miles around. It is situated at the distance of about a mile from the head of Loch Ericht, on the north side of which is the mountain Benalder. A cave exists in this mountain in which Prince Charles Stuart found refuge for a short time after the battle of Culloden. At Dalwhinnie, a road parts off by Laggan and Garviemore, and over the difficult hill of Corryiarick to Fort-Augustus. Leaving Dalwhinnie, at the distance of six miles. the road crosses the Truim, and four miles farther crosses the Spey. At Invernahavon, near the junction of these rivers, a celebrated clan battle was fought in the reign of James I. between the Mackintoshes and Camerons. Glen Truim was the property of the late Col. M'Pherson. The mountains which skirt the road on both sides are bleak and bare, and dull and uninteresting in their forms. Passing the village of Newton of Benchar,* commenced not long

* From Newton of Benchar the road to Fort-William by Loch Laggan strikes

since by the late Mr. M'Pherson of Belleville, the tourist reaches the farm-house of Pitmain, where he will enjoy an extensive view of the valley of the Spey, and of the high black rock of Craig Dhu, the rendezvous of the M'Phersons. Badenoch was anciently the possession of the great family of the Comyns who ruled here during the reigns of the early Scottish sovereigns. The remains of many of their numerous fortresses are still visible. The vast possessions of this family were forfeited on account of the part which they took in the wars between Bruce and Baliol. Badenoch now belongs to various proprietors, the principal of whom are James Evan Baillie, Esq., of Kingussie and Glenelg, (now owner of the greater part of the old Gordon estates,) Cluny Macpherson, Sir George Macpherson Grant of Ballindalloch, and Mackintosh of Mackintosh. A mile beyond Pitmain are the village and inn of Kingussie (the latter a handsome new building erected by Mr. Baillie,) opposite to which, on the other side of the Spey, are the ruins of Ruthven Barracks, destroyed by the Highlanders in 1746. On the same mount once stood one of the castles of the Comyns. It was at this place that the Highlanders reassembled to the number of 8000 two days after their defeat at Culloden, and here they received from Prince Charles the order to disperse. About two miles distant, on the north side of the Spey, is Belleville, the seat of Macpherson, the translator of Ossian, a native of the district, who died here in 1796, now possessed by his daughter, Miss Macpherson. It stands on the site of the ancient castle of Raits, the principal stronghold of the Comyns. A little farther on, a view is obtained of Invereshie, the seat of Sir George Macpherson Grant of Ballindalloch, on the south bank of the Spey of Loch Insh, through which the river passes, and of some of the highest of the Grampians. A short way beyond is Kinrara, the favourite seat of the late Duchess of Gordon, and now the property of the Duke of Richmond. The high rocky crag on the north banks of the Spey is Tor Alvie. On its eastern brow is a rustic hermitage, and at the other

off. Here are relics of a Roman encampment, of which the lines are still discernible.

extremity of the ridge, an enormous cairn of stones, on one side of which is a tablet with an inscription to the memory of the heroes of Waterloo. On the left of the landscape is the beautiful Loch Alvie, with its neat manse and church. The magnificent scenery around Kinrara has been very correctly described by Dr. Macculloch:—"A succession of continuous birch forest, covering Kinrara's rocky hill and its lower grounds, intermixed with open glades, irregular clumps, and scattered trees, produces a scene at once Alpine and dressed, combining the discordant characters of wild mountain landscape, and of ornamental park scenery, while the variety is, at the same time, such as is only found in the most extended domains." Beyond Kinrara, on the right, are the great fir woods of Rothiemurchus* (Sir J. P. Grant,) supposed to cover from fourteen to sixteen square miles. The Spey here takes several majestic sweeps, and supplies a noble foreground to these forests. The road now enters Morayshire, and, thirteen miles from Pitmain, reaches Aviemore Inn, opposite to which is Cairngorm Hill, famous for a peculiar kind of rock crystals.† The mountains on the left are extremely bare and rugged, but towards the west they terminate in the beautiful and bold projecting rock of Craig Ellachie (the *Rock of Alarm*,) the hill of rendezvous of the Grants. "Stand fast Craig Ellachie," is the slogan or war-cry of that clan, the occupants of this

* The reader may, perhaps, recollect Sir Alexander Boswell's lively verses:—

"Come the Grants of Tullochgorum,
Wi' their pipers gaun before 'em,
Proud their mothers are that bore 'em.
Feedle-fa-fum!

Next the Grants of Rothiemurchus,
Every man his sword and dirk has,
Every man as proud's a Turk is.—
Feedle-deedle dum."

strath.—"From its swelling base and rifted precipices the birch trees wave in graceful cluster, their bright and lively green forming a strong contrast in the foreground to the sombre melancholy hue of the pine forests, which in the distance stretch up the sides of the Cairngorms."* At Aviemore a road leads along the banks of the Spey and Grantown to Fochabers, distant forty-nine miles. The road now leaves the Spey, and at the Bridge of Carr, eight miles from Aviemore, crosses the Dulnain; near this place another road strikes off on the right to GRANTOWN.—[*Inns:* The Grant Arms.]—The country around is barren and uninteresting, but a few hoary and stunted pine trees are still to be seen, the solitary remains of those immense forests which once covered the surface of the country. The road now passes through the deep and dangerous pass called Slochmuicht, (the boar's den or hollow,) which was the favourite haunt of banditti even so late as near the close of last century. Four miles from the Bridge of Carr it re-enters Inverness-shire; and two miles farther on crosses the rapid river Findhorn. The banks of the Findhorn are in general highly romantic, but at this spot they are by no means interesting.

In the month of August 1829, the province of Moray, and adjoining districts, were visited by a tremendous flood. Its ravages were most destructive along the course of those rivers which have their source in the Cairngorm Mountains. The waters of the Findhorn and the Spey, and their tributaries, rose to an unexampled height. In some parts of their course these streams rose *fifty feet* above their natural level. Many houses were laid desolate, much agricultural produce was destroyed, and several lives were lost. The woodcut in our text represents the situation of a boatman called Sandy Smith, and his family, in the plains of Forres. "They were huddled together," says the eloquent historian of the Floods, "on a spot of ground a few feet square, some forty or fifty yards below their inundated dwelling. Sandy was sometimes standing and sometimes sitting on a small cask, and, as the beholders fancied,

* ANDERSON'S *Guide to the Highlands*, p. 81.

watching with intense anxiety the progress of the flood, and trembling for every large tree that it brought sweeping past them. His wife, covered with a blanket, sat shivering on a bit of a log, one child in her lap, and a girl of about seventeen, and a boy of about twelve years of age, leaning against her side. A bottle and a glass on the ground, near the man, gave the spectators, as it had doubtless given him, some degree of comfort. About a score of sheep were standing around, or wading or swimming in the shallows. Three cows and a small horse, picking at a broken rick of straw that seemed to be half afloat, were also grouped with the family."* The account of the rescue of the sufferers

afterwards recovered the boat under circumstances almost miraculous, and finally succeeded in rescuing Sandy and his family from their perilous situation.

After crossing the Findhorn, the road passes Corybrough House (Campbell Smith, Esq.,) and a short way beyond reaches the Inn of Freeburn, about nine miles from Bridge of Carr. Near it are the house and plantations of Tomatin (Duncan Macbean, Esq.) The small estate of Free is the property of John Mackintosh, Esq. of Holm. All the rest of the adjoining lands, on the north side of the Findhorn, belong to the Mackintosh estate. Three miles and a half beyond this, on the right, is the castle of Moy, the ancient residence of Mackintosh, the chief of the Clan-Chattan, a confederation of the clans Mackintosh, Macpherson, and others of less consequence. It stands on an island in the midst of a small gloomy lake, called Loch Moy, surrounded by a black wood of Scotch fir, which extends round the lake, and terminates in wild heaths, which are unbroken by any other object as far as the eye can reach. Near the southern end of the lake is a small artificial islet of loose stones, which the former chiefs of Moy used as a place of confinement for their prisoners. On the largest island, a handsome granite obelisk, seventy feet high, has been erected to the memory of the late Sir Æneas Mackintosh, Bart., chief of the clan. On the west side of Loch Moy are the church and manse of Moy, and at the head of the lake, Moy Hall, the family residence of Mackintosh of Mackintosh. Here is preserved the sword of Viscount Dundee, and a sword sent by Pope Leo X. to James V., who bestowed it on the chief of Clan-Chattan, with the privilege of holding the king's sword at coronations. Leaving Loch Moy, the road enters Strathnairn, and passes for three miles through a bleak and heathery plain till it crosses the river Nairn, called in Gaelic *Kis-Nerane*, or the Water of Alders. Six miles from Inverness the road passes, on the right, Daviot House, the residence of Æneas Mackintosh, Esq., (brother of Mackintosh of Mackintosh.) Here are the remains of the ancient castle of Daviot, founded, it is said, by David Earl of Crawford, who, by his marriage with Catherine, daughter of Robert II., acquired possession of the barony of Strathnairn. Passing Leys Castle, the seat of Frederick E. Baillie, Esq. of Leys, the House of Inshes, long occupied by the old family of Robertson of Inshes, and Castlehill, a handsome modern residence belonging to General Sir John Rose of Holme, the tourist enters the royal burgh of

INVERNESS.

[*Inns*:—The Caledonian, Church Street; The Union, High Street; The Private Royal.]

Mail Coaches.

To Perth, Aberdeen, Thurso, by Beauly, Dingwall, Tain, and Dornoch.

Stage Coaches.

To Aberdeen, by Nairn, Forres, Elgin, Fochabers, and Huntly.
To Elgin, by Nairn and Forres.
To Strathpeffer, by Dingwall, during summer.

Steamers.

To Edinburgh, by Cromarty, Nairn, Banff, and Aberdeen.
To Glasgow, by Caledonian Canal, calling at Falls of Foyers.
To London.

Inverness is situated on both sides of the river Ness, at the spot where the basins of the Moray and Beauly Firths and the Great Glen of Scotland meet one another. It is generally considered the capital of the Highlands, and contains a number of well-built streets and elegant houses. A fine stone bridge of seven arches, erected over the Ness in 1685, was swept away by an extraordinary flood in 1849. At the door of the Town-Hall is a strange blue lozenge-shaped stone, called Clach-na-Cudden, or "stone of the tubs," from having served as a resting-place on which the women, in passing from the river, used to set down the deep tubs in which they carried water. It is reckoned the palladium of the town, and is said to have been carefully preserved after the town had been burned by Donald of the Isles in 1410. Inverness contains a flourishing academy, incorporated by Royal Charter, connected with which is a fund amounting to £25,000, left in 1803 by Captain W. Mackintosh of the Hindostan East Indiaman, for the education of boys of certain families of that name. It has also a public seminary, endowed from a bequest of £10,000 made by the late Rev. Dr. Andrew Bell; a public newsroom; six banking-houses; four printing establishments; and two weekly newspapers. The number of vessels belonging to the port is 230, and the tonnage 10,790. In 1841, the population of the parish amounted to 15,308, that of the town alone being 11,575. It unites with Forres, Nairn, and Fortrose, in electing a member of Parliament.

Inverness is a town of great antiquity, but the exact date of its origin is unknown. On an eminence to the south-east of the town stood an ancient castle, in which it is supposed that Duncan was murdered by Macbeth. It is highly probable that Macbeth had possession of this castle, and it is certain that it was destroyed by the son of the murdered king, Malcolm Canmore, who erected a new one on an eminence overhanging the town on the south. This latter edifice continued for several centuries to be a royal fortress. It was repaired by James I., in whose reign a Parliament was held within its walls, to which all the northern chiefs and barons were summoned, three of whom were executed here for treason. In 1562, Queen Mary paid a visit to Inverness, for the purpose of quelling an insurrection of the Earl of Huntly. Being refused admission into the castle by the governor, who held it for the Earl, she took up her residence in a house, part of which is still in existence. The castle was shortly after taken by her attendants and the governor hanged. During the civil wars this castle was repeatedly taken by Montrose and his opponents. In 1715, it was converted into barracks for the Hanoverian soldiers, and in 1746, it was blown up by the troops of Prince Charles Stuart, and not a vestige of it now remains. On the site of this ancient edifice, a handsome castellated building has been erected; from a design by Mr. Burn, architect, consisting of the Court House, County Buildings, and Jail, the whole forming an important feature of the town. The spire of the Old Jail is deservedly admired for its fine proportions. On the north side of the town, near the mouth of the river, Cromwell erected a fort at an expense of £80,000, which was demolished at the Restoration, but a considerable part of the rampart still remains. Within the area of the citadel, a hemp manufactory is carried on. The environs of Inverness are remarkably fine, and the scenery on the banks of the river Ness presents a striking mixture of beauty and grandeur. At a little distance to the west of the town is a singular hill, called Craig Phadric, crowned by a vitrified fort. The view from the summit is varied and extensive. The sides of the hill are covered by fine woods, in the midst of which stands the handsome house of Muirton, the seat of Mr. Huntly Duff, the great-grandson of Catherine Duff, Lady Drummuir, in whose house both Prince Charles and the Duke of Cumberland lodged during their residence in Inverness.*

A mile to the south-west of Inverness is a strange wooded hill, called Tom-na-heurich (the hill of fairies,) shaped like a ship with its keel uppermost. The walks all around it, and on the banks of the Ness, are extremely beautiful. A fine new drive has lately been formed from the Harbour and Cromwell's Fort, along the mouth of the river and adjoining sea-coast.

In the neighbourhoood of Inverness, is Culloden Moor, the scene of the final defeat of the Highland army under Prince Charles Stuart, which lies about five miles south-east of the town. It is a vast and desolate tract of table land, traversed longitudinally by a carriage road, on the side of which are two or three green trenches marking the spot where the heat of the battle took place, and numbers of the slain were interred. On the north it is flanked by the Firth and the table land of the Black Isle. On the south-east by the ridges of Strathnairn, and its extremities are bounded on the westward by the splintered and serrated heights of Stratherrick. In the opposite distance, the moor is lost in a flat bare plain stretching towards Nairn,—one old square tower, the castle of. Dalcross, a hold of the Clan-Chattan, rising upon the open waste with a unique and striking effect. The level na-

* The bustle and confusion occasioned in the house by its distinguished tenants, made the proprietrix very testy. She used to say: "I have had twa kings' bairns for my guests, and trowth I never wish to hae another." This house was at the period in question, the only one in Inverness which contained a parlour without a bed.

ture of the ground rendered it peculiarly unfit for the movements of the Highland army, against cavalry and artillery. According to the general accounts, about 1200 men fell in this engagement. The number killed on both sides was nearly equal.

The victory at Culloden finally extinguished the hopes of the house of Stuart, and secured the liberties of Britain; but the cruelties exercised by the Duke of Cumberland on his helpless foes have stamped his memory with indelible infamy; and there are few who will not join in the sentiments expressed in the concluding stanza of Burns' pathetic song on the battle of Culloden.

" Drummossie muir, Drummossie muir,
A waefu' day it was to me,
For there I lost my father dear,
My father dear and brethren three.

" Their winding-sheet the bluidy clay,
Their graves are growing green to see,
And by them lies the dearest lad
That ever blest a woman's e'e.

" Now wae to thee, thou cruel Duke,
A bluidy man I trow thou be,
For monie a heart thou hast made sair,
That ne'er did wrang to thine or thee."*

On the road leading from the battle-field to Inverness, there is an old farmsteading with trees about it, like a small laird's dwelling. On the day succeeding the battle, the body of a youth of the better class was carried here shrouded in a plaid: "My darling! my darling!" said the pitiful matron, to whom the stranger's corpse was brought, "some mother's heart is lying with thee." It was her own son, whom she fancied safe away with her relations in Glen Urquhart. The following beautiful and pathetic song, of which Culloden is the scene, has never before (as far as we are aware) been in print. It was written, we believe, by a young man of the name of Blair, belonging to Dunfermline.

" Again the lav'rock seeks the skies,
And warbles, dimly seen,
And summer views wi' sunny joys
Her gowanny robe o' green.
But, ah! the summer's blythe return,
In flowery pride array'd,
Nae mair can cheer this heart forlorn
Nor charm the Highland maid.

A mile to the north of Culloden Moor is Culloden House (Forbes, Esq.,) which, at the time of the Rebellion, belonged to the celebrated Duncan Forbes, Lord President of the Court of Session. Here Prince Charles lodged the night before the battle. Since 1745, it has been renewed in a very elegant style. About a mile south-east of the battle-field, on the banks of the river Nairn, is the plain of Clava, a singular spot, covered with circles of stones and cairns, supposed remains of the Celtic Druids. One of these rude cemeteries was lately opened, and in the inner cell, about eighteen inches below the floor, were found two earthen vases containing calcined bones.

Fort-George, distant about twelve miles from Inverness, is another interesting object in this neighbourhood. It is situated on the extremity of a low sandy point which projects far out into the Moray Firth opposite Fortrose. At this spot the breadth of the firth is only about a mile. Fort-George was erected immediately after the suppression of the Rebellion in 1745, for the purpose of keeping the Highlanders in check. The fortifications, which are constructed on the plan of the great fortresses of the Continent cover about fifteen English acres, and afford accommodation for about 3000 men. At the bottom of the peninsula is CAMPBELTON, [*Inns:* The Canteen ; Fort-George ; Commercial] a modern fishing village named from the Campbells of Cawdor. The Earl of Cawdor has an ancient residence

" My father's shielin' on the hill
Is cheerless now and sad,
The breezes round me whisper still,
I've lost my Highland lad.
His bonnet blue has fallen now,
And bloody is the plaid,
Where oft upon the mountain's brow
He row'd his Highland maid.

" The lee-lang night for rest I seek,
The lee-lang day I mourn,
The smile upon my wither'd cheek
Can never mair return.
Upon Culloden's fatal heath
He spak o' me they said ;
And falter'd, wi' his dying breath—
Adieu ! my Highland Maid."

near this place, Cawdor Castle, (erected about the year 1400,) which has still its moat and drawbridge, tower and "donjon keep," as in the days of antiquity. It is the most perfect specimen now remaining of the old feudal fortress. Some ancient and very large oak, elm, and ash trees surround the castle, and the scenery of the neighbourhood is wild and romantic.

Culloden Moor, Cawdor Castle, and Fort-George, can all be combined in one day's delightful excursion of about 35 miles. The better plan is to take them in the above order. At the moor, by walking 100 yards, or more, past a farm-steading, not far from, and to the east of the graves, to indicate which last an abortive monument has been commenced, the stone cairns and circles above alluded can be descried on the opposite side of the river Nairn. On the way to Cawdor we get a glimpse of Kilravock Castle, another edifice also still quite entire, and of similar structure—both being of the middle of the fifteenth century. At Cawdor, where there is a good inn, 14 miles from Inverness, the burn course will be found well worthy of being explored as far as the Hermitage. On the way back to Inverness from Fort-George we pass close by the very picturesque castellated mansion, Castle Stewart, said to have been built by the Regent Moray, and much admired for its symmetry and the gracefulness of its hanging turrets. With the tide at the full, and a favourable day, the approach to Inverness in this direction is among the finest of the many beautiful landscapes by which the scenery around the Highland capital is distinguished.

THE RIVER BEAULY, STRATHGLASS, GLENSTRATHFARAR, GLENCANNICH, STRATH AFFRICK, AND THE FALLS OF GLOMAK.

There is no part of the Highlands where so much of picturesquely beautiful river scenery is to be found as along the course of the Beauly; nor are any of our mountains more gigantic and imposing than those which gird the Alpine lakes and central glens from which it derives its sources. The forenoon's drive from Inverness, by the Aird to the Falls of Kilmorack as far as the island of Aigas, is a verv favourite one. A long day's journey of more than forty miles may be made to Struy on one side, and home by the opposite side of the river. But a tour of two and a-half days to Glenstrathfarar, Strathglass, Loch Affrick, and Loch Benneveian, is now not unfrequent—the small inn of Struy, for want of a better, being the resting-place at night—while a few pedestrians find their way across the country to Loch Duich and Kintail. In either case, Beauly forms a convenient stage. The road to the Falls of Kilmorack and the country beyond strikes off at Beauly Bridge. The lower falls are two miles from Beauly, and are descried from the public road. They are not high but exceedingly picturesque. Above them, the river, for about half-a-mile, works its way in boiling cauldrons and broken cascades, between high rocky banks crowned by birch and pine trees. A pathway leads from the minister's garden (from a summer-house in which one of the best views is to be had) along the edge of the cliffs. Where it rejoins the public road, a longer reach, called the Drhuim, is presented of the river threading its way for two or three miles between more open banks, partly cultivated, and the hill sides clothed to their summits with weeping birches. Fantastic islets and pinnacles of rock jut out in the bed of the river. At the top of the Drhuim the road brings us in front of a round rocky hill in the midst of the valley, beautifully festooned with birches, on both sides of which the river is seen pouring itself down in rocky channels which again exhibit a series of elegant cascades. This eminence is the Island of Eigas—"Eilan Aigas"—and is adorned by a picturesque shooting lodge, in which Sir Robert Peel passed a few quiet months during his last summer's visit to the Highlands. The horses of a party here returning had better be baited at the public-house of Crask of Aigas.

An open glen succeeds, ornamented at the lower end by the mansion-house of Eskadale (Thos. Fraser, Esq.), and the pinnacles of a Roman Catholic chapel, erected by Lord Lovat; and about four miles on by the high old castle and the wooded grounds of Erchless, the seat of "The Chisholm," whose domains stretch far inland, and embrace great mountainous ranges of fine pasture.

Struy Inn, about ten miles from Beauly, and twenty miles from Inverness, stands near the confluence of the rivers Glass and Farar. The ascent of Benevachart just behind, which is upwards of 3000 feet high, may be easily accomplished. Before proceeding up Strathglass, the tourist should proceed for some miles up Glenstrathfarar, which is of varying widths, and more or less wooded with birch. There are two lakes in the glen, a small one, Loch Miulie, and beyond it, Loch Monar, about seven miles long, bordered by lofty mountains, at the lower end of which is Monar House (H. Whyte, Esq). By this route the pedestrian can, across a series of lonely heaths and grassy pastures, reach Attadale, on Loch Carron, and be ferried over to Jeantown, on the Dingwall road. If so disposed, he will probably have to bivouack for the night at the shepherd's hut, at the farther end of Loch Monar.

About ten miles above Struy, up Strathglass, at the bridge of Fasnakyle, a defile opens to the right, down which the waters of the Glass descend from Loch Benneveian and Loch Affrick. The Strath, however, continues right on, and in this direction lies the beautiful Highland residence of Geusachan, the property of Mr. Fraser of Culbockie. Our route, however, lies along the waters of the Glass, and the great central opening to Kintail, in which lie the secluded mountain-girt Lochs Affrick and Beneveian.

Intermediate between, and parallel to Strath Affrick and Glenstrathfarar, stretches another great pastoral valley, Glencannich, presenting yet another passage to the west coast, to visit which the pedestrian strikes off at the Clachan and public-house of Invercannich, seven and a-half miles from Struy. The rich soft pastures of Glencannich are, as the name imports, bedecked with the cotton grass, and by innumerable bright flowering plants. A succession of lakes and tarns occupy, but can scarcely be said to embellish, the surface. At the further end of the longest, Loch Longard, which is seven miles in length, a shepherd's cottage will be found, where to refresh before proceeding, if such be the intention, to Killellan, on Loch Long, about fifteen miles farther.

The traveller's choice will, however, doubtless lead him rather to Strath Affrick. The road slants up the hill from near the bridge of Fasnakyle. Traversing the hill side, along which the river Glass pours its infant floods, this road is cut among the remains of an ancient Caledonian pine forest, of which some magnificent relics may still be seen. A thick underwood of young birch trees surrounds the hoary stems, and spreads itself over all the adjoining heights, producing the richest and most beautiful contrasts. The vistas of thickly wooded declivities are exceedingly extensive and surpassingly beautiful. "The Chisholm's Pass," as it is termed, ushers us on Loch Benneveian, about five miles long and one broad. Here, about fifteen miles from Struy, the carriage road for the present terminates, and the rest of the way must be made out on horseback or on foot, unless the boats, which are kept in these lochs, and hands to man them, happen to be in the way, a matter which a little previous arrangement can ensure, whereby the scenery will be seen to the greater advantage. The woodland around bears a strong resemblance to the best portions of the Trossachs and of the Mar and Rothiemurchus forests. As we near Loch Affrick, the mountain-screens increase in height and grandeur—their long sloping acclivities leading away the eye into distant vistas, which are filled up by the graceful sharp peaks of Kintail. A rocky barrier, mantled over with old pines and birches, separates Loch Benneveian from Loch Affrick, which is about the same length as its neighbour, and from its northern shore rise the beetling crags and far ascending acclivities of Scour na Lapich and Mam Soul.

The wayfarer bound for the west coast will feel thankful for a night's rest at one of the comfortable shepherd's cottages at Culivie or Annamulloch, on the meadow plain at the further end of the loch, and about twenty-five miles from Struy, which are purposely arranged to furnish occasional accommodation.

Should the weather favour, the ascent of Mam Soul, under an experienced guide, is to be recommended. It is almost equal in height to Ben Nevis. It presents the Flora of both coasts, and its summit commands a view of both seas. A great upland pastoral valley succeeds to the lakes. At the farther end of Strath Affrick a wide hollow, running off at right angles towards the north, conducts (four miles distant) to the Falls of Glomak, on the water of that name, and from which a detour westwards again leads, across the bank above, and down the water of Linassie, to Shielhouse. No waterfall in Britain equals Glomak in height, and in the terrific wildness of the gorge below. The waters plunge at once by a fall full 350 feet high into a continuous ravine, cut out to the depth of between 700 and 800 feet! A good view is obtained from the green bank in front, and to the westward of the fall, along which foot-prints will be seen, admitting a cautious descent to a small projecting rock, marked by a single birch and rowan tree, which are just opposite the centre of the fall.

Throughout the whole of this day's walk, the country will be found almost treeless; but the pastures are extremely green and enlivening by their brilliant hues—so different from the heathy brown of the eastern moors. A few alders and birches reappear in Kintail as we attain the shores of Loch Duich (that most magnificent and beautiful of sea lochs, as Dr. M'Culloch thought it), but they seem dwindled down to mere twigs; and an impression of solemn admiration and awe steals over us as the stupendous frontlets and peaks of Ben Attow and Scuir Ouran first burst on the view.

INVERNESS TO FORTROSE AND CROMARTY.

Between the Moray and Cromarty Firths intervenes an extensive peninsular district of country, known as "The Black Isle," and also called, of old, Ardmeanach, or the Monk's Land. There is a considerable thoroughfare across it, in the line from Inverness by Kessock Ferry to Dingwall, which is several miles shorter than the main road round the head of the first mentioned firth by Beauly. The whole of the Black Isle is well peopled; but the portions to the eastward of Kessock Ferry are comparatively little frequented by the tourist. They, however, demand a brief notice.

At Kessock Ferry, about a mile from the town of Inverness, the plain on which it is built, advancing on the waters of the firth, confine them to a width of three quarters of a mile, between it and the continuation of the chain of hills, which, lining the Great Glen of Scotland on the north side, are prolonged along the margin of the Black Isle, and beyond the opening of the Cromarty Firth, forming a continuous stretch of hill coast, of softened outline and highly variegated surface. Beyond Kessock, the sea, having pierced this range of hills, expands into the beauteous basin of the Beauly Firth. The sail across Kessock Ferry is worth taking for the varied and lovely view presented on all sides. The wooded crags of the Ord hill to the east, as those of Craigphadrich to the west, of Kessock, are crowned with the traces of a vitrified fort. On the summit of the ascent from Kessock (two miles from the ferry), the Dingwall and Fortrose and Cromarty roads diverge, the latter following a sloping hollow, which conducts to the bay and village of Munlochy. Here another road ascends across the centre of the Black Isle to Invergordon Ferry, passing a little above Munlochy, below the parks and extensive plantations of Belmadully (Sir Evan Mackenzie of Kilcoy, Bart.); and by a branch of this road, which conducts behind Raddery (Henry Fowler, Esq.), and keeps along the top of the ridge, the distance to Cromarty can be shortened by some miles, the round by Fortrose being avoided.

A few miles beyond Munlochy the mansion-houses of Rosehaugh (Sir James M'Kenzie of Scatwell, Bart.) and of Avoch (Alexander M'Kenzie, Esq.) are passed on the left, and immediately after, the sea-shore is regained at the little fishing village of that name. A mile further on we reach Fortrose, a small burgh, which occupies the root of the northern of two long peninsulas, which, projecting from either side, again confine the firth to a ferry of about a mile in width—the extremity of the southern promontory being occupied by Fort-George, a considerable and very regular fortress erected after the last rebellion. Fortrose was the cathedral town of Ross. It still boasts a fragment—the south aisle—of the cathedral, the rest of the building having been used as a quarry in constructing Cromwell's fort at Inverness. It was of the purest and most elaborate middle-pointed architecture of the early part of the fourteenth century. The sharpness of the mouldings at the present day is remarkable, and the ruin is deservedly admired as betokening a structure of rare ecclesiological merit. There are five lights in the remaining eastern window, and the rood turret is still entire. A canopied tomb, that of the Countess of Ross, who is said to have founded the cathedral, has been a fine work. Here the Mackenzies of Seaforth have their family burying ground. Fortrose has a comfortable inn, and an academy at which several eminent individuals have laid the foundation of their distinction in life—among others, Sir James Mackintosh, a name held in peculiar estimation in the north.

The sea-coast between Fortrose and Cromarty has acquired a geological interest from the writings of Mr. Hugh Miller on the lias deposit and fossil concretions at Eathie, about midway. The cliffs are otherwise interesting both to the geologist and botanist. The burn of Eathie exhibits the junction of the granite and old red sandstone rocks.

The road to Cromarty, passing through the old burgh of Rosemarkie, a mile beyond, and associated with Fortrose, ascends a very deep alluvial gully, which seams the hills behind at right angles, and leads, in a straight line, across the peninsula to the Cromarty Firth, between Newhall (Shaw, Esq.) and Pointzfield (Sir George Gun Munro), whence it skirts, for some miles, a picturesque range of rocks to Cromarty. But two branch roads lead along the summit of the hill—one by Eathie, the other the central road already noticed, from Munlochy below Belmaduthy.

Cromarty has declined much in importance by the rivalry of Invergordon, on the north side of the firth, the latter being more contiguous to the important districts of Easter and Wester Ross. It will, however, ever retain its value as a harbour of refuge, completely sheltered by the headlands called the Sutors of Cromarty, while the roadstead is capacious enough for the largest fleet, and the firth is altogether a very fine sheet of land-locked water. Immediately above the town, Cromarty House (Mrs. Rose Ross) occupies the site of a castle of the old Earls of Ross. There is little to invite a prolonged sojourn in the town, even the inns exhibiting a marked want of the indications of frequent concourse.

DINGWALL TO LOCH CARRON, AND THE DISTRICTS OF LOCHBROOM, GAIRLOCH, LOCH MAREE, TORRIDON, AND APPLECROSS, ON THE WEST COAST OF ROSS-SHIRE.

Ross-shire is intersected by a series of valleys, along which the western post-road to Skye and the sister Hebrides runs, as, in like manner, Inverness-shire is intersected by the Great Glen, or by Strathspey and Badenoch, whence issues the main outlet from the mountains southward. The first of these is Strathpeffer, five miles long, a fine arable flat, bordered on the one hand by the sunny braes which lead up to the higher plateau, whence springs the mighty irregular dome of Ben Wyvis (Ben Uaish, the mountain of storms), and on the opposite by the ridge of Knockfarrel (a large and interesting *vitrified fortress*), which conceals from view the ods and policies of Brahan Castle (the seat of Mackenzie Seaforth), among which, on the high ground, lies the turesque *Italian* looking lake of Loch Ousie. Castle od, an old abode of the Earls of Cromarty, (now repreted by the Marchioness of Stafford), stands near the ther end of the Strath, passing which, the road ascends idge studded with the villas built round the *mineral wells* Strathpeffer (sulphureted hydrogen, like the Harrowgate), and the vicinity of which is noted as having been scene of two desperate clan battles fought in the end of fifteenth century—the one between the Mackenzies and Macdonalds of the Isles, and the other between the forr and the Munros of Ferindonald, in both of which the aberfaeh" was victorious. For the details of those conts, and the analysis of the mineral waters, and statistics Ben Wyvis, and this whole neighbourhood, we must refer r readers to the more enlarged Guide Book to the Highds of Messrs. Anderson.

Quitting the first valley, the road immediately enters on t of Contin and Coul (Sir Alexander Mackenzie, Bart.), ich is encircled by as beautifully clad birch and pine ods, and hills of diversified forms and features, as are to seen in any part of the Highlands ; then, crossing the ackwater at the bridge and snug inn of Contin, and leav- Loch Echiltie on the left (a most enchanting little lake uich the tourist should by all means endeavour to see, th the vale of Comrie and Scatwell, and the falls of the eig and Conon beyond it), our course turns suddenly rthwards, and, after breasting a steepish ascent overhung th oaks and weeping birch trees, and giving us a peep of e Falls of Rogie below on the right, then ushers us on the eat upland moorish pastures, and brings us soon to the el of the large inland reservoir of Loch Garve. Resting at good inn of Garve (fifteen miles from Dingwall), whence e roads proceed either northwards to Loch Broom (as terwards more particularly noticed), or westwards towards ch Carron and Skye, the traveller, keeping the latter, again ascends a little, and soon reaches the large lake called Loch Luichart, around which are the shooting grounds and deer forest of Sir James J. R. Mackenzie of Scatwell, Bart., and at the farther end his beautiful lodge.

Two miles on, at the bridge of Grudic, where the water of that name comes tumbling down on the right from Loch Fannich, a new road will be seen branching northwards which will soon be continued to the *Dirie More* road, and thus supply a short and very convenient access to Loch Broom ; and, immediately thereafter, passing the bridge, the post-road ascends through a small birch wood and the remains of an ancient oak forest, and, emerging from an inclined rocky pass, enters upon Strath Bran, a great open plain, stretching for ten or twelve miles before us, and forming the summit level of the country. Our approach to the soft climate of the west coast here becomes perceptible in the superior greenness of the pastures ; while the mountains also, at the same time, on all hands, become more grand and elegant in their outline. The three peaks of Scuirvullin in Strathconnon bound the view on the left ; those of Foin Bhein (or Fingal's hill), and the clustered alps of Loch Fannich on the right, among which the tourist, if a zealous view hunter and angler, may spend a week or so with great pleasure, making the comfortable Inn of Auchnanault (the most conspicuous and welcome object on the plain before us, eleven miles from Garve Inn) his head quarters during his stay. Five miles on (at Auchnasheen, where there was once a public-house, but none now), another road turns off on the right by Loch Roshk for Loch Maree and Gairloch, after passing which the course of the main post road is found to decline rapidly towards the salt water inlet of Loch Carron. The scenery all along consists of wild open heaths and mountains, nowise remarkable, except for their fine green pastures, and the remains here and there visible of the great oak forest, which at one time appears to have covered the whole country. As we approach the open shores of Loch Carron, numerous beautiful terraces show themselves round all the valley, and then broad patches of corn-land regale the eye, increasing in number and size till we reach the kirk and manse of Loch Carron, and the long straggling fishing village of Jeantown, twenty-five miles from Auchnanault, where the tourist can again enjoy the comforts of a superior inn. He is now in the domains of Mr. Mackenzie of Applecross, and, if desirous of proceeding farther to the west, the mail-car will convey him five miles on to Strome Ferry, from the farther side of which the next stage to Kyleakin, on the way to the Isle of Skye, is twelve miles; or should he intend to return south by Kintail and Glenmoriston, a very delightful route, his course will be to Dornie, on Loch Duich (five miles), and thence to Shielhouse (other ten miles), whence the great falls of Glomak, described at page 402, will form a pleasant day's excursion.

We close this chapter by a short sketch of the other districts mentioned at its commencement, and of the roads leading to them.

1. TO ULLAPOOL ON LOCH BROOM.

An excellent new made district road strikes off from Garve Inn (fifteen miles west of Dingwall, which, after passing the very long upland plain or valley, called *Strath Dirie* and the *Dirie More*, reaches the salt water inlet of Loch Broom (or Bream, the lake of showers), thirty miles off, at Inverbroom, after which a pleasant walk of other seven miles conducts to the village of Ullapool. The whole distance is divided into three stages by two public-houses, one at Glascarnoch, twelve miles from Garve, and another near Fascrinich, or Braemore, about the same distance farther on, where a new road from the district of Dundonald and Groinard joins the main one at the top of Loch Broom. By the branch road just mentioned, the traveller can reach Poolewe in Gairloch, and proceed southwards by the route next to be described; or, after quitting Ullapool, he may proceed northwards into Sutherlandshire by a road sixteen miles long, lately made by the Duke of Sutherland and the Highland Destitution

Board, through Coigach and Strath Cannaird, and by Knockan to Ledmore, on the post road from Bonar Bridge to Loch Inver, whereby a continuous line of communication has thus been at last opened up southwards along the whole western coast of the country. There is nothing at Ullapool to detain the stranger except its dry cheerful situation, its capital bathing, and the fine views which it commands; and that its owner (Sir James Matheson, Bart., M.P. for the county of Ross) has commenced extensive improvements about the place, and will most likely arrange that the mail packet for Stornoway and Lewis will sail from this port. The village contains from 700 to 800 inhabitants, and was commenced by the British Fishery Society about seventy years ago for the encouragement of the fisheries. The herring shoals, however, so frequently shift their ground, and the prosecution of the deep sea or white fisheries is so expensive, or so uncongenial to the habits of the Highlanders, that the village, until very lately, made no progress. A good deal of birch and hazel copse wood occurs round the shores of Loch Broom, which have otherwise much of the features of the south Argyle sea lochs. The surrounding mountains are remarkable for their angular outlines.

2. To Gairloch and Poolewe.

As already mentioned, a good carriage road strikes off the Loch Carron road at Auchnasheen, 5 miles west of the Inn of Achnanault. By a rapid descent through a wild pass, called Glendochart, it lands us at the Inn of Kinlochewe, at the upper end of Loch Maree, whence the road is continued on the left bank of that lake to Slattadale, whence it makes a circuit by Gairloch, where there is a small inn, to Poolewe, while another road branches off from the Inn of Kinlochewe, in a south-westerly direction, to Loch Torridon (distant 12 miles), the group of peaked mountains at the top of which are particularly grand. Ben Eye, which rises up close at hand on the south of Kinlochewe, is also a magnificent mountain of pure white quartz rock; and Slougach, and

Ben Lair, and all the mountain masses around Loch Maree, present scenes of savage barrenness and grandeur not surpassed by any in the Highlands. Towards the middle and upper portions of the lake, the banks exhibit a few stunted relics of an old pine forest, but otherwise there is not a tree, and very little grass to be seen,—the whole country being arid rock (chiefly indurated sandstone), as bare as when first raised out of the deep. On one of a small number of little islets, half way down the loch, a chapel was in ancient days erected with a graveyard around it, dedicated to the great Celtic saint Maolruable, and the founder of which, according to some, was a Culdee saint, Maree, whose name is perpetuated in that of the lake; while others regard it rather as the Gaelic name of the Virgin Mary. In the same islet is a well (still hung round with votive offerings), noted for its healing virtues, and especially, it is believed, for the cure of insanity, when coupled with a good sousing in the waters of the loch.

The shore side of Gairloch, where the basement—mica slate rocks—have been more cleared by denudation of the superincumbent sandstone, contains a good deal of fine pasture and arable ground, and extensive experiments have of late years been tried to introduce the turnip husbandry, and a due rotation of cropping among the crofters and tenantry, but not hitherto, we believe, with any decided success, either as to the landlord's rental or the increased comforts of the people. At Poolewe there is a post-office and inn, and a small village, and the adjoining river Ewe, by which Loch Maree discharges its waters into the sea, is noted as one of the most prolific salmon fishing streams in the north.

3. The Applecross District.

While at Jeantown, on Loch Carron, the tourist should not proceed without devoting a day to the examination of the wilds of Applecross. On reaching Courthill, at the head of Loch Kishorn (5 miles from Jeantown), the road divides into two branches, one turning northwards to the village of

Shieldaig (9 miles off), through a moorish and uninteresting district, while the other goes direct on in a westerly direction, and ascends to the height of 1500 feet along one of the stupendous deer corries of the Bein Bhain of Applecross! This road attains its summit level by a series of corkscrew traverses, and displays along its course one of the wildest pieces of scenery imaginable, scarcely surpassed by that of Loch Coruishk or Glencoe. Its further slope leads rapidly down to the plain of Applecross, a valley encompassed on all sides save one (that next the sea) by high and wild mountains, which completely isolate it from the rest of the world. The road conducts to the village of Milntown, to the church and the fine old mansion-house of the proprietor (Thomas Mackenzie, Esq. of Applecross, late M.P. for Ross-shire), but to no other spot or region. The whole place is as detached and secluded as the happy valley of Rasselas. Yet here, at a very early period, the Culdee monks, probably the contemporaries or immediate successors of St. Columba, and dependants on his chief monastery of Iona, erected a small church and collegiate establishment. It is thus noticed in one of the earliest Irish annals, translated and published by the Iona club in 1835:—"A.D. 673. Malruba founded the church of Aporcrosan." As at I-Columbkil, all barges approaching this sanctuary had to land at a particular spot or harbour, where a cross was erected, and whence a series of other crosses lined or pointed out the way to the church and burying-ground. Some of those crosses (with extremely rude carvings on them) are still extant, but the religious edifices are all gone, and the modern name of Applecross refers to a mere recent monkish tradition, that every apple in the old orchard grew with a cross marked on it! The sanctity of the spot is, however, preserved in the Gaelic patronimic, by which the proprietor is universally recognised by his tenantry as "Fer-na-Comaraich"—"the laird of the sanctuary, or of the land of safety."

SIXTEENTH TOUR.

A Chart of this Tour will be found facing page 294.

INVERNESS—BANKS OF THE CALEDONIAN CANAL—GLEN URQUHART GLEN MORISTON—FORT-AUGUSTUS—FORT-WILLIAM—GLENCOE TYNDRUM.

THE tourist may leave Inverness by a very delightful route, which leads along the banks of the Caledonian Canal. There are two roads along the opposite sides of Loch Ness and Oich, but the north-west road is by far the more picturesque. Leaving Inverness by the old bridge, and leaving the peculiarly-shaped hill called Tom-na-heurich, the tourist, at the distance of about a mile from the town, crosses the canal, and ascends the undulating face of Torvain. On this hill, in 1197, there was fought a desperate battle between Donald Bane of the Isles and a body of troops from the castle of Inverness. Passing the house of Dunain (W. Baillie, Esq.,) the tourist comes in sight of the beautiful little lake Dochfour. On its banks is Dochfour

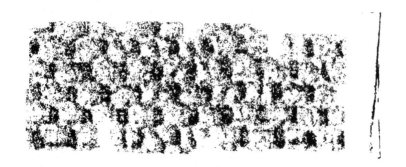

House (Evan Baillie, Esq.,) surrounded by fine parks and magnificent trees. A monumental pillar has lately been erected, near the house, to the memory of the late proprietor, Evan Baillie, Esq., who was at one time M.P. for Bristol, and died in his native glen at the advanced age of ninety-five. Nearly opposite, in a sequestered bay which forms the narrow eastern extremity of Loch Ness, is Aldourie, the seat of W. F. Tytler, Esq., where Sir James Mackintosh was born, and in the immediate neighbourhood of which he spent several years of his childhood. For the first few miles along the shores of Loch Ness, the hills are bare and very steep. They are called Craig Derg, or the Red Rocks, from their reddish tint. The inhabitants of these *braes* were formerly noted for smuggling whisky. About fifteen miles from Inverness, Glen Urquhart opens up from the lake. This glen, which has been pronounced the fairest, the richest, and the most splendid in its beauty among Scotland's glens, is about ten miles in length, and is luxuriantly wooded. At the mouth of the glen there is an excellent inn called Drumnadrochet. In the centre of the vale there is a small but very pretty lake, having the mansions of Lakefield, Lochletter, and Sheuglie, scattered around its borders. About two miles from the inn, a small burn falls over a lofty ledge of rock forming the falls of Divach. A small bay runs up from the loch for about two miles into the valley, receiving the united waters of the Coiltie and Enneric. On the western promontory of this bay are the ruins of the castle of Urquhart, rising finely over the dark waters of the loch, which, at this point, is 125 fathoms in depth. It appears to have been once a strong and extensive building. In 1303 it was besieged and taken by the troops of Edward I. In 1509, it fell, along with the barony of Urquhart, into the hands of the chief of the Clan-Grant, and it still continues in the possession of that family, who have a residence in it called Balmacaan. The road from Drumindrochet to Invermoriston—thirteen miles—is one of remarkable beauty. It is cut in the mountain side, plunging into hollows and climbing sharp acclivities, sometimes bordering the loch, but more frequently proceeding at a considerable elevation above its level, and winding through the most luxuriant woods of oak, birch, alder, and pine. It skirts the base of the high and naked mountain, Mealfourvonie, which separates the two glens of Urquhart and Moriston. Mealfourvonie rises almost perpendicularly from the lake to the height of 3060 feet. The opening of Glen Moriston is a very picturesque scene. In the foreground is the mansion of James Murray Grant, Esq., proprietor of the glen. The situation is very fine. On the opposite side of the river, and twenty-six miles from Inverness, is the inn of Invermoriston, a small but comfortable house. Immediately below it, the river Moriston falls over a considerable precipice, forming a very beautiful and picturesque waterfall. Glen Moriston is a serene and beautiful valley, watered by the Moriston, a wild, foaming, impetuous stream, which has its origin in Loch Cluny, and the distant mountains of Glenshiel.* From Invermoriston a road leads through the glen to Glenelg and the Isle of Skye. Proceeding along the side of Loch Ness, the tourist crosses the river Oich and reaches Fort-Augustus, distant thirty-two miles from Inverness. This fort, which was built shortly after the Rebellion of 1715, is situated at the west end of Loch Ness, on a high peninsula between the rivers Tarff and Oich, and commands a noble sweep of the lake and mountains. It forms a square, with four bastions at the corners, and the barracks are constructed for one field-officer, four captains, twelve subalterns, and 280 rank and file. A few soldiers are stationed in the fort, but the guns have been removed to Fort-George, and the magazine is empty. In the neighbourhood is the pleasant little village of Fort-Augustus.—[*Inns* :—King's Inn.]—From Loch Ness to Loch Oich, the next and smallest of the chain, is a distance of five miles. The old road leads along the south side of Loch Oich, but the tourist should follow the new one on the opposite side. The scenery on the banks of this loch is finer than at any other

* About eight miles from Shielhouse is the waterfall of Glomak, the highest in Scotland. The water falls 350 feet into an awful ravine 700 or 800 feet deep. It can be approached on Highland ponies even by ladies.

part of the Great Glen. Glen Garry, which opens upon Loch Oich, is a charming valley, abounding in the most fascinating scenery. "Less splendid than Glen Urquhart, less diversified than Glen Moriston, it has, in its beautiful Loch Garry, and its endless succession of birch-clad knolls and eminences, and, above all, in the magnificence of the mountain vista to the west, a character quite peculiar." In the birch-woods which adorn this romantic glen the trees have attained a size and luxuriance equal to the finest of the pines of Rothiemurchus, or the beeches of Atholl. Near the mouth of the Garry, and close to the loch, are the ruins of the ancient castle of Invergarry, situated on a rock. It was burnt by the Duke of Cumberland after the Rebellion of 1745. In the immediate neighbourhood of the castle is Invergarry House, lately the residence of the chief of the Macdonells, who, in 1839, sold his estate of Glenquoich to Edward Ellice, Esq., and emigrated, along with a considerable part of his clan, to Australia. Invergarry Inn, one of the best in the Highlands, which stands a little way up the glen, is about seven and a half miles from Fort-Augustus, and about the same distance from Letterfinlay Inn on the banks of Loch Lochy. A little way from Invergarry Castle is a small monument erected by the late Colonel Macdonell of Glengarry over the "well of seven heads," commemorating the summary vengeance inflicted by a former chief of Glengarry, "in the swift course of feudal justice," on the perpetrators of the foul murder of the Keppoch family. This eccentric chief was the original of the character of Fergus M'Ivor, who occupies such a prominent place in the novel of Waverley. The distance between Lochs Oich and Lochy is about two miles. In 1544 Kinloch Lochy was the scene of a bloody encounter between the Frasers and a much superior force of the Macdonalds of Clanranald. On account of the heat of the weather, the combatants threw off their coats and fought in their shirts, whence the battle received the name of "Blar-na-leine," or "the Field of Shirts." Lord Lovat and his eldest son, together with most of the principal gentlemen of the clan, were slain in this engagement. Fourteen miles from Fort-Augustus, on the south side of ch Lochy, is the inn of Letterfinlay. On the opposite e of the Loch is the bay of Arkaig, at a short distance m which, in Glen Arkaig, is Achnacarry, the mansion of chiel, chief of the Clan-Cameron. It is delightfully uated, and completely embosomed in wood.* The hills ich environ Loch Lochy are wild and stupendous, and t scantily wooded. It is ten miles in length, and the pth is, in some places, from seventy to eighty fathoms. ven miles from Letterfinlay the tourist crosses the deep d rocky channel of the Spean by a picturesque-looking idge, called High Bridge, which was built by General ade. At this spot hostilities first commenced in the ebellion of 1745. Here a road strikes off on the left to en Roy, celebrated for its "Parallel Roads." These Roads nsist of a series of terraces or beaches which run through- t the whole glen. The principal terraces are three in mber. The most elevated is stated by Dr. Macculloch to 1262 feet above the level of the sea, and the other two e respectively 82 and 212 feet below the highest. By

'. The district of Lochaber has for ages been the residence of this clan. Their me was originally MacMartin, but they are said to have adopted the name meron on the marriage of a daughter of their chief with a gentleman named marriens or Chambers. MacMartin of Letter Finlay, however, still retains original patronymic.

Close beside the present building are the walls of the old mansion, burned by Duke of Cumberland in 1746.

In the bottom of the valley lies Loch Arkaig, a beautiful sheet of water, out two miles distant from Loch Lochy. It is fourteen or fifteen miles long, d from one to one and a half broad. It is surrounded with dark and lofty untains, and its banks were, till lately, covered with a magnificent oak and e forest, now cut down; but the shoots and saplings rising from the old ck are already covering the sides of the hills. The banks of the lake are fre- ented by herds of Lochiel's celebrated red-deer. A small wooded island, at e lower end of the lake, has been for ages the burying-place of the family of chiel. On the shores of Loch Arkaig Prince Charles more than once found elter after his defeat at Culloden. It was here, too, that after the suppres- n of the rebellion, Major Munro of Culcairn was shot by one of the clan meron in revenge for the death of his son, who had been basely murdered by officer of the name of Grant. Major Munro had unfortunately borrowed e white horse on which Grant rode, and thus met the fate which was intended another. Glen Arkaig is divided at the opening, by a ridge of hills, into two leys of unequal breadth. The southern contains the mansion of Lochiel. e other, which is called Mill-dubh, or the Dark-mill, is a narrow pass, com- tely overshadowed by the branches of the trees by which the perpendicular rriers of rock on each side are clothed to the summit.

numerous observations made upon them they have been proved to be perfectly horizontal or level; and although geologists are still divided in opinion as to their origin, they are generally supposed to be the vestiges of ancient lakes. Proceeding onward, the road opens upon the river Lochy, and, keeping along its banks, the tourist reaches the ruins of Inverlochy Castle, about two miles distant from Fort-William. It consists of four large towers, the western and southern of which are nearly entire. Inverlochy is supposed to have been built by the powerful family of Comyn. It was the scene of a bloody engagement, during the reign of James I., between Donald of the Isles and the Earls of Mar and Caithness, in which the latter were defeated, and the Earl of Caithness slain. Here also, in 1645, the Marquis of Argyle was defeated with great slaughter by the Marquis of Montrose. This engagement is described at great length in the "Legend of Montrose."

A mile and a half from Inverlochy Castle, situated at a bend of Loch Eil, twenty-nine miles from Fort-Augustus, and sixty-one from Inverness, is

FORT-WILLIAM.

[*Inns*:—The Caledonian; The George.]

The fort was erected in the reign of William III., from whom it derived its name. It contains a bomb-proof magazine, and the barracks are intended to accommodate ninety-six private soldiers, with the proper number of officers. In 1715, and again in 1745, the Highlanders besieged it, but without success. The adjacent village of Maryburgh, named in honour of Queen Mary, contains a population of about 1500 persons, who are for the most part engaged in the herring fishery. The two inns are also in this village. The celebrated mountain, Ben Nevis, which rises from the plain to the east of Fort-William, having been already minutely described in the Tenth Tour, demands no additional notice in this place.*

* Glen Roy, in which are the Parallel Roads described in the preceding page, is about sixteen miles distant from Fort-William, where gigs and other vehicles may be engaged by tourists. There is an inn at the bridge of Spean, and another at the bottom of the glen, where horses can be put up.

The road from Fort-William to Oban, along the shores of Lochs Eil and Linnhe, is a continued succession of romantic scenery.

A Parliamentary road leads from Fort-William to Arisaig, distant forty miles, where there is a ferry to Skye. This road passes through the lovely vale of Glenfinnan, in which there is an inn, remarkable as the place where Prince Charles Stuart first raised his standard, August 19, 1745. At Borrodale, on the shore of Loch-na-Naugh, he first disembarked on the mainland of Scotland, and from the same spot he finally embarked for France, after the failure of his unfortunate enterprise. A monument has been erected by the late M'Donald of Glenaladale, on the spot where the standard was unfurled, to the memory of those "who fought and bled" in this rebellion.

Leaving Fort-William, the road proceeds along the south side of Loch Linnhe, and, at the distance of nine miles, reaches Coran Ferry ; thence it leads a short way along the north shore of Loch Leven, a branch of Loch Linnhe, extending in a straight line between the counties of Inverness and Argyle. "From its mouth to its farther extremity," says Dr. Macculloch, "Loch Leven is one continued succession of landscapes." On both sides it is bounded by lofty mountains, which, toward the head of the loch, are grouped in very grand combinations. Fourteen miles from Fort-William, the tourist crosses Loch Leven at Ballachulish Ferry, on each side of which there is an inn. About two miles from the Ferry are the celebrated slate quarries of Ballachulish, which give employment to about 200 people. The road now proceeds for about four miles along the southern shore of Loch Leven, and enters the vale of

GLENCOE,

celebrated both for the grandeur of its scenery and its historical recollections. The lower part of the glen, next Loch Leven, is cultivated and wooded, but the signs of cultivation gradually disappear on approaching the upper portion, which presents a scene of unmingled wildness and grandeur. In the middle of the valley is the small lake

Treachtan, from which issues the wild stream of Cona, celebrated by Ossian, who is said to have been born on its banks. On both sides of this river the hills shoot up perpendicularly to a tremendous height, casting a deep gloom on this wild vale, calculated to strike the traveller with the deepest awe. At the head of the glen the disposition of the mountains becomes peculiarly grand and impressive. Their magnitude, form, and colour, all contribute to the greatness of the effect. In the huge clefts of their rocky and blackened summits, wreaths of snow may be seen all the year round, and the scream of the eagle, and the roar of the mountain torrents are the only sounds heard in "the waste howling wilderness." From one end of the vale to the other only one solitary farm-house is to be seen.* The well-known massacre of Glencoe, which casts so deep a stain on the character of King William and his ministers, happened at the north-west end of the vale. At the farthest extremity of Glencoe is the rugged mountain of Buchael Etive, and on the opposite side of the road is the steep ascent called *The Devil's Staircase*, by which pedestrians may proceed to Fort-William.† Proceeding onward through a barren district, the tourist arrives at King's House Inn, distant twenty-eight miles and a half from Fort-William. The road then crosses a tedious hill called the Black Mount; and, nine and a half miles from the King's House, reaches Inverouran, on the banks of Loch Tulla. Two miles beyond this, the road crosses the river Orchy, which

* As a piece of perfectly wild mountain scenery, Glencoe has no superior that I know of. In the Alps there are many ravines and valleys immensely larger, but I am not aware of any which has better claims to attention in all that relates to the fantastical disposition of barren rocks of great magnitude tossed indiscriminately about by the hand of Nature."—*Captain Basil Hall's Patchwork*, vol. ii., p 268.

† The distance from King's House Inn to Fort-William by the Devil's Staircase is about 23 miles. From the excessive roughness and steepness of a part of the first half of the road, it can be travelled only by pedestrians. The Staircase diverges from the main road at a small cluster of shepherd's houses, called Altnafedh, where it may be well to obtain a guide for the first two miles, the road being scarcely distinguishable among the rocks and loose stones which surround its tract. The only house where any refreshment can be obtained, is one of a very humble order, about twelve miles from Altnafedh, where drovers are accustomed to lodge on their way from the north.

waters the pretty valley of Glenorchy. Seven miles farther, situated at the head of Strathfillan, in Perthshire, is

TYNDRUM.

[*Inns* :—Tyndrum Inn.]

Not far from Tyndrum, at a place called Dalrigh or the King's Field, King Robert Bruce was encountered and repulsed after a very severe engagement, by the Lord of Lorn. "Bruce's personal strength and courage," says Sir Walter Scott, "were never displayed to greater advantage than in this conflict. There is a tradition in the family of the MacDougals of Lorn, that their chieftain engaged in personal battle with Bruce himself, while the latter was employed in protecting the retreat of his men; that MacDougal was struck down by the king, whose strength of body was equal to his vigour of mind, and would have been slain on the spot, had not two of Lorn's vassals, a father and a son, whom tradition terms MacKeoch, rescued him, by seizing the mantle of the monarch, and dragging him from above his adversary. Bruce rid himself of these foes by two blows of his redoubted battle-axe, but was so closely pressed by the other followers of Lorn, that he was forced to abandon the mantle, and brooch which fastened it, clasped in the dying grasp of the MacKeochs."* According to the

* The brooch continued in the MacDougal family till the year 1647, when the castle of Goalen, in the island of Kerrera, having been taken, sacked and burned, by General Leslie's troops, Campbell of Inverawe possessed himself of the valued relic. In that family it remained till about the beginning of the present century, when it passed into the hands of a cadet of the family, who, by his testament, directed it to be sold, and the proceeds divided among his younger children. It was accordingly sent to Rundell and Bridge to be exposed for sale at the price of £1000. The late George IV., then Prince Regent, is said to have offered £500 for it; but the sum was refused, and the brooch withdrawn. Ultimately, in the year 1825, the late General Campbell of Lochnell, anxious to bestow some mark of regard on his friend MacDougal, purchased the brooch, and presented it to him through his chief, the late Duke of Argyle, at a social meeting of the landholders of the county. It was worn by Lieut. Campbell, R.N., when steering the barge that bore her Majesty along Loch Tay, after her visit to Taymouth Castle in 1842. On that occasion it was minutely examined by her Majesty. The encounter between Bruce and the MacDougals is cele-

account given in Barbour, three of the strongest among Lorn's followers resolved to rid their chief of this formidable foe. "They watched their opportunity until Bruce's party had entered a pass between a lake (Loch Dochart probably,) and a precipice, where the King, who was the last of the party, had scarce room to manage his steed. Here his three foes sprung upon him at once. One seized his bridle, but received a wound which hewed off his arm; a second grasped Bruce by the stirrup and leg, and endeavoured to dismount him, but the King, putting spurs to his horse, threw him down, still holding by the stirrup. The third taking advantage of an acclivity, sprung up behind him upon his horse. Bruce, however, whose personal strength is uniformly mentioned as exceeding that of most men, extricated himself from his grasp, threw him to the ground, and cleft his skull with his sword. By similar exertion he drew the stirrup from his grasp, whom he had overthrown, and killed him also with his sword as he lay among the horse's feet."

brated by Sir Walter Scott in the following song, entitled "The Brooch of Lorn," supposed to be sung by the bard of Lorn at his chieftain's request :—

"Whence the brooch of burning gold,
That clasps the chieftain's mantle-fold,
Wrought and chased with rare device,
Studded fair with gems of price,
On the varied tartans beaming,
As, through night's pale rainbow gleaming,
Fainter now, now seen afar,
Fitful shines the northern star?

"Gem! ne'er wrought on Highland mountain,
Did the fairy of the fountain,
Or the mermaid of the wave,
Frame thee in some coral cave?
Did, in Iceland's darksome mine,
Dwarf's swart hands thy metal twine?
Or, mortal-moulded, comest thou here,
From England's love or France's fear?

"No! thy splendours nothing tell
Foreign art or faëry spell.
Moulded thou for monarch's use,
By the overweening Bruce,
When the royal robe he tied
O'er a heart of wrath and pride;
Thence in triumph wert thou torn
By the victor hand of Lorn!

"When the gem was won and lost,
Widely was the war-cry toss'd!
Rung aloud Bendourish fell,
Answer'd Douchart's sounding dell,
Fled the deer from wild Teyndrum,
When the homicide, o'ercome,
Hardly 'scaped with scathe and scorn,
Left the pledge with conquering Lorn.

"Vain was then the Douglas brand,
Vain the Campbell's vaunted hand,
Vain Kirkpatrick's bloody dirk,
Making sure of murder's work;
Barendown fled fast away,
Fled the fiery De la Haye,
When this brooch, triumphant borne,
Beam'd upon the breast of Lorn.

"Farthest fled its former Lord,
Left his men to brand and cord,
Bloody brand of Highland steel,
English gibbet, axe, and wheel,
Let him fly from coast to coast,
Dogg'd by Comyn's vengeful ghost,
While his spoils, in triumph worn,
Long shall grace victorious Lorn!"

Lord of the Isles, canto II., stanza 11, and Notes.

Two miles from Tyndrum is St. Fillan's church. Here there is a linn in the river Ettrick, called St. Fillan's Pool, in which, till lately, a considerable number of lunatics were annually immersed, and then bound hand and foot, and laid all night in the churchyard of St. Fillan's, in the expectation of effecting a cure. Since 1840 there have been only three instances of resort to this barbarous superstition, the last in 1844. Two miles farther is Crianlarich Inn, from which the tourist may either proceed through Glenfalloch to the head of Loch Lomond, or by Glen Dochart and Glen Ogle to Lochearnhead, and join the route described p. 375.

SEVENTEENTH TOUR.

PERTH—CUPAR-ANGUS—FORFAR—MONTROSE—ABERDEEN.

By Scottish Midland and Aberdeen Railways.

About 2 miles from Perth, at the confluence of the Almond and the Tay, on a gently sloping bank, is the PALACE OF SCONE, its massive towers partly concealed in foliage. The woods around, and the general landscape, are very beautiful. At Redgorton the line crosses the Dunkeld turnpike by a skew viaduct. On the opposite bank of the Tay is Oliver Castle. Four miles from Perth is Luncarty Station. The bleachfield in the neighbourhood was the scene of a battle between the Scots and Danes in the reign of Kenneth III. Stanley Station (6½ miles). On the top of a bank to the left is the village of the same name, with its church and tower. By the river-side, surrounded with lofty trees, is Stanley House; and near it is Campsie Linn, a cascade of the Tay. Above the fall is a lofty perpendicular rock, on which are the ruins of an old house connected with Cupar-Angus Abbey. Passing Taymount and Stobball, Cargill Station is reached (11¼ miles from Perth). A little to the left, opposite the confluence of the Isla with the Tay,

SCOTTISH MIDLAND & ABERDEEN RAILWAYS
(PERTH & DUNDEE TO ABERDEEN.)

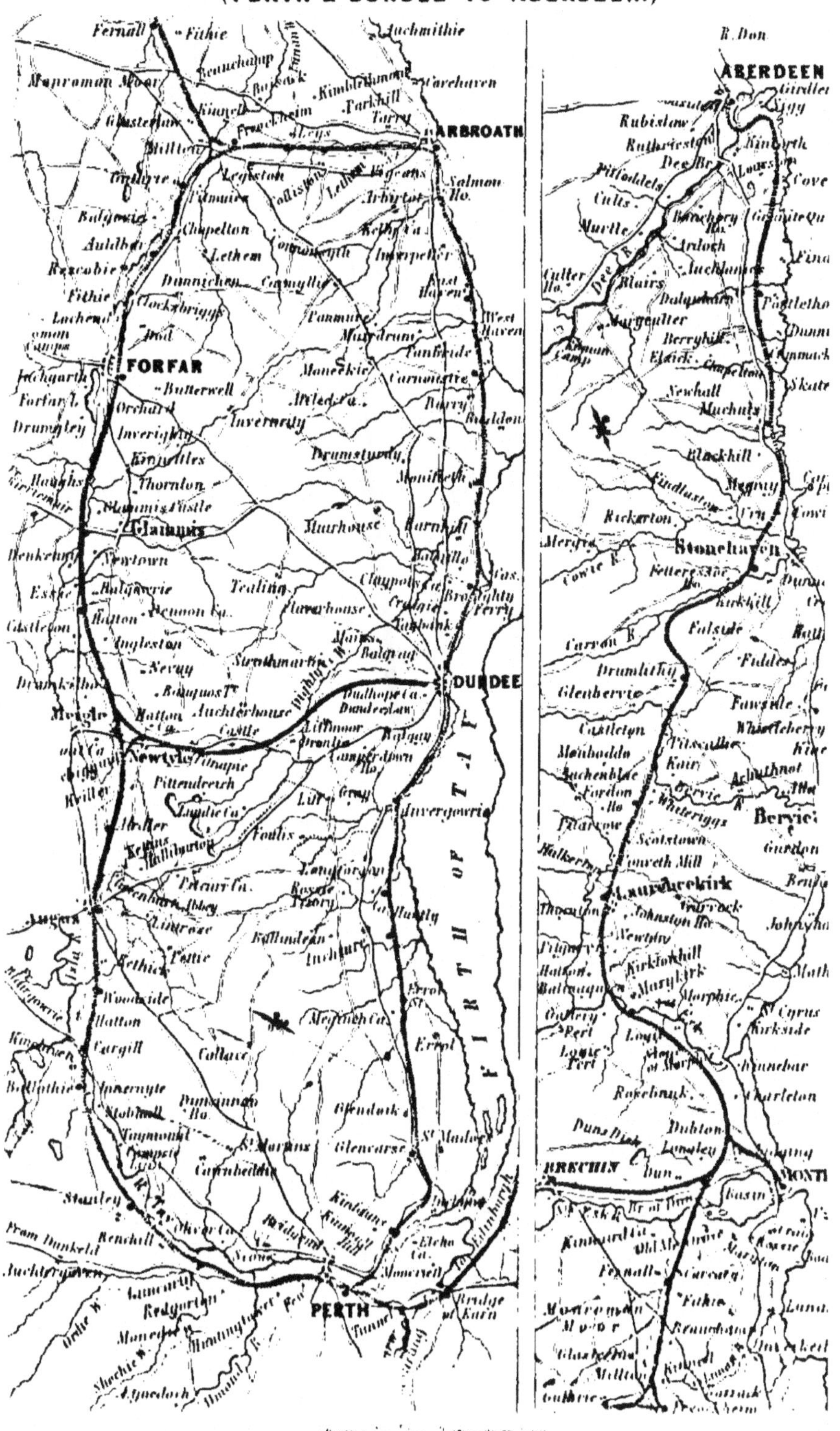

Published by A.&C. Black Edinburgh.

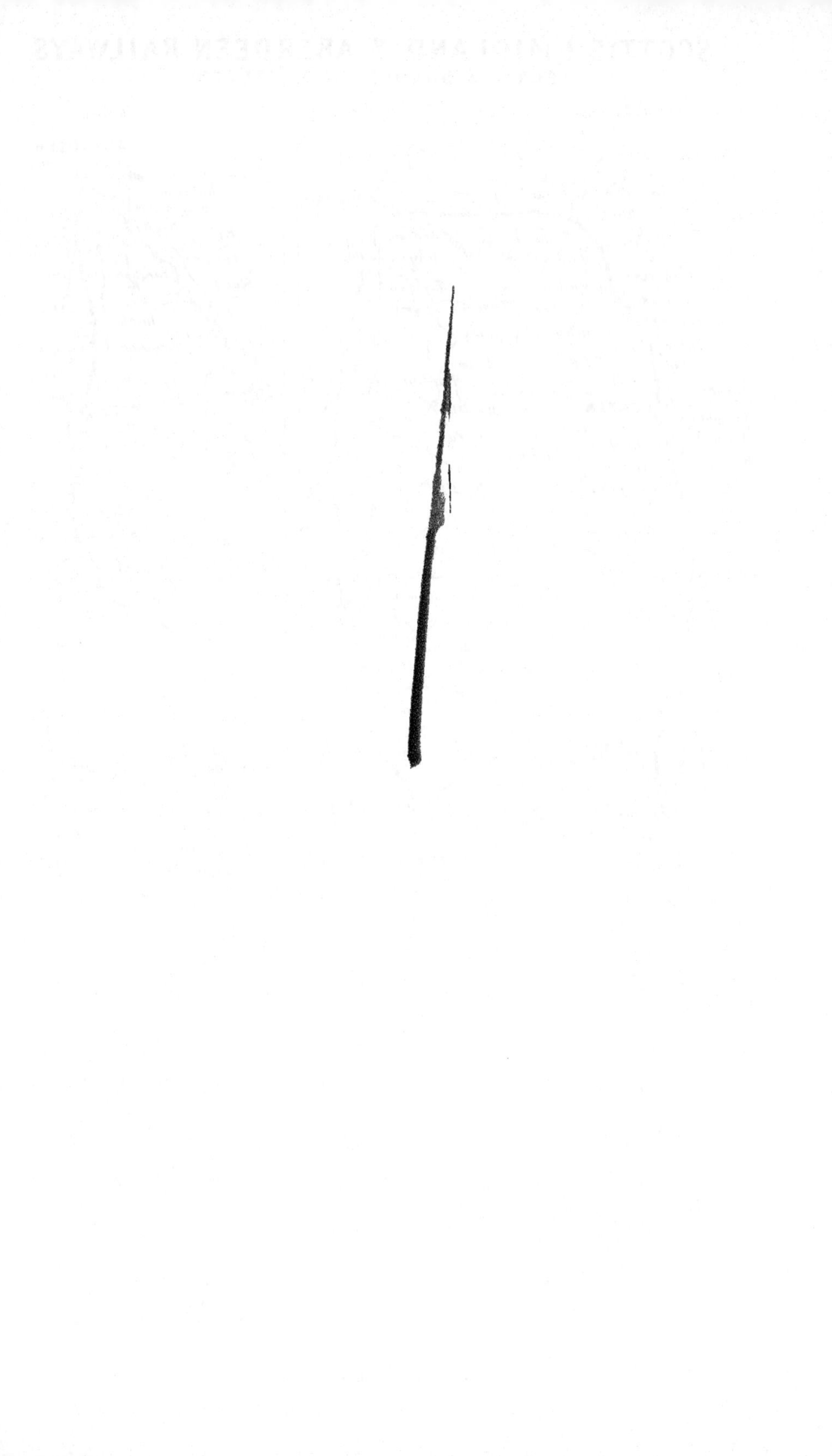

is the ancient castle of Kinclaven. Above it is Mickleour village. Woodside Station ($13\frac{1}{2}$ miles).

Having skirted the luxuriant tract of country known as " the Carse of Gowrie," the scenery loses its peculiar richness of aspect ; bogs, grain-fields, heath and clumps of dark firs diversifying the landscape. Cupar-Angus ($15\frac{3}{4}$ miles), a town of about 6000 inhabitants, is the next station.

About 4 miles to the northward is the village of Blairgowrie, the key to the Highland pass, through the Spittal of Glenshee and Glen Beg, to Braemar.

Ardler Station ($18\frac{1}{4}$ miles), and Meigle Station ($21\frac{1}{4}$ miles). Here a branch-line strikes off, past Newtyle village, to Dundee. The ancient village of Meigle possesses some ancient monuments in the churchyard, said by the common people to mark the grave of Queen Vanore, wife of King Arthur. The stones bear a variety of hieroglyphical figures with representations of men and animals. Close by is Belmont House, a seat of Lord Wharncliffe. Eassie Station, $24\frac{1}{4}$, and Glammis Station, $26\frac{3}{4}$ miles, from Perth.

GLAMMIS CASTLE,

seated in the midst of a park one hundred and sixty acres in extent, is near the latter station.*

* The castle is an edifice of great antiquity, and has a princely appearance. The walls in some places are fifteen feet thick, and the height is such, that the stair which leads to the top contains 143 steps. Glammis was anciently used as a royal residence, and was the scene of the death of Malcolm II., who was mortally wounded by assassins on the Hunter's Hill in this neighbourhood. Macbeth, as the readers of Shakspeare know, was thane of Glammis, and after his death it reverted to the Crown. It was given by Robert II. to John Lyon, who married the king's second daughter by Elizabeth Mure, and became the founder of the present family of Strathmore. On the barbarous execution of the young and beautiful Lady Glammis for witchcraft, in 1537, Glammis was once more forfeited to the Crown, and was for some time a residence of James V., (*the Gudeman of Ballangeich*,) but was afterwards restored to the family. It contains a valuable and extensive museum of ancient curiosities, old armour, and a collection of portraits, amounting to about a hundred in number, principally of the most distinguished characters in the reign of Charles II. The view from the top of the castle is remarkably splendid and extensive. Near the castle stand the figures of four lions rampant, each supporting in their fore-paws a dial facing the four cardinal points. The figures are extremely curious, and well deserve the attention of the tourist.

FORFAR,

[*Inn* :—Morrison's.]

the county town ($32\frac{1}{2}$ miles from Perth), is the terminal station of the railway.* The burgh is of great antiquity, and was a royal residence in the time of Malcolm Canmore.

* In 1728 the Earl of Strathmore was slain in Forfar. That nobleman was returning with a party of gentlemen from attendance upon a *dredgie*, when one of them, Mr. Carnegie of Finhaven, being tossed by another into the gutter rose, bespattered and blinded with mire, and mistaking the Earl for the offender, ran him through the body. He was tried for the crime, and narrowly escaped the gallows. On a mount to the north of the town was the castle in which King Malcolm resided, and his queen lived in a nunnery which stood on a small artificial island near the north side of the loch. In the steeple of Forfar is preserved a curious instrument, called "the Witches' Bridle," which was placed on the head of the miserable creatures burnt in Forfar for the imaginary crime of witchcraft, and acted as a gag to prevent their cries during the dreadful process of incremation. There are a number of pleasant anecdotes connected with Forfar, but it is somewhat curious, as has been noticed by Chambers, that they all refer to drinking or to public-houses. The legal gentlemen of this town, indeed, are characterized as the "drucken writers of Forfar." Their tippling habits are finely illustrated by an anecdote of the late Earl of Strathmore. The town is a good deal annoyed with a lake in its neighbourhood, which the inhabitants have long had it in contemplation to drain, and which would have been drained long ago but for the expensiveness of such an undertaking. At a public meeting held some years ago for the discussion of this measure, the Earl said, that he believed the cheapest method of draining the lake would be, to throw a few hogsheads of good mountain dew into the water, and set the *drucken writers* of Forfar to drink it up.*

The chief magistrate of Forfar, in the time of King James VI., kept an alehouse. His Majesty, in the course of his first journey to London, having been entertained with great splendour by the mayor of an English town, who, in honour of the occasion, kept open house for several days, some of the courtiers hinted that such examples of munificence must be very rare among the civic dignitaries of Scotland. "Fient a bit o' that are they," cried the King; "the provost o' my burgh of Forfar, whilk is by nae means the largest town in Scotland, keeps open house a' the year round, and aye the mae that comes the welcomer."

It was in Forfar that the famous case occurred which led to the decision that no charge could be made for a stirrup-dram. A brewster-wife in Forfar, previous to the Restoration, having one day "brewed a peck o' maut," and set it out to the door to cool, a neighbour's cow passing by drank the whole browst. The injured ale-wife had recourse to the law for satisfaction, when it was decided, that as, by the immemorial custom of the land, nothing is ever charged for a standing-drink, otherwise called a *deoch-an-dorras*, or stirrup-dram, the defendant ought to be absolved from the charge in dependence, seeing that she swallowed the browst standing, and at the door.

* Chambers' Rhymes of Scotland, p. 117. Picture of Scotland, vol. ii., p. 220.

Its inhabitants are principally engaged in weaving and the manufacture of brogues.

Leaving Forfar by the Arbroath and Forfar line, and proceeding eastward, on the left are seen in the distance, the hills of Carse, and in the vicinity of the line the village of Lunanhead, deriving its name from a spring which rises here, and wending its way eastward, flows into the sea at Lunan Bay. On the right is seen the ancient Priory of Restennet, with its Tower; and, passing on the left the house and hill of Pitscandly is Clocksbriggs Station, (35 miles), on the right of which are the hills of Burnside and Dunnichen. The line then passes along the margin of Rescobie Loch on the left, on the opposite shore of which is seen the Parish Church and Manse of Rescobie. To the eastward of this is Turin Hill, famed for its pavement quarries. Proceeding onwards, and skirting Balgavie's Loch on the right, is Auldbar Road Station, (37 miles.) Leaving this Station, on the left is seen the house of Balgavies; and beyond, Guthrie Hill, on the east part of which are the traces of a Roman encampment, carefully preserved. Passing the meal and flour mills of Mill-den on the right, the line is carried across the Lunan Water, and enters a deep cutting, emerging from which is seen a finely wooded district. On the right is Ouchterlony House, and southward from it Dumbarrone Hill. On the left is Guthrie Castle, (John Guthrie, Esq.) The view of this fine building is considerably obstructed by the ancient trees surrounding it. On the right are the policies and House of Pitmunies.

At this point the Aberdeen line properly commences. The Arbroath line proceeds southward, and the Aberdeen northward.

Guthrie Junction, (39¼ miles.) On the left is seen the Kirktown of Guthrie, with the church and manse; on the right is the old Castle of Gardyne, and to the eastward of it Middleton House, and the manufacturing village of Friockheim, with its church and spire.

Glasterlane Junction, (41 miles.) Here a branch line diverges to the right, which is carried over the Lunan

Water by means of a fine stone viaduct of nine arches, and joins the Arbroath and Forfar line at Friockheim.* It has not as yet, however, been used for passenger trains. The line traverses a somewhat bleak district called Monroman Muir, and shortly arrives at Farnell Road Station, (44¼ miles.) The country now becomes finely wooded and fertile. Immediately opposite the station, on the left, are seen the picturesque Church and Manse of Farnell, with the porter's lodge and approach to Kinnaird Castle, (Sir James Carnegie, Bart.), a glimpse of which may be caught after leaving the station, beautifully situated amidst forest and ornamental plantations. Proceeding through finely cultivated fields, with the hills of Carcaray and Bonnyton on the right, the line is carried across the river South Esk by means of a wooden viaduct; it then skirts the left bank of the river, affording a view of the old bridge.

Bridge of Dun Station, (47½ miles.) At this Station a Branch line diverges on the left to Brechin,† which is dis-

* ARBROATH.

[*Inns*:—Bruce's; M'Phail's.]

Arbroath is a neat and thriving seaport. The harbour is an artificial one, and though neither safe nor spacious, possesses considerable trade. Here are the ruins of a magnificent abbey, founded by William the Lion in 1178, and dedicated to the celebrated primate, Thomas-a-Becket. The founder was interred within its precincts, but there are no remains of his tomb. The last abbot was the famous Cardinal Beaton, who was at the same time Archbishop of St. Andrews. King John of England granted this monastery extraordinary privileges, for, by a charter under the Great Seal, he exempted it from taxes in trading to every part of England, except London. The ruins of the abbey are greatly dilapidated. The Scottish nobility met here in 1320, and drew up a spirited remonstrance to the Pope against the claims made by Edward II. upon the sovereignty of the kingdom. Arbroath is a royal burgh, and unites with Forfar, Inverbervie, Montrose and Brechin, in sending a Member to the British Parliament. The population of the burgh within the royalty in 1841 was 8025.

† The ancient royal burgh of Brechin is romantically situated on the banks of the South Esk. In ancient times there was an abbey of Culdees in this place, and a bishoprick was established here by David I. in 1150. On the edge of a precipitous bank descending towards the river, stood the Cathedral, a stately

tant about 8 miles. Leaving the station and proceeding onward along the main line, on the right is seen the town of Montrose, with its chain bridge and capacious basin in view. Passing on the left Dun House, Bromley, and the lime kilns of Hedderwick, we speedily arrive at Dubton Station (50 miles).

Here the branch line to Montrose diverges to the right, and proceeds down the peninsula to that town.*

Adjacent to the station on the right is the ancient mansion of Hedderwick, and beside it Dubton House. On the

* MONTROSE.

[*Inns*:—The Star; M'Laren's Royal; the White Horse; the Commercial.]

Montrose is a remarkably neat town, and carries on a considerable trade. It has been connected with a number of interesting and important events in Scottish history. From this place Sir James Douglas embarked in 1330 on a pilgrimage to the Holy Land, carrying along with him the heart of Robert Bruce. It was the birth-place of the celebrated Marquis of Montrose. It was the first port made by the French fleet in December 1715, with the Chevalier St. George on board; and that personage embarked at the same place 14th February 1716, having spent the previous night in the house in which Montrose was born. The principal public buildings are the town-hall, the parish church, the Episcopal chapel, the public schools, the academy, the lunatic asylum, and the office of the British Linen Company. In 1841, the population of Montrose, within the royalty, was 13,552. Behind the town, which stands on a narrow peninsula, the river expands into a spacious basin which forms a sort of road-stead to the port. At high water, it has a peculiarly striking and beautiful effect. The South Esk is crossed by a very magnificent suspension bridge, the distance between the points of suspension being 432 feet.

Gothic fabric, but its architectural symmetry has of late been almost entirely destroyed by the wretched taste displayed in repairing it as a modern place of worship. Brechin contains one of those round towers, which, like that of Abernethy, is "with great probability ascribed to the Picts, although antiquarians are divided in their opinion concerning them. The tower of Brechin is a circular column, of great beauty and elegance, 80 feet high, with a kind of spire or roof 23 feet more, making the whole height 103, while the diameter is 16 feet." Brechin Castle, the ancient seat of Lord Panmure, stands on a precipitous rock in the immediate neighbourhood of the town. It underwent a siege of twenty days in 1303, from the English army under Edward I., and only surrendered on Sir Thomas Maule, its brave governor, being killed.

left lies the considerable village of Hillside, having some tasteful villas, the residences of parties in Montrose. Leaving Dubton, the line is carried up a high embankment, on the right of which is Charlton House, and on the left Rosemount. The line now enters a deep cutting, on emerging from which is seen, on the right, the river North Esk, and at a distance the spacious stone bridge, on the turnpike road between Montrose and the north. Standing on an eminence beside it is Kirkside House. Skirting the slopes of the valley of the North Esk, passing on the right, are the extensive manufacturing works of Logic and Craigo. Craigo Station (53¼ miles). Leaving this station, on the opposite side of the river, a fine view is obtained of Kirktonhill House (—— Taylor, Esq.), and on the left Craigo, Gallrey, and Balmakewan. We then cross the North Esk by means of an extensive viaduct. Marykirk Station (54½ miles). On the right is the village of Marykirk, and the parish church and manse. The line has now entered Kincardineshire, and on the left, in the distance, appear the Grampians. On the right is seen the Hill of Garvock, with its tower, and in the immediate vicinity is the village of Fettercairn.

Laurencekirk Station (58½ miles). The town of this name, which is scarcely visible from the line, being carried through a deep cutting, was the birthplace of Dr. Beattie, and here the celebrated Ruddiman was once schoolmaster. The place is now chiefly remarkable for the manufacture of snuff-boxes. Leaving Laurencekirk, the line passes through the richly cultivated district known as the "Howe o' the Mearns." Fordoun Station (62 miles). At a short distance from this, to the north, is the village of Auchinblae. The village may partly be seen, with the spire of the church of Fordoun, shortly before reaching the station. George Wishart, the reformer, was a native of this parish, and a monument has recently been erected to his memory by the parishioners of all denominations.

After leaving Fordoun Station, on the left is Monboddo, the seat of the late Lord Monboddo, and on the right the house of Keir. A little beyond, the line is carried across the Water of Bervie at Mondynes, a short way above which is the mansion-house and parish church of Glenbervie ; but these are not seen from the railway. The line shortly reaches Drumlithie Station (66¼ miles). The village of Drumlithie is chiefly inhabited by weavers. On the left of the station is a handsome Free Church and manse. The line is now carried along an extensive viaduct, and turns northwards. On the right, at a considerable distance, may be seen the ancient Castle of Fiddes. On emerging from an immense cutting through the solid rock, the line enters the the valley of the Carron Water, with the woods of Dunnottar and Carmount Hill, on the right, and the lands of Fetteresso on the left. We then cross the Carron near Aquherie, and enter the woods of Fetteresso. On the left is Fetteresso Castle, the ancient residence of the Earls Marischal, situated on the north bank of the Carron, and surrounded with extensive policies. A short way further on, the line again crosses the Carron by a very extensive viaduct, from which a fine view is obtained of the house and extensive enclosures of Ury, the seat of Captain Barclay Allardice. In the valley on the right is the Kirktown and ruins of the old parish church of Fetteresso. On the right, surrounded with trees, is the parish church of Dunnottar, in the churchyard of which there is a grave-stone in memory of certain Covenanters killed in endeavouring to escape from the "Whigs' vault" in Dunnottar Castle. Beyond this is also seen the modern house of Dunnottar. Stonehaven Station (73 miles).—[*Inns:* Finlay's, the Mill ; Melvin's Railway Inn.]—The town of Stonehaven has a safe and commodious harbour, and contains a population of about 2000. To the north of the station stands the parish church of Fetteresso, and at a short distance on the right are the ruins of the celebrated

DUNNOTTAR CASTLE.

the seat of the ancient family of the Keiths, Earls Marischal. The area of the castle measures about three acres, and the rock bears a considerable resemblance to that on which

Edinburgh Castle is built. It is divided from the land by a deep chasm, and the only approach is by a steep path winding round the body of the rock. Dunnottar was built by Sir William Keith, then Great Marischal of Scotland, during the wars between England and Scotland in the reign of Edward I. In 1296 it was taken from the English by Sir William Wallace. Edward III. re-fortified it in his progress through the kingdom in 1336, but as soon as he quitted the kingdom it was again captured by Sir Andrew Murray, Regent of Scotland. During the time of the Commonwealth, it was selected as the strongest place in the kingdom for the preservation of the Regalia. The garrison, under the command of Ogilvy of Barras, made a vigorous resistance to the English army, but were at length compelled to surrender by famine. Previously to this, however, the regalia had been secretly conveyed away, and buried beneath the pulpit of the church of Kinneff, by Mrs. Granger, the wife of the minister of that parish. At the Restoration, all the persons connected with this affair were amply rewarded. Ogilvy was made a baronet; the brother of the Earl Marischal was created Earl of Kintore; and Mrs. Granger was rewarded with a sum of money. During the reign of Charles II. Dunnottar was used as a State prison for confining the Covenanters. It was dismantled soon after the Rebellion of 1715, on the attainder of its proprietor, James, Earl Marischal. "The battlements, with their narrow embrasures, the strong towers and airy turrets, full of loop-holes for the archer and musketeer; the hall for the banquet and the cell for the captive, are all alike entire and distinct. Even the iron rings and bolts that held the culprits for security or torture still remain to attest the different order of things which once prevailed in this country. Many a sigh has been sent from the profound bosom of this vast rock—many a despairing glance has wandered hence over the boundless wave—and many a weary heart has there sunk rejoicing into eternal sleep."

Leaving Stonehaven Station, the line is carried across the Water of Cowie, below Ury, by a viaduct of great length

and height. In the valley is Glenury distillery. The line then passes the House of Cowie, and near the ruins of the church of Cowie approaches the bold sea-cliffs, along which it passes onwards to Aberdeen. The country from Stonehaven to Aberdeen is remarkably bleak and sterile, presenting for the most part barren eminences and cold swampy moorlands. The bold line of coast is the principal object of interest. The stations from Stonehaven to Aberdeen are Muchall's (77½ miles), Newtonhill (78¾ miles), Porblethin (81¼ miles), and Cove (84½ miles). The line passes successively the fishing villages of Skaterow, Portlethen, Findon, or Finnan, and Cove. From the village Finnan the celebrated dried haddocks derive their name. "FINNAN, *magnum et venerabile nomen!* 'To abstract the mind from all local emotion,' says the moralist, 'would be impossible if it were endeavoured, and would be foolish if it were possible. Far from me and from my friends be such frigid philosophy. That man is little to be envied whose patriotism would not gain force upon the plain of *Marathon*,' or whose appetite would not grow keener among the huts of *Finnan*. Its unlettered sages will impart wisdom which will be vainly sought in elaborate dissertations on culinary science."*
After leaving Cove Station, and proceeding for a short distance along the shore, the line sweeps round from Girdleness (the eastern termination of the great chain of the Grampians), and crossing the river Dee by means of an extensive viaduct, reaches Aberdeen.

* From a very amusing and well-written work, entitled "The Book of Bon-Accord; or a Guide to the City of Aberdeen."

ABERDEEN.

[*Hotels:*—The Royal; The North of Scotland; The Aberdeen; The Lemon Tree; The Union; Mollison's.]

Railway to Perth, Edinburgh, Glasgow, &c.

Steamers to Edinburgh, Newcastle, London, also northwards as before mentioned to Banff, Nairn, Cromarty, Invergordon, Fort-George, Inverness, Wick, Thurso, Kirkwall, and Lerwick.

Coach Office, 65 *Union Street.* Coaches to Banff, Ballater, Glens of Foudland Ellon, Fraserburgh, Huntly, by Meldrum, Forgue, and Drumblain; Inverury, Peterhead, Rhynie, Stonehaven; Inverness, by Keith, Elgin, Forres, and Nairn.

Aberdeen ranks next to Edinburgh and Glasgow, in point of general importance, and is considered the capital of the North of Scotland. It is situated on a cluster of eminences, which rise along the northern bank of the river Dee, in the immediate vicinity of its confluence with the German Ocean. On approaching the city, along the principal line of communication from the southward, the tourist is forcibly struck with the scene which bursts upon his view, after a long and rather dreary transit across the Grampians, at a point where their mountainous character is lost, but from which some of their sublimer features are distinctly visible in the far west. The traveller is here suddenly admonished of his approach to an important city; its more prominent buildings, scattered here and there, indicating its magnitude; the numerous vessels in the harbour bearing testimony to the extent of its commerce and trade; while the high cultivation of the surrounding district is evidently tributary to the requirements of a large municipal population. The county of Aberdeen is bounded, on the south, by the Dee, which the tourist crosses by a fine old bridge of seven arches, erected about three centuries ago, by Bishop Dunbar. In the days of the Covenant, this bridge was the scene of more than one tough contest between hostile parties. In 1842 its breadth was nearly doubled, by an addition made to one of its sides. The facing of the side upon which the addition was made, having been removed at the commencement of the work, and afterwards restored to its original position, the character of the structure remains unimpaired by the improvement. A drive of a mile through the western suburbs of the city, which boast many elegant private buildings, brings the traveller to one extremity of Union Street, terminating, at the other, in Castle Street, and presenting a vista which is generally and justly admired, whether regard be had to the spacious dimensions of the street itself, the beauty and regularity of the buildings which line it on each side, the splendour of many of its shops, or the bustle which constantly enlivens it. The two chief inns of the city are situated in it, in any of which, not to mention the attractions of the minor hostelries, the stranger will be comfortably accommodated. Curiosity will probably first direct his steps toward Castle Street, the *Place* of the city. Here he will find the Town House, a plain but commodious building, of date 1730. It contains the Town Hall, Council Chamber, &c., to which ready access may be obtained. The hall is a spacious apartment, and contains one or two good paintings, three superb lustres, and some other matters worthy of inspection. The Council Chamber contains a fine head by Jameson. On the east end of the Town House is a square tower, of ancient date, which has been recently faced up with granite in a very tasteful style. It is surmounted by a spire 120 feet high, of singularly elegant proportions. Contiguous to the tower, on the east, are the new offices of the North of Scotland Banking Company, a fine building in the Grecian style, of beautifully dressed granite. The principal entrance is under a curved portico, supported by granite columns of the Corinthian order, the capitals being executed with a delicacy and precision hitherto deemed unattainable in that stubborn material. On the opposite side of the street stands the Aberdeen Bank, a very chaste building. At the west end of Castle Street is the Athenæum, or Public News Room, to which a stranger may be introduced by any of the subscribers, with free access to it for a fortnight. It is a fine room, liberally supplied with newspapers, and the best periodicals. In the centre of the upper end of Castle Street, stands the cross, a structure well worthy of notice. It was built, in 1686, by John Montgomery, a country mason of the district, and is one of the most beautiful structures of the kind. It is adorned with large medallions of the Scottish monarchs, from James I. to James VII., and from the centre springs a splendid column of the composite order, surmounted by the royal unicorn rampant and bearing a shield. For better effect, it was removed from the place where it originally stood—at the top of a smooth pavement, in the centre of the lower end of Castle Street, opposite to the entrance of the Court House; and in 1842 it was rebuilt where it now stands, in a greatly improved style, being elevated several feet above the level of the street, and surrounded by an iron railing. About 30 feet in front, stands a colossal statue of the late Duke of Gordon, executed in granite, by Mr. Campbell of London. From the centre of Castle Street, there are fine views of Union Street and King Street, which were both laid out, nearly forty years ago, at an expense of about £170,000. In the latter are situated some public buildings, worthy of inspection, viz., the Medical Hall, the North Church and St. Andrew's Chapel. From Union Street, already referred to, diverges, on the south side, a new street, forming a more convenient access to the quay and harbour than any previously existing. In this street are erected a new Post-office, and Public Markets, the latter projected by a joint-stock company to supply what had long been a local desideratum. In the same street is a handsome Coffee-Room, above which there is a Hall for the accommodation of the Agricultural Association of Aberdeenshire, and neighbouring counties. On the north side of Union Street are situated the East and West Churches, surrounded by a cemetery, which is separated from the street by a very beautiful façade of the Ionic order. The West Church is a building in the Italian style, containing a fine monument, in white marble, to the memory of a lady, executed by Bacon, at an expense of £1200: a curious monumental plate of brass, commemorative of the death of Dr. Duncan Liddel, founder of the professorship of Mathematics in Marischal College; and a stone effigy of Sir Robert Davidson, Provost of Aberdeen, who fell at Harlaw in 1411. The East Church is a modern building, in the Gothic style, deservedly much admired. The churches are separated by Drum's Aisle, so called from its being the burial-place of the ancient family of that name. It formed the transept of the original church of St. Nicholas, a fabric of the twelfth century. The only part of the old structure is the central tower, in which hang the bells. The original date of the great bell, Laurence, which weighs 40,000 lbs., is 1352. In the churchyard reposes the hallowed dust of the poet of "The Minstrel," of Principal Campbell, the learned Blackwell, and Dr. Hamilton, the well known author of the work on the National Debt. Part of Union Street is carried over a deep ravine, by means of a magnificent bridge, consisting of one arch of 130 feet span, 44 feet in breadth, and 50 feet above the surface of the ground below. It is built of dressed granite, and surmounted with a cornice, parapet, and balustrades. It cost £13,342. Westward of the bridge, at some distance, are situated the Public Rooms. In beauty of architecture, and splendour of internal decoration, they are inferior to none in the kingdom. The banqueting-room contains a portrait of the late Duke of Gordon, by Lawrence, and another of Provost James Hadden, by Pickersgill. To these has been added another, by the latter artist, of the Hon. Captain Gordon, who has, for many years, represented the county in Parliament. The other public buildings which particularly merit the attention of the stranger, are the New Infirmary, the Lunatic Asylum, Gordon's Hospital, the New Female Orphan Asylum, the Institution for the Blind, the New Hall of the Society of Advocates, the Trades' Hall, and Marischal

College. Gordon's Hospital is an institution similar to that founded in Edinburgh by George Heriot. Upwards of 160 of the sons or grandsons of burgesses are educated in it. It owes its foundation to Robert Gordon, a descendant of the Straloch family, who starved himself, that he might accomplish his charitable design. The Orphan Asylum is a similar institution for females, recently built and endowed by Mrs. Elmslie, a native of Aberdeen, who is understood to have appropriated £30,000 for that purpose. Marischal College was lately rebuilt, partly at the expense of Government, and partly by subscription. It is a building of imposing dimensions, and magnificent architectural effect. It is in the Gothic style, simplified, and adapted to the capabilities of the material (granite) of which it is built. It forms three sides of a quadrangle, and rises to the height of two lofty storeys, presenting unbroken ranges of mullioned windows, which have a fine effect. From the centre of the building springs a splendid tower, to the height of 100 feet from the ground. It contains the principal entry, and the staircase leading to the Hall, Library, and Museum. Each of these rooms is 74 feet long, by 34 feet wide, and upwards of 30 feet in height. There are, besides, a Common Hall and 16 class-rooms, to each of which is attached a private room for the professor. The total expense of the building is estimated at about £30,000. The old buildings, which were mostly of the seventeenth century, were neither elegant nor commodious, and had latterly become ruinous. The College was founded in the sixteenth century by one of the Earls Marischal. It ranks among its alumni many who have distinguished themselves in every department of science and literature. The traveller will, of course, not omit to visit the Harbour, with its noble quays and extensive pier, stretching into the sea upwards of 1200 feet. Vast sums of money have been expended on the improvement of the harbour, and the formation of wet docks, now rapidly approaching completion. The annual revenue, from dues, &c., is about £17,000. The tonnage of vessels registered as belonging to the port is nearly 50,000 tons. There are in the city many extensive manufactories of flax, cotton, wool, and iron, which employ an aggregate number of hands, amounting to about 14,000. We would particularly recommend to the stranger a visit to Banner Mill, one of the most extensive and best arranged cotton manufactories in the kingdom. There are various other branches of commerce and trade successfully prosecuted in the city, the extent of which may be inferred from the fact, that the tonnage of all the vessels actually arriving in the port is about 210,000 tons. Large steamers ply regularly between it and London, Leith, and Hull. The adoption of steam navigation has been of the greatest advantage to the city and county, and particularly to the agriculturist. Cattle are thus shipped in large numbers. and at all seasons, for the London market. The accommodation for passengers is excellent. In the course of three or four days may the care-worn denizen of the metropolis escape from its din and dust, to "the land of the mountain and the flood," there to inhale its invigorating breezes, enjoy the splendid sports offered by its heaths and streams, and admire the magnificent scenery of "dark Lochnagar." The population of the city within the Parliamentary boundary, according to the census of 1841, was 62,900. It is a city of high antiquity, its earliest charter extant being one granted by William the Lion in 1179. Previously to that early period, however, it was a place of comparative importance, and enjoyed, for so remote an age, a rather extensive commerce. At a subsequent period, it stood high in the favour of "The Bruce," who bestowed on it many important privileges, and a large extent of lands in its vicinity, in consequence of the devotion shown by its inhabitants to his cause. The history of Aberdeen exhibits it participating largely in the successive vicissitudes of the times; but, under all circumstances, its inhabitants have generally been distinguished for their loyalty, prudence, and enterprise.

Old Aberdeen, which is situated about a mile to the north of the city, contains the Cathedral and King's College, both of which will amply reward a visit. The nave of the former is used as the parish church, and is in excellent repair.

The style is rather plain, but it boasts a glorious western window, and a carved roof, in the most exquisite style of ancient art. It is a building of the fourteenth century. King's College was founded in 1494 by Bishop Elphinstone. Its buildings are well worthy of notice. It contains a fine Library, Hall, Chapel, and Museum. The Chapel has recently undergone renovation. In it are to be seen the tombs of the founder, and of Hector Boethius, the first Principal. The crown, which surmounts the tower on the west end of the Library, is a perfectly unique specimen of architecture. The top is 100 feet above the ground. For richness of ornament, beauty of design, and general effect, it has, perhaps, no parallel. The tourist must not omit a visit to the far-famed "Brig o' Balgownie," which Byron refers to in a well-known stanza. It was originally built in the twelfth century by Bishop Cheyne. The surrounding scenery is such as was well calculated deeply to impress the mind of the youthful poet; presenting, as it does, a venerable structure, which the lapse of many generations has assimilated with the everlasting rock on which it is founded—a deep and dark stream stealing silently to the blue ocean, descried in the distance, amid the attendant pomp of beetling crag and thick-embowered wood—and the repose of profound seclusion which is breathed over, and hallows the whole!

The Dee, which falls into the sea on the south side of New Aberdeen, is a river of great note in Aberdeenshire. It has its source in Lord Fife's forest, in the parish of Crathy, at the point where the south-western extremity of Aberdeenshire unites with Inverness-shire. The total length of the Dee, from its source to its mouth, following its various windings, is about eighty miles. It is distinguished by its rapidity, its broad and capacious channel, and the limpid clearness of its waters. It is skirted with fine natural forests, and extensive plantations. There is but little alluvial land on its banks, but its salmon-fisheries are very valuable. Hence the old rhyme,—

"A rood o' Don's worth twa o' Dee,
Unless it be for fish and tree."

The Don rises on the skirts of Ben Avon, on the confines of

Aberdeenshire and Banffshire. Its total course is about sixty-one miles. It is a much less rapid river than the Dee, and flows, for a considerable part of its course, through rich valleys. About a mile from Old Aberdeen, the Don is crossed by the "BRIG OF BALGOWNIE," celebrated by Lord Byron in the tenth canto of Don Juan.

"As 'auld lang syne' brings Scotland, one and all,
Scotch plaids, Scotch snoods, the blue hills and clear streams,
The Dee, the Don, Balgownie's Brig's black wall,
All my boy-feelings, all my gentler dreams,
Of what I then dream't cloth'd in their own pall,
Like Banquo's offspring;—floating past me, seems
My childhood, in this childishness of mind:
I care not—'tis a glimpse of 'Auld lang syne.'"

"The Brig of Don," adds the poet in a note, "near the Auld Town of Aberdeen, with its one arch, and its black deep salmon stream below, is in my memory as yesterday. I still remember, though perhaps I may misquote, the awful proverb which made me pause to cross it, and yet lean over it with a childish delight, being an only son, at least by the mother's side. The saying as recollected by me, was this, but I have never heard nor seen it since I was nine years of age:—

"'Brig of Balgownie, black's your wa',
Wi' a wife's ae son, and a mare's ae foal,
Doon ye shall fa'!'"

The bridge was built by Bishop Cheyne, in the time of Robert Bruce, and consists of one spacious Gothic arch, which rests on a rock on each side.

EIGHTEENTH TOUR.

This tour may also be made by railway as far as Aberdeen. The time occupied is nearly the same by either, the express train taking 6½ hours, and the steamer 8 hours in good weather.

The steamers sail in the morning from Granton Pier on the arrival of the trains and coaches from Edinburgh. They do not touch at any of the intervening towns between Edinburgh and Aberdeen. On their way to Inverness they call at Banff, Nairn, Cromarty, Invergordon, and Fort-George. On certain days they proceed to Helmsdale, Wick, Thurso, Stromness, Kirkwall (in Orkney), Lerwick (in Shetland).

STEAMBOAT TOUR FROM GRANTON TO ABERDEEN, INVERNESS, WICK, ORKNEY AND SHETLAND ISLANDS.

After leaving Granton, the first object of interest is the island of Inchkeith, which received its name from the ancient family of Keith, to whom it formerly belonged. It was fortified by the English in the reign of Edward VI., but the fortifications were afterwards demolished by order of the Scottish Parliament. During the regency of Mary of Guise, it was occupied by the French, who designated it L'Isle des Chevaux, because the grass which it produced formed a nutritious food for horses. Inchkeith possesses several fine springs of water, which, from the circumstance of their occurring at an elevated level above the sea and being never dry, it is presumed must obtain their supply by a submarine passage from the high hills of Fife. The

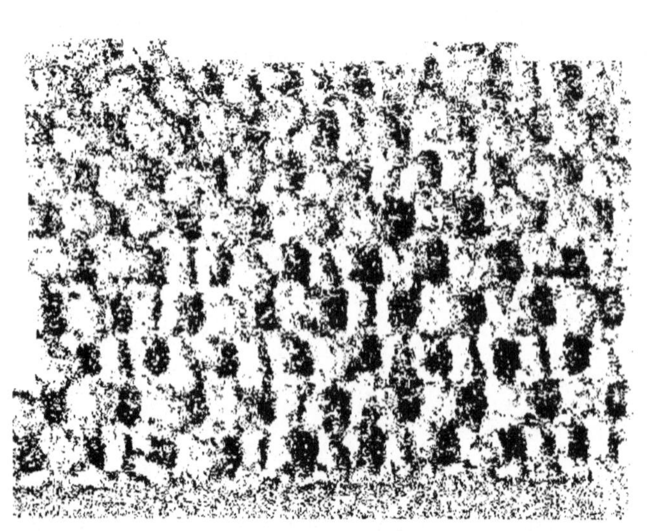

lighthouse on this island is a work of great neatness, and the machinery by which the lights revolve, is very interesting. From the middle of the Firth, a fine view is obtained of the city of Edinburgh, with the harbours of Leith, Newhaven, and Granton, and the coast of Fife, thickly studded with towns. In allusion to this striking characteristic of Fife, King James VI. is said to have likened it to "a grey cloth mantle with a golden fringe." A little to the west is BURNTISLAND.—[*Inns*:—The Forth; The George.]—A little farther east are Pettycur point and the royal burgh of Kinghorn,† which gives the title of Earl to the Earls of Strathmore. About half a mile west of the town is a precipice called the King's Woodend, where Alexander III. was thrown from his horse and killed, 19th March 1285-6. Below Kinghorn is a square tower, the remains of Seafield Castle. A short way farther on is the "lang town of KIRKCALDY," [*Inns*:—The George; The National; Skelton's.] a royal burgh of enterprise and trade. Its streets are extremely irregular, narrow, crooked, ill-paved, and dirty. Dr. Adam Smith, author of the "Wealth of Nations," was a native of this town. Balwearie, in the neighbourhood, was the birthplace of Sir Michael Scott, the famous wizard immortalized in the Lay of the Last Minstrel. The ruins of the old tower of Balwearie are still to be seen. On a rising ground behind Kirkaldy is Raith House, the handsome seat of Colonel Ferguson, M.P. for the Kirkaldy burghs. The situation is commanding, and the pleasure-grounds are extensive and very beautiful. At a short distance is Dunnikier House, the seat of Lady Oswald. To the east of Kirkaldy is Ravenscraig Castle, the property of the Earl of Rosslyn, situated upon a rock overhanging the sea. It has been in the possession of the St. Clair family since the reign of James III., and was entire and habitable till the time of

* Pettycur is supposed to have derived its name (petit corps) from the landing of a small body of French troops during the regency of Mary of Guise.

† The parish church of Kinghorn is without a spire. This, and some other circumstances, supposed to be characteristic of the town, have given rise to the following couplet:—

"Here stands a kirk without a steeple,
A drucken priest, and a graceless people."

Cromwell. About half a mile farther on is Dysart House, a seat of the Earl of Rosslyn, and close to it is the town of Dysart,* a royal burgh of great antiquity, and two or three centuries ago a place of considerable trade. It now exports coals and salt.† Two miles farther on is West Wemyss, a burgh of barony, containing about 600 inhabitants, a dingy, dirty, ruinous looking place. The steamer now passes Wemyss Castle, the seat of Captain Erskine Wemyss, M.P., Lord-Lieutenant of Fife, situated on a steep rock overhanging the sea. In this castle Darnley was first introduced to Queen Mary. Farther on is Easter Wemyss, a burgh of Barony, principally occupied by weavers. Wemyss derives its name from the number of caves on this part of the coast—*Weem* or *Wemyss* being the Gaelic word for a cave. One of these, called the King's Cave, received its designation from an adventure related of James IV. Travelling through Fife on foot, and incognito, that monarch happened to be benighted, and was obliged to enter a cave for shelter. He found it already occupied by a band of robbers, but having gone too far to retreat, he was under the necessity of joining the company. After some time, supper having been served up, two of the gang approached him with a plate on which lay two daggers—a signal that he was to be put to death. He instantly snatched a weapon in each hand, laid the two robbers prostrate at his feet, and rushed through the rest toward the mouth of the cave. Having fortunately succeeded in making his escape,

* "The canty carles o' Dysart,
The merry lads o' Buckhaven,
The saucy limmers o' Largo,
The bonny lasses o' Leven."—*Old Song.*

† "Then from her coal-pits Dysart vomits forth
Her subterranean men of colour dun,
Poor human mould-warps, doom'd to scrape in earth,
Cimmerian people, strangers to the sun;
Gloomy as soot, with faces grim and swarth,
They march most sourly, leering every one,
Yet very keen at Anster loan to share
The merriments and sports to be accomplish'd there.
TENNANT'S *Anster Fair*

he returned next day with a sufficient force, and captured the whole band. A short way farther east are the ruins of Macduff's castle, said to have been built by Macduff, created Thane of Fife about the year 1057. A mile farther down is Buckhaven, a curious antique fishing village, inhabited by a most extraordinary race, supposed to be the descendants of the crew of a vessel from the Netherlands, which was wrecked near this place in the reign of Philip II. They were severely ridiculed more than a century ago in a celebrated satirical pamphlet called the "History of the College of Buckhaven, or the Sayings of Wise Willie and Witty Eppie," well known to the book-stall collectors of pamphlets and broadsides. Buckhaven is, however, a place of considerable wealth. A mile farther on is the small village of Methill, and, at the distance of another mile, the thriving village of Leven, situated at the mouth of the river of the same name, which issues from Loch Leven. Though it has a course of only twelve miles, it receives an immense number of tributary streams. The principal of these are enumerated in the following rhyme:—

> Lochtie, Lochrie, Leven, and Orr,
> Rin a' through Cameron Brig bore.

Leven contains about 1200 inhabitants, who are principally engaged in weaving linen. A short way in the interior is Durie House (C. M. Christie, Esq.) The steamer is now in Largo Bay, familiar to every Scotsman from the allusion made to it in the fine old song, "Weel may the boatie row." In the centre of the bay is the village of Lower Largo, the birth-place of Alexander Selkirk, whose singular adventures form the groundwork of Defoe's charming novel of "Robinson Crusoe." The chest and cup which he used on the uninhabited island are still in possession of his family, and the gun with which he killed his game, now belongs to Major Lumsden of Lathallan. Upper Largo was the birth-place of Sir Andrew Wood, the celebrated Scottish Admiral, who received the barony of Largo from James IV. as a reward for his services at sea against the English.

Largo also gave birth to Sir John Leslie, the celebrated philosopher. Near Upper Largo, in the midst of a beautiful park, and surrounded by trees, stands Largo House, the seat of Sir P. H. C. Durham. To the north of the village, the fine hill called Largo Law rises to the height of 1000 feet above the level of the sea. A short way to the west of Largo, in the midst of a park, are three straight sharp stones, several yards high, called "the Standing Stanes o' Lundie," supposed to be of Roman origin. Four miles east from Largo is ELIE.—[*Inns*:—The Ship.]—Elie House. the seat of Sir W. C. Anstruther, stands close to the town. Two miles farther on is St. Monance, noted for its curious little old Gothic church. The ruins of Newark Castle, the seat of the famous General Leslie, stands on a bold part of the shore, about a mile to the west of the village. A mile to the east is the ancient royal burgh of Pittenweem. Here are the ruins of some curious antique religious buildings. Pittenweem contains the house in which Wilson and Robertson committed the robbery upon the Collector of Excise, which led to the famous Porteous Mob. A mile from Pittenweem, there are two or three towns placed together in a cluster. The first of these are the royal burghs of WESTER and EASTER ANSTRUTHER.—[*Inns*:—Purves'; Robertson's.]—Both go by the name of "Anster," and comprehend a population of about 1420.*

Anstruther was the residence of the renowned "Maggie Lauder," commemorated in the popular song of that name, and "Anster Fair" has been made the subject of an amusing poem by Mr. Tennant, Professor of Oriental Languages in the University of St. Andrews. Opposite to this part of the coast is the Isle of May. It is about three miles in circumference, and was formerly the seat of a considerable religious establishment. It is now inhabited only by the persons who attend upon the lighthouse, which was first

* It is said that a clergyman of Easter Anster, during the last century, used to say of the Magistrates of Wester Anster, that instead of their "being a terror to evil doers," evil doers were a terror to them.

built in the reign of Charles I. A fine view is obtained here of North Berwick Law, the Bass, and the coast of East Lothian. About a mile farther down the coast stands Kilrenny, another royal burgh, with a population of about 1500. The next town to the east is the burgh of CRAIL.—[*Inns:*—Dickson's Golf Inn.]—It contains about 2000 inhabitants. It was in the church of Crail that John Knox, on the 29th of May 1559, preached a sermon against popery, which so inflamed the populace, that they immediately rose, and, in a very short time, demolished all the churches in Crail, Anstruther, and the adjacent towns along the coast. Crail was famous for its *capons*, a kind of dried haddocks prepared by a peculiar mode of cookery.* The well-known Archbishop Sharpe was at one time minister of this parish. About a mile to the east of Crail is the East Neuk of Fife, which gives name to a popular Scottish air. Beyond this promontory is the Carr Rock, on which there is a beacon of iron, after rounding which the coast stretches away towards the north-west, forming the extensive bay called St. Andrew's Bay. At the bottom of this bay, on a ridge of rock projecting into the sea, stands the ancient city of St. Andrews, already described, p. 352.

* "Next from the well-air'd ancient town of Crail,
Go out her craftsmen with tumultuous din;
Her wind-bleach'd fishers sturdy-limb'd and hale;
Her in-kneed tailors garrulous and thin;
And some are flush'd with horns of pithy ale;
And some are fierce with drams of smuggled gin;
While, to augment his drouth, each to his jaws
A good Crail capon holds, at which he rugs and gnaws."

Anster Fair.

There is a strange old song called "Crail Town," of which the following are the introductory stanzas:—

"And was you e'e in Crail toun?
Igo and ago;
And saw ye there Clerk Dishington,
Sing irom igon ago.
His wig was like a doukit hen,
Igo and ago;
The tail o't like a goose pen,
Sing irom igon ago," &c.

It appears to have served as a model for Burns' lines on Captain Grose.

About two miles from St. Andrews is the estuary of the river Eden, and a short distance inland, the village of Leuchars. A little to the East of Leuchars is Tentsmoor Point, the south-eastern point of the firth of the Tay, and on the opposite shore, in Forfarshire, is Button Ness, the north-eastern point of the same estuary. There are two lighthouses on this promontory, and two others on the south shore, nearly opposite to Broughty Ferry, a village. About six miles up the Firth of Tay, on the north shore, is DUNDEE, described page 357.

About twelve miles east from this part of the coast is the famous BELL ROCK,* or Inch Cape Rock, which, from a very remote period, has been the cause of numerous shipwrecks. The top of the rock only being visible at low water, one of the abbots of Aberbrothock attached to it a frame-work and a bell, which, being rung by the waves, warned mariners to avoid the fatal reef. A tradition respecting this bell has been embodied by Dr. Southey in his ballad called "Ralph the Rover." A famous pirate of this name is said to have cut the bell from the frame-work "to plague the Abbot of Abberbrothock," and

* The following beautiful lines were written by Sir Walter Scott in the Album kept by this lighthouse, on his visit to it in the year 1815:—

PHAROS LOQUITUR.

Far on the bosom of the deep,
O'er these wild shelves my watch I keep;
A ruddy gem of changeful light,
Bound on the dusky brow of night;
The seaman bids my lustre hail,
And scorns to strike his tim'rous sail.

sometime after to have received the just punishment of his malice by being shipwrecked on the spot. An elegant lighthouse, 115 feet high, has now been erected by the Commissioners of the Northern Lighthouses at an expense of £60,000. It is one of the most prominent and serviceable beacons on the Scottish shores, and has been the means of preventing innumerable shipwrecks. About nine miles from Button Ness, is ARBROATH, described p. 425.

Leaving Arbroath, at the distance of two miles and a half, is Carlinheugh Bay, and a short way further on, Ethie House, the seat of the Earl of Northesk. About a mile beyond is the promontory of Redhead, 250 feet high. The coast now bends inward, forming the fine bay of Lunan. Six miles from Redhead is the mouth of the South Esk river, and near it the new parish church of Craig, on an elevated situation, and Rossie Castle (Horatio Ross, Esq.) On the north side of the mouth of the South Esk, twelve miles north of Arbroath, stands the royal burgh of MONTROSE, described p. 426.

About four miles and a half from Montrose, the North Esk joins the ocean, and immediately behind it commences Kincardineshire or the Mearns. The scenery along the coast is peculiarly desolate. Passing the fishing village of Milltown, and the manufacturing village of Johnshaven, is INVERBERVIE.—[*Inns:*—The Crown.] This royal burgh received its charter from David II. in 1362, on account of the kindness which the poor fishermen of Bervie displayed to him when forced to land here by stress of weather. About two miles and a half farther on are the remains of Whistleburg Castle, and, in the immediate vicinity, the church of Kinneff, beneath the pulpit of which the regalia of Scotland were concealed, when they had been secretly conveyed from Dunnottar Castle.

All along this district the coast is bold and precipitous. Upon the top of a stupendous insulated rock, 160 feet above the level of the sea, stand the ruins of the celebrated CASTLE OF DUNNOTTAR, the seat of the ancient family of the Keiths, Earls Marischal, already described, p. 428.

About a mile and a half from Dunnottar, at the mouth of a stream called the Carron, is STONEHAVEN.—[*Inns:* Melville's; The Mill.]—a seaport with a safe and commodious harbour. The remaining tract of coast demands no particular description, till the vessel reaches Aberdeen.

After leaving Aberdeen, and passing a number of fishing villages and Cruden Boy, the old castle of Slaines is seen standing on a steep precipice overlooking the sea. This fortress was destroyed in 1594, when James VI. marched north after the battle of Glenlivat, to reduce Huntly and Errol to obedience. The Errol family then removed to their present habitation, a collection of low houses forming a quadrangle, one side of which is built on the very verge of the precipice overhanging the ocean. The coast here is very rocky, but the rocks being soft, are wasted and corroded by the constant action of the waves, and the fragments which remain where the soft parts have been washed away, have assumed the appearance of old Gothic towers. In this neighbourhood is that wonder of nature, the BULLER OF BUCHAN. It is a huge rocky caldron, into which the sea rushes through a natural arch of rock. There is a path around the top which in one place is only two feet wide, with a monstrous precipice on either side. In the side of the caldron there opens a huge black cavern. In high gales the waves rush in with incredible violence, and fly over the natural wall of the Buller, which is at least two hundred feet high. Rounding the promontory of Buchanness,—the most easterly point of land in Scotland—the tourist comes in sight of the seaport of PETERHEAD.—[*Inns:* Fraser's.]—the principal whale-fishing port in the kingdom. It possesses a highly accessible, safe, and commodious harbour, and its inhabitants are remarkable for their activity and public spirit. The Chevalier St. George landed at Peterhead in the disguise of a sailor, on his fruitless expedition to Scotland in 1715. Eighteen miles north from Peterhead is FRASERBURGH.—[*Inns:*—Cruikshanks'.]—Lord Saltoun is superior and chief proprietor of this burgh of regality, which has increased in importance since the construction of a large harbour for the reception of ships of war during the last war. The old castle of Fraserburgh, now converted into a lighthouse, stands on Kinnaird-head, about a mile north of the town. Twenty-one miles from Fraserburgh is the capital of the county and royal burgh of

BANFF.

[*Inns:*—The Banff Hotel, built by the Earl of Fife's Trustees; Cassie's Inn.]

At the distance of a mile, on the opposite bank of the Deveron, is the modern village and seaport of Macduff. In the immediate neighbourhood is Duff House, the magnificent mansion of the Earl of Fife, surrounded by extensive plantations. The park is fourteen miles in circumference. About a century ago Banff was the scene of the execution of a noted robber, named Macpherson, whose "farewell" has been made the subject of a spirited song by Burns.

About seven miles from Banff is Portsoy, a small irregularly built town, with a thriving port. A few miles farther is the royal burgh of Cullen, where the Queen of Robert Bruce died, and was buried in the eastern aisle in the old church. Behind the town is Cullen House, the splendid mansion of the Earl of Seafield. It contains a valuable collection of paintings. The other towns round the coast are Garmouth, a neat modern town on the left bank of the Spey; Burghead, a thriving seaport with a considerable trade in ship-building and herring fishing; and the county town and royal burgh of NAIRN.—[*Inns:*—Anderson's.] —After leaving Aberdeen the Orkney steamer does not touch at any intervening place till it reaches WICK.— [*Inns:* The Caledonian; The Wellington.]—Wick, a royal burgh, and the county town of Caithness, is the principal seat of the herring fishery in the north of Scotland.

After leaving Wick, the steamer proceeds to Kirkwall, the principal town in the ORKNEY ISLANDS. The Orkney and Shetland Islands lie in two groups to the north of Scotland, and form between them a county which returns a member to Parliament. The former, which are the most southerly, are separated from the county of Caithness by the Pentland Firth, which is about six miles broad. Their number is estimated at sixty-seven, of which twenty-seven are inhabited. They comprise an area of about 281,600 acres, and their population, in 1831, amounted to 28,847. The more important islands are about twelve in number, of which Pomona, or the Mainland, is decidedly the largest. Kirkwall, the chief town, contains upwards of 3000 inhabitants. Kirkwall is distant from Edinburgh 241 miles by sea. The most important public building is St. Magnus's Cathedral, a stately pile, which was founded about the year 1138. Under the direction of government, the building has undergone a thorough repair. Many ancient relics have been dug up, and deposited in Kirkwall Museum. Adjoining the Cathedral are the ruins of the Bishop's Palace and of the Earl's Palace, built by the infamous Patrick Stewart, who obtained the earldom in 1600. A pleasant walk may be made to the west, passing Grainbank, the property of Lord Dundas, to Quanterness, at the base of Wideford Hill, where there is a Pict's house. If the day be fine and clear, the traveller should walk up the hill. The ascent is easy, and the view from the *wart* very beautiful. Descending, on the west side, to the road leading to the town, the tourist may take the road to the right leading to Scalpa Bay, distant one mile. To the east the tourist may take another walk by Daisy Bank and Mavis Bank (James Spence, Esq.) to the Braes of Setter, along to the Braes of Bairston (at the top of the fine small bay of Bairston is the seat of Lieutenant William Balfour), and return to Kirkwall by the way of Papdale, a finely situated house, and lately the residence of Samuel Laing, Esq., author of "Scenes in Norway and Sweden." There are three good inns in the town—Kemp's, Brotchie's, and M'Donald's.

EXCURSION FROM KIRKWALL.

1. To the North Isles of Orkney.

Take boat to Shapinshay, three miles. The island is seven miles long, and about three miles broad, and is the property of David Balfour, Esq. The southern portion is well cultivated. On the shore, opposite Stronsay, is a mass of stone, named the Black Stone of Odin. Cross Stronsay Firth, six miles, to the

Island of Stronsay.

This island is about six miles in breadth, and, from its general flatness, is pretty well farmed. It contains a number of Picts' houses. At Whiteball is the first and principal herring-fishing station. At the north side lies the beautiful small island of Papa Stronsay, containing the ruins of two chapels. From this cross to the

Island of Sanday (a distance of Three Miles).

This island is about twelve miles long, and of irregular breadth, and, except at the west side, very flat. The soil is sandy, but fertile, and well cultivated. The farmers are of the better class, and intelligent. There is a good inn at Castlehill. About eight miles from the inn is the Start Point Lighthouse. At Tofts take the ferry to the

Island of North Ronaldshay (a distance of Two Miles).

This is a small flat-lying island, sloping gently down from the middle to the shores on either side. The soil is fertile. Return to Sanday, and cross to the

Island of Eday (Three Miles).

This island is about six miles long, and two or more broad. Although generally hilly, and abounding with peat-moss, there are two or three good farms on the island. The celebrated pirate Gow was captured here. Cross over to Rapuess, in the

Island of Westray (Five Miles).

This island is about nine miles long, and one to four broad. The soil rich. The west side is precipitous and rocky. At Rapness is a cave which afforded shelter to some Orkney gentlemen who joined in the Rebellion of 1745. Walk to Pierowall, five miles, where there is an inn. In the vicinity is Noltland Castle, built for the reception of Bothwell. At the north-east is the small island of Papa Westray, the seat of Thomas Traill, Esq. Cross Westray Firth (seven miles) to the

Island of Rowsay,

Four miles long, and three broad, a fine hilly island, very suitable for sheep walks. One the south side is Westness, the seat of William Traill, Esq., and in the vicinity the ruins of an ancient castle. Cross the small sound of Enhallow to Evie, on the Mainland. Walk to

Rendall, six miles, and cross the beautiful Bay of Firth to Kirkwall, a distance of three miles.

2. From Kirkwall to Westmainland and South Isles.

Take the mail-gig to Firth, seven miles. Walk three miles to Harray, on the east side of the Loch of Stennis. Six miles northwards is Birsay, where the ruins of a palace once the seat of the Earls of Orkney, are beautifully situated. Several lakes are in the neighbourhood. Returning four miles southwards by the coast is Sandwick. The country here is generally bleak looking, although interspersed with some well-cultivated farms. Two miles onward is Skeal House, the residence of William Graham Watt, Esq., and two miles further, Loch of Stennis. The remarkable standing stones here are inferior only to those at Stonehenge. The circle on the west side of the loch is about 360 feet in diameter, formed by a broad ditch on the outside, and on the inside by a range of standing stones, from twelve to sixteen feet high, and four broad. On the east border of the loch is a semicircle 96 feet in diameter, which was formed with stones of larger dimensions. There are several other stones placed irregularly. After a walk of three miles, we again join the main road at

Stromness,

A burgh of barony, very irregularly built, each proprietor having apparantly planted his house to suit his own convenience. It is the chief shipping port of the county. There are two good inns (Flett's and Paterson's). From thence cross by Hoymouth to the

Island of Hoy,

About twelve miles long, and five broad. The hills of Hoy are the highest in Orkney. On one of them is the celebrated "Dwarfie Stone." The climate is considered very healthy. On the southern portion of the island is Melster House, the residence of John Heddle, Esq. Passing the parish of Walls and village of Longhope, cross a small sound to

Flotta,

A small island, with a bold rocky shore, the interior part of which alone is suited for pasture. Crossing three miles to the fishing village of Herston, in the Island of South Ronaldshay, and taking a boat across Wideswell Bay, a walk of about two miles brings us to the

the village of St. Margaret's Hope, where there are two inns (Laird's and Allan's). At the How of Hoxa is a stronghold of great antiquity. At St. Margaret's Hope the traveller may either join the north mail, cross Watersound, walk across Burray, about two miles (a fine dry island, soil sandy), to the ferry-house, and then cross Holm Sound to Holm, walk eight miles to Kirkwall, and return south by either of the steamers; or he may join the south mail, cross the Pentland Firth to Huna, and, proceeding to Wick, get the steamer there.

The SHETLAND or ZETLAND ISLES, supposed to be the *Ultima Thule* of the ancients, are separated from the Orkneys by a channel 48 miles across. They exceed 100 in number, but of these only

Cradle of Noss.

between 30 and 40 are inhabited. "The climate," says Dr. Edmonstone, a native of one of the islands, "is very variable and damp, although by no means generally unwholesome to the inhabitants. Spring can scarcely be said to commence until April, and there is but little general warmth before the middle of June. The summer terminates for the most part with August, though sometimes it continues through September. Autumn is a very uncertain period, and winter commences with the middle of October, and occupies the remaining months of the year." Lerwick, which is the capital, contains about 2700 inhabitants. In the Lowlands it would be only entitled to the name of a thriving village, very irregularly built. "The opposite island of Bressay forms Bressav Sound, one of the finest harbours in the world, and the rendezvous of all the vessels destined for the north and the whale fishery. Off Bressay is the most remarkable of the rock phenomena of Shetland; the Noss, a small high island, with a flat summit, girt on all sides by perpendicular walls of rock."* It is only 500 feet in length, and 170 broad, and rises abruptly from the sea to the height of 160 feet. The communication with the coast of Bressay is maintained by strong ropes stretched across, along which a cradle or wooden chair is run, in which the passenger is seated. It is of a size sufficient for conveying across a man and a sheep at a time. The purpose of this strange contrivance is to give the tenant the benefit of putting a few sheep upon the Holm, the top of which is level, and affords good pasture. The animals are transported in the cradle, one at a time, a shepherd holding them upon his knees in crossing.

"The temptation of getting access to the numberless eggs and young of the sea-fowl which whiten the surface of the Holm, joined to the promised reward of a cow, induced a hardy and adventurous fowler, about two centuries ago, to scale the cliff of the Holm, and establish a connexion by ropes with the neighbouring main island. Having driven two stakes into the rock and fastened his ropes, the desperate man was entreated to avail himself of the communication thus established in returning across the gulf. But this he refused to do, and in attempting to descend the way he had climbed, he fell, and perished by his fool-hardiness."†

In August 1841, Mr. James Wilson and Sir Thomas Dick Lauder crossed the yawning chasm in the cradle above described. The cut with which our text is illustrated represents the adventurers on their aerial journey. The downward view into the gulph below, while thev hung suspended over the abyss, is described by Mr. Wilson as being singularly impressive.‡

* MURRAY'S *Encyclopedia of Geography.* Lond. 1834.

† ANDERSON'S *Guide to the Highlands,* p. 81.

‡ A Voyage round the Coasts of Scotland and the Isles. By James Wilson, F.R.S.E. Vol. ii., pp. 289-298.

There are scarcely any roads in Shetland, and travelling is usually performed on those hardy, spirited little horses, known by the name of *shelties*, which are bred in Shetland, and are exported in considerable numbers.

The trade and exports of Shetland are much the same as those of Orkney. These islands formerly belonged to the kingdom of Denmark, but, in 1468, on the marriage of James III. with the Princess Margaret of Denmark, they were given in pledge for the payment of her dowry, and have never since been disjoined from Scotland. They were at various times bestowed by the Crown on different persons, some of whom subjected the inhabitants to great oppressions. At length in 1707, James Earl of Morton obtained the greater part of them from the Crown in mortgage, which was rendered irredeemable in 1742, and in 1766 he sold the estate for £60,000 to Sir Lawrence Dundas, the ancestor of the Earl of Zetland, their present proprietor.

NINETEENTH TOUR.

ABERDEEN TO THE HIGHLANDS OF DEESIDE, BALMORAL, AND THE CAIRNGORM MOUNTAINS.

On leaving Aberdeen there are two routes as far as Upper Banchory—one on the north, the other on the south side of the Dee. The latter is sometimes adopted by pedestrians and horsemen, but the former is the usual turnpike road, and is not only the shorter but the more interesting of the two in its command of prospect. Opposite the third mile there is the kirk and village of Banchory Devenick on the south bank of the river; and a little farther on is a bridge across the river, built at the private expense of Dr. Morison, the clergyman of the parish, for the use of his parishioners. For several miles after leaving the town there is a succession of small patches of landed property with handsome houses, generally having lawns and pleasure grounds sloping towards the river. Near the sixth milestone, on the south bank, is the Roman Catholic College of Blairs, endowed by the munificent Mr. Menzies of Pitfodels. In its close vicinity the churches of Mary Culter and Peter Culter front each other—the former on the south, the latter on the north side of the river. A little farther on, the road, descending into a ravine, crosses the burn of Culter by a massive stone bridge. The banks are steep and wooded, and refreshing to the tourist's eye, as the first specimen of picturesquely broken ground which he passes on this jaunt. On a bare flat heathy hill, of slight elevation, between this spot and the Dee, the antiquarian will find an object of considerable interest in an undoubted Roman camp in good preservation. It is called Norman Dikes, (supposed to be a corruption of Roman Dikes.) A minute account of it will be found in Chalmers' Caledonia. It has been maintained to be the site of the Roman town and station of Devana, but the ramparts, which are distinctly traceable, are neither in their size nor strength such as to justify the supposition that the Romans had a permanent station within them. In a wooded elevation to the north-east of Norman Dikes there is an oblong space, enclosed by a rampart, which, however, from its irregular construction, appears to be of British origin. It is called Kemp (viz. Camp) Hill. Apropos to this subject, it may be mentioned that the antiquary will find, a

ABERDEEN, BALLATER, BRAEMAR, GLEN TILT, BLAIR ATHOLL.

Drawn & Engd. by J. Bartholomew, Edinr.

Edinburgh, Published July 1. 1846 by Adam & Charles Black 27 North Bridge.

few miles to the north-west, in the vicinity of Skene, one of the most remarkable fortified remains in existence. It consists of five concentric ramparts of stone, enclosing the summit of a steep conical hill, which, in reference to these works, is called the Barmekyne (viz. Barbican) of Echt. The outside ring is nearly a mile in circumference, and the inmost encloses about an acre of level land; after toiling up the steep ascent which leads to it, one is astonished by the traces of the mechanical skill, energy, and patience, which must have been combined in the construction of works so gigantic on such a spot. The whole of this neighbourhood bears traces of ancient and long-forgotten conflict. There are many minor fortifications and camps, and the peasantry frequently turn up flint spear and arrow heads of exquisite proportion and finish, remnants of an ancient and partial civilization, that must have passed away long before the commencement of Scottish history.

At the tenth mile is the house or castle of Drum, (Alex. Irvine, Esq.) boldly looking out from a noble hill slope among scattered forest trees. The most remarkable part of the building is the old keep or donjon, a massive square tower, with rounded corners, which looks as if it had been built to give battle to earthquakes. The walls are twelve feet thick, and thus, though the outside circumference is considerable, the interior merely consists of a small gloomy vaulted chamber in each floor. The family of Drum is of considerable antiquity, and great fame in local history. It is the subject of a multitude of traditions, the more striking of which concern a long deadly feud with the Keith family, and the great battle of Harlaw. A little beyond the tenth mile are Mains of Drum Inn and Drumoak Church and Manse. Opposite the eleventh mile-stone there is, on the south bank of the river, the House of Durris, (Anthony Mactier, Esq.) and a little farther on the Kirk of Durris, or, as it is pronounced in the vicinity, Dores. On the north side of the river, and between it and the road, is Park House, (A. Kinloch, Esq.) a somewhat more dapper and villa looking edifice than the majority of the Deeside buildings. About the 15th mile, Crathes Castle, (Sir Robert Burnett of Leys, Bart.) looks majestically forth from a sloping mass of thick woodland. It is one of those old Flemish buildings which, rising as it were from a solid root and stem, becomes, as it ascends, broken into a varied picturesque cluster of turrets, chimneys, and peaked gables. There are, unfortunately, some modern additions sadly out of keeping with the picturesque character of the older part. Here, as at Drum, there is abundant traditionary lore, both in prose and song.*

At eighteen miles from Aberdeen is the village of Banchory Ternan, or

* Of the latter, there is a somewhat humorous ballad, called "The Baron of Leys," in which a hopeful heir of the family, having got inveigled in some foreign liaison, is represented as mystifying the object of his affections on the

UPPER BANCHORY,

[*Inns:*—The Burnett Arms.]

the first of the genuine pleasure-trip places at Deeside. It enjoys a considerable share of the beauties of water, wood, and mountain. The older part of the village consists of venerable sturdy gloomy houses, that have been built for genuine residenters, and to suit the humours of no capricious city lodger. The newer part contains several stylish "boxes," with gardens, and neat lodging-houses. A new Gothic church, in good taste, terminating the steep bank of the river, along which the straggling village runs, gives a finished landscape air to the whole. The Dee is here joined by the Feugh, an angry moss-stained stream, which comes thundering down from the Braes of Angus, lashing its black waters into foam, as it quarrels with the surly rocks. Near its junction it crosses a stony barrier, where, after a succession of broken foaming torrents and inky pools, it casts itself over the brow of a rock, and makes a stormy cascade—its last act of independent turbulence, before its troublesome spirit is subdued by intermixture with the more dignified and placid waters of the Dee. Looking up in the direction whence this stream runs, the traveller will see the broken outline of the hills from which its waters are supplied, and towering above the others is the characteristic summit of Cloch-na-ben, with a great stone like a gigantic wart projecting from its brow. Four miles north from the village is the Hill of Fare, wide and flat, and not very elevated, presenting little attraction to the searcher after the romantic. A hollow on the north side, however, is not unfrequently visited, from its being the battlefield of Corrichie, where Murray and Huntly fought in 1562, under the eye of Queen Mary. A small fountain near the spot is called Queen Mary's Well. In a densely wooded recess on the northern declivity of this hill rises an oriental looking cluster of turrets, forming the mansion or castle of Midmar.

subject of his identity, by successively representing himself as the proprietor of very grotesque and unreasonable names. The dialogue proceeds thus:—

"Some ca's me this, some ca's me that,
Whatever may best befa' me;
But when I'm in Scotland's King's high court,
Clatter-the-speens they ca' me.

"O waes me now, O Clatter the Speens,
And alas! that ever I saw thee;
For I'm in love, sick sick in love,
And I kenna well fat to ca' thee.

"Some ca's me this, some ca's me that,
I carena what they ca' me;
But when wi' the Earl o' Murray I ride,
Its Scour-the-Braes they ca' me.

"O waes me now, O Scour the Braes," &c.

A little more than a mile beyond Banchory, on the south bank, is the modern castellated mansion of Blackball, (Colonel Campbell,) a parkish looking place, with a long wide avenue, bordered by magnificent trees. On the north bank is Inchmarlo, (D. Davidson, Esq.) About a mile farther on is Woodend Cottage, peeping from a plantation sloping finely to the Dee. At the 24th mile is the Brig of Potarch, where the old south and north road, still used by drovers, crosses to the Cairn o'Mont, Fetter Cairn, and Brechin.* The Dee where it is spanned by this bridge, is hurried between two rocks, which leave a space only of twenty feet for its ample waters. According to Mr. James Brown's Guide Book—of which anon—a caird, or gipsey, called John Young, pursued for murder, escaped, by leaping this wild chasm.† Twenty-six miles from Aberdeen is the village of KINCARDINE O'NEIL.—[*Inns:*—The Gordon Arms.]—Here we could not have wished the traveller better fortune than to find the worthy Mrs. Gordon still presiding over her well-conditioned inn, venerable in the administration of hospitalities, from which the profuseness and cheapness seemed to remove all mercenary character. Mrs. G. has, we understand, retired from her important duties; and we doubt not her successor will feel a stimulus in the ambition to rival so distinguished a predecessor. This remote locality is connected with one of the most remarkable incidents in Scottish history. The pursuit and death of Macbeth, transferred to Perthshire by Boece and the other fabulous annalists whom Shakspeare read, took place, according to the earlier and more credible chroniclers, in the vicinity of Kincardine. Wynton says,

"And ower the mownth thai chast hym than
Til the wode of Lunfanan.
* * *
This Macbeth slewe thai there
Into the wode of Lunfanan,
And his hewyd thai strak off thare,
And that wyth thame fra thair thai bare
Til Kynkardyn, quhare the King
Till thare gayne come made byding."

* If any one wishes to experiment on a really old-fashioned Scottish country inn, equally unknown to tourists and commercial travellers, we would recommend him to the hostel of Cuttles-Hilloc on this road, should it still remain the respectable relic of former hospitality which we remember it to have been but a few years ago.

† Young was a man of many feats in Aberdeenshire story, and is the same to whom was attributed the bold practical joke of releasing all the prisoners in the jail of Aberdeen, (himself included,) and placarding the door with the advertisement "ROOMS TO LET."

It is a singular coincidence between tradition and history, that in the sterile valley of Lumphanan, some miles to the north, where Shakspeare, Boece, and Wynton, are alike unknown, and where neither tourist nor antiquary has taught the simple inhabitants to drive a trade in associating their neighbourhood with great events, a small mound of stones still bears the name of Cairn-beth. The neighbourhood, like that mentioned a little above, is rife with the reliques of ancient warfare. There are several remains of fortification on the hills, and weapons of rude workmanship have frequently been turned up by the plough.*

A little below the twenty-seventh mile-stone the road crosses a stream, on which, some 200 yards or so up, will be found a small cataract called the Slog of Dess. The Parliamentary Road to Bridge of Alford and Huntly here strikes off to the right. 31 miles from Aberdeen is Charleston of ABOYNE.--[*Inns:* The Huntly Arms.]--This village is surrounded by wide stretches of forest land and picturesquely broken ground. Aboyne Castle, one of the seats of the Marquis of Huntly, rears its many heads from the woods on the right. It is an irregular structure, built apparently at different periods, and though imposing in size, scarcely to be characterised as either picturesque or elegant. After leaving the shady woods of Aboyne, the traveller enters a wild and desolate heath, called the Muir of Dinnet, a sort of debateable land, separating the Highlands from the Lowlands, where, to beguile the time, he may speculate on the character of the population he has been passing through. He will have remarked, that on Deeside there are few large farms, and that where the land can be termed fertile, the crofters' and small farmers' houses are numerous. If he be a pedestrian, he will have had many opportunities of personal intercourse with the swains who cultivate these patches, and after he has mastered their energetic northern dialect, will have found them to be a shrewd, civil, and independently courteous people. Interviews are spoken of as a thing that must, in the ordinary course of circumstances, take place, for no man can walk Deeside without either committing a woful breach of etiquette, or

* In the parish of Leochel, immediately adjacent, is the Castle of Craigievar, (Sir John Forbes, Bart.,) a grim old Flemish building, suited to the character of the place, and worth mentioning were it only for the expressive motto in large and very legible characters over the heavy door-way of the keep,

"DO NOT WAKEN SLEEPIN DOUGS."

exchanging courtesies with those he meets. Nor, however humble may be the peasant who says "a fine day," and perhaps offers his "sneeshun mull," will much servility be found in his deportment. There is, in fact, an independence of demeanour in these worthy fellows, which, backed by their energetic accent, has a somewhat repulsive appearance to strangers ; yet, from the genuine kindness met at every turn, wherever there is an opportunity to call it forth, such a feeling must soon disappear. The hospitalities of the Deeside peasantry are, however, by no means of the kind which would generally be called refined in high life. As an illustration of their courtesies, it is said that a weary pedestrian from Aberdeen, who had lost his way, and was kindly provided with a night's lodging, was not a little astonished in stepping out of bed to find himself up to the knees in water—the night had been rainy. On appearing before his entertainers, in a pitiable plight, and representing to them that such an inroad of the element in such a quarter was an uncommon event, which required some peculiar explanation, he met the excuse justificative in these terms, "Oh, man, you surely forgot to look for the stappin' stons."

To the north of the Muir of Dinnet lies the district of Cromar and the village of Tarland. The highest summit in this direction is the Hill of Morven, round, and somewhat flat in its outline ; and a glimpse is just caught from the road of a pretty sedgy sheet of water, called the Loch of Kinnord. The monotony of the progress through the dreary muir is gradually relieved by the opening prospect of the hills, which rise, terrace above terrace, like mounds thrown up for an audience of Titans. Highest of all, a long gracefully waving outline, bending on either side from a sharp peak, characterises the mountain monarch of the district, Lochnagar. If the atmosphere be clear, the line of precipice which constitutes its eastern wall may be seen from summit to base, clear and smooth ; but most generally it suits not the monarch to unveil his fearful beauties, and a mass of black cloud hovers round his summit, within whose mysterious folds proceeds the manufacture of elemental wrath. As the traveller approaches closer to the base of the series of mountain terraces, he perceives a little fertile plain reposing beneath their huge shadows, and edged by the clear waters of the Dee. When the eye is sufficiently accustomed to the large masses by which it is surrounded to detect minuter objects, a small spire may be seen rising very distinct from the plain, round it curls a light smoke, indicative of the dwelling of human beings, and finally, rows of small houses, like so many pebbles that might have rolled from the hills, come into distinct view. This is the village of

BALLATER.

[*Inns*:—The Monaltrie Arms.]

Ballater, forty-two miles from Aberdeen, is a very important place, the Tunbridge Wells and the Keswick of Aberdeenshire, where people resort both to drink the waters and to rove among hills. It has an excellent inn, where there is, or used to be, an ordinary—a shop or two of all wares, a baker, butcher, tailor, and shoemaker, a parish school, manse, lodge, and post-office, besides a commodious church.* The Dee, in its immediate vicinity, was formerly crossed

* To the useful little work called "the Guide to Deeside," by James Brown, formerly car-man on Dee-side, and now, we believe, gardener in the Botanical Garden of Edinburgh, we have, on several occasions, trusted in the above sketch for the spelling of names, or for distances, when our own memory or notes happened to be at fault. We cannot avoid here quoting his description of Ballater, which is in his best and most emphatic manner.

"As Aberdeen is the chief town of the shire, so Ballater is the capital or metropolis of Deeside, an honour which in every respect it is well worthy to enjoy. Though Ballater and Aberdeen are both chief towns, it is altogether out of the question to compare them together in respect of size, number of inhabitants, or stateliness of buildings—for Aberdeen is the capital of a whole shire, with hills, valleys, muirs, and plains, altogether unspeakable, while Ballater is but the metropolis of one single valley, with its parts and pertinents. Surely, therefore, it is a vain thing to think that Ballater should be a town any thing like so large as Aberdeen, or yet so well built; but this I will say, that Ballater, for the extent of ground to which it is the renowned metropolis, is in proportion little behind Aberdeen. As for grandeur and beauty of situation there is no comparison whatsoever—the stance on which Aberdeen stands being just as much inferior to the stance on which Ballater stands, as the Broadhill of the Links is inferior to Lochnagar or Ben-Muick-dhui. And farther, I will take upon me to say, that in point of renown Ballater is very little, if any thing, inferior to Aberdeen—its fame as a fashionable watering place being spread far and wide to the uttermost corners of the earth, as may be known by the number of strangers coming to see it from all parts of the world, and among others from the Isle of Skye and the Cape of Good Hope. As for pleasantness and agreeableness, every one must admit that Ballater has the advantage, else why do such numbers of Aberdeen people leave their homes there and come out here every summer to take up their abode—while few or none of the Ballater people ever visit Aberdeen, except upon urgent business?—a thing which can be accounted for in no way whatever but by allowing Ballater is out of all sight a much more agreeable and pleasant town to dwell in than Aberdeen. What with many Aberdonians is a matter of great reproach to Ballater is, that its steeple is only a timber steeple; but the Ballaterians have no reason to be ashamed of their steeple, and the Aberdonians in objecting to it only show that they can see their neighbour's faults but not their own—for it is perfectly noto-

by a fine stone bridge, which being destroyed by the floods of 1829, has been replaced by a structure partly of wood. The ostensible object of the Ballater visiters (the medicinal wells) are at a spot called Pananich, about two miles to the east, on the south side of the river. Their virtues are long famed in Highland tradition, and bring multitudes from the far off hills to partake of their healing influence; and if the water, unadulterated by any artificial admixture, produced all the joviality that may be witnessed among the groups that sometimes congregate round the brinks of the wells in a sunny evening, it would probably acquire a still more extensive reputation.

From Ballater there are many pleasing detours. The first task of the visiter is invariably to climb Craigendarroch (the rock of oaks), a steep round knob, about the height of Arthur Seat, *i. e.* 800 feet, and rising right up from the village. Its celebrity consists in a rather uncommon qualification to be applied to a hill—its smallness. It is, in fact, the lowest hill in the vicinity that one can get satisfactorily to the top of; and it is many a one's sole premises for the satisfactory conclusion of being "able to say" he has climbed a Highland hill. It is, in this respect, a valuable appendage to Ballater; but it is not without its own merits: the view is magnificent, and few so wide and varied can be purchased with so small an expenditure of climbing. Immediately at its foot is Ballater Cottage, belonging to Mr. Farquharson. To the north, Craigendarroch is separated from a loftier ridge of rock by a precipitous chasm called "The Pass of Ballater." Another rocky hill, about four miles from the village, is frequently scaled, not so much for its own intrinsic merit, perhaps, as because Byron said of it,

> "When I see some dark hill point its crest to the sky,
> I think of the rocks that o'ershadow Culbleen."

From like associations, the farm-house of Ballatrich on the south side

rious that some of the steeples of Aberdeen are timber as well as the Ballater steeple—from which they differ in no respect except that they are covered with lead, and have clocks, which it must be confessed Ballater steeple has not. Nevertheless, for all that, it is as excellent a steeple as any body need wish to look at, and if not covered with lead, is so curiously painted, that it looks just as well as if it were real stone. Indeed, many of those who now scoff at it, at first mistook it for stone. As for other things with which Aberdeen people taunt the Ballaterians—saying that they have no fine streets, or noble buildings, or stately bridges, such as Aberdeen has, we can show hills and mountains, and woods and valleys, and rocks and lochs, with which Aberdeen has nothing to compare, and which every one will allow are much better worth looking at than any streets, bridges, or buildings any where in the whole world, not to speak of Aberdeen. So much for the comparison which has been made between Ballater and Aberdeen."

of the river, where Byron lived, " rude as the rocks where his infancy grew," is often visited. But a spot worthy of admiration on its own account, for ages before the bard existed, and which will continue so when he is forgotten—if the land be inhabited when that comes to pass, is another object of his Highland muse—Lochnagar. From Ballater to the summit is considered about ten miles; but miles where there is no turnpike are terribly long in the Highlands. Those who are not accustomed to hard walking should take Highland ponies with them, and all should make it a day's work, choosing a clear one for the purpose. In itself, the ascent is a stony, boggy, toilsome business; but to all who can admire a run of precipice, varying from 1200 to 900 feet high, with a cold inky lake at its base, and the gorgeous prospect of half Scotland spread below, the toil will not seem misspent. The summit is 3800 feet above the level of the sea. It has been only on a few very warm summers that the snow has ever entirely deserted Lochnagar, and considerable fields of it are generally to be seen in midsummer; it is much prized by knowing tourists as an ingredient in iced grog. Another detour from Ballater is to the Linn and Loch of Muick. This stream joins the Dee at Ballater, and the traveller has but to keep by its rocky banks, along which there is a tolerable road. At the Linn, the Muick, in a considerable body, hurls itself over a precipice into a black hopeless-looking pool. The loch is a considerable sheet of water, but somewhat sombre in its scenery, except in certain spots, where, over its rounded banks, the precipices of Lochnagar may be seen frowning grim and close. The adventurous traveller should not be content with Loch Muick, but ought to ascend a stream at its upper extremity, by which, after passing some miles of wildly broken ground, where cataracts start as it were every now and then at his feet, he will be led to the Dhu Loch, a smaller lake than that of Muick, but incomparably grander in its scenery,—its banks, except where the stream issues, being a circumvallation of huge black precipices, on the same scale with those of Lochnagar. A journey from Ballater of considerable labour, but much interest, is across Mont Keen, (3180 feet above the sea,) to Lochlee, in the Braes of Angus, classical as the residence of Alexander Ross, the author of the Fortunate Shepherdess. The southern descent of Mont Keen is by a serried mass of stones, like a ruined stair-case, not unaptly called " the Ladder," and its descent brings the traveller to a succession of wild narrow broken glens, noisy with a succession of waterfalls, which at last open on the pastoral valley of the North Esk and the pretty lake of Lochlee. It is right to mention that this is a path by which Ballater and the Highlands of Deeside may be reached from the south by way of

Brechin. One more object of interest to be mentioned before we leave Ballater is the Burn of the Vat, so termed from its perforating diagonally a huge natural well of perpendicular rock. The visiter creeps through the channel of the burn by a narrow stony orifice, and looks up astonished through this Barclay-and-Perkins looking freak of nature to the clear heavens, with nothing to interrupt the circular smoothness of the rocks but some birch trees in invisible fissures, that hang from the height like little tendrils.

There are two roads from Ballater up the Dee, one on the north, the other on the south bank—the former is generally preferred. It will be remarked, that the mile-stones on it, (where any happen to remain,) calculated direct from Aberdeen by the old road through the pass, make no allowance for a divergence of a mile and a half at Ballater. Sweeping round Craigendarroch, the water of Gairn is crossed at a point about equidistant from Aberdeen with Ballater. About a mile farther on, on the north side, is Craig Youzie (the rock of firs,) a round knob, something like Craigendarroch. About the forty-fifth mile is a pristine Highland Clachan, not yet brushed up by tourists, called the Micras. Rather more than a mile farther on is Abergeldie Castle (M. F. Gordon, Esq.,) with an old turreted square tower and some modern additions of various dates,—a formidable place in the rieving days, when it was held that

"He should take who had the power,
And he should keep who can."

Hitherto the traveller will have observed the birch trees thickening as he proceeds, and here he will find them at their climax of dense luxuriance and beauty, covering almost every spot, save where the broad river sweeps along the bottom of the glen, or the hills carry their broken rocky heads to the clouds. Abergeldie owes no good turn to Burns, who finding it worthily possessed of the old air of "the Birks of Abergeldie," with the despotism of genius, transferred its leafy honours, without a moment's warning, to his nearer neighbour Aberfeldy. About a mile farther on are two localities respectively bearing the expressive denominations of "The Thief's Pot" and "The Gallow's Hill." These classic spots are held sacred to the memory of that great effort of political subordination and marital affection which prompted the high-souled Highland spouse to say to her rebellious husband, "Get up, John, and be hanged, and dinna anger the laird;" but, as in the case of other heroic acts, Deeside is not without competitors for this honour.

On the north side of the river, between the forty-eighth and forty-ninth mile-stones, are the kirk, manse, school, and post-office of Crathie. Nearly opposite the manse, the river is crossed by an elegant suspension bridge, which conducts the tourist to Crathie Bridge, a pretty little village or clachan, consisting of about twenty cottages, of a class somewhat superior to what might be looked for in this wild and lonely locality. About a quarter of a mile west from this village is

BALMORAL CASTLE,

the Scottish summer residence of her Majesty. The vale or deli in which it stands, is formed by a circumvallation of "the everlasting hills," being, really,

"With rock-wall encircl'd, with precipice crown'd."

To use an apposite Shaksperian word, it is almost completely "circummured" with majestic mountains, by which it is bisectod or severed into two several straths. The southern section, more spacious than the other, is, in superficial shape, a wooded haugh, or natural platform, sloping gently from under the shade of Craig-an-gowan's shaggy side down to the margin of the meandering and sparkling Dee, along which it forms a pleasant, park-like meadow. The other, or opposite section, is a bosky bank, rising abruptly from the rushing tide of the river in the depth of the dell, and anon blending with the steep northern battlement of hills. From the castle, whithersoever the eye is directed, it catches glimpses of the most enchanting scenery, in which the beautiful blends with the sublime, and the picturesque rises to the romantic. Eastward, the view is bounded by Craig-an-darrach (the rock of oaks), and by the precipitous chasm called the Pass of Ballater; westward, beyond the military road from Braemar to Fort-George, which winds by the hoary Cairn-na-cuimhne, may be got some glorious glimpses of the pine-clad haughs of Invercauld; southward, the wearied eye reposes on the soft and fragrant foliage of the birks of Craig-an-gowan, and, northward,

"Dee's silver stream rolls his swift waters near,
Gilt with the golden sunbeams here and there,"

with a hundred heathery hill-tops—a "dark ocean of mountains behind." The prospect all around, instead of being merely beautiful, becomes truly sublime, when we look from the shore of the river up to the distant hills; and the eye is relieved by beholding the immediate and intervening objects, namely, the natural woods on the skirts of the mountains, up to the point where terminates the woody region—a point which, in this latitude, is elevated about

2000 feet above the sea-level. Such, then, is this wild sequestered glen of Balmoral—such is the site of its castle—such are the picturesque beauties of its vicinity. In all our romantic land there is, probably, no region in which the "sublime and beautiful" are more harmoniously and happily blended, than in the environs of the secluded haugh which her Majesty has selected as the site of her Highland Home.

Balmoral Castle is the property of the Earl of Fife, and, previous to its occupation by her Majesty, was held on lease by the late Sir Robert Gordon, brother of the Earl of Aberdeen. The reversion of the lease has been acquired by Prince Albert; and, from being a snug shooting lodge—a long and steep-roofed, high-gabled, small-windowed house—it has, by numerous and various additions, in the form of turrets and erections of almost all shapes and sizes, expanded into a very extensive edifice; and, from being the residence of a retired baronet, has been, unexpectedly, exalted to the dignity of a Palace-Royal. It is an irregular, chateau-like structure, with a venerable Flemish expression about it. Though its dimensions be, of course, dwarfed by the majestic scale of the surrounding scenery, yet the umbrageous, embowering trees by which it is environed, serve, by screening it here and there from the view, to enlarge its extent considerably in appearance. It can be referred to none of the recognised orders of architecture, but is a square-shaped, immethodical mass, or congeries, of successive erections, consisting of towers and turrets, chimneys and peaked gables, built at different periods, as fancy dictated, or increasing wants demanded—and thus presenting a variety of features which, though sufficiently unimposing when viewed separately, produce, when combined in groups, an effect akin to picturesque grandeur. In the recent additions above mentioned, the windows are of proper size, and the rooms good, but still by no means adequate to the requirements of a Court circle. Further additions and improvements are, however, in progress, for the due accommodation of her Majesty and suite. The region around Balmoral comprehends the best deer-stalking and grouse-shooting, with lake and river fishing, in all Scotland, but is subject to the disadvantage of heavy autumnal rains, being on the line of the loftiest Grampian range. The district is about as secluded as Badenoch. Two routes connect it with Perthshire: one through Glen Tilt, from which the present Duke of Atholl unwarrantably attempts to exclude the public; the other by the Spital of Glenshee. The latter was traversed by her Majesty (after visiting Ireland), on taking up her residence at Balmoral in August 1849.

On the 6th September 1850, her Majesty and Prince Albert, accompanied by the eldest son of Prince Leiningen and the Marchioness of Douro, and attended by a few gillies, made an excursion from Balmoral to the summit of Ben-a-bourd. The party started at an early hour in the forenoon, and drove up the south side of the Dee to the Bridge of Invercauld, by which they crossed the river, and after passing up the opposite side for a couple of miles, alighted from their carriages at the Slogan burn. They then mounted ponies, and ascended the Slogan by an excellent pony tract, which carried them up a shoulder of the hill to within about a mile of the top, where the mountain becoming steep and rugged, the ponies were of no farther use, and the party started on foot. During the toilsome ascent her Majesty proved herself to be a first-rate pedestrian, and had the advantage of Prince Albert in more than one contest for superiority in surmounting the more rugged points, where the hands perform fully as important a part of the locomotion as the feet, and eventually the Queen reached the summit the first of the party.

Ben-a-bourd is principally celebrated for the magnificent prospect it commands of the various chains of mountains throughout the Highlands, and although the view over the low country is not very extensive, yet by the help of such a telescope as the deer-stalkers use, a person can distinctly see the ships upon the Firth at Inverness, and even count the windows of some farm-houses in Ross-shire. The summit of the mountain is almost void of vegetation, having the peculiar weather-beaten appearance common to our Scotch mountains of like elevation. The corries near the top are also famous for veins of those beautiful rock crystals, with which we are more familiar as "Cairngorm stones." While the Royal party were in search of specimens of these stones, Prince Albert had the good fortune to pick up what turned out to be an excellent specimen, fully more than sufficient to make a pretty large brooch, and worth two or three days' toil to a "Cairngorm digger."

The Queen conversed very freely with the guides and gillies about her, and appeared to take great interest in the scene, inquiring the names of many of the hills and places round about; and, as exemplifying the interest Her Majesty also takes in the legends and traditions of the country, it may be worth mentioning, that while ascending the Slogan, she requested one of the guides to point out the place where one of the earliest of the Farquharsons of Invercauld ("Fiondladh Mhor") was born, stating that she was aware that it was somewhere in the glen. The guide accordingly pointed out a small ruin among the heather as the spot, and Her Majesty halted and examined it evidently with much interest. "Fiondladh Mhor" is also the hero of a beautiful Gaelic song. After the party had lunched at the "Sappers and Miners" cairn at the top, Her Majesty took a drink from a clear spring well at the top of the "snowy corrie," and shortly after, the Royal strangers left.

the summit, and by six o'clock had safely descended from by far the wildest and sternest region of the Highlands Her Majesty had yet trod.

About a mile beyond the kirk of Crathie, on the north side of the river, a road strikes off, on the right, to Corgarff Tower (a small military station), on the Don, and thence to Fort-George. To the westward are the remains of the House of Monaltrie, which having been burned down in 1745, is now fitted up as a farm-house. A small village in the neighbourhood is called the Street of Monaltrie. A little farther on is the mound called Cairn-a-quheen (the cairn of remembrance,) which was used in the foraying days as the great gathering cry of Deeside when the crossteric passed. A small inn on the way side, called Inver, may here not be without its attractions to the pedestrian. At the fifty-fourth mile-stone, the traveller on the north side of the river will have to cross by the Bridge of Invercauld, thrown over a rapid and rocky strait of the river. It will have been noticed that the soft birch foliage has been gradually giving place to the sturdier and statelier pine, of which there are here many fine trees, masses of which spread up the glens to the south, where they form the great forest of Ballach-bowie. Soon after crossing the bridge, the road winds round the foot of Craig-Cluny, an abrupt ascent clothed with pine much farther up than the eye can individualize single trees, but raising a sharp bare granite peak, that nearly abuts across the road to a much greater height. The foundation of an old tower, called the Laird of Cluny's Charter Chest, about a third of the distance to the top, may be reached by an enterprising scrambler. It is worth visiting, as a specimen of old Highland engineering. How it could have been possible to reach it if any one wished to keep intruders down, none but cats or tigers can tell; from an assault above, it is protected by the superincumbent rock bulging over. At the foot of Craig-Cluny, and on the opposite side of the road, lies a stone about the size of a three-storey house, which has dropped some day or other from the edge of the rock. It would have astonished the outsiders of a stage-coach, if any such had been passing. Beyond Craig-Cluny the strath opens, showing at the bend of the northern sweep Invercauld House, an irregular pile of considerable size, but dwarfed by the majestic scale of the scenery. About the centre of the strath, and on the south side of the river, is Braemar Castle, a high bare walled tower, with a venerable Flemish expression about it, though not dating back so far as "the '15.' Immediately beyond, and fifty-seven miles from Aberdeen, is the village of

CASTLETOWN OF BRAEMAR.

[*Inns:*—The Invercauld Arms.]

This straggling collection of houses stands on a piece of broken rocky ground, where the turbulent stream of the Cluny clatters down into the Dee. The Castletown is in its pristine state as an old Highland village, the capital of the Strath. It has few if any new lodging-houses for health-seeking citizens ; but it has two excellent inns for the tourist, where he may be positively on occasion saturated with venison and grouse. In the close vicinity are the remains, little beyond the foundation, of the old Castle, where the Earl of Mar raised the standard of rebellion in 1715. However adventurously disposed, the traveller should take up his central position in Braemar, as, without crossing the great mountain barriers to the basins of the Tay or the Spey, he will find no other home near the wild scenery of the higher Grampians. It may be mentioned that it is by no means necessary that the journey to Braemar from the south should be made *via* Aberdeen and along Deeside. From Dunkeld or Blairgowrie it may be easily reached through Spital of Glenshee, where there is a good inn. The distance from Blairgowrie to Braemar by this route is about thirty-five miles—viz., Brig O'Cally, (where there is an inn,) six miles ; thence to Spital, fourteen miles ; thence to Braemar, fifteen miles. By another and wilder road, Braemar may be reached through Blair-Athol, by following the Tilt to its source, and descending the streams that run to the Dee. The distance is estimated at twenty-eight miles from Blair-Athol.

To begin with the smaller objects of interest near Braemar : About four miles east, on the declivity of the dusky pine forest of Ballachbowie, is seen a white streak, which forms the cataract of the Garrawalt. It is easily approached by drives constructed along the natural terraces of the forest banks. There is here a considerable supply of water rolling over a bank of great height, which, though not perpendicular, gives a thundering and foamy torrent ; but, as a cataract, it is rather deficient in interest, from its not disgorging itself into one of these black cauldrons, which give a mysterious, frightful, and characteristic feature to most of the Highland falls. It has a rustic bridge, and a fog-house to make it "tural lural" as the cockney said when he tried to utter "truly rural" with his mouth full of strawberries. Between three and four miles west of Braemar, there are two other waterfalls, one on the south, the other on the north side of the river. The former is termed Corramulzie,—exactly the sort of spot where old painters send fawns to sleep in hot days. It is a deep gash in the rock, narrow and precipitous, but having all its asperities softened off by the profusion of birches and creeping plants with which it is matted. The fall (which one often forgets, for it has so little of the terrible in it, though of considerable height, and very steep,) slides down pearly white through a winding slit in the rock, where its gentle surface is in close companionship with the tender wild flowers that are kept in eternal green by its spray. The Linn of Quoich, on the other side of the river (a couple of miles below the Earl of Fife's hunting seat, Mar Lodge,) is of a different character. It is on one of those powerful streams that tumble from the Cairngorm Mountains, and the cataract is formed by a succession of precipitous ledges. The schist rock is perforated in many places by the whirling waters into deep circular holes, from the appearance of which some man of gigantic dram-drinking visions is presumed to have christened the fall by its name of the Quoich. The next waterfall to be visited is the Linn of Dee itself, about eight miles from Braemar. It is not the height of fall, but the contraction of the stream, that is the object of interest; indeed, when the water is swollen, the ledges over which it falls almost disappear, the corners being rounded off as it were by the thickness of the watery drapery. One may descend to the river's edge, and the furious mass of waters, crushed and huddled together by the impregnable granite walls, raves with a wild and deafening fury, that dizzies the brain, and excites a sort of apprehension that the exasperated element may leap from its prison, and overwhelm the spectator as he is coolly gazing on its agony. It is easy to step from the north bank to the south; but the adventurer should adopt the old counsel of looking before leaping. The southern ledge is very narrow, and the rock rises perpendicularly over it. It may happen that, as the leap back is upwards, the adventurer may feel it beyond his power, and there is then nothing for it but climbing up the face of the rock with the hungry Linn below. Instances have been known of lovers of the *juste milieu*—people given to half measures—constituting animal bridges for some length of time across this piece of pleasant scenery.

To conclude with Deeside—we must now give the traveller the briefest possible sketch of the features of that huge mountain desert lying between the Straths of the Dee and Spey, which, presenting a district totally uninhabited, and containing no traces of the foot of man, has more association with the solitudes of distant unpeopled wastes than any one who does not know the place would anticipate in the land of spinning jennies and steam. The mountains, which here rise almost from one root, form the loftiest cluster in the united kingdom. Among them are Ben-muich-dhui, 4390; Bræ-riach, 4280; Cairn-toul, 4230; Cairngorm, 4050; Ben-a-bourd, 3940; and Bena'an, 3920. Their sides present perpendicular precipices of great height, and the valleys between them form gloomy ravines, narrow and dark, from the nearness of the hills to each other. Although no part of this district is within the line of perpetual congelation, the snow lingers in the hollows during the summer in such vast quantities, as to give a perfectly wintry aspect to the higher shaded glens. Down the sides of these mountains there are several cataracts of great height and no small bulk. But the scenery is not without its softer features. Many of the most rugged are relieved by the gentle weeping birch. Glen Lui, one of the entrance avenues from Deeside to this lonely district, presents a wide plain of green turf as bright and almost as smooth as a shaven lawn, while a pellucid stream ripples through it over yellow sand, or among sedges and waterflowers, as gentle and modest as if it could not have come roaring down just ten minutes before from the black precipices of Ben-muich-dhui. The old weather-beaten pines are a curious feature of some of these glens. By Deeside, the trees, lofty and grand as many of them are, have more an air of good keeping about them ; they are more park-like. In Glen Quoich and Glen Derry, they are scarred by centuries of contest with the mountain storms. Some are bowed to the earth, others twisted round and round like the horn of a sea-unicorn, and others stripped bare still stand erect, like mammoth skeletons set on end. On the lower declivities of the hills, and on the skirts of the forest land, may be occasionally seen those noble troops of red-deer, which, since the days of sheep farming and black cattle, are scarcely to be found elsewhere in the Highlands, in their ancient glory. By Deeside you may see a shy stag or so looking down on you from a bank ; but even there the air is tainted to their nice senses ; it is in Glen Lui or Glen Derry that they congregate in droves ; and though they seldom approach very close to the wanderer, he will frequently see their graceful forms and stately antlers on the edges of the heights between him and the setting or rising sun.

To see all the characteristic portions of this wild district, the adventurer should make two or three detours from Braemar, unless he can manage to sleep on the heather, and so take the stages successively. One special object of attention should be Loch A'an. The best means of reaching it is by proceeding up the Glen Lui already mentioned, and at the point where the glen diverges into two others, following that to the right, Glen Derry. When the head of this glen is reached, the mound must be ascended, and then descended on the other side by the stream, the Alt-dhu-lochan, which runs towards the Spey, the mound forming the water-shed between the Straths of Dee and Spey. After descending a considerable way, and winding to the left among precipitous banks, Loch A'an is reached, a sheet of water about two miles long, bedded in the precipices of Ben-muich-dhui and Bena'an, which rise in varied and grotesque forms to the height of from 1000 to 1500 feet. Loch A'an may be reached by following the Quoich instead of the Lui, and crossing the water-shed, as above. It may also be reached by descending Ben-muich-dhui. Near the top, and on the eastern declivity, there is a field of snow, out of which comes a pellucid stream, which, gathering other friendly rills into a considerable torrent, tumbles down into the lake. The descent may be followed by a skilful cragsman; but it is to any one a perilous and tedious business. When the lake is reached, the series of torrents above look like one waterfall from the top to the base of the mountain, and when swollen with melted snow, it must form one of the most stupendous cataracts in Europe. Before this descent is attempted, Ben-muich-dhui must of course have been climbed. With all his ruggedness, this is not a difficult matter, if the old "black hog" (this it seems is the English of his name) be taken in the right way like others of his species. One method is by Glen Lui, the left hand path being taken, up Glen Lui-beg, where the glens diverge, instead of the right hand by Glen Derry. Another method is by ascending right up from the most northern well of the Dee, and there is another by climbing over the banks of the Dee a little above the Linn. Ben-muich-dhui being the centre of the group, and its highest member, cannot easily be mistaken, if the weather be clear, —if it is foul the ascent should not be attempted. The source of the Dee, with Bræ-riach and Cairn-toul deserve a special visit. Where the streams of the Dee beyond the Linn separate,—by keeping all along by the right-hand stream, a circular well is reached, where the water bubbles up clear and full from the interior of the mountains. The stream here passes between what are well called

"The grisly rocks that guard
The infant rills of Highland Dee"—

viz. on the east, Ben-muich-dhui, and on the west, Bræ-riach, which rises in one black smooth perpendicular precipice, extending for two miles, and calculated by Dr. Skene Keith and others at 2000 feet high. By mounting the Garachary, which disputes with the stream just described the title to be the principal source of the Dee, the top of Bræ-riach may be reached. On the way up, the stream is joined by the Guisachan from a small lake on Cairn-toul, called Loch-na-Youan, whence it tumbles by a fall of about 1000 feet, as measured by Dr. Keith. The other branch of the stream then falls over a succession of ledges, making in all 13,000 feet, according to the same authority. The wells at the top were found to be 4068 feet above the sea level. Dr. Keith, who made the ascent in the middle of July, found the stream at its commencement passing under an arch of snow.

TWENTIETH TOUR.

THE GREAT NORTH ROAD FROM INVERNESS THROUGH THE NORTHERN COUNTIES, BY TAIN, DORNOCH, WICK, AND THURSO, TO JOHN O'GROAT'S HOUSE, WITH CROSS ROUTES FROM THE EAST TO THE WEST COAST.

NOT thirty years ago, Inverness was the *Ultima Thule* of the British Tourist; now it is only a resting place whence to start afresh for scenes of great diversity, in which the grand and the beautiful are intermixed, and where the industry of man in reclaiming a naturally barren soil presents as interesting a field for examination by the intelligent stranger as is to be found in any part of the kingdom. We would strongly advise the tourist to follow us throughout this route; and if his time is limited, he will make the most of it by taking a run along the north-eastern or coast road, and diverging thence either from Beauly up Strathglass and Strath Affrick; or from Dingwall by Strathpeffer and the Loch Carron road to Lochs Maree and Torridon, and the splendid scenery of Gairloch, Applecross, and Kintail; or from Bonar Bridge or Golspie, through the interior of Sutherland to the districts of Assynt and Cape Wrath, and thence more or less along the northern coast towards Caithness. Except at the passage of the Ord of Caithness, where the mountain chain separating the county of that name from Sutherland terminates in lofty precipices overhanging the sea, and to avoid which the public road makes an ascent of nearly 1200 feet, the route all along the coast is extremely level, so that the traveller can, with great comfort and safety, either use his own carriage or the public coaches, or disembark from any of the Moray Firth steamers at Invergordon or the Little Ferry in Sutherland, and thence proceed as a pedestrian or by a hired conveyance. In the first stage to Beauly we cross (1 mile from Inverness) the Caledonian Canal, by the Muirtown drawbridge, from which a fine view is obtained of the basin and locks of that great undertaking, and rising above which will be observed the house and grounds of Muirtown (H. Duff, Esq.), and the rocky summit of Craig-phadrick, a vitrified fort, one of the largest and best marked of that singular class of antiquities. Turning the base of this bill at the rough rocks of Clachnaharry (2d mile), 'the watchman's seat,'—where the burghers of Inverness in ancient days kept ward against the marauding clans of the Highlands—the road proceeds westwards along the edge of Loch Beauly, the innermost basin of the Moray Firth. Above the fine cultivated and woodland district which surrounds this beautiful sea-loch, and which the geologist's eye will perceive follows the soft undulating girdle of the *old red sandstone* formation, rises a magnificent amphitheatre of high and rugged mountains, of all shapes and sizes, which terminate towards the north in the huge mass of Ben Wyvis, whose summit seldom wants a cap of snow. The wooded promontory in front is part of the estate of Bunchrew (John Fraser, Esq.), once the favourite retreat of Duncan Forbes of Culloden, President of the Court of Session in 1745, passing which we enter on the estate of Lovat, with the eccentric and cunning old owner of which at that time, the President and Hanoverian Government had so difficult a part to act. Thence to Beauly, the district is called *the Aird*, or *Aird MacShemie* (i.e. Lord Lovat's height, *Simon* being the Gaelic patronimic of the chief of the clan Fraser), and in passing through it will be seen the mansion-houses of several of the principal cadets of the family. Conspicuous on the opposite side of the firth, is Redcastle, the seat of Colonel H. D. Baillie. Crossing the river Beauly by the Lovat bridge—whence a magnificent view is obtained of the surrounding plain, closed in on the south by a terraced bank, on which the chief's residence, Beaufort Castle, is seen, and, further back, the house of Belladrum (John Stewart, Esq.),—the road to the Falls of

Kilmorack and Strathglass deflects on the left, while the main road conducts us to the thriving village of

BEAULY,

[*Inns*:—The Lovat Arms; The Commercial.] Posting Establishments in both.

with its stately old trees, and the ruins of its ancient priory, of which the shell or walls of the chapel alone remain. It was founded by John Bisset of Lovat in 1230, for monks of the order of Valliscaulium, a reform of the Cistercians, following the rule of St. Bennet, and who had similar establishments at Pluscardine, near Elgin, and at Ardchattan, in Argyleshire. At the Reformation, the last prior resigned all his lands and buildings (except the chapel) for *protection sake*, into the hands of Lord Fraser of Lovat. The cloisters and dormitories are all gone; but what remains of the chapel shews it to have been of the most simple and chaste *early English*, with very little of the *decorated* style about it—the windows and arches being all plain and pointed, except three large open trefoil lights on the south side.

Entering now on Ross-shire, a neck of gravelly terrace ground, little more than 2 miles wide, separates the valley of the Beauly from that of the Conon, and prevents Loch Beauly from mingling its waters with those of the Cromarty Firth. On the summit of this flat, the great northern cattle-trysts are held almost monthly, at a place called the Moor of Ord, passing which a beautiful drive of 6 miles overlooking the river Conon, and a rich and very varied amphitheatre of the Ross-shire mountains, conducts the traveller to the town of Dingwall, situated at the junction of the rich valley of Strathpeffer, with the fertile lands around the mouth of the river Conon.

DINGWALL,

[*Inns*:—The National; The Caledonian.]

(a Scandinavian name, importing the *Law* or *Court hill*, and hence not used by the Gaelic population, who call the place Inverphœran) stands in rather a damp situation, which was anciently the site of the moat of one of the largest castles of the Earls of Ross, but is now becoming a clean and thriving town. It contains about 2000 inhabitants, has been a royal burgh since the year 1227, has two banks, a printing-offiee, churches of the Establishment, Free Church and Episcopal communions, a splendid jail, with suitable county and court-rooms, and is amply supplied with gas and water. The lands all around are rich and well wooded, and in almost every direction the huge towering acclivities of Ben Wyvis, (or Ben *Uaish*, the mountain of *Storms*,) form a magnificent background to the view.

For the greater part of the next stage to Invergordon, (13 miles,) the road passes through *Ferrindonald* or the district of the clan Munro, a race distinguished for their military achievements,—especially in the religious wars of our commonwealth and of Germany, in which they always appeared on the *Protestant* or *Covenanting* side—and latterly in the wars which consolidated our Indian empire. This district is nearly bisected at Evantown by the *Aultgraat*, the "terrific" or "ugly burn," which flows from Loch Glass, at the base of Ben Wyvis, and which, for about 2 miles of its course, plunges through a rift or fissure in rough conglomerate rocks upwards of 100 feet deep, and so narrow as to be almost overgrown at top by the trees from the opposite banks. At the mouth of this stream is the house of Balcony, on the foundations of another castle of the old Earls of Ross, and at Invergordon are the ruins of another very old castle, hard by the modern residence of the proprietor, (Mr. M'Leod of Cadboll); and a little further on, Tarbat House, the seat of the Marchioness of Stafford, close upon the foundations of the castle of her ancestors, Mackenzies, Earls of Cromarty.

Invergordon, which is provided with a commodious mole or pier, is becoming the great emporium of trade for Ross-shire, and from its convenient position it attracts most of the steamers and sailing-vessels which were wont to stop

forry, communicating by good roads through the Black Isle with Cromarty, Fortrose and Inverness. A succession of long straggling villages thence extends along the sea side eastwards, on the way to Tain, the houses in which are not occupied by fishermen, but by agricultural labourers and mechanics, (chiefly masons and carpenters,) many of whom migrate every spring southwards in quest of work, and return in winter to spend their earnings with their families. Although from the abundance of good building-stone the cottages are substantial and commodious, yet pauperism is alarmingly on the increase among their inmates, while the depressed state of the agricultural population renders it more difficult for them than heretofore, to bear such an addition to their burdens.

Before plunging into the dark pine woods of Calrossie, the road crosses the Balnagown water, affording a glimpse of the beautiful old baronial residence of the proprietor, Sir Charles Ross of Balnagown, the head of one of the oldest families of the district, if not indeed the representative of the ancient Earls of Ross. From the Alness water to Tarbat Ness, this portion of the country is called EASTER Ross, and is the *locale* of the original Celtic race of Ross; or *Anrias Macbeth*, was probably their ancient Maormor, for he united in his own person, and in right of his wife, the great Gaelic Lordships of Moray, Cromarty and Ross, and was hence a wall of strength against the encroachments of the Scandinavian pirates who had seized all the country north of the Dornoch Firth. His Gaelic successors were ever after prompt and daring warriors, even down to the present generation. How strange, and yet how beautiful the contrast? War is now waged in this district only with the elements, and the difficulties of the soil and climate; for here, on all hands, the drainage of the ground is carried on upon the most extensive scale; farm steadings and enclosures are forming on the most scientific principles; the finest breeds of horses, sheep, and cattle are reared; the tall chimneys of steam thrashing-mills are seen in all directions; and, in short, the agriculture of Easter Ross is now on a par with that of the best portions of the empire. Indeed, the whole eastern coast of Scotland exhibits a belt of cultivated ground, varying from 1 to 10 or 12 miles in breadth, on which a hardy and intelligent tenantry are contending with one another to perfect every kind of husbandry; and the inquisitive stranger will observe that almost the whole of this cultivated zone or belt lies on strata of the old red sandstone, with a subsoil of mixed clay and gravelly beds, and having over them a thin but kindly covering of vegetable loam or mould.

Built along the top, and at the base of a gravel terrace overlooking the Dornoch Firth, which terrace is seen skirting the coast all round, at a height of about 100 feet above the sea, is

TAIN

[*Inn*:—Mrs. Ellison's.]

(*Ting*, a court-place; Gaelic, Baildh Dhuich, the Town of St. Duthus, or Duffus, who was the "godly Bishop of Ross" in the beginning of the thirteenth century), an irregularly built burgh, with one main street and a multitude of cross lanes and alleys. It contains about 2000 inhabitants, with a number of handsome houses, all substantially built of yellow freestone, and having many large gardens attached to them. In the centre of the town there is a fine old tower, surmounted by a spire of polished stone, with smaller ones at each of the angles, connected with an elegant court-house and record rooms; and near it are the British Linen Company and Commercial Banks, the Mason Lodge, and a double row of handsome shops. The prison is an unpretending but neat building, above the town, on the road to the more spacious Poor's House already mentioned, which is in the Elizabethan style! To the north, on an airy and roomy playground, stands an excellent Academy, provided with a rector and two masters, at which a good classical and commercial education is given to about 100 pupils. A flourishing Mechanics' Institution, which is patronized by all the gentry of the neighbourhood, will also soon afford the advantages of a circulating library, literary and scientific. An enormous stretch of flat links ground below the town, called the *Fendom or Morrich More*, used to furnish recreation to the burghers at the game of *golf* and in horse-racing ; but of late it has been partly brought under the plough, while its outer boundary has been greatly encroached upon by sands blowing from the sea, which are spreading to an alarming extent. The Dornoch Firth appears to be rapidly filling up, and as the approach to the town is by a narrow channel, impeded in one place by a bar and sandbanks, over which a tremendous set of breakers, called the "Geygen Briggs," are continually rolling, Tain has no proper harbour, and now gets most of its imports landed at Invergordon. On a little sequestered mount in front of the town is an old burying ground, with the ruins of a very ancient chapel, extremely rude and simple, and massive in its architecture, said to be St. Duthus' original shrine ; and in the centre of the town, surrounded and half hid by large trees, is the collegiate church, erected in 1471 for a provost, eleven prebendaries, and three singing boys. The roof is still entire, and though the windows have been partially injured, this beautiful specimen of middle-pointed or decorated Gothic might be easily restored, though at present it is in a state of neglect and decay. King James V. made a pilgrimage to St. Duthus' shrine in 1527, incited to it, it is said, by Bethune, Archbishop of St. Andrews, that his Majesty might be out of the way at the burning of Patrick Hamilton, Abbot of Fearn, one of the first and holiest martyrs of the Reformation in Scotland.*

* The Abbey Church of Fearn, founded by the first Earl of Ross, in Alexander III.'s reign, though greatly mutilated and decayed, is still used as the parish church. It stands 6 miles south of Tain on the road to Nigg and Cromarty, whither the Abbey was removed by the founder from a site not far eastward of

The mail coach, which north of Tain is drawn only by two horses, used to cross the firth to Dornoch by the Meikle Ferry, a strait 4 miles west of the town ; but it now goes round by Bonar Bridge. The passage of the ferry is sometimes unpleasant, from squalls and the shallowness of the water, and the tourist will not regret the longer round by the head of the firth, as the scenery is rich and lovely in the foreground, and is backed above by varied and picturesque chains of mountains. Near Ardgay Inn (one mile south of Bonar Bridge, an iron structure across a narrow part of the firth 14 miles above Tain) a carriage road 18 miles long, joins from Alness, and which is divided into two nearly equal stages from Dingwall by an excellent inn at Stittenham. At Ardgay, at Dornoch, and at Golspie, carriage and post horses can be hired, but nowhere else between Tain and Wick ; and the tourist who is not a good pedestrian must otherwise depend on the mail coach along the coast road, and the mail cars which proceed from Golspie twice a-week (at present on Monday and Thursday) through the interior of Sutherland, and along the north coast to Thurso, or on the one-horse conveyances which are to be had at most of the Sutherlandshire inns.

The coast road from Bonar Bridge to Helmsdale passes through the most beautiful, at least the most fertile, portions of the county of Sutherland. Two miles and a half from Bonar there is a noted vitrified fort, Dun-creich, on the summit of a hill which juts out into the firth. Five miles farther, the house of Ospisdale (D. Gilchrist, Esq.), is delightfully situated at the foot of wooded heights. A huge pillar of stone, 9 feet high, by the roadside, according to tradition commemorates the death, in battle, of a Danish chief, called Hospis, whence the name of the place. The

Bonar Bridge, where it was found to be too near the turbulent clans of Sutherland. The chancel, nave, and two side chapels still remain, though greatly fallen in, and the windows, the extent of which has been mostly filled up and disfigured by modern masonry. They are almost wholly of the earliest or first pointed style. Fearn Church is within 3 or 4 miles of Hilton and Shandwick, and about the same distance from Nigg Church, at each of which places there is a beautiful and very ancient sculptured cross deserving of the antiquary's notice.

road next passes above Skibo, the delightful residence of G. Dempster, Esq., the abode during Episcopal times of the bishops of Sutherland and Caithness, and always noted for its excellent gardens and orchards.

At the distance of 14 miles from Bonar Bridge, and 5 miles from the Meikle Ferry, is the cathedral town of

DORNOCH,

the Sutherland capital, containing a population of about 800. It is situated immediately in front of a high gravel terrace, on a light sandy soil, bordered by the sea, with extensive sands. The low tower of the cathedral, and the tall square tower still standing of the bishop's palace, give it a pleasing and venerable appearance. The town is clean, regular, and airy. Dornoch was, in Episcopal times, the principal seat of the Bishop of Sutherland and Caithness, and it consequently had the honour of being one of the 14 cities of Scotland. The palace, or castle, was a large building, of most massive structure. In 1570 it was burnt to the ground by banditti under the Master of Caithness and Mackay of Strathnaver, who made an inroad into Sutherland and plundered the town of Dornoch. The whole edifice has recently been removed, with the exception of the picturesque high western tower; and on the site a handsome well-ordered new prison and court-house, with record and county meeting rooms, have been erected.

The cathedral was built by Gilbert de Moravia (bishop from 1223 to 1260), the near kinsman of Andrew de Moravia, who, at the same time, erected, on the opposite side of the firth, the more magnificent minster of Elgin. The Church thus built was "restored" about twelve years ago by the Sutherland family. It consists at present of chancel, nave (but without the aisles), transepts, and central tower. The east window is a triplet, and there is a single lancet in the gable. Both transepts have a small triplet on each side; and at the west end of the nave there is one of those infoliated middle-pointed windows of four lights, so common in the old northern churches. The rest of the windows are lancets. The tower is short and thick, and crowned with a stunted spire.

About 6 or 7 miles from Dornoch, the road crosses Loch Fleet, an arm of the sea, which extends 9 miles inland by a magnificent mole or mound, about 1000 yards in length, having 4 sluices and arches on the north side. This work cost £12,500, but a great deal of land has been reclaimed by means of it. Skelbo Castle, the ruins of which are seen on the southern shore, was formerly the residence of the family of Sutherland, Lord Duffus. Eastward, the tourist will descry, on the summit of Ben Vracky, above Golspie, the colossal statue of the late Duke of Sutherland, erected by the tenantry, after a model by Chantrey.

Hence to Helmsdale, the coast of Sutherland is soft and very beautiful. A range of moderately sized hills, diversified by hanging woods and arable slopes, with a frequent belt of rich level ground in high cultivation, lines the shore. Substantial farm-houses, comfortable stone and lime cottages, a well clad peasantry, and superior farm stock, present themselves as unequivocal signs of a thriving population. But the improved agricultural aspect of the country, as yet, extends to no great distance from the coast. Beyond the first line of hills, which in general border on the sea, and which consist of sandstone and conglomerate rocks, chains of wild and bleak, but in this section of Sutherlandshire not lofty, mountains present themselves, covered with heathy pasture. These mountains are almost all composed of hard gneiss, granite, and quartz rock. Excellent roads, however, now traverse this extensive county, which thirty or forty years ago was utterly inaccessible in all parts away from the east coast. Inns, which might well serve as model inns for many parts of the Highlands, so comfortable, clean, and well conducted are they, are provided in all directions. The tourist has thus many inducements in the way of creature comforts to visit Sutherlandshire, remote though it be.

After resting at Hill's excellent inn of Golspie (25 miles from Bonar Bridge), the tourist will be anxious to have a peep of the Duke of Sutherland's residence, Dunrobin Castle,

DUNROB N CASTLE.

the best view of which is obtained from the sea-side. It is thus described by Sir Robert Gordon, the family historian, who wrote about the year 1630:—"Dunrobin Castle, 'the Erle of Sutherland his speciall residence,' is a house well seated upon a mote hard by the sea, with fair orchards, wher ther be pleasant gardens planted with all kinds of froots, hearbs, and floors used in this kingdom, and abundance of good *saphorn*, *tobacco*, and *rosemarie*, the froot being excellent, and cheeflie the pears and cherries." The castle was founded by Robert, second Earl of Sutherland, A.D. 1097 (whence its name Dunrobin). The country around is well wooded. By recent additions, Dunrobin has become one of the most princely palaces in the kingdom, and undoubtedly one of the most commodious in Scotland. It now exhibits a solid mass of masonry, about 100 feet square by 80 feet in height, of three main storeys, besides the basement and attics, connected by a lower range of buildings with the old structure, itself a large building, which, though modernised and almost lost amidst a multitude of high towers and fretted pinnacles, preserves much of its pristine dignity, forming now the western corner of the building. A magnificent elevation, springing from a terraced basement, and pierced with rows of oriel and plain windows, ornamented with varied tabling, forms an extensive and imposing frontage to the sea, over which rises a series of lofty towers at the angles of the large square mass, while the whole edifice is crowned by numerous turrets and minarets. All the towers have high, sharp, pointed roofs, covered with overlapping plates, or scales of lead; but the main tower at the north-east corner, which is 28 feet square, and rises to a height of 35 feet above the basement terrace, has its roof incurved and truncated. It forms the porte cochér underneath. The general character of the whole building is that of a very large French chateau, or German palace, with details borrowed from the best old Scottish models. The grand entrance and staircase are lined within with polished Caen stone; but the exterior is all of a hard white silicious freestone from Brora and Braamburgh Hill, on the Duke's own property. Internally the private rooms are arranged into numerous suites of apartments, each appropriated to some member of the family, and named accordingly, as the Argyle, the Blantyre, and other apartments, and each suite distinguished by its own peculiar style, coloured decorations, and painting. The state-rooms, specially prepared for her Majesty, command the grand seaward view,—comprehending almost the entire circuit of the Moray Firth. They are done up in the most sumptuous manner, with rich flowered silk, pannelled ceilings, ornamented cornices, and wood work; as, indeed, are the public and the principal private rooms.

Brora, five miles and a half from Golspie, is a little village formerly dependent on the salt and coal-works carried on in its vicinity, now chiefly supported by the produce of the quarries of finely-textured, though rather brittle freestone, and abounding in shells, found in its neighbourhood. The former have been discontinued. To the geologist Brora presents the most interesting appearances, perhaps, in Scotland, by the occurrence of coal and its associated minerals in the immediate neighbourhood of granite. The formation with which the coal is connected is the lias and oolite, the principal bed of coal being about two hundred feet beneath the surface. The freestone or sandstone composing the upper bed is well adapted for building ; and at Helmsdale, and other places along the coast, a fine secondary limestone called cornstone occurs. At Inverbrora, also, there is a small freshwater deposit of the wealden clay formation.

Strathbrora, for several miles up, to the rock Carrol, Kilcalmkill (which still perpetuates St. Columba's name) ; and Cole's Castle, a fortress of enormous strength, built of uncemented stone, on the rocky banks of the Blackwater, will afford an interesting excursion to the tourist when in this neighbourhood.

The distance from Brora to Port Gower, where are a neat little village, a good inn, and the parish school, is ten miles. The secure little bay of Helmsdale, two miles from Port Gower, is frequented by numerous herring busses, its harbour being reckoned the safest station on the coast. The village is thriving and populous, and possesses a sub-branch bank. In front of Helmsdale, and on the west side of the river, are the ruins of a romantic old castle, built by Lady Margaret Baillie, Countess of Sutherland, in the end of the fifteenth century, and "re-edified," says the family genealogist, "the year of God 1615, by Alexander Gordon, son of the Earl."

Between Helmsdale and Berridale (10 miles), the road passes at an elevation of 1200 feet above the sea, along the acclivity of the granitic Ord of Caithness, which is part of a long mountainous range running north-west, separating Caithness from Sutherland. This stage, though tedious, is now comparatively free from danger. Formerly the road proceeded along the edge of a frightful range of precipices overhanging the sea, and of old it was considered unlucky to cross this way on a Monday, as a party of Caithness men passed it on that day on their journey to Flodden field, whence none of them returned.

At Berridale, towards the sea, commence those grand cliffs and stacks, or detached pillars of sandstone rock which are met with from thence round all the coast of Caithness.

Caithness may be described as a broad undulating moorland plain, devoid of trees, and covered in many places by deep peat-mosses. The dwellings of its peasantry are often poor hovels, built of turf and stones, and thatched over with straw or sods. These are made fast by straw ropes thrown across the roof, to the ends of which flat stones are attached as safeguards against the violence of the winds. But Caithness is by no means a poor country; and its agricultural products are greater than those of some others of the northern shires. It has advanced in all sorts of agricultural improvements, and in the feeding of the finest stocks of cattle. Its coasts are highly picturesque. Frequent ancient towers, some of them still habitable, are perched on the cliffs of their rugged shores. The Scandinavian origin, or at least admixture of the people, manifests itself in their tall but strong built forms and smooth fair countenances—the proper names, and many words, betray unequivocal indications of a foreign extraction; and Gaelic is the spoken language nowhere in the county except on the borders of Sutherland.

Wick and Thurso are the only towns in the county: the latter, though possessing the advantage in point of situation, and with more of pretension in appearance, must yield to its rival in mercantile bustle and importance.

Wick (54 miles from Golspie) lies low and in a confined situation; but the adjoining village of Staxigo, which is built on higher ground, and has a more convenient harbour, may be almost reckoned as the port through which Wick conducts its commerce, and with which its streets will soon be united. Though the bay is long and dangerous, and hemmed in on both sides by precipitous rocks, it is the resort of a great many fishing vessels; and in the fishing season the town swarms with crowds of foreigners, as well as strangers from all parts of the country. On a fine summer's morning, from the seaward cliffs, the ocean may be seen bespangled with as many as from 500 to 800 herring-boats, intermingled with larger vessels, and graced by the occasional broad pennon of a revenue cruiser. Indeed, during the fishing season, the busy hand of industry is tried to the utmost, and man, woman, and child are obliged to bear "watching, and labour, and pain."

The town's harbours are extending, and the suburb, Pulteneytown—commenced in 1808 by the British Fishery Society, and built on higher ground than the old town—is a regular and handsome village. The population of the parish had increased from 1831 to 1841 by upwards of 3000: that of the towns had enlarged from 5523 in 1841 to 6698 in 1851.

Wick has been incorporated as a royal burgh since 1589; and since the Union it has been associated with Kirkwall, Dornoch, Tain, and Dingwall (and, since the late Reform Act, with Cromarty) in returning a member to Parliament. The sheriff courts, since 1828, by order of the Court of Session, are held in Wick, and not at Thurso, which was formerly the head burgh of the shire. The custom-house has also been removed to Wick, which likewise possesses a chamber of commerce; and a large trading steamer touches here from Leith once a-week for more than half the year on its passage from that port to Aberdeen and the Orkney and Shetland Isles. Trading smacks ply once a fortnight between Leith and Wick; and an almost constant intercourse is carried on with London, Hull, and other English ports, by means of the vessels which are continually passing along this coast.

Besides the main post road to Thurso, a district road, 27 miles long, leads along the coast to Houna and John O'Groat's House. On the way there is an extensive sweep of sands to pass over, a ferry on Waster Water, and many long stretches of hilly moorland.

The castles of Old Wick, Keiss, Girnigo and Sinclair, with Ackergill and other towers on the verge of the seaward cliffs, give a most picturesque character to the scenery. Ackergill, still habitable, may give a good notion of the rude strongholds which frowned along this ironbound coast. "It is a square tower, 65 feet in height, and in breadth at each angle 45 feet, having three storeys, each of them arched, the walls above 10 feet thick at the butts of the arches. It stands on a rock close to the sea, a few feet above the highest water mark, and is defended by a moat 12 feet deep, and equally broad, extending along each of its angles, except the one facing the sea."

On reaching the inn of Houna, the traveller stands at the land's end, beside John O'Groat's House, upon the rocky shores and shell banks of the Pentland Frith. This far-famed John O'Groat's is merely the site of a house which once stood on a small green knoll close to the beach. John was a Dutchman, who, according to local tradition, settled here about the year 1509, and in erecting his residence, (which seems to have been of very moderate dimensions, in order to set at rest all questions of precedency among the inmates,) constructed it in the form of an octagon, with a door on each side. The bold adjoining headland of Duncansby, the Berubium of Ptolemy, with its numerous deep and lengthened chasms or ghees, and curious detached stacks or columns of rock in the sea, is well deserving of a visit. It is a commanding station whence to behold the Pentland Frith, that great eastern gulf stream of the Atlantic, with the force of all its united tides agonizing through the narrow opening between the mainland and the Orcades. From the Hebrides and Cape Wrath the flow of the Western Ocean comes rolling on in one uniform unbroken stream, which, as it approaches the eastern sea, is dashed and buffeted against the projecting headlands of Caithness and Orkney—the contracted channel imparting to its waters augmented velocity and the utmost agitation. The current then expands, but after crossing the Moray Frith, it again dashes itself with tremendous force on the rocky shores of Aberdeen and Banffshires.

Between Houna and Thurso the road (about 18 miles) proceeds along the margin of the firth. The views of the Isles of Orkney, the Pentland streams, and the projecting points of the mainland of Caithness, are all along grand and varied. Agricultural improvement and the planting and reclaiming of waste lands are also going on in the district with rapid strides. At Castlehill Mr. Traill employs a number of labourers in quarrying pavement flags, of which from three to four thousand square feet are annually exported.

Thurso, or Thor's Town, a burgh of barony holding of Sir George Sinclair as superior, and containing about 2400 inhabitants, is now less than half the size of Wick, and is an irregularly built town. It contains, however, some handsome freestone houses in the suburbs, a neat church, and an excellent inn. East of the town stands a fine old castle (Sir George Sinclair's of Ulbster, Bart.), and further on, in the same direction, Harold's Tower, over the tomb of Earl Harold, the possessor at one time of half of Orkney, Shetland and Caithness, and who fell in battle against his own namesake, Earl Harold the Wicked, in the year 1190. On the west side of the bay are the ruins of Scrabster Castle, a residence of the bishops of Caithness.

Its remoteness from the east coast of Scotland, its proximity to the Pentland Firth, and the want of adequate shelter in the bay, are insuperable obstacles to Thurso becoming a place of much resort for shipping. The bay itself is, however, a delightful object to the view hunter. A magnificent semicircular sweep of sandy beach, on which the long line of breakers yield their power with hollow moan, gives place at either extremity to precipitous rocks forming the sides of the bay, which, converging, terminate in the high bluff promontories of Holborn Head and Dunnet Head. Over these, though upwards of 400 feet in height, the spray dashes during storms. In the opening between, the prodigious western precipices of Hoy present about the most magnificent range of cliff scenery in Britain, and, with other of the Orkney Isles, compose a splendid boundary to the seaward view. Holborn Head itself, with the Clett, a huge detached rock, the boundless expanse and heaving swell of old ocean, and the clouds of screaming sea-birds, exhibits near at hand this style of scenery in great perfection.

TWENTY-FIRST TOUR.

SUTHERLANDSHIRE.

BONAR BRIDGE TO LOCH INVER—SCOURIE—DUIRNESS—TONGUE—LAIRG—AND GOLSPIE.

The extensive county of Sutherland presents the striking peculiarity of having the whole of its surface of 1800 square miles under sheep, with the exception of a narrow border of arable land along its eastern coast. More than four-fifths of this great territory belongs to the Sutherland family, who have recently, too, by marriage, made the large accession of the Cromertie estates adjoining, on the west of Ross-shire—an extent of property altogether unparalleled in this kingdom. In its superficial configuration and aspect, Sutherlandshire is distinguished by several marked features. It is surrounded on three of five sides by the ocean. On the west and north coast, and in the section of country intermediate between the extreme points of these, are assembled groups of huge mountains; while the bulk of the rest of the county is spread out in spacious undulating plains, edged by continuous chains of hills, of comparatively moderate height, while no mountains of corresponding dimensions with those first alluded to stand out in prominent relief, with but one or two exceptions—as, for instance, the imposing central mass of Ben Clibrick. The mountains of Sutherlandshire are characterised by their general isolation from each other—all, however, resting on a general table-land of considerable elevation. They are thus distinguished by boldness of form and outline. Of wood, excepting close by

the eastern shore, and the lower parts of the Oikel river, which falls into the Dornoch Firth, there is not a vestige, saving some recent plantations about Loch Inver and Tongue, a few ancestral trees around the old family seat of the Reay family, at the latter place, patches of copsewood on the banks of some of the lakes, and the fruit trees in an occasional garden enclosure, as at Scourie. From the care, however, taken to keep the heath short, the luxuriant pastures—though wanting the emerald brilliancy of the Argyle Highlands—clothe the landscape in a subdued verdure, redeeming it from the gloom which would otherwise attach to its sequestered and extensive solitudes. The tourist, then, is not to look for woodland beauties, nor for the infinite variety of scenery which gives such a charm to almost all the land of mountain and flood to the south of the bounds of Sutherlandshire. But he will find himself recompensed by the severe grandeur of the majestic mountain forms—by the unbroken stillness of the large inlets of the sea, or of the fresh-water lakes—the impressive altitude of its abrupt and rugged sea-worn cliffs—and even in the solemnity of its pathless waters.

The chief interest, however, with an eye to the picturesque, is confined to the western and northern parts of the county, and is thus still further removed from the ordinary tourist thoroughfares. Yet the means of access are not very inconvenient, and the traveller will find at command accommodations such as are not to be met with in many parts of the Highlands much more accessible ; while there is the further facility in the fact, that the English language is universally understood, and, indeed, well spoken. A daily mail (four horse as far as Tain) traverses the whole distance from Inverness to Thurso; while, during the summer season, a small steamer plies twice a-week between Inverness and the ports on the Moray Firth to the little Ferry near the Mound, and within four miles of Golspie. This steamer can be conveniently joined at Burghead ; or one may proceed by the Leith and Orkney steamer as far as Wick. From Golspie, and also from Bonar, a two-horse open mail-car starts twice a-week—on Monday and Thursday morning—for Lairg, at the lower end of Loch Shin, whence one proceeds to Tongue, and another to Loch Inver. These carry five or six passengers, and return on Wednesdays and Saturdays. A coach runs between Tongue and Thurso thrice a-week. At Innisindamff, within fourteen miles of Loch Inver, a smaller one-horse car, for three passengers, branches off to Kyle Skou, and Scourie. At every inn and public-house some sort of conveyance, phaeton, dog-cart, or swing-cart, is to be had.

The inns in all parts of Sutherlandshire are excellent—clean, comfortable, and well kept—frequently provided with unexpected accessories of progress in the arts of life. Some, however, there are, not yet very commodious, so that, in the height of the travelling season, there may be an occasional scramble for beds. Travelling early in the season is thus advisable, and it has the additional recommendation, that the greater coolness preserves the tourist from the gnats and midges, which are rather troublesome at times. A continuous line of road extends from Lairg, whence it connects with the great north road, by lines to Golspie and Bonar Bridge—to Loch Assynt and Loch Inver on the west, and from Loch Assynt northwards, to Kyle Scou, Scourie, and Duirness ; thence round Loch Eriboll to Tongue and Thurso. From Tongue a road leads right across back to Lairg. A new road, too, is just being completed, from Lairg by the shores of Loch Shin, and of a series of smaller lakes which succeed, to Loch Laxford, shortening the distance by about one half; while it is very level, and also leads through the heart of some of the loftiest mountains, and near the great deer forests. Besides these, a road conducts from Helmsdale, due north, to Bighouse. The only drawback to the Sutherlandshire roads is that they are very narrow—generally 10, and not exceeding 12 feet, including the edging of sward. They are free of toll, as are the Ross-shire roads, in greater measure than in Inverness-shire ; but, even there they are confined to the main thoroughfares. The Sutherlandshire roads are now, too, connected with those on the west of Ross-shire by one from Ledmore, on the way between Oikel Bridge and Loch Assynt, through Strathcannaird, to Ullapool, whence there is a line of communication, not only direct to the Dingwall and Loch Carron road at Strathgarve, but also round by Poolewe, Gairloch, and Kinlochewe, to the same road, at Auçhnasheen. Angling used to be one great attraction of Sutherlandshire. The innkeepers had the privilege of salmon fishing for a period of the year for their inmates. Now the rivers are almost all let, and the right of salmon fishing in them, if to be had at all, must be well paid for. On the lakes there is more license allowed, and trout fishing is unrestricted. Salmon here, as elsewhere, are sensibly on the decrease.

The hanging plantations of fir and larch, which on the Sutherland side skirt the firth for several miles below Bonar Bridge, extend also for some little distance to the west. The Assynt road crosses the Shin at Shin Bridge. The current of the Oikel is sluggish, and the tide flows as far as Rosehall, 12 miles above Bonar Bridge. The water is skirted with meadow ground, chequered with alder and birch. At Rosehall, now the property of Sir James Matheson, of the Lewis, M.P., there are extensive woods and plantations of fir.

Here the road from Golspie, by Lairg to Assynt, joins that from Bonar Bridge. Instead of proceeding from Shin Bridge right on to Rosehall, a detour may be made by Lairg (11 miles from Bonar Bridge), which is very pleasingly situated at the lower end of Loch Shin. This loch is about 20 miles in length, and of a very softened character ; while the new churches and manses, Established and Free, and some scattered cottages, are features quite in keeping with the scene. On the west side of the Shin Sir James Matheson has another fine property, Achany, joining that of Rosehall. The road from Golspie to Lairg, a distance of 19 miles, strikes off from the main north road at the Mound, and leads through Strathfleet, in which are located a considerable number of small tenants, the cultivated spaces around whose dwellings give pleasing indication of industry and enterprise, and earnests of what may be done in the support of a larger population. The river is crossed at Lairg by a ford. When flooded it is necessary to go round by Shin Bridge; but a tiny suspension bridge has been thrown across for pedestrians. The hill ground to Rosehall is a forbidding moorland.

Beyond Rosehall and the river Cassley—which here joins the Oikel—there is little to interest, till the summit level, some miles beyond Oikel Bridge (the latter 15 miles from Lairg) be surmounted. The distant mountain forms, as they come in sight, chiefly occupy the attention as we slowly wend our way,—without, however, anything very notable about them, till we get over the ascent. A series of huge detached mountain masses there suddenly present themselves. All of these spring in strongly defined shapes from the elevated moorland. One of them, Suil Veinn, is called from its remarkable form—though this peculiarity belongs more to its western front—"the sugar loaf." It is *the* feature of this quarter, although its companions, especially Cannishp and Coulmore, are not unworthy compeers,—less fantastic, but also of grand and extraordinary, outline. A series of moorland lochs or lakes—Craggy, Loch-na-Helac, Boarlan, and Loch Awe—serve further to beguile the way as we cross the high ground, and descend the Glen of Assynt. This valley, latterly lined on one hand by a noble range of limestone cliffs, several hundred feet in height, conducts to Loch Assynt, at the east end of which is the Inn of Innisindamff (18 miles from Oikel Bridge), and the church and manse of Assynt. Here we are in the midst of lofty mountains. Cunaig, a mighty mass, stretches along the northern shore, interposing between Loch Assynt, a fine fresh-water lake about 10 miles in length, and Kyle Skou, a far-indenting arm of the sea. About 3 miles down the loch the north road ascends the shoulder of Cunaig. The road to Loch Inver keeps by the side of Loch Assynt, passing by the shell of a large old building, called Edderachalda, and the ruins of an older and more rude and picturesque stronghold, Ardvrock Castle, once the seat of the Macleods of Assyut. It is worthy of note, as the place where Montrose was confined when captured by the Laird of Assynt, as he fled almost alone, after his forces had been surprised and dispersed at Fearn by Colonel Strahan.

At Loch Inver, 14 miles from Innisindamff, and 52 from Bonar Bridge, will be found a capital inn, and the stranger will be gratified by a really fine collection, made and preserved by the innkeeper, Mr. Dunbar, of the birds of the county, comprising many rare and valuable specimens, especially of birds of prey. To get a good view of Suil Veinn will be a chief object with the traveller. A walk of about a mile will accomplish this. But the view from the water is still more striking, and it further commands a prolonged succession of lofty single mountains, all quite apart from each other, resting on an elevated table-land of rugged rocky ground. Suil Veinn is, however, quite distinctive—at first presenting the appearance of a glass house, and, as the distance increases seaward, of a perfect sugar-loaf shaped cone, apparently fully 1500 feet of clear elevation, shooting up at once from the table-land without any supporting base, and certainly a very remarkable looking mass. An extensive trade was at one time carried on here in herring curing, but, like the other establishments along the west and north of Sutherlandshire, it has, after strenuous but hitherto abortive efforts, been abandoned, and the fishing is thus almost at a stand still. Neither is the deep-sea fishing prosecuted to any extent. Lobsters are, however, shipped in great numbers for the southern markets.

Great part of the district of Assyut and of Edderachillis which succeeds—to the north of Kyle Skou, but particularly the latter—is composed of a network of bare rocky eminences, and embedded in the deep hollows between lie innumerable dark motionless tarns or pools, of varying dimensions, frequently margined with water plants. The road, winding up and down among these inequalities, is frequently steep enough ; but there is much of picturesque novelty in the strange ruggedness of the ground ; while here and there the wide ocean or island-studded bays burst on the sight.

Kyle Skou, on the north side of the massive bulk of Cunaig, is a noble inlet, penetrating in its farthest reaches into the recesses of Glen Coul and Glen Dhu, where its waters are closely hemmed in by lofty barriers of rock. These glens are among the most striking scenes on the coast.

At Badcaul, where the parish church and manse of Edderachillis are situated, there is a large store for packing the salmon caught along the west coast.

Scourie is a considerable scattered hamlet or township, with enclosed fields, encircling the termination of a well-indented bay. Among the rocky hills of the more inland mountains, that of Stack is remarkable for its high pyramidal summit. The inn, at present small, though comfortable and soon to be enlarged, is on the south, and on the opposite side of the bay is the local factor's house, a large substantial structure with a good garden. Off the bay the island of Handa presents, in its magnificent range of cliffs, an object well worthy of notice. They extend along nearly the whole of the western side of the island, and rise quite perpendicularly from the sea to a height of 600 or 700 feet. From the rock inclining away landward, the precipices can be approached with some confidence. Myriads of sea fowl tenant the narrow ledges of rock during the breeding season.

Proceeding onwards from Scourie, the road skirts the extremities of two salt-water lochs—Laxford and Inchard. The outline of the former is very irregular. It is at its head that the road in progress from Lairg by Loch Shin reaches the coast. At the end of Loch Inchard is a substantial public house—Rhiconich—12 miles from Scourie. Ascending the course of the Achrisgill, we now round the shoulder of a long ascent, called the Gualin, on which a small public-house has been erected for shelter to the wayfarer. Fronting us, on the further side of the valley, is the massive bulk of Ben Spionnadh, and more to the right, and more removed, the still loftier precipitous summits of Foinne Bhein. By and by the tourist reaches the placid waters of the Kyle of Tongue, and keeping in view for some time the farm-house of Keoldale, he deflects across a fertile table-land of limestone rock which stretches towards the next great arm of the sea—Loch Eriboll—and at length rests from his toils at the comfortable inn of Durin.

From the inn window may be descried, in the distance, the tremendous cliffs of Hoy Head in the Orkneys. The eye, too, ranges along a great line of coast, edged at intervals by lofty mural faces. Close at hand, Farout Head projects into the great north sea. On the bay of Duirness, on the west side of the promontory, stands the old house of Balnakiel, a residence of the Bishops of Sutherland and Caithness, and afterwards of the Reay family, and near it the very old parish church of Duirness. The churchyard is embellished with a monument commemorative of a Gaelic poet of great local celebrity—Rob Donn. In the church is another, with an epitaph which tersely portrays the characteristic qualities of a class of our Highland forefathers, of whom this personage was a noted type. He practised largely the principle,

> "That they should take who have the will,
> And they should keep who can."

The epitaph bears that "*Donald MacMurshov* heir lyis lo; vas ill to his frend and var to his fo, true to his maister in veird and vo. 1623."

Cape Wrath merits its name of warning, and mariners take special care to give it a good berth. This bold headland braves the ocean currents in various grand frontlets—some rising perpendicularly to a height of 600 feet, and others in steep acclivities, surmounted by more precipitous ridges. Sunken rocks cause a turmoil at all times. A reef of perforated rocks run out into the sea. Some desolate islets stud the face of the deep. All around is utter solitude, excepting the durable granite lighthouse, which gives sign that here two individuals of the race of man hold watch and ward to signal vessels off the inhospitable coast. The range of view is magnificent, stretching from the Lewis to the Orkneys, while a grand panorama of mountain screens is spread behind. The distance from Duirness is 13 miles, by a good road, but having a ferry to cross; and though the scenery cannot be viewed to such advantage from the land, it is hardly prudent to venture by boat.

A mile to the east of Durin, and close below the high road, is the cave of Smoo, one of the finest things of the kind in this country, though on a scale not to be compared with similar excavations elsewhere. At the inner end of a narrow creek the limestone rock has been scooped out into a spacious wide-mouthed cavern, having a span of about 110 feet by 53 feet in height. Two subterraneous chambers—one within the other—branch off from the outer cave. The access to the first is over a low ledge of rock, and as the interior of both is filled with water, from a burn which pours into the first, forming a fine cataract, it is necessary to have a boat, which is always to be had on the spot, dragged over. The innermost apartment is attained by the boat making its way under a low bridge of rock, which divides the entrance to it.

The north-east entrance of Loch Erriboll rises into the lofty cliffs of Whitten Head. The road makes a great circuit round the head of the loch. The pedestrian can shorten his distance 10 miles by crossing the wide ferry to the small Inn of Heulim. Here a projecting peninsula affords a sheltered refuge, well known to the tempest-tossed mariner. From Erriboll, a couple of miles from the head of Loch Erriboll, a road leads through Strathmore to Aultnaharrow (18 miles from Erriboll), in the centre of Sutherlandshire, about half-way between Tongue and Lairg. This route is chiefly remarkable for the remains of the celebrated round tower, Dun Dornadilla, at Aultnacaillich, about half-way. It also presents fine views of Loch Hope, a long narrow fresh-water lake parallel to Loch Erriboll, and of the rounded bulk, and imposing precipices of Ben Hope on its eastern margin.

Equally good views are, however, obtained of the loch and mountain from the lower end, where the Tongue road crosses the river by a chain boat. Before quitting Loch Erriboll, however, an admiring parting glance will be cast over the waters of Loch Erriboll and its grand mountain amphitheatre.

Between Loch Hope and the Kyle of Tongue rises a lengthened mossy moorland, called the Moin. Here Ben Loyal, with its four fantastic summits, disputes our notice with Ben Hope. At the Kyle of Tongue is a ferry, about a mile across to the extremity of a projecting promontory, at the landward end of which is situated Tongue House, an old-fashioned mansion, formerly the seat of the Lords of Reay, whose estates were added by purchase to those of Sutherland. It is surrounded by trees and plantations. Towards the head of the Kyle, the square shell of Castle Vairich recals the thoughts to the days of feudal power and strife. A few scattered houses on the hill slope above Tongue House form the village of Kirkiboll, and here will be found a commodious and comfortable inn.*

The drive of 40 miles from Tongue to Lairg is over a tract of country almost uninhabited. Ascending gradually

* There is little of peculiar interest between Tongue and Thurso, a distance of 44 miles. As already mentioned, a coach runs every second day between these places. This route crosses two considerable valleys—Strath Naver and Glen Hallowdale—watered by rivers of some size, which are bordered by fertile meadow land. These rivers are crossed by chain-boats. Between these valleys are several smaller glens, and about half-way Strathy Head projects far into the sea; and at Strathy there is a hamlet, church and manse, and small inn. On the east side of the Naver is the comfortable inn of Bettyhill of Farr, 12 miles, and on the west side of Glen Hallowdale, the scattered township and good inn of Melvich; twenty-eight miles from Tongue, and towards the mouth, and on the further side of the river, is the mansion-house of Bighouse. On the adjacent coast to Melvich is the boat harbour of Port Skerry. A road has been constructed across the country by Auchintoul and Kildonan to Helmsdale, a distance of 30 miles. Four miles beyond the river we pass the house of Sandside (Innes) and the village of Reay, and beyond these the ruins of Castle Down Reay, a still older seat than Tongue of the Reay family. About the middle of the remaining distance of 12 miles, between Reay and Thurso, is the mansion-house of Forss (Sinclair). Of the tract of country just traversed, and on to Thurso Bay, there is a large portion uninteresting moorland, but diversified, as has been indicated, by several

from the coast, and passing two small lakes, our course lies along the shore of Loch Loyal and the eastern base of Ben Loyal, and thence all the rest of the way across elevated moorlands, stretching away to the remote mountains, which loom in the western and northern horizon in the independent masses characteristic of this part of the Highlands. At an interval of several miles south of Ben Loyal rises the great central bulk of Ben Clibrick. At the foot of this latter mountain the peaceful waters of Loch Naver stretch to the north-east, and discharge themselves through the fertile pastures of Strath Naver into the North Sea at Bettyhill of Farr. At Aultnaharrow, near the west end of the loch, and near about half-way to Lairg, is one of the best inns in the county. And here we may bring to a close our rapid survey of Sutherlandshire, as the stage to Lairg is but a repetition of the latter part of that from Tongue, excepting that the moorland wastes are still more extensive than those we have left behind, and more monotonous, though not, therefore, devoid of impressiveness in their tenantless expanse. But the sense of loneliness, however fitted by its very intensity to fill up the thoughts during the journey, is willingly exchanged for the more accustomed impressions produced by the return to human dwellings and their associations, and the marks of human effort, and the indications of daily life, as we regain the shores of Loch Shin. The interval from hence to Golspie we have already briefly noticed in the outset.

For a more detailed description of Sutherlandshire, as of the whole of the Highlands and Islands of Scotland, we beg to refer our readers to Anderson's Guide.

pleasing intervals. The many little bays and the rocky coasts, too, serve to vary the scenery. The vicinity of Thurso Bay becomes well and continuously cultivated. This beautiful and capacious circular expanse is protected by two lofty headlands, Holborn and Dunnet. The former, on the west, shelters the roadstead, near which are the foundations of Scrabster Castle, a residence of the Bishops of Caithness. Not the least distinctive feature of the scene are the grand precipices of Hoy seen in the offing.

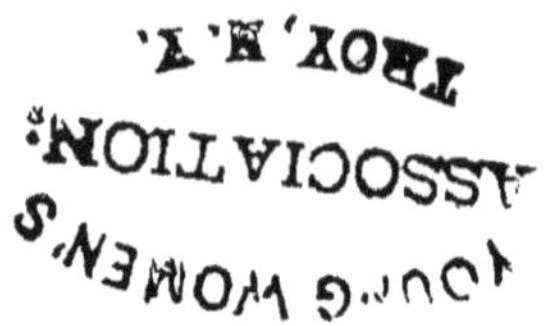

On Right from Edin.	From Jed.	EDINBURGH.		
		Leave Edinburgh by Newington.		
Grange House, Sir Thos. Dick Lauder, Bart.	49	Powburn.	2	
	48	Libberton vill. & Kirk.	3	
	47	Gilmerton.	4	Eldin, ——
In the neighbourhood Roslin Castle and Chapel.	45	Lasswade.	6	Melville Castle, Lo Melville.
Hawthornden, once the seat of Drummond the Poet; under the house are several curious caves.	43	cr. South Esk.	8	Newbattle Abbey, M quis of Lothian.
		Dalhousie.		
	42	Kirkhill vill. & Kirk.	9	Powder Mills, the old in Scotland.
Dalhousie Castle, Earl o Dalhousie, an ancient seat modernized.	39¾	Fushie Bridge.	11¼	Ruins of Borthwi Castle, with Borthw Kirk. The Castle is v entire, and was inhabi for a short time in 1567 Queen Mary and Bothw
	38	Middleton.	13	
Arniston, —— Dundas, Esq.	31	Crookston.		
Heriot House.		cr. Heriot Water.		
Heriot Kirk and Manse. Bowland, —— Walker, Esq.		cr. Crookston Wat.		
	27	Gala bank Inn.	24	Crookston House, Borthwick, Esq.
		Torsonce Inn.	25	
Torwoodlee and Ferniele, —— Pringle, Esq.	25½	Stow vill.	25½	Pirn, —— Tait, Esq.
		Buckholm Farm.		
Galashiels is separated from this line of road by the Gala, which joins the Tweed about a mile below.	20½	Laudhopeburn House.	30½	
		Langhaugh.		Langlee House, Bruce, Esq.
Gala House, —— Scott, Esq.		cr. Allan Water.		Pavillion, L. Somervi The vale of the Alla supposed to be the "G dearg" of the Monaster
Across the river may be seen Abbotsford, the seat of Sir Walter Scott.		cr. Tweed.		
		Darnick vill.		
Melrose Abbey, the finest specimen of Gothic architecture in Scotland.	1	MELROSE.	36	Near Melrose are Eildon Hills, on which the remains of Ro Camps.
		Eildon vill.		
In St. Boswell's Village a great annual fair is held on the 18th of July for horses, cattle, sheep, &c.	13	Newton, Dryburgh.	38	Dryburgh Abbey is be tifully situated on the bank of the Tweed. Walter Scott was inte here. Farther down Tweed is Mertoun, the s of Lord Polwarth.
	10	St. Boswell's.	41	
Ancrum House, Sir Wm. Scott, Bart.	3	Ancrum, where the Ale joins the Teviot.	48	
Near Ancrum the Battle of Lilliards Edge was fought in 1545, where a body of English troops, under Lord Evers and Sir Brian Latoun, were completely defeated by the Earl of Angus.		Teviot Bridge.		
	2	cr. Teviot.		
		Bonjedward.	49	Near Ancrum the Ro road from York to Firth of Forth passes.
		cr. Jed Water.		
		JEDBURGH.	51	

Jedburgh is situated on the west bank of the Jed, in the midst of a country beauti ooded. It is a royal burgh of very ancient erection, and was one of the chief Border to nd a place of considerable importance before the Union. After that period its trade a great measure, destroyed; it has now, however, greatly revived. The remains of bbey form the principal object of curiosity in Jedburgh. It was founded either in 11 147, and, after various damages in the course of the Border wars, was burnt by the Ea Hertford in 1545. It is a magnificent ruin, and is considered the most perfect and b ful specimen of the Saxon and early Gothic in Scotland. Part of the west end is fitte s a parish church. The Castle of Jedburgh, situated on an eminence at the town head, fortress of very great strength. The ground is now occupied by a Jail. The enviro edburgh abound in rich woodland scenes. Some remains of the famous ancient fores be seen in the neighbourhood of the half ruined castle of Ferniehirst, belonging to Marquis of Lothian, and the original seat of his ancestors, the Kers. Jedburgh cont bove 4000 inhabitants, and joins with Haddington, North Berwick, Dunbar, and Laude lecting a member of Parliament.

ON RIGHT FROM EDIN.	From Dumfries.	EDINBURGH. The road leaves Edinburgh by Nicolson Street.	From Edin.	ON LEFT FROM EDIN.
Morton Hall, R. Trotter, Esq.	72	Powburn.	2	At a little distance, th ruins of CraigmillarCastl
	71	Libberton Kirk.	3	Gracemount, Mrs. Ha]
Burdiehouse House, a corruption of Bourdeaux House, some French Protestants having emigrated hither from Bourdeaux after the revocation of the edict of Nantes in 1685.	70½	Burdiehouse.	3½	St. Catherine's.
	69	Straiton vill.	5	Near Straitonwas fough the second of three cor flicts which took place ' one day in 1302, styled th battle of Roslin.
	68	Pass Bilston Toll-bar, where road to Roslin parts off to left.	6	
At a little distance, Woodhouselee, F. Tytler, Esq.	67	Greenlaw.	7	Dryden House, G. Me cer, Esq.
Glencorse House and Church.		Auchindinny.		
	64	Penicuik.	10	Built as a depot fc French prisoners durin the late war, now occu pied as barracks.
Penicuik Ho., Sir George Clerk, Bart.	63	cr. North Esk.	11	
	62	Wellington Inn.	12	
Where the direct road to Dumfries parts off on the right.	61	Leadburn Inn.	13	Pass through a conside able tract of mooris country.
Early Vale.	60	Kingside Edge.	14	
Close to the village is Darnhall, a seat of Lord Elibank.	56	Eddleston vill.	18	Harcus Cottage, Ma kenzie, Esq. of Portmor
An ancient royal burgh beautifully situated on the Tweed. Population of the parish 2750. From this is six miles along the north bank of the Tweed to Innerleithen, a village resorted to for its mineral springs, and for rural recreations.	52	PEEBLES.	22	
	51		23	On the left Nidpat Castle, nearly in ruins, most romantic situation.
	49	cr. Lyne Wat.	25	
	46½	Stobo Kirk.	27½	Barns, Forrester, Esq.
	46	Stobo Castle, G. Montgomery, Bart.	28	Across the Tweed, th Vale of Manor, in whic lived David Ritchie, th original of the Blac Dwarf.
	44½	New Posso, Broughton vill.	29½	
	42½	Drummelzier Kirk.	31½	Oliver Castle ruins.
Drummelzier Castle was formerly the property of the powerful family of Tweedie, from whom it went to the family of the Hays. It is now the property of White, Esq.	37	Crook Inn.	37	Polmood House, Captai Forbes.
		Bield.		
	28	Tweed Shaws.	46	The remarkable hollo called the Devil's Bee stand.
	21	cr. Annan.	48	
		MOFFAT.	53	Moffat is a pleasai town, noted for its med cinal waters. Populatio about 1400.
There is another road from Edinburgh to Moffat and Dumfries, which leads by the Pentland Hills, Glencross, Linton, and Broughton villages, and joins the other road about 31 miles from Edinburgh. The distance between Edinburgh and Dumfries by this road is 71 miles.	19½	Beatock Inn.	54½	
	17½	Kirkpatrick Juxta.	56½	
	6½	cr. Water of Æ.	67½	Amisfield is the seat the ancient family of Ch teris.
	5	Amisfield House, with the old ruined tower of Amisfield.	69	Tinwald was the birtl place of Paterson, the pr jector of the banks of En land and Scotland, an likewise of the Scottish e pedition to Darien.
	3	Tinwald Kirk.	71	
		DUMFRIES. [*Inns*:—King's Arms; Commercial.]	74	

Dumfries was made a royal burgh in the thirteenth century. It contains few mon ments of antiquity, except an excellent bridge of three arches, which has stood for near 600 years. The most interesting circumstance connected with Dumfries is its having bee the residence and burial-place of Burns. St. Michael's church-yard contains an extr ordinary number of monuments of fine proportions and decorations. Dumfries unites wi Annan, Kirkcudbright, Lochmaben, and Sanquhar, in returning a Member of Parliamen

ON RIGHT FROM EDIN.	From Ayr.	EDINBURGH. Leave the city by Princes St.	From Edin.	ON LEFT FROM EDIN.
Near Merchiston Ho., 'alker, Esq.	69½	Gorgie Mills.	½	Dalry House, Walker, Esq.
		cr. Wat. of Leith.		
Saughton Hall, Baird, art.		Loanend.		
Saughton, Watson, Esq.	66	Long Hermandston vill.	6	Riccarton, Sir James Gibson-Craig, Bart.
	64	Addiston. } Earl of		
	63¼	Dalmahoy. } Morton.	7¼	
		cr. Gogar Burn.		
Hatton, Captain David-n ; formerly a resi-ence of the Lauderdale mily.	63	Burn Wynd Inn.	9	
	61¾	Wester Cocksiedean.	10¼	
		East Calder.		
The Church of Mid alder is a fine specimen ' an old parochial place ' worship in the Gothic yle. The father of Arch-shop Spottiswoode offici-ed here, being Minister Calder.	60	MID CALDER.	12	Close to Mid Calder is Calder House, the seat of Lord Torphichen, where John Knox preached, and where the only authentic portrait of him exists. The scenery around Mid Calder is of a very romantic description.
		From Mid Calder proceeds also the southern line of road to Glasgow.		
		cr. Almond Wat.		
	55½	West Calder vill.	16½	
		Here commences an extensive moor, unenlivened by any object of interest. At length, after passing near the extensive iron work of Shotts, the road begins to descend by the minor vale of Calder into the valley of the Clyde.		
A new road leads from is to Strathaven, crossing Clyde by the Garion idge ; another road, mewhat less direct, leads Hamilton. The for-r is used by the stage aches to Ayr.	44	Allanton, Lady Seton Stuart.	28	
	43	Bonkill.	29	
	42	Newmains Inn.	30	
		On left of Garion Bridge the vill. of Dalserf.		
		Stonehouse vill.		The road now passes over a long tract of moorish land, enlivened only by the towering form of London Hill, where Ayrshire is entered.
Vallace's Cairn, marking scene of a conflict be-een that hero and a party English.	32	STRATHAVEN.	40	
	22	Priestland.	50	
mile and a half to the ht is Drumclog, the ne of the battle of that ne, in May 1679, in ich Claverhouse was de-ted by the Covenanters.	21	Darvel vill.	51	The more direct road to Ayr from this point, leads by Fail and St. Quivex, saving two miles.
	17	Newmills vill.	55	
		GALSTON.		
	12	KILMARNOCK.	60	Kilmarnock is eminent as a seat of various branches of woollen manufacture. It now rivals Kidderminster in the manufacture of carpets. The cotton manufacture has also been introduced with marked success, and the town now produces shawls, gauzes, and muslins of the finest quality. The external appearance of Kilmarnock is very pleasing.
oudon Castle, the mag-cent seat of the Mar-s of Hastings.	11	cr. Irvine Water, and pass through	61	
		Riccarton vill.		
	7	Symington Kirk.	65	
	4	Monkton vill.	68	
	2¾	Priestwick vill.	69¼	
		AYR.	72	

From Ayr.	EDINBURGH.	From Edin.	ON LEFT FROM EDIN.
	Leave the city by the Lothian Road and Port-Hopetoun.		Craig Ho., Gordon
	Pass under the Union Canal aqueduct and Railway viaduct.		
73¾	Slateford vill.	3	The Caledonian Railway viaduct crosses the aqueduct of the Union Canal here.
70¾	Currie vill.	6	
69	Ravelrig.	7¾	At a little distance on the left, Colinton village.
65¾	Little Vantage Inn.	11	Lennox Tower in ruins, on a fine situation, commanding an extensive view. It has been a place of great strength.
64¾	Morton Castle Ruins.	12	
62¾	Causewayend Inn.	14	
61¾	cr. Linhouse Wat.	15	
59¼	Crosswood Hill.	17½	Easter Colzium, Linning, Esq.
	cr. Dryburn Burn.		
54¾	cr. Medwen Wat.	22	For many miles before and after this point, the road passes over a dismal moor.
51¾	Carnwath vill.	25	
48¼	Carstairs vill.	28½	Kersewell, Capt. Bertram.
47¼	Ravenstruther Toll.	29½	Carstairs Ho., Monteith, Esq.
	cr. Clyde.		At the distance of 2½ miles is Lanark, an ancient royal burgh; population of the parish 7672. The falls of the Clyde at Bonnington and Cora are about 2 miles from Lanark, approached by a road leading through New Lanark village, where the celebrated cotton mills, formerly conducted by Mr. Robert Owen, are to be seen.
44¾	Hyndford Bridge Inn.	32	
41¼	Hecklebirny.	35½	
38¼	Douglas Mill Inn.	38½	
36¼	Douglas.	40½	
	cr. Douglas Wat.		
25¾	Muirkirk.	51	
	Muirmill Bridge.		Between Cumnock and Muirkirk lies the extensive morass denominated Aird's Moss, where, on July 20, 1680, a skirmish took place between a body of dragoons, commanded by Bruce of Earlshall, and sixty-six Covenanters, under the conduct of Hackstoun of Rathillet and Mr. Richard Cameron.
20¾	cr. Ayr Wat.	56	
15¼	CUMNOCK. [*Inns:*—The Clydesdale Arms.]	61½	
9¾	Ochiltree.	67	
	cr. Burnock Wat.		
5¾	Drongan House.	71	
4¾	cr. Kyle Wat.	72¾	
1	Shawwood.	75¾	
	AYR.	76¾	

Castle,

ristie. Char- family occu- se for some ng quarters.

istance, Ric- -Craig, Bart.

G. Scott. rags, 866 feet

k, Macono- adowbank.

Ho., Sir N. Bart.

the original ily of Doug- cinity of the uglas Castle, Douglas. A ld church is epair, on ac- onuments in ying vault.

celebrated ufacture of ittle cabinets name of Cum- xes.

EDINBURGH—UPHALL

ON RIGHT FROM EDIN.

Murrayfield, W. Murray, Esq.

Beechwood, Dundas, Bart.

Corstorphine House, Keith, Bart.

Clermiston, Paterson, Esq.

Gogar House, Ramsay, Esq.

Ingliston, Gibson, Esq.

Newliston, James Hog, Esq., once the seat of the great Earl of Stair.

Kirkhill, the ancient family seat of the Earl of Buchan.

In Uphall Kirk lie interred the Hon. Henry Erskine and Lord Erskine, his brother.

A burgh of barony, supported mostly by weaving, and partly by the adjacent coal and lime works.

Bedlormie, Livingstone, Bart.

Auchingray, Hallane, Esq.

The road is here skirted by a fine sheet of water, from which the Canal is supplied.

Woodhall, Campbell of Shawfield.

Airdrie is a thriving modern town, which has been called into existence chiefly by the neighbouring iron works and collieries. It is situated between two rivulets on a rising ground, and is a handsome well-built town. The parish of New Monkland, in which Airdrie is situated, contains ... inhabitants.

Summerlee House, ... Baird, Esq.

Bailliestoun Ho., Maxwell, Esq.

Mount Vernon, Buchanan, Esq.

ON RIGHT FROM EDIN.		EDINBURGH. Leave the city by Princes St.		
Murrayfield, W. Murray, Esq.		Coltbridge.	-	Rosebery House, B four, Esq.
Beechwood, Dundas, Bart.		Corstorphine vill.	4	Saughton House, La Aberdour.
Corstorphine House, Keith, Bart.	37¾	North Guile.	5	Milburn Tower.
Clermiston, Paterson, Esq.	36¾	Nether Gogar.	6	Gogar Camp, Osborn Esq.
		cr. Gogar Burn.		
Gogar House, Ramsay, Esq.	36¼	Mount Gogar.	6½	
Ingliston, Gibson, Esq.		Golf Hall.		Wardlaw, Esq.
Newliston, James Hog, Esq., once the seat of the eat Earl of Stair.	35¼	Middle Norton.	7½	Norton House, Norto Esq.
		cr. Almond Wat.		Clifton Hall, Sir A. Gibso Maitland, Bart.
Kirkhill, the ancient mily seat of the Earl of achan.	32¾	cr. Broxburn.	10	
	31¾	Broxburn.	11	
Uphall Kirk lie interred e Hon. Henry Erskine, d Lord Erskine, his other.	30¾	UPHALL.	12	
		West Mains.		Middleton, Maxwell Esq.
A burgh of barony, supported mostly by weaving, d partly by the adjacent al and lime works.	24¾	BATHGATE.	18	Houston, Shairp, Esq. Robert Bruce gave th barony of Bathgate as portion with his daughte Marjory, who marrie Walter, the High Steward in 1315. Walter died a his castle here, the remain of which are still pointe out.
	20¾	Armadale Inn.	22	
Bedlormie, Livingstone, rt.		cr. Craigs Water.		
Auchingray, Haldane, q.		West Craigs Inn.		
The road is here skirted a fine sheet of water, m which the Canal is plied.	18¾	Auchingray.	24	The country is here generally a moorish upland variegated by few objects
		Blackrig.		
Woodhall, Campbell of awfield.	13¾	Pass Calder Water.	29	Moffat Hills in the south
Airdrie is a thriving mo-n town, which has been led into existence chiefly the neighbouring iron rks and collieries. It is ated between two rivu- on a rising ground, and handsomely built town. e parish of New Monk-d, in which Airdrie is ated, contains 9867 inhitants.		Clerkston vill.		Airdrie Place, Mis Mitchelson.
	10¾	AIRDRIE. [*Inns*:—Drummond's.]	32	
	9½	Cairnhall.	33½	
	7¾	Longloan.	35	
	6¾	Drumpellier	36	Drumpellier Ho., Buchannan, Esq.
	3	Shettlestone.	39¾	Barracknie, Hamilton, Esq.
ummerlee House, M'ire, Esq.		Joins the Mid Calder road.		Glenduff Hill, Tod, Esq.
aillieston Ho., Maxl, Esq.		Camlachie.		Larch Grove, Scott, Esq. Wellhouse, Millar, Esq.
Mount Vernon, Buchanan, Esq.		GLASGOW.	42	Greenfield, M'Nairn, Esq. Carntyne House, Gray, Esq.

INBURGH.—QUEENSFERRY.—INVERKEITHING.—KINROSS.— PERTH.—44 Miles.

ROM EDINB.	From Perth.	EDINBURGH.	From Edinb.	ON LEFT FROM EDINB.
's Well. se, Sir J. Nisbet. Park, Bonar, Esq. Quarry.		Leave Edinburgh by Queensferry road. cr. Water of Leith by Dean Bridge, a superb edifice of four arches, each 90 feet in span.		The old road passes between John Watson's Hospital, and the Orphan Hospital; both buildings of great elegance. Ravelston, Lady Murray Keith.
W. R. Ramsay,	40	Barnton.	4	Craigcrook, Lord Jeffrey. Craigiehall, Hope Vere, Esq.
f Cramond on the right.	39	cr. Almond by Cramond Bridge.	5	Dalmeny Kirk.
Park, Earl of Rose-		Hawes Inn.		
the south are the ıdas Castle, a build- t antiquity, which the Dundas family 700 years.	35	QUEENSFERRY. Cross Ferry.	9	Queensferry was erected into a royal burgh by Malcolm Canmore, and derived its name from Margaret his Queen, sister of Edgar Atheling. Here are the ruins of a monastery of Carmelite Friars, erected in 1330.
	33¾	North Queensferry Inn.	10¼	
l Ho. Earl of Moray ne. 11, 1592, of the he Earl of Moray by s of Huntly. This event is commemo- e ballad of "The of Moray."	31½	INVERKEITHING.	12½	A very ancient royal burgh, erected, it is said, by William the Lion. The bay is large and safe. Great quantities of coal and salt are annually exported here.
	27	Crossgates.	17	
o'onel Merce .	25	Cowden Beath Inn.	19	
, Earl of Minto.		cr. Orr.		Kirk of Beath.
Lady Scott.		cr. Kelty Water. Benarty Hill.		Maryburgh, the birth-place of the two brothers Adam, the distinguished architects.
	19	Gairney Bridge hamlet.	25	Blair-Adam, Sir C. Adam, long the seat of the Lord Chief Commissioner Adam, who did much for the improvement of the grounds.
	17	KINROSS. Population, 2017.	27	
Castle.	15	Milnathort.	29	
is situated on the anks of Lochleven. Castle, remarkable t antiquity, and as place where Queen imprisoned. The uced in Lochleven owledged excellence.	11¼	Damhead Inn.	32¾	The road now enters Glenfarg, a beautiful little valley enclosed by the Ochils. To the right Abernethy, the capital of the Pictish kingdom.
		Glen-Farg. Beild Inn.		
	4	Bridge of Earn.	40	In the neighbourhood of Bridge of Earn is Pitcaithly Well, celebrated for its medicinal waters.
		Moncrieffe Hill, On whose shoulder the traveller first comes in sight of Perth.		
		PERTH.	44	

one of the handsomest and most ancient towns in Scotland. It is beautifully situated on the of the Tay, having the spacious plains of the North and South Inches extending on each side t of its importance, and its vicinity to the royal Palace of Scone, it was long considered the cotland, before Edinburgh acquired that distinction. Here, too, the Parliaments and nationa were held, and many of the nobility took up their residence. A splendid bridge of ten arches t in length, leads across the Tay to the north. Perth contains several beautiful streets and nd a number of splendid public buildings. It is peculiarly rich in objects of historic and pic nterest. Of Gowrie House, the scene of a well known mysterious incident in Scottish history tunately not a vestige remains. In Blackfriars Monastery, which once stood at the north town, James I. was assassinated by a band of conspirators. The principal and oldest publi St John's Church, in which the demolitions of the Reformation commenced, in consequenc n preached by John Knox.

PERTH.—DUNKELD.—BLAIR ATHOLL.—INVERNESS.—117 Miles.

RIGHT FROM PERTH.	From Perth.		From Inverness.	ON LEFT FROM PERTH.
		PERTH.	117	Tulloch Printfield.
housie.	2½	Scone Palace.	114½	Earl of Mansfield.
icarty Bleachfield, near ih is the scene of the battle f ncarty, between the Scots a he Danes.	3	cr. Almond Water.	114	Feu House, —— Nicol, Esq.
	4½	cr. Shochie Water.	112½	
	8	New Inn.	109	
ar Stanley Mills, celebrated eir enormous wheels, and inn of Campsie.	9	Auchtergaven village, or Bankfoot.	108	
	12	Murthly Castle.	105	The walks through the policies of Dunkeld are upwards of 50 miles in length.
other road parts off directly to Blairgowrie. The preoute passes for some miles the east bank of the Tay.	14	Pass Birnam Hill and Hotel.	103	From this point a road proceeds by the west side of the river to Logierait, and thence by Aberfeldy to Kenmore.
		cr. the river Tay.		
nkeld is a place of great ity, and was at one time pital of ancient Caledonia.	15	DUNKELD.	102	Eight miles above Dunkeld, the united waters of the Tummel and Garry fall into the Tay.
of the principal objects of ity here, is the ruined dral. It must have been pile of building. The ecture is partly Gothic, Saxon.	20	Dowally Kirk.	97	
	23½	Logierait.	93½	The site of Faskally is of a peculiarly romantic character. It stands at the junction of three deep and confined valleys, and is encircled on all sides by diverging mountains.
	25	Moulinarn Inn.	92	
road now enters the pass lliecrankie, a narrow glen, bottom of which runs the uel water.	28	Pitlochrie.	89	
		cr. the Tilt.		In front, on the ascent to Urrard House, is the scene of the battle of Killiecrankie, fought July 26, 1689, between the Highlanders under Dundee, and the forces of King William under Mackay, the former being killed, and the latter defeated.
vale of the Tilt is celeI for its fine scenery, and ological wonders. At the of Tilt is an excellent	35	BLAIR ATHOL.	82	
	46	Dalnacardoch Inn.	71	
noble old Castle of Blair of Atholl), is in the neighood.	48	Dalnaspidal.	69	
		cr. Edindon Wat.		From Dalwhinnie the mountain of Benalder may be seen, situated on the north side of Loch Ericht.
out two miles from Blair the road crosses the , where that river makes es of cascades, which extensive celebrity.	59	Dalwhinnie Inn.	58	
	66	Etrish.	51	
ar Etrish there is a beautiaterfall.		cr. Truim Water.		Here a road parts off by Laggan and Garvamore, and over the difficult hill of Corrlarrack to Fort Augustus.
oss the Spey, ruins of ven Castle and Barracks, oyed by the Highlanders d.	69	Bridge of Spey.	48	
	72	Pitmain.	45	
	73	Kingussie.	44	From Pitmain may be seen the rocky barrier of Craig Dhu towards the west, the gathering place of the M'Phersons.
oss Spey, Invereshie, Sir M'Pherson Grant of Balloch.	76	Kincraig.	41	
thiemurchus, Sir J. P. t.	84½	Aviemore Inn.	32½	
posite Aviemore is Cairn- Hill.	92	cr. Dolnain Water by Bridge of Carr.	25	Belville, the seat of M'Pherson, the translator of Ossian, now possessed by Miss M'Pherson.
	101	Freeburn Inn.	16	
ar Moy Hall, M'Intosh of tosh. Here Prince Charles t was nearly taken by surin February 1746.	105	Moy Inn.	12	Inverness is a royal burgh of the first reformed class, joining with Forres, Fortrose, and Nairn in electing a Member of Parliament. Population 14,324. Inverness is considered the capital of the Highlands, being the only town of importance beyond Aberdeen.
	111	Daviot Kirk.	6	
	117	INVERNESS.		

GLASGOW.—RUTHERGLEN.—HAMILTON.—LANARK.—PEEBLES SELKIRK—HAWICK.—83½ Miles.

On right from Glasgow.	From Hawick.	GLASGOW. Leave Glasgow by the Calton. At Barrowfield take to the left.		
Near the ancient royal burgh of Rutherglen, of date 1126, now chiefly occupied by weavers.		cr. Clyde at Dalmarnock Bridge.		On the left, at a dis Clyde Iron Works.
	80	Cambuslang vill.	3½	Remarkable for a revival of religion, occurred there in c quence of the preach Whitefield.
Dechmont Hill is here a conspicuous object, it commands a very extensive view.	75½	Blantyre vill. and Priory on the left.	8	The remains of Bla Priory are deligh situated on the ban the Clyde, opposit Bothwell Castle. I neighbourhood there large cotton mill, v gives employment t persons.
Numerous neat villas on both sides of the road.	74¼	HAMILTON.	9¼	
Hamilton unites with Falkirk, Airdrie, Lanark, and Linlithgow in sending a representative to Parliament. Population of the parish in 1831, 9513. Close to the town is Hamilton Palace, the superb seat of the Duke of Hamilton. The interior of the palace is fitted up in the most gorgeous style; and the collection of paintings has long been considered the best in Scotland. Within the grounds, on the banks of the river Avon, the ruin of the ancient Castle of Cadzow is perched on the top of a rock 200 feet above the water.	67	Dalserf vill.	16½	
	60¾	Nethanfoot.	22¾	Near Mauldslie C Nisbet, Esq. once the s the Earls of Hyndfor
		Soon after pass Stonebyres Fall.		Stonebyres Fall, named from the adj estate of Stonebyr cataract of eighty- feet in height.
	59¼	cr. Clyde Water by Lanark Bridge.	24¼	
	58½	LANARK.	25	Lanark is a very an royal burgh conta about 4000 inhabitant
Twenty-two miles from Glasgow stands Craignethan Castle, on a lofty eminence near the conflux of the Nethan and the Clyde. This fortress, now in ruins, was once the seat of the celebrated personage called the Bastard of Arran.		cr. Clyde by Hyndford Bridge.		About a mile from ark, there is a prof ravine through whic Mouse water descen join the Clyde. The cipitous sides of the r are the celebrated land Crags, in Wallace found refu several occasions.
	48	Biggar.	35½	
		cr. Biggar Water.		
	41	Broughton.	42½	
	39½	Stobo Castle.	44	Montgomery, Bart.
Vale of Manor, in which lived David Ritchie, the original of the Black Dwarf.	39	Stobo Kirk.	44½	
		cr. Lyne Water.		Nidpath Castle, nea ruins, a most romantic ation.
	33	PEEBLES.	50½	
Innerleithen, a favourite resort of the citizens of Edinburgh, is a handsome village full of neat houses; its situation is very beautiful.	27	Innerleithen vill. and Mineral Wells.	56½	Horsburgh Castle in r Cardrona, Willian Esq.
	18	Fernalee or Yair Bridge.	65½	
Traquair House, Earl of Traquair.	12	SELKIRK.	71½	
		For the route between Selkirk and Hawick, see No. III.	83½	

GLASGOW.—DUMBARTON.—TARBET.—TYNDRUM.—FORT WILLIAM.—103 MILES.

RIGHT FROM GLASGOW.	From Fort Wil.	GLASGOW.	From Glasgow.	ON LEFT FROM GLASGOW.
		Leave Glasgow by Anderston.		
...nston Hill, Houldsworth, numerous other villas, be...ing to the wealthy citizens.		cr. Kelvin Water.		
	99½	White Inch.	3½	
...rdanhill, Smith, Esq.	93½	Kilpatrick vill.	9½	Dalnottar.
...mbarton is one of the four ...sses stipulated by the arti... of Union to be kept up, and ...dingly is still in repair, ...ccupied by a garrison.	92	Dunglas Castle ruins.	11	Near the termination of the Forth and Clyde Canal.
	88½	DUMBARTON.	14½	
...dale Ho., Stirling, Esq.		cr. Leven Water.		Levenside, Ewing.
...hill, Smollet, Esq. ...loch Castle Stott.	86½	Renton vill.	16¾	Near Smollet's monument, and Dalquhurn House, where he was born.
...h Lomond is on the right ...any miles.	85	Alexandria.	18	Broomley, Miss Alston. Tillichewen Castle.
	84	Lower end of L. Lomond.	19	Woodbank, Miss Scott. Bellretiro, Miss Rowet.
...meron Ho., Smollet, Esq.	82	Arden, Buchannan.	21	
...adow, Colquhoun, Bart.	78	cr. Fruin Water.	25	Glen Fruin was the scene of a bloody conflict between the M'Gregors and Colquhoun in 1603.
...ss is beautifully situated; ... waters of the Luss run ...gh it, and fall into Loch ...ond.	76½	Luss vill. and Inn.	26½	
	72¾	Inveruglas Ferry.	30¼	
...arly opposite Inveruglas ...d, in a hollow above a cascade, are the ruins of ...snaid Fort, an old mili...tation, chiefly designed to ...the Clan Gregor in check.	68½	Tarbet Inn.	34½	For crossing Loch Lomond to Rowardennan, where the ascent to Ben Lomond is usually commenced.
		Keep along the side of Loch Lomond.		Three miles above Tarbet is a small wooded island called Inveruglas, and about two miles farther, another called Ellan; on each of which are the ruins of a stronghold of the family of Macfarlane.
	65	Across the loch is Inversnaid Mill.	38	
	60	Head of Loch Lomond.	43	
	58	Auldtarnan Inn.	45	
...ar half way between ...laroch and Tyndrum, is a linn in the river the Pool of St. Fillan's, is to this day not un...ntly the scene of the ob...ce of a degrading super...s rite. Here St. Fillan, ...ed in the Highlands for ...of piety and sacred gifts, to have lived.	57	Glenfalloch, Campbell.	46	
	52	Proceed up Glenfalloch to Crianlaroch Inn.	51	On the right a road proceeds to Killin.
		Take to the left up Strathfillan.		Strathfillan was the scene of a battle of Robert Bruce.
	47	Tyndrum Inn.	56	Tyndrum Ho., Marquis of Breadalbane.
	38	Inverouran Inn.	65	Between Inverouran and King's House, the road crosses a lofty hill called the Black Mount. From the top an extensive view is obtained of the Moor of Rannoch, the largest tract of the kind in Scotland.
...the neighbourhood of ...hulish, is a cavern of ...ficult access, that no...f late has ventured to ...e it.	28½	Mountainous scenery to King's House Inn.	74½	
	26	Foot of the steep road to Fort William, called the Devil's Staircase.	77	
		Enter Glencoe.		Glencoe is famous for its singularly wild Alpine scenery, and the historical event connected with it. The massacre of Glencoe in King William's reign, took place at the north-west end of the Vale.
	14½	Ballachulish Inn.	88½	
...alled from the tradition ...rick, a Danish Prince, been drowned there.	13	The Ferry of Calas-ic Phatric.	90	Maryburgh contains about 1500 inhabitants, and two respectable inns.
...William is situated on ...re of Loch Eil, at the ...e of about two miles ...the termination of the ...of Corpach. It was ...in the reign of William ...the purpose of keeping ...he Jacobite clans of the	11	ONICH.	92	It contains a bomb-proof magazine, and the barrack is calculated to accommodate 96 men. The fort was besieged in 1745-6 by the Camerons, but without success. It is now almost in a state of disuse.
	7¾	Coran Ferry across Loch Eil.	95¼	
	½	Maryburgh.	102½	
		FORT WILLIAM.	103	

ON RIGHT FROM ABERD.	From Focha.		From Aberd.	ON LEFT FROM A
Mugiemoss, L. Ja. Hay. Caskieben, Dr. Henderson. Glasgowego.		ABERDEEN.* Cross the hill of Tyrebagger, *i.e.* Tirebeggar.	4½	Craibstone, Mrs. Scott. Glasgow Forest, Brebner.
Blackburn Inn. Balbethan, Gordon, Esq. Keith Hall, Earl of Kintore.	45	KINTORE, A borough of considerable antiquity.	12	Benachie rises tc height of 1420 feet. O east end is a remar rock, rising perper larly on three sides 18 it is only accessible o side; it has been fort tradition says, by the
The Bass, a conical mount of considerable elevation, said to be artificial. The river Ury runs close to it. Tradition says the pestilence was buried in it. Thomas the Rhymer has predicted:	41¾	Cross Don by a handsome of 3 arches, built in 1798.	15¼	
"Dee and Don shall run in one, And Tweed shall run in Tay, And the bonnie water of Ury Shall bear the Bass away." The first part of the prediction was fulfilled by the Inverury Canal. Pitcaple, Lumsden, Esq.	41½	INVERURY. Pitcaple Inn. At some distance, on the opposite side of the Ury, the battle of Harlaw was fought. "July 24, St. James's even, Harlaw was fought fourteen hundred and eleven."	15½	A borough of con able antiquity. Here ert Bruce gained a v over the English. in 1745, the rebels def a party of the King's tr Maner, Gordon, Es Balquhain, Leslie, Pittodrie, Erskine.
Logie, Elphinstone, Bart.	36	The Church of Oyne to the west 1 mile.	21	Old castle of Harth
	35	cr. the Gadie. "Oh an I were where Gadie rins, At the back of Benachie."	22	
Pitmachie Inn. Newton, Gordon, Esq.	33		24	
Williamston, Fraser, Esq.	31	Vill. of Old Rain.	26	At a distance ma seen the hill of Duni *i.e.* Dun d'Ore; on th of which are the ruins old castle, said to been the palace of Gregory the Great a 875. It has been surro ed by a double ram The walls, after encou ing 1000 winters, ar hard that the sma stone will break ra than be separated the mass; large mass vitrified stone are sca ed over the level to the hill, and mark many buildings.
Freefield, Gen. Leith.	30½	cr. Kelloch.	26½	
Enter the Glens of Foudland, through which the road passes for some miles. In stormy weather it is frequently shut up.	25	cr. the Ury, Here called the Glen Wat. On the left is the hill of Foudland, celebrated for its slate quarry, some of which are of the finest quality.	32	
Huntly Castle, a ruin partly built by George first Marquis of Huntly, whose name and that of his wife, Hen. Stewart, daughter of Esme Duke of Lennox, are in the hall. The extensive estates of the Gordon family have now devolved upon the Duke of Richmond.	19	cr. Bogie. HUNTLY. [*Inns:*—Gordon Arms.] Once celebrated for its linen manufacture, and still for its bleaching. Huntly Lodge.	38	Many years the resid of the last Duke of don when Mar. of Hu
	18	cr. Deveron.	39	
About a mile distant, the vill. of New Mills.	9	Keith vill. [*Inns:*—Gordon Arms.]	48	A short way below Deveron is joined by Bogie, and afterward the Isla, and after a co of 20 miles it falls into Moray Firth at Banff.
Shortly after leaving Keith, the road enters upon the property of the Duke of Richmond, and continues to Fochabers; close to which stands Gordon Castle, 560 feet in length. The park is 18 miles in circumference.	8	cr. Isla. Fife Keith vill. Barren moor to	49	
		FOCHABERS. [*Inns:*—Gordon Arms.]	57	

* The Great North Road from Aberdeen to Inverness, at the distance of 8½ miles from the fo divided into two, one branch by Turriff, Banff, and Cullen, being 72 miles; the other by Kintore, I ury, Huntly, and Keith, being 57 miles to Fochabers, where the roads again unite. The latter bein shortest line, is the mail coach road, and is now chiefly used by travellers.

..IGHT FROM ABERD.	From Inver.		From Aberd.	ON LEFT FROM ABERD.
..by, Hadden, Esq. ..daide, Kilgour, Esq. ..rton, Pirie, Esq. ..hill, Skene, Esq.	122	ABERDEEN. Leave Aberdeen, and pass for several miles along the bank of the Inverury Canal.		Hilton, Johnston, Bart. Kirkhill, Bannerman, Esq. Fintry House, Forbes, Bart. Kinmundy, Earl of Aberdeen. Elrick House, Burnett, Esq.
	116	cr. the Don by Bridge of Dyce.	6	Straloch, Ramsay, Esq. Barra, Ramsay, Esq. Fingask, Elmslie, Esq
..greig, Harvey, Esq. ..chie, Milne, Esq. ..y Castle, Col. Udney.	111	New Machar Kirk.	11	Tulloch, Kilgour, Esq
..lein, Manson, Esq.	107½	Leithfield.	14½	
..lo House, Earl of Aber-	104½	OLD MELDRUM. Meldrum Ho., Urquhart, Esq.	17½	
	99	Fyvie Kirk and village.	23	
..e Castle is a princely ..building, beautifully ..d on a small eminence ..centre of a large amphi- ..of fine grounds, skirted ..woods on the heights ..and the river winding ..the centre.	97	Fyvie Castle, Gordon of Fyvie, on the right.	25	
	94	Towie, The native place of the ancestor of Barclay de Tolly, i. e., Towie, the Russian general.	28	Gask, Earl of Fife.
..on Castle, Duff, Esq.		cr. Turriff Water.		
..ye're at the Brig o' ..ay, ..half-way between Aber- ..a and Elgin o' Murray."		Muiresk, Spottiswood, Esq. Laithers, Stuart, Esq.		
..atty Castle, Earl of Fife, ..from Turriff; not seen ..he road.	87	TURRIFF. Pronounced Turay.	35	
..gston Castle, Urquhart.		Forglen House, Abercromby, Bart., about a mile from Turriff. On the left Montblairy, Morison, Esq., and Eden, Duff, Esq.		Banff, the county town, agreeably situated on the side of a hill at the mouth of the river Deveron. It was founded by Malcolm Canmore in 1163 There have been large additional piers built to the harbour here, but, owing to the sandy bottom, the bar is often much filled up. On the left on entering the town is Duff House, the elegant mansion of the Earl of Fife.
..len Church on the north ..the river Deveron.		cr. King Edward.		
	76½	cr. Deveron River.	45½	
	70	BANFF.	46	
..een Boyndie and Portsoy ..ns of Boyne Castle, Earl ..ield, once the finest seat ..North of Scotland, but ..ed in the civil war.	72½	Boyndie Kirk.	49½	
		cr. Boyne Streamlet by Bridge of Broadlie.		Park, Gordon, Esq.
..this line of road the ..f Fife and Seafield, and ..e of Richmond, are the ..oprietors.	68	PORTSOY. A small irregularly built town, with a thriving port; population 2000.	54	Durn, Earl of Seafield. Glasshaugh, Abercromby, Esq. Birkenbog, Abercromby, Bart.
..Banff to Fochabers (26 ..the road passes at no ..listance from the sea.	63	CULLEN, A royal burgh in the Elgin district, population 1593.	59	Cullen House, Earl of Seafield, a large and venerable building. The grounds are fine.
..village of Buckle.	59	Letterfourie, Gordon, Bart.	63	Cairnfield, Gordon, Esq.
..village of Port Gordon.	50	FOCHABERS.	72	On the right from Aberdeen, and at the back of Fochabers, is Gordon Castle, Duke of Richmond; a magnificent mansion, erected by Alexander Duke of Gordon, who died in 1827. The ancient seat of the family was Huntly Castle, now in ruins; near it Huntly Lodge, Duchess of Gordon.
..nouth Kirk.		cr. Spey River, enter Morayshire. Innes House. Contown Tower. Kirk of St. Andrews.		
..royal burgh of Elgin is ..ashioned and impressive ..The remains of the ..al form the chief object ..tion in Elgin. It was ..in 1224 by the Bishop ..y. The great tower fell ..The Cathedral, when ..was exactly a model of ..l. Elgin has been much ..d of late years by the ..of various public build-	40	ELGIN. [*Inns:* — Gordon Arms; The Star Inn, called Devie's Hotel.] Joins with Banff, Cullen, Inverury, Kintore, and Peterhead, in electing an M. P.	82	

...M ABERD.	From Inver.		From Aberd.	ON LEFT FROM ABERD.
		[bridge] cr. the Lossie.		
	37	Newton House, Forteath.	85	
		Thunderton, Dunbar, Bart.		
	35	Kirk of Alves.	87	
...e east of Forres, ...road, stands the ...belisk, usually ...Stone; it is ...gh, with a num... ...cut on it, which ...bly distinct.	32	Burgie Castle, Tulloch, Esq. In distance, Abbey of Kinloss.	90	
		Grange Hall, Grant Peterkin, Esq.		Darnaway Castle, Earl ... Moray, not seen from the ro... It is four miles from Forr... The great hall was built by t... celebrated Regent Randol... the nephew of Bruce. It co... tains the *dais* of feudal tim... The original roof, which is ... dark oak, still remains. T... Findhorn flows by it throu... a well-wooded park. Immed... plantations of oak, pine, lar... &c., cover the whole count... side, and conceal the castle fr... view.
	28	FORRES. [*Inns:* Fraser's; M'Garrow's.] A royal burgh, in the Inverness district.	94	
...ruins of Abbey				
	27	Moy, Grant, on the right.	95	
...f Shakspeare has ...e town of Forres. ...ste, two or three ...oad to Inverness, ...nd Banquo were ...met the weird	26	Suspension bridge across River Findhorn.	96	
		Brodie House, Brodie, Esq.		
	24½	Dyke kirk and village.	97½	
...onical hill, about ...Forres, is erected ...mmemorate the ...algar.		Enter Nairnshire.		
	18½	AULDEARN.	103½	Auldearn was the scene of ... victory gained, May 4, 164..., the Marquis of Montrose c... an army of the Covenant... under Sir John Hurry.
		[bridge] cr. Nairn water.		
...distance is Port... ...table as the only ...tion in Britain, ...ete architype in ...e great fortresses ...t. Fort-George ...of Campbelton, ...averness.	16	NAIRN, A royal burgh of very old-fashioned appearance.	106	In the neighbourhood of N... is Cawdor Castle, the seat ... the Earl of Cawdor. It is ... of the most ancient and ent... baronial residences in Scotla... It stands upon a low rock, ov... hanging the bed of a torre... and is surrounded by the larg... sized forest trees. It is enclo... within a moat, and is approa... able only by a draw-brid... Macbeth was "Thane of C... dor."
	15	Firhall.	107	
	9½	Cross roads to Cawdor Castle and Campbelton.	112½	
...and a half miles ...h Castle Stuart, ...a ruin.	6	Castle Stewart.	116	
	4	Culloden House.	118	Cawdor Castle is five mi... from the Cross Roads. Th... is a village and good inn.
	1	Raigmore House.	121	The scene of the battle ... Culloden is a mile to the left ... Culloden House, about six mi... from Inverness.
...ntains a number ...ets, and has the ...dings of a large ... The whole en... ...utiful in a high ...re is no town in ... enjoys so many ...he famous Castle ...hich was the pro... ...ence of Macbeth, ...minence to the ...wn, termed the ...stle was destroy... ...Canmore, who ...another to serve ...idence and for... ...fice was destroy... ...y the troops of ...Stuart, and only ...interior rampart		INVERNESS. The remains of the fort which Oliver Cromwell built at Inverness are to be seen at the place where the Ness joins the sea. The most remarkable natural curiosity in the neighbourhood of Inverness is a strange oblong mound called Tom-na-heurich (hill of the fairies). Inverness joins with Forres,* Nairn, and Fortrose, in electing an M.P.	122	The most distinguished se... in the neighbourhood of Inv... ness are, Culloden House, Ra... more (Mackintosh, Esq.), N... Villa (Lady Saltoun), L... Castle (Mr. Baillie), Muir... (Mr. H. Duff), Dochfour (... Evan Baillie.) The banks ... the river near the town h... lately been ornamented w... tasteful residences, plantati... &c.

ON RIGHT FROM INVERS...

Clachnaharry Basin, the ...nd of the Canal.

Phopachy, Fraser.

Across Beauly Firth. Redcastle, the seat of ... Hugh Baillie.

Near the road, at the point where it enters Ross-shire, are two upright stones, standing in a line east and west, which mark the scene of a conflict between the Frasers and M'Kenzies.

Tarradale, Baillie.

Road to Fortrose.

Highfield, M'Kenzie.

One of the most remarkable things in the eye of a stranger, all through this tract, is the enormous mountain Ben Wyvis. Sir Hector Munro of Foulis, ..., proprietor of the mountain, holds his estate in Ross-shire, by a tenure from one of the early Scottish kings, bound to furnish ... bring three wain-loads of snow from the top of the hill, whenever his majesty shall so desire.*

Dingwall Castle was formerly the residence of the Earls of Ross.

Inchculter, Fraser; and ... Kilcairn and Novar, ... Munro.

Near Castle Leod, the ancient seat of the Cromarty family, and Castle House, M'Kenzie, Bart.

Invergordon Castle, M... Leod, Esq.

Tarbet House was the seat of the Cromarty family, and whence the first Earl took his title of Viscount Tarbet.

* The top of Ben Wyvis was never ..., when it was ...

ON RIGHT FROM INVERN.		INVERNESS. Leave Inverness by the Bridge over the Ness, and cross the Caledonian Canal.	From Invern.	ON LEFT FROM INVERN
hacnnaharry Basin, the d of the Canal. Phopachy, Fraser. Across Beauly Firth, dcastle, the seat of Col. gh Baillie.	173	Bunchrew, Fraser.	2	Muirtown, Duff. Bunchrew, or Bunch rive, was long the res dence of President Forbe
Near the road, at the nt where it enters Ross-re, are two upright nes, standing in a due east and west, which rk the scene of a con-t between the Frasers M'Kenzies.	167½	Kirkhill Kirk.	7½	Near Auchnagairn, Re lig, Warrenfield, and Fi gask.
	165	cr. Beauly river, and enter BEAULY.	10	Beauly, a pleasant vil lage, with the ruins o Beauly Priory, and at n great distance Kilmorac waterfalls. Farther u the Beauly, Beaufort Cas tle, the seat of Lord Lo vat.
Carradale, Baillie. Road to Fortrose. Highfield, M'Kenzie.		Enter Ross-shire.		
One of the most remark-e things in the eye of a nger, all through this ct, is the enormous untain Ben Wyvis. Sir ctor Munro of Foulis, proprietor of this untain, holds his estate Ross-shire, by a tenure n one of the early Scot- kings, binding him to g three wain-loads of w from the top of the whenever his majesty ll so desire. *	163	Gilchrist Kirk.	12	Ord House, M'Kenzie.
	161	Urray Kirk.	14	
	157	Bridgend vill.	18	Brahan Castle, M'Kenzie of Seaforth.
	156	Pitglassie vill.	19	Conon, M'Kenzie.
Dingwall Castle was for-ly the residence of the ls of Ross.	153½	Dingwall.	21½	Dingwall was erected into a royal burgh by Alexander II. in 1226. Near the town are the ruins of the ancient residence of the Earls of Ross. Near the church is an obelisk, fifty-six feet high, though only six feet at the base, intended to distinguish the burial-place of the Cromarty family.
cheulter, Fraser; and cairn and Novar, ro.	151½	Ardulie, and	23½	Near Tulloch, Davidson.
	150	Foulis, Munro, Bart.	25	At the head of Strathpeffer, about four miles from Dingwall, there is an excellent and well-frequented mineral well, round which are congregated a considerable number of buildings.
ear Castle Leod, the ent seat of the Cromarty family, and Coul se, M'Kenzie, Bart.	145½	Alness Kirk.	29½	
	141	Rosskeen Kirk.	34	
vergordon Castle, M'-l, Esq.	139¾	Invergordon vil. & seaport.	35¼	There are some fine views of the opposite coast through the Sutors of Cromarty.
	138	Kilmuir Kirk.	37	
rbet House was once seat of the Cromarty ly, and whence the Earl took his first of Viscount Tarbet.	137	Tarbat House.	38	Balnagown Castle, Sir Chas. Ross, Bart.
	131½	Knockbrake House.	43½	Calrossie, H. R. Ross, Esq.

*The top of Ben Wyvis was never known to be uncovered by snow, till the memorably warm season of when it was quite bare.

ERN.

from Tain to
a very singular
tance between
wns, straight
firth, is only

e of Lochlin is
le building; it
500 years.
'Kenzie, (po-
ominated *The*
enzie,) King's
the reign of
was born there.
dge is a strong
ent structure,
iron. It cost

h Church is an
t feet by four,
memory of a
eftain. Here,
mit of a hill,
out into the
noted vitrified
Dun Creech.

lspie, all the
a, the road is
neat cottages,
by shrubberies
with honey-
ra is one of
lages built by
f Sutherland.
l at the mouth
Brora, which
rough a vale
romantic and
acter.

From Thurso.	TAIN.	From Invern.
	[*Inns:*—The George; The Dragon; Balnagown Arms.]	
128		47
126	On right Meikle Ferry for Dornoch, which, if taken, cuts of 19 miles of road.	49
125	Edderton Kirk.	50
118	West Fearn.	57
116½	Kincardine Inn.	58½
	cr. Firth of Dornoch, by Bonar Bridge.	
115¼	Bonar Inn.	59¾
103¾	Clashmore Inn.	71¼
	Dornoch.	
100¾	[*Inns:*—The Sutherland Arms.]	74¼
98	cr. Loch Fleet, By a stupendous mound, built to dam out the sea—Cost £9600. The Cathedral was fitted up by the late Duchess Countess of Sutherland, at an expense of £6000, as the parish church.	77
89¾	Golspie vill.	85¼
	[*Inns:*—The Sutherland Arms.]	
83¾	Brora.	91¼
82¾	Kirk of Clyne.	92¼
81¾	Kinkradwell.	93¼
77¾	Loth Kirk.	97¼
72	Helmsdale vill. [*Inns:*—The Ross Inn. M'Kay's.]	103

ON LEFT FROM INVERN.

Tain is an irregularly built town, with several new and handsome houses. It is situated on the margin of the Dornoch Firth. The ancient church of Tain was collegiate, and dedicated to St. Duthus. James IV. performed pilgrimage to the shrine of this Saint, to whose honour several churches were at different times built in this place.

Near Fearn, there are the ruins of an abbey of great antiquity, founded by the first Earl of Ross. Patrick Hamilton, an abbot of this place, was the first who suffered in this country for the Reformed religion. Near the abbey is a high square column covered with Saxon characters.

Skibo Castle, G. Dempster, Esq.

Ospisdale, D. Gilchrist, Esq.

Dornoch is one of the most miserable of our royal burghs. It is nevertheless, the county town of Sutherland, and formerly was the seat of the bishopric of Caithness.

Dunrobin Castle, the seat of the Duke of Sutherland, occupies an eminent site upon the shore, a little beyond Golspie, and is surrounded by some fine old wood, besides extensive modern plantations. It is said to have been founded in the 13th century by one of the earliest Earls of Sutherland. About a mile farther on, between the road and the beach, stands one of those unaccountable relics of antiquity, called Picts Houses.

Adjoining Helmsdale are the ruins of a romantic old castle, once the seat of an extensive proprietor of the name of Gordon.

ON RIGHT FROM INVERN.

The Ord Mountains [illegible] lie between [illegible] and Berridale, and the road passes over them, but without danger.

In the immediate neighbourhood of Berridale Inn [illegible] stand the ruins of [illegible] castle, once the residence of the Sutherlands of Langwell, the ancient Lords of Berridale, [illegible] according to tradition, a gigantic race.

Dunbeath Castle, [illegible] Sinclair, Esq.

Latheron House, W. S. [illegible]

Latheron Kirk.

Swiney House, [illegible]

Lybster village.

Lybster Ho., Capt. [illegible]

[illegible] House, Sir G. [illegible]

Thrumster Ho., Sir G. [illegible]

[illegible] House, [illegible] Lady D[illegible]

Castle of Old Wick [illegible]

Ackergill Tower, Sir George [illegible], Bart.

Ruins of Castles Sinclair and Girnigoe, [illegible] two-and-a-half miles from [illegible]

[illegible] Kirk.

[illegible] Ho., Kenneth M'Leay, Esq.

Keiss Castle, ruins, [illegible] seat of the Earls of Caithness.

Ruins of Bucholie Castle, [illegible] the seat of the [illegible]

[illegible] House, J. J. A. [illegible], Esq.

Brabster House, [illegible]

Canisbay Kirk.

John o' Groat's House.

Duncansby Head.

Barrogil Castle, Lord Caithness.

[illegible] House, G. Traill, Esq.

Dunnet Kirk.

Castlehill House, Geo. Traill, Esq., M.P.

Thurso-East Castle, [illegible] Sir George Sinclair [illegible], Baronet.

Thurso is a burgh of barony [illegible]

INVERNESS TO THURSO—*Continued.*

...RIGHT FROM INVERN.	From Thurso.		From Inverness.	ON LEFT FROM INVERN.
...e Ord Mountains (1200 feet ...) lie between Helmsdale ... Berridale, and the road ...s over them, but without ...er.				Scarabin. Maiden Pap. Morven.
...the immediate neighbour... of Berridale Inn, on a ... crag, stand the remains of ...tle, once the residence of ...Sutherlands of Langwell, ...ncient Lords of Berridale, ... according to tradition, a ... gigantic race.	62¼	cr. Berridale water. Berridale vill. [*Inns:*—Berridale Inn.]	112¾	Langwell House, Donald Horne, Esq., W.S.
	56¼	cr. Dunbeath water. Dunbeath Inn.	118½	
...nbeath Castle, J. J. A. ...air, Esq.	52¾	cr. water of Latheronwheel.	122¼	Latheronwheel House, Hon. Captain Dunbar.
...heron House, W. S. Munro,				
...theron Kirk.		Swiney vill. [*Inns:*—Swiney Inn.]		Nottingham House, George Sutherland, Esq. of Forse.
...iney House, Gordon.	49¼		125¼	Stemster and Rangag Lochs. Near the latter is a Druidical temple and the Arch-Druid's house.
...bster village.	48¼	cr. water of Lybster.	126¼	
...bster Ho., Captn. Sinclair.				
...the House, Sir G. Sinclair.	46¾		128¼	Bruan Kirk.
...bster Ho., Sir G. Sinclair.				Thrumster House, Robert Innes, Esq
...mprigg's House, Right ...ourable Lady Duffus.	37¾		137¼	
...stle of Oldwick (a ruin.)				
...kergill Tower, Sir George ...ar, Bart.	35½	cr. water or river of Wick.	139¾	Wick is the principal seat of the herring fishery in Scotland. It is a thriving and fast-increasing town. Piers and other erections have lately been built at the harbour, costing upwards of L.13,000.
...ins of Castles Sinclair and ...ro (south side of Sinclair's ...two-and-a-half miles from ...)	32¾	cr. water of Wester.	142¼	From Wick the mail road to Thurso (21 miles distant) proceeds from a point south of the river, keeping the south side o the Loch of Watten, and passing east of the village of Halkirk.
...iss Kirk.				
...iss Ho., Keir M'Leay, Esq.	25¾		149¼	
...iss Castle, ruins, formerly ... of the Earls of Caithness.		Nybster Inn.		
...ns of Bucholly Castle, for... the seat of the Mowats.				
...swick House, J. J. A. Sin... Esq.	23¾	Freswick. Prince Albert's Inn.	151¼	Wester House and Loch.
...bster House, Sinclair.				
...nisbay Kirk. ...n o' Groat's House ...ncansbay Head. ...rrogil Castle, Lord Caith...	18¾	Huna Inn.	156½	
...tter House, G. Trail, Esq.				
...nnet Kirk.	8¾	Dunnet Inn. Castletown. Castletown Inn.	166¼	
...tlehill House, Geo Trail, M.P.				Castletown Kirk. Olrig House James Smith, Esq. Murkle House.
...rso-East Castle, residence ...r George Sinclair of Ulb... Baronet.	1	THURSO. [*Inns:*—Mackay's; Kelly's.]	175	

...hurso is a burgh of barony, holding of Sir George Sinclair of Ulbster. In the neighbourhood is a highly ...mental structure which the late Sir John built to the memory of Harrold, Earl of Caithness, who was slain ...buried on the spot upwards of six centuries ago. The coast to the west increases in terrific wildness and ...deur, till it terminates at Cape Wrath.

I.—CALEDONIAN RAILWAY.—(Edinburgh Branch.)

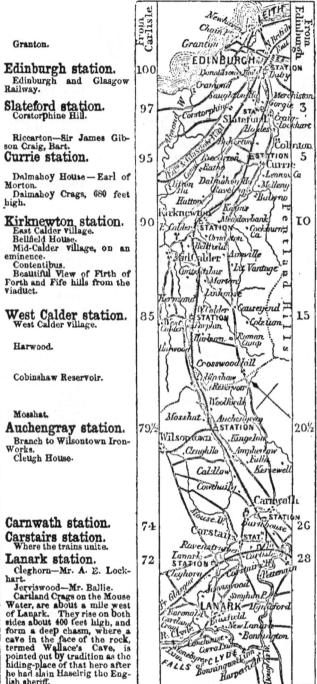

ON RIGHT FROM EDINBURGH.	From Carlisle	EDINBURGH—LANARK.	From Edinburgh	ON LEFT FROM
Granton.				North British Railway.
Edinburgh station. Edinburgh and Glasgow Railway.	100			**Edinburgh statio** Dalry village.
				Merchiston.
Slateford station. Corstorphine Hill.	97		3	**Slateford station.** Viaduct over Water of I Hailes House.
Riccarton—Sir James Gibson Craig, Bart.				Baberton House — Ca Christie.
Currie station.	95		5	**Currie station.** Currie village. Ruins of Lennox Castl Ravelrig Hill.
Dalmahoy House—Earl of Morton. Dalmahoy Crags, 680 feet high.				Balerno—Lord Cockbu Meadowbank — Lord dowbank.
Kirknewton station. East Calder village. Bellfield House. Mid-Calder village, on an eminence. Contentibus. Beautiful View of Firth of Forth and Fife hills from the viaduct.	90		10	**Kirknewton stati** Kirknewton village. Ormiston village.
				Viaduct over the Lin w in 6 arches of 60 feet span 103 feet above the stream
West Calder station. West Calder village.	85		15	**West Calder stati**
Harwood.				Harburn—Mr. Cochran
Cobinshaw Reservoir.				The surrounding count this part is bleak and uni esting.
Mosshat.				Woolfords.
Auchengray station. Branch to Wilsontown Iron-Works. Cleugh House.	79½		20½	**Auchengray stati** Ampherlaw—Dr Some
				Carnwath village.
Carnwath station.	74		26	**Carnwath station**
Carstairs station. Where the trains unite.				**Carstairs station,** Where the trains unite.
Lanark station. Cleghorn—Mr. A. E. Lockhart. Jerviswood—Mr. Ballie. Cartland Crags on the Mouse Water, are about a mile west of Lanark. They rise on both sides about 400 feet high, and form a deep chasm, where a cave in the face of the rock, termed Wallace's Cave, is pointed out by tradition as the hiding-place of that hero after he had slain Haselrig the English sheriff.	72		28	**Lanark station.** In the vicinity of La are the Falls of the Clyde. Bonnington Linn (the u most fall) the water is th over a perdendicular about 30 feet in height i deep hollow or basin. C Linn, the largest of the is half a mile below the fo The river here makes distinct leaps, in height gether of about 84 feet.

r.

by
be
ect
ic-

al

th

r.

l.

ON RI

Grar

Edin

Edin
Railwa

Slate

Cors

Ricc
son Cr

Curri

Dalm
Morton
Dalm
high.

Kirk

East
Bellfi
Mid-
eminen
Cont
Beau
Forth a
viaduct

West

West

Harw

Cobir

Mossl

Auch

Bran
Works.
Cleug

Carn

Carst

Wher

Lana

Clegl
hart.
Jervi
Cartl
Water,
of Lan
sides al
form a
cave in
termed
pointed
hiding-
he had
lish she

CALEDONIAN RAILWAY.—(GLASGOW FORK.)

RIGHT FROM GLASGOW.	From Carlisle	GLASGOW—CRAWFORD.	From Glasgow	ON LEFT FROM GLASGOW.
asgow station. utherglen. ambuslang.	101			**Glasgow station.** The temporary route by the Garnkirk Railway will be supplanted by the more direct line of the Clydesdale Junction.
rnkirk station. e Priory—Lord Blantyre. dins of Bothwell Castle.				**Garnkirk station.**
tbridge station. othwell village. amilton.			9½	**Coatbridge station.** Cross the Monkland Canal by a wooden viaduct. Woodhall in the distance.
lytown station.				**Holytown station.**
therwell station. lziel House—Mr J. G. C. ilton.	89		12	**Motherwell station.** Cleland House—Hon. North Dalrymple, Esq.
shaw station.	86		15	**Wishaw station.** Wishaw Castle—Lord Belhaven.
rtown station. lserf village. auldslie Castle. lton—Mr. Wm. Lockhart,	84½		16½	**Overtown station.**
luke station.	82		19	**Carluke station.** Carluke village.
	80½		20½	
House—Sir N. M. Lockhart, Bart. viswood—Mr. G. Baillie. wn of Lanark.				Kilcadzow village.
ark station. of the Clyde.	76		25	**Lanark station.** Viaduct over Mouse Water. Carstairs village.
tairs junction st. tairs House—Mr. Henry ith.	73½		27½	**Carstairs junction st.** Branch to Edinburgh.
tairs junction st. luct over the Clyde. nain House. ngrife House. michael House—Sir W. ther, Bart.	73½		27½	**Carstairs junction st.** Carnwath village. Liberton village. Covington Castle—ruins.
kerton station. o Hill, 2300 feet high. ips Castle.	68½		32½	**Thankerton station.** Symington village.
ngton station. on village. gavel Hill. lington—Mr. R. Mac-	66½		34½	**Symington station—for Biggar.**
rton village.	64		37	Lamington village. Woodend. Clyde's Bridge. Duneaton.
gton station.	57½		43½	**Abington station.** Crawford village. Castle in ruins.
	56		45	

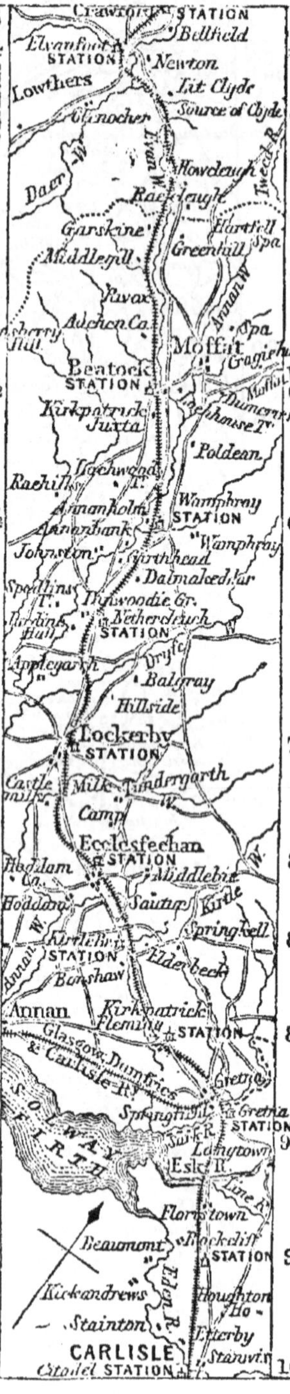

ON RIGHT FROM GLASGOW.	From Carlisle	CRAWFORD—CARLISLE.	From Glasgow	ON LEFT FROM GLA
	56	Crawford STATION	45	
Elvanfoot station. The Lowther hills, 3150 feet high. Glenocher. Garskine. Middlegill. Rivax. Auchen Castle. Queensberry Hill, 2260 feet high.	54	Elvanfoot STATION	47	**Elvanfoot statio** Newton. Source of Clyde. Howcleugh. Raecleugh. Greenhill. Moffat village.
Beatock station—for Moffat. Kirkpatrick Juxta. Lochwood Tower. Rachills—J. J. H. Johnston, Esq., M.P.	39½	Beatock STATION	61½	**Beatock station Moffat.** Lochhouse Tower. Poldean. Viaduct over the Water, 350 feet in lengt
Wamphray station. Johnston village. Spedlin's Tower. Dinwoodie—A. Maxwell.	34½	Wamphray STATION	66½	**Wamphray stati** Oblique bridge over phray Water. Wamphray village. Dalmakeddar.
Nethercleuch station. Jardine Hall—Sir W. Jardine, Bart Applegarth village. Viaduct over Dryfe Water	29	Nethercleuch STATION	72	**Nethercleuch sta** Millkbank—Wm. Roy Hillside—C. Stewart.
Lockerby station. Lockerby village. Castlemilk—Mrs. Hart.	26	Lockerby STATION	75	**Lockerby station** Bridge of 6 arches ov Milk Water. Fine vie both sides.
Ecclefechan station. Hoddam Castle—Lieut.-General Sharpe. Hoddam village.	20	Ecclefechan STATION	81	**Ecclefechan stati** Viaduct over Main W Bridge over the cross 120 feet in length.
Kirtle Bridge station. Bonshaw Tower. Beautiful scenery along the banks of the Kirtle Water.	17	Kirtle Bri. STATION	84	**Kirtle Bridge sta** Viaduct over Kirtle W Elderbeck.
Kirkpatrick station. Branch to Annan and Dumfries. Springfield village.	13	Kirkpatrick Fleming STATION	88	**Kirkpatrick stati**
Gretna station. Bridge over the river Sark, the boundary between England and Scotland. Viaduct over the Esk river.	8½	Gretna STATION	92½	**Gretna station.** Skiddaw and Keswick of mountains seen from point. Floristown village.
Rockcliff station. Stainton village. Viaduct over the river Eden.	4	Rockcliff STATION	97	**Rockcliff station.** Houghton House.
Carlisle station.		CARLISLE Citadel STATION	101	**Carlisle station.**

II. DUNDEE, ARBROATH, AND FORFAR RAILWAY.

IGHT FROM DUNDEE.	DUNDEE TO ARBROATH AND FORFAR. From Forfar	From Dundee	ON LEFT FROM DUNDEE.
Dundee station. principal objects to be n Dundee, are the Town Exchange, Academy, the or Burying-Ground and ower of the Old Church.	32		**Dundee station.** Dundee is the chief seat of the linen manufacture, and one of the most prosperous towns in Britain.
roughty station. ughty Ferry, a sea-bathllage. Near it are the of an ancient fortress, was occupied by the h after the battle of .	29	3	**Broughty station.**
onifieth station.	27	5	**Monifieth station.** Monifieth is a small village of thatched houses, and contains a somewhat extensive iron foundry.
			Barry village.
noustie station.	22	10	**Carnoustie station.** Panbride village contains an ancient church. Hector Boece is generally supposed to have been a native of this village.
Havenstation.	20	12	**East Haven station.**
			Arbirlot village, near which are the ruins of Kelly Castle, standing on a rock.
broath station. onth is a royal burgh. ns of its extensive Ab. much admired. It was about the year 1178 liam I., and dedicated mas à Becket.	15¾	16¾	**Arbroath station.**
			Lethem village, standing on the summit of a table land, commanding an extensive prospect.
lliston station. ell.	11	21	**Colliston station.**
eockheim sta. to Aberdeen branches	8½	23½	**Freockheim sta.**
uthrie station.	6½	25½	**Guthrie station.** Kirkden village. Dunnichen village.
ne village. is a royal burgh, and f great antiquity. **orfar station.**		32	In the castle of Forfar, no vestige of which now remains, Malcolm Canmore is said to have held a Parliament in the year 1057.

III.—DUNDEE, NEWTYLE, CUPAR-ANGUS RAILWAY, 15 MILES,

With Branch to Glammis.

Dundee station.

Claverhouse, a modern erection, built on the site of the ncient residence of Viscount undee.

Strathmartin village.
Strathmartin House.

Auchterhouse village.

Auchterhouse Castle, (Lady . Wedderburn.)

Ruins of Hatton Castle, built n 1575 by Lawrence, Lord Oliphaut.

Newtyle station.

Belmont Castle, the seat of ord Wharncliffe, is an eleant quadrangular mansion, rrounded with gardens, oods, and lawns, and companding an extensive view. In he park is a tumulus assigned y tradition as the scene of he combat between Macbeth nd Macduff.

Cupar-Angus sta.

Kinpirnie Hill, 1151 feet high.

Banquo tower.

Nevay village.

Denoon Castle, supposedly esigned as a place of retreat n times of danger.

Glammis Castle, the property f the Earl of Strathmore, is a ajestic pile of great antiquity.

Glammis station.

Dundee station.

Dudhope Castle.
Dundee Law.

Camperdown House, seat of the Earl of Camdown,) so named from Adral Lord Duncan's victor 1797, and built for that gal officer by government. N it is Gray House, the fa mansion of Lord Gray

Lundie Castle (Cap Wemyss.)

Lundie village, situated a small loch.

Newtyle station.

Newtyle has lately risen fr obscurity to the importance a bustling town.

Auchtertyre, where there traces of a camp said to been occupied by the Mar of Montrose.

Hallyburton House (L Hallyburton, M.P.)

Kettins village, near wh on the summit of a hill, st the Castle of Dores, traditio ly reported to have been residence of Macbeth.

Cupar-Angus sta

Belmont Castle.

Meigle, an insignificant lage. The churchyard conta a very antique and curious m nument, upon which are presented some of the scene the life of King Arthur's fa less queen, Vanora. Most the carvings are now defaced destroyed.

Castleton village.

Essie village.

Glammis station.

The village of Glammis c sists of an old and new to and is of considerable size.

NR.

) the

Lord

a.

Ca-

ban-
the
Er-
Lord
iter-

ON.

ross-
-five
and
feet

the
ches

tion

1.
one
sta-
ius.

pert

Var-
a

nd
vay

Du

Clav
tion, t
aucien
Dunde

Strat
Stra

Auc

Auc
H. W

Rui
in 157
phaut

N

Bel
Lord
gant
surro
wood
mand
the p
by tr
the c
and l

C

Kin

Ba

Ne

De
desig
In th

Gla
of th
maje

G

IV.—EDINBURGH AND GLASGOW RAILWAY.

EDINBURGH.—LINLITHGOW.—FALKIRK.—GLASGOW.—46 Miles.

...HT FROM EDINR.	From Glasgow.	GLASGOW TO EDINBURGH.	From Edinr.	ON LEFT FROM EDINR.
...dinr. station. ...son's Hospital.	46			**Edinr. station.** Pentland Hills seen to the left.
...phine Hill, richly ...nd covered with villas. ...ood, (Sir George ...s.)				Saughton House, (Lord Aberdour.
...storphine sta. ...n Tower, (Mrs. Lis...erly the residence of ...ous ambassador Sir ...ton.	43		3	**Corstorphine sta.**
...ogar station.	41½		4½	**Gogar station.** Ratho House, (Robert Cadell, Esq.)
...atho station. ...on, (J. M. Hog, Esq.) ... Castle, where Queen ... slept after her escape ...hleven.	39			**Ratho station.** Ratho village. Tunnel.
...nchburgh sta. ...of Winchburgh, where ...II. first halted in his ...n Bannockburn. ... Tower, on a range of ... to the right.	35		11	**Winchburgh sta.** Uphall village. In the chancel of the parish church, the celebrated barrister Henry Erskine, and his brother, Lord Chancellor Erskine, lie interred.
...nlithgow sta. ...gow Palace was a ...ience, and the birth... Queen Mary. In ...h James IV. saw the ... which warned him ... at Flodden Field.	29½		16½	**Linlithgow station.** The River Avon is here crossed by a viaduct of twenty-five arches, each fifty feet span, and from seventy to eighty feet high.
...mont station. ... Village. ...r House, (William ...sq., M.P.) formerly ... the Earls of Callan...nlithgow.	24½		21½	**Polmont station.** From near Polmont, the Slamannan Railway branches off to Airdrie.
...kirk station. ...is noted for its great ...ket. The battle of ...as fought in 1298. ...e, Prince Charles ... defeated General ...1746.	21½		24½	**Falkirk station.** Viaduct over the Union Canal, 102 yards long.
...stlecary sta. ...h Central Railway ...ff from this station ... Perth, &c.	15		31	**Castlecary station.** Where are the ruins of one of the Præsidia or principal stations on the wall of Antoninus.
...roy station. ... a village of about ...itants. Here was ... battle of Kilsyth, ...Montrose and the ...s, in 1645. The ruins ...Castle, anciently the ...f the Kilsyth and ... families.	11½		34½	**Croy station.** Dumbreck House, (Robert Scott, Esq.) Garnkirk Railway to Carluke, from which there is a coach to Lanark.
...intilloch sta. ...loch, an old Roman	6½		39½	**Kirkintilloch sta.** From which the Monkland and Kirkintilloch Railway branches off.
...bridge sta.	3½		42½	**Bishopbridge sta.**
Tunnel. **...gow station.**			46	Tunnel. **Glasgow station.**

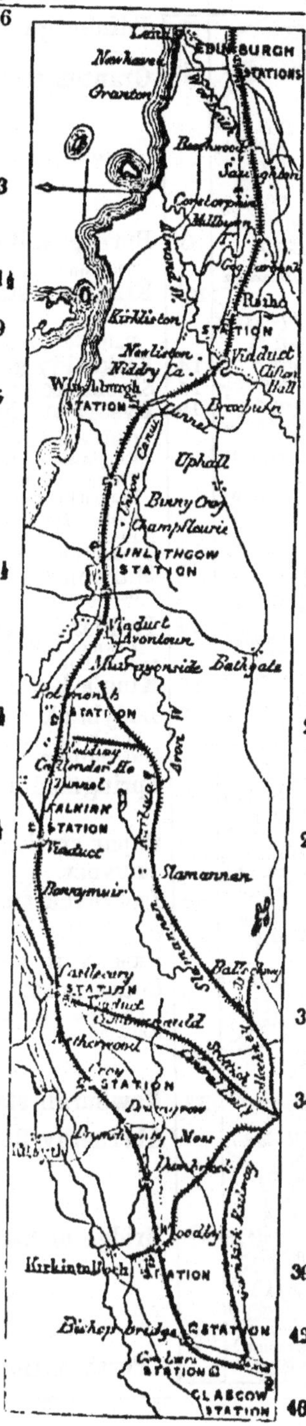

'ant of space the continuation of the route from Cupar to Dundee is not given.

OM EDINBURGH.	From Perth.	EDINBURGH — CUPAR — DUNDEE — PERTH.	From Edinb.	ON LEFT FROM EDINBURGH
station.	45			Edinburgh station.
tation.	41		7	Granton station.
'th of Forth.				Cross the Firth of Forth.
and and Light-				
d station. r.	36		8	Burntisland station
station.	33½		10½	The Binn and King's Crag. Kinghorn station.
'er, ancient re- Moutries.				Raith—Colonel Ferguson.
station.	30		14	Kirkcaldy station.
station.	29		15	Sinclairtown statio
tion.	28		16	Dysart station.
village.				Gallowton village.
stle — Captain				Kinglassie village.
duff Castle. tle.				Thornton village. Branch line to Dunfermli
use—Drinkwa- sq.				Leslie House — Earl Rothes. Viaduct over the Leven.
station.	22½		21½	Markinch station. Balbirnie House.
tation.	20		24	Falkland station. Town of Falkland, with ancient Palace.
ttle sta.	18		26	King's Kettle sta.
junction.	17		27	Ladybank junction For branch to Perth lower division.
station.	14		30	Springfield station
ion.				Cupar station.
				DUNDEE.
station.	17		27	Ladybank station.
Mr. Macgill				
l of Melville.				Kinloch—Mr Kinnear.
ation.	14		30	Collessie station.
y—Mr. Wilson.				Lindores House — L Maitland.
	11¾		32¼	
lores Abbey. station.	10		34	Newburgh station
Road sta.				Abernethy Road s
se — Mr. Hay				
Lord Elcho. arn sta.	4		41	Bridge of Earn st
			45	Scottish Central line.
tion.				Perth station.

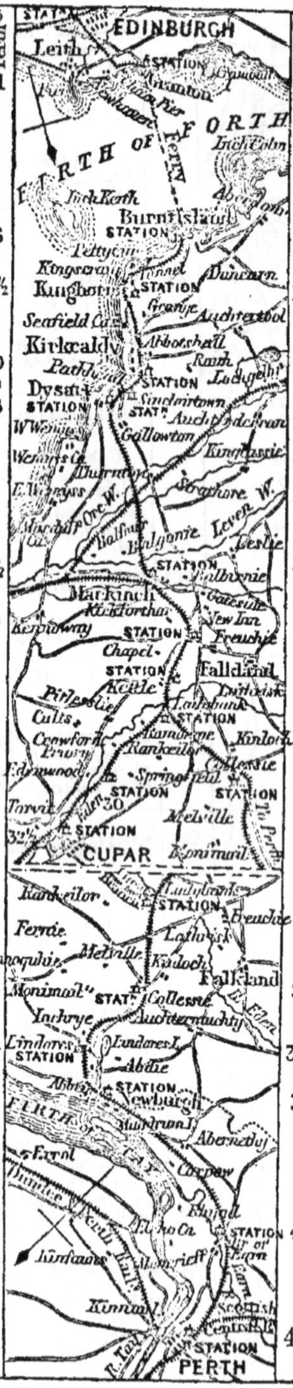

NGHT FROM GLASG

Glasgow station.

Govan village contains a celebrated ... factory, and ... furnaces for ... pig and bar iron.

Renfrew, the capital of the county. It was long the chief residence of the Royal ... Stewart. It is a small town, and has no manufactures.

Paisley station

Paisley is a town of great antiquity; ...

Johnstone station.

Kilbarchan is a pleasantly situated village. ...

Castle Semple, ...

Lochwinnoch sta

Beith station.

Kilbirnie station

Kilbirnie, a small village, containing ...

Dalry station.

Dalry is situate ... of the Garnock ...

Kilwinning sta

Irvine station

Troon station

Monkton station

Ayr station.

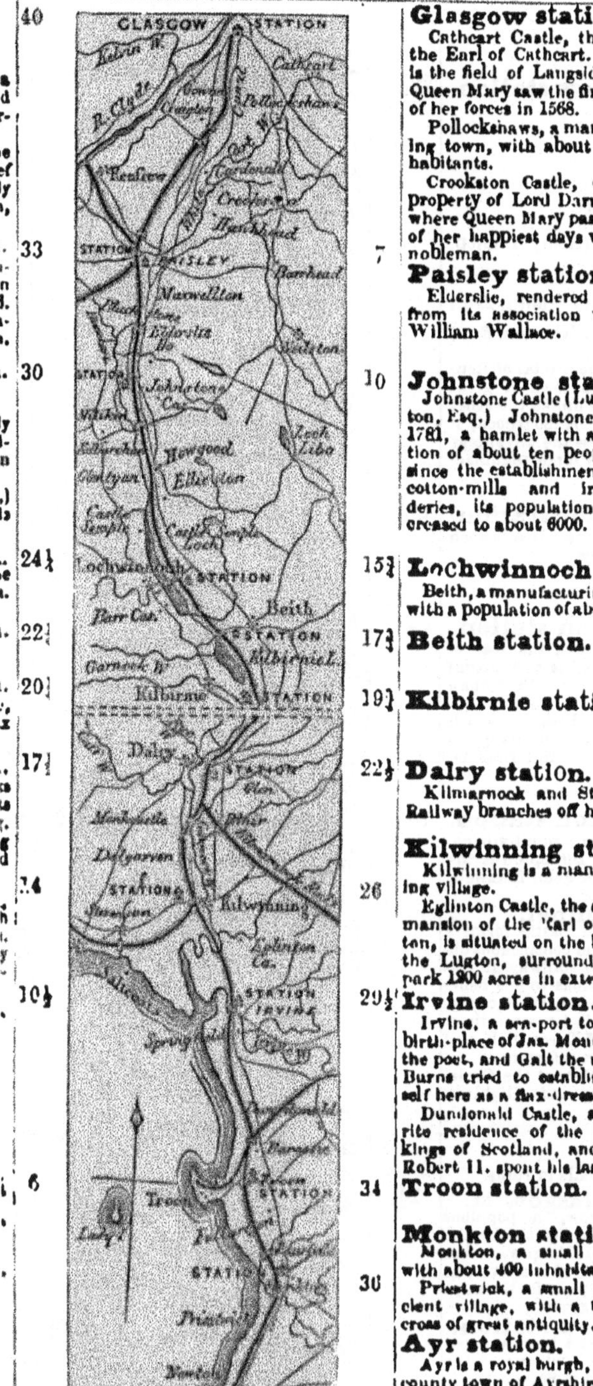

40 **Glasgow station.**

Cathcart Castle, the seat of the Earl of Cathcart. Near it is the field of Langside, where Queen Mary saw the final defeat of her forces in 1568.

Pollockshaws, a manufacturing town, with about 5000 inhabitants.

Crookston Castle, once the property of Lord Darnley, and where Queen Mary passed some of her happiest days with that nobleman.

33 **Paisley station.** 7

Elderslie, rendered classical from its association with Sir William Wallace.

30 **Johnstone station.** 10

Johnstone Castle (Lud. Houston, Esq.) Johnstone was, till 1781, a hamlet with a population of about ten people; but since the establishment of the cotton-mills and iron-founderies, its population has increased to about 6000.

24½ **Lochwinnoch sta.** 15¾

Beith, a manufacturing town, with a population of about 3000.

22¼ **Beith station.** 17¾

20¼ **Kilbirnie station.** 19¾

17½ **Dalry station.** 22½

Kilmarnock and Stewarton Railway branches off here.

14 **Kilwinning sta.** 26

Kilwinning is a manufacturing village.

Eglinton Castle, the splendid mansion of the Earl of Eglinton, is situated on the banks of the Lugton, surrounded by a park 1200 acres in extent.

10½ **Irvine station.** 29½

Irvine, a sea-port town, the birth-place of Jas. Montgomery the poet, and Galt the novelist. Burns tried to establish himself here as a flax-dresser.

Dundonald Castle, a favourite residence of the Stewart kings of Scotland, and where Robert II. spent his last days.

6 **Troon station.** 34

Monkton station. 36

Monkton, a small village, with about 400 inhabitants.

Priestwick, a small but ancient village, with a market-cross of great antiquity.

Ayr station. 40

Ayr is a royal burgh, and the county town of Ayrshire.

• Steamboats

ON RIGHT FROM GLASGOW. Greenock. GLASGOW TO GREENOCK.

Glasgow station. 22½

Govan village.

Craigton, (Henry Dunlop, Esq.)

Jordanhill, (J. Smith, Esq.)

Shielhall, (A. Johnston, Esq.)

Renfrew, the capital of Renfrewshire, is a town of great antiquity, but unlike the other towns in its neighbourhood, it does not possess the advantage of having any large manufactories.

Paisley station. 15½

From which there is a branch line to Renfrew.

Houston station. 13

Erskine House, the seat of Lord Blantyre, is a beautiful structure in the Elizabethan style. The estate and old mansion house of Erskine, which still remains, were long the property of the Lords Erskine, Earls of Mar.

Bishopton station. 10

Bishopton is a small village. The estate of Bishopton is the property of Sir John Maxwell, Bart.

Tunnel.

Dumbarton Castle forms a prominent and conspicuous object from the Railway at this point. Previous to his being sent to England, Wallace was confined in it for some time. The rock is 560 feet high, and a mile in circumference.

Beautiful View of the Clyde, the Garloch, and Highland Hills.

Newark Castle in ruins.

Port-Glasgow st. 2½

Port-Glasgow, a populous sea-port town, erected by the merchants of Glasgow, before the deepening of the river, as a convenient place for the shipping of their goods.

Greenock station.

Greenock is a large and populous town, and one of the first sea-ports in Scotland.

ON LEFT FROM GREENOCK.

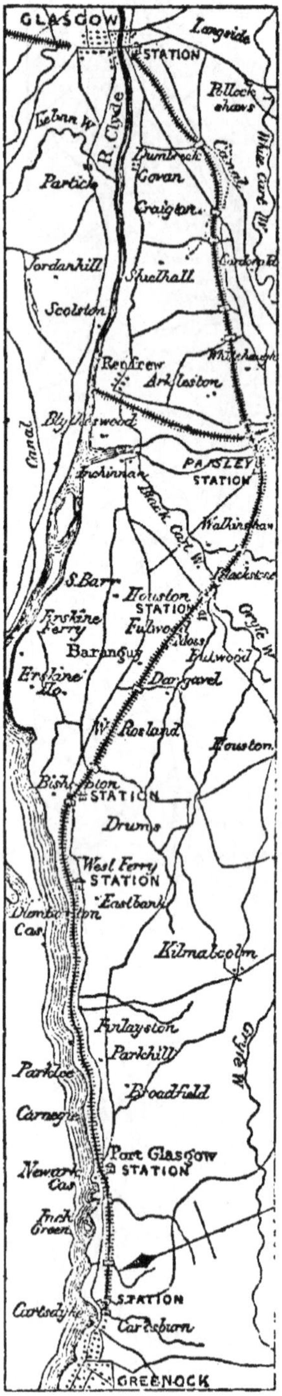

Glasgow stati

Pollockshaws, a b rony situated in a val banks of the Cart. to the last census, it 5007 inhabitants, chiefly engaged in t factories of the place.

Cardonald, an anti ture, embowered in been in the possessi Blantyre family since of James VI.

Paisley, a celebra manufacturing indus Abbey Church is an i object.

7 **Paisley statio**

There is a small c tached to the Abb Marjory, daughter of bert Bruce, is interr chapel possesses a re echo.

9½ **Houston stati**

Houston is a neat vi derives its name f Houston family, who the neighbourhood.

Dargavel House, (Esq.)

12½ **Bishopton sta**

Tunnel

Through Bishopton R yards long, with an o of 100 yards long in th It is 70 feet below the and cost £12,000 in struction.

20 **Port-Glasgo**

22½ **Greenock sta**

The situation of Gr very beautiful. Its House and Exchange ings of considerable e

VIII.—NORTH BRITISH RAILWAY.

EDINBURGH.—DUNBAR.—BERWICK-ON-TWEED.—58 MILES.
WITH BRANCH LINE TO HADDINGTON.—17 MILES.

EDINBURGH TO DUNBAR.

ON RIGHT FROM EDIN.	Berwick.	From Edinr	ON LEFT FROM EDIN.
Edinr. station. Holyrood Palace, St Anthony's Chapel, and Arthur's Seat. Piershill barracks, with accommodation for 1000 cavalry.	58		**Edinr. station.** Waterloo Bridge. Jail and Calton Hill. Restalrig village.
Portobello station.	55	3	**Portobello station.** Portobello, much frequented by the inhabitants of Edinburgh for sea-bathing. Inveresk church and village.
Musselburgh stat. A little to the right, Carberry Hill, where Queen Mary surrendered herself to the confederated Lords. Tranent, an ancient village, chiefly inhabited by colliers.	51½	6½	**Musselburgh stat.** On Musselburgh Links the Edinburgh races are run. In their vicinity, the battle of Pinkie was fought in 1547. House where Col. Gardiner fell, and ruins of Preston tower.
Tranent station. Scene of the battle of Prestonpans, where Prince Charles Stuart routed the forces of Sir John Cope in 1745.	47½	10½	**Tranent station.** Seton House, for many centuries the residence of the Setons, Earls of Wintoun.
Longniddry stat. Gladsmuir, the birth-place of George Heriot.	44½	13½	**Longniddry station.** Longniddry, interesting from its association with John Knox. Near the coast, is Gosford House, a mansion of the Earl of Wemyss.
Gullane station.	42½	15½	**Gullane station.** Ballencrieff, the property of Lord Elibank. From this Station, there are coaches for Aberlady and Gullane.
Haddington station. Haddington, the county town of East Lothian, distant seventeen miles from Edinburgh. On the south side of the town are the ruins of a Franciscan church. John Knox is said to have been born in a house near the church. A mile to the south, is Lethington, a seat of Lord Blantyre's. Hailes Castle, (Sir C. Ferguson, Bart.,) was the chief residence of Queen Mary during her union with Bothwell.	40½	17½	**Drem station.** From which a coach runs to Dirleton and North Berwick. North Berwick Law and the Bass Rock, which rises 400 feet sheer out of the sea. It was long a stronghold of the Lauders. It is covered with sea-fowl of all kinds.
Linton station. Linton, a populous village, on the banks of the Tyne, which sweeps round its northern side, and falls into a large and deep ... Smeaton House, (James Hamilton, Esq.) ...l, (Mrs. Ferguson,) with extensive plantations and charming walks. ...ton Place, (Captain Hay, ...) ...chend House, (Sir George ...render, Bart.)	34½	23½	**Linton station.** Phantassie, (T. M. Innes, Esq.) Tyningham House, the mansion of the Earl of Haddington. Beltonford village. West Barns village. Beautiful village of Belhaven.
Dunbar station.	29	29	**Dunbar station.** Half-way.

NORTH BRITISH RAILWAY.—*Continued.*

	From Berwick.	DUNBAR TO BERWICK.	From Edinr.	ON LEFT FROM EDIN.
r station. historical asso-	29		29	**Dunbar station.** Dunbar Castle, where Black Agnes, (Countess of March,) signalized herself.
J. Henderson,				Broxmouth Park, a seat of the Duke of Roxburgh. Barryhill, (Capt. Sandilands.)
				East Barns village.
erwick Castle. e of the Glen is , the former the milton, and the				Skateraw.
				Thornton Loch.
use, (Sir John ed amid beau-				Bitsdean.
spath sta.	21		37	**Cockburnspath sta.**
of Cockburns- rty of Sir John				Peas Bridge, 123 feet high, and 300 feet long. In former times was an important pass. Oliver Cromwell described it as a place "where one man to hinder another is better than twelve to make way."
ouse sta. nse.	16½		41½	**Grant's House sta.**
				Renton Inn.
				South Renton.
				Greenwood. Houndwood. Houndwood House, (Mrs. Coulson.)
n station. ere are coaches	11½		46½	**Reston station.** Coldingham, near the sea, with the ruins of a priory celebrated in Border history. Near Coldingham is St. Abb's Head and Fast Castle, the wolf's crag of "the Bride of Lammermoor."
n station.	7½		50½	**Ayton station.** Ayton village on the banks of the Eye, and Ayton House (Mitchell Innes, Esq.) Burnmouth, a romantic little fishing village, formerly a frequented haunt of the smuggler
mberton Kirk, t, daughter of as married by IV., a marriage ly led to the wns.				Beautiful View of the sea.
ated on a gentle well built town, streets, and is walls, which sed to be regu-				Berwick Castle, so celebrated in early history, is now shapeless ruin.
k station.			58	**Berwick station.**

STATION DUNBAR, Broxburn, Chesterhall, Broxmouth, Oxwell Mains, Barryhill, East Barns, Innerwick, Skateraw, Crowhill, Thorntonloch, Palmerton, Bitsdean, Dunglass Mains, Dunglass, Cockburnspath STATION, Cove, Tower, Pathhead, Peas Bridge, Tunnel, Penmanshiel Woods, Grants House STATION, from Dunse, Renton Inn, South Renton, Greenwood, Houndwood, Houndwood Ho, Lemanton, Coveyheugh, Reston STATION, West Reston, Coldingham, Reston Hill, East Reston, Peelwall, Ayton, Prendergust, STATION, Flemington, Burnmouth, Greystonelees, Ross, Lamberton Shiels, from Lamberton, Dunse, Marshall Meadows, R. Tweed, from Kelso, Tweedmouth, STATION, BERWICK on Tweed

NORTH BRITISH ...
N RIGHT FROM EDINBURGH.

Edinburgh station.
Portobello station.
Niddrie Station. Pentland Hills.
Dalkeith station.
Dalhousie station. Cockpen Church. Dalhousie Castle—Earl Dalh.
Gorebridge station. Arniston House—Dundas.
Fushiebridge station. Borthwick Castle ... Currie House—Mr Brown.
Tynehead station. ... Manse—Rev. G. ...
Heriot station. Hallree.
Fountainhall station. Fountainhall. Pirnplyth. ...—Captain Tait. E. N. ... Castle.
Stow station. Ferniehirst. Gala Water.
Bowland Bridge sta. Bowland—Mr Walker. Torwoodlee—Mr. ...
Galashiels station. Galashiels town. Abbotsford. Cross the Tweed. Eildon Hills.
Melrose station.
Newstead station.
Newton St. Boswell sta. ... ...
New Belses station FOR JEDBURGH.
Hassendean station.
Hawick station.

NORTH BRITISH RAILWAY—*Continued.* HAWICK BRANCH.

RIGHT FROM EDINBURGH.	From Hawick	EDINBURGH—GALASHIELS—MELROSE—HAWICK. From Edin.	ON LEFT FROM EDINBURGH.
inburgh station.	53		**Edinburgh station.**
rtobello station.	50	3	**Portobello station.**
iddrie Station. 'entland Hills.	48½	4½	**Niddrie station.** Beautiful new church and town of Dalkeith.
lkeith station.	45	8	**Dalkeith station.**
lhousie station. ockpen Church. alhousie Castle—Earl Dalh.	44	9	**Dalhousie station.** Ruins of Newbyres Castle.
rebridge station. rniston House—Dundas.	41	12	**Gorebridge station.**
ishiebridge station. orthwick Castle (ruins). urrie House—Mr. Brown.	40	13	**Fushiebridge station.** Crichton Castle (ruins).
nehead station. leriot Manse—Rev. G. S. ith.	37	16	**Tynehead station.** Hangingshaw village.
eriot station. alltree.	33½	19½	**Heriot station.** Crookston—Mr. Borthwick.
untainhall station. rntaiton. lenploth. irn—Captain Tait, R.N. ugate Castle.	30½	22½	**Fountainhall station.** Burnhouse—Lord Wood. Watherston.
ow station. ernichirst. ala Water.	26	27	**Stow station.** Stow village. Torsonce.
owland Bridge sta. owland—Mr. Walker. Torwoodlee—Mr. Meikleham.	23	30	**Bowland Bridge sta.** Gala Water.
alashiels station. Galashiels town. Abbotsford. Cross the Tweed. Eildon Hills.	19½	33½	**Galashiels station.** The Pavilion—Lord Somerville. Gattonside village. Melrose town and Abbey.
elrose station.	15½	37	**Melrose station.**
ewstead station.	14½	38½	**Newstead station.**
ewton St. Bosw. sta. Elliestoun. Longnewton village.	12½	40½	**Newton St. Bosw. sta.**
ew Belses station, FOR JEDBURGH.	7½	45½	**New Belses station,** FOR JEDBURGH.
assendean station.	4	49	**Hassendean station.** Minto Castle—Earl of Minto.
awick station.		53	**Hawick station.**

IX.—SCOTTISH CENTRAL RAILWAY.

Coaches in connection with this line run from Stirling to Callander; from Greenloaning to Crieff, Abe and Amulree; from Dunblane to Doune; and from Blackford to Rumbling Bridge.

ON RIGHT FROM PERTH.	From Castlecary.	PERTH STIRLING— CASTLECARY COATBRIDGE.	From Perth.	
Perth station.	45			Perth station.
Aberdalgie village.				Pitcathly Wells.
Forgandenny station.	41		4	Forgandenny sta
Forteviot station.	38		7	Forteviot station. Invermay—Mr. Belshe
Dunning station. Gask House—Mr. J. B. Oliphant.	35½		9½	Dunning station. Duncrab—Lord Rollo.
Aberruthven.				Ternavie.
Auchterarder village. Auchterarder station. Tullibardine Castle—ruins.	31½		13½	Auchterarder sta Kincardine Castle — Johnstone. Gleneagles House — Camperdown.
Orchil. Blackford station. Roman Camp. Ardoch.	27		18	Blackford station Bittergask.
Greenloaning station.	23		22	Greenloaning sta
Kinbuck station.	19½		25½	Kinbuck station. Sheriff Muir, where a was fought in 1715.
Dunblane station. Keir—Mr. A. Stirling.	17		28	Dunblane station Dunblane Village. Kippenross—Mr. J. St
Lecropt. Bridge of Allan sta.	15		30	Bridge of Allan s
Stirling. Stirling station.	12		33	Stirling station. River Forth.
Bannockburn station. Bannockburn village, and field of battle, fought 1514.	9½		35½	Bannockburn sta Bruce Castle.
Larbert village. Larbert station.	4		41	Larbert station. Camelon village.
Denny village. Loanhead village.			45	Greenhill junc. st Change here for Edinb Glasgow, or Carlisle.
Castlecary station. Kilsyth village.	103½			
The Scottish Central here joins the Caledonian and Edinburgh and Glasgow Railways.	From Carlisle.			Glenhove—Mr. Marsh
Coatbridge station.	94½		52	Airdrie village. Coatbridge statio

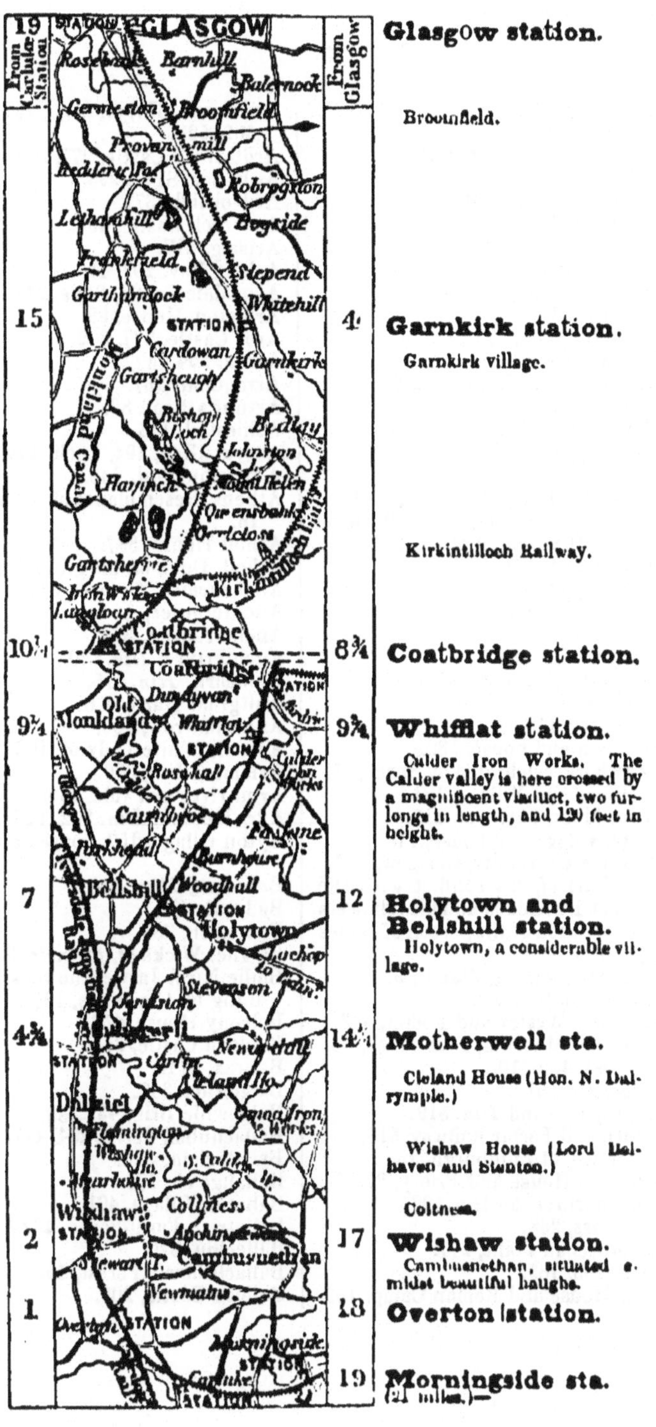

From Carlisle Station	From Glasgow	
19		**Glasgow station.**
		Broomfield.
15	4	**Garnkirk station.** Garnkirk village.
		Kirkintilloch Railway.
10¼	8¾	**Coatbridge station.**
9¼	9¾	**Whifflat station.** Calder Iron Works. The Calder valley is here crossed by a magnificent viaduct, two furlongs in length, and 120 feet in height.
7	12	**Holytown and Bellshill station.** Holytown, a considerable village.
4¾	14¼	**Motherwell sta.** Cleland House (Hon. N. Dalrymple.) Wishaw House (Lord Belhaven and Stenton.) Coltness.
2	17	**Wishaw station.** Cambusnethan, situated amidst beautiful haughs.
1	18	**Overton station.**
	19	**Morningside sta.** (21 miles.)—

INDEX.

EDINBURGH: PRINTED BY ROBERT CLARK.

Lightning Source UK Ltd.
Milton Keynes UK
UKOW05f0615091216
289556UK00014B/439/P

9 781332 003297